CONCISE CONCORDANCE

to the Revised Standard Version

of the Holy Bible

650

THOMAS NELSON & SONS

EDINBURGH   NEW YORK   TORONTO

Explanatory Notes
on the RSV Concise Concordance

Wherever an asterisk (*) immediately follows a key word it indicates that all occurrences in the Bible of that word have been listed.

Where possible, verbal forms have been combined. The singular and plural forms of nouns are also listed together. All entries referring to the first key word are listed in the order of the books of the Bible, followed by entries referring to the second key word, etc. For example: under "abase —d —s*" the first entry refers to *abase,* the second to *abased,* and the third to *abases.* Under "abomination —s" the first seven entries refer to *abomination,* the last entry to *abominations.*

Nouns and verbs are always separated so there is one listing "abuse —d (v)" and another "abuse (n)." In some cases, even though *only* the verb or *only* the noun of an ambiguous word is listed, the "(v)" or "(n)" is still used to avoid confusion; e.g., "bridle (v)."

Other distinctions of this kind have sometimes been made, e.g., "divine" as a *verb* and as an *adjective.* Usually no distinction is made between nouns and adjectives. Occasionally, also, an *adverb* is designated as such. Where the same word is listed under several forms, the following sequence is used, with these abbreviations:

> verb (v)
> adverb (adv)
> noun (n)
> adjective (adj)

Verse references between 1 and 9 are preceded by a 0 except for the one-chapter books, Obadiah (Ob), Philemon (Phm), 2nd John (2Jn), 3rd John (3Jn), and Jude (Jud). Thus, under "ambassador —s" the verse reference for one entry reads "Is 18.02," and for another, "Phm 9."

In some cases it has seemed well to include in the heading a *phrase* instead of a *single word.* In these instances, the listing will be found under the *first* word in the phrase. E.g., "steadfast love" translates only one Hebrew word. Thus there is one listing for "steadfast —ly," another for "steadfast love."

When the entry refers to a footnote an asterisk (*) is placed beside the verse number. Under "ground" the entry for John 8.6 is in a footnote and therefore is listed as "*Jn 8.6."

The Proper Names: A high degree of selectivity has been maintained in the choice of proper names, only the most important or familiar names having been included. References given under each name have been selected on the basis (1) of their value in describing or defining the name; (2) of their usefulness in specifying the major passages where the person or place figures in the Bible; and (3) of their helpfulness in locating verses or events of special interest or significance.

If there are several Biblical persons who bear the same name and more than one of them are listed, the numbers (1), (2), etc., follow the key name.

3

ABBREVIATIONS

The abbreviations used for the books of the Bible in this Concise Concordance are as follows:

Gen	Genesis	Nah	Nahum
Ex	Exodus	Hab	Habakkuk
Lev	Leviticus	Zep	Zephaniah
Num	Numbers	Hag	Haggai
Deu	Deuteronomy	Zec	Zechariah
Jos	Joshua	Mal	Malachi
Ju	Judges	Mt	Matthew
Ru	Ruth	Mk	Mark
1Sa	1 Samuel	Lk	Luke
2Sa	2 Samuel	Jn	John
1Ki	1 Kings	Ac	Acts of the Apostles
2Ki	2 Kings	Rom	Romans
1Ch	1 Chronicles	1Co	1 Corinthians
2Ch	2 Chronicles	2Co	2 Corinthians
Ez	Ezra	Gal	Galatians
Neh	Nehemiah	Eph	Ephesians
Est	Esther	Php	Philippians
Job	Job	Col	Colossians
Ps	Psalms	1Th	1 Thessalonians
Pro	Proverbs	2Th	2 Thessalonians
Ecc	Ecclesiastes	1Ti	1 Timothy
Sol	Song of Solomon	2Ti	2 Timothy
Is	Isaiah	Tit	Titus
Jer	Jeremiah	Phm	Philemon
Lam	Lamentations	Heb	Hebrews
Eze	Ezekiel	Jas	James
Dan	Daniel	1Pe	1 Peter
Hos	Hosea	2Pe	2 Peter
Joe	Joel	1Jn	1 John
Amo	Amos	2Jn	2 John
Ob	Obadiah	3Jn	3 John
Jon	Jonah	Jud	Jude
Mic	Micah	Rev	Revelation

A

ABANDON —ED
The LORD will not a. him to his	Ps 37.33
For thou wilt not a. my soul to	Ac 2.27
'You a. me, so I have a. you to	2Ch 12.05
that he was not a. to Hades,	Ac 2.31
that you have a. the love you had	Rev 2.04

ABASE —D —S*
one that is proud, and a. him.	Job 40.11
I know how to be a., and I	Php 4.12
For God a. the proud, but he saves	Job 22.29

ABBA*
And he said, "A., Father, all things	Mk 14.36
When we cry, "A.! Father!"	Rom 8.15
Son into our hearts, crying, "A.!	Gal 4.06

ABHOR —RED
pit, and my own clothes will a. me.	Job 9.31
I hate and a. falsehood, but I love	Ps 119.163
You who a. idols, do you rob	Rom 2.22
cursed by peoples, a. by nations;	Pro 24.24

ABIDE —S
shall not a. in man for ever, for	Gen 6.03
their heritage will a. for ever;	Ps 37.18
Man cannot a. in his pomp, he is	49.12
the arrogant man shall not a.	Hab 2.05
A. in me, and I in you.	Jn 15.04
So faith, hope, love a., these three;	1Co 13.13
heard from the beginning a. in you,	1Jn 2.24
who a. in the shadow of the Almighty,	Ps 91.01
flesh and drinks my blood a. in me,	Jn 6.56
for God's nature a. in him,	1Jn 3.09

ABIDING
like a shadow, and there is no a.	1Ch 29.15
a better possession and an a. one.	Heb 10.34
the living and a. word of God;	1Pe 1.23

ABILITY
I have given to all able men a.,	Ex 31.06
LORD has put a. and intelligence	36.01
for they were men of great a.	1Ch 26.06
according to their a. they gave to	Ez 2.69
one, to each according to his a.	Mt 25.15
every one according to his a.,	Ac 11.29
to another the a. to distinguish	1Co 12.10

ABLE
"Who is a. to stand before the LORD,	1Sa 6.20
"The LORD is a. to give you much	2Ch 25.09
he will not be a. to deliver you.	Is 36.14
God is a. from these stones to	Mt 3.09
Are you a. to drink the cup that I	20.22
cast it out, and they were not a."	Mk 9.18
to build, and was not a. to finish.'	Lk 14.30
which is a. to build you up and to	Ac 20.32
will be a. to separate us from the	Rom 8.39
Now to him who is a. to strengthen	16.25
within us is a. to do far more	Eph 3.20
Now to him who is a. to keep you	Jud 24

ABLUTIONS*
with instruction about a., the laying	Heb 6.02
with food and drink and various a.,	9.10

ABODE
by thy strength to thy holy a.	Ex 15.13
From thy lofty a. thou waterest the	Ps 104.13
he blesses the a. of the righteous	Pro 3.33

ABOLISH —ED* —ES* —ING*
and I will a. the bow, the sword, and	Hos 2.18
I have come to a. the law and the	Mt 5.17
who a. death and brought life and	2Ti 1.10
He a. the first in order to	Heb 10.09
by a. in his flesh the law of	Eph 2.15

ABOMINABLE
"You shall not eat any a. thing.	Deu 14.03
she had an a. image made for	1Ki 15.13
put away the a. idols from all the	2Ch 15.08
they do a. deeds, there is none that	Ps 14.01
they made their a. images and	Eze 7.20

ABOMINATION —S
it shall be an a., and he who	Lev 7.18
for it is an a. to the LORD your	Deu 7.25
perverse man is an a. to the LORD,	Pro 3.32
The sacrifice of the wicked is an a.;	21.27
incense is an a. to me. New moon	Is 1.13
set up the a. that makes desolate.	Dan 11.31
among men is an a. in the sight of	Lk 16.15
there are seven a. in his heart;	Pro 26.25

ABOUND —ED —ING
and peace a., till the moon be no	Ps 72.07
continue in sin that grace may a.?	Rom 6.01
your love may a. more and more,	Php 1.09
one man Jesus Christ a. for many.	Rom 5.15
always a. in the work of the LORD,	1Co 15.58

ABROAD
abundance, O God, thou didst shed a.;	Ps 68.09
his sheep have been scattered a.,	Eze 34.12
the report went a. concerning him;	Lk 5.15

ABSENT
when we are a. one from the other.	Gen 31.49
For though a. in body I am present	1Co 5.03

ABSTAIN —S
to them to a. from the pollutions	Ac 15.20
that you a. from immorality;	1Th 4.03
and exiles to a. from the passions	1Pe 2.11
him who eats despise him who a.,	Rom 14.03

ABUNDANCE
and the a. of the everlasting hills,	Deu 33.15
Israel gave in a. the first fruits	2Ch 31.05
But I through the a. of thy steadfast	Ps 5.07
Rain in a., O God, thou didst shed	68.09
but in an a. of counselors there is	Pro 11.14
a. of salvation, wisdom, and	Is 33.06
For out of the a. of the heart the	Mt 12.34
all contributed out of their a.;	Mk 12.44

ABUNDANCE (cont.)
consist in the a. of his possessions." Lk 12.15
plenty and hunger, a. and want. Php 4.12

ABUNDANT —LY
O how a. is thy goodness, which thou Ps 31.19
according to thy a. mercy blot out 51.01
you know the a. love that I have 2Co 2.04
bring forth a. on the earth and Gen 9.07
to our God, for he will a. pardon. Is 55.07
they may have life, and have it a. Jn 10.10
to do far more a. than all that we Eph 3.20

ABUSE —ED (v)
you, pray for those who a. you. Lk 6.28
when you are a., those who revile 1Pe 3.16

ABUSE (n)
and quarreling and a. will cease. Pro 22.10
He considered a. suffered for the Heb 11.26

ABYSS*
command them to depart into the a. Lk 8.31
or "Who will descend into the a.?" Rom 10.07

ACCEPT —ED
and a. the work of his hands; Deu 33.11
A. my offerings of praise, O Lord, Ps 119.108
Listen to advice and a. instruction, Pro 19.20
therefore the Lord does not a. them, Jer 14.10
the word and a. it and bear fruit, Mk 4.20
you not to a. the grace of God in 2Co 6.01
and the Lord a. Job's prayer. Job 42.09
sake and have a. nothing from the 3Jn 7

ACCEPTABLE
of my heart be a. in thy sight, Ps 19.14
The sacrifice a. to God is a broken 51.17
Your burnt offerings are not a., Jer 6.20
to proclaim the a. year of the Lord." Lk 4.19
no prophet is a. in his own country. 4.24
holy and a. to God, which is your Rom 12.01
"At the a. time I have listened to 2Co 6.02
let us offer to God a. worship, Heb 12.28

ACCEPTANCE
what will their a. mean but life Rom 11.15
is sure and worthy of full a., 1Ti 1.15

ACCOMPLISH —ED —ES*
but it shall a. that which I Is 55.11
which he was to a. at Jerusalem. Lk 9.31
who sent me, and to a. his work. Jn 4.34
pass from the law until all is a. Mt 5.18
when these things are all to be a.?" Mk 13.04
I am constrained until it is a.! Lk 12.50
having a. the work which thou Jn 17.04
of him who a. all things according Eph 1.11

ACCORD —ANCE
Yea, they conspire with one a.; Ps 83.05
the Lord and serve him with one a. Zep 3.09
Son can do nothing of his own a., Jn 5.19
But I have not come of my own a.; 7.28
All these with one a. devoted Ac 1.14

What a. has Christ with Belial? 2Co 6.15
being in full a. and of one mind. Php 2.02
in a. with these words I have made Ex 34.27
in a. with the word of the Lord." 2Ki 9.26
third day in a. with the scriptures, 1Co 15.04

ACCORDING
each a. to its kind, upon the earth." Gen 1.11
careful to do a. to all the law Jos 1.07
For a. to the work of a man he will Job 34.11
and a. to his ways he will make it 34.11
a. to thy steadfast love remember Ps 25.07
on me, O God, a. to thy steadfast love; 51.01
"A. to your faith be it done to you." Mt 9.29
one, to each a. to his ability. 25.15
not live a. to the tradition of Mk 7.05
depart in peace, a. to thy word; Lk 2.29
You judge a. to the flesh, I judge Jn 8.15
delivered up a. to the definite Ac 2.23
every one a. to his ability, to send 11.29
descended from David a. to the flesh Rom 1.03
who walk not a. to the flesh but 8.04
who are called a. to his purpose. 8.28
each a. to the measure of faith 12.03
by us to live a. to scripture, 1Co 4.06
For they gave a. to their means, as 2Co 8.03
need of yours a. to his riches in Php 4.19
unless he competes a. to the rules. 2Ti 2.05
But a. to his promise we wait for 2Pe 3.13
and do not live a. to the truth; 1Jn 1.06

ACCOUNT
"Behold, I am of small a.; Job 40.04
is breath, for of what a. is he? Is 2.22
Turn in the a. of your stewardship, Lk 16.02
us shall give a. of himself to God. Rom 14.12
you anything, charge that to my a. Phm 8

ACCURSED
who do not know the law, are a." Jn 7.49
love for the Lord, let him be a. 1Co 16.22

ACCUSATION —S*
"What a. do you bring against this Jn 18.29
here before you and to make an a., Ac 24.19
against all the a. of the Jews, 26.02

ACCUSE
In return for my love they a. me, Ps 109.04
so that they might a. him. Mt 12.10
that I shall a. you to the Father; Jn 5.45

ACCUSER —S
I must appeal for mercy to my a. Job 9.15
Make friends quickly with your a., Mt 5.25
May my a. be put to shame and Ps 71.13
accused met the a. face to face, Ac 25.16

ACKNOWLEDGE
they turn again and a. thy name, 2Ch 6.24
In all your ways a. him, Pro 3.06
all who see them shall a. them, Is 61.09
We a. our wickedness, O Lord, and Jer 14.20
they did not see fit to a. God, Rom 1.28

ACQUIRE
Do not toil to a. wealth; be wise Pro 23.04
until we a. possession of it, to Eph 1.14

ACQUIT —TED
for I will not a. the wicked. Ex 23.07
and a. yourselves like men, O 1Sa 4.09
myself, but I am not thereby a. 1Co 4.04

ACT —ED —S (v)
if there are any that a. wisely, Ps 14.02
It is time for the LORD to a., 119.126
a., O LORD, for thy name's sake; Jer 14.07
of Israel, that I am about to a., Eze 36.22
is appointed to a. on behalf of Heb 5.01
So speak and so a. as those who are Jas 2.12
if you then have a. in good faith Ju 9.19
I know that you a. in ignorance, Ac 3.17
a prudent man a. with knowledge, Pro 13.16
that forgets but a doer that a., Jas 1.25

ACT —S (n)
been caught in the a. of adultery. *Jn 8.4
so one man's a. of righteousness Rom 5.18
arm and with great a. of judgment, Ex 6.06
his a. to the people of Israel. Ps 103.07
may know the saving a. of the LORD." Mic 6.05
of good works and a. of charity. Ac 9.36
he who does a. of mercy, with Rom 12.08

ADD —ED
You shall not a. to the word which Deu 4.02
who a. field to field, until there Is 5.08
that they may a. sin to sin; 30.01
anxious can a. one cubit to his Mt 6.27
and years will be a. to your life. Pro 9.11
the LORD has a. sorrow to my pain; Jer 45.03
And the Lord a. to their number day Ac 2.47
It was a. because of transgressions, Gal 3.19

ADDRESS —ED —ES* —ING*
could not a. you as spiritual men, 1Co 3.01
Pilate a. them once more, desiring Lk 23.20
when Peter saw it he a. the people, Ac 3.12
exhortation which a. you as sons?— Heb 12.05
a. one another in psalms and hymns Eph 5.19

ADJUSTED*
But God has so a. the body. 1Co 12.24

ADMINISTRATORS*
a., speakers in various kinds of 1Co 12.28

ADMONISH
Hear, O my people, while I a. you! Ps 81.08
night or day to a. every one with Ac 20.31
you teach and a. one another in Col 3.16

ADOPTION*
inwardly as we wait for a. as sons, Rom 8.23
that we might receive a. as sons. Gal 4.05

ADORN —ED
prophets and a. the monuments of Mt 23.29

women should a. themselves modestly 1Ti 2.09
as a bride a. for her husband; Rev 21.02

ADULTERESS
but an a. stalks a man's very life. Pro 6.26
beloved of a paramour and is an a.; Hos 3.01
of unchastity, makes her an a.; Mt 5.32

ADULTEROUS
"An evil and a. generation seeks Mt 12.39
God will judge the immoral and a. Heb 13.04

ADULTERY
"You shall not commit a. Ex 20.14
"If a man commits a. with the wife Lev 20.10
committing a. with stone and tree. Jer 3.09
and her a. from between her breasts; Hos 2.02
committed a. with her in his heart. Mt 5.28
"You shall not commit a., Rom 13.09
They have eyes full of a., 2Pe 2.14

ADVANCE —D
really served to a. the gospel, Php 1.12
and I a. in Judaism beyond many of Gal 1.14

ADVANTAGE
and man has no a. over the beasts; Ecc 3.19
it is to your a. that I go away, for Jn 16.07
Then what a. has the Jew? Or what Rom 3.01
Christ will be of no a. to you. Gal 5.02

ADVERSARIES —Y
him, "Are you for us, or for our a.?" Jos 5.13
The a. of the LORD shall be broken 1Sa 2.10
thou didst exalt me above my a.; Ps 18.48
And the waters covered their a.; 106.11
all his a. were put to shame; Lk 13.17
to me, and there are many a. 1Co 16.09
my a. sharpens his eyes against me. Job 16.09
Who is my a.? Let him come Is 50.08
Your a. the devil prowls around 1Pe 5.08

ADVERSITIES* —Y
thou hast taken heed of my a., Ps 31.07
redeemed my life out of every a., 2Sa 4.09
affliction, and opens their ear by a. Job 36.15
and a brother is born for a. Pro 17.17

ADVOCATE* (n)
we have an a. with the Father, Jesus 1Jn 2.01

AFAR
Why dost thou stand a. off, O LORD? Ps 10.01
discernest my thoughts from a. 139.02
Lo, these shall come from a., Is 49.12
the LORD, and not a God a. off? Jer 23.23
women there, looking on from a., Mt 27.55
And when he saw Jesus from a., Mk 5.06
seen it and greeted it from a., Heb 11.13

AFFAIRS
who conducts his a. with justice. Ps 112.05
anxious about the a. of the Lord, 1Co 7.32
live quietly, to mind your own a., 1Th 4.11

AFFECTION —S*
love one another with brotherly a.;	Rom 12.10
you are restricted in your own a.	2Co 6.12

AFFLICT —ED
You shall not a. any widow or	Ex 22.22
thou didst a. the peoples, but them	Ps 44.02
you who a. the righteous, who take a	Amo 5.12
but thinking to a. me in my	Php 1.17
with affliction those who a. you,	2Th 1.06
But the LORD a. Pharaoh and his	Gen 12.17
and a. Job with loathsome sores	Job 2.07
does not forget the cry of the a.	Ps 9.12
in faithfulness thou hast a. me.	119.75
LORD maintains the cause of the a.,	140.12
stricken, smitten by God, and a.	Is 53.04
me to bring good tidings to the a.;	61.01
In all their affliction he was a.;	63.09
they are a. for want of a shepherd.	Zec 10.02
those a. with various diseases and	Mt 4.24
We are a. in every way, but not	2Co 4.08
destitute, a., ill-treated—	Heb 11.37

AFFLICTION —S
God saw my a. and the labor of my	Gen 31.42
"I have seen the a. of my people	Ex 3.07
the bread of a.—for you came out	Deu 16.03
and caught in the cords of a.,	Job 36.08
but he raises up the needy out of a.,	Ps 107.41
this is vanity; it is a sore a.	Ecc 6.02
tried you in the furnace of a.	Is 48.10
Remember my a. and my bitterness,	Lam 3.19
who comforts us in all our a.,	2Co 1.04
to comfort those who are in any a.,	1.04
momentary a. is preparing for us	4.17
publicly exposed to abuse and a.,	Heb 10.33
Many are the a. of the righteous;	Ps 34.19
in Christ's a. for the sake of his	Col 1.24

AFRAID
and I was a., because I was naked;	Gen 3.10
Then Moses was a., and thought,	Ex 2.14
face, for he was a. to look at God.	3.06
Saul was a. of David, because the	1Sa 18.12
And David was a. of the LORD that	2Sa 6.09
When I am a., I put my trust in	Ps 56.03
heart is steady, he will not be a.,	112.08
I will trust, and will not be a.;	Is 12.02
Fear not, nor be a.; have I not	44.08
Be not a. of them, for I am with you	Jer 1.08
he was a. to go there, and being	Mt 2.22
"Why are you a., O men of little	8.26
they were a., and they glorified	9.08
so I was a., and I went and hid	25.25
said to the women, "Do not be a.;	28.05
And the angel said to them, "Be not a.;	Lk 2.10
troubled, neither let them be a.	Jn 14.27
for they were a. of being stoned by	Ac 5.26
I am a. I have labored over you in	Gal 4.11
is my helper, I will not be a.;	Heb 13.06

AGE —S
and Sarah were old, advanced in a.;	Gen 18.11
cast me off in the time of old a.;	Ps 71.09

for ever, a joy from a. to a.	Is 60.15
you were at the a. for love;	Eze 16.08
the youths who are of your own a.	Dan 1.10
either in this a. or in the a. to come.	Mt 12.32
you always, to the close of the a."	28.20
and in the a. to come eternal life.	Mk 10.30
was about thirty years of a.,	Lk 3.23
Where is the debater of this a.?	1Co 1.20
us from the present evil a.,	Gal 1.04
A. ago I was set up, at the first,	Pro 8.23
was kept secret for long a.	Rom 16.25
before the a. for our glorification.	1Co 2.07

AGONY
And being in an a. he prayed more	Lk 22.44

AGREE
"A. with God, and be at peace;	Job 22.21
if two of you a. on earth about	Mt 18.19
a. with one another, live in peace,	2Co 13.11

AGREEMENT
and with Sheol we have an a.;	Is 28.15
What a. has the temple of God with	2Co 6.16

AHEAD
and Jesus was walking a. of them;	Mk 10.32
each one goes a. with his own meal,	1Co 11.21
straining forward to what lies a.,	Php 3.13

AIM (v)
who a. bitter words like arrows,	Ps 64.03
a. at righteousness, godliness, faith,	1Ti 6.11

AIM (n)
Make love your a., and earnestly	1Co 14.1
whereas the a. of our charge is	1Ti 1.5
my a. in life, my faith, my patience,	2Ti 3.10

AIR
sea, and over the birds of the a.,	Gen 1.26
birds of the a. have their habitation;	Ps 104.12
Look at the birds of the a.:	Mt 6.26
and threw dust into the a.,	Ac 22.23
I do not box as one beating the a.;	1Co 9.26
you will be speaking into the a.	14.09
the prince of the power of the a.,	Eph 2.02

ALARMED
see that you are not a.;	Mt 24.06
and rumors of wars, do not be a.;	Mk 13.07

ALARM (n)
Sound the a. at Bethaven;	Hos 5.08
sound the a. on my holy mountain!	Joe 2.01
what a., what longing, what zeal,	2Co 7.11

ALIEN —S
and the a., may be refreshed.	Ex 23.12
an a. to my mother's sons.	Ps 69.08
and set out slips of an a. god,	Is 17.10
do no wrong or violence to the a.,	Jer 22.03
for they have borne a. children.	Hos 5.07
A. shall stand and feed your flocks,	Is 61.05
beseech you as a. and exiles to	1Pe 2.11

ALIVE

Joseph my son is still a.;	Gen 45.28
I kill and I make a.;	Deu 32.39
behold, the LORD has kept me a.,	Jos 14.10
"Am I God, to kill and to make a.,	2Ki 5.07
He does not keep the wicked a.,	Job 36.06
and he who cannot keep himself a.	Ps 22.29
which today is a. and tomorrow is	Mt 6.30
my son was dead, and is a. again;	Lk 15.24
presented himself a. after his	Ac 1.03
dead to sin and a. to God in	Rom 6.11
spirits are a. because of righteousness.	8.10
in Christ shall all be made a.	1Co 15.22
long as the one who made it is a.	Heb 9.17

ALLEGORY

Now this is an a.: these women are	Gal 4.24

ALLOW —ED

nor a. those who would enter to go	Mt 23.13
Spirit of Jesus did not a. them;	Ac 16.07
Am I not a. to do what I choose	Mt 20.15

ALMIGHTY

and said to him, "I am God A.;	Gen 17.01
for the A. has dealt very bitterly	Ru 1.20
you find out the limit of the A.?	Job 11.07
But I would speak to the A.,	13.03
Will he take delight in the A.?	27.10
"Shall a faultfinder contend with the A.?	40.02
abides in the shadow of the A.,	Ps 91.01
holy, holy, is the Lord God A.,	Rev 4.08
the Lord God the A. and the Lamb	21.22

ALMS

when you give a., sound no trumpet	Mt 6.02
But give for a. those things which	Lk 11.41
one who sat for a. at the Beautiful	Ac 3.10
and your a. have ascended as a	10.04

ALONE

not good that the man should be a.;	Gen 2.18
Moses a. shall come near to the	Ex 24.02
that man does not live by bread a.,	Deu 8.03
"Upon me a., my lord, be the guilt;	1Sa 25.24
know that thou, O LORD, art God a."	2Ki 19.19
Let me a., for my days are a breath	Job 7.16
Behold, this a. I found, that God	Ecc 7.29
"I have trodden the wine press a.,	Is 63.03
Let him sit a. in silence when he	Lam 3.28
'Man shall not live by bread a.' "	Lk 4.04
he was praying a. the disciples	9.18
No one is good but God a.	18.19
he has not left me a.,	Jn 8.29
by works and not by faith a.	Jas 2.24

ALOUD

"Cry a., for he is a god;	1Ki 18.27
I cry a. to the LORD, and he answers	Ps 3.04
Wisdom cries a. in the street;	Pro 1.20
"Cry a., spare not, lift up your	Is 58.01
Now why do you cry a.?	Mic 4.09
crying a., "Have mercy on us, Son of	Mt 9.27
Blessed is he who reads a. the	Rev 1.03

ALTAR —S

Then Noah built an a. to the LORD,	Gen 8.20
him, Abraham built an a. there,	22.09
And Moses built an a. and called	Ex 17.15
You shall build an a. to the LORD	Deu 27.06
Then Joshua built an a. in Mount	Jos 8.30
Then Gideon built an a. there to	Ju 6.24
the LORD standing beside the a.	Amo 9.01
gift there before the a. and go;	Mt 5.24
swears by the a., it is nothing;	23.18
I found also an a. with this	Ac 17.23
serve at the a. share in the	1Co 9.13
We have an a. from which those	Heb 13.10
You shall tear down their a.,	Ex 34.13
thy covenant, thrown down thy a.,	1Ki 19.10
at thy a., O LORD of hosts, my king	Ps 84.03

ALTOGETHER

LORD are true, and righteous a.	Ps 19.09
lo, O LORD, thou knowest it a.	139.04

ALWAYS

learn to fear the LORD your God a.	Deu 14.23
I am with you a., to the close of	Mt 28.20
that they ought a. to pray and not	Lk 18.01
I mention you a. in my prayers,	Rom 1.09

AMAZED

And all the people were a.,	Mt 12.23
the disciples were a. at his words.	Mk 10.24
And he said to them, "Do not be a.;	16.06
And they were a. and wondered,	Ac 2.07

AMBASSADOR* —S*

for which I am an a. in chains;	Eph 6.20
I, Paul, an a. and now a prisoner	Phm 9
which sends a. by the Nile, in	Is 18.02
rebelled against him by sending a. to	Eze 17.15
So we are a. for Christ, God making	2Co 5.20

AMBUSH

and set them in a. between Bethel	Jos 8.12
they set an a. for their own lives.	Pro 1.18
of Paul's sister heard of their a.;	Ac 23.16

AMEN

people shall answer and say, 'A.'	Deu 27.15
"A., A.," lifting up their hands;	Neh 8.06
say the "A." to your thanksgiving	1Co 14.16
is why we utter the A. through him,	2Co 1.20
write: 'The words of the A.,	Rev 3.14

AMEND

A. your ways and your doings, and I	Jer 7.03
that you might a. what was defective,	Tit 1.05

ANCIENT OF DAYS*

he came to the A. o. D. and was	Dan 7.13
until the A. o. D. came, and judgment	7.22

ANEW*

say to you, unless one is born a.,	Jn 3.03
said to you, 'You must be born a.'	3.07

ANEW (cont.)

have been born a. to a living hope	1Pe 1.03
You have been born a.,	1.23

ANGEL —S

in my sight as an a. of God;	1Sa 29.09
And God sent the a. to Jerusalem to	1Ch 21.15
If there be for him an a.,	Job 33.23
and the a. of his presence saved	Is 63.09
He strove with the a. and prevailed,	Hos 12.04
But the a. said to the women, "Do	Mt 28.05
And an a. of the Lord appeared to	Lk 2.09
face was like the face of an a.	Ac 6.15
disguises himself as an a. of light.	2Co 11.14
but received me as an a. of God,	Gal 4.14
the a. of God were ascending and	Gen 28.12
will give his a. charge of you to	Ps 91.11
The Son of man will send his a.,	Mt 13.41
When the a. went away from them	Lk 2.15
and the a. of God ascending and	Jn 1.51
as delivered by a. and did not	Ac 7.53
nor a., nor principalities, nor	Rom 8.38
in the tongues of men and of a.,	1Co 13.01
seen by a., preached among the	1Ti 3.16
For it was not to a. that God	Heb 2.05
some have entertained a. unawares.	13.02
things into which a. long to look.	1Pe 1.12
stars are the a. of the seven	Rev 1.20
Michael and his a. fighting	12.07

ANGER

Moses' a. burned hot, and he threw	Ex 32.19
'The Lord is slow to a.,	Num 14.18
"God will not turn back his a.;	Job 9.13
O Lord, rebuke me not in thy a.,	Ps 6.01
Turn not thy servant away in a.,	27.09
For his a. is but for a moment, and	30.05
Pour out thy a. on the nations that	79.06
slow to a. and abounding in steadfast	145.08
who is slow to a. quiets contention.	Pro 15.18
A fool gives full vent to his a.,	29.11
I trod down the peoples in my a.,	Is 63.06
I will not execute my fierce a.,	Hos 11.09
slow to a., and abounding in	Joe 2.13
repent and turn from his fierce a.,	Jon 3.09
And he looked around at them with a.,	Mk 3.05
let the sun go down on your a.	Eph 4.26
hear, slow to speak, slow to a.,	Jas 1.19

ANGRY

So Cain was very a.,	Gen 4.05
Therefore the Lord was very a. with	2Ki 17.18
of the family of Ram, became a.	Job 32.02
Be a., but sin not; commune	Ps 4.04
I will not be a. for ever.	Jer 3.12
one who is a. with his brother	Mt 5.22
are you a. with me because on the	Jn 7.23
Now Herod was a. with the people of	Ac 12.20

ANGUISH

will speak in the a. of my spirit;	Job 7.11
Trouble and a. have come upon me,	Ps 119.143
they will be in a. like a woman in	Is 13.08
My a., my a.! I writhe	Jer 4.19

for I am in a. in this flame.'	Lk 16.24
and unceasing a. in my heart.	Rom 9.02
affliction and a. of heart and	2Co 2.04

ANIMAL —S

of every clean a. and of every	Gen 8.20
Every a. which parts the hoof but	Lev 11.26
you seven pairs of all clean a.,	Gen 7.02
another for a., another for birds,	1Co 15.39
But these, like irrational a.,	2Pe 2.12

ANNOUNCE —D

watchman, let him a. what he sees.	Is 21.06
a. to Jerusalem, "Besiegers come	Jer 4.16
those who a. beforehand the coming	Ac 7.52
have now been a. to you by those	1Pe 1.12

ANNUL —LED —S*

does not a. a covenant previously	Gal 3.17
covenant with death will be a.,	Is 28.18
no one a. even a man's will, or adds	Gal 3.15

ANOINT —ED —EST* (v)

And you shall a. Aaron and his sons,	Ex 30.30
Wash therefore and a. yourself,	Ru 3.03
and a. themselves with the finest	Amo 6.06
a. your head and wash your face,	Mt 6.17
servant Jesus, whom thou didst a.,	Ac 4.27
and there they a. David king over	2Sa 2.04
the Lord has a. me to bring good	Is 61.01
she has a. my body beforehand for	Mk 14.08
because he has a. me to preach	Lk 4.18
how God a. Jesus of Nazareth with	Ac 10.38
thou a. my head with oil, my cup	Ps 23.05

ANOINTED (n)

"Surely the Lord's a. is before him."	1Sa 16.06
the a. of the God of Jacob, the	2Sa 23.01
and shows steadfast love to his a.,	Ps 18.50
the Lord and against his A.'—	Ac 4.26

ANOTHER

to their own country by a. way.	Mt 2.12
to come, or shall we look for a.?"	11.03
not be left here one stone upon a.,	Mk 13.02
Jesus, and so did a. disciple.	Jn 18.15
and 'His office let a. take.'	Ac 1.20
that there is a. king, Jesus."	17.07
in my members a. law at war with	Rom 7.23
the glory of the terrestrial is a.	1Co 15.40
from one degree of glory to a.;	2Co 3.18
not that there is a. gospel,	Gal 1.07
Therefore confess your sins to one a.,	Jas 5.16
we have fellowship with one a.,	1Jn 1.07

ANSWER —ED (v)

until noon, saying, "O Baal, a. us!"	1Ki 18.26
is there any one who will a. you?	Job 5.01
Though I am innocent, I cannot a. him;	9.15
"Should a wise man a. with windy	15.02
let the Almighty a. me!)	31.35
Consider and a. me, O Lord my God;	Ps 13.03
I cry by day, but thou dost not a.;	22.02
When he calls to me, I will a. him;	91.15

ANSWER —ED (v) (cont.)
A. a fool according to his folly,   Pro 26.05
I called, was there no one to a.?   Is 50.02
Before they call I will a.,   65.24
I will a. the heavens and they   Hos 2.21
And no one was able to a. him a word,   Mt 22.46
Then the righteous will a. him,   25.37
what you are to a. or what you are   Lk 12.11
"Is that how you a. the high priest?"   Jn 18.22
are you, a man, to a. back to God?   Rom 9.20
the LORD a. me and set me free.   Ps 118.05
And Jesus a. him, "Blessed are you,   Mt 16.17
Peter a. him, "You are the Christ."   Mk 8.29

ANSWER —S (n)
A soft a. turns away wrath, but a   Pro 15.01
To make an apt a. is a joy to a man,   15.23
who, when I ask, gives an a.   Is 41.28
and said, "Have you no a. to make?   Mt 26.62
But he gave him no a.,   27.14
Let us have an a. for those who   Jn 1.22
granted us in a. to many prayers.   2Co 1.11
at his understanding and his a.   Lk 2.47

ANTICHRIST* —S*
you have heard that a. is coming,   1Jn 2.18
This is the a., he who denies the   2.22
This is the spirit of a.,   4.03
one is the deceiver and the a.   2Jn 7
coming, so now many a. have come;   1Jn 2.18

ANXIETY
A. in a man's heart weighs him down,   Pro 12.25
in this tent, we sigh with a.;   2Co 5.04
Have no a. about anything, but in   Php 4.06

ANXIOUS
rest, eating the bread of a. toil;   Ps 127.02
do not be a. about your life, what   Mt 6.25
do not be a. beforehand what you   Mk 13.11
you are a. and troubled about many   Lk 10.41
unmarried man is a. about the   1Co 7.32
be genuinely a. for your welfare.   Php 2.20

APART
I have no good a. from thee."   Ps 16.02
and set them a. for the day of   Jer 12.03
in a boat to a lonely place a.   Mt 14.13
for a. from me you can do nothing.   Jn 15.05
"Set a. for me Barnabas and Saul   Ac 13.02
set a. for the gospel of God   Rom 1.01
by faith a. from works of law.   3.28

APOSTASIES* —Y*
are many, their a. are great.   Jer 5.06
and your a. will reprove you.   2.19
if they then commit a.,   Heb 6.06

APOSTLE —S
of Jesus Christ, called to be an a.,   Rom 1.01
then as I am an a. to the Gentiles,   11.13
Am I not an a.?   1Co 9.01
The signs of a true a. were performed   2Co 12.12
Paul an a.—not from men nor   Gal 1.01

the a. and high priest of our   Heb 3.01
The names of the twelve a. are these: Mt 10.02
'I will send them prophets and a.,   Lk 11.49
they arrested the a. and put them   Ac 5.18
The a. and the elders were gathered   15.06
they are men of note among the a.,   Rom 16.07
appointed in the church first a.,   1Co 12.28
For such men are false a.,   2Co 11.13
foundation of the a. and prophets,   Eph 2.20
O saints and a. and prophets, for   Rev 18.20

APPAREL
Why is thy a. red, and thy garments   Is 63.02
men stood by them in dazzling a.;   Lk 24.04
modestly and sensibly in seemly a.,   1Ti 2.09

APPEAL (v)
up to them. I a. to Caesar."   Ac 25.11
I a. to you therefore, brethren, by   Rom 12.01

APPEAL (n)
God making his a. through us.   2Co 5.20
For our a. does not spring from   1Th 2.03
body but as an a. to God for a   1Pe 3.21

APPEAR —ED —S
one place, and let the dry land a."   Gen 1.09
And none shall a. before me empty.   Ex 34.20
for today the LORD will a. to you.' "   Lev 9.04
you also will a. with him in glory.   Col 3.04
will a. a second time, not to deal   Heb 9.28
it does not yet a. what we shall be,   1Jn 3.02
I a. to Abraham, to Isaac, and to   Ex 6.03
from them what time the star a.;   Mt 2.07
John the baptizer a. in the wilderness,   Mk 1.04
And an angel of the Lord a. to them,   Lk 2.09
risen indeed, and has a. to Simon!"   24.34
And a vision a. to Paul in the   Ac 16.09
and that he a. to Cephas, then to   1Co 15.05
of God has a. for the salvation of   Tit 2.11
he has a. once for all at the end   Heb 9.26
and who can stand when he a.?   Mal 3.02
and when the Christ a.,   Jn 7.27
When Christ who is our life a.,   Col 3.04
are a mist that a. for a little   Jas 4.14
that when he a. we shall be like   1Jn 3.02

APPLIED —Y
And I a. my mind to seek and to   Ecc 1.13
I have a. all this to myself and   1Co 4.06
be careful to a. themselves to   Tit 3.08

APPOINT —ED —S
time which I a. I will judge with   Ps 75.02
kingdom for me, so do I a. for you   Lk 22.29
to a. you to serve and bear witness   Ac 26.16
and a. elders in every town as I   Tit 1.05
And he a. twelve, to be with him, and   Mk 3.14
I chose you and a. you that you   Jn 15.16
And God has a. in the church first   1Co 12.28
whom he a. the heir of all things,   Heb 1.02
the law a. men in their weakness as   7.28

APPROVAL
good, and you will receive his a.,   Rom 13.03
it patiently, you have God's a.   1Pe 2.20

APPROVE —D
his will and a. what is excellent,   Rom 2.18
as we have been a. by God to be   1Th 2.04
present yourself to God as one a.,   2Ti 2.15

ARGUE —ED —S* —ING
and I desire to a. my case with   Job 13.03
came and began to a. with him,   Mk 8.11
And they a. with one another, "If   Mt 21.25
three weeks he a. with them from   Ac 17.02
He who a. with God, let him answer   Job 40.02
a. and pleading about the kingdom   Ac 19.08

ARISE
A., O God, judge the earth;   Ps 82.08
A., shine; for your   Is 60.01
. "A., go to Nineveh, that great city,   Jon 1.02
queen of the South will a. at the   Mt 12.42
"Little girl, I say to you, a."   Mk 5.41
said, "Young man, I say to you, a.`   Lk 7.14
I will a. and go to my father, and I   15.18
and a. from the dead, and Christ   Eph 5.14
priest to a. after the order of   Heb 7.11

ARK
Make yourself an a. of gopher wood;   Gen 6.14
Philistines captured the a. of God,   1Sa 5.01
put out his hand to hold the a.,   1Ch 13.09
"Put the holy a. in the house which   2Ch 35.03
incense and the a. of the covenant   Heb 9.04

ARM (v)*
"A. men from among you for the   Num 31.03
a. yourselves with the same thought,   1Pe 4.01

ARM —S (n)
Have you an a. like God, and can you   Job 40.09
Thou didst with thy a. redeem thy   Ps 77.15
and his holy a. have gotten him   98.01
so my own a. brought me victory, and   Is 63.05
to whom has the a. of the Lord   Jn 12.38
with uplifted a. he led them out   Ac 13.17
underneath are the everlasting a.   Deu 33.27
to walk, I took them up in my a.;   Hos 11.03
and taking him in his a., he said   Mk 9.36
them in his a. and blessed them,   10.16

ARMOR
darkness and put on the a. of light;   Rom 13.12
Put on the whole a. of God.   Eph 6.11

AROUSE* —D
to a. you by way of reminder,   2Pe 1.13
This city has a. my anger and wrath,   Jer 32.31
Then all the city was a.,   Ac 21.30

ARRAY (n)
Worship the Lord in holy a.;   1Ch 16.29
of the earth set themselves in a.,   Ac 4.26

ARRAYED
glory was not a. like one of these   Mt 6.29
and a. him in a purple robe;   Jn 19.02

ARREST —ED
in order to a. Jesus by stealth   Mt 26.04
So they sought to a. him;   Jn 7.30
he proceeded to a. Peter also.   Ac 12.03
he heard that John had been a.,   Mt 4.12
but no one a. him, because his hour   Jn 8.20
they a. the apostles and put them   Ac 5.18

ARROGANCE
Pride and a. and the way of evil   Pro 8.13
me and your a. has come to my ears,   Is 37.29
As it is, you boast in your a.   Jas 4.16

ARROGANT
Some are a., as though I were not   1Co 4.18
it is not a. or rude.   13.05
he must not be a. or quick-tempered   Tit 1.07

ASCEND —ED —ING
Who shall a. the hill of the Lord?   Ps 24.03
If I a. to heaven, thou art there!   139.08
heart, "Who will a. into heaven?"   Rom 10.06
Who has a. to heaven and come down?   Pro 30.04
No one has a. into heaven but he   Jn 3.13
"When he a. on high he led a host   Eph 4.08
of God were a. and descending on   Gen 28.12
angels of God a. and descending   Jn 1.51

ASHAMED
were both naked, and were not a.   Gen 2.25
"Fear not, for you will not be a.;   Is 54.04
For whoever is a. of me and of my   Mk 8.38
For I am not a. of the gospel: it is   Rom 1.16
I do not write this to make you a.,   1Co 4.14
to do with him, that he may be a.   2Th 3.14
But I am not a., for I know whom I   2Ti 1.12
a workman who has no need to be a.,   2.15
as a Christian, let him not be a.,   1Pe 4.16

ASHES
the Lord, I who am but dust and a.   Gen 18.27
Your maxims are proverbs of a.,   Job 13.12
give them a garland instead of a.,   Is 61.03
long ago in sackcloth and a.   Mt 11.21

ASIDE
have not turned a. to uncleanness,   Num 5.19
and you turn a. and serve other   Deu 11.16
to turn a. the needy from justice   Is 10.02
he took the twelve disciples a.,   Mt 20.17
laid a. his garments, and girded   Jn 13.04
All have turned a.,   Rom 3.12
put something a. and store it up,   1Co 16.02
this he set a., nailing it to the   Col 2.14
let us also lay a. every weight,   Heb 12.01

ASKS
For every one who a. receives,   Mt 7.08
an embassy and a. terms of peace.   Lk 14.32

ASLEEP

Your shepherds are a., O king	Nah 3.18
the waves; but he was a.	Mt 8.24
who had fallen a. were raised,	27.52
said to Peter, "Simon, are you a.?	Mk 14.37
"Our friend Lazarus has fallen a.,	Jn 11.11
alive, though some have fallen a.	1Co 15.06
concerning those who are a.,	1Th 4.13

ASS

And the a. saw the angel of the	Num 22.23
plow with an ox and an a. together.	Deu 22.10
said, "With the jawbone of an a.,	Ju 15.16
immediately you will find an a. tied,	Mt 21.02
having an a. or an ox that has	Lk 14.05
a dumb a. spoke with human voice	2Pe 2.16

ASSEMBLIES —Y

take no delight in your solemn a.	Amo 5.21
when the whole a. of the congregation	Ex 12.06
David said to all the a. of Israel,	1Ch 13.02
And all the a. said "Amen" and	Neh 5.13
Sanctify a fast, call a solemn a.	Joe 1.14
the a. of the elders of the people	Lk 22.66
and the a. was divided.	Ac 23.07
and to the a. of the first-born who	Heb 12.23

ASSIGNED

when he a. to the sea its limit, so	Pro 8.29
of faith which God has a. him.	Rom 12.03
believed, as the Lord a. to each.	1Co 3.05
life which the Lord has a. to him,	7.17

ASSOCIATE (v)

therefore do not a. with one who	Pro 20.19
be haughty, but a. with the lowly;	Rom 12.16

ASSURANCE

he has given a. to all men by	Ac 17.31
the full a. of hope until the end,	Heb 6.11
Now faith is the a. of things hoped	11.01

ASTONISHED

As many were a. at him—his appearance	Is 52.14
the crowds were a. at his teaching,	Mt 7.28
I am a. that you are so quickly	Gal 1.06

ASTRAY

They have all gone a., they are	Ps 14.03
I have gone a. like a lost sheep;	119.176
and your knowledge led you a.,	Is 47.10
All we like sheep have gone a.;	53.06
their shepherds have led them a.,	Jer 50.06
going a. from me after their idols	Eze 44.10
sheep, and one of them has gone a.,	Mt 18.12
"Take heed that no one leads you a.	24.04
"No, he is leading the people a."	Jn 7.12
you were led a. to dumb idols,	1Co 12.02
'They always go a. in their hearts;	Heb 3.10

ASUNDER

"Let us burst their bonds a.,	Ps 2.03
joined together, let no man put a."	Mt 19.06

ATONE* —D*

upon you, for which you cannot a.;	Is 47.11
and to a. for iniquity, to bring in	Dan 9.24
faithfulness iniquity is a. for,	Pro 16.06

ATONEMENT

a bull as a sin offering for a.	Ex 29.36
Aaron shall make a. upon its horns	30.10
in to make a. in the holy place,	Lev 16.27
to make a. for the house of Israel.	Eze 45.17

ATTAIN —ED

it is high, I cannot a. it.	Ps 139.06
until we all a. to the unity of the	Eph 4.13
possible I may a. the resurrection	Php 3.11
us hold true to what we have a.	3.16

ATTEND

a. to my cry! Give ear	Ps 17.01
Till I come, a. to the public	1Ti 4.13

ATTENTIVE

Let thy ears be a. to the voice of	Ps 130.02
My son, be a. to my words; incline	Pro 4.20

AUTHOR*

and killed the A. of life, whom God	Ac 3.15

AUTHORITIES —Y

synagogues and the rulers and the a.,	Lk 12.11
and the city a. were disturbed	Ac 17.08
be subject to the governing a.	Rom 13.01
dominions or principalities or a.—	Col 1.16
for he taught them as one who had a.,	Mt 7.29
For I am a man under a.,	8.09
Son of man has a. on earth to	9.06
"All a. in heaven and on earth has	28.18
and has given him a. to execute	Jn 5.27
"I can do nothing on my own a.;	5.30
"let the men of a. among you go	Ac 25.05
For there is no a. except from God,	Rom 13.01
Do I say this on human a.?	1Co 9.08
our God and the a. of his Christ	Rev 12.10

AVENGE —D

he said, "May the LORD see and a.!"	2Ch 24.22
Beloved, never a. yourselves, but	Rom 12.19
oppressed man and a. him by striking	Ac 7.24

AVENGER

the Lord is an a. in all these	1Th 4.06

AVOID

not only to a. God's wrath but also	Rom 13.05
A. the godless chatter and	1Ti 6.20
power of it. A. such people.	2Ti 3.05

AWAKE

A., my soul! A., O harp and lyre!	Ps 57.08
When I a., I am still with thee.	139.18
I slept, but my heart was a.	Sol 5.02
A., a., put on strength, O arm of	Is 51.09
a., as in days of old, the generations	51.09

AWAKE (cont.)

him who says to a wooden thing, A.;	Hab 2.19
the master finds a. when he comes;	Lk 12.37
but let us keep a. and be sober.	1Th 5.06
Blessed is he who is a., keeping	Rev 16.15

AWE —SOME*

and stand in a. of him, all you sons	Ps 22.23

faces, and were filled with a.	Mt 17.06
not become proud, but stand in a.	Rom 11.20
worship, with reverence and a.;	Heb 12.28
and said, "How a. is this place!	Gen 28.17

AXE

Shall the a. vaunt itself over him	Is 10.15
Even now the a. is laid to the root	Mt 3.10

B

BABE —S

the b. leaped in her womb;	Lk 1.41
you will find a b. wrapped in	2.12
by the mouth of b. and infants,	Ps 8.02
and b. shall rule over them.	Is 3.04
understanding and revealed them to b.;	Mt 11.25
men of the flesh, as b. in Christ.	1Co 3.01
be b. in evil, but in thinking be	14.20

BAD

a good for a b., or a b. for a good;	Lev 27.10
"It is b., it is b.," says the buyer;	Pro 20.14
and the b. figs very b., so b. that	Jer 24.03
but the b. tree bears evil fruit.	Mt 7.17
make the tree b., and its fruit b.;	12.33
into vessels but threw away the b.	13.48
whom they found, both b. and good;	22.10
"B. company ruins good morals."	1Co 15.33
will go on from b. to worse,	2Ti 3.13

BAG

would be sealed up in a b.,	Job 14.17
no b. for your journey, nor two	Mt 10.10

BAKER —S*

whose b. ceases to stir the fire,	Hos 7.04
to be perfumers and cooks and b.	1Sa 8.13

BALANCE —S

A just b. and scales are the LORD's;	Pro 16.11
You shall have just b.,	Lev 19.36
weighed in the b. and found	Dan 5.27

BALD —NESS

or make himself b. for them.	Jer 16.06
Make yourselves b. and cut off your	Mic 1.16
On every head is b., every beard	Is 15.02
B. has come upon Gaza, Ashkelon has	Jer 47.05

BALM

Is there no b. in Gilead?	Jer 8.22

BAND —S

a b. of ruthless men seek my life,	Ps 86.14
A b. of drunkards, they give themselves	Hos 4.18
procuring a b. of soldiers and some	Jn 18.03
with the b. of love, and I became to	Hos 11.04

BANK

down the steep b. into the sea,	Mt 8.32
you not put my money into the b.,	Lk 19.23

BANNER

the name of it, The LORD is my b.,	Ex 17.15
and his b. over me was love.	Sol 2.04

BAPTISM

and Sadducees coming for b.,	Mt 3.07
The b. of John, whence was it?	21.25
preaching a b. of repentance for	Mk 1.04
with the b. with which I am	10.38
therefore with him by b. into death,	Rom 6.04
one Lord, one faith, one b.,	Eph 4.05
and you were buried with him in b.,	Col 2.12
B., which corresponds to this, now	1Pe 3.21

BAPTIZE —D —S* —ING

"I b. you with water for repentance,	Mt 3.11
(although Jesus himself did not b.,	Jn 4.02
not send me to b. but to preach	1Co 1.17
And when Jesus was b.,	Mt 3.16
I have a baptism to be b. with;	Lk 12.50
you shall be b. with the Holy	Ac 1.05
Rise and be b., and wash away your	22.16
Or were you b. in the name of Paul?	1Co 1.13
we were all b. into one body—	12.13
of you as were b. into Christ have	Gal 3.27
this is he who b. with the Holy Spirit.'	Jn 1.33
b. them in the name of the Father	Mt 28.19
was making and b. more disciples	Jn 4.01

BARE

foundations of the world were laid b.,	2Sa 22.16
Lift up your eyes to the b. heights,	Jer 3.02
but a b. kernel, perhaps of wheat or	1Co 15.37
open and laid b. to the eyes of	Heb 4.13

BARLEY

a land of wheat and b., of vines	Deu 8.08
who has five b. loaves and two	Jn 6.09
three quarts of b. for a denarius;	Rev 6.06

BARN —S

but gather the wheat into my b.' "	Mt 13.30
sow nor reap nor gather into b.,	6.26

BARRACKS

him to be brought into the b.	Ac 21.34
and entered the b. and told Paul.	23.16

BARREN

Now Sarai was b.; she had no	Gen 11.30
For the company of the godless is b.,	Job 15.34
"Sing, O b. one, who did not bear;	Is 54.01

BARREN (cont.)

| they will say, 'Blessed are the b., | Lk 23.29 |
| that faith apart from works is b.? | Jas 2.20 |

BASKET —S

she saw the b. among the reeds and	Ex 2.05
One b. had very good figs, like	Jer 24.02
a b. of summer fruit.	Amo 8.01
the wall, lowering him in a b.	Ac 9.25
let down in a b. through a window	2Co 11.33
took up twelve b. full of the	Mt 14.20

BATHE —D —ING*

and b. himself in water, and he	Lev 14.08
he will b. his feet in the blood of	Ps 58.10
that you may b. your feet in blood,	68.23
"He who has b. does not need to	Jn 13.10
he saw from the roof a woman b.;	2Sa 11.02

BATTLE

for the b. is not yours but God's.	2Ch 20.15
He smells the b. from afar,	Job 39.25
gird me with strength for the b.;	Ps 18.39
and mighty, the LORD, mighty in b.!	24.08
nor the b. to the strong, nor bread	Ecc 9.11
The noise of b. is in the land, and	Jer 50.22
sound, who will get ready for b.?	1Co 14.08

BEAM —S

| a b. shall be pulled out of his | Ez 6.11 |
| who hast laid the b. of thy chambers | Ps 104.03 |

BEAR —ING —S (v)

"You shall not b. false witness	Ex 20.16
curses his God shall b. his sin.	Lev 24.15
the priests who b. the ark of the	Jos 3.08
root downward, and b. fruit upward;	2Ki 19.30
How long must I b. pain in my soul,	Ps 13.02
but a broken spirit who can b.?	Pro 18.14
woman shall conceive and b. a son,	Is 7.14
virgin shall conceive and b. a son,	Mt 1.23
B. fruit that befits repentance,	3.08
that does not b. good fruit is cut	3.10
A sound tree cannot b. evil fruit,	7.18
How long am I to b. with you?	17.17
hard to b., and lay them on men's	23.04
because you b. the name of Christ,	Mk 9.41
Whoever does not b. his own cross	Lk 14.27
to b. witness to the light, that all	Jn 1.07
If I b. witness to myself, my	5.31
that you b. much fruit, and so prove	15.08
so you must b. witness also at Rome."	Ac 23.11
strong ought to b. with the	Rom 15.01
B. one another's burdens, and so	Gal 6.02
offered once to b. the sins of	Heb 9.28
b. his own cross, to the place	Jn 19.17
Spirit himself b. witness with our	Rom 8.16
will be saved through b. children,	1Ti 2.15
Blessed be the Lord, who daily b. us	Ps 68.19
A man who b. false witness against	Pro 25.18
the tree b. its fruit, the fig tree	Joe 2.22
there is another who b. witness to me,	Jn 5.32
conscience also b. witness and	Rom 2.15
any one who b. the name of brother	1Co 5.11

| Love b. all things, believes all | 13.07 |
| of God and b. the very stamp of | Heb 1.03 |

BEAR (n)

who made the B. and Orion, the	Job 9.09
or a charging b. is a wicked ruler	Pro 28.15
The cow and the b. shall feed;	Is 11.07
fled from a lion, and a b. met him;	Amo 5.19

BEARD

or mar the edges of your b.	Lev 19.27
and shaved off half the b. of each,	2Sa 10.04
is shaved and every b. cut off;	Jer 48.37

BEAST —S

formed every b. of the field and	Gen 2.19
or an unclean b. or any unclean	Lev 7.21
the likeness of any b. that is on	Deu 4.17
For every b. of the forest is mine,	Ps 50.10
him on his own b. and brought him	Lk 10.34
For every kind of b. and bird,	Jas 3.07
reckon the number of the b.,	Rev 13.18
The b. that you saw was, and is not,	17.08
worshiped the b. or its image and	20.04
And God made the b. of the earth	Gen 1.25
But wild b. will lie down there, and	Is 13.21
And four great b. came up out of	Dan 7.03
Even the wild b. cry to thee	Joe 1.20
and he was with the wild b.,	Mk 1.13
I fought with b. at Ephesus?	1Co 15.32

BEAT —ING (v)

winds blew and b. upon that house,	Mt 7.25
and begins to b. his fellow servants,	24.49
And they took him and b. him,	Mk 12.03
but b. his breast, saying, 'God, be	Lk 18.13
they b. them and charged them not	Ac 5.40
and b. him in front of the tribunal.	18.17
I do not box as one b. the air;	1Co 9.26

BEAUTIFUL

that you are a woman b. to behold;	Gen 12.11
and the woman was very b.	2Sa 11.02
"Let b. young virgins be sought out	Est 2.02
you are b., my beloved, truly lovely.	Sol 1.16
the LORD shall be b. and glorious,	Is 4.02
How b. upon the mountains are the	52.07
tombs, which outwardly appear b.,	Mt 23.27
For she has done a b. thing to me.	26.10
which is called B. to ask alms of	Ac 3.02

BEAUTY

to behold the b. of the LORD, and to	Ps 27.04
strength and b. are in his sanctuary.	96.06
and b. is vain, but a woman who	Pro 31.30
and no b. that we should desire him.	Is 53.02
"But you trusted in your b.,	Eze 16.15
his b. shall be like the olive, and	Hos 14.06
one vessel for b. and another for	Rom 9.21
flower falls, and its b. perishes.	Jas 1.11

BECAME

| and man b. a living being. | Gen 2.07 |
| And the Word b. flesh and dwelt | Jn 1.14 |

BECAME (cont.)

To the Jews I b. as a Jew, in order	1Co 9.20
the law I b. as one under	9.20
first man Adam b. a living being";	15.45

BED —S

'My b. will comfort me, my couch	Job 7.13
night I flood my b. with tears;	Ps 6.06
If I make my b. in Sheol, thou art	139.08
For the b. is too short to stretch	Is 28.20
"Rise, take up your b. and go home."	Mt 9.06
or under a b., and not on a stand?	Mk 4.21
down with his b. through the tiles	Lk 5.19
and my children are with me in b.;	11.07
there will be two men in one b.;	17.34
let the marriage b. be undefiled;	Heb 13.04
rest in their b. who walk in their	Is 57.02
Woe to those who lie upon b. of ivory,	Amo 6.04
and work evil upon their b.!	Mic 2.01

BEFALL

Does not calamity b. the unrighteous,	Job 31.03
no evil shall b. you, no scourge	Ps 91.10
befalls the fool will b. me also;	Ecc 2.15
Does evil b. a city, unless the LORD	Amo 3.06

BEFIT* —S

Bear fruits that b. repentance,	Lk 3.08
Praise b. the upright.	Ps 33.01
her in the Lord as b. the saints,	Rom 16.02
you, teach what b. sound doctrine.	Tit 2.01

BEFOREHAND

Lo, I have told you b.	Mt 24.25
anointed my body b. for burying.	Mk 14.08
Spirit spoke b. by the mouth of	Ac 1.16
which he has prepared b. for glory,	Rom 9.23

BEG —S

May his children wander about and b.;	Ps 109.10
And they began to b. Jesus to	Mk 5.17
b. you to lead a life worthy of the	Eph 4.01
Give to him who b. from you,	Mt 5.42

BEGAN

that time men b. to call upon the	Gen 4.26
When men b. to multiply on the face	6.01
From that time Jesus b. to preach,	Mt. 4.17
he b. to be sorrowful and troubled	26.37
Jesus, when he b. his ministry, was	Lk 3.23
Never since the world b. has it	Jn 9.32
that he who b. a good work in you	Php1.06

BEGGAR*

a blind b., the son of Timaeus, was	Mk 10.46
who had seen him before as a b.,	Jn 9.08

BEGIN

For behold, I b. to work evil at the	Jer 25.29
for judgment to b. with the	1Pe 4.17

BEGINNING (n)

In the b. God created the heavens	Gen 1.01
is only the b. of what they will	11.06
days of Job more than his b.;	Job 42.12
of the LORD is the b. of wisdom;	Ps 111.10
The b. of wisdom is this: Get wisdom,	Pro 4.07
Better is the end of a thing than its b.;	Ecc 7.08
it not been told you from the b.?	Is 40.21
Who declared it from the b.,	41.26
The b. of the gospel of Jesus	Mk 1.01
In the b. was the Word, and the Word	Jn 1.01
That which was from the b.,	1Jn 1.01
and the Omega, the b. and the end.	Rev 21.06

BEGOTTEN

are my son, today I have b. you.	Ps 2.07

BEHALF

yet something to say on God's b.	Job 36.02
We beseech you on b. of Christ,	2Co 5.20
has gone as a forerunner on our b.,	Heb 6.20

BEHAVE —D —ING

one ought to b. in the household	1Ti 3.15
that we have b. in the world,	2Co 1.12
and b. like ordinary men?	1Co 3.03

BEHEADED

and had John b. in the prison,	Mt 14.10
who had been b. for their testimony	Rev 20.04

BEHELD

Then I b., and, lo, a form that had	Eze 8.02
we have b. his glory, glory as of	Jn 1.14

BEHIND

But Lot's wife b. him looked back,	Gen 19.26
and you cast my words b. you.	Ps 50.17
Thou dost beset me b. and before,	139.05
hast cast all my sins b. thy back.	Is 38.17
said to Peter, "Get b. me, Satan!	Mt 16.23
boy Jesus stayed b. in Jerusalem.	Lk 2.43
what lies b. and straining forward	Php 3.13

BEHOLD

and b., it was very good.	Gen 1.31
I b. him, but not nigh: a star shall	Num 24.17
Come, b. the works of the LORD, how	Ps 46.08
"B., we are going up to Jerusalem;	Mt 20.18
B., your king is coming to you,	21.05
"B., the Lamb of God, who takes away	Jn 1.29
to his mother, "Woman, b. your son!"	19.26
"B., I make all things new."	Rev 21.05

BEING —S (n)

and man became a living b.	Gen 2.07
praise to my God while I have b.	Ps 104.33
in bondage to b. that by nature	Gal 4.08

BELIEVE —S

"that they may b. that the LORD, the	Ex 4.05
b. them not, though they speak fair	Jer 12.06
"Do you b. that I am able to do	Mt 9.28
the cross, and we will b. in him.	27.42
repent, and b. in the gospel."	Mk 1.15
the child cried out and said, "I b.;	9.24
"If I tell you, you will not b.;	Lk 22.67

BELIEVE —S (cont.)

that all might b. through him.	Jn 1.07
b. in God, b. also in me.	14.01
my hand in his side, I will not b."	20.25
"B. in the Lord Jesus, and you will	Ac 16.31
So we know and b. the love God has	1Jn 4.16
he who b. in me, though he die, yet	Jn 11.25
"He who b. in me, b. not in me	12.44
b. all things, hopes all things,	1Co 13.07
Every one who b. that Jesus is the	1Jn 5.01

BELIEVER —S

Or what has a b. in common with an	2Co 6.15
a sign not for b. but for unbelievers,	1Co 14.22
of God, which is at work in you b.	1Th 2.13

BELLY

upon your b. you shall go, and dust	Gen 3.14
was in the b. of the fish three	Jon 1.17
out of the b. of Sheol I cried, and	2.02
nights in the b. of the whale,	Mt 12.40
destruction, their god is the b.,	Php 3.19

BELONG —S

LORD your God b. heaven and the	Deu 10.14
for to thee b. all the nations!	Ps 82.08
The plans of the mind b. to man,	Pro 16.01
because you do not b. to my sheep.	Jn 10.26
God to whom I b. and whom I	Ac 27.23
"I b. to Paul," or "I b. to Apollos,"	1Co 1.12
I do not b. to the body," that would	12.15
better things that b. to salvation.	Heb 6.09
Deliverance b. to the LORD;	Ps 3.08
for to such b. the kingdom of	Mt 19.14
the one hope that b. to your call,	Eph 4.04
but the substance b. to Christ.	Col 2.17

BELOVED

My b. is mine and I am his, he	Sol 2.16
Let me sing for my b. a love song	Is 5.01
"This is my b. Son, with whom I am	Mt 3.17
"This is my b. Son, with whom I am	17.05
To all God's b. in Rome, who are	Rom 1.07
Luke the b. physician and Demas	Col 4.14
B., we are God's children now;	1Jn 3.02

BELOW

The shades b. tremble, the waters	Job 26.05
of the earth b. can be explored,	Jer 31.37
"You are from b., I am from above;	Jn 8.23

BENEATH

above, or that is in the earth b.,	Ex 20.04
with which he toils b. the sun?	Ecc 2.22
return and dwell b. my shadow,	Hos 14.07

BENEFIT —S (n)

I say this for your own b.,	1Co 7.35
I want some b. from you in the Lord.	Phm 20
soul, and forget not all his b.,	Ps 103.02

BEREFT

my soul is b. of peace, I have	Lam 3.17
in mind and b. of the truth,	1Ti 6.05

BESEECH

Save us, we b. thee, O LORD!	Ps 118.25
We b. you on behalf of Christ, be	2Co 5.20
Brethren, I b. you, become as I am,	Gal 4.12

BESET

They b. me with words of hate, and	Ps 109.03
Thou dost b. me behind and before,	139.05

BESIDE —S

He leads me b. still waters;	Ps 23.02
was standing b. a wall built with	Amo 7.07
for they said, "He is b. himself."	Mk 3.21
Again he began to teach b. the sea.	4.01
there is no other b. him.	Deu 4.35
and b. me there is no savior.	Hos 13.04

BESOUGHT

But Moses b. the LORD his God, and	Ex 32.11
and b. him that they might only	Mt 14.36
Three times I b. the Lord about	2Co 12.08

BEST

feasts and the b. seats in the	Mt 23.06
servants, 'Bring quickly the b. robe,	Lk 15.22

BESTOW —ED —S

and majesty thou dost b. upon him.	Ps 21.05
understand the gifts b. on us by God.	1Co 2.12
exalted him and b. on him the name	Php 2.09
Lord of all and b. his riches upon	Rom 10.12

BETRAY —ED

he sought an opportunity to b. him.	Mt 26.16
would you b. the Son of man with a	Lk 22.48
For he knew who was to b. him;	Jn 13.11
man by whom the Son of man is b.!	Mt 26.24
whom you have now b. and murdered,	Ac 7.52
night when he was b. took bread,	1Co 11.23

BETRAYER

but one who utters lies is a b.	Pro 14.25
see, my b. is at hand."	Mt 26.46

BETTER

to obey is b. than sacrifice, and to	1Sa 15.22
for I am no b. than my fathers."	1Ki 19.04
thy steadfast love is b. than life,	Ps 63.03
thy courts is b. than a thousand	84.10
Two can be b., because they	Ecc 4.09
it is b. that you lose one of your	Mt 5.29
Are we Jews any b. off?	Rom 3.09
For it is b. to marry than to be	1Co 7.09
be with Christ, for that is far b.	Php 1.23
count others b. than yourselves.	2.03
a b. hope is introduced, through	Heb 7.19

BEWARE

"B. of practicing your piety before	Mt 6.01
b. lest you be carried away with	2Pe 3.17

BID —DEN

b. my brother divide the inheritance	Lk 12.13
I now b. you take heart; for there	Ac 27.22

BID —DEN (cont.)

given to me I b. every one among   Rom 12.03
I say as the Father has b. me."   Jn 12.50

BIND —S

B. them upon your heart always;   Pro 6.21
B. up the testimony, seal the   Is 8.16
has sent me to b. up the brokenhearted,   61.01
'B. him hand and foot, and cast him   Mt 22.13
unless he first b. the strong man?   12.29
which b. everything together in   Col 3.14

BIRD —S

every winged b. according to its   Gen 1.21
"Flee like a b. to the mountains;   Ps 11.01
In them the b. build their nests;   104.17
Look at the b. of the air: they   Mt 6.26
and b. of the air have nests;   8.20

BIRTH —RIGHT

you forgot the God who gave you b.   Deu 32.18
mouth and cursed the day of his b.   Job 3.01
the untimely b. that never sees   Ps 58.08
day of death, than the day of b.   Ecc 7.01
Now the b. of Jesus Christ took   Mt 1.18
And she gave b. to her first-born   Lk 2.07
powerful, not many were of noble b.;   1Co 1.26
Jacob said, "First sell me your b."   Gen 25.31
who sold his b. for a single meal.   Heb 12.16

BITTER —LY

who aim b. words like arrows,   Ps 64.03
who put b. for sweet and sweet for b.!   Is 5.20
Almighty has dealt very b. with me.   Ru 1.20
And he went out and wept b.   Mt 26.75

BITTERNESS

He has filled me with b., he has   Lam 3.15
Let all b. and wrath and anger and   Eph 4.31
that no "root of b." spring up and   Heb 12.15

BLACK

cannot make one hair white or b.   Mt 5.36
a b. horse, and its rider had a   Rev 6.05

BLAMELESS —LY*

b. in his generation;   Gen 6.09
You shall be b. before the LORD   Deu 18.13
and that man was b. and upright,   Job 1.01
Blessed are those whose way is b.,   Ps 119.01
and ordinances of the Lord b.   Lk 1.06
should be holy and b. before him.   Eph 1.04
to righteousness under the law b.   Php 3.06
if any man is b., the husband of   Tit 1.06
He who walks b., and does what is   Ps 15.02

BLASPHEME —D —S —ING

Is it not they who b. that honorable   Jas 2.07
name of God is b. among the   Rom 2.24
but whoever b. against the Holy   Mk 3.29
said to themselves, "This man is b."   Mt 9.03
b. his name and his dwelling, that   Rev 13.06

BLEMISH

Your lamb shall be without b.,   Ex 12.05
youths without b., handsome and   Dan 1.04
she might be holy and without b.   Eph 5.27
offered himself without b. to God,   Heb 9.14

BLESS —ED (v)

and I will b. you, and make your   Gen 12.02
The LORD b. you and keep you: Num 6.24
"Stand up and b. the LORD your God   Neh 9.05
I will b. the LORD at all times;   Ps 34.01
B. the LORD, O my soul; and all   103.01
Come, b. the LORD, all you servants   134.01
b. those who curse you, pray for   Lk 6.28
When reviled, we b.; when   1Co 4.12
if you b. with the spirit, how can   14.16
And God b. them, saying, "Be fruitful   Gen 1.22
So God b. the seventh day and   2.03
B. is the man who walks not in the   Ps 1.01
"B. are the poor in spirit, for   Mt 5.03
And b. is he who takes no offense   Mt 11.06
O b. of my Father, inherit the   25.34
'It is more b. to give than to   Ac 20.35
awaiting our b. hope, the appearing   Tit 2.13
B. are the dead who die in the Lord   Rev 14.13

BLESSING —S (n)

our God turned the curse into a b.   Neh 13.02
The b. of the LORD makes rich, and   Pro 10.22
in the fulness of the b. of Christ.   Rom 15.29
The cup of b. which we bless, is it   1Co 10.16
B. and glory and wisdom and   Rev 7.12
to share in their spiritual b.,   Rom 15.27

BLIND

the LORD opens the eyes of the b.   Ps 146.08
Then the eyes of the b. shall be   Is 35.05
the b. receive their sight and the   Mt 11.05
Let them alone; they are b. guides.   15.14
"Woe to you, b. guides, who say, 'If   23.16
that though I was b., now I see."   Jn 9.25

BLOOD

your brother's b. is crying to me   Gen 4.10
that was in the Nile turned to b.   Ex 7.20
And Moses took the b. and threw it   24.08
Only you shall not eat the b.:   Deu 12.16
do not delight in the b. of bulls,   Is 1.11
Their land shall be soaked with b.,   34.07
who build Zion with b. and Jerusalem   Mic 3.10
because of the b. of my covenant   Zec 9.11
For flesh and b. has not revealed   Mt 16.17
for this is my b. of the covenant,   26.28
called the Field of B. to this day.   27.08
"I am innocent of this man's b.;   27.24
had a flow of b. for twelve years,   Mk 5.25
Galileans whose b. Pilate had   Lk 13.01
great drops of b. falling down   22.44
of the Son of man and drink his b.,   Jn 6.53
we are now justified by his b.,   Rom 5.09
cup is the new covenant in my b.   1Co 11.25
did not confer with flesh and b.,   Gal 1.16
much more shall the b. of Christ,   Heb 9.14
and for sprinkling with his b.:   1Pe 1.02

BLOOD (cont.)
and the b. of Jesus his Son cleanses   1Jn 1.07
them white in the b. of the Lamb.   Rev 7.14

BLOODGUILT —INESS*
LORD will leave his b. upon him,   Hos 12.14
Deliver me from b., O God,   Ps 51.14

BLOODSHED
looked for justice, but behold, b.;   Is 5.07
who keeps back his sword from b.   Jer 48.10

BLOSSOM (v)
the desert shall rejoice and b.;   Is 35.01
he shall b. as the lily, he shall   Hos 14.05

BLOT —S (v)
"I will b. out man whom I have   Gen 6.07
abundant mercy b. out my   Ps 51.01
and I will not b. his name out of   Rev 3.05
I am He who b. out your transgressions   Is 43.25

BLOW —S (v)
God made a wind b. over the earth,   Gen 8.01
b. the trumpet among the nations;   Jer 51.27
B. the trumpet in Zion; sound the   Joe 2.01
the breath of the LORD b. upon it;   Is 40.07
The wind b. where it wills, and you   Jn 3.08

BOAST (v)
"Let him who boasts, b. of the Lord."   1Co 1.31
of works, lest any man should b.   Eph 2.09
do not b. and be false to the truth.   Jas 3.14

BOAST —ING (n)
My soul makes its b. in the LORD;   Ps 34.02
their hope and of Egypt their b.   Is 20.05
this b. of mine shall not be   2Co 11.10
Then what becomes of our b.? It is   Rom 3.27

BOAT
in the b. with Zebedee their father,   Mt 4.21
so that the b. was being swamped by   8.24
he got into a b. and sat there;   13.02

BODIES —Y
their b. are sound and sleek.   Ps 73.04
although your b. are dead because   Rom 8.10
to present your b. as a living   12.01
know that your b. are members of   1Co 6.15
celestial b. and there are terrestrial b.;   15.40
that your whole b. be thrown into   Mt 5.29
"The eye is the lamp of the b.   6.22
you shall drink, nor about your b.,   6.25
who kill the b. but cannot kill   10.28
came and took the b. and buried it;   14.12
Wherever the b. is, there the eagles   24.28
"Take, eat; this is my b."   26.26
And Joseph took the b.,   27.59
went in they did not find the b.   Lk 24.03
deliver me from this b. of death?   Rom 7.24
are one b. in Christ, and individually   12.05
So glorify God in your b.   1Co 6.20
"This is my b. which is for you.   11.24

we were all baptized into one b.—   12.13
Now you are the b. of Christ and   12.27
with what kind of b. do they come?"   15.35
always carrying in the b. the death   2Co 4.10
There is one b. and one Spirit, just   Eph 4.04
He is the head of the b., the church;   Col 1.18
For as the b. apart from the spirit   Jas 2.26

BODILY
descended upon him in b. form,   Lk 3.22
but his b. presence is weak, and his   2Co 10.10
whole fulness of deity dwells b.,   Col 2.09

BOLD —LY —NESS
A wicked man puts on a b. face,   Pro 21.29
have such a hope, we are very b.,   2Co 3.12
are much more b. to speak the word   Php 1.14
And Paul and Barnabas spoke out b.,   Ac 13.46
they saw the b. of Peter and John,   4.13
in whom we have b. and confidence   Eph 3.12

BOND —S
of the Spirit in the b. of peace.   Eph 4.03
having canceled the b. which stood   Col 2.14
to loose the b. of wickedness, to   Is 58.06
bring them in b. to Jerusalem to   Ac 22.05

BONDAGE
of Israel groaned under their b.,   Ex 2.23
from Egypt, out of the house of b.,   13.03
God has not forsaken us in our b.,   Ez 9.09
free from its b. to decay and   Rom 8.21
you were in b. to beings that by   Gal 4.08

BONES
and all my b. are out of joint;   Ps 22.14
said to me, "Prophesy to these b.,   Eze 37.04
not flesh and b. as you see that I   Lk 24.39

BOOK —S
Then he took the b. of the covenant,   Ex 24.07
written in the B. of the Chronicles   1Ki 14.19
in the b. of Moses, where the LORD   2Ch 25.04
found the b. of the law of the   34.14
And Ezra opened the b. in the sight   Neh 8.05
Write in a b. all the words that I   Jer 30.02
is inscribed in the b. of truth: Dan 10.21
The b. of the genealogy of Jesus   Mt 1.01
to him the b. of the prophet   Lk 4.17
which are not written in this b.;   Jn 20.30
In the first b., O Theophilus, I   Ac 1.01
whose names are in the b. of life.   Php 4.03
who keep the words of this b.   Rev 22.09
Of making many b. there is no end,   Ecc 12.12

BOOTHS
is the feast of b. to the LORD.   Lev 23.34
wish, I will make three b. here,   Mt 17.04

BORN
"Let the day perish wherein I was b.,   Job 3.03
but man is b. to trouble as the   5.07
and a brother is b. for adversity.   Pro 17.17
a time to be b., and a time to die;   Ecc 3.02

BORN (cont.)

For to us a child is b., to us a	Is 9.06
before you were b. I consecrated	Jer 1.05
Cursed be the day on which I was b.!	20.14
of Mary, of whom Jesus was b.,	Mt 1.16
Now when Jesus was b. in Bethlehem	2.01
who were b., not of blood nor of	Jn 1.13
unless one is b. anew, he cannot see	3.03
For this I was b., and for this	18.37
Last of all, as to one untimely b.,	1Co 15.08
b. of woman, b. under the law,	Gal 4.04
being b. in the likeness of men.	Php 2.07
we have been b. anew to a living	1Pe 1.03
he who loves is b. of God and	1Jn 4.07

BORNE

to us who have b. the burden of	Mt 20.12
seen and have b. witness that this	Jn 1.34
and for the witness they had b.;	Rev 6.09

BOSOM

arms, he will carry them in his b.,	Is 40.11
by the angels to Abraham's b.	Lk 16.22
who is in the b. of the Father, he	Jn 1.18

BOTTOMLESS

the key of the shaft of the b. pit;	Rev 9.01

BOUGHT

"And I b. the field at Anathoth	Jer 32.09
and sold all that he had and b. it.	Mt 13.46
all who sold and b. in the temple,	21.12
you were b. with a price. So glorify	1Co 6.20

BOUND

and b. Isaac his son, and laid him	Gen 22.09
seized John and b. him and put him	Mt 14.03
on earth shall be b. in heaven,	16.19
and they b. him and led him away	27.02
b. in the Spirit, not knowing what	Ac 20.22
woman is b. by law to her husband	Rom 7.02
that he is b. to keep the whole	Gal 5.03

BOUNDS

hast fixed all the b. of the earth;	Ps 74.17
They know no b. in deeds of wickedness;	Jer 5.28

BOW —ED (v)

Mordecai did not b. down or do	Est 3.02
all the proud of the earth b. down;	Ps 22.29
you shall not b. down to a foreign	81.09
O come, let us worship and b. down,	95.06
B. thy heavens, O LORD, and come down!	144.05
name of Jesus every knee should b.,	Php 2.10
and he b. his head and gave up his	Jn 19.30

BOW (n)

I set my b. in the cloud, and it	Gen 9.13
For not in my b. do I trust, nor can	Ps 44.06

BOX (n)

had the money b. he used to take	Jn 12.06
because Judas had the money b.,	13.29

BOY —S

And the b. Samuel grew in the	1Sa 2.21
and the b. was cured instantly.	Mt 17.18
the b. Jesus stayed behind in	Lk 2.43
be full of b. and girls playing in	Zec 8.05

BRANCH

raise up for David a righteous B.,	Jer 23.05
Every b. of mine that bears no	Jn 15.02

BREACH —ES

one commits a b. of faith and sins	Lev 5.15
be called the repairer of the b.,	Is 58.12
And you shall go out through the b.,	Amo 4.03

BREAD

you shall eat b. till you return	Gen 3.19
Seven days you shall eat unleavened b.;	Ex 12.15
I will rain b. from heaven for you;	16.04
who ate of my b., has lifted his	Ps 41.09
Can he also give b., or provide meat	78.20
Man ate of the b. of the angels;	78.25
eating the b. of anxious toil;	127.02
Cast your b. upon the waters, for	Ecc 11.01
give you the b. of adversity and	Is 30.20
to the sower and b. to the eater,	55.10
No one shall break b. for the	Jer 16.07
As they ate b. together there at	41.01
and eat b. there, and prophesy there;	Amo 7.12
stones to become loaves of b."	Mt 4.03
'Man shall not live by b. alone,	4.04
Give us this day our daily b.;	6.11
of you, if his son asks him for b.,	7.09
God and ate the b. of the Presence,	12.04
they had forgotten to bring any b.	16.05
Jesus took b., and blessed, and	26.26
no b., no bag, no money in their	Mk 6.08
come eating no b. and drinking no	Lk 7.33
'He gave them b. from heaven to eat.'"	Jn 6.31
Jesus said to them, "I am the b. of life;	6.35
the breaking of b. and the prayers.	Ac 2.42
the unleavened b. of sincerity and	1Co 5.08
The b. which we break, is it not a	10.16
when he was betrayed took b.,	11.23
eat any one's b. without paying,	2Th 3.08

BREADTH

what is the b. and length and	Eph 3.18

BREAK —ING —S (v)

commandments, but b. my covenant,	Lev 26.15
you shall b. down their altars.'	Ju 2.02
and b. me in pieces with words?	Job 19.02
You shall b. them with a rod of	Ps 2.09
b. forth into joyous song and sing	98.04
a time to b. down, and a time to	Ecc 3.03
they b. forth into singing.	Is 14.07
go free, and to b. every yoke?	58.06
kingdoms, to pluck up and to b. down,	Jer 1.10
So will I b. this people and this	19.11
Can he b. the covenant and yet	Eze 17.16
and where thieves b. in and steal,	Mt 6.19
dead, they did not b. his legs.	Jn 19.33
but if you b. the law, your circumcision	Rom 2.25

BREAK —ING —S (v) (cont.)
and as their nets were b., Lk 5.06
as one b. a potter's vessel, so that Jer 19.11

BREAKING (n)
to the b. of bread and the prayers. Ac 2.42
do you dishonor God by b. the law? Rom 2.23

BREAST —PLATE
but beat his b., saying, 'God, be Lk 18.13
was lying close to the b. of Jesus; Jn 13.23
He put on righteousness as a b., Is 59.17
put on the b. of righteousness, Eph 6.14
and put on the b. of faith and 1Th 5.08

BREATH
into his nostrils the b. of life; Gen 2.07
"Remember that my life is a b.; Job 7.07
surely every man is a mere b.! Ps 39.11
Man is like a b., his days are like 144.04
the b. of the LORD, like a stream of Is 30.33
and the b. came into them, and they Eze 37.10
all men life and b. and everything. Ac 17.25

BRETHREN
And if you salute only your b., Mt 5.47
one teacher, and you are all b. 23.08
to one of the least of these my b., 25.40
apostles, "B., what shall we do?" Ac 2.37
"B. and fathers, hear me. The God 7.02
be the first-born among many b. Rom 8.29
made like his b. in every respect, Heb 2.17
to lay down our lives for the b. 1Jn 3.16

BRIBE
who acquit the guilty for a b., Is 5.23
who take a b., and turn aside the Amo 5.12

BRICKS
let us make b., and burn them Gen 11.03
yet they say to us, 'Make b.!' Ex 5.16

BRIDE —S
Come with me from Lebanon, my b.; Sol 4.08
bridegroom rejoices over the b., Is 62.05
He who has the b. is the bridegroom; Jn 3.29
you as a pure b. to her one 2Co 11.02
The Spirit and the B. say, "Come." Rev 22.17
and your b. commit adultery. Hos 4.13

BRIDEGROOM
as long as the b. is with them? Mt 9.15
lamps and went to meet the b. 25.01

BRIDLE* (v)
I will b. my mouth, so long as the Ps 39.01
and does not b. his tongue but Jas 1.26
able to b. the whole body also. 3.02

BRIGHT
thee, the night is b. as the day; Ps 139.12
a b. cloud overshadowed them, and a Mt 17.05
of David, the b. morning star." Rev 22.16

BRIMSTONE
and Gomorrah b. and fire from the Gen 19.24

Sodom fire and b. rained from Lk 17.29
lake of fire that burns with b. Rev 19.20

BROAD
of that land to a good and b. land, Ex 3.08
phylacteries b. and their fringes Mt 23.05

BROKE —N
and b. and gave the loaves to the Mt 14.19
given thanks he b. them and gave 15.36
and b. it, and gave it to the 26.26
and she b. the jar and poured it Mk 14.03
the stream b. against that house, Lk 6.48
he not only b. the sabbath but Jn 5.18
he b. it, and said, "This is my body 1Co 11.24
his people; he has b. my covenant." Gen 17.14
"We have b. faith with our God and Ez 10.02
My spirit is b., my days are Job 17.01
My heart is b. within me, all my Jer 23.09
some of the branches were b. off, Rom 11.17
and has b. down the dividing wall Eph 2.14
when earthen pots are b. in pieces, Rev 2.27

BRONZE
Instead of b. I will bring gold, and Is 60.17
its belly and thighs of b., Dan 2.32
of cups and pots and vessels of b.) Mk 7.04
his feet were like burnished b., Rev 1.15

BROOD
he said to them, "You b. of vipers! Mt 3.07
hen gathers her b. under her wings, 23.37

BROTHER —S
and a b. is born for adversity. Pro 17.17
first be reconciled to your b., Mt 5.24
"If your b. sins against you, go and 18.15
Whoever does the will of God is my b., Mk 3.35
the b. for whom Christ died. 1Co 8.11
and wrong his b. in this matter, 1Th 4.06
as an enemy, but warn him as a b. 2Th 3.15
If a b. or sister is ill-clad and Jas 2.15
loves God should love his b. also 1Jn 4.21
it is when b. dwell in unity! Ps 133.01
All a poor man's b. hate him; Pro 19.07
mother and his b. stood outside, Mt 12.46
said, "Here are my mother and my b.! 12.49
For even his b. did not believe in Jn 7.05
with the Twin B. as figurehead. Ac 28.11
a father; treat younger men like b., 1Ti 5.01

BUILD —ING —S (v)
let us b. ourselves a city, and a Gen 11.04
"B. yourself a house in Jerusalem, 1Ki 2.36
Solomon desired to b. in Jerusalem, 9.19
but we alone will b. to the LORD, Ez 4.03
Come, let us b. the wall of Jerusalem, Neh 2.17
those who b. it labor in vain. Ps 127.01
Foreigners shall b. up your walls, Is 60.10
They shall not b. and another 65.22
B. houses and live in them; Jer 29.05
on this rock I will b. my church, Mt 16.18
and to b. it in three days.' " 26.61
down my barns, and b. larger ones; Lk 12.18
desiring to b. a tower, does not 14.28

BUILD —ING —S (v) (cont.)

is able to b. you up and to give	Ac 20.32
lest I b. on another man's foundation,	Rom 15.20
one another and b. one another up,	1Th 5.11
he is like a man b. a house,	Lk 6.48
to excel in b. up the church.	1Co 14.12
for b. up the body of Christ,	Eph 4.12
Unless the LORD b. the house,	Ps 127.01
Wisdom b. her house, but folly with	Pro 14.01
man take care how he b. upon it.	1Co 3.10
"Knowledge" puffs up, but love b. up.	8.01

BUILDER —S

skilled master b. I laid a foundation,	1Co 3.10
whose b. and maker is God.	Heb 11.10
And when the b. laid the foundation	Ez 3.10
The stone which the b. rejected has	Ps 118.22
stone which the b. rejected has	Mt 21.42

BUILDING —S (n)

you are God's field, God's b.	1Co 3.09
we have a b. from God, a house not	2Co 5.01
out to him the b. of the temple.	Mt 24.01

BUILT

So he b. there an altar to the LORD,	Gen. 12.07
And Moses b. an altar and called	Ex 17.15
you have b. houses of hewn stone,	Amo 5.11
my house shall be b. in it,	Zec 1.16
and he b. us our synagogue."	Lk 7.05
they sold, they planted, they b.,	17.28
you also are b. into it for a	Eph 2.22
rooted and b. up in him and established	Col 2.07
(For every house is b. by some one,	Heb 3.04

BURDEN —S (n)

Cast your b. on the LORD, and he	Ps 55.22
And in that day his b. will depart	Is 10.27
you, 'What is the b. of the LORD?'	Jer 23.33
yoke is easy, and my b. is light."	Mt 11.30
They bind heavy b., hard to	23.04
Bear one another's b., and so	Gal 6.02

BURIED —Y

came and took the body and b. it;	Mt 14.12
David that he both died and was b.,	Ac 2.29
We were b. therefore with him by	Rom 6.04
that he was b., that he was raised	1Co 15.04
and you were b. with him in baptism,	Col 2.12
the dead to b. their own dead."	Mt 8.22
potter's field, to b. strangers in.	27.07

BURN —ED —ING

from me, and my bones b. with heat.	Job 30.30
thy jealous wrath b. like fire?	Ps 79.05

you who b. with lust among the oaks,	Is 57.05
b. incense to Baal, and go after	Jer 7.09
chaff he will b. with unquenchable	Mt 3.12
not our hearts b. within us while	Lk 24.32
If any man's work is b. up,	1Co 3.15
and if I deliver my body to be b.,	13.03
the bush was b., yet it was not	Ex 3.02
loins be girded and your lamps b.,	Lk 12.35
you will heap b. coals upon his	Rom 12.20

BURNING (n)

as a brand plucked out of the b.;	Amo 4.11

BURNT (adj)

and offered b. offerings on the	Gen 8.20
Your b. offerings are not acceptable,	Jer 6.20
of God, rather than b. offerings.	Hos 6.06
than all whole b. offerings and	Mk 12.33
in b. offerings and sin offerings	Heb 10.06

BURST

new wineskins, it is ready to b.	Job 32.19
the skins b., and the wine is	Mt 9.17
headlong he b. open in the middle	Ac 1.18

BUSH

to him out of the b., "Moses, Moses!"	Ex 3.04
Moses, in the passage about the b.,	Mk 12.26
Sinai, in a flame of fire in a b.	Ac 7.30

BUSHEL*

light a lamp and put it under a b.	Mt 5.15
brought in to be put under a b.,	Mk 4.21
puts it in a cellar or under a b.,	Lk 11.33

BUSINESS

is an unhappy b. that God has	Ecc 1.13
to his farm, another to his b.,	Mt 22.05
and the money-changers at their b.	Jn 2.14
no little b. to the craftsmen.	Ac 19.24

BUY

to Egypt to Joseph to b. grain,	Gen 41.57
"B. what we need for the feast"; or,	Jn 13.29
and those who b. as though they had	1Co 7.30
counsel you to b. from me gold	Rev 3.18
so that no one can b. or sell	13.17

BYSTANDERS

saw him, and she said to the b.,	Mt 26.71
And some of the b. hearing it said,	27.47

BYWORD

and a b., among all the peoples	Deu 28.37
Thou has made us a b. among the	Ps 44.14

C

CALAMITIES —Y

in afflictions, hardships, c.,	2Co 6.04
hardships, persecutions, and c.;	12.10
and all my c. laid in the balances!	Job 6.02
Does not c. befall the unrighteous,	31.03

They came upon me in the day of my c.;	Ps 18.18
I also will laugh at your c.;	Pro 1.26

CALF

graving tool, and made a molten c.;	Ex 32.04

CALF (cont.)

They made a c. in Horeb and	Ps 106.19
and bring the fatted c. and kill it,	Lk 15.23
And they made a c. in those days,	Ac 7.41

CALL —ED —S (v)

I c. you by your name, I surname you,	Is 45.04
c. upon him while he is near;	55.06
Before they c. I will answer, while	65.24
and you shall c. his name Jesus, for	Mt 1.21
For I came not to c. the righteous,	9.13
"Why do you c. me 'Lord, Lord,' and	Lk 6.46
But how are men to c. upon him in	Rom 10.14
God c. the light Day, and the	Gen 1.05
The man c. his wife's name Eve,	3.20
c. to be an apostle, set apart for	Rom 1.01
who are c. according to his purpose.	8.28
For God has c. us to peace.	1Co 7.15
is the hope to which he has c. you,	Eph 1.18
who saved us and c. us with a holy	2Ti 1.09
For to this you have been c.,	1Pe 2.21
and he c. his own sheep by name and	Jn 10.03
be that whoever c. on the name of	Ac 2.21
He who c. you is faithful, and he	1Th 5.24

CALL —ING (n)

his angels with a loud trumpet c.,	Mt 24.31
of works but because of his c.,	Rom 9.11
gifts and the c. of God are	11.29
For consider your c., brethren;	1Co 1.26
one hope that belongs to your c.,	Eph 4.04
of the upward c. of God in Christ	Php 3.14
command, with the archangel's c.,	1Th 4.16
God may make you worthy of his c.,	2Th 1.11
brethren, who share in a heavenly c.,	Heb 3.01
to confirm your c. and election,	2Pe 1.10
Here is a c. for the endurance and	Rev 13.10
us and called us with a holy c.,	2Ti 1.09

CAMEL —S

is easier for a c. to go through	Mt 19.24
out a gnat and swallowing a c.!	23.24
'Drink, and I will water your c.'—	Gen 24.14

CAMP

stench of your c. go up into your	Amo 4.10
us go forth to him outside the c.,	Heb 13.13

CANOPY

his c. thick clouds dark with water.	Ps 18.11
will spread his royal c. over them.	Jer 43.10

CAPTAIN —S

and their c. and the officers of	Jn 18.12
priests and the c. of the temple	Ac 4.01
attention to the c. and to the	27.11
priests and c. how he might betray	Lk 22.04
the flesh of c., the flesh of	Rev 19.18

CAPTIVE —S

carried the people c. to Assyria.	2Ki 15.29
Babylon brought c. to Babylon all	24.16
treacherous are taken c. by their lust.	Pro 11.06
O c. Jerusalem; loose the	Is 52.02

the LORD's flock has been taken c.	Jer 13.17
and be led c. among all nations;	Lk 21.24
law, dead to that which held us c.,	Rom 7.06
and making me c. to the law of sin	7.23
every thought c. to obey Christ,	2Co 10.05
on high he led a host of c.,	Eph 4.08

CAPTIVITY

for they shall go into c.	Deu 28.41
to c. those who are doomed to c.,	Jer 43.11
they shall go into exile, into c.'	Eze 12.11
they go into c. before their	Amo 9.04
to be taken captive, to c. he goes;	Rev 13.10

CAPTURED

for the ark of God has been c."	1Sa 4.22
David also c. all the flocks and	30.20
Then they c. the king, and brought	Jer 52.09
And the beast was c., and with	Rev 19.20

CARE —S (v)

of man that thou dost c. for him?	Ps 8.04
the shepherds who c. for my people:	Jer 23.02
God truthfully, and c. for no man;	Mt 22.16
on him, for he c. about you.	1Pe 5.07

CARE —S (n)

each man take c. how he builds	1Co 3.10
Only take c. lest this liberty of	8.09
have the same c. for one another.	12.25
Take c., brethren, lest there be in	Heb 3.12
When the c. of my heart are many,	Ps 94.19
but the c. of the world and the	Mt 13.22
drunkenness and c. of this life,	Lk 21.34

CAREFUL —LY

Therefore be c. lest the light in	Lk 11.35
in God may be c. to apply themselves	Tit 3.08
Look c. then how you walk, not as	Eph 5.15

CARRIED —Y

our griefs and c. our sorrows;	Is 53.04
c. into exile to Babylon the rest	Jer 39.09
because they c. into exile a whole	Amo 1.06
Yet was c. away, she went into	Nah 3.10
to him a paralytic c. by four men.	Mk 2.03
died and was c. by the angels to	Lk 16.22
to and fro and c. about with every	Eph 4.14
waterless clouds, c. along by winds;	Jud 12
And he c. me away in the Spirit	Rev 17.03
shepherd, and c. them for ever.	Ps 28.09
"who c. out a plan, but not mine;	Is 30.01
sandals I am not worthy to c.;	Mt 3.11
man they compelled to c. his cross.	27.32
C. no purse, no bag, no sandals;	Lk 10.04
lawful for you to c. your pallet."	Jn 5.10
of mine to c. my name before the	Ac 9.15
their hearts to c. out his purpose	Rev 17.17

CARVED

He c. all the walls of the house	1Ki 6.29
and the nave were c. likenesses	Eze 41.17
c. in letters on stone, came with	2Co 3.07

CASE —S

Moses brought their c. before the	Num 27.05
I desire to argue my c. with God.	Job 13.03
I would lay my c. before him and	23.04
the governor their c. against Paul;	Ac 24.01
laid Paul's c. before the king,	25.14
In their c. the god of this world	2Co 4.04
you incompetent to try trivial c.?	1Co 6.02
so as to help c. of urgent need, and	Tit 3.14

CAST —ING —S

and I will c. lots for you here	Jos 18.08
C. me not away from thy presence,	Ps 51.11
C. your burden on the LORD, and he	55.22
C. your bread upon the waters, for	Ecc 11.01
and c. out demons in your name,	Mt 7.22
Spirit of God that I c. out demons,	12.28
'Be taken up and c. into the sea,'	21.21
'Be taken up and c. into the sea,'	Mk 11.23
"I came to c. fire upon the earth;	Lk 12.49
And they c. him out of the vineyard	20.15
who comes to me I will not c. out.	Jn 6.37
Let us then c. off the works of	Rom 13.12
C. all your anxieties on him, for he	1Pe 5.07
but c. them into hell and committed	2Pe 2.04
and c. them to the earth. And the	Rev 12.04
c. a net into the sea; for they	Mt 4.18
his garments among them by c. lots;	27.35
c. up the foam of their own shame;	Jud 13
a workman c. it, and a goldsmith	Is 40.19
and if Satan c. out Satan, he is	Mt 12.26
love, but perfect love c. out fear.	1Jn 4.18

CATCH —ES (v)

slothful man will not c. his prey,	Pro 12.27
They set a trap; they c. men.	Jer 5.26
"He c. the wise in their craftiness,"	1Co 3.19

CATTLE

c. and creeping things and beasts	Gen 1.24
Now Abram was very rich in c.,	13.02
himself, and his sons, and his c.?"	Jn 4.12

CAUGHT

hid has their own foot been c.	Ps 9.15
woman who had been c. in adultery,	*Jn 8.03
but that night they c. nothing.	21.03
Spirit of the Lord c. up Philip;	Ac 8.39
years ago was c. up to the third	2Co 12.02
shall be c. up together with them	1Th 4.17

CAUSE —S (v)

what you eat c. the ruin of one	Rom 14.15
If your right eye c. you to sin,	Mt 5.29
but whoever c. one of these little	18.06

CAUSE (n)

to divorce one's wife for any c.?"	Mt 19.03
law, 'They hated me without a c.'	Jn 15.25
may have ample c. to glory in	Php 1.26
in it there is no c. for stumbling.	1Jn 2.10

CEASE —D —S

day and night, shall not c."	Gen 8.22

He makes wars c. to the end of the	Ps 46.09
they did not c. teaching and	Ac 5.42
as for tongues, they will c.;	1Co 13.08
I do not c. to give thanks for you,	Eph 1.16
and night they never c. to sing,	Rev 4.08
got into the boat, the wind c.	Mt 14.32
in the flesh has c. from sin,	1Pe 4.01
steadfast love of the LORD never c.,	Lam 3.22
God's rest also c. from his labors	Heb 4.10

CEDAR

"See now, I dwell in a house of c.,	2Sa 7.02
from the c. that is in Lebanon to	1Ki 4.33
for the c. has fallen, for the	Zec 11.02

CENSUS

"When you take the c. of the people	Ex 30.12
the days of the c. and drew away	Ac 5.37

CENTURION

a c. came forward to him, beseeching	Mt 8.05
When the c. and those who were with	27.54
a c. of what was known as the Italian	Ac 10.01
prisoners to a c. of the Augustan	27.01

CEREAL OFFERING —S

offer with it a c. o. and its libation,	Ex 29.41
Because c. o. and drink offering are	Joe 1.13
offer me your burnt offerings and c. o.,	Amo 5.22

CHAFF

and like c. that the storm carries	Job 21.18
but are like c. which the wind	Ps 1.04
but the c. he will burn with	Mt 3.12

CHAIN —S

that I am bound with this c."	Ac 28.20
the bottomless pit and a great c.	Rev 20.01
"Can you bind the c. of the Pleiades,	Job 38.31
gold, and casts for it silver c.	Is 40.19
he has put heavy c. on me;	Lam 3.07
such as I am—except for these c."	Ac 26.29
for which I am an ambassador in c.;	Eph 6.20

CHAMBER —S

he entered his c. and wept there.	Gen 43.30
men lying in wait in an inner c.	Ju 16.09
like a bridegroom leaving his c.,	Ps 19.05
house, into the secretary's c.;	Jer 36.12
in the upper c. where we were	Ac 20.08
going down to the c. of death.	Pro 7.27
enter your c., and shut your doors	Is 26.20

CHANCE (n)

but time and c. happen to them all.	Ecc 9.11
Now by c. a priest was going down	Lk 10.31

CHANGE —D —S (v)

Can the Ethiopian c. his skin or	Jer 13.23
"For I the LORD do not c.; therefore	Mal 3.06
and will c. the customs which Moses	Ac 6.14
with you now and to c. my tone,	Gal 4.20
who will c. our lowly body to be	Php 3.21
all sleep, but we shall all be c.,	1Co 15.51

CHANGE —D —S (v) (cont.)

are being c. into his likeness from	2Co 3.18
He c. times and seasons;	Dan 2.21

CHARGE —D (v)

did not sin or c. God with wrong.	Job 1.22
Like warriors they c., like soldiers	Joe 2.07
I c. you in the presence of God and	2Ti 4.01
anything, c. that to my account.	Phm 18
And Jesus sternly c. them, "See that	Mt 9.30
with them he c. them not to depart	Ac 1.04
"We strictly c. you not to teach in	5.28
but c. with nothing deserving death	23.29

CHARGE —S (n)

Who gave him c. over the earth and	Job 34.13
give his angels c. of you to guard	Ps 91.11
no answer, not even to a single c.;	Mt 27.14
this c. I have received from my	Jn 10.18
to know the c. on which they	Ac 23.28
Who shall bring any c. against God's	Rom 8.33
I may make the gospel free of c.,	1Co 9.18
whereas the aim of our c. is love	1Ti 1.05
This c. I commit to you, Timothy, my	1.18
tend the flock of God that is your c.,	1Pe 5.02
See how many c. they bring against	Mk 15.04
not to indicate the c. against him."	Ac 25.27

CHARIOT —S

'Why is his c. so long in coming?	Ju 5.28
David hamstrung all the c. horses,	2Sa 8.04
to Philip, "Go up and join this c."	Ac 8.29
who trust in c. because they are	Is 31.01
his c. like the whirlwind;	Jer 4.13
trusted in your c. and in the	Hos 10.13
overthrow the c. and their riders;	Hag 2.22
noise of many c. with horses	Rev 9.09

CHASTEN —ED

Blessed is the man whom thou dost c.,	Ps 94.12
Your wickedness will c. you, and your	Jer 2.19
Those whom I love, I reprove and c.;	Rev 3.19
stricken and c. every morning.	Ps 73.14
we are c. so that we may not be	1Co 11.32

CHASTENING (n)

despise not the c. of the Almighty.	Job 5.17

CHASTISE —D —S*

I will therefore c. him and release	Lk 23.16
My father c. you with whips, but I	1Ki 12.11
and c. every son whom he receives."	Heb 12.06

CHASTISEMENT

it, but folly is the c. of fools.	Pro 16.22
him was the c. that made us whole,	Is 53.05

CHEEK

let him give his c. to the smiter,	Lam 3.30
one strikes you on the right c.,	Mt 5.39

CHEERFUL —NESS*

A glad heart makes a c. countenance,	Pro 15.13
compulsion, for God loves a c. giver.	2Co 9.07
he who does acts of mercy, with c.	Rom 12.08

CHERUB —IM

And a c. stretched forth his hand	Eze 10.07
garden of Eden he placed the c.,	Gen 3.24
He sits enthroned upon the c.;	Ps 99.01
who art enthroned above the c.,	Is 37.16
above it were the c. of glory	Heb 9.05

CHIEF

assembling all the c. priests and	Mt 2.04
the elders and c. priests and	16.21
Iscariot, went to the c. priests	26.14
he was a c. tax collector, and rich.	Lk 19.02
And when the c. Shepherd is manifested	1Pe 5.04

CHILD —REN

"Shall a c. be born to a man who is	Gen 17.17
like a c. quieted at its mother's	Ps 131.02
Train up a c. in the way he should	Pro 22.06
Do not withhold discipline from a c.;	23.13
For to us a c. is born, to us a son	Is 9.06
and a little c. shall lead them.	11.06
When Israel was a c., I loved	Hos 11.01
and search diligently for the c.,	Mt 2.08
to death, and the father his c.,	10.21
And calling to him a c., he put	18.02
this c. is set for the fall and	Lk 2.34
And the c. grew and became strong,	2.40
When I was a c., I spoke like a c.,	1Co 13.11
in pain you shall bring forth c.,	Gen 3.16
upon the c. and the children's c.,	Ex 34.07
Moses set before the c. of Israel;	Deu 4.44
upon the c. to the third and	5.09
"When your c. ask their fathers in	Jos 4.21
The c. of men take refuge in the	Ps 36.07
As a father pities his c., so the	103.13
May you see your children's c.!	128.06
like the glory of the c. of Israel,	Is 17.03
stones to raise up c. to Abraham.	Mt 3.09
how to give good gifts to your c.,	7.11
It is like c. sitting in the market	11.16
"Let the c. come to me, and do not	19.14
and having no c. left his wife to	22.25
Yet wisdom is justified by all her c."	Lk 7.35
Little c., yet a little while I am	Jn 13.33
our spirit that we are c. of God,	Rom 8.16
and not all are c. of Abraham	9.07
do not be c. in your thinking;	1Co 14.20
C., obey your parents in the Lord,	Eph 6.01
Beloved, we are God's c. now;	1Jn 3.02

CHOOSE

your God will c. out of all your	Deu 12.05
c. this day whom you will serve,	Jos 24.15
C. a man for yourselves, and let him	1Sa 17.08
Let us c. what is right; let us	Job 34.04
to refuse the evil and c. the good.	Is 7.15
"Is not this the fast that I c.:	58.06
"Did I not c. you, the twelve, and	Jn 6.70
You did not c. me, but I chose you	15.16
to c. men from among them and send	Ac 15.22
Yet which I shall c. I cannot tell.	Php 1.22

CHOSE —N

but I c. you out of the world,	Jn 15.19

CHOSE —N (cont.)

and they c. Stephen, a man full of	Ac 6.05
but God c. what is foolish in the	1Co 1.27
even as he c. us in him before the	Eph 1.04
because God c. you from the beginning	2Th 2.13
your God has c. you to be a people	Deu 7.06
yourselves that you have c. the LORD,	Jos 24.22
where I have c. to put my name.	1Ki 11.36
The LORD is my c. portion and my	Ps 16.05
made a covenant with my c. one,	89.03
I have c. the way of faithfulness, I	119.30
Holy One of Israel, who has c. you."	Is 49.07
For many are called, but few are c."	Mt 22.14
Mary has c. the good portion, which	Lk 10.42
I know whom I have c.; it is that	Jn 13.18
for he is a c. instrument of mine	Ac 9.15
as God's c. ones, holy and beloved,	Col 3.12
a cornerstone c. and precious, and	1Pe 2.06
him are called and c. and faithful."	Rev 17.14

CHRIST

"You are the C., the Son of the	Mt 16.16
saying, "What do you think of the C.?	22.42
God has made him both Lord and C.,	Ac 2.36
For C. is the end of the law, that	Rom 10.04
C. the power of God and the wisdom	1Co 1.24
God was in C. reconciling the world	2Co 5.19
as C. loved us and gave himself up	Eph 5.02
knowledge of God's mystery, of C.,	Col 2.02
Jesus C. is the same yesterday and	Heb 13.08
are reproached for the name of C.,	1Pe 4.14
he who denies that Jesus is the C.?	1Jn 2.22
kingdom of our Lord and of his C.,	Rev 11.15

CHRISTIAN* —S*

time you think to make me a C.!"	Ac 26.28
yet if one suffers as a C.,	1Pe 4.16
were for the first time called C.	Ac 11.26

CHURCH —ES

on this rock I will build my c.,	Mt 16.18
But Saul laid waste the c.,	Ac 8.03
called to him the elders of the c.	20.17
teach them everywhere in every c.	1Co 4.17
to excel in building up the c.	14.12
head over all things for the c.,	Eph 1.22
be glory in the c. and in Christ	3.21
as Christ is the head of the c.,	5.23
He is the head of the body, the c.;	Col 1.18
which is the c. of the living God,	1Ti 3.15
me of my anxiety for all the c.	2Co 11.28
John to the seven c. that are in	Rev 1.04
what the Spirit says to the c.	2.07

CIRCUMCISE —D

C. therefore the foreskin of your	Deu 10.16
Every male among you shall be c.	Gen 17.10
when he was c., he was called Jesus,	Lk 2.21
c. and uncircumcised, barbarian,	Col 3.11

CIRCUMCISION

the c. party criticized him,	Ac 11.02
nor is true c. something external	Rom 2.28
He received c. as a sign or seal of	4.11

For neither c. counts for anything	1Co 7.19
For we are the true c., who worship	Php 3.03

CISTERN —S

Drink water from your own c.,	Pro 5.15
or the wheel broken at the c.,	Ecc 12.06
had put Jeremiah into the c.—	Jer 38.07
and hewed out c. for themselves,	2.13

CITIES —Y

"Until c. lie waste without inhabitant,	Is 6.11
say to the c. of Judah, "Behold your	40.09
and against all the c. of Judah.	Jer 1.15
as many as your c. are your gods,	2.28
Her c. have become a horror, a land	51.43
went about all the c. and villages,	Mt 9.35
to teach and preach in their c.	11.01
persecuted them even to foreign c.	Ac 26.11
"Come, let us build ourselves a c.,	Gen 11.04
up and rebuilds this c., Jericho.	Jos 6.26
of Israel, "Go every man to his c."	1Sa 8.22
there is a man of God in this c.,	9.06
of Zion, that is, the c. of David.	2Sa 5.07
streams make glad the c. of God,	Ps 46.04
the LORD watches over the c.,	127.01
shall be called the faithful c.,	Zec 8.03
and dwelt in a c. called Nazareth,	Mt 2.23
A c. set on a hill cannot be hid.	5.14
all the c. came out to meet Jesus;	8.34
all the c. was stirred, saying, "Who	21.10
and saw the c. he wept over it,	Lk 19.41
was crucified was near the c.;	Jn 19.20
So there was much joy in that c.	Ac 8.08
and they are disturbing our c.	16.20
for he has prepared for them a c.	Heb 11.16
and the name of the c. of my God,	Rev 3.12
And I saw the holy c., new	21.02

CLAY

that thou hast made me of c.;	Job 10.09
the potter be regarded as the c.;	Is 29.16
Does the c. say to him who fashions	45.09
we are the c., and thou art our	64.08
Jesus made c. and anointed my eyes	Jn 9.11
Has the potter no right over the c.,	Rom 9.21

CLEAN

every c. animal and of every c. bird,	Gen 8.20
the priest shall pronounce him c.	Lev 13.23
can he who is born of woman be c.?	Job 25.04
He who has c. hands and a pure	Ps 24.04
Create in me a c. heart, O God, and	51.10
that the outside also may be c.	Mt 23.26
(Thus he declared all foods c.)	Mk 7.19
behold, everything is c. for you.	Lk 11.41
already made c. by the word which	Jn 15.03
Everything is indeed c., but it is	Rom 14.20

CLEANSE —D

for you c. the outside of the cup	Mt 23.25
C. out the old leaven that you may	1Co 5.07
C. your hands, you sinners, and	Jas 4.08
our sins and c. us from all	1Jn 1.09
"What God has c., you must not call	Ac 10.15
that he was c. from his old sins.	2Pe 1.09

CLEAR

C. thou me from hidden faults.	Ps 19.12
and I will not c. the guilty,	Joe 3.21
and he will c. his threshing floor	Mt 3.12
what eagerness to c. yourselves,	2Co 7.11
This is a c. omen to them of their	Php 1.28
and keep your conscience c.,	1Pe 3.16

CLEAVE —S

Let my tongue c. to the roof of my	Ps 137.06
and his mother and c. to his wife,	Gen 2.24
Because he c. to me in love, I will	Ps 91.14

CLEFT —S (n)

hide it there in a c. of the rock."	Jer 13.04
the rocks and the c. of the cliffs,	Is 2.21

CLIMB —ED —S

though they c. up to heaven, from	Amo 9.02
on ahead and c. up into a sycamore	Lk 19.04
by the door but c. in by another	Jn 10.01

CLING* —S*

My soul c. to thee;	Ps 63.08
the waistcloth c. to the loins of	Jer 13.11
and sin which c. so closely, and let	Heb 12.01

CLOAK

coat, let him have your c. as well;	Mt 5.40
And they clothed him in a purple c.,	Mk 15.17
bring the c. that I left with	2Ti 4.13

CLOSE —D (v)

They c. their hearts to pity;	Ps 17.10
'Do not c. thine ear to my cry for	Lam 3.56
of his ribs and c. up its place	Gen 2.21
and their eyes they have c.,	Mt 13.15
And he c. the book, and gave it back	Lk 4.20

CLOSE (n)

the harvest is the c. of the age,	Mt 13.39
you always, to the c. of the age."	28.20

CLOTH —S

of unshrunk c. on an old garment,	Mt 9.16
left the linen c. and ran away	Mk 14.52
and his face wrapped with a c.	Jn 11.44
and wrapped him in swaddling c.,	Lk 2.07
it in linen c. with the spices, as	Jn 19.40

CLOTHE —D

oven, will he not much more c. you,	Mt 6.30
welcome thee, or naked and c. thee?	25.38
C. yourselves, all of you, with	1Pe 5.05
Thou art c. with honor and majesty,	Ps 104.01
but that we would be further c.,	2Co 5.04

CLOTHES —ING (n)

on your best c. and go down to the	Ru 3.03
a pit, and my own c. will abhor me.	Job 9.31
food, and the body more than c.?	Mt 6.25
you in sheep's c. but inwardly are	7.15
them, and for my c. they cast lots."	Jn 19.24
but if we have food and c., with these	1Ti 6.08

CLOUD —S

I set my bow in the c.,	Gen 9.13
in a pillar of c. to lead them	Ex 13.21
And Moses entered the c.,	24.18
a little c. like a man's hand is	1Ki 18.44
As the c. fades and vanishes, so he	Job 7.09
In the daytime he led them with a c.,	Ps 78.14
over her assemblies a c. by day,	Is 4.05
Your love is like a morning c.,	Hos 6.04
them, and a voice from the c. said,	Mt 17.05
"When you see a c. rising in the	Lk 12.54
man coming in a c. with power and	21.27
our fathers were all under the c.,	1Co 10.01
by so great a c. of witnesses.	Heb 12.01
sat upon the c. swung his sickle	Rev 14.16
C. and thick darkness are round	Ps 97.02
who makest the c. thy chariot,	104.03
coming on the c. of heaven with	Mt 24.30
them in the c. to meet the Lord in	1Th 4.17
Behold, he is coming with the c.,	Rev 1.07

CLUSTER

"As the wine is found in the c.,	Is 65.08

COAL —S

hand a burning c. which he had	Is 6.06
No c. for warming oneself is this,	47.14
Let burning c. fall upon them!	Ps 140.10
will heap burning c. upon his head."	Rom 12.20

COASTLANDS

let the many c. be glad!	Ps 97.01
Listen to me in silence, O c.;	Is 41.01

COAT —S

himself with cursing as his c.,	Ps 109.18
one would sue you and take your c.,	Mt 5.40
answered them, "He who has two c.,	Lk 3.11
and showing c. and garments which	Ac 9.39

COCK

before the c. crows, you will deny	Mt 26.34
And immediately the c. crowed.	26.74

COIN —S

And they brought him a c.	Mt 22.19
silver coins, if she loses one c.,	Lk 15.08
came, and put in two copper c.,	Mk 12.42
poured out the c. of the money-changers	Jn 2.15

COLD

even a cup of c. water because he	Mt 10.42
most men's love will grow c.	24.12
without food, in c. and exposure.	2Co 11.27
and neither c. nor hot, I will spew	Rev 3.16

COLLECTOR —S

Thomas and Matthew the tax c.;	Mt 10.03
a Pharisee and the other a tax c.	Lk 18.10
Do not even the tax c. do the same?	Mt 5.46
a friend of tax c. and sinners!'	11.19

COLT

an ass, on a c. the foal of an ass.	Zec 9.09
an ass tied, and a c. with her;	Mt 21.02

COMELY
c. as Jerusalem, terrible as an army — Sol 6.04

COMFORT —ED (v)
'My bed will c. me, my couch will — Job 7.13
How then will you c. me with empty — 21.34
thy rod and thy staff, they c. me. — Ps 23.04
C., c.. my people, says your God. — Is 40.01
For the LORD will c. Zion; he will — 51.03
rather turn to forgive and c. him, — 2Co 2.07
Therefore c. one another with these — 1Th 4.18
LORD, hast helped me and c. me. — Ps 86.17
For the LORD has c. his people. — Is 49.13
you shall be c. in Jerusalem. — 66.13
who mourn, for they shall be c. — Mt 5.04

COMFORT (n)
Lord and in the c. of the Holy — Ac 9.31
we share abundantly in c. too. — 2Co 1.05
gave us eternal c. and good hope — 2Th 2.16

COMMAND —ED (v)
You shall speak all that I c. you; — Ex 7.02
c. these stones to become loaves of — Mt 4.03
my friends if you do what I c. you. — Jn 15.14
This I c. you, to love one another. — 15.17
"Have you c. the morning since your — Job 38.12
he has c. his covenant for ever. — Ps 111.09
For he c. and they were created. — 148.05
Jesus c. them, "Tell no one the — Mt 17.09
to observe all that I have c. you; — 28.20
but I do as the Father has c. me, — Jn 14.31
For so the Lord has c. us, — Ac 13.47
the Lord c. that those who proclaim — 1Co 9.14
one another, just as he has c. us. — 1Jn 3.23

COMMAND (n)
The Lord gives the c.; great is — Ps 68.11
by the way of concession, not of c. — 1Co 7.06
I have no c. of the Lord, but I give — 7.25

COMMANDMENT —S
the c. of the LORD is pure, enlightening — Ps 19.08
but thy c. is exceedingly broad. — 119.96
My son, keep your father's c., — Pro 6.20
He who keeps the c. keeps his life; — 19.16
transgress the c. of God for the — Mt 15.03
This is the great and first c. — 22.38
they rested according to the c. — Lk 23.56
A new c. I give to you, that you — Jn 13.34
he had given c. through the Holy — Ac 1.02
sin, finding opportunity in the c., — Rom 7.08
you to keep the c. unstained and — 1Ti 6.14
those who love me and keep my c. — Ex 20.06
words of the covenant, the ten c. — 34.28
my delight in thy c., which I love. — Ps 119.47
Fear God, and keep his c.; for this — Ecc 12.13
O that you had hearkened to my c.! — Is 48.18
you would enter life, keep the c." — Mt 19.17
On these two c. depend all the law — 22.40
You know the c.: 'Do not kill, Do not — Mk 10.19
"If you love me, you will keep my c. — Jn 14.15
If you keep my c., you will abide — 15.10
The c., "You shall not commit — Rom 13.09

love of God, that we keep his c. — 1Jn 5.03
is love, that we follow his c.; — 2Jn 6

COMMEND —ED
And now I c. you to God and to the — Ac 20.32
Food will not c. us to God. — 1Co 8.08
Are we beginning to c. ourselves — 2Co 3.01
The master c. the dishonest steward — Lk 16.08

COMMISSION —ED (v)
and you shall c. him in their sight. — Num 27.19
with you in Christ, and has c. us; — 2Co 1.21
as c. by God, in the sight of God we — 2.17

COMMIT —S —TED
"You shall not c. adultery. — Ex 20.14
and to God would I c. my cause; — Job 5.08
Into thy hand I c. my spirit; — Ps 31.05
C. your way to the LORD; trust — 37.05
said, 'You shall not c. adultery,' — Mt 5.27
into thy hands I c. my spirit!" — Lk 23.46
This charge I c. to you, Timothy, my — 1Ti 1.18
you c. sin, and are convicted by the — Jas 2.09
every one who c. sin is a slave to — Jn 8.34
No one born of God c. sin; — 1Jn 3.09
for my people have c. two evils: — Jer 2.13
who had c. murder in the insurrection. — Mk 15.07
they c. them to the LORD in whom — Ac 14.23

COMMON
between the holy and the c., and — Lev 10.10
together and had all things in c.; — Ac 2.44
c. men, they wondered; and they — 4.13
has cleansed, you must not call c." — 10.15
write to you of our c. salvation, — Jud 3

COMPANION —S
his brother, and every man his c., — Ex 32.27
I am a c. of all who fear thee, of — Ps 119.63
My friends and c. stand aloof from — 38.11
who were Paul's c. in travel. — Ac 19.29

COMPANY
in the c. of the upright, in the — Ps 111.01
not sit in the c. of merrymakers, — Jer 15.17
of Herodias danced before the c., — Mt 14.06
to be in the c. they went a day's — Lk 2.44
Moreover, some women of our c. amazed — 24.22
Now the c. of those who believed — Ac 4.32
deceived: "Bad c. ruins good morals." — 1Co 15.33

COMPARE —D —ING*
toward us; none can c. with thee! — Ps 40.05
God, or what likeness c. with him? — Is 40.18
"But to what shall I c. this — Mt 11.16
heaven shall be c. to ten maidens — 25.01
are not worth c. with the glory — Rom 8.18

COMPASSION
Has he in anger shut up his c.?" — Ps 77.09
and his c. is over all that he has — 145.09
my c. grows warm and tender. — Hos 11.08
he had c. for them, because they — Mt 9.36
and he had c. on them, and healed — 14.14

COMPASSION (cont.)

"I have c. on the crowd, because | Mt 15.32
and I will have c. on whom I have c." | Rom 9.15
c., kindness, lowliness, meekness, and | Col 3.12

COMPASSIONATE

how the Lord is c. and merciful. | Jas 5.11

COMPEL —LED

and c. people to come in, that my | Lk 14.23
how can you c. the Gentiles to live | Gal 2.14
Young men are c. to grind at the | Lam 5.13
this man they c. to carry his cross. | Mt 27.32

COMPLAIN —ING*

Why should a living man c., | Lam 3.39
Not that I c. of want; for I have | Php 4.11
Who has c.? Who has wounds | Pro 23.29

COMPLAINT

"Today also my c. is bitter, his | Job 23.02
Hear my voice, O God, in my c.; | Ps 64.01
with him have a c. against any one, | Ac 19.38
if one has a c. against another, | Col 3.13

COMPLETE —ED (v)

"C. your work, your daily task, as | Ex 5.13
c. my joy by being of the same mind, | Php 2.02
in my flesh I c. what is lacking | Col 1.24
works, and faith was c. by works, | Jas 2.22

COMPLETE (adj)

that the man of God may be c., | 2Ti 3.17
this that our joy may be c. | 1Jn 1.04

CONCEAL —ED —S

he will c. me under the cover of | Ps 27.05
It is the glory of God to c. things, | Pro 25.02
and it was c. from them, that they | Lk 9.45
A prudent man c. his knowledge, but | Pro 12.23

CONCEIT —S*

any who are wise in their own c." | Job 37.24
Do nothing from selfishness or c., | Php 2.03
Lest you be wise in your own c., | Rom 11.25

CONCEIVE —D

and in sin did my mother c. me. | Ps 51.05
woman shall c. and bear a son, | Is 7.14
"Behold, a virgin shall c. and bear a son, | Mt 1.23
ear heard, nor the heart of man c., | 1Co 2.09
when it has c. gives birth to sin; | Jas 1.15

CONCERNED —ING

Is it for oxen that God is c.? | 1Co 9.09
the gospel c. his Son, who was | Rom 1.03

CONDEMN —ED —S

and they will c. him to death, | Mt 20.18
c. not, and you will not be condemned; | Lk 6.37
not to c. the world, but that the | Jn 3.17
who is to c.? Is it Christ | Rom 8.34
whenever our hearts c. us; | 1Jn 3.20
But he who has doubts is c., | Rom 14.23

lest you come together to be c. | 1Co 11.34
by this he c. the world and became | Heb 11.07
Your own mouth c. you, and not I; | Job 15.06

CONDITION —S

and though my c. was a trial to you, | Gal 4.14
containing the terms and c., | Jer 32.11

CONDUCT (n)

but wise c. is pleasure to a man of | Pro 10.23
to a base mind and to improper c. | Rom 1.28
give you in our c. an example to | 2Th 3.09
Maintain good c. among the Gentiles, | 1Pe 2.12

CONFER*

I did not c. with flesh and blood, | Gal 1.16

CONFESS —ING

he shall c. the sin he has committed, | Lev 5.05
any one should c. him to be Christ, | Jn 9.22
if you c. with your lips that Jesus | Rom 10.09
and every tongue c. that Jesus | Php 2.11
Therefore c. your sins to one | Jas 5.16
If we c. our sins, he is faithful | 1Jn 1.09
in the river Jordan, c. their sins. | Mt 3.06

CONFESSION

made the good c. in the presence | 1Ti 6.12

CONFIDENCE

Is not your fear of God your c., | Job 4.06
but the upright are in his c. | Pro 3.32
what do you rest this c. of yours? | Is 36.04
Such is the c. that we have through | 2Co 3.04
I have c. in the Lord that you will | Gal 5.10
boldness and c. of access through | Eph 3.12
Jesus, and put no c. in the flesh. | Php 3.03
Let us then with c. draw near to | Heb 4.16
since we have c. to enter the | 10.19
Through him you have c. in God, | 1Pe 1.21
condemn us, we have c. before God; | 1Jn 3.21

CONFINED

we were c. under the law, kept under | Gal 3.23

CONFIRM —S*

and will c. my covenant with you. | Lev 26.09
in order to c. the promises given | Rom 15.08
more zealous to c. you call and | 2Pe 1.10
who c. the word of his servant, and | Is 44.26

CONFOUND —ED

Then the moon will be c., | Is 24.23
also, because its hopes are c. | Zec 9.05
and c. the Jews who lived in | Ac 9.22

CONFUSED

there the LORD c. the language of | Gen 11.09

CONFUSION

stretch the line of c. over it, | Is 34.11
So the city was filled with the c.; | Ac 19.29
is not a God of c. but of peace. | 1Co 14.33

CONGREGATION
sinners in the c. of the righteous;	Ps 1.05
midst of the c. I will praise thee:	22.22
Remember thy c., which thou hast	74.02
who was in the c. in the wilderness	Ac 7.38
midst of the c. I will praise thee."	Heb 2.12

CONQUER —ED
he went our conquering and to c.	Rev 6.02
Lamb, and the Lamb will c. them,	17.14
who through faith c. kingdoms,	Heb 11.33
And they have c. him by the blood	Rev 12.11

CONSCIENCE
while their c. also bears witness	Rom 2.15
my c. bears me witness in the Holy	9.01
wrath but also for the sake of c.	13.05
and their c., being weak, is defiled.	1Co 8.07
to every man's c. in the sight of	2Co 4.02
and a good c. and sincere faith.	1Ti 1.05
purify your c. from dead works to	Heb 9.14
and keep your c. clear, so that, when	1Pe 3.16

CONSECRATE —D
"C. to me all the first-born;	Ex 13.02
Aaron also and his sons I will c.,	29.44
c. yourselves therefore, and be holy,	Lev 11.44
And for their sake I c. myself,	Jn 17.19
whom the Father c. and sent into	10.36
husband is c. through his wife, and	1Co 7.14
for then it is c. by the word of	1Ti 4.05
c. and useful to the master of the	2Ti 2.21

CONSENT —ING*
if sinners entice you, do not c.	Pro 1.10
witnesses and c. to the deeds of	Lk 11.48
And Saul was c. to his death.	Ac 8.01

CONSENT (n)
without your c. no man shall lift	Gen 41.44

CONSIDER —ED —S
C. and answer me, O LORD my God;	Ps 13.03
C. the work of God; who can	Ecc 7.13
C. the lilies of the field, how they	Mt 6.28
So you also must c. yourselves dead	Rom 6.11
For c. your call, brethren; not many	1Co 1.26
I do not c. that I have made it my	Php 3.13
c. Jesus, the apostle and high	Heb 3.01
C. him who endured from sinners	12.03
c. the outcome of their life, and	13.07
Then I c. all that my hands had	Ecc 2.11
rule well be c. worthy of double	1Ti 5.17
He c. abuse suffered for the Christ	Heb 11.26
No one c., nor is there knowledge	Is 44.19

CONSOLATION —S
him the cup of c. to drink for his	Jer 16.07
looking for the c. of Israel,	Lk 2.25
for you have received your c.	6.24
upbuilding and encouragement and c.	1Co 14.03
Are the c. of God too small for you,	Job 15.11

CONSPIRACY
"Do not call c. all that this	Is 8.12
more than forty who made this c.	Ac 23.13

CONSTANT*
in tribulation, be c. in prayer.	Rom 12.12

CONSULT
be a priest to c. Urim and Thummim.	Ez 2.63
and they will c. the idols and the	Is 19.03
Whom did he c. for his enlightenment,	40.14

CONSUME —D —ING
but the lips of a fool c. him.	Ecc 10.12
moth and rust c. and where thieves	Mt 6.19
"Zeal for thy house will c. me."	Jn 2.17
fire which will c. the adversaries.	Heb 10.27
For zeal for thy house has c. me,	Ps 69.09
My soul is c. with longing for thy	119.20
Egypt shall be c. by the sword and	Jer 44.27
women and were c. with passion for	Rom 1.27
that you are not c. by one another.	Gal 5.15
for our God is a c. fire.	Heb 12.29

CONTEMPT
he pours c. upon princes and makes	Ps 107.40
When wickedness comes, c. comes	Pro 18.03
treated him with c. and mocked him;	Lk 23.11
own account and hold him up to c.	Heb 6.06

CONTEND —ING
Why do you c. against him, saying,	Job 33.13
"Shall a faultfinder c. with the	40.02
to you to c. for the faith which	Jud 3
For we are not c. against flesh and	Eph 6.12

CONTENT
accusation, and be c. with your wages."	Lk 3.14
in whatever state I am, to be c.	Php 4.11
clothing, with these we shall be c.	1Ti 6.08
and be c. with what you have;	Heb 13.05

CONTINUAL —LY
A c. dripping on a rainy day and a	Pro 27.15
will wear me out by her c. coming.'"	Lk 18.05
of his heart was only evil c.	Gen 6.05
his praise shall c. be in my mouth.	Ps 34.01
May prayer be made for him c.,	72.15
And the LORD will guide you c.,	Is 58.11
justice, and wait c. for your God."	Hos 12.06
and were c. in the temple blessing	Lk 24.53
Through him then let us c. offer up	Heb 13.15

CONTINUE —D —S
"If you c. in my word, you are truly	Jn 8.31
exhorting them to c. in the faith,	Ac 14.22
Are we to c. in sin that grace may	Rom 6.01
And what I do I will c. to do,	2Co 11.12
C. steadfastly in prayer, being	Col 4.02
Let brotherly love c.	Heb 13.01
The flood c. forty days upon the	Gen 7.17
all night he c. in prayer to God.	Lk 6.12
Son of God he c. a priest for ever.	Heb 7.03

CONTRARY
to a disobedient and c. people."	Rom 10.21
to you a gospel c. to that which	Gal 1.08
whatever else is c. to sound	1Ti 1.10

CONTRIBUTE* —D —S*
C. to the needs of the saints,	Rom 12.13
For they all c. out of their	Mk 12.44
he who c., in liberality; he who gives	Rom 12.08

CONTRIBUTION —S
to make some c. for the poor among	Rom 15.26
Now concerning the c. for the saints:	1Co 16.01
generosity of your c. for them and	2Co 9.13
so that c. need not be made when I	1Co 16.02

CONTRITE*
a broken and c. heart, O God, thou	Ps 51.17
him who is of a c. and humble	Is 57.15
and to revive the heart of the c.	57.15
he that is humble and c. in spirit,	66.02

CONTROL —S* (v)
the younger men to c. themselves.	Tit 2.06
For the love of Christ c. us,	2Co 5.14

CONTROVERSIES —Y
all customs and c. of the Jews;	Ac 26.03
But avoid stupid c., genealogies,	Tit 3.09
craving for c. and for disputes	1Ti 6.04

CONVERSION*
reporting the c. of the Gentiles,	Ac 15.03

CONVERT* —S* (n)
was the first c. in Asia for	Rom 16.05
He must not be a recent c., or he	1Ti 3.06
Jews and devout c. to Judaism	Ac 13.43
were the first c. in Achaia,	1Co 16.15

CONVICTION*
the Holy Spirit and with full c.	1Th 1.05
hoped for, the c. of things not seen.	Heb 11.01

CONVINCE —D
he will c. the world of sin and of	Jn 16.08
and trying to c. them about Jesus	Ac 28.23
And some were c. by what he said,	28.24
fully c. that God was able to do	Rom 4.21
because we are c. that one has	2Co 5.14
C. of this, I know that I shall	Php 1.25

COPY (n)
They serve a c. and shadow of the	Heb 8.05

CORD —S
this scarlet c. in the window	Jos 2.18
before the silver c. is snapped,	Ecc 12.06
Pleiades, or loose the c. of Orion?	Job 38.31
lengthen your c. and strengthen	Is 54.02
I led them with c. of compassion,	Hos 11.04
And making a whip of c., he drove	Jn 2.15

CORNER —S
has become the head of the c.;	Mt 21.42
has become the head of the c.	Ac 4.11
for this was not done in a c.	26.26
has become the head of the c.,"	1Pe 2.07
synagogues and at the street c.,	Mt 6.05
at the four c. of the earth, holding	Rev 7.01

CORNERSTONE
Christ Jesus himself being the c.,	Eph 2.20

CORRECTION
for c., and for training in righteousness,	2Ti 3.16

CORRUPTION
Hades, nor let thy Holy One see c.	Ac 2.27
the dead, no more to return to c.,	13.34
flesh will from the flesh reap c.;	Gal 6.08

COST
first sit down and count the c.,	Lk 14.28
God's gospel without c. to you?	2Co 11.07

COSTLY
very c., and she broke the jar and	Mk 14.03
or gold or pearls or c. attire	1Ti 2.09

COUCH —ES (n)
I drench my c. with my weeping.	Ps 6.06
stretch themselves upon their c.,	Amo 6.04

COUCHES —ING* (v)
of the deep that c. beneath,	Gen 49.25
not do well, sin is c. at the door;	4.07

COUNCIL —S
brother shall be liable to the c.,	Mt 5.22
and the whole c. sought false	26.59
together the c. and all the senate	Ac 5.21
Pharisee in the c. named Gamaliel,	5.34
And Paul, looking intently at the c.,	23.01
found when I stood before the c.,	24.20
when he had conferred with his c.,	25.12
for they will deliver you up to c.,	Mt 10.17

COUNSEL —S (n)
The c. of the wicked is far from me.	Job 21.16
walks not in the c. of the wicked,	Ps 1.01
I bless the LORD who gives me c.;	16.07
"Give c., grant justice; make your	Is 16.03
counselors of Pharaoh give stupid c.	19.11
Has c. perished from the prudent?	Jer 49.07
went out and took c. against him,	Mt 12.14
the people took c. against Jesus	27.01
declaring to you the whole c. of God.	Ac 20.27
according to the c. of his will,	Eph 1.11
let them fall by their own c.;	Ps 5.10
hearts, to follow their own c.	81.12
the c. of the wicked are treacherous.	Pro 12.05

COUNSELOR
name will be called "Wonderful C.,	Is 9.06
or as his c. has instructed him?	40.13
among these there is no c. who,	41.28

COUNSELOR (cont.)

and he will give you another C.,   Jn 14.16
But when the C. comes, whom I shall   15.26
the Lord, or who has been his c.?"   Rom 11.34

COUNT —ED

I can c. all my bones—they stare   Ps 22.17
If I would c. them, they are more   139.18
not first sit down and c. the cost,   Lk 14.28
but in humility c. others better   Php 2.03
did not c. equality with God a   2.06
his promise as some c. slowness,   2Pe 3.09
that they were c. worthy to suffer   Ac 5.41
but sin is not c. where there is   Rom 5.13
Yet Jesus has been c. worthy of as   Heb 3.03

COUNTENANCE

The LORD lift up his c. upon you,   Num 6.26
A glad heart makes a cheerful c.,   Pro 15.13
At that saying his c. fell, and he   Mk 10.22

COUNTRY

as his c. improved he improved his   Hos 10.01
to their own c. by another way.   Mt 2.12
honor, except in his own c., and   Mk 6.04
and took his journey into a far c.,   Lk 15.13
But as it is, they desire a better c.,   Heb 11.16

COURAGE

Be strong, and let your heart take c.,   Ps 31.24
took c. and went to Pilate, and   Mk 15.43
"Take c., for as you have testified   Ac 23.11
So we are always of good c.; we know   2Co 5.06
we had c. in our God to declare to   1Th 2.02
nor lose c. when you are punished   Heb 12.05

COURSE

a strong man runs its c. with joy.   Ps 19.05
and the third day I finish my c.   Lk 13.32
And as John was finishing his c.,   Ac 13.25
accomplish my c. and the ministry   20.24

COURT —S

"You shall make the c. of the   Ex 27.09
Daniel remained at the king's c.   Dan 2.49
while you are going with him to c.,   Mt 5.25
he entered the c. of the high   Jn 18.15
a member of the c. of Herod the   Ac 13.01
judged by you or by any human c.   1Co 4.03
it not they who drag you into c.?   Jas 2.06
not measure the c. outside the   Rev 11.02
yea, faints for the c. of the LORD;   Ps 84.02
For a day in thy c. is better than   84.10
live in luxury are in king's c.   Lk 7.25

COURTYARD

as far as the c. of the high priest,   Mt 26.58
was sitting outside in the c.   26.69

COVENANT —S

But I will establish my c. with you;   Gen 6.18
the sign of the c. which I make   9.12
God remembered his c. with Abraham,   Ex 2.24
the ark of the c. of the LORD went   Num 10.33
God who keeps c. and steadfast   Deu 7.09

So Joshua made a c. with the people   Jos 24.25
shall make no c. with the inhabitants   Ju 2.02
Then Jonathan made a c. with David,   1Sa 18.03
the book of the c. which had been   2Ch 34.30
"I have made a c. with my eyes;   Job 31.01
He is mindful of his c. for ever,   Ps 105.08
will make a new c. with the house   Jer 31.31
an everlasting c. which will never   50.05
not remember the c. of brotherhood.   Amo 1.09
of the blood of my c. with you,   Zec 9.11
My c. with him was a c. of life and   Mal 2.05
for this is my blood of the c.,   Mt 26.28
"This cup is the new c. in my blood   1Co 11.25
us to be ministers of a new c.,   2Co 3.06
not annul a c. previously ratified   Gal 3.17
Jesus the surety of a better c.   Heb 7.22
Therefore he is the mediator of a new c.,   9.15
by the blood of the eternal c.,   13.20
with empty oaths they make c.;   Hos 10.04
allegory: these women are two c.   Gal 4.24
and strangers to the c. of promise,   Eph 2.12

COVER —ED —EST* —S (v)

If I say, "Let only darkness c. me,   Ps 139.11
darkness shall c. the earth, and thick   Is 60.02
and to c. his face, and to strike   Mk 14.65
For a man ought not to c. his head,   1Co 11.07
death and will c. a multitude of   Jas 5.20
for nothing is c. that will not be   Mt 10.26
field, which a man found and c. up;   13.44
forgiven, and whose sins are c.;   Rom 4.07
who c. thyself with light as with a   Ps 104.02
since love c. a multitude of sins.   1Pe 4.08

COVERING (n)

He made darkness his c. around him,   Ps 18.11
He spread a cloud for a c., and fire   105.39
and the c. too narrow to wrap   Is 28.20

COVET

"You shall not c. your neighbor's   Ex 20.17
shall you c. your neighbor's wife;   Deu 5.21
you shall not c. the silver or the   7.25
They c. fields, and seize them;   Mic 2.02
not have known what it is to c. if   Rom 7.07
You shall not c.," and any other   13.09
And you c. and cannot obtain;   Jas 4.02

COVETOUSNESS

"Take heed, and beware of all c.;   Lk 12.15
of wickedness, evil, c., malice.   Rom 1.29

CRAFTSMAN —MEN

a thing made by the hands of a c.,   Deu 27.15
out a skilful c. to set up an   Is 40.20
to shame, and the c. are but men;   44.11
silver, all of them the work of c.   Hos 13.02
no little business to the c.   Ac 19.24
Demetrius and the c. with him have   19.38

CRAVING (n)

had a wanton c. in the wilderness,   Ps 106.14
he thwarts the c. of the wicked.   Pro 10.03
he has a morbid c. for controversy   1Ti 6.04

CREATE —D

C. in me a clean heart, O God, and	Ps 51.10
Then the LORD will c. over the	Is 4.05
he did not c. it a chaos, he formed	45.18
of those who c. dissensions and	Rom 16.17
that he might c. in himself one new	Eph 2.15
beginning God c. the heavens and	Gen 1.01
So God c. man in his own image, in	1.27
eyes on high and see: who c. these?	Is 40.26
the LORD has c. a new thing on the	Jer 31.22
Has not one God c. us? Why then	Mal 2.10
creation which God c. until now,	Mk 13.19
c. in Christ Jesus for good works,	Eph 2.10
c. after the likeness of God in	4.24
For everything c. by God is good,	1Ti 4.04
the world was c. by the word of	Heb 11.03
who c. heaven and what is in it, the	Rev 10.06

CREATION

But from the beginning of c.,	Mk 10.06
Ever since the c. of the world his	Rom 1.20
For the c. waits with eager longing	8.19
depth, nor anything else in all c.,	8.39
one is in Christ, he is a new c.;	2Co 5.17
nor uncircumcision, but a new c.	Gal 6.15
God, the first-born of all c.;	Col 1.15

CREATOR

Remember also your C. in the days	Ecc 12.01
entrust their souls to a faithful C.	1Pe 4.19

CREATURE —S

is not his like, a c. without fear.	Job 41.33
and served the c. rather than the	Rom 1.25
preached to every c. under heaven,	Col 1.23
And before him no c. is hidden,	Heb 4.13
the first living c. like a lion,	Rev 4.07
And I heard every c. in heaven and	5.13
bring forth swarms of living c.,	Gen 1.20
the earth is full of thy c.	Ps 104.24
c. of instinct, born to be caught	2Pe 2.12

CREEP —ING

the beasts of the forest c. forth.	Ps 104.20
and over every c. thing that creeps	Gen 1.26

CRIED —IES —Y (v)

because I delivered the poor who c.,	Job 29.12
to my God I c. for help. From his	Ps 18.06
This poor man c., and the LORD	34.06
and beginning to sink he c. out,	Mt 14.30
hour Jesus c. with a loud voice,	27.46
And they c. out again, "Crucify him."	Mk 15.13
But Paul c. with a loud voice, "Do	Ac 16.28
Once more they c., "Hallelujah!	Rev 19.03
And if he c. to me, I will hear, for	Ex 22.27
Wisdom c. aloud in the street;	Pro 1.20
A voice c.: "In the wilderness	Is 40.03
and in his temple all c., "Glory!"	Ps 29.09
Out of the depths I c. to thee,	130.01
A voice says, "C.!" And I said,	Is 40.06
He will not c. or lift up his voice,	42.02
who c. "Peace" when they have	Mic 3.05
who c. to him day and night?	Lk 18.07

the very stones would c. out."	19.40
When we c., "Abba! Father!"	Rom 8.15

CRIES —Y (n)

with loud c. that he should be	Lk 23.23
Surely God does not hear an empty c.,	Job 35.13
attend to my c.! Give ear	Ps 17.01
he inclined to me and heard my c.	40.01
For a c. has gone round the land of	Is 15.08
But at midnight there was a c.,	Mt 25.06
And Jesus uttered a loud c.,	Mk 15.37
from heaven with a c. of command,	1Th 4.16

CRIME

multitudes, "I find no c. in this man."	Lk 23.04
matter of wrongdoing or vicious c.,	Ac 18.14

CROOKED

are a perverse and c. generation.	Deu 32.05
Put away from you c. speech,	Pro 4.24
A man of c. mind does not prosper,	17.20
The way of the guilty is c.,	21.08
What is c. cannot be made straight,	Ecc 1.15
and the c. shall be made straight,	Lk 3.05
yourselves from this c. generation."	Ac 2.40

CROP —S

thresh in hope of a share in the c.	1Co 9.10
for I have nowhere to store my c.?'	Lk 12.17
to have the first share of the c.	2Ti 2.06

CROSS (n)

not take his c. and follow me is	Mt 10.38
and take up his c. and follow me.	16.24
man they compelled to carry his c.	27.32
Son of God, come down from the c."	27.40
let him come down now from the c.,	27.42
Alexander and Rufus, to carry his c.	Mk 15.21
he went out, bearing his own c.,	Jn 19.17
wrote a title and put it on the c.;	19.19
standing by the c. of Jesus were	19.25
remaining on the c. on the sabbath	19.31
lest the c. of Christ be emptied of	1Co 1.17
For the word of the c. is folly to	1.18
block of the c. has been removed.	Gal 5.11
to God in one body through the c.,	Eph 2.16
unto death, even death on a c.	Php 2.08
was set before him endured the c.,	Heb 12.02

CROWD —S

said, "I have compassion on the c.,	Mt 15.32
And commanding the c. to sit down	15.35
Jericho, a great c. followed him.	20.29
him a great c. with swords and	26.47
and washed his hands before the c.,	27.24
not get near him because of the c.,	Mk 2.04
a woman in the c. raised her voice	Lk 11.27
could not, on account of the c.,	19.03
Paul wished to go in among the c.,	Ac 19.30
And great c. followed him from	Mt 4.25
Seeing the c., he went up on the	5.01
the c. were astonished at his	7.28
and the c. marveled, saying, "Never	9.33

CROWD —S (cont.)
Jesus said to the c. in parables; Mt 13.34
stirring up and inciting the c. Ac 17.13

CROWN* —ED —EST* —S (v)
and dost c. him with glory and Ps 8.05
An athlete is not c. unless he 2Ti 2.05
c. with glory and honor because of Heb 2.09
Thou c. the year with thy bounty; Ps 65.11
who c. you with steadfast love and 103.04

CROWN —S (n)
Grandchildren are the c. of the aged. Pro 17.06
and does a c. endure to all generations? 27.24
of hosts will be a c. of glory, Is 28.05
The c. has fallen from our head; Lam 5.16
and plaiting a c. of thorns they Mt 27.29
my joy and c., stand firm thus in Php 4.01
hope or joy or c. of boasting 1Th 2.19
obtain the unfading c. of glory. 1Pe 5.04
and I will give you the c. of life. Rev 2.10
on her head a c. of twelve stars; 12.01
they cast their c. before the 4.10

CRUCIFIED —Y
to be mocked and scourged and c., Mt 20.19
man will be delivered up to be c." 26.02
They all said, "Let him be c." 27.22
And when they had c. him, they divided 27.35
that you seek Jesus who was c. 28.05
where Jesus was c. was near the Jn 19.20
you c. and killed by the hands of Ac 2.23
and Christ, this Jesus whom you c." 2.36
whom you c., whom God raised from 4.10
old self was c. with him so that Rom 6.06
but we preach Christ c., a stumbling 1Co 1.23
For he was c. in weakness, but lives 2Co 13.04
I have been c. with Christ; Gal 2.20
some of whom you will kill and c., Mt 23.34
"C. him, c. him!" Pilate said Jn 19.06
with him, away with him, c. him!" 19.15
since they c. the Son of God on Heb 6.06

CRUSH —ED
it shall c. the forehead of Moab, Num 24.17
the crowd, lest they should c. him; Mk 3.09
peace will soon c. Satan under Rom 16.20
brokenhearted, and saves the c. in spirit. Ps 34.18
unbearably c. that we despaired of 2Co 1.08
afflicted in every way, but not c.; 4.08

CUBIT
can add one c. to his span of life? Mt 6.27

CULT
and sacrifice with c. prostitutes, Hos 4.14

CUNNING
to practice c. or to tamper with 2Co 4.02
the serpent deceived Eve by his c., 11.03
by the c. of men, by their craftiness Eph 4.14

CUP
my head with oil, my c. overflows. Ps 23.05

lift up the c. of salvation and 116.13
of the LORD the c. of his wrath, Is 51.17
give him the c. of consolation to Jer 16.07
Babylon was a golden c. in the 51.07
but to you also the c. shall pass; Lam 4.21
ones even a c. of cold water Mt 10.42
to drink the c. that I am to drink?" 20.22
outside of the c. and of the plate, 23.25
And he took a c., and when he had 26.27
possible, let this c. pass from me; 26.39
I not drink the c. which the Jn 18.11
The c. of blessing which we bless, 1Co 10.16
eat this bread and drink the c., 11.26
unmixed into the c. of his anger, Rev 14.10

CURE —D
is not able to c. you or heal your Hos 5.13
all demons and to c. diseases, Lk 9.01
him, and the boy was c. instantly. Mt 17.18
Jews said to the man who was c., Jn 5.10
had diseases also came and were c. Ac 28.09

CURSE —D (v)
never again c. the ground because Gen 8.21
your integrity? C. God, and die." Job 2.09
bless those who c. you, Lk 6.28
bless and do not c. them. Rom 12.14
c. is the ground because of you; Gen 3.17
"C. is the man who trusts in man Jer 17.05
C. be the day on which I was born! 20.14
you c., into the eternal fire Mt 25.41
fig tree which you c. has withered." Mk 11.21
of God ever says "Jesus be c.!" 1Co 12.03

CURSE —S (n)
to invoke a c. on himself and to Mt 26.74
on works of the law are under a c.; Gal 3.10
redeemed us from the c. of the law, 3.13
with all the c. of the covenant Deu 29.21
mouth is full of c. and bitterness." Rom 3.14

CURTAIN
stretches out the heavens like a c., Is 40.22
the c. of the temple was torn in Mt 27.51
the inner shrine behind the c., Heb 6.19

CUSTOM —S
as his c. was, he taught them. Mk 10.01
old, they went up according to c.; Lk 2.42
But you have a c. that I should Jn 18.39
They advocate c. which it is not Ac 16.21

CUT
good fruit is c. down and thrown Mt 3.10
c. it off and throw it from you; 18.08
high priest, and c. off his ear. 26.51
At Cenchreae he c. his hair, for he Ac 18.18
accursed and c. off from Christ Rom 9.03
then she should c. off her hair; 1Co 11.06

CYMBAL*
I am a noisy gong or a clanging c. 1Co 13.01

D

DAILY
Blessed be the Lord, who d. bears us up; Ps 68.19
Yet they seek me d., and delight   Is 58.02
Give us this day our d. bread;   Mt 6.11
take up his cross d. and follow me.   Lk 9.23
And he was teaching d. in the temple.   19.47
the scriptures d. to see if these   Ac 17.11
there is the d. pressure upon me of   2Co 11.28

DANCE —D —ING
time to mourn, and a time to d.;   Ecc 3.04
'We piped to you, and you did not d.;   Mt 11.17
to eat and drink and rose up to d."   1Co 10.07
And David d. before the Lord with   2Sa 6.14
of Herodias d. before the company,   Mt 14.06
singing and d., to meet King Saul,   1Sa 18.06

DANCING (n)
Let them praise his name with d.,   Ps 149.03
our d. has been turned to mourning.   Lam 5.15
the house, he heard music and d.   Lk 15.25

DANGER
man sees d. and hides himself;   Pro 22.03
filling with water, and were in d.   Lk 8.23
For we are in d. of being charged   Ac 19.40

DARE
day did any one d. to ask him any   Mt 22.46
a good man one will d. even to die.   Rom 5.07

DARK (n)
They grope in the d. without light;   Job 12.25
What I tell you in the d., utter   Mt 10.27

DARK (adj)
even the darkness is not d. to thee,   Ps 139.12
tomb early, while it was still d.,   Jn 20.01
as to a lamp shining in a d. place,   2Pe 1.19

DARKENED
Let their eyes be d., so that   Ps 69.23
The sun and the moon are d.,   Joe 2.10
of those days the sun will be d.,   Mt 24.29
and their senseless minds were d.   Rom 1.21
let their eyes be d. so that they   11.10
they are d. in their understanding,   Eph 4.18

DARKNESS
and d. was upon the face of the   Gen 1.02
to separate the light from the d.   1.18
voice out of the midst of the d.,   Deu 5.23
noonday, as the blind grope in d.,   28.29
that he would dwell in thick d.   1Ki 8.12
He made d. his covering around him,   Ps 18.11
the Lord my God lightens my d.   18.28
"Let only d. cover me, and the light   139.11
who walked in d. have seen a great   Is 9.02
I form light and create d.,   45.07
For behold, d. shall cover the earth,   60.02
who makes the morning d.,   Amo 4.13
Is not the day of the Lord d.,   5.20
who sat in d. have seen a great   Mt 4.16
and cast him into the outer d.;   22.13
hour there was d. over all the   27.45

and men loved d. rather than light,   Jn 3.19
believes in me may not remain in d.   12.46
the works of d. and put on the   Rom 13.12
what fellowship has light with d.?   2Co 6.14
the dominion of d. and transferred   Col 1.13
we are not of the night or of d.   1Th 5.05
you out of d. into his marvelous   1Pe 2.09
light and in him is no d. at all.   1Jn 1.05

DASH —ED —ES
and d. them in pieces like a   Ps 2.09
And I will d. them one against   Jer 13.14
and d. you to the ground, you and   Lk 19.44
little ones shall be d. in pieces,   Hos 13.16
it seizes him, it d. him down;   Mk 9.18

DAUB —ED
these prophets d. it with whitewash;   Eze 13.10
prophets have d. for them with   22.28

DAUGHTER —S
and said, "Tell me whose d. you are.   Gen 24.23
Now the d. of Pharaoh came down to   Ex 2.05
"When a man sells his d. as a slave,   21.07
And she said to her, "Go, my d."   Ru 2.02
gates of the d. of Zion I may   Ps 9.14
O d. of Babylon, you devastator!   137.08
Say to the d. of Zion, "Behold, your   Is 62.11
I will destroy the d. of Zion.   Jer 6.02
destruction of the d. of my people,   Lam 2.11
about you, 'Like mother, like d.'   Eze 16.44
She conceived again and bore a d.   Hos 1.06
Sing aloud, O d. of Zion; shout,   Zep 3.14
him, saying, "My d. has just died;   Mt 9.18
and a d. against her mother, and a   10.35
the d. of Herodias danced before   14.06
"Tell the d. of Zion, Behold, your   21.05
a d. of Abraham whom Satan bound   Lk 13.16
"Fear not, d. of Zion;   Jn 12.15
saw that the d. of men were fair;   Gen 6.02
lest the d. of the Philistines   2Sa 1.20
Jerusalem, repaired, he and his d.   Neh 3.12
"Your sons and d. were eating and   Job 1.18
were no women so fair as Job's d.;   42.15
Take wives and have sons and d.;   Jer 29.06
Therefore your d. play the harlot,   Hos 4.13
sons and your d. shall prophesy,   Joe 2.28
"D. of Jerusalem, do not weep for me,   Lk 23.28
sons and your d. shall prophesy,   Ac 2.17
and you shall be my sons and d.,   2Co 6.18

DAUGHTER-IN-LAW
Ruth the Moabitess her d. with her,   Ru 1.22
and a d. against her mother-in-law;   Mt 10.35

DAWN* —ED —S
the day shall d. upon us from on   Lk 1.78
As day was about to d., Paul urged   Ac 27.33
and shadow of death light has d."   Mt 4.16
until the day d. and the morning   2Pe 1.19

DAY —S
God called the light D., and the   Gen 1.05
the greater light to rule the d.,   1.16

35

DAY —S (cont.)

the seventh d. and hallowed it,	Gen 2.03
"This d. shall be for you a memorial d.,	Ex 12.14
"Here is the d. of which the LORD	1Sa 24.04
This d. is a d. of good news;	2Ki 7.09
of his salvation from d. to d.	1Ch 16.23
"This d. is holy to the LORD your	Neh 8.09
and cursed the d. of his birth.	Job 3.01
Let that d. be darkness!	3.04
his law he meditates d. and night.	Ps 1.02
D. to d. pours forth speech, and	19.02
and of thy praise all the d. long	35.28
have been my food d. and night,	42.03
Thine is the d., thine also the	74.16
For a d. in thy courts is better	84.10
This is the d. which the LORD has	118.24
The sun shall not smite you by d.,	121.06
the night is bright as the d.;	139.12
not know what a d. may bring forth.	Pro 27.01
the d. of death, than the d. of birth.	Ecc 7.01
O D. Star, son of Dawn! How you	Is 14.12
in a d. of salvation I have helped	49.08
Shall a land be born in one d.?	66.08
Cursed be the d. on which I was	Jer 20.14
covenant with d. and night and the	33.25
Bring thou the d. thou hast announced,	Lam 1.21
"Behold, the d.! Behold, it	Eze 7.10
three times a d. and prayed and	Dan 6.10
a d. of darkness and gloom, a d. of	Joe 2.02
Is not the d. of the LORD darkness,	Amo 5.20
Give us this d. our daily bread;	Mt 6.11
trouble be sufficient for the d.	6.34
tolerable on the d. of judgment for	10.15
and on the third d. be raised.	16.21
the laborers for a denarius a d.,	20.02
he will be raised on the third d."	20.19
"But of that d. and hour no one	24.36
Now on the first d. of Unleavened	26.17
dawn of the first d. of the week,	28.01
is born this d. in the city of	Lk 2.11
and that d. come upon you suddenly	21.34
The next d. he saw Jesus coming	Jn 1.29
me, but raise it up at the last d.	6.39
In that d. you will know that I am	14.20
When the d. of Pentecost had come,	Ac 2.01
yourself on the d. of wrath when	Rom 2.05
are being killed all the d. long;	8.36
ourselves becomingly as in the d.,	13.13
on the third d. in accordance with	1Co 15.04
Jesus our Lord, I die every d.!	15.31
nature is being renewed every d.	2Co 4.16
sealed for the d. of redemption.	Eph 4.30
gospel from the first d. until now.	Php 1.05
we worked night and d.,	1Th 2.09
But, since we belong to the d.,	5.08
supplications and prayers night and d.;	1Ti 5.05
on the d. of testing in the wilderness,	Heb 3.08
was in the Spirit on the Lord's d.,	Rev 1.10
"For ask now of the d. that are past,	Deu 4.32
Remember the d. of old, consider the	32.07
My d. are swifter than a weaver's	Job 7.06
for our d. on earth are a shadow.	8.06
follow me all the d. of my life;	Ps 23.09
hast made my d. a few handbreadths,	39.05

to number our d. that we may get a	90.12
My d. are like an evening shadow;	102.11
As for man, his d. are like grass;	103.15
I remember the d. of old, I meditate	143.05
For by me your d. will be multiplied,	Pro 9.11
Creator in the d. of your youth,	Ecc 12.01
"But in the latter d. I will	Jer 49.39
allotted place at the end of the d."	Dan 12.13
the fish three d. and three nights.	Jon 1.17
And he fasted forty d. and forty	Mt 4.02
From the d. of John the Baptist	11.12
the elect those d. will be shortened.	24.22
As were the d. of Noah, so will be	24.37
God, and to build it in three d.' "	26.61
'After three d. I will rise again.'	27.63
another man esteems all d. alike.	Rom 14.05
You observe d., and months, and	Gal 4.10
the time, because the d. are evil.	Eph 5.16
but in these last d. he has spoken	Heb 1.02
laid up treasure for the last d.	Jas 5.03

DEACONS

Philippi, with the bishops and d.:	Php 1.01

DEAD

for they said, "We are all d. men."	Ex 12.33
not forsaken the living or the d.!"	Ru 2.20
After a d. dog! After a flea!	1Sa 24.14
Saul is d.,' and thought he was	2Sa 4.10
out of mind like one who is d.;	Ps 31.12
The d. do not praise the LORD, nor	115.17
dog is better than a d. lion.	Ecc 9.04
D. flies make the perfumer's ointment	10.01
Thy d. shall live, their bodies	Is 26.19
Weep not for him who is d.,	Jer 22.10
valley of the d. bodies and the	31.40
and leave the d. to bury their own d."	Mt 8.22
the girl is not d. but sleeping."	9.24
raise the d., cleanse lepers, cast	10.08
Son of man is raised from the d."	17.09
And as for the resurrection of the d.,	22.31
He is not God of the d., but of	22.32
people, 'He has risen from the d.,'	27.64
And the d. man sat up, and began to	Lk 7.15
you seek the living among the d.?	24.05
raises the d. and gives them life,	Jn 5.21
life, whom God raised from the d.	Ac 3.15
whom God raised from the d., by him	4.10
be judge of the living and the d.	10.42
raised from the d. Jesus our Lord,	Rom 4.24
yourselves d. to sin and alive to	6.11
Apart from the law sin lies d.	7.08
your bodies are d. because of sin,	8.10
For if the d. are not raised, then	1Co 15.16
Christ has been raised from the d.,	15.20
will ask, "How are the d. raised?	15.35
and the d. will be raised imperishable,	15.52
O sleeper, and arise from the d.,	Eph 5.14
beginning, the first-born from the d.,	Col 1.18
repentance from d. works and of	Heb 6.01
again from the d. our Lord Jesus,	13.20
so faith apart from works is d.	Jas 2.26
gospel was preached even to the d.,	1Pe 4.06
Blessed are the d. who die in the	Rev 14.13

DEAF

and the ears of the d. unstopped;	Is 35.05
are cleansed and the d. hear,	Mt 11.05
"You dumb and d. spirit, I command	Mk 9.25

DEAL —T

May the LORD d. kindly with you, as	Ru 1.08
He does not d. with us according to	Ps 103.10
the LORD will d. with us according	Jer 21.02
Therefore I will d. in wrath;	Eze 8.18
for they d. falsely, the thief	Hos 7.01
and those who d. with the world as	1Co 7.31
He can d. gently with the ignorant	Heb 5.02
not to d. with sin but to save	9.28
I have d. with all that Jesus began	Ac 1.01
He d. craftily with our race and	7.19

DEALING

He is not weak in d. with you,	2Co 13.03

DEATH

I do not know the day of my d.	Gen 27.02
Let me die the d. of the righteous,	Num 23.10
also if even d. parts me from you."	Ru 1.17
who long for d., but it comes not,	Job 3.21
Have the gates of d. been revealed	38.17
eyes, lest I sleep the sleep of d.;	Ps 13.03
the valley of the shadow of d.,	23.04
D. shall be their shepherd;	49.14
What man can live and never see d.?	89.48
hast delivered my soul from d.,	116.08
but he has not given me over to d.	118.18
but the way of error leads to d.	Pro 12.28
for love is strong as d.,	Sol 8.06
"We have made a covenant with d.,	Is 28.15
he poured out his soul to d.,	53.12
the powers of d. shall not prevail	Mt 16.18
will not taste d. before they see	16.28
soul is very sorrowful, even to d.;	26.38
against Jesus to put him to d.;	27.01
darkness and in the shadow of d.,	Lk 1.79
but has passed from d. to life.	Jn 5.24
to show by what d. he was to die.	12.33
up, having loosed the pangs of d.,	Ac 2.24
And Saul was consenting to his d.	8.01
who was put to d. for our trespasses	Rom 4.25
Yet d. reigned from Adam to Moses,	5.14
so that, as sin reigned in d.,	5.21
with him by baptism into d.,	6.04
The d. he died he died to sin, once	6.10
For the wages of sin is d.,	6.23
deliver me from this body of d.?	7.24
For I am sure that neither d.,	8.38
the Lord's d. until he comes.	1Co 11.26
For as by a man came d.,	15.21
"O d., where is thy victory?	15.55
O d., where is thy sting?"	15.55
The sting of d. is sin, and the	15.56
Now if the dispensation of d.,	2Co 3.07
So d. is at work in us, but life in	4.12
obedient unto d., even d. on a cross.	Php 2.08
becoming like him in his d.,	3.10
Put to d. therefore what is earthly	Col 3.05
who abolished d. and brought life	2Ti 1.10

we have passed out of d. into life,	1Jn 3.14
Be faithful unto d., and I will	Rev 2.10
horse, and its rider's name was D.,	6.08
such the second d. has no power,	20.06

DEBT —S

released him and forgave him the d.	Mt 18.27
and indeed they are in d. to them,	Rom 15.27
And forgive us our d.,	Mt 6.12

DEBTOR —S

with the creditor, so with the d.	Is 24.02
As we also have forgiven our d.;	Mt 6.12
"A certain creditor had two d.;	Lk 7.41
we are d., not to the flesh, to live	Rom 8.12

DECEIT —FULNESS*

D. is in the heart of those who	Pro 12.20
Bread gained by d. is sweet to a	20.17
and there was no d. in his mouth.	Is 53.09
of you by philosophy and empty d.,	Col 2.08
may be hardened by the d. of sin.	Heb 3.13

DECEITFUL

The heart is d. above all things,	Jer 17.09
d. workmen, disguising themselves as	2Co 11.13
by their craftiness in d. wiles.	Eph 4.14

DECEIVE —D —S —ING

king: 'Do not let Hezekiah d. you,	Is 36.14
they use their tongues to d."	Rom 3.13
Let no one d. himself. If any one	1Co 3.18
Let no one d. you with empty words,	Eph 5.06
we d. ourselves, and the truth is	1Jn 1.08
Why then have you d. me?"	Gen 29.25
The pride of your heart has d. you,	Ob 3
d. me and by it killed me.	Rom 7.11
Do not be d.; neither the	1Co 6.09
as the serpent d. Eve by his	2Co 11.03
Do not be d.; God is not	Gal 6.07
when he is nothing, he d. himself.	6.03
not hearers only, d. yourselves.	Jas 1.22

DECEIVER* —S*

the d. of the whole world—he was	Rev 12.09

DECIDE —D

and shall d. for many peoples;	Is 2.04
to d. what each should take.	Mk 15.24
wise enough to d. between members	1Co 6.05
For I d. to know nothing among you	2.02

DECISION —S

but the d. is wholly from the LORD.	Pro 16.33
LORD is near in the valley of d.	Joe 3.14
custody for the d. of the emperor,	Ac 25.21
Inspired d. are on the lips of a	Pro 16.10

DECLARE —D —S —ING

D. his glory among the nations, his	1Ch 16.24
and what I have seen I will d.	Job 15.17
The heavens d. his righteousness,	Ps 50.06
D. his glory among the nations, his	96.03
come, let us d. in Zion the work of	Jer 51.10

DECLARE —D —S —ING (cont.)

And then will I d. to them,	Mt 7.23
and d. how much God has done for	Lk 8.39
and I d. to the world what I have	Jn 8.26
worship God and d. that God is	1Co 14.25
that I may d. it boldly, as I ought	Eph 6.20
to d. the mystery of Christ, on	Col 4.03
D. these things; exhort and	Tit 2.15
that you may d. the wonderful deeds	1Pe 2.09
my name may be d. throughout all	Ex 9.16
I first have d. it to Zion, and I	Is 41.27
Who d. it of old? Was it not	45.21
(Thus he d. all foods clean.)	Mk 7.19
together and d. all that God had	Ac 14.27
It was d. at first by the Lord, and	Heb 2.03
and night to night d. knowledge.	Ps 19.02
and d. to man what is his thought;	Amo 4.13
exhorting and d. that this is the	1Pe 5.12

DECREE —D (v)

Woe to those who d. iniquitous	Is 10.01
which God d. before the ages for	1Co 2.07

DECREE —S (n)

In those days a d. went out from	Lk 2.01
Though they know God's d. that those	Rom 1.32
Thy d. are very sure; holiness	Ps 93.05
acting against the d. of Caesar,	Ac 17.07

DEDICATE —D

the battle and another man d. it.	Deu 20.05
of Israel d. the house of the LORD.	1Ki 8.63

DEDICATION

And at the d. of the wall of	Neh 12.27
the feast of the D. at Jerusalem;	Jn 10.22

DEED —S

what good d. must I do, to have	Mt 19.16
mighty in d. and word before God	Lk 24.19
"I did one d., and you all marvel	Jn 7.21
from the Gentiles, by word and d.,	Rom 15.18
disobedient, unfit for any good d.	Tit 1.16
or speech but in d. and in truth.	1Jn 3.18
in glorious d., doing wonders?	Ex 15.11
Tell among the peoples his d.!	Ps 9.11
By dread d. thou dost answer us	65.05
I still proclaim thy wondrous d.	71.17
Praise him for his mighty d.;	150.02
Yet wisdom is justified by her d."	Mt 11.19
They do all their d. to be seen by	23.05
consent to the d. of your fathers;	Lk 11.48
light, because their d. were evil.	Jn 3.19
to death the d. of the body you	Rom 8.13
to do good, to be rich in good d.,	1Ti 6.18
God, but they deny him by their d.;	Tit 1.16
in all respects a model of good d.,	2.07
not because of d. done by us in	3.05
see your good d. and glorify God	1Pe 2.12
is the righteous d. of the saints.	Rev 19.08

DEEP

was upon the face of the d.;	Gen 1.02
"Can you find out the d. things of God?	Job 11.07

D. calls to d. at the thunder of	Ps 42.07
O LORD! Thy thoughts are very d.!	92.05
is, is far off, and d., very d.;	Ecc 7.24
who dwelt in a land of d. darkness,	Is 9.02
who says to the d., "Be dry,	44.27
out into the d. and let down your	Lk 5.04
to draw with, and the well is d.;	Jn 4.11
for us with sighs too d. for words.	Rom 8.26
some call the d. things of Satan,	Rev 2.24

DEFEND —ING*

May he d. the cause of the poor of	Ps 72.04
d. the fatherless, plead for the	Is 1.17
we have been d. ourselves before	2Co 12.19

DEFENSE

God has shown himself a sure d.	Ps 48.03
wishing to make a d. to the people.	Ac 19.33
And as he thus made his d., Festus	26.24
This is my d. to those who would	1Co 9.03
put here for the d. of the gospel;	Php 1.16

DEFILE —D —S

you shall not d. yourselves with	Lev 11.43
in their dreamings d. the flesh,	Jud 8
For your hands are d. with blood	Is 59.03
They have d. my holy name by their	Eze 43.08
played the harlot, Israel is d.	Hos 5.03
of his disciples ate with hands d.,	Mk 7.02
and he has d. this holy place."	Ac 21.28
conscience, being weak, is d.	1Co 8.07
and by it the many become d.;	Heb 12.15
who have not d. themselves with	Rev 14.04
not what goes into the mouth d. a man,	Mt 15.11

DEFRAUD —ED

Do not d., Honor your father and	Mk 10.19
and if I have d. any one of anything	Lk 19.08

DEITY

whole fulness of d. dwells bodily,	Col 2.09

DELAY (v)

and do not d. to keep thy	Ps 119.60
night? Will he d. long over them?	Lk 18.07

DELIGHT —S (v)

servants who d. to fear thy name;	Neh 1.11
I d. to do thy will, O my God;	Ps 40.08
I do not d. in the blood of bulls,	Is 1.11
of the covenant in whom you d.,	Mal 3.01
world and the d. in riches choke	Mt 13.22
art not a God who d. in wickedness;	Ps 5.04
my chosen, in whom my soul d.;	Is 42.01

DELIGHT (n)

and that it was a d. to the eyes,	Gen 3.06
but his d. is in the law of the	Ps 1.02
For thou hast no d. in sacrifice;	51.16
And his d. shall be in the fear of	Is 11.03
and I take no d. in your solemn	Amo 5.21

DELIVER —ED —S

come down to d. them out of the	Ex 3.08
and I will d. you from their	6.06

DELIVER —ED —S (cont.)

Thou dost d. a humble people, but	2Sa 22.28
thou didst d. them according to	Neh 9.28
D. me, O my God!	Ps 3.07
let him d. him, let him rescue him,	22.08
D. me from all my transgressions.	39.08
For he will d. you from the snare	91.03
and will defend and d. them.	Is 19.20
saying, "The LORD will surely d. us;	36.15
them, for I am with you to d. you,	Jer 1.08
and I will d. them by the LORD	Hos 1.07
temptation, But d. us from evil.	Mt 6.13
for they will d. you up to councils,	10.17
Brother will d. up brother to death,	10.21
and d. him to the Gentiles to be	20.19
let God d. him now, if he desires	27.43
Who will d. me from this body of	Rom 7.24
and if I d. my body to be burned,	1Co 13.03
our hope that he will d. us again.	2Co 1.10
for our sins to d. us from the	Gal 1.04
and d. all those who through fear	Heb 2.15
because I d. the poor who cried, and	Job 29.12
For thou hast d. my soul from death,	Ps 56.13
and he d. them from their distress;	107.06
He who walks in integrity will be d.,	Pro 28.18
Have the gods of the nations d. them,	Is 37.12
have been d. to me by my Father;	Mt 11.27
of man will be d. up to be crucified."	26.02
him away and d. him to Pilate the	27.02
just as they were d. to us by those	Lk 1.02
the time came for her to be d.	2.06
therefore he who d. me to you has	Jn 19.11
this Jesus, d. up according to the	Ac 2.23
the customs which Moses d. to us."	6.14
the Lord what I also d. to you,	1Co 11.23
For I d. to you as of first importance	15.03
he d. us from so deadly a peril, and	2Co 1.10
was once for all d. to the saints.	Jud 3
but righteousness d. from death.	Pro 10.02
when he d. the kingdom to God the	1Co 15.24
Jesus who d. us from the wrath to	1Th 1.10

DELIVERANCE

the LORD has wrought d. in Israel."	1Sa 11.13
D. belongs to the LORD; thy	Ps 3.08
I bring near my d., it is not	Is 46.13
this will turn out for my d.,	Php 1.19

DELIVERER

raised up a d. for the people of	Ju 3.09
my d., my God, my rock, in whom I	Ps 18.02
"The D. will come from Zion, he	Rom 11.26

DELUSION

men of high estate are a d.; in the	Ps 62.09
God sends upon them a strong d.,	2Th 2.11

DEMAND —ED* (v)

For Jews d. signs and Greeks seek	1Co 1.22
Satan d. to have you, that he might	Lk 22.31

DEMANDS* (n)

stood against us with its legal d.;	Col 2.14
might have made d. as apostles of	1Th 2.06

DEMON —S

and they say, 'He has a d.';	Mt 11.18
and the d. came out of him, and the	17.18
Jesus answered, "I have not a d.;	Jn 8.49
and cast out d. in your name, and do	Mt 7.22
"He casts out d. by the prince of d."	9.34
prince of d., that this man casts out d."	12.24
Spirit of God that I cast out d.,	12.28
they offer to d. and not to God.	1Co 10.20
cup of the Lord and the cup of d.	10.21
spirits and doctrines of d.,	1Ti 4.01
Even the d. believe—and shudder.	Jas 2.19
has become a dwelling place of d.,	Rev 18.02

DEMONIAC —S

a dumb d. was brought to him.	Mt 9.32
d., epileptics, and paralytics, and	4.24

DEN

shall be cast into the d. of lions.	Dan 6.07
a young lion cry out from his d.,	Amo 3.04
but you make it a d. of robbers."	Mt 21.13

DENARII —IUS

servants who owed him a hundred d.;	Mt 18.28
"Two hundred d. would not buy	Jn 6.07
with the laborers for a d. a day,	Mt 20.02
saying, "A quart of wheat for a d.,	Rev 6.06

DENIED —IES —Y

But he d. it before them all, saying,	Mt 26.70
And again he d. it with an oath, "I	26.72
men will be d. before the angels	Lk 12.09
But you d. the Holy and Righteous	Ac 3.14
but whoever d. me before men, I also	Mt 10.33
No one who d. the Son has the	1Jn 2.23
let him d. himself and take up his	Mt 16.24
die with you, I will not d. you."	26.35
he did not d., but confessed, "I am	Jn 1.20
if we d. him, he also will d. us;	2Ti 2.12
but they d. him by their deeds;	Tit 1.16
and you did not d. my faith even	Rev 2.13

DENOUNCED

why am I d. because of that for	1Co 10.30

DEPART —ED

The scepter shall not d. from Judah,	Gen 49.10
and to d. from evil is understanding.' "	Job 28.28
D. from evil and do good; seek	Ps 34.14
d. from me, you evildoers."	Mt 7.23
"D. from me, for I am a sinful man, O	Lk 5.08
had come to d. out of this world	Jn 13.01
them not to d. from Jerusalem,	Ac 1.04
My desire is to d. and be with	Php 1.23
times some will d. from the faith	1Ti 4.01
name of the Lord d. from iniquity."	2Ti 2.19
I have not d. from the commandment	Job 23.12
its glory which has d. from it.	Hos 10.05
they d. to their own country by	Mt 2.12
and d., leaving him half dead.	Lk 10.30

DEPEND* —ED* —S*

commandments d. all the law and	Mt 22.40

DEPEND —ED —S (cont.)

That is why it d. on faith, in order	Rom 4.16
righteousness from God that d. on	Php 3.09

DEPTH —S

up, since they had no d. of soil,	Mt 13.05
to be drowned in the d. of the sea.	18.06
nor d., nor anything else in all	Rom 8.39
O the d. of the riches and wisdom	11.33
and length and height and d.,	Eph 3.18
In his hand are the d. of the earth;	Ps 95.04
Out of the d. I cry to thee, O LORD!	130.01
everything, even the d. of God.	1Co 2.10

DESCEND —ED —ING

saw the Spirit d. as a dove from	Jn 1.32
or "Who will d. into the abyss?"	Rom 10.07
himself will d. from heaven with a	1Th 4.16
And the LORD d. in the cloud and	Ex 34.05
that the Christ is d. from David,	Jn 7.42
not all who are d. from Israel	Rom 9.06
He who d. is he who also ascended	Eph 4.10
of God were ascending and d. on it!	Gen 28.12

DESCENDANT —S

a d. of Abraham, a member of the	Rom 11.01
with you and your d. after you,	Gen 9.09
you and your d. after you throughout	17.09
to David, and his d. for ever."	2Sa 22.51
I will pour my Spirit upon your d.,	Is 44.03
"We are d. of Abraham, and have	Jn 8.33
Are they d. of Abraham? So am I.	2Co 11.22
concerned but with the d. of Abraham.	Heb 2.16

DESCRIBE —D

Who can d. his generation? For his	Ac 8.33
he d. to them how the Lord had	12.17

DESERT (n)

and put God to the test in the d.;	Ps 106.14
He turns a d. into pools of water, a	107.35
the d. shall rejoice and blossom;	Is 35.01
wilderness, and streams in the d.;	35.06
Be like a wild ass in the d.!	Jer 48.06
enough in the d. to feed so great	Mt 15.33
driven by the demon into the d.)	Lk 8.29

DESERTED —ING

but a poor man is d. by his friend.	Pro 19.04
Her cities will be d. for ever;	Is 17.02
has d. me and gone to Thessalonica;	2Ti 4.10
No one took my part; all d. me.	4.16
are so quickly d. him who called	Gal 1.06

DESERVE —D —S —ING

nothing to d. death or imprisonment."	Ac 26.31
those who do such things d. to die,	Rom 1.32
to each of you as your works d.	Rev 2.23
think will be d. by the man who	Heb 10.29
staff; for the laborer d. his food.	Mt 10.10
and, "The laborer d. his wages."	1Ti 5.18
they all condemned him as d. death.	Mk 14.64

DESIGNATED

and d. Son of God in power according	Rom 1.04
being d. by God a high priest after	Heb 5.10
long ago were d. for this condemnation,	Jud 4

DESIRE —D —S —ST* —ING (v)

Sacrifice and offering thou dost not d.;	Ps 40.06
no beauty that we should d. him.	Is 53.02
For I d. steadfast love and not	Hos 6.06
And what does he d.? Godly	Mal 2.15
'I d. mercy, and not sacrifice.'	Mt 9.13
Father, I d. that they also, whom	Jn 17.24
But earnestly d. the higher gifts.	1Co 12.31
you who d. to be under law, do you	Gal 4.21
they d. a better country, that is, a	Heb 11.16
More to be d. are they than gold,	Ps 19.10
and kings d. to see what you see,	Lk 10.24
So when God d. to show more	Heb 6.17
who d. all men to be saved and to	1Ti 2.04
of bishop, he d. a noble task.	3.01
Behold, thou d. truth in the inward	Ps 51.06
But he, d. to justify himself, said	Lk 10.29

DESIRE (n)

yet your d. shall be for your	Gen 3.16
May he grant you your heart's d.,	Ps 20.04
but a d. fulfilled is a tree of	Pro 13.12
my beloved's, and his d. is for me.	Sol 7.10
my heart's d. and prayer to God for	Rom 10.01
but having his d. under control,	1Co 7.37
My d. is to depart and be with	Php 1.23
do not gratify the d. of the flesh.	Gal 5.16

DESOLATE —ING*

and that the land may not be d."	Gen 47.19
he has made d. all my company.	Job 16.07
streets of Jerusalem that are d.,	Jer 33.10
the transgression that makes d.,	Dan 8.13
up the abomination that makes d.	11.31
D.! Desolation and ruin!	Nah 2.10
Behold, your house is forsaken and d.	Mt 23.38
"I will not leave you d.; I will	Jn 14.18
for the d. hath more children than	Gal 4.27
they will make her d. and naked,	Rev 17.16
you see the d. sacrilege spoken of	Mt 24.15
you see the d. sacrilege set up	Mk 13.14

DESOLATION —S

know that its d. has come near.	Lk 21.20
how he has wrought d. in the earth.	Ps 46.08

DESPAIR (n)

my heart up to d. over all the	Ecc 2.20
perplexed, but not driven to d.;	2Co 4.08

DESPISE —D —S —ING

God is mighty, and does not d. any;	Job 36.05
heart, O God, thou wilt not d.	Ps 51.17
My son, do not d. the LORD's discipline	Pro 3.11
"I hate, I d. your feasts, and I take	Amo 5.21
to the one and d. the other.	Mt 6.24
"See that you do not d. one of	18.10
Or do you d. the church of God and	1Co 11.22
do not d. prophesying,	1Th 5.20

DESPISE —D —S —ING (cont.)

Let no one d. your youth, but set	1Ti 4.12
Thus Esau d. his birthright.	Gen 25.34
they have d. the Holy One of Israel,	Is 1.04
He was d. and rejected by men;	53.03
they were righteous and d. others:	Lk 18.09
what is low and d. in the world,	1Co 1.28
A fool d. his father's instruction,	Pro 15.05
d. the shame, and is seated at the	Heb 12.02

DESTINED

He d. us in love to be his sons	Eph 1.05
For God has not d. us for wrath,	1Th 5.09
chosen and d. by God the Father and	1Pe 1.02
He was d. before the foundation of	1.20

DESTROY —ED —ING —S

I will d. them with the earth.	Gen 6.13
Wilt thou d. the whole city for	18.28
D. their plans, O Lord, confuse their	Ps 55.09
And he will d. on this mountain the	Is 25.07
shepherds who d. and scatter the	Jer 23.01
midst, and I will not come to d.	Hos 11.09
to search for the child, to d. him."	Mt 2.13
him who can d. both soul and body	10.28
'I am able to d. the temple of God,	26.61
d. the work of God. Everything	Rom 14.20
"I will d. the wisdom of the wise,	1Co 1.19
God's temple, God will d. him.	3.17
he who is able to save and to d.	Jas 4.12
and the flood came and d. them all.	Lk 17.27
that the sinful body might be d.,	Rom 6.06
did and were d. by the Destroyer.	1Co 10.10
The last enemy to be d. is death.	15.26
forsaken; struck down, but not d.;	2Co 4.09
the earthly tent we live in is d.,	5.01
those who shrink back and are d.,	Heb 10.39
Father after d. every rule and	1Co 15.24
no thief approaches and no moth d.	Lk 12.33
If any one d. God's temple, God will	1Co 3.17

DESTROYER

did and were destroyed by the D.	1Co 10.10
so that the D. of the first-born	Heb 11.28

DESTROYING (n)

building you up and not for d. you,	2Co 10.08

DESTRUCTION

they are doomed to d. for ever,	Ps 92.07
them, and delivered them from d.	107.20
Pride goes before d., and a	Pro 16.18
cry out, I shout, "Violence and d.!"	Jer 20.08
they made idols for their own d.	Hos 8.04
that leads to d., and those who	Mt 7.13
the vessels of wrath made for d.,	Rom 9.22
a clear omen to them of their d.,	Php 1.28
then sudden d. will come upon	1Th 5.03
of eternal d. and exclusion from	2Th 1.09
and unstable twist to their own d.,	2Pe 3.16

DETERMINE —D —S*

were going to d. his case more	Ac 23.15
Son of man goes as it has been d.;	Lk 22.22

my liberty be d. by another man's	1Co 10.29
He d. the number of the stars, he	Ps 147.04

DETESTABLE

and became d. like the thing they	Hos 9.10
they are d., disobedient, unfit for	Tit 1.16

DEVASTATION —S

d. and destruction, famine and	Is 51.19
they shall raise up the former d.;	61.04

DEVICES

He frustrates the d. of the crafty,	Job 5.12
not good, following their own d.;	Is 65.02

DEVIL

wilderness to be tempted by the d.	Mt 4.01
the enemy who sowed them is the d.;	13.39
prepared for the d. and his angels;	25.41
the twelve, and one of you is a d.?"	Jn 6.70
and give no opportunity to the d.	Eph 4.27
reproach and the snare of the d.	1Ti 3.07
power of death, that is, the d.,	Heb 2.14
Resist the d. and he will flee from	Jas 4.07
adversary the d. prowls around	1Pe 5.08
He who commits sin is of the d.;	1Jn 3.08
Michael, contending with the d.,	Jud 9
who is called the D. and Satan,	Rev 12.09

DEVISE —D

to d. artistic designs, to work in	Ex 31.04
Do they not err that d. evil?	Pro 14.22
yet they d. evil against me.	Hos 7.15
follow cleverly d. myths when we	2Pe 1.16

DEVISING

The d. of folly is sin, and the	Pro 24.09

DEVOTE —D

But we will d. ourselves to prayer	Ac 6.04
that you may d. yourselves to	1Co 7.05
d. yourself to them, so that all may	1Ti 4.15
or he will be d. to the one and	Mt 6.24
and they have d. themselves to the	1Co 16.15

DEVOUR —ED —ING —S

Joab, "Shall the sword d. for ever?	2Sa 2.26
You love all words that d.,	Ps 52.04
who d. widows' houses and for a	Mk 12.40
But if you bite and d. one another	Gal 5.15
lion, seeking some one to d.	1Pe 5.08
a wild beast has d. him; Joseph is	Gen 37.33
and the birds came and d. them.	Mt 13.04
who has d. your living with harlots,	Lk 15.30
For the LORD your God is a d. fire,	Deu 4.24
and his tongue is like a d. fire;	Is 30.27
each d. his neighbor's flesh,	9.20
of the LORD d. from one end of the	Jer 12.12

DEVOUT

and this man was righteous and d.,	Lk 2.25
d. men from every nation under	Ac 2.05
D. men buried Stephen, and made	8.02
many of the d. Greeks and not a	17.04
a d. man according to the law, well	22.12

DEW

rain, my speech distil as the d.,	Deu 32.02
favor is like d. upon the grass.	Pro 19.12
for my head is wet with d.,	Sol 5.02
like the d. that goes early away.	Hos 6.04

DIADEMS

horns, and seven d. upon his heads.	Rev 12.03

DICTATION

a scroll at the d. of Jeremiah all	Jer 36.04

DIE —S

that you eat of it you shall d."	Gen 2.17
said to the woman, "You will not d.	3.04
Let me d. the death of the righteous,	Num 23.10
For I must d. in this land, I must	Deu 4.22
where you d. I will d., and there	Ru 1.17
integrity? Curse God, and d."	Job 2.09
If a man d., shall he live again?	14.14
I shall not d., but I shall live,	Ps 118.17
a time to be born, and a time to d.;	Ecc 3.02
eat and drink, for tomorrow we d."	Is 22.13
to him, "Even if I must d. with you,	Mt 26.35
for they cannot d. any more,	Lk 20.36
a man may eat of it and not d.	Jn 6.50
will seek me and d. in your sin;	8.21
and believes in me shall never d.	11.26
one man should d. for the people,	11.50
Why, one will hardly d. for a	Rom 5.07
according to the flesh you will d.,	8.13
and if we d., we d. to the Lord;	14.08
For as in Adam all d., so also	1Co 15.22
Jesus our Lord, I d. every day!	15.31
live is Christ, and to d. is gain.	Php 1.21
it is appointed for men to d. once,	Heb 9.27
that we might d. to sin and live to	1Pe 2.24
the dead who d. in the Lord	Rev 14.13
that he may bless you before he d."	Gen 27.10
and none of us d. to himself.	Rom 14.07
does not come to life unless it d.	1Co 15.36

DIFFERENT

For who sees anything d. in you?	1Co 4.07
you receive a d. spirit from the	2Co 11.04
of Christ and turning to a d. gospel—	Gal 1.06
not to teach any d. doctrine,	1Ti 1.03

DIM

his eyes were d. so that he could	Gen 27.01
his eye was not d., nor his	Deu 34.07
My eye has grown d. from grief,	Job 17.07
My eyes grow d. with waiting for my	Ps 69.03

DINNER

Behold, I have made ready my d.,	Mt 22.04
he did not first wash before d.	Lk 11.38
invites you to d. and you are	1Co 10.27

DIPPED —ING*

"He who has d. his hand in the dish	Mt 26.23
He is clad in a robe d. in blood,	Rev 19.13
one who is d. bread in the same	Mk 14.20

DIRECT —ED —S

Therefore I d. my steps by all thy	Ps 119.128
our Lord Jesus, d. our way to you;	1Th 3.11
May the Lord d. your hearts to the	2Th 3.05
Who has d. the Spirit of the LORD,	Is 40.13
went and did as Jesus had d. them;	Mt 21.06
as I d. the churches of Galatia, so	1Co 16.01
elders in every town as I d. you,	Tit 1.05
his way, but the LORD d. his steps.	Pro 16.09
wherever the will of the pilot d.	Jas 3.04

DIRECTIONS

of their four d. without turning	Eze 10.11
things I will give d. when I come.	1Co 11.34
and gave d. concerning his burial.	Heb 11.22

DISASTER

hand, and in his d. cry for help?	Job 30.24
D. follows hard on d., the	Jer 4.20

DISCERN —ED* —EST* —ING

angel of God to d. good and evil.	2Sa 14.17
Cannot my taste d. calamity?	Job 6.30
They know not, nor do they d.;	Is 44.18
because they are spiritually d.	1Co 2.14
thou d. my thoughts from afar.	Ps 139.02
drinks without d. the body eats	1Co 11.29
and d. the thoughts and intentions	Heb 4.12

DISCERNMENT

For this is a people without d.;	Is 27.11
more, with knowledge and all d.,	Php 1.09

DISCIPLE —S

"A d. is not above his teacher, nor	Mt 10.24
As this d. was known to the high	Jn 18.15
and the d. whom he loved standing	19.26
an early d., with whom we should	Ac 21.16
seal the teaching among my d.	Is 8.16
he sat down his d. came to him.	Mt 5.01
Then the d. of John came to him,	9.14
him his twelve d. and gave them	10.01
"Why do your d. transgress the	15.02
Then the d. came to Jesus privately	17.19
And he came to the d. and found	26.40
Then all the d. forsook him and	26.56
therefore and make d. of all nations,	28.19
and baptizing more d. than John	Jn 4.01
many of his d. drew back and no	6.66
in my word, you are truly my d.,	8.31
His d. did not understand this at	12.16
His d. said, "Ah, now you are speaking	16.29
Jesus often met there with his d.	18.02
days when the d. were increasing	Ac 6.01
in Antioch the d. were for the	11.26
And some of the d. from Caesarea	21.16

DISCIPLINE —S (v)

D. your son while there is hope;	Pro 19.18
fathers to d. us and we respected	Heb 12.09
For the Lord d. him whom he loves,	12.06
but he d. us for our good, that we	12.10

DISCIPLINE (n)
Whoever loves d. loves knowledge,	Pro 12.01
Do not withhold d. from a child;	23.13
their God, and did not accept d.;	Jer 7.28
them up in the d. and instruction	Eph 6.04
regard lightly the d. of the Lord,	Heb 12.05
For the moment all d. seems painful	12.11

DISCLOSE —D
for the Day will d. it, because it	1Co 3.13
and will d. the purposes of the	4.05
but is now d. and through the	Rom 16.26
the secrets of his heart are d.;	1Co 14.25

DISCRETION
LORD grant you d. and understanding,	1Ch 22.12
My son, keep sound wisdom and d.;	Pro 3.21

DISCUSS —ED —ING
why do you d. among yourselves the	Mt 16.08
way they had d. with one another	Mk 9.34
them, "What were you d. on the way?"	9.33

DISEASE —S
By d. his skin is consumed, the	Job 18.13
healing every d. and every infirmity	Mt 4.23
our infirmities and bore our d."	8.17
island who had d. also came and	Ac 28.09

DISGRACE
and thus put d. upon all Israel."	1Sa 11.02
All day long my d. is before me,	Ps 44.15
because I bore the d. of my youth.'	Jer 31.19

DISGUISE —S —ING
servants also d. themselves as	2Co 11.15
for even Satan d. himself as an	11.14
d. themselves as apostles of Christ.	11.13

DISH
dipped his hand in the d. with me,	Mt 26.23
outside of the cup and of the d.,	Lk 11.39

DISHONEST
and heart only for your d. gain,	Jer 22.17
commended the d. steward for his	Lk 16.08

DISHONOR —ED* —S (v)
I honor my Father, and you d. me.	Jn 8.49
do you d. God by breaking the law?	Rom 2.23
But you have d. the poor man.	Jas 2.06
be he who d. his father or his	Deu 27.16
with his head covered d. his head,	1Co 11.04

DISHONOR —ING* (n)
worthy to suffer d. for the name.	Ac 5.41
It is sown in d., it is raised in	1Co 15.43
in honor and d., in ill repute and	2Co 6.08
to the d. of their bodies among	Rom 1.24

DISMAY —ED
by them, lest I d. you before them.	Jer 1.17
be not d., for I am your God;	Is 41.10
says the LORD, nor be d., O Israel;	Jer 30.10
And your mighty men shall be d.,	Ob 9

DISOBEDIENCE
For as by one man's d. many were	Rom 5.19
For God has consigned all men to d.,	11.32
is now at work in the sons of d.	Eph 2.02
failed to enter because of d.,	Heb 4.06

DISOBEDIENT
I was not d. to the heavenly vision,	Ac 26.19
my hands to a d. and contrary	Rom 10.21
you were once d. to God but now	11.30
d., unfit for any good deed.	Tit 1.16

DISOBEY* —ED —S*
king, and do not d. either of them;	Pro 24.21
stumble because they d. the word,	1Pe 2.08
you, and I never d. your command;	Lk 15.29
"I know him" but d. his	1Jn 2.04

DISPUTE —D* —ING (v)
is not able to d. with one stronger	Ecc 6.10
the LORD and to decide d. cases.	2Ch 19.08
The Jews then d. among themselves,	Jn 6.52
Asia, arose and d. with Stephen.	Ac 6.09
he spoke and d. against the Hellenists;	9.29
d. about the body of Moses, he did	Jud 9
and heard them d. with one another,	Mk 12.28

DISPUTE —S —ING (n)
It is beyond d. that the inferior	Heb 7.07
controversy and for d. about words,	1Ti 6.04
in all their d. an oath is final	Heb 6.16
the Lord to avoid d. about words,	2Ti 2.14

DISSENSION —S
selfishness, d., party spirit,	Gal 5.20
who create d. and difficulties, in	Rom 16.17
d., and quarrels over the law, for	Tit 3.09

DISTANCE
But Peter followed him at a d.,	Mt 26.58
But while he was yet at a d.,	Lk 15.20
by ten lepers, who stood at a d.	17.12

DISTINCTION —S*
LORD makes a d. between the	Ex 11.07
have made no d. between the holy	Eze 22.26
and he made no d. between us and	Ac 15.09
who believe. For there is no d.;	Rom 3.22
For there is no d. between Jew and	10.12
have you not made d. among yourselves,	Jas 2.04

DISTINGUISH —ED
You are to d. between the holy and	Lev 10.10
the ability to d. between spirits,	1Co 12.10
by practice to d. good from evil.	Heb 5.14
Daniel became d. above all the	Dan 6.03

DISTRESS (n)
In my d. I called upon the LORD;	Ps 18.06
In d. you called, and I delivered	81.07
Nevertheless he regarded their d.,	106.44
be no cry of d. in our streets!	144.14
the land, behold, darkness and d.;	Is 5.30
O LORD, in d. they sought thee, they	26.16

DISTRESS (n) (cont.)
For great d. shall be upon the	Lk 21.23
tribulation and d. for every human	Rom 2.09
or d., or persecution, or famine, or	8.35
the impending d. it is well for a	1Co 7.26
in all our d. and affliction we	1Th 3.07

DISTRIBUTE —D
that you have and d. to the poor,	Lk 18.22
He has d. freely, he has given to	Ps 112.09
he d. them to those who were seated;	Jn 6.11
and goods and d. them to all, as any	Ac 2.45
the Holy Spirit d. according to	Heb 2.04

DISTRICT
he withdrew to the d. of Galilee.	Mt 2.22
of this went through all that d.	9.26
came into the d. of Caesarea	16.13
and drove them out of their d.	Ac 13.50

DISTURBED —ING*
authorities were d. when they heard	Ac 17.08
are Jews and they are d. our city.	16.20

DIVIDE —D —ING
they d. my garments among them, and	Ps 22.18
Thou didst d. the sea by thy might;	74.13
bid my brother d. the inheritance	Lk 12.13
"Take this, and d. it among yourselves;	22.17
they cast lots to d. his garments.	23.34
and there it d. and became four	Gen 2.10
dry land, and the waters were d.	Ex 14.21
He d. the sea and let them pass	Ps 78.13
who d. the waters before them to	Is 63.12
of iron, it shall be a d. kingdom;	Dan 2.41
"Every kingdom d. against itself is	Mt 12.25
they d. his garments among them by	27.35
And he d. his living between them.	Lk 15.12
Sadducees; and the assembly was d.	Ac 23.07
Is Christ d.? Was Paul crucified	1Co 1.13
and his interests are d. And the	7.34
broken down the d. wall of hostility,	Eph 2.14

DIVINE —D* —S* (v)
that such a man as I can indeed d.?"	Gen 44.15
And he said, "D. for me by a spirit,	1Sa 28.08
hire, its prophets d. for money;	Mic 3.11
have spoken falsehoods and d. a lie;	Eze 13.06
drinks, and by this that he d.?	Gen 44.05

DIVINE (adj)
Your d. throne endures for ever and	Ps 45.06
because in his d. forbearance he	Rom 3.25
but have d. power to destroy	2Co 10.04
rather than the d. training that	1Ti 1.04
men of old received d. approval.	Heb 11.02
become partakers of the d. nature.	2Pe 1.04

DIVISION —S
No, I tell you, but rather d.;	Lk 12.51
So there was a d. among the people	Jn 7.43
piercing to the d. of soul and	Heb 4.12
I hear that there are d. among you;	1Co 11.18
It is these who set up d.,	Jud 19

DIVORCE (v)
shame, resolved to d. her quietly.	Mt 1.19
"Is it lawful to d. one's wife for	19.03
Moses allowed you to d. your wives,	19.08

DIVORCE (n)
her a bill of d. and puts it in	Deu 24.01
"For I hate d., says the LORD the	Mal 2.16
him give her a certificate of d.'	Mt 5.31
one to give a certificate of d.,	19.07

DOCTRINE —S
'My d. is pure, and I am clean in	Job 11.04
opposition to the d. which you have	Rom 16.17
about with every wind of d.,	Eph 4.14
not to teach any different d.,	1Ti 1.03
may adorn the d. of God our Savior.	Tit 2.10
teaching as d. the precepts of men.' "	Mt 15.09
according to human precepts and d.?	Col 2.22
the elementary d. of Christ and go	Heb 6.01

DOERS*
but the d. of the law who will be	Rom 2.13
But be d. of the word, and not	Jas 1.22

DOG —S
who takes a passing d. by the ears.	Pro 26.17
for a living d. is better than a dead	Ecc 9.04
The d. turns back to his own vomit,	2Pe 2.22
Yea, d. are round about me; a company	Ps 22.16
they are all dumb d., they cannot	Is 56.10
"Do not give d. what is holy;	Mt 7.06
bread and throw it to the d."	15.26
moreover the d. came and licked his	Lk 16.21
Look out for the d., look out	Php 3.02
Outside are the d. and sorcerers	Rev 22.15

DOMINION —S
let them have d. over the fish of	Gen 1.26
"D. and fear are with God;	Job 25.02
Thou hast given him d. over the	Ps 8.06
For d. belongs to the LORD, and he	22.28
and thy d. endures throughout all	145.13
his d. is an everlasting d., which	Dan 7.14
death no longer has d. over him.	Rom 6.09
and authority and power and d.,	Eph 1.21
us from the d. of darkness and	Col 1.13
glory and d. for ever and ever.	1Pe 4.11
to him be the d. for ever and ever.	5.11
d., and authority, before all time	Jud 25
be glory and d. for ever and ever.	Rev 1.06
thrones or d. or principalities or	Col 1.16

DOOMED
power preserve those d. to die!	Ps 79.11
this age, who are d. to pass away.	1Co 2.06
them, thus he is d. to be killed.	Rev 11.05

DOOR —S
do well, sin is couching at the d.;	Gen 4.07
As a d. turns on its hinges, so does	Pro 26.14
the Valley of Achor a d. of hope.	Hos 2.15
and shut the d. and pray to your	Mt 6.06
great stone to the d. of the tomb,	27.60

DOOR —S (cont.)
for them, not even about the d.;   Mk 2.02
"Strive to enter by the narrow d.;   Lk 13.24
to you, I am the d. of the sheep.   Jn 10.07
I am the d.; if any one   10.09
maid who kept the d. said to Peter,   18.17
he had opened a d. of faith to the   Ac 14.27
for a wide d. for effective work   1Co 16.09
a d. was opened for me in the Lord;   2Co 2.12
may open to us a d. for the word,   Col 4.03
I have set before you an open d.,   Rev 3.08
Behold, I stand at the d. and knock;   3.20
"Or who shut in the sea with d.,   Job 38.08
and be lifted up, O ancient d.!   Ps 24.07
above, and opened the d. of heaven;   78.23
The d. were shut, but Jesus came and   Jn 20.26
saw that the prison d. were open,   Ac 16.27
the Judge is standing at the d.   Jas 5.09

DOORPOSTS
it on the two d. and the lintel of   Ex 12.07

DOUBLE
lips and a d. heart they speak.   Ps 12.02
that you might have a d. pleasure;   2Co 1.15
be considered worthy of d. honor,   1Ti 5.17
your hearts, you men of d. mind.   Jas 4.08

DOUBT —S* (v)
of little faith, why did you d.?"   Mt 14.31
if you have faith and never d.,   21.21
and does not d. in his heart, but   Mk 11.23
And convince some, who d.;   Jud 22
for he who d. is like a wave of the   Jas 1.06

DOUBTS* (n)
But he who has d. is condemned, if   Rom 14.23

DOUGH
took their d. before it was   Ex 12.34
If the d. offered as first fruits   Rom 11.16

DOVE —S
sent forth the d. out of the ark;   Gen 8.10
say, "O that I had wings like a d.!   Ps 55.06
My d., my perfect one, is only one,   Sol 6.09
Ephraim is like a d., silly and   Hos 7.11
Spirit of God descending like a d.,   Mt 3.16
as serpents and innocent as d.   10.16

DRAG —GED —GING
lest he d. you to the judge, and the   Lk 12.58
and you will be d. before governors   Mt 10.18
stoned Paul and d. him out of the   Ac 14.19
d. the net full of fish, for they   Jn 21.08

DRAGON
will slay the d. that is in the   Is 27.01
behold a great red d., with seven   Rev 12.03
Men worshiped the d., for he had   13.04

DRANK
it to them, and they all d. of it.   Mk 14.23
'We ate and d. in your presence, and   Lk 13.26

They ate, they d., they married, they   17.27
they d. from the supernatural Rock   1Co 10.04

DRAW —ING —S
"Can you d. out Leviathan with a   Job 41.01
D. near to me, redeem me, set me free   Ps 69.18
of the Holy One of Israel d. near,   Is 5.19
she does not d. near to her God.   Zep 3.02
"Then I will d. near to you for   Mal 3.05
a woman of Samaria to d. water.   Jn 4.07
with confidence d. near to the   Heb 4.16
through which we d. near to God.   7.19
let us d. near with a true heart in   10.22
D. near to God and he will d. near   Jas 4.08
because your redemption is d. near."   Lk 21.28
more as you see the Day d. near.   Heb 10.25
My deliverance d. near speedily, my   Is 51.05
the Father who sent me d. him;   Jn 6.44

DREAD (n)
of you and the d. of you shall be   Gen 9.02
Terror and d. fall upon them;   Ex 15.16
your fear, and let him be your d.   Is 8.13

DREAM —S (n)
Then God said to him in the d.,   Gen 20.06
Now Joseph had a d., and when   37.05
to Solomon in a d. by night; and God   1Ki 3.05
In a d., in a vision of the night,   Job 33.15
They are like a d. when one awakes,   Ps 73.20
"I had a d., and my spirit is   Dan 2.03
Daniel had a d. and visions of his   7.01
the Lord appeared to him in a d.,   Mt 1.20
warned in a d. not to return to   2.12
warned in a d. he withdrew to the   2.22
For when d. increase, empty words   Ecc 5.07
and your old men shall dream d.;   Ac 2.17

DRESS —ED
shall plant vineyards and d. them,   Deu 28.39
"D. yourself and put on your   Ac 12.08
but we will build with d. stones;   Is 9.10
d. in a white robe;   Mk 16.05

DREW
he d. me out of many waters.   Ps 18.16
Then they d. Jeremiah up with ropes   Jer 38.13
And when they d. near to Jerusalem   Mt 21.01
out his hand and d. his sword,   26.51
his disciples d. back and no   Jn 6.66
as the time of the promise d. near,   Ac 7.17
they came he d. back and separated   Gal 2.12

DRIED
the waters were d. up from the   Gen 8.07
my strength is d. up like a potsherd,   Ps 22.15
they say, 'Our bones are d. up,   Eze 37.11

DRINK —ING (v)
Moses, saying, "What shall we d.?"   Ex 15.24
"D. no wine nor strong d., you nor   Lev 10.09
D. water from your own cistern,   Pro 5.15
it is not for kings to d. wine,   31.04
is to eat and d. and find enjoyment   Ecc 5.18

DRINK —ING (v) (cont.)

and d. your wine with a merry heart;	Ecc 9.07
"Let us eat and d., for tomorrow	Is 22.13
to d. the waters of the Nile?	Jer 2.18
D., be drunk and vomit, fall and	25.27
who d. wine in bowls, and anoint	Amo 6.06
you shall eat or what you shall d.,	Mt 6.25
able to d. the cup that I am to d.?"	20.22
"D. of it, all of you;	26.27
you I shall not d. again of this	26.29
if this cannot pass unless I d. it,	26.42
do you eat and d. with tax collectors	Lk 5.30
You cannot d. the cup of the Lord	1Co 10.21
So, whether you eat or d.,	10.31
you eat this bread and d. the cup,	11.26
all were made to d. of one Spirit.	12.13
No longer d. only water, but use a	1Ti 5.23
he also shall d. the wine of God's	Rev 14.10
the Son of man came eating and d.,	Mt 11.19
And no one after d. old wine	Lk 5.39
eating and d. what they provide, for	10.07

DRINK (n)

Wine is a mocker, strong d. a brawler;	Pro 20.01
that they may run after strong d.,	Is 5.11
wine and stagger with strong d.;	28.07
I was thirsty and you gave me d.,	Mt 25.35
Jesus said to her, "Give me a d."	Jn 4.07
mean food and d. but righteousness	Rom 14.17
all drank the same supernatural d.	1Co 10.04
to be slanderers or slaves to d.;	Tit 20.3
with food and d. and various	Heb 9.10

DRIP (v)

the lips of a loose woman d. honey,	Pro 5.03
the mountains shall d. sweet wine,	Amo 9.13

DRIPPING (n)

A continual d. on a rainy day and a	Pro 27.15

DRIVE —N —S

and began to d. out those who sold	Mk 11.15
"D. out the wicked person from	1Co 5.13
thou hast d. me this day away from	Gen 4.14
Wilt thou frighten a d. leaf and	Job 13.25
you like chaff d. by the wind from	Jer 13.24
kind cannot be d. out by anything	Mk 9.29
perplexed, but not d. to despair;	2Co 4.08
the sea that is d. and tossed by	Jas 1.06
Nimshi; for he d. furiously."	2Ki 9.20
like chaff which the wind d. away.	Ps 1.04
which the wind of the LORD d.	Is 59.19

DROSS

Take away the d. from the silver,	Pro 25.04
Your silver has become d., your	Is 1.22

DROVE

and the LORD d. the sea back by a	Ex 14.21
to him and d. the peg into his	Ju 4.21
of God and d. out all who sold and	Mt 21.12
and d. us out, and displease God and	1Th 2.15

DRUNK

Be d., but not with wine;	Is 29.09
I made them d. in my wrath, and I	63.06
and to eat and drink and get d.,	Lk 12.45
For these men are not d., as you	Ac 2.15
one is hungry and another is d.	1Co 11.21
And do not get d. with wine, for	Eph 5.18
those who get d. are d. at night.	1Th 5.07
d. with the blood of the saints and	Rev 17.06

DRUNKARD —S

say, 'Behold, a glutton and a d.,	Mt 11.19
d., or robber—not even to eat with	1Co 5.11
no d., not violent but gentle, not	1Ti 3.03
nor d., nor revilers, nor robbers	1Co 6.10

DRUNKENNESS

time, for strength, and not for d.!	Ecc 10.17
dissipation and d. and cares of	Lk 21.34
in the day, not in reveling and d.,	Rom 13.13
envy, d., carousing, and the like.	Gal 5.21

DRY

God called the d. land Earth, and	Gen 1.10
as in a d. and weary land where no	Ps 63.01
He turned the sea into d. land;	66.06
the Red Sea, and it became d.;	106.09
and like a root out of d. ground;	Is 53.02
O d. bones, hear the word of the	Eze 37.04

DUE (n)

it is your d. and your sons' d.,	Lev 10.13
to drink. It is their d.!"	Rev 16.06

DUE (adj)

holy things which are d. from you,	Deu 12.26
render them their d. reward.	Ps 28.04
Praise is d. to thee, O God, in Zion;	65.01
give them their food in d. season.	104.27
receiving the d. reward of our	Lk 23.41
own persons the d. penalty for	Rom 1.27
for in d. season we shall reap, if	Gal 6.09
that in d. time he may exalt you.	1Pe 5.06

DULL

For this people's heart has grown d.,	Mt 13.15
you have become d. of hearing.	Heb 5.11

DUMB

the tongue of the d. sing for joy.	Is 35.06
that before its shearers is d.,	53.07
to a d. stone, Arise! Can this	Hab 2.19
a d. demoniac was brought to him.	Mt 9.32
when they saw the d. speaking,	15.31
the deaf hear and the d. speak."	Mk 7.37
you were led astray to d. idols,	1Co 12.02
a d. ass spoke with human voice and	2Pe 2.16

DUST

formed man of d. from the ground,	Gen 2.07
you are d., and to d. you shall return."	3.19
Lord, I who am but d. and ashes.	18.27
bow all who go down to the d.,	Ps 22.29
Will the d. praise thee? Will it	30.09

DUST (cont.)

accounted as the d. on the scales; Is 40.15
he takes up the isles like fine d. 40.15
the clouds are the d. of his feet. Nah 1.03
shake off the d. from your feet as Mt 10.14
shook off the d. from their feet Ac 13.51
was from the earth, a man of d.; 1Co 15.47

DUTIES —Y

the rights and d. of the kingship; 1Sa 10.25
Practice these d., devote yourself 1Ti 4.15
beloved. Teach and urge these d. 6.02
tent, performing their ritual d.; Heb 9.06
we have only done what was our d.' " Lk 17.10
their religious d. to their own 1Ti 5.04

DWELL —S

of those who d. in tents and have Gen 4.20
their possession, cities to d. in; Num 35.02
choose, to make his name d. there, Deu 12.11
"But will God indeed d. on the earth? 1Ki 8.27
Who shall d. on thy holy hill? Ps 15.01
and I shall d. in the house of the 23.06
that the LORD God may d. there. 68.18
of my God than d. in the tents of 84.10

him, that glory may d. in our land. 85.09
the morning and d. in the uttermost 139.09
and I d. in the midst of a people Is 6.05
The wolf shall d. with the lamb, and 11.06
Then justice will d. in the wilderness, 32.16
and I will make them d. in safety. Jer 32.37
and Jerusalem will d. securely. 33.16
D. in the land, and serve the king 40.09
and I will d. in the midst of you, Zec 2.11
upon all who d. upon the face of Lk 21.35
moreover my flesh will d. in hope. Ac 2.26
High does not d. in houses made 7.48
and that Christ may d. in your Eph 3.17
fulness of God was pleased to d., Col 1.19
word of Christ d. in you richly, 3.16
He will d. with them, and they shall Rev 21.03
and the place where thy glory d. Ps 26.08
He who d. in the shelter of the 91.01
the Father who d. in me does his Jn 14.10
that nothing good d. within me, Rom 7.18
the Spirit of God really d. in you. 8.09
through his Spirit which d. in you. 8.11
immortality and d. in unapproachable 1Ti 6.16
earth in which righteousness d. 2Pe 3.13
killed among you, where Satan d. Rev 2.13

E

EAGER —LY

so I am e. to preach the gospel to Rom 1.15
waits with e. longing for the 8.19
which very thing I was e. to do. Gal 2.10
e. to maintain the unity of the Eph 4.03
as it is my e. expectation and hope Php 1.20
the more e. and with great desire 1Th 2.17
searched for me e. and found me— 2Ti 1.17
those who are e. waiting for him. Heb 9.28

EAGLE —S

the way of an e. in the sky, the way Pro 30.19
make yourselves as bald as the e., Mic 1.16
and I heard an e. crying with a Rev 8.13
shall mount up with wings like e., Is 40.31
there the e. will be gathered Mt 24.28

EAR —S

let thy e. be attentive, and thy Neh 1.06
Give e. to my words, O LORD; give Ps 5.01
incline thy e. to me, hear my words. 17.06
He who closes his e. to the cry of Pro 21.13
Hear, O heavens, and give e., O earth; Is 1.02
The Lord GOD has opened my e., 50.05
high priest, and cut off his e. Mt 26.51
the e., then the full grain in the e. Mk 4.28
nor e. heard, nor the heart of man 1Co 2.09
And if the e. should say, "Because I 12.16
seven e. of grain, plump and good, Gen 41.05
We have heard with our e., Ps 44.01
Let thy e. be attentive to the 130.02
and the e. of the deaf unstopped; Is 35.05
He who has e. to hear, let him hear. Mt 11.15
And his e. were opened, his tongue Mk 7.35

not see and e. that should not Rom 11.08
having itching e. they will 2Ti 4.03

EARTH

God created the heavens and the e. Gen 1.01
While the e. remains, seedtime and 8.22
Now the whole e. had one language 11.01
Most High, maker of heaven and e.; 14.19
the Judge of all the e. do right?" 18.25
and as all the e. shall be filled Num 14.21
LORD will judge the ends of the e.; 1Sa 2.10
"But will God indeed dwell on the e.? 1Ki 8.27
And the whole e. sought the presence 10.24
no God in all the e. but in Israel; 2Ki 5.15
rain upon the e. and sends waters Job 5.10
I laid the foundation of the e.? 38.04
All the ends of the e. shall Ps 22.27
The e. is the LORD's and the fulness 24.01
Let all the e. fear the LORD, let 33.08
he utters his voice, the e. melts. 46.06
For God is the king of all the e.; 47.07
go down into the depths of the e.; 63.09
The e. has yielded its increase; 67.06
may his glory fill the whole e.! 72.19
When the e. totters, and all its 75.03
tremble before him, all the e.! 96.09
the heavens are high above the e., 103.11
Thou didst set the e. on its 104.05
I am a sojourner on e.; hide not 119.19
God is in heaven, and you upon e.; Ecc 5.02
the business that is done on e., 8.16
sits above the circle of the e., Is 40.22
I made the e., and created man upon 45.12
the heavens are higher than the e., 55.09
not thither but water the e., 55.10

EARTH (cont.)

proclaimed to the end of the e.:	Is 62.11
I create new heavens and a new e.;	65.17
throne and the e. is my footstool;	66.01
Do I not fill heaven and e.?	Jer 23.24
lifted me up between e. and heaven,	Eze 8.03
who dwell at the center of the e.	38.12
of all the families of the e.;	Amo 3.02
He stood and measured the e.;	Hab 3.06
nations of the e. will come	Zec 12.03
for they shall inherit the e.	Mt 5.05
you, till heaven and e. pass away,	5.18
On e. as it is in heaven.	6.10
up for yourselves treasures on e.,	6.19
I have come to bring peace on e.;	10.34
you bind on e. shall be bound in	16.19
Heaven and e. will pass away, but my	24.35
The e. produces of itself, first the	Mk 4.28
"I came to cast fire upon the e.;	Lk 12.49
wheat falls into the e. and dies,	Jn 12.24
I glorified thee on e., having	17.04
Samaria and to the end of the e."	Ac 1.08
may be proclaimed in all the e."	Rom 9.17
voice has gone out to all the e.,	10.18
man was from the e., a man of dust;	1Co 15.47
into the lower parts of the e.?	Eph 4.09
heaven and on e. and under the e.,	Php 2.10
not on things that are on e.	Col 3.02
strangers and exiles on the e.	Heb 11.13
and an e. formed out of water and	2Pe 3.05
Then I saw a new heaven and a new e.;	Rev 21.01

EARTHEN

take holy water in an e. vessel,	Num 5.17
have this treasure in e. vessels,	2Co 4.07

EARTHLY

If I have told you e. things and	Jn 3.12
not by e. wisdom but by the grace	2Co 1.12
that if the e. tent we live in is	5.01
shame, with minds set on e. things.	Php 3.19
for worship and an e. sanctuary.	Heb 9.01

EARTHQUAKE —S

but the LORD was not in the e.;	1Ki 19.11
And behold, there was a great e.;	Mt 28.02
and suddenly there was a great e.,	Ac 16.26
be famines and e. in various places;	Mt 24.07

EASE (n)

"Woe to those who are at e. in Zion,	Amo 6.01
take your e., eat, drink, be merry.'	Lk 12.19
that you put him at e. among you.	1Co 16.10

EASIER

For which is e., to say, 'Your sins	Mt 9.05
it is e. for a camel to go through	19.24
But it is e. for heaven and earth	Lk 16.17

EAST

a garden in Eden, in the e.;	Gen 2.08
as far as the e. is from the west,	Ps 103.12
the God of Israel came from the e.;	Eze 43.02
men from the E. came to Jerusalem,	Mt 2.01
will come from e. and west and sit	8.11

EASY

the gate is wide and the way is e.,	Mt 7.13
For my yoke is e., and my burden is	11.30

EAT —EN —ING

'You shall not e. of any tree of	Gen 3.01
"You shall not e. any flesh with	Lev 19.26
Only you shall not e. the blood;	Deu 12.16
"E. no bread, and drink no water";	1Ki 13.22
who e. up my people as they e. bread,	Ps 14.04
For they e. the bread of wickedness	Pro 4.17
"Come, e. of my bread and drink of	9.05
"E. and drink!" he says	23.07
Go, e. your bread with enjoyment, and	Ecc 9.07
"Let us e. and drink, for tomorrow	Is 22.13
plant vineyards and e. their fruit.	65.21
e. this scroll, and go, speak to the	Eze 3.01
They shall e. their bread with	12.19
the youths who e. the king's rich	Dan 1.13
be made to e. grass like an ox, and	4.25
and e. bread there, and prophesy	Amo 7.12
You shall e., but not be satisfied,	Mic 6.14
what you shall e. or what you	Mt 6.25
your teacher e. with tax collectors	9.11
you give them something to e."	14.16
not wash their hands when they e."	15.02
even the dogs e. the crumbs that	15.27
prepare for you to e. the passover?"	26.17
the disciples and said, "Take, e.;	26.26
receive you, e. what is set before you;	Lk 10.08
take your ease, e., drink, be merry.'	12.19
"I have food to e. of which you do	Jn 4.32
unless you e. the flesh of the Son	6.53
is being injured by what you e.,	Rom 14.15
it is right not to e. meat or drink	14.21
not even to e. with such a one.	1Co 5.11
to e. food offered to idols?	8.10
I will never e. meat, lest I cause	8.13
E. whatever is sold in the meat	10.25
whether you e. or drink, or whatever	10.31
not the Lord's supper that you e.	11.20
and so e. of the bread and drink of	11.28
"Let us e. and drink, for tomorrow	15.32
one will not work, let him not e.	2Th 3.10
I will grant to e. of the tree of	Rev 2.07
come in to him and e. with him,	3.20
and bread e. in secret is pleasant."	Pro 9.17
'The fathers have e. sour grapes,	Jer 31.29
e. and drinking and dancing, because	1Sa 30.16
the Son of man came e. and drinking,	Mt 11.19
flood they were e. and drinking,	24.38
Now as they were e., Jesus took	26.26

EDGE —S

the children's teeth are set on e.'	Jer 31.29
children's teeth are set on e.'?	Eze 18.02
temples or mar the e. of your beard.	Lev 19.27

EDICT

were not afraid of the king's e.	Heb 11.23

EDIFIED —Y*

so that the church may be e.	1Co 14.05
neighbor for his good, to e. him.	Rom 15.02

EDIFYING* (n)
but only such as is good for e.,   Eph 4.29

EGG* —S
or if he asks for an e., will give   Lk 11.12
They hatch adders' e., they weave the   Is 59.05

ELDER —S
"Now his e. son was in the field;   Lk 15.25
"The e. will serve the younger."   Rom 9.12
against an e. except on the   1Ti 5.19
as a fellow e. and a witness of the   1Pe 5.01
Go and gather the e. of Israel   Ex 3.16
Then Moses called all the e. of Israel,   12.21
transgress the tradition of the e.?   Mt 15.02
things from the e. and chief   16.21
with the e. and taken counsel, they   28.12
had appointed e. for them in every   Ac 14.23
apostles and the e. about this   15.02
called to him the e. of the church.   20.17
when the e. laid their hands upon   1Ti 4.14
Let the e. who rule well be considered   5.17
and appoint e. in every town as I   Tit 1.05
are younger be subject to the e.   5.05
on the thrones were twenty-four e.,   Rev 4.04

ELECT
the sake of the e. those days will   Mt 24.22
And will not God vindicate his e.,   Lk 18.07
bring any charge against God's e.?   Rom 8.33
The e. obtained it, but the rest   11.07
and of the e. angels I charge you   1Ti 5.21
faith of God's e. and their   Tit 1.01

ELECTION
God's purpose of e. might continue,   Rom 9.11

ELEVEN
Now the e. disciples went to   Mt 28.16
was enrolled with the e. apostles.   Ac 1.26

EMBODIMENT*
in the law the e. of knowledge and   Rom 2.20

EMBRACE —D
a time to e., and a time to refrain   Ecc 3.05
and ran and e. him and kissed him.   Lk 15.20
all wept and e. Paul and kissed   Ac 20.37

EMPTIED
cross of Christ be e. of its power.   1Co 1.17
but e. himself, taking the form of a   Php 2.07

EMPTY (adj)
it shall not return to me e.,   Is 55.11
with e. oaths they make covenants;   Hos 10.04
do not heap up e. phrases as the   Mt 6.07
and when he comes he finds it e.,   12.44
and the rich he has sent e. away.   Lk 1.53
Let no one deceive you with e. words,   Eph 5.06
of you by philosophy and e. deceit,   Col 2.08

EMPTY-HANDED
None shall appear before me e.   Ex 23.15
and beat him, and sent him away e.   Mk 12.03

ENCAMP —S*
Though a host e. against me, my   Ps 27.03
of the LORD e. around those who   34.07

ENCOMPASS —ED —ES
thou dost e. me with deliverance.   Ps 32.07
Now their deeds e. them,   Hos 7.02
The cords of death e. me,   Ps 18.04
he e. him all the day long, and   Deu 33.12

ENCOURAGE —D —S* —ING*
and that he may e. your hearts.   Eph 6.22
Therefore e. one another and build   1Th 5.11
e. the fainthearted, help the weak,   5.14
may be mutually e. by each other's   Rom 1.12
The craftsman e. the goldsmith, and   Is 41.07
but e. one another, and all the more   Heb 10.25

ENCOURAGEMENT
and by the e. of the scriptures we   Rom 15.04
upbuilding and e. and consolation.   1Co 14.03
So if there is any e. in Christ,   Php 2.01
have strong e. to seize the hope   Heb 6.18

END —ED —ING —S (v)
same, and thy years will never e."   Heb 1.12
cry to her that her warfare is e.,   Is 40.02
my deliverance will never be e.   51.06
and when the feast was e., as they   Lk 2.43
Spirit, are you now e. with the flesh?   Gal 3.03
Love never e.; as for prophecy,   1Co 13.08

END —S (n)
determined to make an e. of all flesh;   Gen 6.13
Shall windy words have an e.?   Job 16.03
"LORD, let me know my e.,   Ps 39.04
but its e. is the way to death.   Pro 14.12
Better is the e. of a thing than   Ecc 7.08
making many books there is no e.,   12.12
and of peace there will be no e.,   Is 9.07
declaring the e. from the beginning   46.10
endures to the e. will be saved.   Mt 10.22
take place, but the e. is not yet.   24.06
sat with the guards to see the e.   26.58
of his kingdom there will be no e."   Lk 1.33
Samaria and to the e. of the earth."   Ac 1.08
sanctification and its e., eternal life.   Rom 6.22
For Christ is the e. of the law,   10.04
For to this e. Christ died and   14.09
who will sustain you to the e.,   1Co 1.08
upon whom the e. of the ages has   10.11
Then comes the e., when he delivers   15.24
Their e. will correspond to their   2Co 11.15
bringing the hostility to an e.   Eph 2.16
Their e. is destruction, their god   Php 3.19
The e. of all things is at hand;   1Pe 4.07
Omega, the beginning and the e.   Rev 21.06
the Creator of the e. of the earth.   Is 40.28
their words to the e. of the world."   Rom 10.18

ENDURANCE
By your e. you will gain your lives.   Lk 21.19
knowing that suffering produces e.,   Rom 5.03
for all e. and patience with joy,   Col 1.11

ENDURANCE (cont.)

For you have need of e., so that you	Heb 10.36
faith and service and patient e.,	Rev 2.19
a call for the e. and faith of the	13.10

ENDURE —D —S —ING

May his name e. for ever, his fame	Ps 72.17
But who can e. the day of his	Mal 3.02
we bless; when persecuted, we e.;	1Co 4.12
but we e. anything rather than put	9.12
if we e., we shall also reign with	2Ti 2.10
e. suffering, do the work of an	4.05
for discipline that you have to e.	Heb 12.07
thus Abraham, having patiently e.,	6.15
thy name e. to all generations.	Ps 102.12
and his righteousness e. for ever.	111.03
Thy faithfulness e. to all generations;	119.90
the food which e. to eternal life,	Jn 6.27
hopes all things, e. all things.	1Co 13.07
Blessed is the man who e. trial,	Jas 1.12
of the LORD is clean, e. for ever;	Ps 19.09

ENEMIES —Y

before me in the presence of my e.;	Ps 23.05
Deliver me from my e., O my God,	59.01
a man's e. are the men of his own	Mic 7.06
Love your e. and pray for those who	Mt 5.44
till I put thy e. under thy feet'?	22.44
while we were e. we were reconciled	Rom 5.10
the gospel they are e. of God,	11.28
live as e. of the cross of Christ.	Php 3.18
wait until his e. should be made a	Heb 10.13
his e. came and sowed weeds among	Mt 13.25
No, "if your e. is hungry, feed him;	Rom 12.20
The last e. to be destroyed is	1Co 15.26
become your e. by telling you the	Gal 4.16
Do not look on him as an e., but	2Th 3.15
and give the e. no occasion to	1Ti 5.14
world makes himself an e. of God.	Jas 4.04

ENJOY

"Then the land shall e. its sabbaths	Lev 26.34
and another man e. its fruit.	Deu 20.06
test of pleasure; e. yourself."	Ecc 2.01
E. life with the wife whom you love,	9.09
furnishes us with everything to e.	1Ti 6.17
of God than to e. the fleeting	Heb 11.25

ENJOYMENT

And I commend e., for man has no	Ecc 8.15
Go, eat your bread with e., and drink	9.07

ENLARGE —D —ST*

E. the place of your tent, and let	Is 54.02
that you e. your eyes with paint?	Jer 4.30
field among you may be greatly e.,	2Co 10.15
when thou e. my understanding!	Ps 119.32

ENLIGHTENED —ING* —S*

a zeal for God, but it is not e.	Rom 10.02
having the eyes of your hearts e.,	Eph 1.18
of the LORD is pure, e. the eyes;	Ps 19.08
The true light that e. every man	Jn 1.09

ENMITY

I will put e. between you and the	Gen 3.15
had been at e. with each other.	Lk 23.12
e., strife, jealousy, anger, selfishness,	Gal 5.20
with the world is e. with God?	Jas 4.04

ENOUGH

he might die, saying, "It is e.;	1Ki 19.04
and the fire which never says, "E."	Pro 30.16
it is e. for the disciple to be	Mt 10.25
It is e.; the hour has come;	Mk 14.41
servants have bread e. and to spare,	Lk 15.17
may always have e. of everything	2Co 9.08

ENRICHED —EST

A liberal man will be e., and one	Pro 11.25
way you were e. in him with all	1Co 1.05
You will be e. in every way for	2Co 9.11
waterest it, thou greatly e. it;	Ps 65.09

ENROL* —LED

But refuse to e. younger widows;	1Ti 5.11
that all the world should be e.	Lk 2.01
and he was e. with the eleven	Ac 1.26
first-born who are e. in heaven,	Heb 12.23

ENROLLMENT

This was the first e., when	Lk 2.02

ENSLAVE —D

so that no one should e. a Jew,	Jer 34.09
we might no longer be e. to sin.	Rom 6.06
but I will not be e. by anything.	1Co 6.12
overcomes a man, to that he is e.	2Pe 2.19

ENSNARE —D

Though the cords of the wicked e. me,	Ps 119.61
An evil man is e. in his transgression,	Pro 29.06

ENTANGLE —D

counsel how to e. him in his talk.	Mt 22.15
the cords of Sheol e. me, the snares	Ps 18.05
on service gets e. in civilian	2Ti 2.04

ENTER —ED —S

E. his gates with thanksgiving, and	Ps 100.04
you will never e. the kingdom of	Mt 5.20
"E. by the narrow gate; for the gate	7.13
and e. no town of the Samaritans,	10.05
Or how can one e. a strong man's	12.29
you will never e. the kingdom of	18.03
If you would e. life, keep the	19.17
a rich man to e. the kingdom of	19.24
e. into the joy of your master.'	25.21
you may not e. into temptation;	26.41
God like a child shall not e. it."	Mk 10.15
these things and e. into his glory?"	Lk 24.26
Can he e. a second time into his	Jn 3.04
tribulations we must e. the kingdom	Ac 14.22
'They shall never e. my rest.'"	Heb 3.11
the Spirit e. into me and set me	Eze 2.02
no church e. into partnership with	Php 4.15
For Christ has e., not into a sanctuary	Heb 9.24
Blessed be he who e. in the name of	Ps 118.26

ENTER —ED —S (cont.)
when he e. the inner court. Eze 44.21
and an unbeliever or outsider e., 1Co 14.24

ENTHRONED
But thou, O LORD, art e. for ever; Ps 102.12
O thou who art e. in the heavens! 123.01

ENTICE —D
if sinners e. you, do not consent. Pro 1.10
They e. unsteady souls. They have 2Pe 2.14
he is lured and e. by his own Jas 1.14

ENTREAT
"E. me not to leave you or to Ru 1.16
I e. thy favor with all my heart; Ps 119.58
we e. you not to accept the grace 2Co 6.01
myself e. you, by the meekness and 10.01

ENTRUST —ED —ING*
who will e. to you the true riches? Lk 16.11
do right and e. their souls to a 1Pe 4.19
servants and e. to them his property; Mt 25.14
own will, I am e. with a commission. 1Co 9.17
that I had been e. with the gospel Gal 2.07
guard what has been e. to you. Avoid 1Ti 6.20
e. to us the message of reconciliation. 2Co 5.19

ENVOY* —S
but a faithful e. brings healing. Pro 13.17
you sent your e. far off, and sent Is 57.09

ENVY (v)
Let not your heart e. sinners, Pro 23.17

ENVY (n)
it was out of e. that they had Mt 27.18
Full of e., murder, strife, deceit, Rom 1.29
e., drunkenness, carousing, and the Gal 5.21
preach Christ from e. and rivalry, Php 1.15
passing our days in malice and e., Tit 3.03

EPHAH
(An omer is the tenth part of an e.) Ex 16.36
a just e., and a just hin: I am the Lev 19.36
a just e., and a just bath. Eze 45.10

EQUAL
have made them e. to us who have Mt 20.12
Father, making himself e. with God. Jn 5.18
plants and he who waters are e., 1Co 3.08
a faith of e. standing with ours 2Pe 1.01

EQUIPMENT
for the e. of the saints, for the Eph 4.12
feet with the e. of the gospel of 6.15

EQUITY
he judges the peoples with e. Ps 9.08
and decide with e. for the meek of Is 11.04
abhor justice and pervert all e., Mic 3.09

ERECT —ED
no idols and e. no graven image or Lev 26.01

Moses was about to e. the tent, Heb 8.05
There he e. an altar and called it Gen 33.20

ERROR —S
but the way of e. leads to death. Pro 12.28
and no e. or fault was found in him. Dan 6.04
the due penalty for their e. Rom 1.27
not spring from e. or uncleanness, 1Th 2.03
of truth and the spirit of e. 1Jn 4.06
and for the e. of the people. Heb 9.07

ESCAPE (v)
to e. the waters of the flood. Gen 7.07
And we, how shall we e.?' " Is 20.06
Can a man e. who does such things? Eze 17.15
how are you to e. being sentenced Mt 23.33
to die, I do not seek to e. death; Ac 25.11
lest any should swim away and e.; 27.42
you will e. the judgment of God? Rom 2.03
how shall we e. if we neglect such Heb 2.03
these you may e. from the corruption 2Pe 1.04

ESCAPE (n)
will also provide the way of e., 1Co 10.13
child, and there will be no e. 1Th 5.03

ESTABLISH —ED —S
But I will e. my covenant with you; Gen 6.18
and e. thou the work of our hands Ps 90.17
God, and seeking to e. their own, Rom 10.03
to e. you in your faith and to 1Th 3.02
when I will e. a new covenant with Heb 8.08
E. your hearts, for the coming of Jas 5.08
and the stars which thou hast e.; Ps 8.03
Yea, the world is e.; it shall never 93.01
A man is not e. by wickedness, but Pro 12.03
Plans are e. by counsel; by wise 20.18
Who has e. all the ends of the 30.04
believe, surely you shall not be e.' " Is 7.09
LORD shall be e. as the highest of Mic 4.01
But whoever is firmly e. in his heart, 1Co 7.37
But it is God who e. us with you in 2Co 1.21

ESTATE
said, "Go to Anathoth, to your e.; 1Ki 2.26
Men of low e. are but a breath, men Ps 62.09
he who remembered us in our low e., 136.23
regarded the low e. of his handmaiden. Lk 1.48
he is the owner of all the e.; Gal 4.01

ESTEEM —ED (v)
and to e. them very highly in love 1Th 5.13
he was despised, and we e. him not. Is 53.03
who are least e. by the church? 1Co 6.04

ESTRANGED
He who is e. seeks pretexts to Pro 18.01
who once were e. and hostile in Col 1.21

ETERNAL
the blessings of the e. mountains, Gen 49.26
The e. God is your dwelling place, Deu 33.27
feet to be thrown into the e. fire. Mt 18.08
deed must I do, to have e. life?" 19.16

ETERNAL (cont.)
but the righteous into e. life."   Mt 25.46
you into the e. habitations.   Lk 16.09
should not perish but have e. life.   Jn 3.16
of water welling up to e. life."   4.14
You have the words of e. life;   6.68
and I give them e. life, and they   10.28
And this is e. life, that they know   17.03
his e. power and deity, has been   Rom 1.20
gift of God is e. life in Christ   6.23
for us an e. weight of glory beyond   2Co 4.17
the things that are unseen are e.   4.18
made with hands, e. in the heavens.   5.01
according to the e. purpose which   Eph 3.11
us and gave us e. comfort and good   2Th 2.16
hold of the e. life to which you   1Ti 6.12
become heirs in hope of e. life.   Tit 3.07
the source of e. salvation to all   Heb 5.09
by the blood of the e. covenant,   13.20
undergoing a punishment of e. fire.   Jud 7
with an e. gospel to proclaim to   Rev 14.06

ETERNITY
also he has put e. into man's mind,   Ecc 3.11

EUNUCH —S
And the e. said to Philip, "About   Ac 8.34
For there are e. who have been so   Mt 19.12

EVENING
And there was e. and there was   Gen 1.05
E. and morning and at noon I utter   Ps 55.17
My days are like an e. shadow;   102.11
for the shadows of e. lengthen!"   Jer 6.04
for at e. time there shall be light.   Zec 14.07
When e. came, he was there alone,   Mt 14.23
"When it is e., you say, 'It will be   16.02
When it was e., he sat at table   26.20
to them from morning till e., testifying   Ac 28.23

EVER
life, and eat, and live for e."—   Gen 3.22
shall not abide in man for e.,   6.03
The LORD is king for e. and e.;   Ps 10.16
in the house of the LORD for e.   23.06
Wilt thou hide thyself for e.?   89.46
He is mindful of his covenant for e.,   105.08
cannot be moved, but abides for e.   125.01
for riches do not last for e.;   Pro 27.24
No one has e. seen God: the only   Jn 1.18
"No man e. spoke like this man!"   7.46
the Creator, who is blessed for e.!   Rom 1.25
place, "Thou art a priest for e.,   Heb 5.06
yesterday and today and for e.   13.08

EVERLASTING
remember the e. covenant between   Gen 9.16
and the abundance of the e. hills,   Deu 33.15
and underneath are the e. arms.   33.27
of Israel, from e. to e.!   Ps 41.13
from e. to e. thou art God.   90.02
LORD is from e. to e. upon those who   103.17
in me, and lead me in the way e.!   139.24
Thy kingdom is an e. kingdom,   145.13

God, E. Father, Prince of Peace."   Is 9.06
The LORD is the e. God, the Creator   40.28
I have loved you with an e. love;   Jer 31.03

EVERMORE
be glory for e. through Jesus Christ!   Rom 16.27
died, and behold I am alive for e.,   Rev 1.18

EVERYTHING
And God saw e. that he had made,   Gen 1.31
Let e. that breathes praise the   Ps 150.06
The LORD has made e. for its   Pro 16.04
For e. there is a season, and a time   Ecc 3.01
we have left e. and followed you.   Mt 19.27
he said to him, "Lord, you know e.;   Jn 21.17
We know that in e. God works for   Rom 8.28
E. is indeed clean, but it is wrong   14.20
For the Spirit searches e., even the   1Co 2.10
that God may be e. to every one.   15.28
do e. in the name of the Lord Jesus,   Col 3.17
but test e.; hold fast what   1Th 5.21

EVIDENCE
On the e. of two witnesses or of   Deu 17.06
confirmed by the e. of two or three   Mt 18.16
This is e. of the righteous judgment   2Th 1.05

EVIL
of the knowledge of good and e.   Gen 2.09
his heart was only e. continually.   6.05
man's heart is e. from his youth: 8.21
to depart from e. is understanding,' "   Job 28.28
But when I looked for good, e. came;   30.26
Keep your tongue from e., and your   Ps 34.13
Incline not my heart to any e.,   141.04
A righteous man turns away from e.,   Pro 12.26
There is a grievous e. which I have   Ecc 5.13
those who call e. good and good e.,   Is 5.20
to refuse the e. and choose the   7.15
I will punish the world for its e.,   13.11
They are skilled in doing e.,   Jer 4.22
I begin to work e. at the city   25.29
Hate e., and love good, and establish   Amo 5.15
all kinds of e. against you falsely   Mt 5.11
temptation, But deliver us from e.   6.13
A sound tree cannot bear e. fruit,   7.18
you speak good, when you are e.?   12.34
"An e. and adulterous generation   12.39
For out of the heart come e. thoughts,   15.19
who are e., know how to give good   Lk 11.13
one who does e. hates the light,   Jn 3.20
But the e. spirit answered them,   Ac 19.15
And why not do e. that good may   Rom 3.08
do right, he. lies close at hand.   7.21
hate what is e., hold fast to what   12.09
be babes in e., but in thinking be   1Co 14.20
the time, because the days are e.   Eph 5.16
abstain from every form of e.   1Th 5.22
practice to distinguish good from e.   Heb 5.14
your freedom as a pretext for e.;   1Pe 2.16
Beloved, do not imitate e. but   3Jn 11

EVILDOER —S
him, "If this man were not an e.,   Jn 18.30

EVILDOER —S (cont.)

Let the e. still do evil, and the	Rev 22.11
The face of the LORD is against e.,	Ps 34.16
Fret not yourself because of e.,	Pro 24.19
knew you; depart from me, you e.'	Mt 7.23
all causes of sin and all e.,	13.41

EXALT —ED —S

and let us e. his name together!	Ps 34.03
e. that which is low, and abase that	Eze 21.26
Christ did not e. himself to be	Heb 5.05
before the Lord and he will e. you.	Jas 4.10
that in due time he may e. you.	1Pe 5.06
Be e., O God, above the heavens!	Ps 57.05
he shall be e. and lifted up, and	Is 52.13
whoever humbles himself will be e.	Mt 23.12
Being therefore e. at the right	Ac 2.33
God e. him at his right hand as	5.31
myself so that you might be e.,	2Co 11.07
Therefore God has highly e. him and	Php 2.09
from sinners, e. above the heavens.	Heb 7.26
with unutterable and e. joy.	1Pe 1.08
Righteousness e. a nation, but sin	Pro 14.34

EXAMINE —D

Let us test and e. our ways,	Lam 3.40
Let a man e. himself, and so eat of	1Co 11.28
E. yourselves, to see whether you	2Co 13.05
if we are being e. today concerning	Ac 4.09

EXAMPLE —S*

For I have given you an e., that you	Jn 13.15
also follow the e. of the faith	Rom 4.12
and made a public e. of them,	Col 2.15
you became an e. to all the believers	1Th 1.07
believers an e. in speech and conduct,	1Ti 4.12
suffered for you, leaving you an e.,	1Pe 2.21
charge but being e. to the flock	5.03

EXCELLENT

because an e. spirit was in him;	Dan 6.03
for you, most e. Theophilus,	Lk 1.03
most e. Felix, reforms are introduced	Ac 24.02
his will and approve what is e.,	Rom 2.18
will show you a still more e. way.	1Co 12.31
so that you may approve what is e.,	Php 1.10
is as much more e. than the old as	Heb 8.06

EXCHANGE —D (v)

and make merry and e. presents,	Rev 11.10
They e. the glory of God for the	Ps 106.20
and e. the glory of the immortal	Rom 1.23
because they e. the truth about God	1.25

EXCHANGE (n)

you, peoples in e. for your life.	Is 43.04

EXCLUDE* —D

and when they e. you and revile you,	Lk 6.22
It is e. On what principle?	Rom 3.27

EXECUTE —S

gods of Egypt I will e. judgments:	Ex 12.12
He will e. judgment among the nations,	Ps 110.06
" 'E. justice in the morning, and	Jer 21.12

I will not e. my fierce anger, I	Hos 11.09
given him authority to e. judgment,	Jn 5.27
of God to e. his wrath on the	Rom 13.04
to e. judgment on all, and to	Jud 15
he that e. his word is powerful.	Joe 2.11

EXERCISE —S

their great men e. authority over	Mt 20.25
But if they cannot e. self-control,	1Co 7.09
was allowed to e. authority for	Rev 13.05
Every athlete e. self-control in	1Co 9.25

EXHORT—ING

you in your faith and to e. you,	1Th 3.02
we command and e. in the Lord	2Th 3.12
older man but e. him as you would	1Ti 5.01
and e., be unfailing in patience	2Ti 4.02
e. and reprove with all authority.	Tit 2.15
So I e. the elders among you, as a	1Pe 5.01
e. and declaring that this is the	5.12

EXHORTATION —S*

have any word of e. for the people,	Ac 13.15
he who exhorts, in his e.; he who	Rom 12.08
brethren, bear with my word of e.,	Heb 13.22
So, with many other e., he preached	Lk 3.18

EXILE —S (n)

He took into e. in Babylon those	2Ch 36.20
of Israel who had returned from e.,	Ez 6.21
people go into e. for want of	Is 5.13
taken into e., wholly taken into e.	Jer 13.19
had taken into e. from Jerusalem	24.01
saying, "Your e. will be long;	29.28
Prepare yourselves baggage for e.,	46.19
Judah has gone into e. because of	Lam 1.03
sent them into e. among the nations,	Eze 39.28
must go into e. away from his land.' "	Amo 7.11
and became an e. in the land of	Ac 7.29
throughout the time of your e.	1Pe 1.17
faithlessness of the returned e.,	Ez 9.04
build my city and set my e. free,	Is 45.13
"Send to all the e., saying 'Thus	Jer 29.31
I was among the e. by the river	Eze 1.01
were strangers and e. on the earth.	Heb 11.13
To the e. of the dispersion in	1Pe 1.01
as aliens and e. to abstain from	2.11

EXIST —ED —S*

existence the things that do not e.	Rom 4.17
for whom and by whom all things e.,	Heb 2.10
word of God heavens e. long ago,	2Pe 3.05
thy will they e. and were created."	Rev 4.11
believe that he e. and that he	Heb 11.06

EXPECT —ING

is coming at an hour you do not e.	Mt 24.44
e. nothing in return; and your	Lk 6.35

EXPIATION

sprinkle the water of e. upon them,	Num 8.07
put forward as an e. by his blood,	Rom 3.25
to make e. for the sins of the	Heb 2.17
and he is the e. for our sins, and	1Jn 2.02
his Son to be the e. for our sins.	4.10

EXPLAIN —ED —ING*

Moses undertook to e. this law,	Deu 1.05
and to whom will he e. the message?	Is 28.09
"E. to us the parable of the weeds	Mt 13.36
said to him, "E. the parable to us."	15.15
much to say which is hard to e.,	Heb 5.11
his own disciples he e. everything.	Mk 4.34
e. and proving that it was necessary	Ac 17.03

EXPOSE —D

of darkness, but instead e. them.	Eph 5.11
light, lest his deeds should be e.	Jn 3.20
anything is e. by the light it	Eph 5.13
sometimes being publicly e. to	Heb 10.33

EXTEND —ED —S

be none to e. kindness to him, nor	Ps 109.12
the Lord will e. his hand yet a	Is 11.11
and who e. to me his steadfast love	Ez 7.28
e. to the heavens, thy faithfulness	Ps 36.05
that as grace e. to more and more	2Co 4.15

EXTORTION

Put no confidence in e., set no vain	Ps 62.10
they are full of e. and rapacity.	Mt 23.25

EXULT —S

I would even e. in pain unsparing;	Job 6.10
let not my enemies e. over me.	Ps 25.02
how long shall the wicked e.?	94.03
Let the faithful e. in glory;	149.05
joy, O heavens, and e., O earth;	Is 49.13
E. not like the peoples; for you have	Hos 9.01
Rejoice and e. with all your heart,	Zep 3.14
their hearts shall e. in the LORD.	Zec 10.07
Let us rejoice and e. add give him	Rev 19.07
and said, "My heart e. in the LORD;	1Sa 2.01
her throng and he who e. in her.	Is 5.14

EYE —S

e. for e., tooth for tooth, hand for	Ex 21.24
My e. has grown dim from grief, and	Job 17.07
Keep me as the apple of the e.;	Ps 6.07
Behold, the e. of the LORD is on	33.18
The hearing ear and the seeing e.,	Pro 20.12
no e. has seen a God besides thee,	Is 64.04
face to face and see him e. to e.;	Jer 32.04
If your right e. causes you to sin,	Mt 5.29
'An e. for an e. and a tooth for a	5.38
"The e. is the lamp of the body.	6.22
speck that is in your brother's e.,	7.03
go through the e. of a needle than	19.24
Your e. is the lamp of your body;	Lk 11.34
"What no e. has seen, nor ear heard,	1Co 2.09

If the whole body were an e., where	12.17
moment, in the twinkling of an e.,	15.52
and every e. will see him, every one	Rev 1.07
eat of it your e. will be opened,	Gen 3.05
Then the e. of both were opened, and	3.07
his e. shall be red with wine, and	49.12
Then the LORD opened the e. of	Num 22.31
"Why have I found favor in your e.,	Ru 2.10
was a small thing in thy e., O God;	1Ch 17.17
Hast thou e. of flesh? Dost thou see	Job 10.04
pure, and I am clean in God's e.'	11.04
I was e. to the blind, and feet to	29.15
"I have made a covenant with my e.;	31.01
LORD is pure, enlightening the e.;	Ps 19.08
Turn my e. from looking at vanities;	119.37
I lift up my e. to the hills.	121.01
Thy e. beheld my unformed substance;	139.16
Be not wise in your own e.; fear the	Pro 3.07
He who winks his e. plans perverse	16.30
The e. of the LORD keep watch over	22.12
A rich man is wise in his own e.,	28.11
LORD gives light to the e. of both.	29.13
And whatever my e. desired I did	Ecc 2.10
Your e. are doves behind your veil.	Sol 4.01
hands, I will hide my e. from you;	Is 1.15
and the e. of the haughty are humbled.	5.15
for my e. have seen the King, the	6.05
Then the e. of the blind shall be	35.05
Because you are precious in my e.,	43.04
Lift up your e. round about and see;	49.18
we grope like those who have no e.;	59.10
LORD, do not thy e. look for truth?	Jer 5.03
Our e. failed, ever watching vainly	Lam 4.17
rims were full of e. round about.	Eze 1.18
And their e. were opened. And Jesus	Mt 9.30
But blessed are your e., for they see,	13.16
than with two e. to be thrown into	18.09
to him, "Lord, let our e. be opened."	20.33
doing, and it is marvelous in our e.'?	21.42
sleeping, for their e. were heavy.	26.43
for mine e. have seen thy salvation	Lk 2.30
and the e. of all in the synagogue	4.20
not even lift up his e. to heaven	18.13
lifted up his e. to heaven and	Jn 17.01
let their e. be darkened so that	Rom 11.10
Look at what is before your e. If	2Co 10.07
before whose e. Jesus Christ was	Gal 3.01
out your e. and given them to me.	4.15
having the e. of your hearts	Eph 1.18
bare to the e. of him with whom we	Heb 4.13
For the e. of the Lord are upon the	1Pe 3.12
They have e. full of adultery,	2Pe 2.14
which we have seen with our e.,	1Jn 1.01
with seven horns and with seven e.,	Rev 5.06

F

FACE —S

sweat of your f. you shall eat	Gen 3.19
Abraham fell on his f. and laughed,	17.17
"For I have seen God f. to f.,	32.30
And Moses hid his f., for he was	Ex 3.06
used to speak to Moses f. to f.,	33.11

the skin of his f. shone because	34.29
with them, he put a veil on his f.;	34.33
and honor the f. of an old man, and	Lev 19.32
The LORD make his f. to shine upon	Num 6.25
I will defend my ways to his f.	Job 13.15
He covers the f. of the moon, and	26.09

FACE —S (cont.)

Who can open the doors of his f.?	Job 41.14
the upright shall behold his f.	Ps 11.07
long wilt thou hide thy f. from me?	13.01
Hide not thy f. from me. Turn not	27.09
Hide thy f. from my sins, and blot	51.09
light of a king's f. there is life,	Pro 16.15
understanding sets his f. toward wisdom,	17.24
A wicked man puts on a bold f.,	21.29
As in water f. answers to f., so the	27.19
wings: with two he covered his f.,	Is 6.02
to me their back and not their f.;	Jer 32.33
beryl, his f. like the appearance of	Dan 10.06
anoint your head and wash your f.,	Mt 6.17
I send my messenger before thy f.,	11.10
and his f. shone like the sun, and	17.02
Then they spat in his f., and struck	26.67
he set his f. to go to Jerusalem.	Lk 9.51
saw that his f. was like the f. of an	Ac 6.15
mirror dimly, but then f. to f. Now I	1Co 13.12
look at Moses' f. because of its	2Co 3.07
with unveiled f., beholding the glory	3.18
glory of God in the f. of Christ.	4.06
observes his natural f. in a mirror;	Jas 1.23
But the f. of the Lord is against	1 Pe 3.12
and his f. was like the sun shining	Rev 1.16
creature with the f. of a man, and the	4.07
they shall see his f., and his	22.04
fell on their f. before the throne	7.11
fell on their f. and worshiped God,	11.16

FACT —S*

And as for the f. that he raised	Ac 13.34
But in f. Christ has been raised	1Co 15.20
They deliberately ignore this f.,	2Pe 3.05
not learn the f. because of the	Ac 21.34

FADE —S —ING

For they will soon f. like the grass,	Ps 37.02
the rich man f. away in the midst	Jas 1.11
As the cloud f. and vanishes, so he	Job 7.09
The grass withers, the flower f.;	Is 40.08
not see the end of the f. splendor.	2Co 3.13

FAIL —ED —S

he will not f. you or destroy you	Deu 4.31
My flesh and my heart may f., but	Ps 73.26
He will not f. or be discouraged	Is 42.04
spring of water, whose waters f. not.	58.11
How is it that you f. to perceive	Mt 16.11
in the heavens that does not f.,	Lk 12.33
for you that your faith may not f.;	22.32
indeed you f. to meet the test!	2Co 13.05
it that no one f. to obtain the grace	Heb 12.15
"I will never f. you nor forsake	13.05
and my close friends have f. me;	Job 19.14
When the wine f., the mother of	Jn 2.03
as though the word of God had f.	Rom 9.06
Israel f. to obtain what it sought.	11.07
whole law but f. in one point has	Jas 2.10
is right to do and f. to do it,	4.17

FAINT —ING —S (v)

He does not f. or grow weary, his	Is 40.28

weary, they shall walk and not f.	40.31
Hearts f. and knees tremble, anguish	Nah 2.10
hungry, lest they f. on the way."	Mt 15.32
men f. with fear and with foreboding	Lk 21.26
not another. My heart f. within me!	Job 19.27
f. for the courts of the LORD; my heart	Ps 84.02

FAINT

When my spirit is f., thou knowest	Ps 142.03
He gives power to the f., and to him	Is 40.29

FAIR —LY*

that the daughters of men were f.;	Gen 6.02
her beauty; for she was f. to behold.	Est 1.11
no women so f. as Job's daughters;	Job 42.15
f. as the moon, bright as the sun,	Sol 6.10
Yea, how good and how f. it shall be!	Zec 9.17
"It is not f. to take the children's	Mt 15.26
Masters, treat your slaves justly and f.,	Col 4.01

FAITH

a breach of f. and sins unwittingly	Lev 5.15
because you broke f. with me in the	Deu 32.51
"We have broken f. with our God	Ez 10.02
Do you have f. in him that he will	Job 39.12
because they had no f. in God,	Ps 78.22
I kept my f., even when I said, "I	116.10
the righteous shall live by his f.	Hab 2.04
clothe you, O men of little f.?	Mt 6.30
your f. has made you well." And	9.22
to them, "Because of your little f.	17.20
if you have f. and never doubt, you	21.21
answered them, "Have f. in God.	Mk 11.22
He said to them, "Where is your f.?"	Lk 8.25
comes, will he find f. on earth?"	18.08
a man full of f. and the Holy	Ac 6.05
priests were obedient to the f.	6.07
but cleansed their hearts by f.	15.09
him speak upon f. in Christ Jesus.	24.24
who are sanctified by f. in me.'	26.18
salvation to every one who has f.,	Rom 1.16
of God through f. in Jesus Christ	3.22
We say that f. was reckoned to Abraham	4.09
Therefore, since we are justified by f.,	5.01
the word of f. which we preach);	10.08
So f. comes from what is heard, and	10.17
the measure of f. which God has	12.03
bring about the obedience of f.—	16.26
So f., hope, love abide, these three;	1Co 13.13
is in vain and your f. is in vain.	15.14
for we walk by f., not by sight.	2Co 5.07
flesh I live by f. in the Son of	Gal 2.20
of the law, or by hearing with f.?	3.02
but the law does not rest on f.,	3.12
But now that f. has come, we are no	3.25
Spirit, by f., we wait for the hope of	5.05
to those who are of the household of f.	6.10
you have been saved through f.;	Eph 2.08
dwell in your hearts through f.;	3.17
one Lord, one f., one baptism,	4.05
above all taking the shield of f.,	6.16
the firmness of your f. in Christ.	Col 2.05
your work of f. and labor of love	1Th 1.03
supply what is lacking in your f.?	3.10

FAITH (cont.)

because your f. is growing abundantly,	2Th 1.03
and evil men; for not all have f.	3.02
a good conscience and sincere f.	1Ti 1.05
have made shipwreck of their f.,	1.19
mystery of the f. with a clear	3.09
disowned the f. and is worse than	5.08
Fight the good fight of the f.;	6.12
a f. that dwelt first in your	2Ti 1.05
finished the race, I have kept the f.	4.07
dead works and of f. toward God.	Heb 6.01
Now f. is the assurance of things	11.01
By f. we understand that the world	11.03
These all died in f., not having	11.13
pioneer and perfecter of our f.,	12.02
to be rich in f. and heirs of the	Jas 2.05
so f. apart from works is dead.	2.26
guarded through f. for a salvation	1Pe 1.05
to supplement your f. with virtue,	2Pe 1.05
that overcomes the world, our f.	1Jn 5.04
contend for the f. which was once	Jud 3
commandments of God and the f. of	Rev 14.12

FAITHFUL

the f. God who keeps covenant and	Deu 7.09
The LORD preserves the f., but	Ps 31.23
"Who then is the f. and wise servant,	Mt 24.45
'Well done, good and f. servant; you	25.21
all to remain f. to the Lord with	Ac 11.23
God is f., by whom you were called	1Co 1.09
He is a f. minister of Christ on	Col 1.07
he judged me f. by appointing me	1Ti 1.12
but temperate, f. in all things.	3.11
but Christ was f. over God's house	Heb 3.06
entrust their souls to a f. Creator.	1Pe 4.19
he is f. and just, and will forgive	1Jn 1.09
and from Jesus Christ the f. witness,	Rev 1.05
sat upon it is called F. and True,	19.11

FAITHFULNESS

A God of f. and without iniquity,	Deu 32.04
Steadfast love and f. will meet;	Ps 85.10
and the f. of the LORD endures for	117.02
Thy f. endures to all generations;	119.90
I will betroth you to me in f.;	Hos 2.20
faithlessness nullify the f. of God?	Rom 3.03
patience, kindness, goodness, f.,	Gal 5.22

FAITHLESS —LY —NESS

he overthrows the words of the f.	Pro 22.12
"F. Israel has shown herself less	Jer 3.11
why then are we f. to one another,	Mal 2.10
"O f. and perverse generation, how	Mt 17.17
my side; do not be f., but believing."	Jn 20.27
if we are f., he remains faithful—	2Ti 2.13
They have dealt f. with the LORD;	Hos 5.07
I will heal their f.; I will love	14.04

FALL —EN —ING —S

May all kings f. down before him,	Ps 72.11
A thousand may f. at your side, ten	91.07
hate the work of those who f. away;	101.03
All their host shall f., as leaves f.	Is 34.04
and young men shall f. exhausted;	40.30

Shall I f. down before a block of	44.19
When men f., do they not rise again?	Jer 8.04
they shall f. among the fallen;	8.12
if you will f. down and worship me."	Mt 4.09
upon that house, but it did not f.,	7.25
blind man, both will f. into a pit."	15.14
the crumbs that f. from their	15.27
And then many will f. away, and betray	24.10
"You will all f. away because of me	26.31
of you, I will never f. away."	26.33
"I saw Satan f. like lightning from	Lk 10.18
say to the mountains, 'F. on us';	23.30
have sinned and f. short of the	Rom 3.23
a rock that will make them f.;	9.33
to make others f. by what he eats;	14.20
lest I cause my brother to f.	1Co 8.13
Who is made to f., and I am not	2Co 11.29
thing to f. into the hands of the	Heb 10.31
for if you do this you will never f.;	2Pe 1.10
twenty-four elders f. down before	Rev 4.10
of the saints who had f. asleep were	Mt 27.52
severity toward those who have f.,	Rom 11.22
also who have f. asleep in Christ	1Co 15.18
by the law; you have f. away from	Gal 5.04
with him those who have f. asleep	1Th 4.14
I saw a star f. from heaven to earth,	Rev 9.01
"F., f. is Babylon the great, she who	14.08
like leaves f. from the fig tree.	Is 34.04
and the stars will be f. from heaven,	Mk 13.25
drops of blood f. down upon the	Lk 22.44
keep you from f. and to present	Jud 24
so that his rider f. backward.	Gen 49.17
there is no guidance, a people f.;	Pro 11.14
Do not rejoice when your enemy f.,	24.17
graven image and f. down before it.	Is 44.15
sheep and it f. into a pit on the	Mt 12.11
waste, and house f. upon house.	Lk 11.17
share of property that f. to me.'	15.12
grain of wheat f. into the earth	Jn 12.24
grass; its flower f., and its beauty	Jas 1.11
grass withers, and the flower f.,	1Pe 1.24

FALSE —LY

"You shall not bear f. witness against	Ex 20.16
They went after f. idols, and became f.,	2Ki 17.15
therefore I hate every f. way.	Ps 119.104
A f. balance is an abomination to	Pro 11.01
any among the f. gods of the	Jer 14.22
"Beware of f. prophets, who come to	Mt 7.15
You shall not bear f. witness,	19.18
For f. Christs and f. prophets	24.24
God be true though every man be f.,	Rom 3.04
For such men are f. apostles,	2Co 11.13
But because of f. brethren secretly	Gal 2.04
to make them believe what is f.,	2Th 2.11
impossible that God should prove f.,	Heb 6.18
for many f. prophets have gone out	1Jn 4.01
the beast and the f. prophet were,	Rev 20.10
evil against you f. on my account.	Mt 5.11
of what is f. called knowledge,	1Ti 6.20

FALSEHOOD

who draw iniquity with cords of f.,	Is 5.18
is true, and in him there is no f.	Jn 7.18

FALSEHOOD (cont.)
But if through my f. God's truthfulness Rom 3.07
putting away f., let every one speak Eph 4.25

FAME
his f. continue as long as the sun! Ps 72.17
pour forth the f. of thy abundant 145.07
not heard my f. or seen my glory; Is 66.19
So his f. spread throughout all Mt 4.24
tetrarch heard about the f. of Jesus; 14.01

FAMILIES —Y
went forth by f. out of the ark. Gen 8.19
by their f., in their nations. 10.05
by you all the f. of the earth 12.03
and all the f. of the nations shall Ps 22.27
O f. of the peoples, ascribe to the 96.07
and makes their f like flocks. 107.41
and all the f. of the house of Jer 2.04
shall all the f. of the earth be Ac 3.25
upsetting whole f. by teaching for Tit 1.11
And is not my f. the humblest of 1Sa 9.21
in every f., province, and city, and Est 9.28
sons of the f. of Abraham, and those Ac 13.26
baptized at once, with all his f. 16.33
from whom every f. in heaven and on Eph 3.15
to their own f. and make some return 1Ti 5.04

FAMINE —S
east wind are also seven years of f. Gen 41.27
Before the year of f. came, Joseph 41.50
In f. he will redeem you from death, Job 5.20
but I will kill your root with f., Is 14.30
those who are for f., to f., and those Jer 15.02
not a f. of bread, nor a thirst for Amo 8.11
came a great f. over all the land; Lk 4.25
a great f. arose in that country, 15.14
or f., or nakedness, or peril, or Rom 8.35
sword and with f. and with pestilence Rev 6.08
there will be f. and earthquakes Mt 24.07

FAR
"We have come from a f. country; Jos 9.06
withdraw thy hand f. from me, Job 13.21
f. be it from God that he should do 34.10
Be not f. from me, for trouble is Ps 22.11
O God, be not f. from me; O my God, 71.12
thou art exalted f. above all gods. 97.09
as f. as the east is from the west, 103.12
Salvation is f. from the wicked, for 119.155
so is good news from a f. country. Pro 25.25
She is f. more precious than jewels. 31.10
is f. off, and deep, very deep; Ecc 7.24
it is not f. off, and my salvation Is 46.13
Therefore justice is f. from us, 59.09
but their heart is f. from me; Mt 15.08
"You are not f. from the kingdom of Mk 12.34
took his journey into a f. country, Lk 15.13
standing f. off, would not even lift 18.13
children and to all that are f. off,. Ac 2.39
Yet he is not f. from each one of 17.27
so f. as it depends upon you, live Rom 12.18
But f. be it from me to glory except Gal 6.14
who once were f. off have been Eph 2.13
is able to do f. more abundantly 3.20
but they will not get very f., 2Ti 3.09

FARMER —S
hard-working f. who ought to have 2Ti 2.06
Behold, the f. waits for the precious Jas 5.07
and the f. and those who wander Jer 31.24

FASHION* —ED*
and did not one f. us in the womb? Job 31.15
Thy hands have made and f. me; Ps 119.73
no weapon that is f. against you Is 54.17

FAST —ED (v)
"And when you f., do not look dismal, Mt 6.16
"Why do we and the Pharisees f., 9.14
bridegroom with them, they cannot f. Mk 2.19
I f. twice a week, I give tithes of Lk 18.12
'Why have we f., and thou seest it Is 58.03
And he f. forty days and forty Mt 4.02

FAST —ING —S* (n)
Is such the f. that I choose, a day Is 58.05
Sanctify a f., call a solemn Joe 1.14
My knees are weak through f.; my Ps 109.24
that your f. may not be seen by men Mt 6.18
comes out except by prayer and f." * 17.21
with regard to their f. and their Est 9.31

FAT —TED
you shall eat the f. of the land.' Gen 45.18
their heart is gross like f., Ps 119.70
Make the heart of this people f., Is 6.10
my oxen and my f. calves are Mt 22.04
love is than a f. ox and hatred Pro 15.17
and bring the f. calf and kill it, Lk 15.23

FATE
This is the f. of those who have Ps 49.13
that one f. comes to all of them. Ecc 2.14
For the f. of the sons of men and 3.19

FATHER —S
man leaves his f. and his mother Gen 2.24
"Honor your f. and your mother, Ex 20.12
he was the f. of Jesse, the f. of David. Ru 4.17
O LORD, the God of Israel our f., 1Ch 29.10
I was a f. to the poor, and I Job 29.16
"Has the rain a f., or who has 38.28
F. of the fatherless and protector Ps 68.05
'Thou art my F., my God, and the 89.26
As a f. pities his children, so the 103.13
A wise son makes a glad f., but a Pro 10.01
A foolish son is ruin to his f., 19.13
If one curses his f. or his mother, 20.20
who loves wisdom makes his f. glad, 29.03
how to cry 'My f.' or 'My mother,' Is 8.04
Everlasting F., Prince of Peace." 9.06
For thou art our F., though Abraham 63.16
Yet, O LORD, thou art our F.; we are 64.08
My F., and would not turn from Jer 3.19
Have we not all one f.? Has not one Mal 2.10
glory to your F. who is in heaven. Mt 5.16
be sons of your F. who is in heaven; 5.45

FATHER —S (cont.)

Our F. who art in heaven, Hallowed	Mt 6.09
let me first go and bury my f."	8.21
He who loves f. or mother more than	10.37
F., Lord of heaven and earth, that	11.25
the will of my F. in heaven is my	12.50
or sisters or f. or mother or children	19.29
And call no man your f. on earth,	23.09
hands, 'Come, O blessed of my F., inherit	25.34
My F., if it be possible, let this	26.39
F., all things are possible to thee;	Mk 14.36
And his f. and his mother marveled	Lk 2.33
What f. among you, if his son asks	11.11
I will arise and go to my f., and I will	15.18
'F. Abraham, have mercy upon me, and	16.24
"My F. is working still, and I am	Jn 5.17
sabbath but also called God his F.,	5.18
For the F. loves the Son, and shows	5.20
to him therefore, "Where is your F.?"	8.19
He who has seen me has seen the F.;	14.09
Holy F., keep them in thy name which	17.11
to wait for the promise of the F.,	Ac 1.04
from God our F. and the Lord Jesus	Rom 1.07
When we cry, "Abba! F.!"	8.15
access in one Spirit to the F.	Eph 2.18
shall leave his f. and mother and	5.31
like a f. with his children, we	1Th 2.11
whose f. I have become in my	Phm 1.10
Or again, "I will be to him a f.,	Heb 1.05
subject to the F. of spirits and	12.09
down from the F. of lights with	Jas 1.17
See what love the F. has given us,	1Jn 3.01
sat down with my F. on his throne.	Rev 3.21
you shall go to your f. in peace;	Gen 15.15
'The God of your f. has sent me to	Ex 3.13
LORD swore to give to your f.	Deu 6.18
In thee our f. trusted; they trusted,	Ps 22.04
Both we and our f. have sinned;	106.06
Kings shall be your foster f., and their	Is 49.23
f. and sons together, neighbor and	Jer 6.21
'The f. have eaten sour grapes, and	31.29
O God of my f., I give thanks and	Dan 2.23
the hearts of f. to their children	Mal 4.06
Fill up, then, the measure of your f.	Mt 23.32
for so their f. did to the prophets.	Lk 6.23
consent to the deeds of your f.;	11.48
Our f. worshiped on this mountain;	Jn 4.20
Our f. ate the manna in the wilderness;	6.31
and of Jacob, the God of our f.,	Ac 3.13
The God of our f. raised Jesus whom	5.30
'I am the God of your f., the God of	7.32
"Brethren and f., hear the defense	22.01
in Christ, you do not have many f.	1Co 4.15
F., do not provoke your children to	Eph 6.04

FATHERLESS

justice for the f. and the widow,	Deu 10.18
Father of the f. and protector of	Ps 68.05

FAULT —S

but the f. is in your own people."	Ex 5.16
you, go and tell him his f.,	Mt 18.15
me then, "Why does he still find f.?	Rom 9.19
so that no f. may be found with our	2Co 6.03

For he finds f. with them when he	Heb 8.08
errors? Clear thou me from hidden f.	Ps 19.12

FAVOR

But Noah found f. in the eyes of	Gen 6.08
Esther found f. in the eyes of all	Est 2.15
cover him with f. as with a shield.	Ps 5.12
scornful, but to the humble he shows f.	Pro 3.34
Many seek the f. of a generous man,	19.06
but his f. is like dew upon the	19.12
"In a time of f. I have answered	Is 49.08
stature, and in f. with God and man.	Lk 2.52
be puffed up in f. of one against	1Co 4.06
Am I now seeking the f. of men,	Gal 1.10

FEAR —ED —ING —S (v)

f. not, for I am with you and will	Gen 26.24
you do not yet f. the LORD God."	Ex 9.30
to f. me and to keep all my	Deu 5.29
"You shall not f. other gods or bow	2Ki 17.35
LORD, "Does Job f. God for nought?	Job 1.09
the LORD is for those who f. him,	Ps 25.14
whom shall I f.? The LORD is	27.01
Why should I f. in times of trouble,	49.05
words grow many: but do you f. God.	Ecc 5.07
F. God, and keep his commandments;	12.13
a fearful heart, "Be strong, f. not!	Is 35.04
f. not, for I am with you, be not	41.10
F. not, for I am with you; I will bring	43.05
and I f. the LORD, the God of heaven,	Jon 1.09
And do not f. those who kill the	Mt 10.28
synagogue, "Do not f., only believe."	Mk 5.33
"F. not, little flock, for it is your	Lk 12.32
I neither f. God nor regard man,	18.04
"Men of Israel, and you that f. God,	Ac 13.16
F. God. Honor the emperor.	1Pe 1.17
"F. God and give him glory, for the	Rev 14.07
judgment; the earth f. and was still,	Ps 76.08
he is to be f. above all gods.	96.04
he f. the people, because they held	Mt 14.05
for Herod f. John, knowing that he	Mk 6.20
who neither f. God nor regarded	Lk 18.02
said this because they f. the Jews,	Jn 9.22
a devout man who f. God with all	Ac 10.02
himself, f. the circumcision party.	Gal 2.12
singleness of heart, f. the Lord.	Col 3.22
Who is the man that f. the LORD?	Ps 25.12
Who among you f. the LORD and obeys	Is 50.10

FEAR (n)

There is no f. of God at all in	Gen 20.11
God of Abraham and the F. of Isaac,	31.42
Is not your f. of God your confidence,	Job 4.06
Serve the LORD with f., with trembling	Ps 2.11
the f. of the LORD is clean, enduring	19.09
in God I trust without a f. What can	56.04
The f. of the LORD is the beginning	111.10
The f. of the LORD leads to life;	Pro 19.23
I will put the f. of me in their	Jer 32.40
"Take heart, it is I; have no f."	Mt 14.27
the tomb with f. and great joy,	28.08
f. fell upon them all; and the name	Ac 19.17
of slavery to fall back into f.,	Rom 8.15
and in much f. and trembling;	1Co 2.03

FEAR (n) (cont.)

knowing the f. of the Lord, we	2Co 5.11
turn—fighting without and f. within.	7.05
speak the word of God without f.	Php 1.14
salvation with f. and trembling;	2.12
and he was heard for his godly f.	Heb 5.07
but perfect love casts out f.	1Jn 4.18

FEAST —S (n)

they may hold a f. to me in the	Ex 5.01
shall keep it as a f. to the LORD;	12.14
You shall keep the f. of unleavened	23.15
And you shall observe the f. of weeks,	34.22
days is the f. of booths to the	Lev 23.34
among the Jews, a f. and a holiday.	Est 8.17
were invited to the marriage f.;	Mt 22.03
Now at the f. the governor was	27.15
Passover and the f. of Unleavened	Mk 14.01
were looking for him at the f.,	Jn 7.11
It was the f. of the Dedication at	10.22
"Let their f. become a snare and a	Rom 11.09
are the appointed f. of the LORD,	Lev 23.04
let their sacrificial f. be a trap.	Ps 69.22
your appointed f. my soul hates;	Is 1.14
"I hate, I despise your f., and I take	Amo 5.21
of honor at f. and the best seats	Mt 23.06
These are blemishes on your love f.,	Jud 12

FED

Thou hast f. them with the bread of	Ps 80.05
the shepherds have f. themselves,	Eze 34.08
her, "Let the children first be f.,	Mk 7.27
I f. you with milk, not solid food;	1Co 3.02

FEEBLE

"What are these f. Jews doing?	Neh 4.02
you have made firm the f. knees.	Job 4.04
hands, and make firm the f. knees.	Is 35.03
All hands are f., and all knees	Eze 7.17

FEED —S

I will again f. your flock and keep	Gen 30.31
the mouths of fools f. on folly.	Pro 15.14
f. me with the food that is needful	30.08
The cow and the bear shall f.;	Is 11.07
He will f. his flock like a shepherd,	40.11
should not shepherds f. the sheep?	Eze 34.02
They f. on the sin of my people;	Hos 4.08
the desert to f. so great a crowd?"	Mt 15.33
did we see thee hungry and f. thee,	25.37
He said to him, "F. my lambs,"	Jn 21.15
Jesus said to him, "F. my sheep.	21.17
to f. the church of the Lord which	Ac 20.28
No, "if your enemy is hungry, f. him;	Rom 12.20
He f. on ashes; a deluded mind	Is 44.20
yet your heavenly Father f. them.	Mt 6.26

FEEL

that I may f. you, my son, to know	Gen 27.21
They have hands, but do not f.;	Ps 115.07
to those who f. secure on the	Amo 6.01
that they might f. after him and	Ac 17.27
we f. sure of better things that	Heb 6.09

FEET

put off your shoes from your f.,	Ex 3.05
So she lay at his f. until the	Ru 3.14
a son who was crippled in his f.	2Sa 4.04
He made my f. like hinds' f., and	22.34
Thou puttest my f. in the stocks,	Job 13.27
hast put all things under his f.,	Ps 8.06
have pierced my hands and f.—	22.16
and set my f. upon a rock, making my	40.02
my f. from falling, that I may walk	56.13
is a lamp to my f. and a light to	119.105
f. that make haste to run to evil,	Pro 6.18
and with two he covered his f.,	Is 6.02
Their f. run to evil, and they make	59.07
me "Son of man, stand upon your f.,	Eze 2.01
and put your shoes on your f.;	24.17
its f. partly of iron and partly of	Dan 2.33
dust from your f. as you leave	Mt 10.14
and they put them at his f., and he	15.30
hands or two f. to be thrown into	18.08
I put thy enemies under thy f.'?	22.44
hold of his f. and worshiped him.	28.09
to guide our f. into the way of	Lk 1.79
began to wet his f. with her tears,	7.38
See my hands and my f., that it is I	24.39
began to wash the disciples' f.,	Jn 13.05
one at the head and one at the f.	20.12
and laid it at the apostles' f.;	Ac 4.35
beautiful are the f. of those who	Rom 10.15
soon crush Satan under your f.	16.20
you," nor again the head to the f.,	1Co 12.21
shod your f. with the equipment of	Eph 6.15
washed the f. of the saints, relieved	1Ti 5.10
come and bow down before your f.,	Rev 3.09

FELL

very angry, and his countenance f.	Gen 4.05
And rain f. upon the earth forty	7.12
beat against that house, and it f.;	Mt 7.27
some seeds f. along the path, and	13.04
At that saying his countenance f.,	Mk 10.22
and as they sailed he f. asleep.	Lk 8.23
and he f. among robbers, who stripped	10.30
tower in Siloam f. and killed them,	13.04
like scales f. from his eyes and	Ac 9.18
the Holy Spirit f. on all who	10.44
he f. down from the third story and	20.09
twenty-four elders f. down before	Rev 5.08

FELLOW

they fall, one will lift up his f.;	Ecc 4.10
every man his f. and every man his	Is 3.05
have had mercy on your f. servant,	Mt 18.33
"This f. said, 'I am able to destroy	26.61
have found this man a pestilent f.,	Ac 24.05
of God and f. heirs with Christ,	Rom 8.17
Aquila, my f. workers in Christ Jesus,	16.03
Timothy, my f. worker, greets you;	16.21
For we are f. workers for God; you	1Co 3.09
but you are f. citizens with the	Eph 2.19
every one his f. or every one his	Heb 8.11
you foolish f., that faith apart	Jas 2.20

FELLOWSHIP

within God's house we walked in f.	Ps 55.14
to the apostles' teaching and f.,	Ac 2.42
were called into the f. of his Son,	1Co 1.09
Or what f. has light with darkness?	2Co 6.14
of God and the f. of the Holy	13.14
and Barnabas the right hand of f.,	Gal 2.09
you may have f. with us; and our f. is	1Jn 1.03

FEMALE

male and f. he created them.	Gen 1.27
male and f., went into the ark with	7.09
beginning made them male and f.,	Mt 19.04
free, there is neither male nor f.;	Gal 3.28

FESTAL

Bind the f. procession with branches,	Ps 118.27
innumerable angels in f. gathering,	Heb 12.22

FESTIVAL

thanksgiving, a multitude keeping f.	Ps 42.04
release one man to them at the f.	*Lk 23.17
celebrate the f., not with the old	1Co 5.08
regard to a f. or a new moon or a	Col 2.16

FETCH —ED

I will f. my knowledge from afar,	Job 36.03
and they f. Uriah from Egypt and	Jer 26.23

FETTERS

bound him in f. to take him to	Jer 39.07
been bound with f. and chains,	Mk 5.04
and every one's f. were unfastened.	Ac 16.26
with my own hand. Remember my f.	Col 4.18
I am suffering and wearing f.	2Ti 2.09

FEVER

mother-in-law lying sick with a f.;	Mt 8.14
the seventh hour the f. left him."	Jn 4.52
lay sick with f. and dysentery;	Ac 28.08

FIELD —S

beast of the f. and every bird of	Gen 2.19
you shall eat the plants of the f.	3.18
And when they were in the f., Cain rose	4.08
said to Naomi, "Let me go to the f.,	Ru 2.02
So David hid himself in the f.;	1Sa 20.24
let the f. exult, and everything in	Ps 96.12
flourishes like a flower of the f.;	103.15
Zion shall be plowed as a f.;	Jer 26.18
'Buy my f. which is at Anathoth, for	32.07
lilies of the f., how they grow;	Mt 6.28
man who sowed good seed in his f.;	13.24
the f. is the world, and the good	13.38
is like treasure hidden in a f.,	13.44
Then two men will be in the f.;	24.40
been called the F. of Blood to	27.08
there were shepherds out in the f.,	Lk 2.08
him who is in the f. not turn back.	17.31
you are God's f., God's building.	1Co 3.09
work already done in another's f.	2Co 10.16
they sow f., and plant vineyards,	Ps 107.37
F. shall be bought in this land of	Jer 32.43
which they had cut from the f.	Mk 11.08

sent him into his f. to feed swine.	Lk 15.15
and see how the f. are already	Jn 4.35

FIERCE

that the f. anger of the LORD may	Num 25.04
the lion, the voice of the f. lion,	Job 4.10
He let loose on them his f. anger,	Ps 78.49
for the f. anger of the LORD has	Jer 4.08
I will not execute my f. anger,	Hos 11.09
so f. that no one could pass that	Mt 8.28
my departure f. wolves will come	Ac 20.29
profligates, f., haters of good,	2Ti 3.03
men were scorched by the f. heat,	Rev 16.09

FIERY

Then the LORD sent f. serpents	Num 21.06
weapons, making his arrows f. shafts.	Ps 7.13
be cast into a burning f. furnace."	Dan 3.06
surprised at the f. ordeal which	1Pe 4.12

FIFTY-TWO

number was f. thousand seven	Num 26.34

FIG

and they sewed f. leaves together	Gen 3.07
The f. tree puts forth its figs, and	Sol 2.13
a first-ripe f. before the summer:	Is 28.04
And seeing a f. tree by the wayside	Mt 21.19
"From the f. tree learn its lesson:	24.32
when you were under the f. tree,	Jn 1.48
Can a f. tree, my brethren, yield	Jas 3.12
earth as the f. tree sheds its	Rev 6.13

FIGHT (v)

f. against those who f. against me!	Ps 35.01
this world, my servants would f.,	Jn 18.36
F. the good f. of the faith;	1Ti 6.12
I have fought the good f., I have	2Ti 4.07
so you f. and wage war. You do not	Jas 4.02
beast, and who can f. against it?"	Rev 13.04

FIGHTING —S* (n)

every turn—f. without and fear within.	2Co 7.05
wars, and what causes f. among you?	Jas 4.01

FIGURE —S

to understand a proverb and a f.,	Pro 1.06
he shapes it into the f. of a man,	Is 44.13
This f. Jesus used with them, but	Jn 10.06
speaking plainly, not in any f.!	16.29
with carved f. of cherubim and	1Ki 6.29
the f. which you made to worship;	Ac 7.43

FILL —ED —S (v)

and f. the earth and subdue it;	Gen 1.28
F. me with joy and gladness; let the	Ps 51.08
may his glory f. the whole earth!	72.19
F. their faces with shame, that they	83.16
for Fortune and f. cups of mixed	Is 65.11
Do I not f. heaven and earth? says	Jer 23.24
F. up, then, the measure of your	Mt 23.32
"F. the jars with water." And they	Jn 2.07
May the God of hope f. you with	Rom 15.13
heavens, that he might f. all things.)	Eph 4.10

FILL —ED —S (v) (cont.)

so as always to f. up the measure of	1Th 2.16
and I have f. him with the Spirit	Ex 31.03
glory of the LORD f. the tabernacle.	40.34
earth shall be f. with the glory	Num 14.21
I am f. with power, with the Spirit	Mic 3.08
their faces, and were f. with awe.	Mt 17.06
wedding hall was f. with guests.	22.10
Elizabeth was f. with the Holy	Lk 1.41
Zechariah was f. with the Holy	1.67
them, and they were f. with fear.	2.09
and became strong, f. with wisdom;	2.40
Every valley shall be f., and every	3.05
And they were all f. with the Holy	Ac 2.04
Then Peter, f. with the Holy Spirit,	4.08
f. with all knowledge, and able to	Rom 15.14
Already you are f.! Already you have	1Co 4.08
debauchery; but be f. with the Spirit,	Eph 5.18
and more; I am f., having received	Php 4.18
that you may be f. with the knowledge	Col 1.09
be warmed and f.," without giving	Jas 2.16
and the temple was f. with smoke	Rev 15.08
Let the sea roar, and all that f. it;	Ps 98.07
the hungry he f. with good things.	107.09
fulness of him who f. all in all.	Eph 1.23

FILL (n)

Come, let us take our f. of love	Pro 7.18
you ate your f. of the loaves.	Jn 6.26

FILTHINESS

Let there be no f., nor silly talk,	Eph 5.04
Therefore put away all f. and rank	Jas 1.21

FIND —ING —S

"Can we f. such a man as this, in	Gen 41.38
"Can you f. out the deep things of	Job 11.07
Oh, that I knew where I might f. him,	23.03
me diligently but will not f. me.	Pro 1.28
but a faithful man who can f.?	20.06
A good wife who can f.? She is far	31.10
that he cannot f. out what God has	Ecc 3.11
very deep; who can f. it out?	7.24
and f. rest for your souls. But they	Jer 6.16
You will seek me and f. me; when you	29.13
seek, and you will f.; knock,	Mt 7.07
his life for my sake will f. it.	10.39
and you will f. rest for your souls.	11.29
immediately you will f. an ass tied,	21.02
comes, will he f. faith on earth?"	Lk 18.08
"I f. no crime in this man."	23.04
went in they did not f. the body.	24.03
mercy and f. grace to help in time	Heb 4.16
But sin, f. opportunity in the	Rom 7.08
Even the sparrow f. a home, and the	Ps 84.03
seek diligently until she f. it?	Lk 15.08
because my word f. no place in you.	Jn 8.37

FINE

they than gold, even much f. gold;	Ps 19.10
F. speech is not becoming to a fool;	Pro 17.07
he takes up the isles like f. dust.	Is 40.15
rings and in f. clothing comes	Jas 2.02

FINGER —S

to Pharaoh, "This is the f. of God."	Ex 8.19
stone, written with the f. of God.	31.18
But if it is by the f. of God that	Lk 11.20
wrote with his f. on the ground.	*Jn 8.06
"Put your f. here, and see my hands;	20.27
at thy heavens, the work of thy f.,	Ps 8.03
the burdens with one of your f.	Lk 11.46

FINISH —ED

and the third day I f. my course.	Lk 13.32
seventh day God f. his work which	Gen 2.02
the vinegar, he said, "It is f.";	Jn 19.30
I have f. the race, I have kept the	2Ti 4.07
his works were f. from the foundation	Heb 4.03
And when they have f. their testimony,	Rev 11.07

FIRE

in a flame of f. out of the midst	Ex 3.02
in a pillar of f. to give them	13.21
is a devouring f., a jealous God.	Deu 4.24
and after the earthquake a f.,	1Ki 19.12
will heap coals of f. on his head,	Pro 25.22
The light of Israel will become a f.,	Is 10.17
"For behold, the LORD will come in f.,	66.15
making my words in your mouth a f.,	Jer 5.14
Is not my word like f., says the LORD,	23.29
You shall be fuel for the f.;	Eze 21.32
cast three men bound into the f.?"	Dan 3.24
whose baker ceases to stir the f.,	Hos 7.04
with the Holy Spirit and with f.	Mt 3.11
shall be liable to the hell of f.	5.22
is cut down and thrown into the f.	7.19
to be thrown into the eternal f.	18.08
die and the f. is not quenched.	*Mk 9.44
and warming himself at the f.	14.54
"I came to cast f. upon the earth;	Lk 12.49
appeared to them tongues as of f.,	Ac 2.03
Sinai, in a flame of f. in a bush.	7.30
for our God is a consuming f.	Heb 12.29
And the tongue is a f. The tongue	Jas 3.06
though perishable is tested by f.,	1Pe 1.07
the second death, the lake of f.;	Rev 20.14

FIRM

yea, the world stands f., never to be	1Ch 16.30
this we make a f. covenant and	Neh 9.38
faithfulness is f. as the heavens.	Ps 89.02
root of the righteous stands f.	Pro 12.12
stand f. in your faith, be courageous,	1Co 16.13
that you stand f. in one spirit,	Php 1.27
stand f. and hold to the traditions	2Th 2.15
first confidence f. to the end,	Heb 3.14

FIRMAMENT

"Let there be a f. in the midst of	Gen 1.06
and the f. proclaims his handiwork.	Ps 19.01

FIRST

of the f. fruits of your labor, of	Ex 23.16
two tables of stone like the f.,	Deu 10.01
the f. of his acts of old.	Pro 8.22
who states his case f. seems right,	18.17
the f., and with the last; I am He.	Is 41.04

FIRST (cont.)

I am the f., and I am the last.	Is 48.12
f. be reconciled to your brother,	Mt 5.24
But seek f. his kingdom and his	6.33
f., Simon, who is called Peter, and	10.02
that man becomes worse than the f.	12.45
But many that are f. will be last,	19.30
This is the great and f. commandment	22.38
the dawn of the f. day of the week,	28.01
"The f. is 'Hear, O Israel: The Lord	Mk 12.29
But f. he must suffer many things	Lk 17.25
He f. found his brother Simon, and	Jn 1.41
This, the f. of his signs, Jesus did	2.11
be the f. to throw a stone at her."	*8.07
In the f. book, O Theophilus, I have	Ac 1.01
were for the f. time called Christians.	11.26
to the Jew f. and also to the Greek.	Rom 1.16
appointed in the church f. apostles,	1Co 12.28
to you as of f. importance what I	15.03
"The f. man Adam became a living	15.45
we who f. hoped in Christ have been	Eph 1.12
For Adam was formed f., then Eve;	1Ti 2.13
We love, because he f. loved us.	1Jn 4.19
not, I am the f. and the last,	Rev 1.17

FIRST-BORN

birth to her f. son and wrapped	Lk 2.07
he might be the f. among many	Rom 8.29
invisible God, the f. of all creation;	Col 1.15
he brings the f. into the world,	Heb 1.06

FISH

dominion over the f. of the sea,	Gen 1.26
And the f. in the Nile died;	Ex 7.21
their f. stink for lack of water,	Is 50.02
belly of the f. three days and	Jon 1.17
Or if he asks for a f., will give him	Mt 7.10
only five loaves here and two f."	14.17
take the first f. that comes up,	17.27
They gave him a piece of broiled f.,	Lk 24.42
for birds, and another for f.	1Co 15.39

FISHERS*

"Behold, I am sending for many f.,	Jer 16.16
me, and I will make you f. of men."	Mt 4.19
I will make you become f. of men."	Mk 1.17

FIT —TING

looks back is f. for the kingdom	Lk 9.62
It is f. neither for the land nor	14.35
did not see f. to acknowledge God,	Rom 1.28
talk, nor levity, which are not f.;	Eph 5.04
husbands, as is f. in the Lord.	Col 3.18
as is f., because your faith is	2Th 1.03
For it was f. that he, for whom and	Heb 2.10
For it was f. that we should have	7.26

FIXED

means that the thing is f. by God,	Gen 41.32
of Queen Esther f. these practices	Est 9.32
Thou hast f. all the bounds of the	Ps 74.17
word is firmly f. in the heavens.	119.89
"If this f. order departs from	Jer 31.36
because he has f. a day on which he	Ac 17.31

FLAME —S (n)

to him in a f. of fire out of the	Ex 3.02
a fire, and his Holy One a f.;	Is 10.17
for I am in anguish in this f.'	Lk 16.24
the LORD flashes forth f. of fire.	Ps 29.07
winds, and his servants f. of fire."	Heb 1.07

FLAMING

and a f. sword which turned every	Gen 3.24
quench all the f. darts of the	Eph 6.16
with his mighty angels in f. fire,	2Th 1.07

FLASH —ED —ES —ING

F. forth the lightning and scatter	Ps 144.06
a light from heaven f. about him.	Ac 9.03
the lightning f. and lights up the	Lk 17.24
and fire f. forth continually, and	Eze 1.04

FLATTER —ING

they f. with their tongue.	Ps 5.09
with f. lips and a double heart	12.02
and by fair and f. words they	Rom 16.18
f. people to gain advantage.	Jud 16

FLEE —S

and you shall f. when none pursues	Lev 26.17
"F. like a bird to the mountains;	Ps 11.01
What ails you, O sea, that you f.?	114.05
whither shall I f. from thy presence?	139.07
day breathes and the shadows f.,	Sol 2.17
To whom will you f. for help,	Is 10.03
and f. to Egypt, and remain there	Mt 2.13
warned you to f. from the wrath to	3.07
you in one town, f. to the next;	10.23
are in Judea f. to the mountains;	24.16
the devil and he will f. from you.	Jas 4.07
coming and leaves the sheep and f.;	Jn 10.12

FLEET (n)

King Solomon built a f. of ships at	1Ki 9.26
Moreover the f. of Hiram, which	10.11

FLESH

his wife, and they become one f.	Gen 2.24
And all f. died that moved upon the	7.21
Whatever touches its f. shall be holy;	Lev 6.27
For the life of the f. is in the	17.11
My f. and my heart may fail, but God	Ps 73.26
My f. trembles for fear of thee, and	119.120
and let all f. bless his holy name	145.21
study is a weariness of the f.	Ecc 12.12
All f. is grass, and all its	Is 40.06
stone and give you a heart of f.	Eze 36.26
will pour out my spirit on all f.;	Joe 2.28
For f. and blood has not revealed	Mt 16.17
is willing, but the f. is weak."	26.41
and all f. shall see the salvation	Lk 3.06
And the Word became f. and dwelt	Jn 1.14
you eat the f. of the Son of man	6.53
moreover my f. will dwell in hope.	Ac 2.26
While we were living in the f.,	Rom 7.05
sin, he condemned sin in the f.,	8.03
To set the mind on the f. is death,	8.06
and make no provision for the f.,	13.14

FLESH (cont.)

spiritual men, but as men of the f.,	1Co 3.01
For not all f. is alike, but there	15.39
f. and blood cannot inherit the	15.50
a thorn was given me in the f.,	2Co 12.07
now live in the f. I live by faith	Gal 2.20
not gratify the desires of the f.	5.16
Now the works of the f. are plain:	5.19
and put no confidence in the f.	Php 3.03
He was manifested in the f.,	1Ti 3.16
In the days of his f., Jesus	Heb 5.07
curtain, that is, through his f.,	10.20
therefore Christ suffered in the f.,	1Pe 4.01

FLOCK

firstlings of his f. and of their	Gen 4.04
was keeping the f. of his father-in-law,	Ex 3.01
He will feed his f. like a shepherd,	Is 40.11
the LORD's f. has been taken captive.	Jer 13.17
him as a shepherd keeps his f.'	31.10
in pieces the shepherd and his f.;	51.23
LORD took me from following the f.,	Amo 7.15
sheep of the f. will be scattered.'	Mt 26.31
watch over their f. by night.	Lk 2.08
little f., for it is your Father's	12.32
shall be one f., one shepherd.	Jn 10.16
in among you, not sparing the f.;	Ac 20.29
Who tends a f. without getting some	1Co 9.07
Tend the f. of God that is your	1Pe 5.02

FLOOD —S (n)

I will bring a f. of waters upon	Gen 6.17
The f. continued forty days upon	7.17
The LORD sits enthroned over the f.;	Ps 29.10
days before the f. they were	Mt 24.38
he brought a f. upon the world of	2Pe 2.05
Let the f. clap their hands; let the hills	Ps 98.08
love, neither can f. drown it.	Sol 8.07

FLOW —ED —ING

for from it f. the springs of life.	Pro 4.23
his heart shall f. rivers of	Jn 7.38
A river f. out of Eden to water the	Gen 2.10
a land f. with milk and honey, to	Ex 3.08
As a hart longs for f. streams,	Ps 42.01
f. from the throne of God and of	Rev 22.01

FLOW (n)

who had had a f. of blood for	Mk 5.25

FLOWER

The grass withers, the f. fades;	Is 40.08
its f. falls, and its beauty perishes.	Jas 1.11
all its glory like the f. of grass.	1Pe 1.24

FLUTE

and saw the f. players, and the	Mt 9.23
such as the f. or the harp, do not	1Co 14.07
of f. players and trumpeters, shall	Rev 18.22

FOE —S

How long, O God, is the f. to scoff?	Ps 74.10
O LORD, how many are my f.!	3.01
But thou hast saved us from our f.,	44.07

and rescued us from our f., for his	136.24
and a man's f. will be those of his	Mt 10.36

FOLD

I will bring them back to their f.,	Jer 23.03
them together like sheep in a f.,	Mic 2.12
sheep, that are not of this f.;	Jn 10.16

FOLLOW —ED —ING

and mercy shall f. me all the days	Ps 23.06
"F. me, and I will make you fishers	Mt 4.19
"F. me, and leave the dead to bury	8.22
and he said to him, "F. me."	9.09
his cross and f. me is not worthy	10.38
and take up his cross and f. me.	16.24
in heaven; and come, f. me."	19.21
A stranger they will not f.,	Jn 10.05
If any one serves me, he must f. me;	12.26
I am going you cannot f. me now;	13.36
but also f. the example of the	Rom 4.12
that you should f. in his steps.	1Pe 2.21
that we f. his commandments;	2Jn 6
it is these who f. the Lamb wherever	Rev 14.04
labors, for their deeds f. them!"	14.13
And great crowds f. him from	Mt 4.25
But Peter f. him at a distance, as	26.58
we have left everything and f. you."	Mk 10.28
And a young man f. him, with nothing	14.51
She f. Paul and us, crying, "These	Ac 16.17
supernatural Rock which f. them,	1Co 10.04
f. the course of this world, f. the prince	Eph 2.02

FOLLOWING (n)

the LORD took me from f. the flock.	Amo 7.15

FOLLY

O God, thou knowest my f.; the wrongs	Ps 69.05
F. is a joy to him who has no sense,	Pro 15.21
of the cross is f. to those who	1Co 1.18
God through the f. of what we	1.21
of this world is f. with God.	3.19
for their f. will be plain to all,	2Ti 3.09

FOOD —S

fruit; you shall have them for f.	Gen 1.29
have been my f. day and night,	Ps 42.03
Is not life more than f., and the body	Mt 6.25
for the laborer deserves his f.	10.10
villages and buy f. for themselves."	14.15
for I was hungry and you gave me f.,	25.35
"I have f. to eat of which you do	Jn 4.32
does not mean f. and drink but	Rom 14.17
I fed you with milk, not solid f.;	1Co 3.02
Now concerning f. offered to idols:	8.01
all ate the same supernatural f.	10.03
ill-clad and in lack of daily f.,	Jas 2.15
(Thus he declared all f. clean.)	Mk 7.19

FOOL —S

behold, I have played the f.,	1Sa 26.21
The f. says in his heart, "There is	Ps 14.01
The f. folds his hands, and eats his	Ecc 4.05
The prophet is a f., the man of	Hos 9.07
council, and whoever says, 'You f.!'	Mt 5.22

FOOL—S (cont.)

But God said to him, 'F.! This night	Lk 12.20
to boast of—I am speaking as a f.—	2Co 11.21
I have been a f.! You forced me	12.11
of the people! F., when will you be wise?	Ps 94.08
You blind f.! for which is greater,	Mt 23.17
Claiming to be wise, they became f.,	Rom 1.22
We are f. for Christ's sake, but you	1Co 4.10

FOOLISH

you f. and senseless people?	Deu 32.06
A f. son is a grief to his father	Pro 17.25
will be like a f. man who built	Mt 7.26
Five of them were f., and five were	25.02
both to the wise and to the f.:	Rom 1.14
not God made f. the wisdom of the	1Co 1.20
O f. Galatians! Who has bewitched	Gal 3.01
For we ourselves were once f.,	Tit 3.03
to silence the ignorance of f. men.	1Pe 2.15

FOOLISHNESS

licentiousness, envy, slander, pride, f.	Mk 7.22
For the f. of God is wiser than men,	1Co 1.25
would bear with me in a little f.	2Co 11.01

FOOT

My f. has held fast to his steps;	Job 23.11
He will not let your f. be moved,	Ps 121.03
out and trodden under f. by men.	Mt 5.13
hand or your f. causes you to sin,	18.08
If the f. should say, "Because I am	1Co 12.15

FOOTSTOOL

worship at his f.! Holy is he!	Ps 99.05
for it is his f., or by Jerusalem,	Mt 5.35
'Heaven is my throne, and earth my f.	Ac 7.49

FORBEARANCE

in his divine f. he had passed	Rom 3.25
Let all men know your f. The Lord	Php 4.05

FORBID —DING*

rebuke him, saying, "God f., Lord!	Mt 16.22
"Can any one f. water for baptizing	Ac 10.47
and do not f. speaking in tongues;	1Co 14.39
who f. marriage and enjoin abstinence	1Ti 4.03
and f. us to give tribute to Caesar,	Lk 23.02

FORCE (n)

and men of violence take it by f.	Mt 11.12

FORCED —S (v)

our race and f. our fathers to	Ac 7.19
You f. me to it, for I ought to have	2Co 12.11
and if any one f. you to go one	Mt 5.41

FOREFATHER —S

our f. according to the flesh?	Rom 4.01
remember the covenant with their f.,	Lev 26.45

FOREHEAD —S

It shall be upon Aaron's f., and Aaron	Ex 28.38
struck the Philistine on his f.;	1Sa 17.49
marked on the right hand or the f.,	Rev 13.16

and on her f. was written a name of	17.05
a mark upon the f. of the men who	Eze 9.04

FOREIGN

"Put away the f. gods that are	Gen 35.02
sing the LORD's song in a f. land?	Ps 137.04
be a preacher of f. divinities"—	Ac 17.18
as in a f. land, living in tents	Heb 11.09

FOREIGNER —S

I shall be a f. to the speaker and	1Co 14.11
Athenians and the f. who lived	Ac 17.21

FORESKIN —S

flesh of his f. shall be cut off	Gen 17.14
remove the f. of your hearts, O men	Jer 4.04
of a hundred f. of the Philistines."	2Sa 3.14

FOREST

For every beast of the f. is mine,	Ps 50.10
How great a f. is set ablaze by a	Jas 3.05

FORFEIT —ED

the whole world and f. his life?	Mk 8.36
many peoples; you have f. your life.	Hab 2.10

FORGAVE

released him and f. him the debt.	Mt 18.27
another, as God in Christ f. you.	Eph 4.32

FORGET —TING

"Take heed lest you f. the LORD	Deu 8.11
Wilt thou f. me for ever? How long	Ps 13.01
If I f. you, O Jerusalem, let my	137.05
My son, do not f. my teaching, but	Pro 3.01
Even these may f., yet I will not f. you.	Is 49.15
f. what lies behind and straining	Php 3.13

FORGIVE —N —S —ING

F., O LORD, thy people Israel, whom	Deu 21.08
But thou art a God ready to f.,	Neh 9.17
then thou didst f. the guilt of my	Ps 32.05
And f. us our debts, As we also have	Mt 6.12
authority on earth to f. sins"—	9.06
Who can f. sins but God alone?"	Mk 2.07
And Jesus said, "Father, f. them;	Lk 23.34
Any one whom you f., I also f.	2Co 2.10
forgiven you, so you also must f.	Col 3.13
and will f. our sins and cleanse us	1Jn 1.09
Blessed is he whose transgression is f.,	Ps 32.01
will not be f. you till you die,"	Is 22.14
easier, to say, 'Your sins are f.,'	Mt 9.05
against the Spirit will not be f.	12.31
are those whose iniquities are f.,	Rom 4.07
as the Lord has f. you, so you also	Col 3.13
who f. all your iniquity, who heals	Ps 103.03
"Who is this, who even f. sins?"	Lk 7.49
thou wast a f. God to them, but an	Ps 99.08
f. one another, as God in Christ	Eph 4.32

FORGIVENESS

But there is f. with thee, that thou	Ps 130.04
out for many for the f. of sins.	Mt 26.28
Christ for the f. of your sins;	Ac 2.38

FORGIVENESS (cont.)
we have redemption, the f. of sins. Col 1.14
Where there is f. of these, there is Heb 10.18

FORGOTTEN
"Why hast thou f. me? Why go I Ps 42.09
Has God f. to be gracious? Has he in 77.09
For you have f. the God of your Is 17.10
and have f. the LORD, your Maker, who 51.13
And have you f. the exhortation Heb 12.05

FORM —ED —S (v)
For thou didst f. my inward parts, Ps 139.13
I f. light and create darkness, I Is 45.07
then the LORD God f. man of dust Gen 2.07
I too was f. from a piece of clay. Job 33.06
ever thou hadst f. the earth and Ps 90.02
for his hands f. the dry land. 95.05
plans f. of old, faithful and sure. Is 25.01
"Before I f. you in the womb I knew Jer 1.05
he is the one who f. all things, 51.19
travail until Christ be f. in you! Gal 4.19
For Adam was f. first, then Eve; 1Ti 2.13
and an earth f. out of water and by 2Pe 3.05
For lo, he who f. the mountains, and Amo 4.13

FORM (n)
The earth was without f. and void, Gen 1.02
and he beholds the f. of the LORD. Num 12.08
in the f. of any figure, the likeness Deu 4.16
and their f. shall waste away; Ps 49.14
he had no f. or comeliness that we Is 53.02
likeness as it were of a human f. Eze 1.26
descended upon him in bodily f., Lk 3.22
his f. you have never seen; Jn 5.37
For the f. of this world is passing 1Co 7.31
who, though he was in the f. of God, Php 2.06
abstain from every f. of evil. 1Th 5.22
holding the f. of religion but 2Ti 3.05
of the true f. of these realities, Heb 10.01

FORNICATION
f., theft, false witness, slander. Mt 15.19
to him, "We were not born of f.; Jn 8.41
earth have committed f. with her, Rev 18.03

FORSAKE —N —ING
he will not fail you or f. you." Deu 31.06
and I will f. them and hide my face 31.17
f. me not, O God of my salvation! Ps 27.09
For the LORD will not f. his people; 94.14
Do not f. the work of thy hands. 138.08
the God of Israel will not f. them. Is 41.17
to those who f. the holy covenant. Dan 11.30
"I will never fail you nor f. you." Heb 13.05
My God, my God, why hast thou f. me? Ps 22.01
You shall no more be termed F., Is 62.04
Behold, your house is f. and desolate. Mt 23.38
God, my God, why hast thou f. me?" 27.46
persecuted, but not f.; struck down, 2Co 4.09
played the harlot, f. your God. Hos 9.01
F. the right way they have gone 2Pe 2.15

FORSOOK
is because they f. the covenant of Deu 29.25

They f. the LORD, and served the Ju 2.13
For a brief moment I f. you, but with Is 54.07
all the disciples f. him and fled. Mt 26.56

FORTRESS —ES
and my f., and my deliverer, my God, Ps 18.02
Yea, thou art my rock and my f.; 31.03
is my rock and my salvation, my f.; 62.02
and all your f. shall be destroyed, Hos 10.14
All your f. are like fig trees with Nah 3.12

FORTUNE —S
set a table for F. and fill cups Is 65.11
And the LORD restored the f. of Job, Job 42.10
God restores the f. of his people, Ps 53.06

FORTY
The flood continued f. days upon Gen 7.17
of Israel ate the manna f. years. Ex 16.35
shepherds in the wilderness f. years, Num 14.33
for f. years I loathed that generation Ps 95.10
he fasted f. days and f. nights, Mt 4.02
appearing to them during f. days. Ac 1.03
And for about f. years he bore with 13.18
There were more than f. who made 23.13
of the Jews the f. lashes less one. 2Co 11.24

FORWARD
Let your eyes look directly f., Pro 4.25
and went backward and not f. Jer 7.24
And they put f. two, Joseph called Ac 1.23
whom God put f. as an expiation by Rom 3.25
and straining f. to what lies Php 3.13
For he looked f. to the city which Heb 11.10

FOUGHT
I f. with beasts at Ephesus? If the 1Co 15.32
I have f. the good fight, I have 2Ti 4.07

FOUL
My wounds grow f. and fester Ps 38.05
slander, and f. talk from your mouth. Col 3.08
three f. spirits like frogs; Rev 16.13

FOUND —ED
But Noah f. favor in the eyes of Gen 6.08
"I have f. the book of the law in 2Ki 22.08
a scroll was f. on which this was Ez 6.02
"But where shall wisdom be f.? And Job 28.12
this alone I f., that God made man Ecc 7.29
"Seek the LORD while he may be f., Is 55.06
you f. new life for your strength, 57.10
I will be f. by you, says the LORD, Jer 29.14
in Israel have I f. such faith. Mt 8.10
and f. Mary and Joseph, and the babe Lk 2.16
he was lost, and is f.' And they 15.24
I f. also an altar with this Ac 17.23
And being f. in human form he Php 2.08
and be f. in him, not having a 3.09
didst f. the earth in the beginning, Heb 1.10
for he has f. it upon the seas, and Ps 24.02
earth, which he has f. for ever. 78.69
The LORD by wisdom f. the earth; Pro 3.19
because it had been f. on the rock. Mt 7.25

FOUNDATION —S

fourth year the f. of the house of	1Ki 6.37
when I laid the f. of the earth?	Job 38.04
justice are the f. of thy throne;	Ps 89.14
am laying in Zion for a f. a stone,	Is 28.16
My hand laid the f. of the earth,	48.13
hidden since the f. of the world."	Mt 13.35
Otherwise, when he has laid a f.,	Lk 14.29
for me before the f. of the world.	Jn 17.24
lest I build on another man's f.,	Rom 15.20
For no other f. can any one lay	1Co 3.11
built upon the f. of the apostles	Eph 2.20
But God's firm f. stands, bearing	2Ti 2.19
laying again a f. of repentance	Heb 6.01
Thou didst set the earth on its f.,	Ps 104.05
And the f. of the thresholds shook	Is 6.04
so that the f. of the prison were	Ac 16.26
forward to the city which has f.,	Heb 11.10

FOUNTAIN —S

For with thee is the f. of life;	Ps 36.09
The fear of the LORD is a f. of life,	Pro 14.27
or the pitcher is broken at the f.,	Ecc 12.06
he established the f. of the deep,	Pro 8.28
and f. in the midst of the valleys;	Is 41.18

FOX —ES

said to them, "Go and tell that f.,	Lk 13.32
went and caught three hundred f.,	Ju 15.04
"F. have holes, and birds of the air	Mt 8.20

FRAGRANCE

filled with the f. of the ointment.	Jn 12.03
us spreads the f. of the knowledge	2Co 2.14
to one a f. from death to death, to	2.16

FRAGRANT

a f. offering and sacrifice to God.	Eph 5.02
a f. offering, a sacrifice acceptable	Php 4.18

FRAME —S (v)

thee, who f. mischief by statute?	Ps 94.20
evil, and your tongue f. deceit	50.19

FRAME (n)

mighty strength, or his goodly f.	Job 41.12
For he knows our f.; he remembers	Ps 103.14
my f. was not hidden from thee, when	139.15

FRANKINCENSE

They shall bring gold and f.,	Is 60.06
him gifts, gold and f. and myrrh.	Mt 2.11
f., wine, oil, fine flour and wheat,	Rev 18.13

FREE

you will be f. from this oath of	Gen 24.08
the LORD answered me and set me f.	Ps 118.05
The LORD sets the prisoners f.;	146.07
every one would set f. his slave,	Jer 34.10
said to him, "Then the sons are f.	Mt 17.26
and the truth will make you f."	Jn 8.32
But the f. gift is not like the	Rom 5.15
and, having been set f. from sin,	6.18

has set me f. from the law of sin	8.02
I want you to be f. from anxieties.	1Co 7.32
Am I not f.? Am I not an apostle?	9.01
there is neither slave nor f.,	Gal 3.28
For freedom Christ has set us f.;	5.01
Lord, whether he is a slave or f.	Eph 6.08
Keep your life f. from love of	Heb 13.05
Live as f. men, yet without using	1Pe 2.16

FREED

you are f. from your infirmity,"	Lk 13.12
believes is f. from everything	Ac 13.39
For he who has died is f. from sin.	Rom 6.07
us and has f. us from our sins by	Rev 1.05

FREEDOM

Spirit of the Lord is, there is f.	2Co 3.17
For you were called to f., brethren;	Gal 5.13
using your f. as a pretext for	1Pe 2.16

FREELY

"You may f. eat of every tree of	Gen 2.16
I will love them f., for my anger	Hos 14.04
out and began to talk f. about it,	Mk 1.45
grace which he f. bestowed on us	Eph 1.06

FRESH

thou hast poured over me f. oil.	Ps 92.10
new wine is put into f. wineskins,	Mt 9.17
leaven that you may be f. dough,	1Co 5.07
No more can salt water yield f.	Jas 3.12

FRIEND —S

to face, as a man speaks to his f.	Ex 33.11
A f. loves at all times, and a	Pro 17.17
every one is a f. to a man who	19.06
a f. of tax collectors and sinners!'	Mt 11.19
for a f. of mine has arrived on a	Lk 11.06
the f. of the bridegroom, who stands	Jn 3.29
this man, you are not Caesar's f.;	19.12
and he was called the f. of God.	Jas 2.23
wishes to be a f. of the world	4.04
Job's three f. heard of all this	Job 2.11
My f. and companions stand aloof	Ps 38.11
Wealth brings many new f., but a poor	Pro 10.04
'Your trusted f. have deceived you	Jer 38.22
Make f. quickly with your accuser,	Mt 5.25
make f. for yourselves by means of	Lk 16.09
a man lay down his life for his f.	Jn 15.13
but I have called you f., for all	15.15
to go to his f. and be cared for.	Ac 27.03

FRIGHTEN —ED —ING*

Wilt thou f. a driven leaf and	Job 13.25
and as they were f. and bowed their	Lk 24.05
near to the boat. They were f.,	Jn 6.19
and not f. in anything by your	Php 1.28
you, and its appearance was f.	Dan 2.31
not seem to be f. you with letters.	2Co 10.09

FROGS

plague all your country with f.;	Ex 8.02
prophet, three foul spirits like f.;	Rev 16.13

FRONT

each had the face of a man in f.;	Eze 1.10
And those who were in f. rebuked him,	Lk 18.39
and beat him in f. of the tribunal.	Ac 18.17
full of eyes in f. and behind:	Rev 4.06

FRUIT —S

shall not eat of the f. of the tree	Gen 3.03
shall count their f. as forbidden;	Lev 19.23
Cursed shall be the f. of your body,	Deu 28.18
that yields its f. in its season,	Ps 1.03
The f. of the righteous is a tree	Pro 11.30
root downward, and bear f. upward;	Is 37.31
and yield your f. to my people	Eze 36.08
you have eaten the f. of lies.	Hos 10.13
me: behold, a basket of summer f.	Amo 8.01
the f. of my body for the sin of my	Mic 6.07
Bear f. that befits repentance,	Mt 3.08
A sound tree cannot bear evil f.,	7.18
the tree good, and its f. good;	12.33
again of this f. of the vine until	26.29
and blessed is the f. of your womb!	Lk 1.42
and gathers f. for eternal life, so	Jn 4.36
but if it dies, it bears much f.	12.24
go and bear f. and that your f.	15.16
order that we may bear f. for God.	Rom 7.04
without eating any of its f.?	1Co 9.07
But the f. of the Spirit is love,	Gal 5.22
bearing f. in every good work and	Col 1.10
the f. of lips that acknowledge his	Heb 13.15
twelve kinds of f., yielding its f.	Rev 22.02
of the first f. of your labor, of	Ex 23.16
You will know them by their f.	Mt 7.16
have the first f. of the Spirit,	Rom 8.23
dough offered as first f. is holy,	11.16
his own order; Christ the first f.,	1Co 15.23
filled with the f. of righteousness	Php 1.11
as first f. for God and the Lamb,	Rev 14.04

FRUITFUL

"Be f. and multiply and fill the	Gen 1.22
And the Lord made his people very f.,	Ps 105.24
flesh, that means f. labor for me.	Php 1.22

FRUSTRATED*

us and that God had f. their plan,	Neh 4.15
He f. the devices of the crafty, so	Job 5.12

FUGITIVE

you shall be a f. and a wanderer on	Gen 4.12

FULFIL —LED

The LORD will f. his purpose for me;	Ps 138.08
took place to f. what the Lord had	Mt 1.22
not to abolish them but to f. them.	5.17
This took place to f. what was	21.04
This was to f. the word which Jesus	Jn 18.32
and so f. the law of Christ.	Gal 6.02
"See that you f. the ministry which	Col 4.17
of an evangelist, f. your ministry.	2Ti 4.05
A desire f. is sweet to the soul;	Pro 13.19
"The time is f., and the kingdom of	Mk 1.15
has been f. in your hearing."	Lk 4.21
it until it is f. in the kingdom	22.16

may have my joy f. in themselves.	Jn 17.13
"Brethren, the scripture had to be f.,	Ac 1.16
loves his neighbor has f. the law.	Rom 13.08
For the whole law is f. in one word,	Gal 5.14

FULL —Y

And you shall eat and be f., and you	Deu 8.10
is f. of thy steadfast love; teach me	Ps 119.64
man who has his quiver f. of them!	127.05
All things are f. of weariness;	Ecc 1.08
the whole earth is f. of his glory."	Is 6.03
earth shall be f. of the knowledge	11.09
whole body will be f. of light;	Mt 6.22
twelve baskets f. of the broken	14.20
inside they are f. of extortion	23.25
then the f. grain in the ear.	Mk 4.28
And Jesus, f. of the Holy Spirit,	Lk 4.01
"Woe to you that are f. now,	6.25
f. of grace and truth; we have beheld	Jn 1.14
f. of the Spirit and of wisdom, whom	Ac 6.03
how it is f. time now for you to	Rom 13.11
being in f. accord and of one mind	Php 2.02
I have received f. payment, and more;	4.18
realizing the f. assurance of hope	Heb 6.11
for my time has not yet f. come."	Jn 7.08
f. convinced that God was able to	Rom 4.21
Illyricum I have f. preached the	15.19
in part; then I shall understand f.,	1Co 13.12
But when the time had f. come,	Gal 4.04
to make the word of God f. known,	Col 1.25
strength to proclaim the word f.,	2Ti 4.17
set your hope f. upon the grace	1Pe 1.13

FULNESS

in thy presence there is f. of joy,	Ps 16.11
is the LORD's and the f. thereof,	24.01
And from his f. have we all received,	Jn 1.16
as a plan for the f. of time, to unite	Eph 1.10
the f. of him who fills all in all.	1.23
be filled with all the f. of God.	3.19
of the stature of the f. of Christ;	4.13
him the whole f. of deity dwells	Col 2.09

FURNACE

smoke, and my bones burn like a f.	Ps 102.03
be cast into a burning fiery f."	Dan 3.06
and throw them into the f. of fire;	Mt 13.42
smoke like the smoke of a great f.,	Rev 9.02

FURNISHED —S*

a large upper room f. and ready;	Mk 14.15
God who richly f. us with everything	1Ti 6.17

FURY

he has poured out his f. like fire.	Lam 2.04
Thou didst bestride the earth in f.,	Hab 3.12
filled with f. and discussed with	Lk 6.11
wickedness, there will be wrath and f.	Rom 2.08
the cup of the f. of his wrath.	Rev 16.19

FUTILE

but they became f. in their thinking	Rom 1.21
your faith is f. and you are still	1Co 15.17

FUTURE
Surely there is a f., and your hope   Pro 23.18
for the evil man has no f.; the lamp   24.20

evil, to give you a f. and a hope.   Jer 29.11
present or the f., all are yours;   1Co 3.22
a good foundation for the f., so that   1Ti 6.19

G

GAIN —ED (v)
understanding, and he will g.   Pro 19.25
What does man g. by all the toil at   Ecc 1.03
to g. the whole world and forfeit   Mk 8.36
Whoever seeks to g. his life will   Lk 17.33
endurance you will g. your lives.   21.19
burned, but have not love, I g. nothing.   1Co 13.03
to you, you have g. your brother.   Mt 18.15

GAIN (n)
ways of all who get g. by violence;   Pro 1.19
hates unjust g. will prolong his   28.16
every one is greedy for unjust g.;   Jer 6.13
live is Christ, and to die is g.   Php 1.21
But whatever g. I had, I counted as   3.07
that godliness is a means of g.   1Ti 6.05
a year there are trade and get g.";   Jas 4.13

GARDEN
the LORD God planted a g. in Eden,   Gen 2.08
A g. locked is my sister, my bride, a   Sol 4.12
and you shall be like a watered g.,   Is 58.11
You were in Eden, the g. of God; every   Eze 28.13
they shall flourish as a g.; they shall   Hos 14.07
a man took and sowed in his g.   Lk 13.19
valley, where there was a g., which he   Jn 18.01
he was crucified there was a g.,   19.41

GARLAND
wisdom, but folly is the g. of fools.   Pro 14.24
to give them a g. instead of ashes,   Is 61.03

GARMENT —S
shall a man put on a woman's g.;   Deu 22.05
every man of them took his g.,   2Ki 9.13
when I made clouds its g., and thick   Job 38.09
they will all wear out like a g.   Ps 102.26
Now John wore a g. of camel's hair,   Mt 3.04
of unshrunk cloth on an old g.,   9.16
and touched the fringe of his g.;   9.20
there a man who had no wedding g.;   22.11
they will all grow old like a g.,   Heb 1.11
hating even the g. spotted by the   Jud 23
and his g. became white as light.   Mt 17.02
crowd spread their g. on the road,   21.08
divided his g. among them by   27.35
rose from supper, laid aside his g.,   Jn 13.04
laid down their g. at the feet of   Ac 7.58
coats and g. which Dorcas made while   9.39
rotted and your g. are moth-eaten.   Jas 5.02
shall be clad thus in white g., and I   Rev 3.05

GATE —S
God, and this is the g. of heaven."   Gen 28.17
talk of those who sit in the g.,   Ps 69.12
This is the g. of the LORD;   118.20
for him who reproves in the g.,   Is 29.21

"Stand in the g. of the LORD's house,   Jer 7.02
and turn aside the needy in the g.   Amo 5.10
and establish justice in the g.;   5.15
"Enter by the narrow g.;   Mt 7.13
And at his g. lay a poor man named   Lk 16.20
Jerusalem by the Sheep G. a pool,   Jn 5.02
outside the g. in order to sanctify   Heb 13.12
sojourner who is within your g.;   Ex 20.10
of your house and on your g.   Deu 6.09
Lift up your heads, O g.! and be lifted   Ps 24.07
Enter his g. with thanksgiving, and   100.04
Open to me the g. of righteousness,   118.19
Your g. shall be open continually;   Is 60.11
Salvation, and your g. Praise.   60.18
Jerusalem, who enter by these g.   Jer 17.20
that has no g. or bars, that dwells   49.31
that he is near, at the very g.   Mt 24.33
twelve g., and at the g. twelve angels,   Rev 21.12

GATEWAY
entrance of the g. of the inner   Eze 8.03
mean." And he went out into the g.   Mk 14.68
he knocked at the door of the g.,   Ac 12.13

GATHER —ED —S
Go and g. the elders of Israel   Ex 3.16
g. your men at Mount Tabor, taking   Ju 4.06
and will g. all Israel to my lord   2Sa 3.21
"Go, g. all the Jews to be found in   Est 4.16
of the peoples g. as the people of   Ps 47.09
"G. to me my faithful ones, who made   50.05
he will g. the lambs in his arms, he   Is 40.11
and from the west I will g. you;   43.05
I am coming to g. all nations and   66.18
The children g. wood, the fathers   Jer 7.18
Then I will g. the remnant of my   23.03
Behold, I will g. them from all the   32.37
"G. yourselves together and come   49.14
I will g. you from the peoples, and   Eze 11.17
When I g. the house of Israel from   28.25
For my decision is to g. nations,   Zep 3.08
sow nor reap nor g. into barns,   Mt 6.26
he who does not g. with me scatters.   12.30
and they will g. out of his kingdom   13.41
and they will g. his elect from the   24.31
and g. where I have not winnowed?   25.26
but to g. into one the children of   Jn 11.52
g. for the great supper of God,   Rev 19.17
to g. them for battle; their number   20.08
the heavens g. together into   Gen 1.09
He g. the waters of the sea as in a   Ps 33.07
Are grapes g. from thorns, or figs   Mt 7.16
the sea and g. fish of every kind;   13.47
two or three are g. in my name,   18.20
the eagles will be g. together.   24.28
who g. the outcasts of Israel, I   Is 56.08
he g. them in his seine; so he rejoices   Hab 1.15

GATHER —ED —S (cont.)

as a hen g. her brood under her Mt 23.37
and g. fruit for eternal life, so Jn 4.36

GAZE —D —ING

who g. at the stars, who at the new Is 47.13
and nations g. at their dead bodies Rev 11.09
g. into heaven and saw the glory of Ac 7.55
he sat in the light and g. at him, Lk 22.56
And while they were g. into heaven Ac 1.10

GAZELLE

save yourself like a g. from the Pro 6.05
My beloved is like a g., or a young Sol 2.09
Tabitha, which means Dorcas or G. Ac 9.36

GENEALOGIES —Y

and endless g. which promote 1Ti 1.04
The book of the g. of Jesus Christ, Mt 1.01
He is without father or mother or g., Heb 7.03

GENERATION —S

righteous man, blameless in his g.; Gen 6.09
and the fourth g. of those who Ex 20.05
Such is the g. of those who seek Ps 24.06
to the coming g. the glorious 78.04
from g. to g. we will recount 79.13
One g. shall laud thy works to 145.04
A g. goes, and a g. comes, but the Ecc 1.04
kingdom endures from g. to g.; Dan 4.34
"But to what shall I compare this g.? Mt 11.16
and adulterous g. seeks for a sign; 12.39
"O faithless and perverse g., 17.17
this g. will not pass away till all 24.34
world, may be required of this g., Lk 11.50
in their own g. than the sons of 16.08
the counsel of God in his own g., Ac 13.36
midst of a crooked and perverse g., Php 2.15
Therefore I was provoked with that g., Heb 3.10
These are the g. of the heavens and Gen 2.04
This is the book of the g. of Adam. 5.01
been our dwelling place in all g. Ps 90.01
thy name endures to all g. 102.12
and does a crown endure to all g.? Pro 27.24
henceforth all g. will call me Lk 1.48
In past g. he allowed all the Ac 14.16
and in Christ Jesus to all g., Eph 3.21
for ages and g. but now made Col 1.26

GENTILE —S

be to you as a G. and a tax Mt 18.17
live like a G. and not like a Jew, Gal 2.14
Do not even the G. do the same? Mt 5.47
heap up empty phrases as the G. do; 6.07
them, "Go nowhere among the G., 10.05
and in his name will the G. hope." 12.21
'Why did the G. rage, and the Ac 4.25
had been poured out even on the G. 10.45
opened a door of faith to the G. 14.27
how God first visited the G., 15.14
When G. who have not the law do by Rom 2.14
Is he not the God of G. also? Yes, of G. 3.29
salvation has come to the G., 11.11
Now I am speaking to you G. 11.13

block to Jews and folly to G., 1Co 1.23
I might preach him among the G., Gal 1.16
God would justify the G. by faith, 3.08
great among the G. are the riches Col 1.27
Maintain good conduct among the G., 1Pe 2.12

GENTLE

A g. tongue is a tree of life, but Pro 15.04
But I was like a g. lamb led to the Jer 11.19
for I am g. and lowly in heart, and Mt 11.29
But we were g. among you, like a 1Th 2.07
g., open to reason, full of mercy Jas 3.17

GENTLENESS

or with love in a spirit of g.? 1Co 4.21
by the meekness and g. of Christ— 2Co 10.01
restore him in a spirit of g. Gal 6.01

GENUINE

Let love be g.; hate what is Rom 12.09
kindness, the Holy Spirit, g. love, 2Co 6.06

GIFT —S

offer it as a g. to the LORD Lev 17.04
I give your priesthood as a g., Num 18.07
Or has he given us any g.?" 2Sa 19.42
Have I said, 'Make me a g.'? Job 6.22
in his toil—this is the g. of God. Ecc 5.19
are offering your g. at the altar, Mt 5.23
the g. or the altar that makes the g. 23.19
her, "If you knew the g. of God, Jn 4.10
receive the g. of the Holy Spirit. Ac 2.38
obtain the g. of God with money! 8.20
gave the same g. to them as he 11.17
are justified by his grace as a g., Rom 3.24
But the free g. is not like the 5.15
but the free g. of God is eternal 6.23
"Or who has given a g. to him that 11.35
has his own special g. from God, 1Co 7.07
to carry your g. to Jerusalem. 16.03
as an exaction but as a willing g. 2Co 9.05
according to the g. of God's grace Eph 3.07
Not that I seek the g.; but I seek Php 4.17
Do not neglect the g. you have, 1Ti 4.14
to rekindle the g. of God that is 2Ti 1.06
who have tasted the heavenly g., Heb 6.04
As each has received a g., employ it 1Pe 4.10
to give good g. to your children, Mt 7.11
For the g. and the call of God are Rom 11.29
Having g. that differ according to 12.06
Now concerning spiritual g., 1Co 12.01
But earnestly desire the higher g. 12.31
And his g. were that some should be Eph 4.11
to offer g. and sacrifices for sins. Heb 5.01

GIRD —ED

G. up your loins like a man, I will Job 38.03
For thou didst g. me with strength Ps 18.39
the hills g. themselves with joy, 65.12
I g. you, though you do not know me, Is 45.05
he will g. himself and have them Lk 12.37
another will g. you and carry you Jn 21.18
Therefore g. up your minds, be sober, 1Pe 1.13
is robed, he is g. with strength. Ps 93.01

GIRD —ED (cont.)

"Let your loins be g. and your	Lk 12.35
and g. himself with a towel.	Jn 13.04
having g. your loins with truth, and	Eph 6.14

GIRDLE

and instead of a g., a rope;	Is 3.24
Righteousness shall be the g. of his waist,	11.05
and a leather g. around his waist;	Mt 3.04
he took Paul's g. and bound his	Ac 21.11

GIRL —S

for the g. is not dead but sleeping."	Mt 9.24
met by a slave g. and who had a spirit	Ac 16.16
and if a g. marries she does not	1Co 7.28
of boys and g. playing in its	Zec 8.05

GLAD —LY

Be g. in the LORD, and rejoice, O	Ps 32.11
I have told the g. news of deliverance	40.09
Let the nations be g. and sing for	67.04
Let the heavens be g., and let the	96.11
I was g. when they said to me, "Let	122.01
Let Israel be g. in his Maker, let	149.02
A wise son makes a g. father,	Pro 10.01
let us be g. and rejoice in his	Is 25.09
Rejoice and be g., for your reward	Mt 5.12
And when they heard it they were g.,	Mk 14.11
fitting to make merry and be g.,	Lk 15.32
your sake I am g. that I was not	Jn 11.15
of food with g. and generous	Ac 2.46
For we are g. when we are weak and	2Co 13.09
I am g. and rejoice with you all.	Php 2.17
rejoice and be g. when his glory	1Pe 4.13
perplexed; and yet he heard him g.	Mk 6.20
And the great throng heard him g.	12.37
I will most g. spend and be spent	2Co 12.15

GLADNESS

Serve the LORD with g.! Come into	Ps 100.02
The hope of the righteous ends in g.,	Pro 10.28
And joy and g. are taken away from	Is 16.10
they shall obtain joy and g.,	35.10
And you will have joy and g.,	Lk 1.14
with the oil of g. beyond thy	Heb 1.09

GLOOM

Let g. and deep darkness claim it.	Job 3.05
There is no g. or deep darkness	34.22
and your g. be as the noonday.	Is 58.10
pits of nether g. to be kept until	2Pe 2.04

GLORIFIED —Y —ING

before all the people I will be g.' "	Lev 10.03
and they g. God, who had given such	Mt 9.08
because Jesus was not yet g.	Jn 7.39
come for the Son of man to be g.	12.23
said, "Now is the Son of man g.,	13.31
I g. thee on earth, having accomplished	17.04
g. his servant Jesus, whom you	Ac 3.13
If I g. myself, my glory is nothing;	Jn 8.54
He will g. me, for he will take what	16.14
by what death he was to g. God.)	21.19
Gentiles might g. God for his	Rom 15.09
a price. So g. God in your body.	1Co 6.20

good deeds and g. God on the day	1Pe 2.12
but under that name let him g. God.	4.16
g. and praising God for all they	Lk 2.20

GLORIOUS —LY

g. in power, thy right hand, O LORD,	Ex 15.06
Blessed be his g. name for ever;	Ps 72.19
G. things are spoken of you, O city	87.03
and the g. splendor of thy kingdom.	145.12
to magnify his law and make it g.	Is 42.21
and I will glorify my g. house.	60.07
the east, and toward the g. land.	Dan 8.09
of man shall sit on his g. throne,	Mt 19.28
and obtain the g. liberty of the	Rom 8.21
praise of his g. grace which he	Eph 1.06
lowly body to be like his g. body,	Php 3.21
power, according to his g. might,	Col 1.11
with the g. gospel of the blessed	1Ti 1.11
not afraid to revile the g. ones,	2Pe 2.10
the LORD, for he has triumphed g.;	Ex 15.01
to the LORD, for he has done g.;	Is 12.05

GLORY

and I will get g. over Pharaoh and	Ex 14.04
you shall see the g. of the LORD,	16.07
the g. of the LORD appeared in the	16.10
The g. of the LORD settled on Mount	24.16
Moses said, "I pray thee, show me thy g."	33.18
and the g. of the LORD filled the	40.34
dost crown him with g. and honor.	Ps 8.05
The heavens are telling the g. of God;	19.01
that the King of g. may come in.	24.07
Ascribe to the LORD the g. of his name;	29.02
Let thy g. be over all the earth!	57.05
May the g. of the LORD endure for	104.31
They exchanged the g. of God for	106.20
This is g. for all his faithful	149.09
A hoary head is a crown of g.;	Pro 16.31
And the g. of the LORD shall be	Is 40.05
My g. I will not give to another.	48.11
and the g. of the LORD has risen	60.01
and your God will be your g.	60.19
And the g. of the LORD went up	Eze 10.04
and the earth shone with his g.	43.02
works and give g. to your Father	Mt 5.16
kingdom and the power and the g.,	*6.13
in all his g. was not arrayed like	6.29
"When the Son of man comes in his g.,	25.31
"G. to God in the highest, and on	Lk 2.14
and truth; we have beheld his g.,	Jn 1.14
do not seek the g. that comes from	5.44
Yet I do not seek my own g.;	8.50
it is for the g. of God, so that the	11.04
The God of g. appeared to our	Ac 7.02
exchanged the g. of the immortal	Rom 1.23
and fall short of the g. of God,	3.23
our hope of sharing the g. of God.	5.02
with the g. that is to be revealed	8.18
all things. To him be g. for ever.	11.36
not have crucified the Lord of g.	1Co 2.08
you do, do all to the g. of God.	10.31
but the g. of the celestial is one,	15.40
from one degree of g. to another;	2Co 3.18
weight of g. beyond all comparison,	4.17

GLORY (cont.)

to live for the praise of his g.	Eph 1.12
to him be g. in the church and in	3.21
his riches in g. in Christ Jesus.	Php 4.19
is Christ in you, the hope of g.	Col 1.27
you into his own kingdom and g.	1Th 2.12
on in the world, taken up in g.	1Ti 3.16
He reflects the g. of God and bears	Heb 1.03
the spirit of g. and of God rests	1Pe 4.14
obtain the unfading crown of g.	5.04
presence of his g. with rejoicing,	Jud 24
to receive g. and honor and power,	Rev 4.11
voice, "Fear God and give him g.,	14.07

GLUTTON —S

a g. and a drunkard, a friend of tax	Mt 11.19
always liars, evil beasts, lazy g."	Tit 1.12

GNASH —ES —ING*

men will weep and g. their teeth."	Mt 8.12
the righteous, and g. his teeth at him;	Ps 37.12
and more, g. at me with their teeth.	35.16

GNAT*

straining out a g. and swallowing	Mt 23.24

GOATS

separates the sheep from the g.,	Mt 25.32
the blood of g. and calves but his	Heb 9.12
about in skins of sheep and g.,	11.37

GOD

When G. created man, he made him in	Gen 5.01
"I am the G. of Abraham your father;	26.24
G. said to Moses, "I AM WHO I AM."	Ex 3.14
the G. of Abraham, of Isaac, and of	3.16
G. is not man, that he should lie, or	Num 23.19
and Israel, 'What has G. wrought!'	23.23
The LORD our G. is one LORD;	Deu 6.04
LORD your G. is G. of gods and Lord	10.17
O give thanks to the G. of gods,	Ps 136.02
Consider the work of G.; who can	Ecc 7.13
"Behold, G. is my salvation;	Is 12.02
The LORD is the everlasting G.,	40.28
'Let us fear the LORD our G.,	Jer 5.24
for I am G. and not man, the Holy	Hos 11.09
whose name is the G. of hosts.	Amo 5.27
and to walk humbly with your G.?	Mic 6.08
Who is a G. like thee, pardoning	7.18
You cannot serve G. and mammon.	Mt 6.24
"My G., my G., why hast thou forsaken	27.46
No one has ever seen G.;	Jn 1.18
G. is spirit, and those who worship	4.24
but also called G. his Father,"	5.18
we have one Father, even G."	8.41
answered him, "My Lord and my G.!"	20.28
name of G. is blasphemed among	Rom 2.24
But G. shows his love for us in	5.08
G. is faithful, by whom you were	1Co 1.09
and that "there is no G. but one."	8.04
In their case the g. of this world	2Co 4.04
for G. is at work in you, both to	Php 2.13
But the word of G. is not fettered.	2Ti 2.09
of our great G. and Savior Jesus	Tit 2.13

therefore G., thy G., has anointed	Heb 1.09
not ashamed to be called their G.,	11.16
You believe that G. is one;	Jas 2.19
that G. is light and in him is no	1Jn 1.05
"Fear G. and give him glory, for the	Rev 14.07
I will be his G. and he shall be	21.07

GODLESS

the hope of the g. man shall perish.	Job 8.13
that a g. man shall not come before	13.16
For the company of the g. is barren,	15.34
Against a g. nation I send him, and	Is 10.06
to do with g. and silly myths.	1Ti 4.07
Avoid the g. chatter and contradictions	6.20

GODLINESS

silly myths. Train yourself in g.;	1Ti 4.07
the truth which accords with g.,	Tit 1.01
and g. with brotherly affection, and	2Pe 1.07

GODLY

with holiness and g. sincerity,	2Co 1.12
for you felt a g. grief,	7.09
to live a g. life in Christ Jesus	2Ti 3.12
and he was heard for his g. fear.	Heb 5.07

GODS

stole her father's household g.	Gen 31.19
the LORD is greater than all g.,	Ex 18.11
"You shall have no other g. before me.	20.03
back to her people and to her g.;	Ru 1.15
"Their g. are g. of the hills, and	1Ki 20.23
all g. bow down before him.	Ps 97.07
to molten images, "You are our g."	Is 42.17
For your g. have become as many as	Jer 11.13
among the false g. of the nations	14.22
'Make for us g. to go before us;	Ac 7.40
that g. made with hands are not g.	19.26
be so-called g. in heaven or on	1Co 8.05
to beings that by nature are no g.;	Gal 4.08

GOLD

and if the Almighty is your g.,	Job 22.25
tried me, I shall come forth as g.	23.10
"If I have made g. my trust,	31.24
More to be desired are they than g.,	Ps 19.10
Their idols are silver and g.,	115.04
commandments above g., above fine g.	119.127
knowledge rather than choice g.;	Pro 8.10
Like a g. ring in a swine's snout is	11.22
a goldsmith overlays it with g.,	Is 40.19
Instead of bronze I will bring g.,	60.17
worth their weight in fine g.,	Lam 4.02
The head of this image was of fine g.,	Dan 2.32
Nebuchadnezzar made an image of g.,	3.01
g. and frankincense and myrrh.	Mt 2.11
Take no g., nor silver, nor copper	10.09
to think that the Deity is like g.,	Ac 17.29
builds on the foundation with g.,	1Co 3.12
braided hair or g. or pearls or	1Ti 2.09
For if a man with g. rings and in	Jas 2.02
Your g. and silver have rusted, and	5.03
to buy from me g. refined by fire,	Rev 3.18
the street of the city was pure g.,	21.21

GOLDSMITH

and a g. overlays it with gold, and	Is 40.19
every g. is put to shame by his	Jer 10.14

GONG*

I am a noisy g. or a clanging	1Co 13.01

GOOD —S (n)

be like God, knowing g. and evil."	Gen 3.05
'Why have you returned evil for g.?	44.04
of God to discern g. and evil.	2Sa 14.17
we receive g. at the hand of God,	Job 2.10
But when I looked for g., evil came;	30.26
I have no g. apart from thee."	Ps 16.02
Depart from evil, and do g.;	34.14
but one sinner destroys much g.	Ecc 9.18
Is evil a recompense for g.?	Jer 18.20
Seek g., and not evil, that you may	Amo 5.14
You who hate the g. and love the	Mic 3.02
For I do not do the g. I want,	Rom 7.19
God works for g. with those who	8.28
by evil, but overcome evil with g.	12.21
Let no one seek his own g.,	1Co 10.24
do not imitate evil but imitate g.	3Jn 11
When g. increase, they increase who	Ecc 5.11
man's house and plunder his g.,	Mt 12.29
you have ample g. laid up for many	Lk 12.19
the half of my g. I give to the	19.08
possessions and g. and distributed	Ac 2.45
has the world's g. and sees his	1Jn 3.17

GOOD (adj)

made, and behold, it was very g.	Gen 1.31
Be strong and of g. courage,	Deu 31.06
if you acted in g. faith and honor	Ju 9.16
This day is a day of g. news;	2Ki 7.09
O taste and see that the LORD is g.!	Ps 34.08
For the LORD is g.; his steadfast	100.05
but a g. word makes him glad.	Pro 12.25
G. sense makes a man slow to anger,	19.11
O Zion, herald of g. tidings;	Is 40.09
said, "Figs, the g. figs very g., and	Jer 24.03
He has showed you, O man, what is g.;	Mic 6.08
The LORD is g., a stronghold in the	Nah 1.07
Yea, how g. and how fair it shall be!	Zec 9.17
does not bear g. fruit is cut down	Mt 3.10
may see your g. works and give	5.16
Other seeds fell on g. soil and	13.08
'Well done, g. and faithful servant;	25.21
"G. Teacher, what must I do to	Mk 10.17
No one is g. but God alone.	10.18
me to preach g. news to the poor.	Lk 4.18
Mary has chosen the g. portion,	10.42
your Father's g. pleasure to give	12.32
I am the g. shepherd. The g. shepherd	Jn 10.11
but be of g. cheer, I have overcome	16.33
as he preached g. news about the	Ac 8.12
feet of those who preach g. news?"	Rom 10.15
"Bad company ruins g. morals."	1Co 15.33
So we are always of g. courage;	2Co 5.06
in abundance for every g. work.	9.08
and to work for his g. pleasure.	Php 2.13
everything; hold fast what is g.,	1Th 5.21
comfort and g. hope through grace,	2Th 2.16

For everything created by God is g.,	1Ti 4.04
you will be a g. minister of Christ	4.06
Fight the g. fight of the faith;	6.12
I have fought the g. fight, I have	2Ti 4.07
a shadow of the g. things to come	Heb 10.01

GOOD-LOOKING*

Now Joseph was handsome and g.	Gen 39.06

GOODNESS

Surely g. and mercy shall follow me	Ps 23.06
O how abundant is thy g., which	31.19
that you yourselves are full of g.,	Rom 15.14
a lover of g., master of himself,	Tit 1.08
and have tasted the g. of the word	Heb 6.05

GOSPEL

preaching the g. of the kingdom	Mt 4.23
wherever this g. is preached in the	26.13
beginning of the g. of Jesus Christ,	Mk 1.01
And the g. must first be preached	13.10
set apart for the g. of God	Rom 1.01
For I am not ashamed of the g.:	1.16
me to baptize but to preach the g.,	1Co 1.17
to me if I do not preach the g.!	9.16
And even if our g. is veiled,	2Co 4.03
may preach the g. in lands beyond	10.16
not that there is another g.,	Gal 1.07
the equipment of the g. of peace;	Eph 6.15
to proclaim the mystery of the g.,	6.19
life be worthy of the g. of Christ,	Php 1.27
in the word of the truth, the g.	Col 1.05
for our g. came to you not only in	1Th 1.05
the glorious g. of the blessed God	1Ti 1.11
immortality to light through the g.	2Ti 1.10
during my imprisonment for the g.;	Phm 13
For this is why the g. was preached	1Pe 4.06

GOVERN —ING

us a king to g. us like all the	1Sa 8.05
understanding mind to g. thy people,	1Ki 3.09
Shall one whom hates justice g.?	Job 34.17
ruler who will g. my people Israel.' "	Mt 2.06
be subject to the g. authorities.	Rom 13.01

GOVERNOR —S

Now Joseph was g. over the land;	Gen 42.06
Babylon had appointed Gedaliah g.,	2Ki 25.23
and delivered him to Pilate the g.	Mt 27.02
when Quirinius was g. of Syria.	Lk 2.02
bring him safely to Felix the g."	Ac 23.24
dragged before g. and kings for my	Mt 10.18
or to g. as sent by him to punish	1Pe 2.14

GRACE

the sword found g. in the wilderness;	Jer 31.02
And I took my staff G., and I broke	Zec 11.10
among us, full of g. and truth;	Jn 1.14
have we all received, g. upon g.	1.16
to the gospel of the g. of God.	Ac 20.24
have received g. and apostleship	Rom 1.05
they are justified by his g. as a gift,	3.24
continue in sin that g. may abound?	6.01
there is a remnant, chosen by g.	11.05

GRACE (cont.)

But by the g. of God I am what I am,	1Co 15.10
"My g. is sufficient for you, for my	2Co 12.09
and has called me through his g.,	Gal 1.15
according to the riches of his g.	Eph 1.07
strong in the g. that is in Christ	2Ti 2.01
draw near to the throne of g.,	Heb 4.16
But grow in the g. and knowledge of	2Pe 3.18

GRACIOUS

and I will be g. to whom I will be g.,	Ex 33.19
g. and merciful, slow to anger and	Neh 9.17
May God be g. to us and bless us	Ps 67.01
Has God forgotten to be g.? Has he in	77.09
The Lord is merciful and g., slow to	103.08
Therefore the Lord waits to be g. to you;	Is 30.18
complete among you this g. work.	2Co 8.06
whatever is g., if there is any	Php 4.08
Let your speech always be g.,	Col 4.06

GRAIN

seven ears of g., plump and good,	Gen 41.05
came to Egypt to Joseph to buy g.,	41.57
The first fruits of your g., of your	Deu 18.04
tenth of your g. and of your	1Sa 8.15
people curse him who holds back g.,	Pro 11.26
the Lord will thresh out the g.,	Is 27.12
I will take back my g. in its time,	Hos 2.09
to pluck ears of g. and to eat.	Mt 12.01
on good soil and brought forth g.,	13.08
is like a g. of mustard seed which	13.31
disciples began to pluck ears of g.	Mk 2.23
unless a g. of wheat falls into the	Jn 12.24
of wheat or of some other g.	1Co 15.37

GRANT —ED —ING

Only g. two things to me, then I	Job 13.20
O Lord, and g. us thy salvation.	Ps 85.07
and at my left is not mine to g.,	Mt 20.23
May the Lord g. mercy to the	2Ti 1.16
I will g. him to sit with me on my	Rev 3.21
Thou hast g. me life and steadfast	Job 10.12
was dead, he g. the body to Joseph.	Mk 15.45
so he has g. the Son also to have	Jn 5.26
g. signs and wonders to be done by	Ac 14.03

GRAPES

'The fathers have eaten sour g.,	Jer 31.29
you shall tread g., but not drink	Mic 6.15
Are g. gathered from thorns, or figs	Mt 7.16
of the earth, for its g. are ripe."	Rev 14.18

GRASS

he makes g. grow upon the hills.	Ps 147.08
All flesh is g., and all its	Is 40.06
bones shall flourish like the g.;	66.14
he was fed g. like an ox, and his	Dan 5.21
God so clothes the g. of the field,	Mt 6.30
the crowds to sit down on the g.;	14.19
the flower of g. The g. withers,	1Pe 1.24

GRAVE —S (n)

carried from the womb to the g.	Job 10.19
death, jealousy is cruel as the g.	Sol 8.06

And they made his g. with the	Is 53.09
"Their throat is an open g.,	Rom 3.13
you are like g. which are not seen,	Lk 11.44

GRAVEN

shall not make for yourself a g. image,	Ex 20.04
to jealousy with their g. images.	Ps 78.58
who trust in g. images, who say to	Is 42.17
Behold, I have g. you on the palms	49.16

GREAT —ER —EST

and I will make him a g. nation.	Gen 17.20
turn aside and see this g. sight	Ex 3.03
arm and with g. acts of judgment,	6.06
who does g. things and unsearchable,	Job 5.09
Behold, God is g., and we know him	36.26
"G. is the Lord, who delights in the	Ps 35.27
faithfulness from the g. congregation.	40.10
G. is the Lord and greatly to be	48.01
Thou who hast done g. things, O God,	71.19
is holy. What god is g. like our God?	77.13
For the Lord is a g. God, and a g. King	95.03
who plays the g. man but lacks	Pro 12.09
in darkness have seen a g. light;	Is 9.02
the shade of a g. rock in a weary	32.02
rejoiced exceedingly with g. joy;	Mt 2.10
shall be called g. in the kingdom	5.19
her, "O woman, g. is your faith!	15.28
This is the g. and first commandment.	22.38
And behold, there was a g. earthquake;	28.02
from the tomb with fear and g. joy,	28.08
He will be g., and will be called	Lk 1.32
good news of a g. joy which will	2.10
"A g. prophet has arisen among us!"	7.16
This is a g. mystery, and I take it	Eph 5.32
if we neglect such a g. salvation?	Heb 2.03
Since then we have a g. high priest	4.14
the g. shepherd of the sheep, by the	13.20
The g. city was split into three	Rev 16.19
were the g. men of the earth, and	18.23
the g. light to rule the day, and	Gen 1.16
risen no one g. than John the	Mt 11.11
something g. than the temple is	12.06
For which is g., the gift or the	23.19
no other commandment g. than these."	Mk 12.31
for the Father is g. than I.	Jn 14.28
G. love has no man than this, that a	15.13
servant is not g. than his master.'	15.20
swear by a g. than themselves, and	Heb 6.16
for God is g. than our hearts, and	1Jn 3.20
No g. joy can I have than this, to	3Jn 4
"Who is the g. in the kingdom of	Mt 18.01
He who is g. among you shall be	23.11
but the g. of these is love.	1Co 13.13
from the least of them to the g.	Heb 8.11

GREATNESS

God has shown us his glory and g.,	Deu 5.24
thou hast redeemed through thy g.,	9.26
and his g. is unsearchable.	Ps 145.03
acts, and I will declare thy g.	145.06
"Whom are you like in your g.?	Eze 31.02
immeasurable g. of his power in us	Eph 1.19

GREED
His g. is as wide as Sheol;	Hab 2.05
And in their g. they will exploit	2Pe 2.03
They have hearts trained in g.	2.14

GREEDY
He who is g. for unjust gain makes	Pro 15.27
g. to practice every kind of	Eph 4.19

GREEN
the hills and under every g. tree;	Deu 12.02
he searches after every g. thing.	Job 39.08
he makes me lie down in g. pastures.	Ps 23.02
the oaks, under every g. tree;	Is 57.05
they do this when the wood is g.,	Lk 23.31

GRIEF —S*
My eye has grown dim from g.,	Job 17.07
A stupid son is a g. to a father;	Pro 17.21
My g. is beyond healing, my heart is	Jer 8.18
poured out in g. because of the	Lam 2.11
for you felt a godly g., so that you	2Co 7.09
has borne our g. and carried our	Is 53.04

GRIEVE —D
And do not g. the Holy Spirit of	Eph 4.30
you may not g. as others do who	1Th 4.13
g. at their hardness of heart, and	Mk 3.05
for I see that that letter g. you,	2Co 7.08

GRIND —ING —S*
are compelled to g. at the mill;	Lam 5.13
Two women will be g. at the mill;	Mt 24.41
he foams and g. his teeth and	Mk 9.18

GROAN —ING (v)
g. inwardly as we wait for adoption	Rom 8.23
Here indeed we g., and long to put	2Co 5.02
has been g. in travail together	Rom 8.22

GROANING (n)
And God heard their g., and God	Ex 2.24
I am weary with my g.,	Jer 45.03

GROPE —ING
we g. like those who have no eyes;	Is 59.10
wearied themselves g. for the door.	Gen 19.11

GROUND —ED (v)
and he g. at the mill in the prison.	Ju 16.21
you, being rooted and g. in love	Eph 3.17

GROUND (n)
God formed man of dust from the g.,	Gen 2.07
bread till you return to the g.,	3.19
When you till the g., it shall no longer	4.12
which you are standing is holy g."	Ex 3.05
walked on dry g. through the sea,	14.29
My foot stands on level g.;	Ps 26.12
thou renewest the face of the g.	104.30
but on the g. of thy great mercy.	Dan 9.18
and the g. shall give its increase,	Zec 8.12
except on the g. of unchastity,	Mt 5.32
Other seeds fell on rocky g., where they	13.05

went and hid your talent in the g.	25.25
a house on the g. without a foundation;	Lk 6.49
and wrote with his finger on the g.	*Jn 8.06
where you are standing is holy g.	Ac 7.33
deprive me of my g. for boasting.	1Co 9.15
question on the g. of conscience.	10.25

GROW —ING —S
God made to g. every tree that is	Gen 2.09
Though its root g. old in the earth,	Job 14.08
empty words g. many: but do you fear	Ecc 5.07
He does not faint or g. weary,	Is 40.28
lilies of the field, how they g.;	Mt 6.28
Let both g. together until the	13.30
most men's love will g. cold.	24.12
And let us not g. weary in well-doing,	Gal 6.09
we are to g. up in every way into	Eph 4.15
by it you may g. up to salvation;	1Pe 2.02
But g. in the grace and knowledge	2Pe 3.18
and good, were g. on one stalk.	Gen 41.05
your faith is g. abundantly,	2Th 1.03
my compassion g. warm and tender.	Hos 11.08
it is sown it g. up and becomes	Mk 4.32
together and g. into a holy temple	Eph 2.21

GROWTH
watered, but God gave the g.	1Co 3.06
makes bodily g. and upbuilds itself	Eph 4.16
grows with a g. that is from God.	Col 2.19

GUARD —ED —ING —S (v)
"He will g. the feet of his faithful	1Sa 2.09
Oh g. my life, and deliver me;	Ps 25.20
of a priest should g. knowledge,	Mal 2.07
angels charge of you, to g. you,'	Lk 4.10
four squads of soldiers to g. him,	Ac 12.04
strengthen you and g. you from evil.	2Th 3.03
O Timothy, g. what has been entrusted	1Ti 6.20
he is able to g. until that Day	2Ti 1.12
g. the truth that has been entrusted	1.14
I have g. them, and none of them is	Jn 17.12
by himself, with the soldier that g. him.	Ac 28.16
God's power are g. through faith	1Pe 1.05
g. the paths of justice and preserving	Pro 2.08
before the door were g. the prison;	Ac 12.60
Righteousness g. him whose way is	Pro 13.06
g. his own palace, his goods are in	Lk 11.21

GUARD —S (n)
Set a g. over my mouth, O LORD, keep	Ps 141.03
Jeremiah from the court of the g.	Jer 39.14
The captain of the g. took Jeremiah	40.02
sealing the stone and setting a g.	Mt 27.66
he sat with the g. to see the end.	26.58

GUARDING (n)
By g. it according to thy word.	Ps 119.09

GUEST* —S
in to be the g. of a man who is a	Lk 19.07
"Can the wedding g. mourn as long	Mt 9.15
wedding hall was filled with g.	22.10
she pleased Herod and his g.;	Mk 6.22

GUIDE —D —S (v)

And the LORD will g. you continually,	Is 58.11
to g. our feet into the way of	Lk 1.79
he will g. you into all the truth;	Jn 16.13
and g. them in the wilderness like	Ps 78.52
they are g. by a very small rudder	Jas 3.04
"How can I, unless some one g. me?"	Ac 8.31

GUIDE* —S (n)

ever and ever. He will be our g. for ever.	Ps 48.14
Judas who was g. to those who	Ac 1.16
that you are a g. to the blind,	Rom 2.19
they are blind g. And if a blind	Mt 15.14
you have countless g. in Christ,	1Co 4.15

GUILE

Israelite indeed, in whom is no g.!"	Jn 1.47
and got the better of you by g.	2Co 12.16
committed no sin; no g. was found on	1Pe 2.22

GUILT

shall purge the g. of innocent	Deu 19.13
But if there is g. in me, slay me	1Sa 20.08
we are before thee in our g.,	Ez 9.15
Make them bear their g., O God;	Ps 5.10
pardon my g., for it is great.	25.11
your g. is taken away, and your sin	Is 6.07
Only acknowledge your g., that you	Jer 3.13
from all the g. of their sin	33.08

is full of g. against the Holy One	51.05
now they must bear their g. The LORD	Hos 10.02
you say, 'We see,' your g. remains.	Jn 9.41

GUILTLESS

not hold him g. who takes his name	Ex 20.07
profane the sabbath, and are g.?	Mt 12.05
g. in the day of our Lord Jesus	1Co 1.08
proved yourselves g. in the matter.	2Co 7.11

GUILTY

When a man is g. in any of these, he	Lev 5.05
he will by no means clear the g.,	Num 14.18
who acquit the g. for a bribe, and	Is 5.23
who will declare me g.? Behold, all of	50.09
All who ate of it became g.;	Jer 2.03
but is g. of an eternal sin"—	Mk 3.29
find this man g. of any of your	Lk 23.14
If he is g. of immorality or greed,	1Co 5.11
manner will be g. of profaning the	11.27
point has become g. of all of it.	Jas 2.10
commits sin is g. of lawlessness;	1Jn 3.04

GUSH* —ED —ING*

Thou makest springs g. forth in the	Ps 104.10
and our eyelids g. with water.	Jer 9.18
the rock and the water g. out.	Is 48.21
middle and all his bowels g. out.	Ac 1.18
fountain of wisdom is a g. stream.	Pro 18.04

H

HABITATION —S

Look down from thy holy h.,	Deu 26.15
I love the h. of thy house, and the	Ps 26.08
refuge, the Most High your h.,	91.09
O h. of righteousness, O holy hill?'	Jer 31.23
their true h., the LORD, the hope of	50.07
'Let his h. become desolate, and let	Ac 1.20
leave to find a h. for the God of	7.46
receive you into the eternal h.	Lk 16.09

HAIL (n)

I will cause very heavy h. to fall,	Ex 9.18
He destroyed their vines with h.,	Ps 78.47
He gave them h. for rain, and	105.32
and there followed h. and fire,	Rev 8.07

HAIR —S

"Do not let the h. of your heads	Lev 10.06
not let the h. of his head hang	21.10
But the h. of his head began to	Ju 16.22
beauty of old men is their gray h.	Pro 20.29
instead of well-set h., baldness;	Is 3.24
Cut off your h. and cast it away;	Jer 7.29
John wore a garment of camel's h.,	Mt 3.04
tears and wiped them with her h.	Lk 7.44
But not a h. of your head will	21.18
At Cenchreae he cut his h.,	Ac 18.18
but if a woman has long h.,	1Co 11.15
with braided h. or gold or pearls	1Ti 2.09
his head and his h. were white as	Rev 1.14

are more than the h. of my head;	Ps 40.12
But even the h. of your head are	Mt 10.30

HALLOW —ED

and h. my sabbaths that they may be	Eze 20.20
blessed the seventh day and h. it.	Gen 2.03
who art in heaven, H. be thy name.	Mt 6.09

HAMMER —S

and took a h. in her hand, and went	Ju 4.21
and like a h. which breaks the rock	Jer 23.29
How the h. of the whole earth is	50.23
he shapes it with h., and forges it	Is 44.12

HAND —S

"Put your h. under my thigh,	Gen 24.02
and his h. had taken hold of Esau's	25.26
tooth, h. for h., foot for foot.	Deu 19.21
"Our h. is triumphant, the LORD has	32.27
The h. of God was very heavy there;	1Sa 5.11
I have taken my life in my h.,	28.21
said, "If it is, give me your h."	2Ki 10.15
"The h. of our God is for good upon	Ez 8.22
each with one h. labored on the	Neh 4.17
your own right h. can give you	Job 40.14
My times are in thy h.; deliver	Ps 31.15
Thy right h. is filled with victory;	48.10
For in the h. of the LORD there is	75.08
In his h. are the depths of the	95.04
His right h. and his holy arm have	98.01
Whatever your h. finds to do, do it	Ecc 9.10

HAND —S (cont.)

will extend his h. yet a second	Is 11.11
His h. is stretched out, and who	14.27
My h. laid the foundation of the	48.13
in the shadow of his h. he hid me;	49.02
So I took the cup from the LORD's h.,	Jer 25.17
form of a human h. under their	Eze 10.08
line, with a plumb line in his h.	Amo 7.07
with a measuring line in his h.!	Zec 2.01
for the kingdom of heaven is at h."	Mt 3.02
And if your right h. causes you to	5.30
let your left h. know what your	6.03
there was a man with a withered h.	12.10
sit at my right h. and at my left	20.23
will say to those at his right h.,	25.34
one shall snatch them out of my h.	Jn 10.28
and place my h. in his side, I will	20.25
exalted at the right h. of God,	Ac 2.33
to do right, evil lies close at h.	Rom 7.21
The eye cannot say to the h.,	1Co 12.21
write this greeting with my own h.	16.21
Barnabas the right h. of fellowship,	Gal 2.09
therefore under the mighty h. of God,	1Pe 5.06
But he laid his right h. upon me,	Rev 1.17
mark on his forehead or on his h.,	14.09
work and from the toil of our h."	Gen 5.29
voice, but the h. are the h. of Esau."	27.22
for Moses had laid his h. upon him;	Deu 34.09
Now therefore let your h. be strong,	2Sa 2.07
now, O God, strengthen thou my h.	Neh 6.09
"Amen, Amen," lifting up their h.;	8.06
Thy h. fashioned and made me;	Job 10.08
dominion over the works of thy h.;	Ps 8.06
I wash my h. in innocence, and go	26.06
as I lift up my h. toward thy most	28.02
Clap your h., all peoples!	47.01
the work of our h. establish thou	90.17
the heavens are the work of thy h.	102.25
The works of his h. are faithful	111.07
Lift up your h. to the holy place,	134.02
Therefore all h. will be feeble, and	Is 13.07
I spread out my h. all the day to a	65.02
our hearts and h. to God in heaven	Lam 3.41
"Clap your h., and stamp your foot,	Eze 6.11
'Our God,' to the work of our h.	Hos 14.03
and 'On their h. they will bear	Mt 4.06
with unwashed h. does not defile a	15.20
be delivered into the h. of men,	17.22
than with two h. or two feet to be	18.08
And he laid his h. on them an went	19.15
and washed his h. before the crowd,	27.24
mighty works are wrought by his h.!	Mk 6.02
into thy h. I commit my spirit!"	Lk 23.46
See my h. and my feet, that it is I	24.39
had given all things into his h.,	Jn 13.03
I see in his h. the print of the	20.25
the laying on of the apostles' h.,	Ac 8.18
Paul had laid his h. upon them,	19.06
know that these h. ministered to	20.34
held out my h. to a disobedient	Rom 10.21
and we labor, working with our own h.	1Co 4.12
from God, a house not made with h.,	2Co 5.01
the elders laid their h. upon you.	1Ti 4.14
be hasty in the laying on of h.,	5.22

more perfect tent (not made with h.,	Heb 9.11
fall into the h. of the living God.	10.31
Cleanse your h., you sinners, and	Jas 4.08

HANDLE —S —ING

h. me, and see; for a spirit	Lk 24.39
"Do not h., Do not taste, Do not	Col 2.21
he who h. the bow shall not stand,	Amo 2.15
rightly h. the word of truth.	2Ti 2.15

HANDMAID —EN*

"Behold I am the h. of the Lord;	Lk 1.38
regarded the low estate of his h.	1.48

HANDSOME*

Now Joseph was h. and good-looking	Gen 39.06
name was Saul, a h. young man.	1Sa 9.02
people of Israel more h. than he;	9.02
He was also a very h. man;	1Ki 1.06
h. and skilful in all wisdom,	Dan 1.04

HANG —ED —ING —S

h. you on a tree; and the birds	Gen 40.19
death, and you h. him on a tree,	Deu 21.22
your life shall h. in doubt before	28.66
And the king said, "H. him on that."	Est 7.10
for a h. man is accursed by God;	Deu 21.23
And he h. the king of Ai on a tree	Jos 8.29
and he went and h. himself.	Mt 27.05
criminals who were h. railed at him,	Lk 23.39
and he was left h. between heaven	2Sa 18.09
and h. the earth upon nothing.	Job 26.07
be every one who h. on a tree"—	Gal 3.13

HANGING (n)

you killed by h. him on a tree	Ac 5.30

HAPPY

"Behold, h. is the man whom God	Job 5.17
H. the people to whom such blessings	Ps 144.15
H. is he whose help is the God of	146.05
and h. is he who trusts in the LORD.	Pro 16.20
h. is he who has no reason to judge	Rom 14.22
we call those h. who were steadfast.	Jas 5.11

HARASS —ED

to h. me, to keep me from being too	2Co 12.07
because they were h. and helpless,	Mt 9.36

HARD

Is anything too h. for the LORD?	Gen 18.14
h. cases they brought to Moses, but	Ex 18.26
"Has not man a h. service upon	Job 7.01
gate is narrow and the way is h.,	Mt 7.14
it will be h. for a rich man to	19.23
h. to bear, and lay them on men's	23.04
'Master, I knew you to be a h. man,	25.24
it, said, "This is a h. saying;	Jn 6.60
But by your h. and impenitent heart	Rom 2.05
I am h. pressed between the two.	Php 1.23
much to say which is h. to explain,	Heb 5.11
things in them h. to understand,	2Pe 3.16

HARDEN —ED —S

but I will h. his heart, so that he	Ex 4.21

HARDEN —ED —S (cont.)

you shall not h. your heart or shut	Deu 15.07
H. not your hearts, as at Meribah, as	Ps 95.08
do not h. your hearts as in the	Heb 3.08
Still Pharaoh's heart was h.,	Ex 7.13
or understand? Are your hearts h.?	Mk 8.17
But their minds were h.;	2Co 3.14
and he h. the heart of whomever he	Rom 9.18

HARDENING* (n)

a h. has come upon part of Israel,	Rom 11.25

HARLOT —S

they play the h. after their gods	Ex 34.15
You shall not bring the hire of a h.,	Deu 23.18
only Rahab the h. and all who are	Jos 6.17
and played the h. after the Baals,	Ju 8.33
For a h. is a deep pit;	Pro 23.27
How the faithful city has become a h.,	Is 1.21
Though you play the h., O Israel,	Hos 4.15
By faith Rahab the h. did not	Heb 11.31
also Rahab the h. justified by	Jas 2.25
of the great h. who is seated upon	Rev 17.01
collectors and the h. go into the	Mt 21.31
has devoured your living with h.,	Lk 15.30

HARLOTRIES —Y

your lewd h., on the hills in the	Jer 13.27
For a spirit of h. has led them	Hos 4.12

HARM (n)

the sabbath to do good or to do h.,	Mk 3.04
out of him, having done him no h.	Lk 4.35

HARP —S

praise him with lute and h.!	Ps 150.03
such as the flute or the h.,	1Co 14.07
before the Lamb, each holding a h.,	Rev 5.08
to Sheol, the sound of your h.;	Is 14.11
of harpers playing on their h.,	Rev 14.02

HARSH —LY

but a h. word stirs up anger.	Pro 15.01
wives, and do not be h. with them.	Col 3.19
Then Sarai dealt h. with her,	Gen 16.06

HARVEST (n)

seedtime and h., cold and heat,	Gen 8.22
You shall keep the feast of h.,	Ex 23.16
"The h. is past, the summer is ended,	Jer 8.20
Put in the sickle, for the h. is ripe.	Joe 3.13
"The h. is plentiful, but the	Mt 9.37
pray therefore the Lord of the h. to	9.38
the h. is the close of the age, and	13.39
fields are already white for h.	Jn 4.35
I may reap some h. among you as	Rom 1.13

HASTEN —ED —ING

in its time I will h. it.	Is 60.22
and my foot has h. to deceit;	Job 31.05
the LORD is near, near and h. fast;	Zep 1.14
waiting for and h. the coming of	2Pe 3.12

HASTY

he who has a h. temper exalts	Pro 14.29
Do not be h. in the laying on of	1Ti 5.22

HATE —D —S

"You shall not h. your brother in	Lev 19.17
generation of those who h. me,	Deu 5.09
righteousness and h. wickedness.	Ps 45.07
The LORD loves those who h. evil;	97.10
I h. double-minded men, but I love	119.113
Do I not h. them that h. thee, O LORD?	139.21
a time to love, and a time to h.;	Ecc 3.08
I h. robbery and wrong; I will	Is 61.08
H. evil, and love good, and establish	Amo 5.15
"I h., I despise your feasts, and I	5.21
your neighbor and h. your enemy.'	Mt 5.43
either he will h. the one and love	6.24
"Blessed are you when men h. you,	Lk 6.22
me and does not h. his own father	14.26
The world cannot h. you, but it	Jn 7.07
want, but I do the very thing I h.	Rom 7.15
So I h. life, because what is done	Ecc 2.17
I h. all my toil in which I had	2.18
and you will be h. by all for my	Mt 10.22
that it has h. me before it h. you.	Jn 15.18
the world has h. them because they	17.14
h. by men and hating one another;	Tit 3.03
There are six things which the LORD h.,	Pro 6.16
one who does evil h. the light, and does	Jn 3.20
and he who h. his life in this world	12.25
He who h. me h. my Father also.	15.23
For no man ever h. his own flesh,	Eph 5.29
But he who h. his brother is in the	1Jn 2.11

HATRED

I hate them with perfect h.; I count	Ps 139.22
H. stirs up strife, but love covers	Pro 10.12

HAUGHTY

and the eyes of the h. are humbled.	Is 5.15
do not be h., but associate with	Rom 12.16
world, charge them not to be h.,	1Ti 6.17

HEAD —S

he shall bruise your h., and you shall	Gen 3.15
Sisera a blow, she crushed his h.,	Ju 5.26
Behold, God is with us at our h.,	2Ch 13.12
A hoary h. is a crown of glory;	Pro 16.31
will heap coals of fire on his h.,	25.22
And do not swear by your h.,	Mt 5.36
of man has nowhere to lay his h."	8.20
"Give me the h. of John the Baptist	14.08
has become the h. of the corner;	21.42
he bowed his h. and gave up his	Jn 19.30
that the h. of every man is Christ,	1Co 11.03
and the h. of Christ is God.	11.03
For a man ought not to cover his h.,	11.07
you," nor again the h. to the feet,	12.21
husband is the h. of the wife as	Eph 5.23
as Christ is the h. of the church,	5.23
cloud, with a rainbow over his h.,	Rev 10.01
Lift up your h., O gates! and be lifted	Ps 24.07
derided him, wagging their h.	Mt 27.39
place, look up and raise your h.,	Lk 21.28

HEAD —S (cont.)

them, "Your blood be upon your h.!	Ac 18.06
so that they may shave their h.	21.24

HEAL —ED —S

O LORD, h. me, for my bones are	Ps 6.02
I will h. your faithlessness."	Jer 3.22
H. the sick, raise the dead, cleanse	Mt 10.08
"Is it lawful to h. on the sabbath?"	12.10
disciples, and they could not h. him."	17.16
proverb, "Physician, h. yourself;	Lk 4.23
and with his stripes we are h.	Is 53.05
they did not know that I h. them.	Hos 11.03
with a word, and h. all who were sick.	Mt 8.16
compassion on them, and h. their sick.	14.14
him in the temple, and he h. them.	21.14
And he touched his ear and h. him.	Lk 22.51
what means this man has been h.,	Ac 4.09
put out of joint but rather be h.	Heb 12.13
By his wounds you have been h.	1Pe 2.24
wound, but its mortal wound was h.,	Rev 13.03
iniquity, who h. all your diseases,	Ps 103.03
He h. the brokenhearted, and binds	147.03

HEALTH

to the soul and h. to the body.	Pro 16.24
restore me to h. and make me live!	Is 38.16

HEAP —ED (v)

praying do not h. up empty phrases	Mt 6.07
doing you will h. burning coals	Rom 12.20
for her sins are h. high as heaven,	Rev 18.05

HEAP (n)

made the waters stand like a h.	Ps 78.13
For thou hast made the city a h.,	Is 25.02

HEAR —D —S

the people may h. when I speak	Ex 19.09
"H., O Israel, the statutes and the	Deu 5.01
"H., O Israel: The LORD our God is	6.04
"H. my prayer, O LORD, and give ear	Ps 39.12
They have ears, but do not h.;	115.06
'H. and h., but do not understand;	Is 6.09
bones, h. the word of the LORD.	Eze 37.04
and tell John what you h. and see:	Mt 11.04
He who has ears to h., let him h.	11.15
And when you h. of wars and tumults,	Lk 21.09
and you h. the sound of it, but you	Jn 3.08
"We will h. you again about this."	Ac 17.32
are they to h. without a preacher?	Rom 10.14
And they h. the sound of the LORD	Gen 3.08
And God h. their groaning, and God	Ex 2.24
I had h. of thee by the hearing of	Job 42.05
he inclined to me and h. my cry.	Ps 40.01
As we have h., so have we seen in	48.08
the turtledove is h. in our land.	Sol 2.12
And I h. the voice of the Lord	Is 6.08
"You have h. that it was said to	Mt 5.21
they will be h. for their many	6.07
speak of what we have seen and h."	Ac 4.20
in him of whom they have never h.?	Rom 10.14
nor ear h., nor the heart of man	1Co 2.09
which we have h., which we have	1Jn 1.01

'Speak, LORD, for thy servant h.' "	1Sa 3.09
And every one who h. these words of	Mt 7.26
this is he who h. the word and	13.23
He who is of God h. the words of	Jn 8.47
we know that he h. us in whatever	1Jn 5.15

HEARER —S

For if any one is a h. of the word	Jas 1.23
For it is not the h. of the law who	Rom 2.13
save both yourself and your h.	1Ti 4.16
did not meet with faith in the h.	Heb 4.02
and not h. only, deceiving yourselves.	Jas 1.22

HEARKEN

spoke to you, and you would not h.;	Deu 1.43
But if they do not h., they perish	Job 36.12
H. to the sound of my cry, my King	Ps 5.02

HEART —S

thoughts of his h. was only evil	Gen 6.05
But I will harden Pharaoh's h.,	Ex 7.03
with all your h. and with all your	Deu 4.29
therefore the foreskin of your h.,	10.16
"My h. exults in the LORD;	1Sa 2.01
"Is your h. true to my h. as mine	2Ki 10.15
Behold, my h. is like wine that has	Job 32.19
their h. is destruction, their	Ps 5.09
The fool says in his h., "There is no God."	14.01
He who has clean hands and a pure h.,	24.04
For he knows the secrets of the h.	44.21
Create in me a clean h., O God,	51.10
Search me, O God, and know my h.!	139.23
them on the tablet of your h.	Pro 3.03
Anxiety in a man's h. weighs him	12.25
Hope deferred makes the h. sick,	13.12
The king's h. is a stream of water	21.01
drink your wine with a merry h.;	Ecc 9.07
I slept, but my h. was awake.	Sol 5.02
Make the h. of this people fat, and	Is 6.10
My h. is beating wildly; I cannot keep	Jer 4.19
of Israel is uncircumcised in h."	9.26
My h. is broken within me, all my	23.09
give them a h. to know that I am	24.07
when you seek me with all your h.,	29.13
I will give them one h. and one way,	32.39
flesh and give them a h. of flesh,	Eze 11.19
A new h. I will give you, and a new	36.26
"Blessed are the pure in h.,	Mt 5.08
adultery with her in his h.	5.28
is, there will your h. be also.	6.21
for I am gentle and lowly in h.,	11.29
For this people's h. has grown dull,	13.15
For out of the h. come evil thoughts,	15.19
and slow of h. to believe all that	Lk 24.25
uncircumcised in h. and ears,	Ac 7.51
circumcision is a matter of the h.,	Rom 2.29
believe in your h. that God raised	10.09
nor the h. of man conceived, what	1Co 2.09
the secrets of his h. are disclosed;	14.25
mercy of God, we do not lose h.	2Co 4.01
to you, Corinthians; our h., is wide.	6.11
doing the will of God from the h.,	Eph 6.06
from a pure h. and a good conscience	1Ti 1.05
I am he who searches mind and h.,	Rev 2.23

HEART —S (cont.)

and I will write it upon their h.;	Jer 31.33
put the fear of me in their h.,	32.40
Let us lift up our h. and hands to	Lam 3.41
"Why do you think evil in your h.?	Mt 9.04
in the imagination of their h.,	Lk 1.51
"Let not your h. be troubled;	Jn 14.01
searches the h. of men knows what	Rom 8.27
Spirit in our h. as a guarantee.	2Co 1.22
stone but on tablets of human h.	3.03
having the eyes of your h. enlightened,	Eph 1.18
may dwell in your h. through faith;	3.17
peace of Christ rule in your h.,	Col 3.15
with our h. sprinkled clean from an	Heb 10.22
you sinners, and purify your h.,	Jas 4.08
but in your h. reverence Christ as	1Pe 3.15
for God is greater than our h.,	1Jn 3.20

HEAVEN —S

And God called the firmament H.	Gen 1.08
Most High, maker of h. and earth;	14.19
"Look toward h., and number the	15.05
Out of h. he let you hear his voice,	Deu 4.36
God belong h. and the h. of h.,	10.14
say, 'Who will go up for us to h.,	30.12
he makes peace in his high h.	Job 25.02
temple, the LORD's throne is in h.;	Ps 11.04
Whom have I in h. but thee?	73.25
They mounted up to h., they went	107.26
If I ascend to h., thou art there!	139.08
Who has ascended to h. and come	Pro 30.04
a time for every matter under h.:	Ecc 3.01
for God is in h., and you upon	5.02
it be deep as Sheol or high as h."	Is 7.11
"Repent, for the kingdom of h. is at	Mt 3.02
a voice from h., saying, "This is my	3.17
for your reward is great in h.,	5.12
till h. and earth pass away, not an	5.18
this: Our Father who art in h.,	6.09
H. and earth will pass away, but my	24.35
gazed into h. and saw the glory of	Ac 7.55
let down from h. by four corners;	11.05
revealed from h. against all	Rom 1.18
of dust; the second man is from h.	1Co 15.47
ago was caught up to the third h.—	2Co 12.02
in h. and on earth and under the	Php 2.10
But our commonwealth is in h.,	3.20
because of the hope laid up for you in h.	Col 1.05
and to wait for his Son from h.,	1Th 1.10
descend from h. with a cry of	4.16
looked, and lo, in h. an open door!	Rev 4.01
Then I saw a new h. and a new earth;	21.01
"The LORD has set the sun in the h.,	1Ki 8.12
who alone stretched out the h.,	Job 9.08
Look at the h., and see; and behold	35.05
When I look at thy h., the work of	Ps 8.03
The h. are telling the glory of God;	19.01
The h. are thine, the earth also is	89.11
For as the h. are high above the	103.11
thy word is firmly fixed in the h.	119.89
and marked off the h. with a span,	Is 40.12
For as the h. are higher than the	55.09
I created new h. and a new earth;	65.17
"For as the new h. and the new	66.22

the h. were opened and he saw the	Mt 3.16
powers of the h. will be shaken;	24.29
treasure in the h. that does not	Lk 12.33
made with hands, eternal in the h.	2Co 5.01
who has passed through the h.,	Heb 4.14
the word of God h. existed long	2Pe 3.05

HEAVENLY

O h. beings, ascribe to the LORD	Ps 29.01
Who among the h. beings is like the	89.06
as your h. Father is perfect.	Mt 5.48
multitude of the h. host praising	Lk 2.13
believe if I tell you h. things?	Jn 3.12
not disobedient to the h. vision,	Ac 26.19
long to put on our h. dwelling,	2Co 5.02
brethren, who share in a h. call,	Heb 3.01
copies of the h. things to be	9.23
the h. Jerusalem, and to innumerable	12.22

HEAVY

his hand is h. in spite of my	Job 23.02
Thy wrath lies h. upon me, and thou	Ps 88.07
songs to a h. heart is like one	Pro 25.20
man's trouble lies h. upon him.	Ecc 8.06
you made your yoke exceedingly h.	Is 47.06
to me, all who labor and are h. laden,	Mt 11.28
They bind h. burdens, hard to bear,	23.04
sleeping, for their eyes were h.	26.43

HEED —ED

but the sheep did not h. them.	Jn 10.08
h. my appeal, agree with one another,	2Co 13.11
But they have not all h. the gospel;	Rom 10.16

HEED (n)

"Take h. lest you forget the LORD	Deu 8.11
Give h., O house of Israel!	Hos 5.01
he stands take h. lest he fall.	1Co 10.12

HEEL

head, and you shall bruise his h."	Gen 3.15
hand had taken hold of Esau's h.;	25.26

HEIFER

"A beautiful h. is Egypt, but a	Jer 46.20
Like a stubborn h., Israel is	Hos 4.16
the ashes of a h. sanctifies for	Heb 9.13

HEIR —S

"Has Israel no sons? Has he no h.?	Jer 49.01
to themselves, 'This is the h.;	Mt 21.38
I mean that the h., as long as he	Gal 4.01
he appointed the h. of all things,	Heb 1.02
h. of God and fellow h. with Christ,	Rom 8.17
offspring, h. according to promise.	Gal 3.29
is, how the Gentiles are fellow h.,	Eph 3.06
you are joint h. of the grace of	1Pe 3.07

HELL

shall be liable to the h. of fire.	Mt 5.22
killed, has power to cast into h.;	Lk 12.05

HELMET

and a h. of salvation upon his head;	Is 59.17

HELMET (cont.)
And take the h. of salvation, and	Eph 6.17
and for a h. the hope of salvation.	1Th 5.08

HELP —ED —S (v)
God will h. her right early.	Ps 46.05
to you, "Fear not, I will h. you."	Is 41.13
before him, saying, "Lord, h. me."	Mt 15.25
and said, "I believe; h. my unbelief!"	Mk 9.24
"Come over to Macedonia and h. us."	Ac 16.09
You also must h. us by prayer, so	2Co 1.11
prayers and the h. of the Spirit	Php 1.19
h. the weak, be patient with them	1Th 5.14
find grace to h. in time of need.	Heb 4.16
I was falling, but the LORD h. me.	Ps 118.13
A brother h. is like a strong city,	Pro 18.19
He has h. his servant Israel, in	Lk 1.54
Every one h. his neighbor, and says	Is 41.06
Likewise the Spirit h. us in our	Rom 8.26

HELP (n)
In truth I have no h. in me,	Job 6.13
me, there is no h. for him in God.	Ps 3.02
They cried for h., but there was	18.41
a very present h. in trouble.	46.01
My h. comes from the LORD, who made	121.02
Our h. is in the name of the LORD,	124.08
To whom will you flee for h.,	Is 10.03

HELPER —S
I will make him a h. fit for him."	Gen 2.18
Behold, God is my h.; the Lord is	Ps 54.04
confidently say, "The Lord is my h.,	Heb 13.06
h., administrators, speakers in	1Co 12.28

HEN
together as a h. gathers her brood	Mt 23.37

HERALD
to Jerusalem a h. of good tidings.	Is 41.27

HERD —S
Now a h. of many swine was feeding	Mt 8.30
also had flocks and h. and tents,	Gen 13.05
and give attention to your h;	Pro 27.23
H. shall lie down in the midst of	Zep 2.14

HERDSMAN* —MEN
but I am a h., and a dresser of	Amo 7.14
between your h. and my h.; for we are	Gen 13.08
The h. fled, and going into the city	Mt 8.33

HERITAGE
For they are thy people and thy h.,	Deu 9.29
and my h. from the Almighty on high?	Job 31.02
he will not abandon his h.;	Ps 94.14
Thy testimonies are my h. for ever;	119.111
Lo, sons are a h. from the LORD, the	127.03
He who conquers shall have this h.,	Rev 21.07

HEW —ED —N
'H. two tables of stone like the	Deu 10.01
you who h. a tomb on the height, and	Is 22.16
and h. out cisterns for themselves,	Jer 2.13

to the rock from which you were h.,	Is 51.01
you have built houses of h. stone,	Amo 5.11
tomb, which he had h. in the rock;	Mt 27.60

HID —DEN
and his wife h. themselves from	Gen 3.08
And Moses h. his face, for he was	Ex 3.06
"My way is h. from the LORD, and my	Is 40.27
in the shadow of his hand he h. me;	49.02
for thou hast h. thy face from us,	64.07
Compassion is h. from my eyes.	Hos 13.14
a city set on a hill cannot be h.	Mt 5.14
woman took and h. in three measures	13.33
and I went and h. your talent in	25.25
For there is nothing h., except to	Mk 4.22
in whom are h. all the treasures of	Col 2.03
your life is h. with Chris tin God.	3.03
Clear thou me from h. faults.	Ps 19.12
Better is open rebuke than h. love.	Pro 27.05
that thou hast h. these things	Mt 11.25
what has been h. since the foundation	13.35
is like treasure h. in a field,	13.44
a secret and h. wisdom of God,	1Co 2.07
of the mystery h. for ages in God	Eph 3.09

HIDE —ST
Oh that thou wouldest h. me in Sheol,	Job 14.13
long wilt thou h. thy face from me?	Ps 13.01
h. me in the shadow of thy wings,	17.08
"Fall on us and h. us from the face	Rev 6.16
Truly, thou art a God who h. thyself,	Is 45.15

HIGH —ER —EST —LY
away from the dew of heaven on h.	Gen 27.39
And I will destroy your h. places,	Lev 26.30
he that vouches for me is on h.	Job 16.19
"Is not God h. in the heavens?	22.12
The LORD is h. above all nations,	Ps 113.04
Get you up to a h. mountain,	Is 40.09
They built the h. places of Baal in	Jer 32.35
is low, and abase that which is h.	Eze 21.26
took him to a very h. mountain,	Mt 4.08
led them up a h. mountain apart	17.01
led him to Caiaphas the h. priest,	26.57
devout women of h. standing and	Ac 13.50
he ascended on h. he led a host of	Eph 4.08
me to the rock that is h. than I;	Ps 61.02
But earnestly desire the h. gifts.	1Co 12.31
established as the h. of the mountains,	Is 2.02
name of the Lord! Hosanna in the h.!"	Mt 21.09
"Glory to God in the h., and on earth	Lk 2.14
Peace in heaven and glory in the h.!"	19.38
of himself more h. than he ought	Rom 12.03
Therefore God has h. exalted him	Php 2.09

HIGHWAY —S
And a h. shall be there, and it	Is 35.08
in the desert a h. for our God.	40.03
'Go out to the h. and hedges,	Lk 14.23

HILL —S
Who shall dwell on thy holy h.?	Ps 15.01
Who shall ascend the h. of the LORD?	24.03
every mountain and h. be made low;	Is 40.04

HILL —S (cont.)

A city set on a h. cannot be hid.	Mt 5.14
the brow of the h. on which their	Lk 4.29
abundance of the everlasting h.,	Deu 33.15
I lift up my eyes to the h.	Ps 121.01
before the h., I was brought forth;	Pro 8.25
us, and to the h., Fall upon us.	Hos 10.08
the everlasting h. sank low.	Hab 3.06
up into the h. by himself to pray.	Mt 14.23
'Fall on us'; and to the h., 'Cover us.'	Lk 23.30
heads are seven h. on which the	Rev 17.09

HINDER —ED

who can h. him? Who will say	Job 9.12
come to me, and do not h. them;	Mt 19.14
so often been h. from coming to	Rom 15.22
again and again—but Satan h. us.	1Th 2.18

HIRE —D

the morning to h. laborers for his	Mt 20.01
wandering alone; Ephraim has h.	Hos 8.09
in the boat with the h. servants,	Mk 1.20
of my father's h. servants have	Lk 15.17

HISS —ED

they h. and wag their heads at the	Lam 2.15
a thing to be h. at for ever.	Jer 18.16

HOLD —ING

"Do you still h. fast your integrity?	Job 2.09
I h. fast my righteousness, and will	27.06
Why dost thou h. back thy hand, why	Ps 74.11
H. me up, that I may be safe and	119.117
me, and thy right hand shall h. me.	139.10
"Let your heart h. fast my words;	Pro 4.04
h. fast to love and justice, and	Hos 12.06
h. it fast in an honest and good	Lk 8.15
"Do not h. me, for I have not yet	Jn 20.17
is evil, h. fast to what is good;	Rom 12.09
Only let us h. true to what we have	Php 3.16
and in him all things h. together.	Col 1.17
take h. of the eternal life to	1Ti 6.12
let us h. fast our confession.	Heb 4.14
each h. twenty or thirty gallons.	Jn 2.06
h. fast the word of life, so that in	Php 2.16
and not h. fast to the Head, from	Col 2.19
h. the form of religion but denying	2Ti 3.05

HOLES

to put them into a bag with h.	Hag 1.06
"Foxes have h., and birds of the	Mt 8.20

HOLINESS

majestic in h., terrible in glorious	Ex 15.11
h. befits thy house, O LORD, for	Ps 93.05
so communicate h. to the people."	Eze 46.20
in h. and righteousness before him	Lk 1.75
the Spirit of h. by his resurrection	Rom 1.04
unblamable in h. before our God	1Th 3.13
wife for himself in h. and honor,	4.04
our good, that we may share his h.	Heb 12.10

HOLY

you are standing is h. ground."	Ex 3.05

"Remember the sabbath day, to keep it h.	20.08
therefore, and be h., for I am h.	Lev 11.44
for I the LORD your God am h.	19.02
are a people h. to the LORD your	Deu 7.06
for he is a h. God; he is a jealous	Jos 24.19
Worship the LORD in h. array;	1Ch 16.29
The LORD is in his h. temple,	Ps 11.04
Thy way, O God, is h.	77.13
Lift up your hands to the h. place,	134.02
"H., h., h., is the LORD of hosts;	Is 6.03
"I dwell in the high and h. place,	57.15
rebelled and grieved his h. spirit;	63.10
But the LORD is in his h. temple;	Hab 2.20
conceived in her is of the H. Spirit;	Mt 1.20
you with the H. Spirit and with	3.11
"Do not give dogs what is h.;	7.06
against the H. Spirit will not be	12.32
child to be born will be called h.,	Lk 1.35
H. Father, keep them in thy name	Jn 17.11
to them, "Receive the H. Spirit.	20.22
the promise of the H. Spirit,	Ac 2.33
full of the H. Spirit and of faith,	11.24
you receive the H. Spirit when you	19.02
his prophets in the h. scriptures,	Rom 1.02
and if the root is h., so are the	11.16
Greet one another with a h. kiss.	16.16
For God's temple is h., and that	1Co 3.17
to present you h. and blameless	Col 1.22
lifting h. hands without anger or	1Ti 2.08
us and called us with a h. calling,	2Ti 1.09
but as he who called you is h.,	1Pe 1.15
to be a h. priesthood, to offer	2.05
a h. nation, God's own people, that	2.09
"H., h., h., is the Lord God Almighty,	Rev 4.08
For thou alone art h. All nations	15.04
And I saw the h. city, new Jerusalem,	21.02

HOME —S

I may go to my own h. and country.	Gen 30.25
The LORD grant that you may find a h.,	Ru 1.09
Even the sparrow finds a h.,	Ps 84.03
because man goes to his eternal h.,	Ecc 12.05
At that time I will bring you h.,	Zep 3.20
"Rise, take up your bed and go h."	Mt 9.06
And when he came h., Jesus spoke to	17.25
it was reported that he was at h.	Mk 2.01
when he leaves h. and puts his	13.34
master to come h. from the marriage	Lk 12.36
And when he comes h., he calls together	15.06
He came to his own h.,	Jn 1.11
to him and make our h. with him.	14.23
one is hungry, let him eat at h.—	1Co 11.34
let them ask their husbands at h.	14.35
the body and at h. with the Lord.	2Co 5.08
send them away hungry to their h.,	Mk 8.03
disciples went back to their h.	Jn 20.10
and breaking bread in their h.,	Ac 2.46

HONEST

How forceful are h. words!	Job 6.25
it fast in an h. and good heart,	Lk 8.15
doing h. work with his hands, so	Eph 4.28
obedient, to be ready for any h. work,	Tit 3.01

HONEY

a land flowing with milk and h.,	Ex 3.08
in the body of the lion, and h.	Ju 14.08
taste, sweeter than h. to my mouth!	Ps 119.103
For the lips of a loose woman drip h.,	Pro 5.03
his food was locusts and wild h.	Mt 3.04

HONOR —ED —S (v)

"H. your father and your mother,	Ex 20.12
He who does not h. the Son does not	Jn 5.23
with all joy; and h. such men,	Php 2.29
Fear God. H. the emperor.	1Pe 2.17
if one member is h., all rejoice	1Co 12.26
Christ will be h. in my body,	Php 1.20
'This people h. me with their lips,	Mt 15.08

HONOR (n)

my h. is pursued as by the wind, and	Job 30.15
dost crown him with glory and h.	Ps 8.05
H. and majesty are before him;	96.06
and humility goes before h.	Pro 15.33
is not without h. except in his	Mt 13.57
the place of h. at feasts and the	23.06
outdo one another in showing h.	Rom 12.10
You are held in h., but we in	1Co 4.10
the greater h. to the inferior	12.24
be considered worthy of double h.,	1Ti 5.17
to receive glory and h. and power,	Rev 4.11

HONORABLE

we think less h. we invest with	1Co 12.23
aim at what is h. not only in the	2Co 8.21
whatever is h., whatever is just,	Php 4.08
blaspheme that h. name by which	Jas 2.07

HOOF —S

Whatever parts the h. and is	Lev 11.03
parts the h. and has the h. cloven	Deu 14.06
their horses' h. seem like flint,	Is 5.28

HOOK —S

He brings all of them up with a h.,	Hab 1.15
them, go to the sea and cast a h.,	Mt 17.27
and their spears into pruning h.;	Is 2.04
and your pruning h. into spears;	Joe 3.10

HOPE —D —S (v)

O Israel, h. in the LORD!	Ps 130.07
and in his name will the Gentiles h."	Mt 12.21
because I have h. in thy word.	Ps 119.74
But we had h. that he was the one	Lk 24.21
life only we have h. in Christ,	1Co 15.19
we who first h. in Christ have been	Eph 1.12
is the assurance of things h. for,	Heb 11.01
h. all things, endures all things.	1Co 13.07
one who thus h. in him purifies	1Jn 3.03

HOPE (n)

now there is h. for Israel in	Ez 10.02
the integrity of your ways your h.?	Job 4.06
so thou destroyest the h. of man.	14.19
and my h. has he pulled up like a	19.10
for what do I wait? My h. is in thee.	Ps 39.07
H. deferred makes the heart sick,	Pro 13.12

O thou h. of Israel, its savior in	Jer 14.08
We set our h. on thee, for thou	14.22
to give you a future and a h.	29.11
There is h. for your future, says	31.17
you, on whom you set your h.	Jn 5.45
respect to the h. and the resurrection	Ac 23.06
our twelve tribes h. to attain,	26.07
In h. he believed against h., that	Rom 4.18
rejoice in our h. of sharing the	5.02
and h. does not disappoint us,	5.05
Now h. that is seen is not h.	8.24
of the scriptures we might have h.	15.04
should plow in h. and the thresher	1Co 9.10
So faith, h., love abide, these three;	13.13
we wait for the h. of righteousness.	Gal 5.05
having no h. and without God in the	Eph 2.12
because of the h. laid up for you	Col 1.05
is Christ in you, the h. of glory.	1.27
For what is our h. or joy or crown	1Th 2.19
grieve as others do who have no h.	4.13
for a helmet the h. of salvation.	5.08
a better h. is introduced, through	Heb 7.19
to a living h. through the resurrection	1Pe 1.03
account for the h. that is in you,	3.15

HORN —S

He has raised up a h. for his people,	Ps 148.14
this h. made war with the saints,	Dan 7.21
Blow the h. in Gibeah, the trumpet	Hos 5.08
and has raised up a h. of salvation	Lk 1.69
And you shall make h. for it on its	Ex 27.02
were before it; and it had ten h.	Dan 7.07
with seven h. and with seven eyes,	Rev 5.06

HORROR

And you shall become a h., a proverb,	Deu 28.37
My mind reels, h. has appalled me;	Is 21.04
A cup of h. and desolation, is the	Eze 23.33

HORSE —S

the h. and his rider he has thrown	Ex 15.01
Be not like a h. or a mule, without	Ps 32.09
The war h. is a vain hope for	33.17
behold, a man riding upon a red h.!	Zec 1.08
opened, and behold, a white h.!	Rev 19.11
Some boast of chariots, and some of h.;	Ps 20.07
to Egypt for help and rely on h.,	Is 31.01
the mouths of h. that they may	Jas 3.03
and pure, followed him on white h.	Rev 19.14

HORSEMEN

on Egypt for chariots and for h.?	Is 36.09
with seventy h. and two hundred	Ac 23.23

HOSANNA

"H. to the Son of David! Blessed be he	Mt 21.09

HOST —S

Though a h. encamp against me, my	Ps 27.03
who brings out their h. by number,	Is 40.26
the moon and all the h. of heaven,	Jer 8.02
of the heavenly h. praising God	Lk 2.13
on high he led a h. of captives,	Eph 4.08
The LORD of h., he is the King of	Ps 24.10

HOST —S (cont.)

The LORD of h. is with us;	Ps 46.07
the spiritual h. of wickedness in	Eph 6.12

HOT

My heart became h. within me.	Ps 39.03
was strict and the furnace very h.,	Dan 3.22
works: you are neither cold nor h.	Rev 3.15

HOUR

will be given to you in that h.;	Mt 10.19
"But of that day and h. no one knows,	24.36
Behold, the h. is at hand, and the	26.45
And about the ninth h. Jesus cried	27.46
Could you not watch one h.?	Mk 14.37
known at what h. the thief was	Lk 12.39
My h. has not yet come."	Jn 2.04
But the h. is coming, and now is,	4.23
"The h. has come for the Son of man	12.23
Besides this you know what h. it is,	Rom 13.11
Why am I in peril every h.?	1Co 15.30
Children, it is the last h.;	1Jn 2.18
for the h. of his judgment has come;	Rev 14.07

HOUSE —S

is none other than the h. of God,	Gen 28.17
out of the h. of bondage, for by	Ex 13.03
The h. which King Solomon built for	1Ki 6.02
the LORD filled the h. of the LORD.	8.11
"Why is the h. of God forsaken?"	Neh 13.11
dwell in the h. of the LORD for	Ps 23.06
within God's h. we walked in fellowship.	55.14
For zeal for thy h. has consumed me,	69.09
doorkeeper in the h. of my God than	84.10
holiness befits thy h., O LORD, for	93.05
"Let us go to the h. of the LORD!"	122.01
Unless the LORD builds the h.,	127.01
Wisdom has built her h., she has	Pro 9.01
my h. shall be called a h. of prayer	Is 56.07
for they are a rebellious h.	Eze 2.06
the winter h. with the summer h.;	Amo 3.15
while this h. lies in ruins?	Hag 1.04
it gives light to all in the h.	Mt 5.15
man who built his h. upon the rock;	7.24
And when Jesus entered Peter's h.,	8.14
As you enter the h., salute it.	10.12
a strong man's h. and plunder his	12.29
'My h. shall be called a h. of prayer';	21.13
passover at your h. with my disciples.' "	26.18
And if a h. is divided against	Mk 3.25
who has left h. or brothers or	10.29
that I must be in my Father's h.?"	Lk 2.49
he is like a man building a h.,	6.48
and sweep the h. and seek diligently	15.08
housetop, with his goods in the h.,	17.31
not make my Father's h. a h. of trade."	Jn 2.16
In my Father's h. are many rooms;	14.02
filled all the h. where they were	Ac 2.02
greet also the church in their h.	Rom 16.05
a h. not made with hands, eternal in	2Co 5.01
gadding about from h. to h., and not	1Ti 5.13
In a great h. there are not only	2Ti 2.20
faithful over God's h. as a son.	Heb 3.06
yourselves built into a spiritual h.,	1Pe 2.05

I built h. and planted vineyards	Ecc 2.04
They shall build h. and inhabit	Is 65.21
Build h. and live in them;	Jer 29.05
'The time is not near to build h.;	Eze 11.03
and the h. of ivory shall perish,	Amo 3.15
Though they build h., they shall not	Zep 1.13
who has left h. or brothers or	Mt 19.29
who devour widows' h. and for a	Mk 12.40
not dwell in h. made with hands;	Ac 7.48
Do you not have h. to eat and drink	1Co 11.22

HOUSEHOLD

into the ark, you and all your h.,	Gen 7.01
foes will be those of his own h.	Mt 10.36
will be saved, you and all your h.'	Ac 11.14
you will be saved, you and your h."	16.31
those who are of the h. of faith.	Gal 6.10
and members of the h. of God,	Eph 2.19
especially those of Caesar's h.	Php 4.22
He must manage his own h. well,	1Ti 3.04
an ark for the saving of his h.;	Heb 11.07

HOUSEHOLDER

servants of the h. came and said	Mt 13.27
is like a h. who went out early in	20.01
There was a h. who planted a	21.33
and tell the h., 'The Teacher says	Lk 22.11

HOUSETOP —S

who is on the h. not go down to	Mt 24.17
Peter went up on the h. to pray,	Ac 10.09
whispered, proclaim upon the h.	Mt 10.27

HUMAN

beyond h. semblance, and his form	Is 52.14
no h. being would be saved; but for the	Mt 24.22
nor is he served by h. hands,	Ac 17.25
for every h. being who does evil,	Rom 2.09
wrath on us? (I speak in a h. way.)	3.05
I am speaking in h. terms, because of	6.19
so that no h. being might boast in	1Co 1.29
not taught by h. wisdom but taught	2.13
judged by you or by any h. court.	4.03
stone but on tablets of h. hearts.	2Co 3.03
Christ from a h. point of view,	5.16
And being found in h. form he	Php 2.08
but no h. being can tame the tongue—	Jas 3.08
ass spoke with h. voice and	2Pe 2.16
and slaves, that is, h. souls.	Rev 18.13

HUMBLE —D —S (v)

H. yourselves therefore under the	1Pe 5.06
and the pride of men shall be h.;	Is 2.11
whoever exalts himself will be h.,	Mt 23.12
human form he h. himself and became	Php 2.08
Whoever h. himself like this child,	Mt 18.04

HUMBLE

h., and mounted on an ass, and on a	Mt 21.05
I who am h. when face to face with	2Co 10.01
proud, but gives grace to the h."	Jas 4.06

HUMILITY

in wisdom, and h. goes before honor.	Pro 15.33

HUMILITY (cont.)

Lord with all h. and with tears	Ac 20.19
but in h. court others better than	Php 2.03

HUNG

willows there we h. up our lyres.	Ps 137.02
millstone were h. round his neck	Mk 9.42

HUNGER (v)

"Blessed are those who h. and	Mt 5.06
he who comes to me shall not h.,	Jn 6.35
To the present hour we h. and thirst,	1Co 4.11
They shall h. no more, neither	Rev 7.16

HUNGRY

and the h. he fills with good	Ps 107.09
If your enemy is h., give him	Pro 25.21
As when a h. man dreams he is	Is 29.08
his disciples were h., and they began	Mt 12.01
am unwilling to send them away h.,	15.32
for I was h. and you gave me food, I	25.35
he has filled the h. with good	Lk 1.53
No, "if your enemy is h., feed him;	Rom 12.20
if any one is h., let him eat at	1Co 11.34

HURT —S (v)

the enemy; and nothing shall h. you.	Lk 10.19
It h. you to kick against the goads.'	Ac 26.14

HURT (n)

LORD binds up the h. of his people,	Is 30.26
Your h. is incurable, and your wound	Jer 30.12

HUSBAND —S

your desire shall be for your h.,	Gen 3.16
A good wife is the crown of her h.,	Pro 12.04
For your Maker is your h., the LORD	Is 54.05
and her h. Joseph, being a just man	Mt 1.19
divorces her h. and marries	Mk 10.12
"Go, call your h., and come here."	Jn 4.16
out and buried her beside her h.	Ac 5.10
But if her h. dies she is free from	Rom 7.03
own wife and each woman her own h.	1Co 7.02
is bound to her h. as long as he	7.39
the head of a woman is her h.,	11.03
you as a pure bride to her one h.	2Co 11.02
children than she who hath a h."	Gal 4.27
as a bride adorned for her h.;	Rev 21.02
Wives, be subject to your h.,	Eph 5.22
H., love your wives, as Christ loved	5.25

HYMN —S

And when they had sung a h.,	Mt 26.30
were praying and singing h. to God,	Ac 16.25

HYPOCRITE —S

You h., first take the log out of	Mt 7.05
as the h. do in the synagogues and	6.02
"Why put me to the test, you h.?	22.18
Woe to you, scribes and Pharisees, h.!	23.15

HYSSOP

Purge me with h., and I shall be	Ps 51.07
the vinegar on h. and held it to	Jn 19.29
with water and scarlet wool and h.,	Heb 9.19

I

IDLE —Y*

who sing i. songs to the sound of	Amo 6.05
others standing i. in the market	Mt 20.03
words seemed to them an i. tale,	Lk 24.11
admonish the i., encourage the	1Th 5.14
your own pleasure, or talking i.;	Is 58.13

IDOL —S

The i.! a workman casts it,	Is 40.19
What profit is an i, when its maker	Hab 2.18
we know that "an i. has no real	1Co 8.04
anything, or that an i. is anything?	10.19
Do not turn to i. or make for	Lev 19.04
all the gods of the peoples are i.;	Ps 96.05
Their i. are like scarecrows in a	Jer 10.05
Repent and turn away from your i.;	Eze 14.06
Ephraim, what have I to do with i.?	Hos 14.08
saw that the city was full of i.	Ac 17.16
You who abhor i., do you rob	Rom 2.22
Now concerning food offered to i.:	1Co 8.01
you were led astray to dumb i.,	12.02
has the temple of God with i.?	2Co 6.16
and how you turned to God from i.,	1Th 1.09
Little children, keep yourselves from i.	1Jn 5.21
and to eat food sacrificed to i.	Rev 2.20

IDOLATERS

Do not be i. as some of them were:	1Co 10.07

IDOLATRY

stubbornness is as iniquity and i.	1Sa 15.23
i., sorcery, enmity, strife, jealousy,	Gal 5.20

IGNORANCE

The times of i. God overlooked, but	Ac 17.30
to the passions of your former i.,	1Pe 1.14

IGNORANT

For, being i. of the righteousness	Rom 10.03
For we do not want you to be i.,	2Co 1.08
But we would not have you i.,	1Th 4.13

IGNORE —ING*

They deliberately i. this fact,	2Pe 3.05
But i. what they said, Jesus said to	Mk 5.36

ILL

told, "Behold, your father is i.";	Gen 48.01
mother-in-law was i. with a high	Lk 4.38
"Lord, he whom you love is i."	Jn 11.03
is why many of you are weak and i.,	1Co 11.30
in i. repute and good repute.	2Co 6.08
because you heard that he was i.	Php 2.26

IMAGE —S

So God created man in his own i.,	Gen 1.27
to set up an i. that will not move.	Is 40.20

IMAGE —S (cont.)
be conformed to the i. of his Son,   Rom 8.29
since he is the i. and glory of   1Co 11.07
have borne the i. of the man of   15.49
He is the i. of the invisible God,   Col 1.15
not worship the i. of the beast to   Rev 13.15
All worshipers of i. are put to   Ps 97.07
their molten i. are empty wind.   Is 41.29
immortal God for i. resembling   Rom 1.23

IMAGINATION
proud in the i. of their hearts,   Lk 1.51

IMITATE
Beloved, do not i. evil but i. good.   3Jn 11

IMITATING* (n)
join in i. me, and mark those who so   Php 3.17

IMITATORS
Be i. of me, as I am of Christ.   1Co 11.01
but i. of those who through faith   Heb 6.12

IMMORAL —LY*
but the i. man sins against his own   1Co 6.18
that no i. or impure man, or one who   Eph 5.05
i. persons, sodomites, kidnapers,   1Ti 1.10
that no one be i. or irreligious   Heb 12.16
likewise acted i. and indulged in   Jud 7

IMMORALITY
reported that there is i. among you,   1Co 5.01
The body is not meant for i.,   6.13
i., impurity, licentiousness,   Gal 5.19
But i. and all impurity or covetousness   Eph 5.03
sanctification: that you abstain from i.;   1Th 4.03
she refuses to repent of her i.   Rev 2.21

IMMORTALITY
this mortal nature must put on i.   1Co 15.53
life and i. to light through the   2Ti 1.10

IMMOVABLE
i., always abounding in the work of   1Co 15.58

IMPART
that I may i. to you some spiritual   Rom 1.11
But we i. a secret and hidden   1Co 2.07

IMPERISHABLE
a perishable wreath, but we an i.   1Co 9.25
perishable, what is raised is i.   15.42
perishable nature must put on the i.,   15.53
and to an inheritance which is i.,   1Pe 1.04

IMPOSSIBLE
and nothing will be i. to you."   Mt 17.20
said to them, "With men this is i.,   19.26
For it is i. to restore again to   Heb 6.04

IMPRISONMENT —S
every city that i. and afflictions   Ac 20.23
with nothing deserving death or i.   23.29
the rest that my i. is for Christ;   Php 1.13

behalf during my i. for the gospel;   Phm 13
beatings, i., tumults, labors, watching,   2Co 6.05

IMPURITY
shall be in her i. for seven days,   Lev 15.19
your members to i. and to greater   Rom 6.19
and have not repented of the i.,   2Col 12.21
immorality, i., licentiousness,   Gal 5.19
immorality and all i. or covetousness   Eph 5.03
i., passion, evil desire, and covetousness,   Col 3.05

INCLINE —D —S
I. thy ear, O LORD, and answer me, for   Ps 86.01
I i. my heart to perform thy   119.112
he i. to me and heard my cry.   40.01
man's heart i. him toward the   Ecc 10.02

INCREASE —D —S —ING (v)
When goods i., they i. who eat them;   Ecc 5.11
said to the Lord, "I. our faith!"   Lk 17.05
He must i., but I must decrease."   Jn 3.30
Law came in, to i. the trespass;   Rom 5.20
more people it may i. thanksgiving,   2Co 4.15
And Jesus i. in wisdom and in   Lk 2.52
And the word of God i.; and the number   Ac 6.07
but where sin i., grace abounded   Rom 5.20
our hope is that as your faith i.,   2Co 10.15
good work and i. in the knowledge   Col 1.10

INCREASE (n)
The earth has yielded its i.;   Ps 67.06
May the LORD give you i.,   115.14
Of the i. of his government and of   Is 9.07

INCUR —RED —S*
those who resist will i. judgment.   Rom 13.02
and so they i. condemnation for   1Ti 5.12
never offset the guilt he has i.   Hos 12.08
reproves a wicked man i. injury.   Pro 9.07

INDIGNANT
they were i. at the two brothers.   Mt 20.24
they were i., saying, "Why this   26.08
is made to fall, and I am not i.?   2Co 11.29

INDIGNATION
Hot i. seizes me because of the   Ps 119.53
Who can stand before his i.?   Nah 1.06
what i., what alarm, what longing,   2Co 7.11

INFERIOR
the greater honor to the i. part,   1Co 12.24
in the least i. to these superlative   2Co 11.05
that the i. is blessed by the   Heb 7.07

INFIRMITIES —Y
"He took our i. and bore our   Mt 8.17
healing every disease and every i.   9.35

INFLICT —ING*
God is unjust to i. wrath on us?   Rom 3.05
i. vengeance upon those who do not   2Th 1.08

INHABITANTS
let all the i. of the world stand — Ps 33.08
known to all the i. of Jerusalem, — Ac 1.19
earth and its i. worship the first — Rev 13.12

INHERIT
and they shall i. it for ever.' " — Ex 32.13
my chosen shall i. it, and my servants — Is 65.09
meek, for they shall i. the earth. — Mt 5.05
a hundredfold, and i. eternal life. — 19.29
i. the kingdom prepared for you — 25.34
that they should i. the world, — Rom 4.13
nor robbers will i. the kingdom of God. — 1Co 6.10
blood cannot i. the kingdom of God, — 15.50
faith and patience i. the promises. — Heb 6.12

INHERITANCE
to give you their land for an i., — Deu 4.38
let us kill him and have his i.' — Mt 21.38
he gave them their land as an i., — Ac 13.19
For if the i. is by the law, it is — Gal 3.18
guarantee of our i. until we acquire — Eph 1.14
will receive the i. as your reward; — Col 3.24
receive the promised eternal i., — Heb 9.15
and to an i. which is imperishable, — 1Pe 1.04

INIQUITIES —Y
him all the i. of the people of — Lev 16.21
Thou hast set our i. before thee, — Ps 90.08
shouldst mark i., Lord, who could — 130.03
you have wearied me with your i. — 43.24
transgressions, he was bruised for our i.; — Is 53.05
righteous; and he shall bear their i. — 53.11
but your i. have made a separation — 59.02
I will be merciful toward their i., — Heb 8.12
visiting the i. of the fathers upon — Ex 20.05
those who plow i. and sow trouble — Job 4.08
I confess my i., I am sorry for my — Ps 38.18
Wash me thoroughly from my i., and — 51.02
that her i. is pardoned, that she — Is 40.02
has laid on him the i. of us all. — 53.06
Lord, and remember not i. for ever. — 64.09
for I will forgive their i., — Jer 31.34
and end to sin, and to atone for i., — Dan 9.24
You have plowed i., you have reaped — Hos 10.13
you are full of hypocrisy and i., — Mt 23.28
and to greater and greater i., — Rom 6.19
partnership have righteousness and i.? — 2Co 6.14

INJUSTICE
hope, and i. shuts her mouth. — Job 5.16
He who sows i. will reap calamity, — Pro 22.08
Is there i. on God's part? — Rom 9.14

INK
not with i. but with the Spirit of — 2Co 3.03

INNER —MOST
our i. nature is being renewed — 2Co 4.16
through his Spirit in the i. man, — Eph 3.16
enters into the i. shrine behind — Heb 6.19
Lord, searching all his i. parts. — Pro 20.27
who is in the i. parts of the — Amo 6.10

INNOCENT
"Lord, wilt thou slay an i. people? — Gen 20.04
Though I am i., I cannot answer him; — Job 9.15
He delivers the i. man; you will be — 22.30
wise as serpents and i. as doves. — Mt 10.16
"I am i. of this man's blood; — 27.24
said, "Certainly this man was i.!" — Lk 23.47
that you may be blameless and i., — Php 2.15

INQUIRE —D
"Go, i. of the Lord for me, and for — 2Ki 22.13
If you will i., i.; come back again." — Is 21.12
My people i. of a thing of wood, and — Hos 4.12
do not seek the Lord or i. of him." — Zep 1.06
were going to i. somewhat more — Ac 23.20
he i. of them where the Christ was — Mt 2.04
going by, he i. what this meant. — Lk 18.36
they i., "By what power or by what — Ac 4.07
searched and i. about this salvation; — 1Pe 1.10

INSCRIBE* —D
and i. it in a book, that it may be — Is 30.08
Oh that they were i. in a book! — Job 19.23
And this is the writing that was i.: — Dan 5.25
he has a name i. which no one — Rev 19.12

INSCRIPTION
"Whose likeness and i. is this?" — Mt 22.20
There was also an i. over him, — Lk 23.38
I found also an altar with this i., — Ac 17.23

INSIDE
cleanse the i. of the cup and of — Mt 23.26
Is it not those i. the church whom — 1Co 5.12

INSIGHT
and whatever you get, get i. — Pro 4.07
knowledge of the Holy One is i. — 9.10
all wisdom and i. the mystery of — Eph 1.09
can perceive my i. into the — 3.04

INSIST
Love does not i. on its own way; — 1Co 13.05

INSOLENT —LY
on high, or speak with i. neck." — Ps 75.05
i., haughty, boastful, inventors of — Rom 1.30
that they acted i. against our — Neh 9.10

INSPIRED —S*
I. decisions are on the lips of a — Pro 16.10
i. by the Spirit, calls him Lord, — Mt 22.43
All these are i. by one and the — 1Co 12.11
with joy i. by the Holy Spirit; — 1Th 1.06
All scripture is i. by God and — 2Ti 3.16
same God who i. them all in every — 1Co 12.06
which he mightily i. within me. — Col 1.29

INSTRUCT —ED
I will i. you and teach you the way — Ps 32.08
mind of the Lord so as to i. him?" — 1Co 2.16
are able to i. you for salvation — 2Ti 3.15
or as his counselor has i. him? — Is 40.13

INSTRUCT —ED (cont.)

He had been i. in the way of the	Ac 18.25
he was i. by God, saying, "See that	Heb 8.05

INSTRUCTION —S

former days was written for our i.,	Rom 15.04
they were written down for our i.,	1Co 10.11
be able to give i. in sound	Tit 1.09
the following i. I do not commend	1Co 11.17
For you know what i. we gave you	1Th 4.02

INSTRUMENT —S

he is a chosen i. of mine to carry	Ac 9.15
to God as i. of righteousness.	Rom 6.13
If even lifeless i., such as the flute	1Co 14.07

INSULTS (n)

and the i. of those who insult thee	Ps 69.09
i., hardships, persecutions, and	2Co 12.10

INTEGRITY

He still holds fast his i.,	Job 2.03
May i. and uprightness preserve me,	Ps 25.21
He who walks in i. will be delivered,	Pro 28.18
in your teaching show i., gravity,	Tit 2.07

INTERCEDE —S

then let them i. with the LORD of	Jer 27.18
Spirit himself i. for us with	Rom 8.26

INTEREST —S

Take no i. from him or increase, but	Lev 25.36
To a foreigner you may lend upon i.,	Deu 23.20
who does not put out his money at i.,	Ps 15.05
received what was my own with i.	Mt 25.27
and his i. are divided. And the	1Co 7.34
but also to the i. of others.	Php 2.04

INTERPRET —ED —ING*

You know how to i. the appearance	Mt 16.03
all speak with tongues? Do all i.?	1Co 12.30
should pray for the power to i.	14.13

he i. to them in all the scriptures	Lk 24.27
i. spiritual truths to those who	1Co 2.13

INTERPRETATION —S

show me the dream and its i."	Dan 2.06
This is the i. of the matter: MENE,	5.26
to another the i. of tongues.	1Co 12.10
is a matter of one's own i.,	2Pe 1.20
to them, "Do not i. belong to God?	Gen 40.08

INVISIBLE

He is the image of the i. God,	Col 1.15

INVITE —D —S

and i. to the marriage feast as	Mt 22.09
And he i. Philip to come up and	Ac 8.31
those who are i. to the marriage	Rev 19.09
one of the unbelievers i. you to dinner	1Co 10.27

INVOKE —D

Then he began to i. a curse on	Mt 26.74
And if you i. as Father him who	1Pe 1.17
By faith Isaac i. future blessings	Heb 11.20

INWARD —LY

desirest truth in the i. being;	Ps 51.06
For thou didst form my i. parts,	139.13
clothing but i. are ravenous	Mt 7.15
He is a Jew who is one i., and real	Rom 2.29
groan i. as we wait for adoption as	8.23

IRON

You shall break them with a rod of i.,	Ps 2.09
image on its feet of i. and clay,	Dan 2.34
shall rule them with a rod of i.,	Rev 2.27

ISLAND

people on the i. who had diseases	Ac 28.09
was on the i. called Patmos on	Rev 1.09

ITCHING

but having i. ears they will	2Ti 4.03

J

JACKALS

I am a brother of j., and a companion	Job 30.29
It shall be the haunt of j.,	Is 34.13

JAR —S

let down your j. that I may drink,'	Gen 24.14
"Every j. shall be filled with wine." '	Jer 13.12
an alabaster j. of very expensive	Mt 26.07
man carrying a j. of water will	Mk 14.13
So the woman left her water j.,	Jn 4.28
Now six stone j. were standing	2.06

JEALOUS —LY*

And his brothers were j. of him,	Gen 37.11
I the LORD your God am a j. God,	Ex 20.05
"I have been very j. for the LORD,	1Ki 19.10
But the Jews were j., and taking some	Ac 17.05
Gentiles, so as to make Israel j.	Rom 11.11

love is not j. or boastful;	1Co 13.04
"He yearns j. over the spirit which	Jas 4.05

JEALOUSY

For j. makes a man furious, and he	Pro 6.34
I, the LORD, have spoken in my j.,	Eze 5.13
licentiousness, not in quarreling and j.	Rom 13.13
Shall we provoke the Lord to j.?	1Co 10.22
I feel a divine j. for you,	2Co 11.02
j., anger, selfishness, dissension,	Gal 5.20

JESUS

book of the genealogy of J. Christ,	Mt 1.01
and you shall call his name J.,	1.21
"This man was with J. of Nazareth."	26.71
"This is J. the King of the Jews."	27.37
"This J., whom I proclaim to you, is	Ac 17.03
"J. I know, and Paul I know; but	19.15

JESUS (cont.)

'I am J. of Nazareth whom you are	Ac 22.08
your lips that J. is Lord and	Rom 10.09
the life of J. may be manifested	2Co 4.11
that at the name of J. every knee	Php 2.10

JEWEL —S

lips of knowledge are a precious j.	Pro 20.15
imperishable j. of a gentle and	1Pe 3.04
for wisdom is better than j.,	Pro 8.11
a bride adorns herself with her j.	Is 61.10

JOIN —ED —S*

Philip, "Go up and j. this chariot."	Ac 8.29
he attempted to j. the disciples;	9.26
Brethren, j. in imitating me, and	Php 3.17
you do not now j. them in the same	1Pe 4.04
Ephraim is j. to idols, let him	Hos 4.17
What therefore God has j. together,	Mt 19.06
But some men j. him and believed,	Ac 17.34
The Jews also j. in the charge,	24.09
structure is j. together and grows	Eph 2.21
and mother and be j. to his wife,	5.31
that he who j. himself to a prostitute	1Co 6.16

JOINT

was put out of j. as he wrestled	Gen 32.25
by every j. with which it is	Eph 4.16

JOURNEY —S

Then Jacob went on his j.,	Gen 29.01
no bag for your j., nor two tunics,	Mt 10.10
man going on a j. called his	25.14
the company they went a day's j.,	Lk 2.44
and took his j. into a far country,	15.13
Jerusalem, a sabbath day's j. away;	Ac 1.12
to be sped on my j. there by you,	Rom 15.24
speed me on my j., wherever I go.	1Co 16.06
on frequent j., in danger from	2Co 11.26

JOURNEYED

And Abram j. on, still going toward	Gen 12.09
and j. into the wilderness in the	Deu 2.01
and I j. to Damascus to take those	Ac 22.05

JOY

for the j. of the LORD is your	Neh 8.10
he comes into his presence with j.	Job 33.26
Thou hast put more j. in my heart	Ps 4.07
Shout to God with loud songs of j.!	47.01
Restore to me the j. of thy salvation,	51.12
flesh sing for j. to the living	84.02
let the hills sing for j. together	98.08
So he led forth his people with j.,	105.43
yea, they are the j. of my heart.	119.111
is sad, and the end of j. is grief.	Pro 14.13
all j. has reached its eventide;	Is 24.11
everlasting j. shall be upon their	35.10
everlasting j. shall be upon their	51.11
"For you shall go out in j., and be	55.12
yours shall be everlasting j.	61.07
rejoiced exceedingly with great j.;	Mt 2.10
then in his j. he goes and sells	13.44
enter into the j. of your master.'	25.21
the tomb with fear and great j.,	28.08

The seventy returned with j.,	Lk 10.17
there is j. before the angels of	15.10
therefore this j. of mine is now	Jn 3.29
that my j. may be in you, and that	15.11
but your sorrow will turn into j.	16.20
So there was much j. in that city.	Ac 8.08
filled with j. and with the Holy	13.52
and peace and j. in the Holy	Rom 14.17
we work with you for your j.,	2Co 1.24
j., peace, patience, kindness, goodness,	Gal 5.22
complete my j. by being of the same	Php 2.02
my j. and crown, stand firm thus in	4.01
is our hope or j. or crown of	1Th 2.19
who for the j. that was set before	Heb 12.02
Count it all j., my brethren, when	Jas 1.02
this that our j. may be complete.	1Jn 1.04

JOYFUL

Make a j. noise to God, all the	Ps 66.01
let us make a j. noise to the rock	95.01
In the day of prosperity be j.,	Ecc 7.14

JUDGE —D —S —ING (v)

May the LORD j. between you and	Gen 16.05
May he j. thy people with righteousness,	Ps 72.02
He will j. the world with righteousness,	98.09
He shall j. between many peoples,	Mic 4.03
"J. not, that you be not judged.	Mt 7.01
"And why do you not j. for yourselves	Lk 12.57
but j. with right judgment."	Jn 7.24
You j. according to the flesh, I j. no one.	8.15
and j. yourselves unworthy of eternal	Ac 13.46
human court. I do not even j. myself.	1Co 4.03
not know that we are to j. angels?	6.03
J. for yourselves; is it proper	11.13
Jesus who is to j. the living and	2Ti 4.01
who is ready to j. the living and	1Pe 4.05
said to him, "You have j. rightly."	Lk 7.43
because he j. me faithful by appointing	1Ti 1.12
and all were j. by what they had	Rev 20.13
The Father j. no one, but has given	Jn 5.22
God j. the secrets of men by Christ	Rom 2.16
he trusted to him who j. justly.	1Pe 2.23
j. the twelve tribes of Israel.	Mt 19.28

JUDGE —S (n)

be acquitted for ever by my j.	Job 23.07
God is a righteous j., and a God	Ps 7.11
accuser hand you over to the j.,	Mt 5.25
"Hear what the unrighteous j. says.	Lk 18.06
by God to be j. of the living and	Ac 10.42
and to a j. who is God of all, and	Heb 12.23
There is one lawgiver and j.,	Jas 4.12
behold, the J. is standing at the	5.09
"You shall appoint j. and officers	Deu 16.18
Then the LORD raised up j., who saved	Ju 2.16
he gave them j. until Samuel the	Ac 13.20

JUDGMENT —S

face of man, for the j. is God's;	Deu 1.17
that you may know there is a j."	Job 19.29
From the heavens thou didst utter j.;	Ps 76.08
by a spirit of j. and by a spirit	Is 4.04
For by fire will the LORD execute j.,	66.16
For with the j. you pronounce you	Mt 7.02

JUDGMENT —S (cont.)

arise at the j. with this generation	Mt 12.41
he was sitting on the j. seat,	27.19
And this is the j., that the light	Jn 3.19
but has given all j. to the Son,	5.22
Now is the j. of this world, now	12.31
you will escape the j. of God?	Rom 2.03
us no more pass j. on one another,	14.13
eats and drinks j. upon himself.	1Co 11.29
of the dead, and eternal j.	Heb 6.02
die once, and after that comes j.,	9.27
mercy; yet mercy triumphs over j.	Jas 2.13
has come for j. to begin with the	1Pe 4.17
have confidence for the day of j.,	1Jn 4.17
God has given j. for you against	Rev 18.20
I will execute j.: I am the LORD.	Ex 12.12
unsearchable are his j. and how	Rom 11.33
for his j. are true and just;	Rev 19.02

JUST

You shall have j. balances, j.	Lev 19.36
But how can a man be j. before God?	Job 9.02
The LORD is j. in all his ways, and	Ps 145.17
rain on the j. and on the unjust.	Mt 5.45
at the resurrection of the j."	Lk 14.14
with saying. Their condemnation is j.	Rom 3.08
commandment is holy and j. and good.	7.12
in order that the j. requirement of	8.04
whatever is j., whatever is pure,	Php 4.08
God deems it j. to repay with	2Th 1.06
the spirits of j. men made perfect,	Heb 12.23
our sins, he is faithful and j.,	1Jn 1.09

JUSTICE

J., and only j., you shall follow,	Deu 16.20

I call aloud, but there is no j.	Job 19.07
For the LORD loves j.; he will not	Ps 37.28
Give the king thy j., O God,	72.01
Righteousness and j. are the foundation	89.14
When j. is done, it is a joy to the	Pro 21.15
By j. a king gives stability to the	29.04
and he looked for j., but behold,	Is 5.07
And I will make j. the line,	28.17
J. is turned back, and righteousness	59.14
For I the LORD love j., I hate	61.08
But let j. roll down like waters,	Amo 5.24
LORD require of you but to do j.,	Mic 6.08
j. and mercy and faith; these you ought	Mt 23.23
In his humiliation j. was denied him.	Ac 8.33
he argued about j. and self-control	24.25
serves to show the j. of God,	Rom 3.05
enforced j., received promises,	Heb 11.33

JUSTIFIED —S —Y

Yet wisdom is j. by her deeds."	Mt 11.19
for by your words you will be j.,	12.37
to his house j. rather than the	Lk 18.14
they are j. by his grace as a gift,	Rom 3.24
that a man is j. by faith apart	3.28
since we are j. by faith, we have	5.01
those whom he called he also j.;	8.30
every one who has faith may be j.	10.04
a man is not j. by works of the	Gal 2.16
came, that we might be j. by faith.	3.24
we might be j. by his grace and	Tit 3.07
that a man is j. by works and not	2.24
God's elect? It is God who j.;	8.33
desiring to j. himself, said to	Lk 10.29
are those who j. yourselves before	16.15
that God would j. the Gentiles by	Gal 3.08

K

KEEP —ING —S

You shall therefore k. this ordinance	Ex 13.10
commandments and k. all his statutes,	15.26
"Remember the sabbath day, to k. it holy.	20.08
that you may k. the commandments of	Deu 4.02
fear me and to k. all my commandments,	5.29
love him and k. his commandments,	7.09
fail they would k. these two days	Est 9.27
K. back thy servant also from	Ps 19.13
They did not k. God's covenant, but	78.10
The LORD will k. your going out and	121.08
a time to k., and a time to cast	Ecc 3.06
a time to k. silence, and a time to	3.07
Fear God, and k. his commandments;	12.13
Thou dost k. him in perfect peace,	Is 26.03
"Be ready and k. ready, you and all	Eze 38.07
all the earth k. silence before	Hab 2.20
enter life, k. the commandments."	Mt 19.17
God, in order to k. your tradition!	Mk 7.09
this world will k. it for eternal	Jn 12.25
If you k. my commandments, you will	15.10
Holy Father, k. them in thy name	17.11
k. between yourself and God;	Rom 14.22
will k. your hearts and your minds	Php 4.07
love of God, that we k. his	1Jn 5.03

who is able to k. you from falling	Jud 24
Now Moses was k. the flock of his	Ex 3.01
k. watch over their flock by night.	Lk 2.08
He who k. the commandment k. his	Pro 19.16
but He who was born of God k. him,	1Jn 5.18

KEEPER

"I do not know; am I my brother's k.?"	Gen 4.09
The LORD is your k.; the LORD is your	Ps 121.05

KEY —S

taken away the k. of knowledge;	Lk 11.52
give you the k. of the kingdom of	Mt 16.19

KID

not boil a k. in its mother's milk.	Ex 23.19
leopard shall lie down with the k.,	Is 11.06
yet you never gave me a k.,	Lk 15.29

KILL —ED —ING —S

let us k. him and throw him into	Gen 37.20
"You shall not k.	Ex 20.13
the men of old, 'You shall not k.;	Mt 5.21
the body but cannot k. the soul;	10.28
and Jesus said, "You shall not k.,	19.18

KILL —ED —ING —S (cont.)

come, let us k. him and have his	Mt 21.38
of whom you will k. and crucify,	23.34
arrest Jesus by stealth and k. him.	26.04
to do harm, to save life or to k.?"	Mk 3.04
do not fear those who k. the body,	Lk 12.04
to him. "Rise, Peter; k. and eat."	Ac 10.13
You shall not k., You shall not	Rom 13.09
them and conquer them and k. them,	Rev 11.07
his brother Abel, and k. him.	Gen 4.08
to kill me as you k. the Egyptian?"	Ex 2.14
And Moses k. it, and took the blood,	Lev 8.15
struck the Philistine, and k. him;	1Sa 17.50
and be k., and on the third day be	Mt 16.21
and k. the Author of life, whom God	Ac 3.15
Jesus whom you k. by hanging him	5.30
nor drink till they had k. Paul.	23.12
we are being k. all the day long;	Rom 8.36
they have k. thy prophets, they have	11.03
who k. both the Lord Jesus and the	1Th 2.15
k. the prophets and stoning those	Mt 23.37
The LORD k. and brings to life;	1Sa 2.06
and whoever k. shall be liable to	Mt 5.21
for the written code k., but the Spirit	2Co 3.06

KIN

his next of k. shall come and	Lev 25.25
own country, and among his own k.,	Mk 6.04

KIND —LY

A man who is k. benefits himself,	Pro 11.17
happy is he who is k. to the poor.	14.21
for he is k. to the ungrateful and	Lk 6.35
Love is patient and k.; love is not	1Co 13.04
and be k. to one another,	Eph 4.32
k., and submissive to their husbands,	Tit 2.05
not only to the k. and gentle but	1Pe 2.18
May the LORD deal k. with you,	Ru 1.08
be quarrelsome but k. to every one,	2Ti 2.24

KINDLED

LORD your God be k. against you,	Deu 6.15
For a fire is k. by my anger, and it	32.22
He has k. his wrath against me, and	Job 19.11
and would that it were already k.!	Lk 12.49
heavens will be k. and dissolved,	2Pe 3.12

KINDNESS

made this last k. greater than the	Ru 3.10
"He who withholds k. from a friend	Job 6.14
There is no faithfulness or k.,	Hos 4.01
and loving k. of God our Savior	Tit 3.04
you have tasted the k. of the Lord.	1Pe 2.03

KING —S

Now there arose a new k. over Egypt,	Ex 1.08
days there was no k. in Israel;	Ju 17.06
he will give strength to his k.,	1Sa 2.10
people shouted, "Long live the k.!"	10.24
that the K. of glory may come in.	Ps 24.07
LORD sits enthroned as k. for ever.	29.10
For God is the k. of all the earth;	47.07
Give the k. thy justice, O God, and	72.01
sons of Zion rejoice in their K.!	149.02

decisions are on the lips of a k.;	Pro 16.10
In the year that K. Uzziah died I	Is 6.01
for my eyes have seen the K.,	6.05
Behold, a k. will reign in righteousness,	32.01
the Creator of Israel, your K."	43.15
the K. of Israel and his Redeemer,	44.06
who has been born k. of the Jews?	Mt 2.02
for it is the city of the great K.	5.35
your k. is coming to you, humble, and	21.05
The k. was angry, and he sent his	22.07
Then the K. will say to those at	25.34
him, "Are you the K. of the Jews?"	27.11
"This is Jesus the K. of the Jews."	27.37
He is the K. of Israel; let him come	27.42
saying, "Blessed be the K. who comes	Lk 19.38
that he himself is Christ a k."	23.02
You are the K. of Israel!"	Jn 1.49
take him by force to make him k.,	6.15
answered, "You say that I am a k.	18.37
answered, "We have no k. but Caesar."	19.15
To the K. of ages, immortal, invisible,	1Ti 1.17
the K. of kings and Lord of lords,	6.15
K. of kings and Lord of lords.	Rev 19.16
The k. of the earth set themselves,	Ps 2.02
All the k. of the earth shall	138.04
From whom do k. of the earth take	Mt 17.25
"The k. of the Gentiles exercise	Lk 22.25
Without us you have become k.!	1Co 4.08

KINGDOM —S

not come to the k. for such a time	Est 4.14
Thy k. is an everlasting k.,	Ps 145.13
They shall name it No K. There,	Is 34.12
the God of heaven has given the k.,	Dan 2.37
Most High God rules the k. of men,	5.21
for the k. of heaven is at hand."	Mt 3.02
called least in the k. of heaven;	5.19
Thy k. come, Thy will be done, On	6.10
But seek first his k. and his	6.33
while the sons of the k. will be	8.12
and preaching the gospel of the k.,	9.35
"Every k. divided against itself is	12.25
the secrets of the k. of heaven,	13.11
"The k. of heaven may be compared	13.24
you the keys of the k. of heaven,	16.19
to such belongs the k. of heaven."	19.14
and one at your left, in your k."	20.21
"You are not far from the k. of God."	Mk 12.34
I drink it new in the k. of God."	14.25
and of his k. there will be no end."	Lk 1.33
you, go and proclaim the k. of God."	9.60
the k. of God is in the midst of	17.21
as my Father appointed a k. for me,	22.29
anew, he cannot see the k. of God."	Jn 3.03
this time restore the k. to Israel?"	Ac 1.06
For the k. of God does not mean	Rom 14.17
For the k. of God does not consist	1Co 4.20
he delivers the k. to God the	15.24
blood cannot inherit the k. of God,	15.50
inheritance in the k. of Christ and	Eph 5.05
the eternal k. of our Lord and	2Pe 1.11
and made us a k., priests to his	Rev 1.06
"The k. of the world has become the k.	11.15
Sing to God, O k. of the earth;	Ps 68.32

KINGDOM —S (cont.)

him all the k. of the world and	Mt 4.08
who through faith conquered k.,	Heb 11.33

KINGSHIP

"My k. is not of this world;	Jn 18.36

KINSMAN —MEN

a k. of the man whose ear Peter had	Jn 18.26
brothers or your k. or rich neighbors,	Lk 14.12
sake of my brethren, my k. by race.	Rom 9.03

KISS —ED (v)

O that you would k. me with the	Sol 1.02
"The one I shall k. is the man;	Mt 26.48
and k. his feet, and anointed them	Lk 7.38
ran and embraced him and k. him.	15.20
wept and embraced Paul and k. him,	Ac 20.37

KISS —ES (n)

betray the Son of man with a k.?"	Lk 22.48
Greet one another with a holy k.	Rom 16.16
profuse are the k. of an enemy.	Pro 27.06
and your k. like the best wine that	Sol 7.09

KNEE —S

name of Jesus every k. should bow,	Php 2.10
reason I bow my k. before the	Eph 3.14
hands and strengthen your weak k.,	Heb 12.12

KNEW

and they k. that they were naked;	Gen 3.07
"Before I formed you in the womb I k.	Jer 1.05
I declare to them, 'I never k. you;	Mt 7.23
him, yet the world k. him not.	Jn 1.10
for although they k. God they did	Rom 1.21

KNOCK

k., and it will be opened to you.	Mt 7.07
Behold, I stand at the door and k.;	Rev 3.20

KNOW —EST —ING —N

and you shall k. that I am the LORD	Ex 6.07
Now Samuel did not yet k. the LORD,	1Sa 3.07
"Behold, I k. your thoughts, and your	Job 21.27
"Be still, and k. that I am God.	Ps 46.10
And they say, "How can God k.?	73.11

Search me, O God, and k. my heart!	139.23
Then you will k. that I am the LORD;	Is 49.23
Is not this to k. me? says the LORD.	Jer 22.16
your left hand k. what your right	Mt 6.03
You will k. them by their fruits.	7.16
Did you not k. that I must be in my	Lk 2.49
we worship what we k., for salvation	Jn 4.22
and you will k. the truth, and the	8.32
I k. my own and my own k. me,	10.14
that they k. thee the only true God,	17.03
We k. that in everything God works	Rom 8.28
world did not k. God through	1Co 1.21
For I decided to k. nothing among	2.02
for I k. whom I have believed and I	2Ti 1.12
'K. the Lord,' for all shall k. me,	Heb 8.11
By this we k. love, that he laid	1Jn 3.16
"'I k. your works, your toil and	Rev 2.02
lo, O LORD, thou k. it altogether.	Ps 139.04
who k. the hearts of all men, show	Ac 1.24
will be like God, k. good and evil."	Gen 3.05
worth of k. Christ Jesus my Lord.	Php 3.08
The LORD has made himself k.,	Ps 9.16
thou hast searched me and k. me!	139.01
Have you not k.? Have you not	Is 40.21
"You only have I k. of all the	Amo 3.02
if one loves God, one is k. by him.	1Co 8.03
to be k. and read by all men;	2Co 3.02
God, or rather to be k. by God,	Gal 4.09

KNOWLEDGE

the tree of the k. of good and	Gen 2.09
for the LORD is a God of k.,	1Sa 2.03
Will any teach God k., seeing that	Job 21.22
Is there k. in the Most High?"	Ps 73.11
Such k. is too wonderful for me;	139.06
Whoever loves discipline loves k.,	Pro 12.01
the spirit of k. and the fear of	Is 11.02
of salvation, wisdom, and k.;	33.06
Every man is stupid and without k.;	Jer 10.14
to give k. of salvation to his	Lk 1.77
you have taken away the key of k.;	11.52
a rather accurate k. of the Way,	Ac 24.22
through the law comes k. of sin.	Rom 3.20
"K." puffs up, but love builds up.	1Co 8.01
For our k. is imperfect and our	13.09
love of Christ which surpasses k.,	Eph 3.19
of what is falsely called k.,	1Th 6.20
the grace and k. of our Lord and	2Pe 3.18

L

LABOR —ED (v)

Six days you shall l., and do all	Ex 20.09
why then do I l. in vain?	Job 9.29
those who build it l. in vain.	Ps 127.01
all who l. and are heavy laden, and	Mt 11.28
Do not l. for the food which	Jn 6.27
those who l. in preaching and	1Ti 5.17
others have l., and you have	Jn 4.38
afraid I have l. over you in vain.	Gal 4.11

LABOR —S (n)

were bowed down with hard l.;	Ps 107.12

and your l. for that which does not	Is 55.02
his wages according to his l.	1Co 3.08
in the Lord your l. is not in vain.	15.58
of faith and l. of love and	1Th 1.03
with toil and l. we worked night	2Th 3.08
and toil of my l. under the sun,	Ecc 2.19
tumults, l., watching, hunger;	2Co 6.05
that they may rest from their l.,	Rev 14.13

LABORER —S

Sweet is the sleep of a l.,	Ecc 5.12
for the l. deserves his food.	Mt 10.10

LABORER —S (cont.)

and to every fellow worker and l.	1Co 16.16
is plentiful, but the l. are few;	Mt 9.37
wages of the l. who mowed your	Jas 5.04

LACK —ING (v)

observed; what do I still l.?"	Mt 19.20
supply what is l. in your faith?	1Th 3.10

LAMB —S

Your l. shall be without blemish, a	Ex 12.05
like a l. that is led to the slaughter,	Is 53.07
they sacrificed the passover l.,	Mk 14.12
the L. of God, who takes away the	Jn 1.29
our paschal l., has been sacrificed.	1Co 5.07
I saw a L. standing, as though it	Rev 5.06
Lord God the Almighty and the L.	21.22
send you out as l. in the midst of	Lk 10.03
He said to him, "Feed my l."	Jn 21.15

LAME

then shall the l. man leap like a	Is 35.06
their sight and the l. walk,	Mt 11.05
to enter life l. than with two	Mk 9.45

LAMP —S

the l. of God had not yet gone out,	1Sa 3.03
Thy word is a l. to my feet and a	Ps 119.105
Nor do men light a l. and put it	Mt 5.15
"The eye is the l. of the body.	6.22
He was a burning and shining l.,	Jn 5.35
its light, and its l. is the Lamb.	Rev 21.23
For when the foolish took their l.,	Mt 25.03

LANGUAGE

confused the l. of all the earth;	Gen 11.09
Jacob from a people of strange l.,	Ps 114.01
heard them speaking in his own l.	Ac 2.06
do not know the meaning of the l.,	1Co 14.11

LAST

But many that are first will be l.,	Mt 19.30
and the l. fraud will be worse than	27.64
a loud cry, and breathed his l.	Mk 15.37
me, but raise it up at the l. day.	Jn 6.39
'And in the l. days it shall be, God	Ac 2.17
The l. enemy to be destroyed is	1Co 15.26
of an eye, at the l. trumpet.	15.52
but in these l. days he has spoken	Heb 1.02
'The words of the first and the l.,	Rev 2.08

LAUGH —ED —S

that weep now, for you shall l.	Lk 6.21
Then Abraham fell on his face and l.,	Gen 17.17
but sleeping." And they l. at him.	Mt 9.24
but the LORD l. at the wicked, for	Ps 37.13

LAUGHINGSTOCK

I am a l. to my friends; I, who called	Job 12.04

LAUGHTER

Sarah said, "God has made l. for me;	Gen 21.06
Even in l. the heart is sad, and the	Pro 14.13
Let your l. be turned to mourning	Jas 4.09

LAW —S

There shall be one l. for the	Ex 12.49
This is the l. which Moses set	Deu 4.44
delight is in the l. of the LORD,	Ps 1.02
The l. of the LORD is perfect,	19.07
wondrous things out of thy l.	119.18
I will put my l. within them, and I	Jer 31.33
according to the l. of the Medes	Dan 6.08
to abolish the l. and the prophets;	Mt 5.17
depend all the l. and the prophets."	22.40
the weightier matters of the l.,	23.23
For the l. was given through Moses;	Jn 1.17
"We have a l., and by that l. he	19.07
but keep the l. will condemn you	Rom 2.27
through the l. comes nowledge of	3.20
by faith apart from works of l.	3.28
L. came in, to increase the trespass;	5.20
But now we are discharged from the l.,	7.06
That the l. is sin? By no means!	7.07
So the l. is holy, and the commandment	7.12
free from the l. of sin and death.	8.02
For Christ is the end of the l.,	10.04
love is the fulfilling of the l.	13.10
For I through the l. died to the l.,	Gal 2.19
So that the l. was our custodian	3.24
righteousness under the l. blameless.	Php 3.06
For since the l. has but a shadow	Heb 10.01
my statutes, and my l."	Gen 26.05
I will put my l. into their minds,	Heb 8.10

LAWFUL

"Is it l. to heal on the sabbath?"	Mt 12.10
"All things are l. for me," but not	1Co 6.12

LAWLESS

And then the l. one will be revealed,	2Th 2.08
the error of l. men and lose your	2Pe 3.17

LAWYER —S

a l., asked him a question, to test	Mt 22.35
Pharisees and the l. rejected the	Lk 7.30

LEAD —S

of cloud to l. them along the way,	Ex 13.21
L. me in thy truth, and teach me, for	Ps 25.05
L. thou me to the rock that is	61.02
and l. me in the way everlasting!	139.24
And I will l. the blind in a way	Is 42.16
So thou didst l. thy people, to make	63.14
And l. us not into temptation, But	Mt 6.13
"Can a blind man l. a blind man?	Lk 6.39
let every one l. the life which the	1Co 7.17
that we may l. a quiet and peaceable	1Ti 2.02
that l. to destruction, and those	Mt 7.13
own sheep by name and l. them out.	Jn 10.03
in Christ always l. us in triumph,	2Co 2.14
repentance that l. to salvation	7.10

LEADER —S

and the l. as one who serves.	Lk 22.26
at his right hand as L. and Savior,	Ac 5.31
Remember your l., those who spoke	Heb 13.07

LEAF

and its l. does not wither. In all that he   Ps 1.03
We all fade like a l., and our iniquities   Is 64.06
in the distance a fig tree in l.,   Mk 11.13

LEAN —ING

will no more l. upon him that   Is 10.20
yet they l. upon the LORD and say,   Mic 3.11
like a l. wall, a tottering fence?   Ps 62.03

LEAP —ED —ING

then shall the lame man l. like a hart,   Is 35.06
and l. for joy, for behold, your   Lk 6.23
the babe in my womb l. for joy.   1.44
saw King David l. and dancing   2Sa 6.16

LEARN —ED

Take my yoke upon you, and l. from   Mt 11.29
You did not so l. Christ!   Eph 4.20
And let our people l. to apply   Tit 3.14
has heard and l. from the Father   Jn 6.45
What you have l. and received and   Php 4.09
circumstances I have l. the secret   4.12
he l. obedience through what he   Heb 5.08

LEAST

shall be called l. in the kingdom   Mt 5.19
from the l. to the greatest, saying,   Ac 8.10
For I am the l. of the apostles,   1Co 15.09

LEAVEN

heaven is like l. which a woman   Mt 13.33
beware of the l. of the Pharisees   16.06
Cleanse out the old l. that you may   1Co 5.07

LEND

"You shall not l. upon interest to   Deu 23.19
and l., expecting nothing in return;   Lk 6.35

LENGTH

l. of days for ever and ever.   Ps 21.04
the breadth and l. and height and   Eph 3.18

LEPER —S

"The l. who has the disease shall   Lev 13.45
and behold, a l. came to him and   Mt 8.02
in the house of Simon the l.,   26.06
l. are cleansed and the deaf hear,   11.05
a village, he was met by ten l.,   17.12

LEPROSY

"When a man is afflicted with l.,   Lev 13.09
immediately his l. was cleansed.   Mt 8.03

LETTER —S

words of the l. which Jeremiah the   Jer 29.01
with the following l.: "The brethren   Ac 15.23
that you are a l. from Christ   2Co 3.03
And when this l. has been read   Col 4.16
Lord that this l. be read to all   1Th 5.27
or by l. purporting to be from us,   2Th 2.02
is the mark in every l. of mine;   3.17
"His l. are weighty and strong, but   2Co 10.10
See with what large l. I am writing   Gal 6.11

LEVEL

the uneven ground shall become l.,   Is 40.04
with them and stood on a l. place,   Lk 6.17

LIAR —S

disobeys his commandments is a l.,   1Jn 2.04
and hates his brother, he is a l.;   4.20
l., perjurers, and whatever else is   1Ti 1.10

LIBATION —S

be poured as a l. upon the sacrificial   Php 2.17
They shall not pour l. of wine to   Hos 9.04

LIBERTY

and proclaim l. throughout the land   Lev 25.10
to proclaim l. to the captives, and   Is 61.01
to set at l. those who are oppressed,   Lk 4.18
the glorious l. of the children of   Rom 8.21
why should my l. be determined by   1Co 10.29
to be judged under the law of l.   Jas 2.12

LICENTIOUSNESS

l., envy, slander, pride, foolishness.   Mk 7.22
not in debauchery and l.,   Rom 13.13
and l. which they have practiced.   2Co 12.21
plain: immorality, impurity, l.,   Gal 5.19

LIFE

into his nostrils the breath of l.;   Gen 2.07
to guard the way to the tree of l.   3.24
I have set before you l. and death,   Deu 30.19
now, O LORD, take away my l.;   1Ki 19.04
"Remember that my l. is a breath;   Job 7.07
LORD is the stronghold of my l.;   Ps 27.01
For with thee is the fountain of l.;   36.09
O Lord, what the measure of l. is,   89.47
give me l., O LORD, according to thy   119.107
The wage of the righteous leads to l.,   Pro 10.16
The fear of the LORD prolongs l.,   10.27
A gentle tongue is a tree of l.;   15.04
The fear of the LORD leads to l.;   19.23
during the few days of their l.   Ecc 2.03
In my vain l. I have seen everything;   7.15
all these is the l. of my spirit.   Is 38.16
you found new l. for your strength,   57.10
their l. shall be like a watered   Jer 31.12
O Lord, thou hast redeemed my l.   Lam 3.58
awake, some to everlasting l.,   Dan 12.02
do not be anxious about your l.,   Mt 6.25
He who finds his l. will lose it,   10.39
deed must I do, to have eternal l.?"   19.16
was l., and the l. was the light of men.   Jn 1.04
said to them, "I am the bread of l.;   6.35
It is the spirit that gives l.,   6.63
You have the words of eternal l.;   6.68
lays down his l. for the sheep.   10.11
"I am the resurrection and the l.;   11.25
the way, and the truth, and the l.;   14.06
lay down his l. for his friends.   15.13
And this is eternal l., that they know   17.03
and killed the Author of l.,   Ac 3.15
to eternal l. through Jesus Christ   Rom 5.21
but the l. he lives he lives to God.   6.10
sanctification and its end, eternal l.   6.22

LIFE (cont.)

the Spirit of l. in Christ Jesus	Rom 8.02
one lead the l. which the Lord has	1Co 7.17
does not come to l. unless it dies.	15.36
kills, but the Spirit gives l.	2Co 3.06
mortal may be swallowed up by l.	5.04
and the l. I now live in the flesh	Gal 2.20
whose names are in the book of l.	Php 4.03
When Christ who is our l. appears,	Col 3.04
consider the outcome of their l.,	Heb 13.07
the crown of l. which God has	Jas 1.12
By his good l. let him show his	3.13
hands, concerning the word of l.—	1Jn 1.01
He who has the Son has l.;	5.12
grant to eat of the tree of l.,	Rev 2.07

LIFT —ED

The LORD l. up his countenance upon	Num 6.26
I cannot l. up my head, for I am	Job 10.15
L. up your heads, O gates! and be	Ps 24.07
I l. up my eyes to the hills.	121.01
L. up your hands to the holy place,	134.02
l. up your voice with strength, O	Is 40.09
would not even l. up his eyes to	Lk 18.13
Therefore l. your drooping hands	Heb 12.12
And as Moses l. up the serpent in	Jn 3.14
that the Son of man must be l. up?	12.34
then they l. up their voices and	Ac 22.22

LIGHT —S

God called the l. Day, and the	Gen 1.05
I waited for l., darkness came.	Job 30.26
Lift up the l. of thy countenance	Ps 4.06
Oh send out thy l. and thy truth;	43.03
is God, and he has given us l.	118.27
to my feet and a l. to my path.	119.105
let us walk in the l. of the LORD.	Is 2.05
I form l. and create darkness, I	45.07
Then shall your l. break forth like	58.08
for your l. has come, and the glory	60.01
in darkness have seen a great l.,	Mt 4.16
"You are the l. of the world.	5.14
a l. for revelation to the Gentiles,	Lk 2.32
The l. shines in the darkness, and	Jn 1.05
that the l. has come into the world,	3.19
saying, "I am the l. of the world;	8.12
While you have the l., believe in the l.,	12.36
set you to be a l. for the Gentiles,	Ac 13.47
I saw on the way a l. from heaven,	26.13
darkness and put on the armor of l.;	Rom 13.12
to give the l. of the knowledge of	2Co 4.06
dead, and Christ shall give you l."	Eph 5.14
immortality to l. through the	2Ti 1.10
that God is l. and in him is no	1Jn 1.05
loves his brother abides in the l.,	2.10
By its l. shall the nations walk;	Rev 21.24
for the Lord God will be their l.,	22.05
And God made the two great l.,	Gen 1.16
whom you shine as l. in the world,	Php 2.15
the Father of l. with whom there	Jas 1.17

LIGHTNING —S

For as the l. comes from the east	Mt 24.27
His appearance was like l.,	28.03

saw Satan fall like l. from heaven.	Lk 10.18
His l. lighten the world; the earth sees	Ps 97.04

LIKENESS

man in our image, after our l.;	Gen 1.26
or what l. compare with him?	Is 40.18
"Whose l. and inscription is this?"	Mt 22.20
come down to us in the l. of men!"	Ac 14.11
own Son in the l. of sinful flesh	Rom 8.03
of Christ, who is the l. of God.	2Co 4.04
being born in the l. of men.	Php 2.07

LILIES

Consider the l. of the field, how	Mt 6.28

LIMIT (n)

find out the l. of the Almighty?	Job 11.07
I have seen a l. to all perfection,	Ps 119.96

LINE

Or who stretched the l. upon it?	Job 38.05
His l. shall endure for ever, his	Ps 89.36
l. upon l., l. upon l., here a little,	Is 28.10
and I will make justice the l.,	28.17
And the measuring l. shall go out	Jer 31.39
a wall built with a plumb l.,	Amo 7.07
with a measuring l. in his hand!	Zec 2.01

LINEN

wrapped it in a clean l. shroud,	Mt 27.59
but he left the l. cloth and ran	Mk 14.52
lying with the l. cloths but rolled	Jn 20.07
plagues, robed in pure bright l.,	Rev 15.06

LION —S

What is stronger than a l.?"	Ju 14.18
dog is better than a dead l.	Ecc 9.04
the LORD, he will roar like a l.;	Hos 11.10
prowls around like a roaring l.,	1Pe 5.08
lo, the L. of the tribe of Judah, the	Rev 5.05
promises, stopped the mouths of l.,	Heb 11.33

LIPS

than life, my l. will praise thee.	Ps 63.03
Lying l. are an abomination to the	Pro 12.22
are smooth l. with an evil heart.	26.23
for I am a man of unclean l.,	Is 6.05
'This people honors me with their l.,	Mt 15.08
with your l. that Jesus is Lord	Rom 10.09
the fruit of l. that acknowledge	Heb 13.15
sin; no guile was found on his l.	1Pe 2.22

LISTEN —ED —ING —S

Give heed, O Job, l. to me; be	Job 33.31
Hear my cry, O God, l. to my prayer;	Ps 61.01
L. to advice and accept instruction,	Pro 19.20
Do not l. to them; serve the king of	Jer 27.17
melody of your harps I will not l.	Amo 5.23
"This is my beloved Son; l. to him!"	Mk 9.07
that God does not l. to sinners,	Jn 9.31
sent to the Gentiles; they will l."	Ac 28.28
Have you l. in the council of God?	Job 15.08
and the prisoners here l. to them,	Ac 16.25
If he l. to you, you have gained	Mt 18.15
Whoever knows God l. to us, and he	1Jn 4.06

LITTLE

hast made him l. less than God,	Ps 8.05
Yet a l. while, and the wicked will	37.10
so a l. folly outweighs wisdom and	Ecc 10.01
and a l. child shall lead them.	Is 11.06
upon line, here a l. there a l."	28.10
yet a l. while and the time of her	Jer 51.33
You have sown much, and harvested l.;	Hag 1.06
more clothe you, O men of l. faith?	Mt 6.30
but he who is forgiven l., loves l."	Lk 7.47
"Fear not, l. flock, for it is your	12.32
"I shall be with you a l. longer,	Jn 7.33
"What does he mean by 'a l. while'?	16.18
not know that a l. leaven ferments	1Co 5.06
A l. yeast leavens the whole lump.	Gal 5.09
"For yet a l. while, and the coming	Heb 10.37
My l. children, I am writing this to	1Jn 2.01

LIVE —D —S

tree of life, and eat, and l. for ever"—	Gen 3.22
a man shall l.: I am the LORD.	Lev 18.05
If a man die, shall he l. again?	Job 14.14
What man can l. and never see death?	Ps 89.48
Let me l., that I may praise thee,	119.175
house of Israel: "Seek me and l.;	Amo 5.04
'Man shall not l. by bread alone,	Mt 4.04
of God, and those who hear will l.	Jn 5.25
for 'In him we l. and move and have	Ac 17.28
through faith is righteous shall l."	Rom 1.17
If we l., we l. to the Lord, and if	14.08
that those who l. might l. no longer	2Co 5.15
as dying, and behold we l.;	6.09
it is no longer I who l., but Christ	Gal 2.20
If we l. by the Spirit, let us also	5.25
For to me to l. is Christ, and to	Php 1.21
Jesus the Lord, so l. in him,	Col 2.06
this end Christ died and l. again,	Rom 14.09
we all once l. in the passions of	Eph 2.03
wounded by the sword and yet l.;	Rev 13.14
For I know that my Redeemer l.,	Job 19.25
The LORD l.; and blessed be	Ps 18.46
but l. by the power of God. For we are	2Co 13.04

LIVING

the Christ, the Son of the l. God."	Mt 16.16
not God of the dead, but of the l."	22.32
do you seek the l. among the dead?	Lk 24.05
I am the l. bread which came down	Jn 6.51
shall flow rivers of l. water.' "	7.38
first man Adam became a l. being";	1Co 15.45
we are the temple of the l. God;	2Co 6.16
For the word of God is l. and active,	Heb 4.12
fall into the hands of the l. God.	10.31
born anew to a l. hope through the	1Pe 1.03
to that l. stone, rejected by men	2.04

LOAD* —S* (n)

man will have to bear his own l.	Gal 6.05
goods of Damascus, forty camel l.	2Ki 8.09
and boys stagger under l. of wood.	Lam 5.13

LOAVES

these stones to become l. of bread."	Mt 4.03
have only five l. here and two	14.17

he took the seven l. and the fish,	15.36
to him, 'Friend, lend me three l.;	Lk 11.05

LOATHE —S

I l. my life; I would not live	Job 7.16
Does thy soul l. Zion?	Jer 14.19
He who is sated l. honey, but to one	Pro 27.07

LOCUST —S

not a single l. was left in all the	Ex 10.19
at evening; I am shaken off like a l.	Ps 109.23
I will bring l. into your country,	Ex 10.04
and his food was l. and wild honey.	Mt 3.04

LOG —S

first take the l. out of your own	Mt 7.05
he who splits l. is endangered by	Ecc 10.09

LOINS

Gird up your l. like a man, I will	Job 38.03
faithfulness the girdle of his l.	Is 11.05
But you, gird up your l.;	Jer 1.17
"Let your l. be girded and your	Lk 12.35
having girded your l. with truth,	Eph 6.14

LONELY

I am like a l. bird on the housetop.	Ps 102.07
in a boat to a l. place apart.	Mt 14.13

LONG —ED —S (v)

I l. for thy salvation, O LORD, and	Ps 119.174
For I l. to see you, that I may	Rom 1.11
and l. to put on our heavenly	2Co 5.02
brethren, whom I love and l. for,	Php 4.01
into which angels l. to look.	1Pe 1.12
they will l. to die, and death flies	Rev 9.06
righteous men l. to see what you	Mt 13.17
Like a slave who l. for the shadow,	Job 7.02
My soul l., yea, faints for the	Ps 84.02

LOOK —ED —S

do not l. back or stop anywhere in	Gen 19.17
for he was afraid to l. at God.	Ex 3.06
L. at the heavens, and see;	Job 35.05
When I l. at thy heavens, the work	Ps 8.03
their eyes will l. to the Holy One	Is 17.07
"I will quietly l. from my dwelling	18.04
we l. for justice, but there is none;	59.11
L. at the birds of the air: they	Mt 6.26
'L., here is the Christ!' or 'L., there	Mk 13.21
l., the world has gone after him."	Jn 12.19
L. at what is before your eyes.	2Co 10.07
into which angels long to l.	1Pe 1.12
But when I l. for good, evil came;	Job 30.26
The sea l. and fled, Jordan turned	Ps 114.03
But Jesus l. at them and said to	Mt 19.26
And he l. around at them with anger,	Mk 3.05
And the Lord turned and l. at Peter.	Lk 22.61
which we have l. upon and touched	1Jn 1.01
every one who l. at a woman	Mt 5.28

LOOSE —D

to l. the bonds of wickedness, to	Is 58.06
whatever you l. on earth shall be	Mt 16.19

LOOSE —D (cont.)

be l. from this bond on the	Lk 13.16
having l. the pangs of death,	Ac 2.24
Satan will be l. from his prison	Rev 20.07

LORD

The L. passed before him, and	Ex 34.06
you might know that the L. is God;	Deu 4.35
Israel: The L. our God is one L.;	6.04
said: "Thou art the L., thou alone;	Neh 9.06
For who is God, but the L.? And who	Ps 18.31
'L., L.,' shall enter the kingdom	Mt 7.21
Son of man is l. even of the	Mk 2.28
told him, "We have seen the L."	Jn 20.25
has made him both L. and Christ,	Ac 2.36
the same L. is L. of all and	Rom 10.12
not have crucified the L. of glory.	1Co 2.08
say "Jesus is L." except by the	12.03
one L., one faith, one baptism,	Eph 4.05
confess that Jesus Christ is L.,	Php 2.11
King of kings and L. of lords.	Rev 19.16

LOSE —S

better that you l. one of your	Mt 5.29
He who finds his life will l. it,	10.39
would save his life will l. it,	16.25
mercy of God, we do not l. heart.	2Co 4.01
if she l. one coin, does not light a	Lk 15.08

LOSS

that you suffered no l. through us.	2Co 7.09
I counted as l. for the sake of	Php 3.07

LOST

I have gone astray like a l. sheep;	Ps 119.176
For I am l.; for I am a man	Is 6.05
"My people have been l. sheep;	Jer 50.06
rather to the l. sheep of the	Mt 10.06
he was l., and is found.' And they	Lk 15.24
none of them is l. but the son of	Jn 17.12

LOTS

and for my raiment they cast l.	Ps 22.18
garments among them by casting l.;	Mt 27.35
And they cast l. for them, and	Ac 1.26

LOVE —D —S (v)

but you shall l. your neighbor as	Lev 19.18
L. the LORD, all you his saints! The	Ps 31.23
Therefore l. thy commandments	119.127
For I the LORD l. justice, I hate	Is 61.08
L. your enemies and pray for those	Mt 5.44
"You shall l. the Lord your God	22.37
"Lord, he whom you l. is ill."	Jn 11.03
"If you l. me, you will keep my	14.15
This I command you, to l. one another.	15.17
do you l. me more than these?"	21.15
l. one another with brotherly	Rom 12.10
whom I l. and long for, my joy and	Php 4.01
Husbands, l. your wives, and do not	Col 3.19
L. the brotherhood. Fear God. Honor	1Pe 2.17
Do not l. the world or the things	1Jn 2.15
let us not l. in word or speech but	3.18
Those whom I l., I reprove and	Rev 3.19

I l. him, and out of Egypt I called	Hos 11.01
And Jesus looking upon him l. him,	Mk 10.21
For God so l. the world that he	Jn 3.16
As the Father has l. me, so have I l. you;	15.09
conquerors through him who l. us.	Rom 8.37
who l. me and gave himself for me.	Gal 2.20
We love, because he first l. us.	1Jn 4.19
Whoever l. discipline l. knowledge,	Pro 12.01
as the LORD l. the people of	Hos 3.01
He who l. father or mother more	Mt 10.37
the Father l. the Son, and has given	Jn 3.35
He who l. his life loses it, and he	12.25
But if one l. God, one is known by	1Co 8.03
He who l. his wife l. himself.	Eph 5.28
Lord disciplines him whom he l.,	Heb 12.06
If anyone l. the world, love for	1Jn 2.15

LOVE (n)

compassion, with the bands of l.,	Hos 11.04
hold fast to l. and justice, and	12.06
I loved you; abide in my l.	Jn 15.09
Greater l. has no man than this,	15.13
But God shows his l. for us in that	Rom 5.08
separate us from the l. of Christ?	8.35
Let l. be genuine; hate what is	12.09
therefore l. is the fulfilling of	13.10
Christ and by the l. of the Spirit,	15.30
but have not l., I am a noisy gong	1Co 13.01
but the greatest of these is l.	13.13
For the l. of Christ controls us,	2Co 5.14
But the fruit of the Spirit is l.,	Gal 5.22
He destined us in l. to be his sons	Eph 1.05
in Christ, any incentive of l.,	Php 2.01
since l. covers a multitude of sins.	1Pe 4.08
know God; for God is l.	1Jn 4.08
In this is l., not that we loved	4.10
but perfect l. casts out fear.	4.18

LOVELY

How l. is thy dwelling place, O LORD	Ps 84.01
whatever is l., whatever is gracious,	Php 4.08

LOVER —S

Mighty King, l. of justice, thou hast	Ps 99.04
a l. of goodness, master of himself,	Tit 1.08
and drink: drink deeply, O l.!	Sol 5.01
Your l. despise you; they seek your	Jer 4.30
alone; Ephraim has hired l.	Hos 8.09
who were l. of money, heard all this,	Lk 16.14
For men will be l. of self,	2Ti 3.02

LOW —LY

every mountain and hill be made l.;	Is 40.04
and exalted those of l. degree;	Lk 1.52
God chose what is l. and despised	1Co 1.28
LORD is high, he regards the l.;	Ps 38.06
for I am gentle and l. in heart,	Mt 11.29
haughty, but associate with the l.;	Rom 12.16
who will change our l. body to be	Php 3.21
Let the l. brother boast in his	Jas 1.09

LOWER

into the l. parts of the earth?	Eph 4.09
while was made l. than the angels,	Heb 2.09

LOYALTY
I will sing of l. and of justice; Ps 101.01
What is desired in a man is l., Pro 19.22
vain idols forsake their true l. Jon 2.08

LUMP
a little leaven leavens the whole l.? 1Co 5.06

LUST —S*
the passion of l. like heathen who 1Th 4.05
l. of the flesh and the l. of the eyes 1Jn 2.16

them up in the l. of their hearts Rom 1.24
is corrupt through deceitful l., Eph 4.22

LYING
swaddling clothes and l. in a manger. Lk 2.12
was l. close to the breast of Jesus; Jn 13.23

LYRE —S
My l. is turned to mourning, and my Job 30.31
Praise the LORD with the l., Ps 33.02
willows there we hung up our l. 137.02

M

MAD
said, "He has a demon, and he is m.; Jn 10.20
a loud voice, "Paul, you are m.; Ac 26.24
will they not say that you are m.? 1Co 14.23

MADE
This is the day which the LORD has m.; Ps 118.24
He has m. everything beautiful in Ecc 3.11
that God m. man upright, but they 7.29
them, "The sabbath was m. for man, Mk 2.27
all things were m. through him, Jn 1.03
For our sake he m. him to be sin 2Co 5.21
m. us alive together with Christ Eph 2.05
Christ Jesus has m. me his own. Php 3.12

MAGICIAN —S
But Elymas the m. (for that is the Ac 13.08
Then the king commanded that the m., Dan 2.02
father, made him chief of the m., 5.11

MAGISTRATE* —S
go with your accuser before the m., Lk 12.58
brought them to the m. they said, Ac 16.20

MAGNIFIED —IES* —Y
Then the he-goat m. himself Dan 8.08
And Mary said, "My soul m. the Lord, Lk 1.46
O m. the LORD with me, and let us Ps 34.03
to the Gentiles, I m. my ministry Rom 11.13

MAID —S
And a m. came up to him, and said, Mt 26.69
When Esther's m. and her eunuchs Est 4.04

MAIDEN —S
The m. was very fair to look upon, a Gen 24.16
A m. or two for every man; Ju 5.30
are, O loved one, delectable m.! Sol 7.06
Can a m. forget her ornaments, or a Jer 2.32
Young men and m. together, old men Ps 148.12
compared to ten m. who took their Mt 25.01

MAIDSERVANTS
to beat the menservants and the m., Lk 12.45
menservants and my m. in those days Ac 2.18

MAIMED
the m., the blind, the dumb, and many Mt 15.30
to enter life m. or lame than with 18.08

MAINTAIN —S
everything and m. the traditions 1Co 11.02
eager to m. the unity of the Spirit Eph 4.03
M. good conduct among the Gentiles, 1Pe 2.12
that the LORD m. the cause of the Ps 140.12

MAJESTIC
m. in holiness, terrible in glorious Ex 15.11
how m. is thy name in all the earth! Ps 8.01
I will make you m. for ever, Is 60.15
was borne to him by the M. Glory, 2Pe 1.17

MAJESTY
God is clothed with terrible m. Job 37.22
Honor and m. are before him; Ps 96.06
On the glorious splendor of thy m., 145.05
were astonished at the m. of God. Lk 9.43
the right hand of the M. on high, Heb 1.03
but we were eyewitnesses of his m. 2Pe 1.16
m., dominion, and authority, before Jud 25

MAKER
Can a man be pure before his M.? Job 4.17
us kneel before the LORD, our M.! Ps 95.06
He who mocks the poor insults his M.; Pro 17.05
For Israel has forgotten his M., Hos 8.14
whose builder and m. is God. Heb 11.10

MALICE
But Jesus, aware of their m., Mt 22.18
the leaven of m. and evil, but with 1Co 5.08
be put away from you, with all m., Eph 4.31

MAN
God is not m., that he should lie, Num 23.19
but m. is born to trouble as the Job 5.07
"M. that is born of a woman is of 14.01
answer you. God is greater than m. 33.12
Blessed is the m. who walks not in Ps 1.01
what is m. that thou art mindful of 8.04
Let not m. prevail; let the nations 9.19
So m. is humbled, and men are Is 2.09
a word make a m. out to be an 29.21
He saw that there was no m., 59.16
Every m. is stupid and without Jer 10.14
for I am God and not m., the Holy Hos 11.09
'M. shall not live by bread alone, Mt 4.04
"What sort of m. is this, that even 8.27
There was a m. sent from God, whose Jn 1.06

MAN (cont.)

"Stand up; I too am a m."	Ac 10.26
"The voice of a god, and not of m.!"	12.22
the head of every m. is Christ,	1Co 11.03

MANIFEST —ED

nothing hid, except to be made m.;	Mk 4.22
on the third day and made him m.;	Ac 10.40
the life was made m.,	1Jn 1.02
of God has been m. apart from law,	Rom 3.21
Jesus may also be m. in our bodies.	2Co 4.10
He was m. in the flesh, vindicated	1Ti 3.16

MANNA

house of Israel called its name m.;	Ex 16.31
Our fathers ate the m. in the	Jn 6.31
I will give some of the hidden m.,	Rev 2.17

MANNER

"My m. of life from my youth, spent	Ac 26.04
in an unworthy m. will be guilty	1Co 11.27
Only let your m. of life be worthy	Php 1.27

MANTLE

red, all his body like a hairy m.;	Gen 25.25
And he took up the m. of Elijah	2Ki 2.13
field not turn back to take his m.	Mt 24.18
no sword sell his m. and buy one.	Lk 22.36
like a m. thou wilt roll them up,	Heb 1.12

MARCH —ED —ING

when thou didst m. through the	Ps 68.07
second day they m. around the city	Jos 6.14
And they m. up over the broad earth	Rev 20.09
m. in the greatness of his strength?	Is 63.01
As they were m. out, they came upon	Mt 27.32

MARK —S (n)

And the LORD put a m. on Cain,	Gen 4.15
my finger in the m. of the nails,	Jn 20.25
This is the m. in every letter of	2Th 3.17
have missed the m. as regards the	1Ti 6.21
and receives a m. on his forehead	Rev 14.09
to remove the m. of circumcision.	1Co 7.18
I bear on my body the m. of Jesus.	Gal 6.17

MARKET

and salutations in the m. places,	Mt 23.07
in the meat m. without raising any	1Co 10.25

MARRIAGE

king who gave a m. feast for his	Mt 22.02
neither marry nor are given in m.,	22.30
went in with him to the m. feast;	25.10
refrains from m. will do better.	1Co 7.38
Let m. be held in honor among all,	Heb 13.04
for the m. of the Lamb has come, and	Rev 19.07

MARRIED —IES —Y

the men who had m. foreign women.	Ez 10.17
the first m., and died, and having	Mt 22.25
To the m. I give charge, not I but	1Co 7.10
and m. another, commits adultery	Mt 19.09
they neither m. nor are given in	22.30
But if you m., you do not sin, and	1Co 7.28

MARVEL —ED (v)

Do not m. that I said to you, 'You	Jn 3.07
When the disciples saw it they m.,	Mt 21.20
and to be m. at in all who have	2Th 1.10

MARVELOUS

song, for he has done m. things!	Ps 98.01
LORD's doing; it is m. in our eyes.	118.23
things too great and too m. for me,	131.01
doing, and it is m. in our eyes'!	Mt 21.42
out of darkness into his m. light.	1Pe 2.09

MASONS

carpenters and m. who built David	2Sa 5.11
and to the m. and the stonecutters,	2Ki 12.12

MASTER —S (n)

And if I am a m., where is my fear?	Mal 1.06
teacher, nor a servant above his m.;	Mt 10.24
for you have one m., the Christ.	23.10
to himself, 'My m. is delayed,'	24.48
to Jesus at once and said, "Hail M.!"	26.49
is both their M. and yours is in	Eph 6.09
m. of himself, upright, holy, and	Tit 1.08
denying the M. who bought them,	1Pe 2.01
"No one can serve two m.; for either	Mt 6.24
Neither be called m., for you have	23.10
M., do the same to them, and forbear	Eph 6.09

MATTER —S

'The root of the m. is found in him';	Job 19.28
circumcision is a m. of the heart,	Rom 2.29
the weightier m. of the law,	Mt 23.23
m. pertaining to this life!	1Co 6.03

MATURE

Yet among the m. we do impart	1Co 2.06
in evil, but in thinking be m.	14.20
to m. manhood, to the measure of the	Eph 4.13
of us who are m. be thus minded;	Php 3.15
may present every man m. in Christ.	Col 1.28

MEAL

and hid in three measures of m.,	Mt 13.33
one goes ahead with his own m.,	1Co 11.21
his birthright for a single m.	Heb 12.16

MEASURE —D (v)

"To m. Jerusalem, to see what is its	Zec 2.02
But when they m. themselves by one	2Co 10.12
"Rise and m. the temple of God and	Rev 11.01
Who has m. the waters in the hollow	Is 40.12
"If the heavens above can be m.,	Jer 31.37
He stood and m. the earth;	Hab 3.06

MEASURE —S (n)

Correct me, O LORD, but in just m.;	Jer 10.24
the m. you give will be the m. you get.	Mt 7.02
up, then, the m. of your fathers.	23.32
good m., pressed down, shaken	Lk 6.38
according to the m. of faith which	Rom 12.03
to the m. of the stature of the	Eph 4.13
to fill up the m. of their sins.	1Th 2.16
took and hid in three m. of meal,	Mt 13.33

MEASURING LINE
And the m. l. shall go out farther,	Jer 31.39
a man with a m. l. in his hand!	Zec 2.01

MEAT
no m. or wine entered my mouth, nor	Dan 10.03
not to eat m. or drink wine or do	Rom 14.21
falling, I will never eat m.,	1Co 8.13

MEDITATE —S*
went out to m. in the field in the	Gen 24.63
that I may m. upon thy promise.	Ps 119.148
not to m. beforehand how to answer;	Lk 21.14
and on his law he m. day and night.	Ps 1.02

MEDITATION
mouth and the m. of my heart be	Ps 19.14
May my m. be pleasing to him, for I	104.34
thy law! It is my m. all the day.	119.97

MEDIUM —S
"Behold, there is a m. at Endor."	1Sa 28.07
"Consult the m. and the wizards who	Is 8.19

MEEK
But the m. shall possess the land,	Ps 37.11
"Blessed are the m., for they shall	Mt 5.05

MEEKNESS
by the m. and gentleness of Christ—	2Co 10.01

MEET
and went to m. the bridegroom.	Mt 25.01
When you m. together, it is not the	1Co 11.20
the clouds to m. the Lord in the	1Th 4.17

MEETING
In the tent of m., outside the veil	Ex 27.21
burned all the m. places of God in	Ps 74.08
And when the m. of the synagogue	Ac 13.43

MELODY
I will make m. to the Lord, the God	Ju 5.03
will sing and make m. to the Lord.	Ps 27.06
and making m. to the Lord with all	Eph 5.19

MELT
The mountains m. like wax before	Ps 97.05
and the elements will m. with fire!	2Pe 3.12

MEMBER —S
not consist of one m. but of many.	1Co 12.14
If one m. suffers, all suffer	12.26
one of your m. than that your	Mt 5.29
Do not yield your m. to sin as	Rom 6.13
and individually m. one of another.	12.05
that your bodies are m. of Christ?	1Co 6.15
the saints and m. of the household	Eph 2.19

MEMORIAL
"This day shall be for you a m. day,	Ex 12.14
have ascended as a m. before God.	Ac 10.04

MEMORY
His m. perishes from the earth, and	Job 18.17
has done will be told in m. of her."	Mt 26.13

MEN
nations know that they are but m.!	Ps 9.20
"M. are all a vain hope."	116.11
the hearts of m. are full of evil,	Ecc 9.03
The Egyptians are m., and not God;	Is 31.03
He was despised and rejected by m.;	53.03
foolishness of God is wiser than m.,	1Co 1.25
not to please m., but to please God	1Th 2.04
spirits of just m. made perfect,	Heb 12.23
Honor all m. Love the brotherhood.	1Pe 2.17

MEND—ED —ING
M. your ways, heed my appeal, agree	2Co 13.11
wineskins, worn-out and torn and m.,	Jos 9.04
m. their nets, and he called them.	Mt 4.21

MERCHANT —S
is like a m. in search of fine	Mt 13.45
and the m. of the earth have grown	Rev 18.03

MERCIES —Y
by the m. of God, to present your	Rom 12.01
the Father of m. and God of all	2Co 1.03
shall make a m. seat of pure gold;	Ex 25.17
Surely goodness and m. shall follow	Ps 23.06
Have m. on me, O God, according to	51.01
Have m. upon us, O Lord, have m.	123.03
it known; in wrath remember m.	Hab 3.02
merciful, for they shall obtain m.	Mt 5.07
'I desire m., and not sacrifice.'	9.13
the law, justice and m. and faith;	23.23
"I will have m. on whom I have m.,	Rom 9.15
he who does acts of m.,	12.08
by the Lord's m. is trustworthy.	1Co 7.25
this ministry by the m. of God,	2Co 4.01
But God, who is rich in m.,	Eph 2.04
of glory overshadowing the m. seat.	Heb 9.05
yet m. triumphs over judgment.	Jas 2.13
By his great m. we have been born	1Pe 1.03

MERCIFUL
Be m. to me, O God, be m. to me,	Ps 57.01
The Lord is m. and gracious, slow to	103.08
"Blessed are the m., for they	Mt 5.07
saying, 'God, be m. to me a sinner!'	Lk 18.13

MERE —LY
every man stands as a m. breath!	Ps 39.05
They utter m. words; with empty	Hos 10.04
m. busybodies, not doing any work.	2Th 3.11
to Apollos," are you not m. men?	1Co 3.04

MERRY
drink your wine with a m. heart;	Ecc 9.07
take your ease, eat, drink, be m.'	Lk 12.19

MESSAGE
been sent the m. of this salvation.	Ac 13.26
speech and my m. were not in	1Co 2.04
to us the m. of reconciliation.	2Co 5.19
For if the m. declared by angels	Heb 2.02
This is the m. we have heard from	1Jn 1.05

MESSENGER —S
is a faithful m. to those who send	Pro 25.13

MESSENGER —S (cont.)

the m. of the covenant in whom you	Mal 3.01
I send my m. before thy face, who	Mt 11.10
a m. of Satan, to harass me, to keep	2Co 12.07
and your m. and minister to my need,	Php 2.25
And he sent m. ahead of him,	Lk 9.51
they are m. of the churches, the	2Co 8.23

MESSIAH*

have found the M." (which means	Jn 1.41
"I know that M. is coming (he who	4.25

MIDST

am the LORD in the m. of the earth.	Ex 8.22
Moses out of the m. of the cloud.	24.16
in the m. of the congregation I	Ps 22.22
salvation in the m. of the earth.	74.12
I will dwell in their m. for ever.	Eze 43.09
"Is not the LORD in the m. of us?	Mic 3.11
out as sheep in the m. of wolves;	Mt 10.16
name, there am I in the m. of them."	18.20
kingdom of God is in the m. of you."	Lk 17.21
in the m. of the congregation I	Heb 2.12
For the Lamb in the m. of the	Rev 7.17

MIGHT (n)

your soul, and with all your m.	Deu 6.05
"With God are wisdom and m.;	Job 12.13
But I will sing of thy m.;	Ps 59.16
Behold, the Lord GOD comes with m.,	Is 40.10
Not by m., nor by power, but by my	Zec 4.06
Lord and in the strength of his m.	Eph 6.10
according to his glorious m.,	Col 1.11
Lord and from the glory of his m.,	2Th 1.09

MIGHTIER

M. than the thunders of many waters,	Ps 93.04
is coming after me is m. than I,	Mt 3.11

MIGHTY

"Like Nimrod a m. hunter before the	Gen 10.09
thy high places! How are the m. fallen!	2Sa 1.19
strong and m., the LORD, m. in battle!	Ps 24.08
M. God, Everlasting Father, Prince of	Is 9.06
The LORD goes forth like a m. man,	42.13
your Redeemer, the M. One of Jacob."	49.26
announcing vindication, m. to save."	63.01
most of his m. works had been done,	Mt 11.20
And he did not do many m. works	13.58
own tongues the m. works of God."	Ac 2.11
signs and wonders and m. works.	2Co 12.12
therefore under the m. hand of God,	1Pe 5.06

MILK

not boil a kid in its mother's m.	Ex 23.19
buy wine and m. without money and	Is 55.01
I fed you with m., not solid food;	1Co 3.02
without getting some of the m.?	9.07
who lives on m. is unskilled in	Heb 5.13
long for the pure spiritual m.,	1Pe 2.02

MILLSTONE

to have a great m. fastened round	Mt 18.06
like a great m. and threw it into	Rev 18.21

MIND —S (n)

not given you a m. to understand,	Deu 29.04
test my heart and my m.	Ps 26.02
For the inward m. and heart of a	64.06
A man's m. plans his way, but the	16.09
Many are the plans in the m. of a man,	19.21
who trusts in his own m. is a fool;	28.26
And I applied my m. to know wisdom	Ecc 1.17
he has put eternity into man's m.,	3.11
LORD search the m. and try the	Jer 17.10
and set your m. upon all that I	Eze 40.04
your soul, and with all your m.	Mt 22.37
are to drink, nor be of anxious m.	Lk 12.29
up to a base m. and to improper	Rom 1.28
To set the m. on the flesh is death,	8.06
knows what is the m. of the Spirit,	8.27
"For who has known the m. of the Lord,	11.34
But we have the m. of Christ.	1Co 2.16
Have this m. among yourselves, which	Php 2.05
a tender heart and a humble m.	1Pe 3.08
This calls for a m. with wisdom:	Rev 17.09
closed their m. to understanding,	Job 17.04
thou who triest the m. and hearts,	Ps 7.09
Then he opened their m. to understand	Lk 24.45
is read a veil lies over their m.;	2Co 3.15
Set your m. on things that are	Col 3.02
I will put my laws into their m.,	Heb 8.10

MINISTER —ED —ING (v)

in prison, and did not m. to thee?'	Mt 25.44
your messenger and m. to my need,	Php 2.25
behold, angels came and m. to him.	Mt 4.11
Are they not all m. spirits sent	Heb 1.14

MINISTER —S (n)

to be a m. of Christ Jesus to the	Rom 15.16
I was made a m. according to the	Eph 3.07
will be a good m. of Christ Jesus,	1Ti 4.06
a m. in the sanctuary and the true	Heb 8.02
for the authorities are m. of God,	Rom 13.06
us to be m. of a new covenant, not	2Co 3.06

MINISTRY

Jesus, when he began his m.,	Lk 3.23
place in this m. and apostleship	Ac 1.25
prayer and to the m. of the word."	6.04
Gentiles, I magnify my m.	Rom 11.13
having this m. by the mercy of God,	2Co 4.01
and gave us the m. of reconciliation;	5.18
you fulfil the m. which you have	Col 4.17
of an evangelist, fulfil your m.	2Ti 4.05
has obtained a m. which is as much	Heb 8.06

MIRACLES

extraordinary m. by the hands of	Ac 19.11
to another the working of m.,	1Co 12.10

MISERIES* —Y

howl for the m. that are coming	Jas 5.01
You will forget your m.;	Job 11.16
in their paths are ruin and m.,	Rom 3.16

MISFORTUNE

at ease there is contempt for m.;	Job 12.05

MISFORTUNE (cont.)
M. pursues sinners, but prosperity   Pro 13.21
time and saw no m. come to him,   Ac 28.06

MISLEAD —S
your leaders m. you, and confuse the   Is 3.12
He who m. the upright into an evil   Pro 28.10

MIST —S
but a m. went up from the earth and   Gen 2.06
For you are a m. that appears for a   Jas 4.14
springs and m. driven by a storm;   2Pe 2.17

MIX —ED
m. a double draught for her in the   Rev 18.06
fill cups of m. wine for Destiny;   Is 65.11
m. with blood, which fell on the   Rev 8.07

MOAN —S (v)
I think of God, and I m.;   Ps 77.03
Therefore my heart m. for Moab like   Jer 48.36

MOANING (n)
I am weary with my m.; every night   Ps 6.06

MOCK —ED
All who see me m. at me, they make   Ps 22.07
and they will m. him, and spit upon   Mk 10.34
your servants you have m. the Lord,   Is 37.24
And when they had m. him,   Mt 27.31
The soldiers also m. him,   Lk 23.36
resurrection of the dead, some m.;   Ac 17.32
God is not m., for whatever a man   Gal 6.07

MOCKING (n)
Others suffered m. and scourging,   Heb 11.36

MOLTEN
a graving tool, and made a m. calf;   Ex 32.04
shall make for yourself no m. gods.   34.17
their m. images are empty wind.   Is 41.29

MOMENT
For his anger is but for a m.,   Ps 30.05
of the world in a m. of time,   Lk 4.05
in a m., in the twinkling of an eye,   1Co 15.52
not yield submission even for a m.,   Gal 2.05
For the m. all discipline seems   Heb 12.11

MONEY
are lending them m. and grain.   Neh 5.10
you shall be redeemed without m.   Is 52.03
and he who has no m., come, buy   55.01
Show me the m. for the tax."   Mt 22.19
no bag, no m. in their belts;   Mk 6.08
The Pharisees, who were lovers of m.,   Lk 16.14
that, because Judas had the m. box,   Jn 13.29
obtain the gift of God with m.!   Ac 8.20
For the love of m. is the root of   1Ti 6.10
Keep your life free from love of m.,   Heb 13.05

MONEY-CHANGERS*
tables of the m. and the seats of   Mt 21.12
tables of the m. and the seats of   Mk 11.15

and the m. at their business.   Jn 2.14
coins of the m. and overturned   2.15

MONTHS
and m., and seasons, and years!   Gal 4.10

MOON —S
He covers the face of the m.,   Job 26.09
the m. and the stars which thou   Ps 8.03
and the m. will not give its light,   Mt 24.29
sun, and another glory of the m.,   1Co 15.41
festival or a new m. or a sabbath.   Col 2.16
with the m. under her feet, and on   Rev 12.01
her new m., her sabbaths, and all   Hos 2.11

MORNING
nor see the eyelids of the m.;   Job 3.09
dost visit him every m., and test   7.18
when the m. stars sang together, and   38.07
Evening and m. and at noon I utter   Ps 55.17
in the m. my prayer comes before   88.13
M. by m. I will destroy all the   101.08
In the m. sow your seed, and at   Ecc 11.06
Be our arm every m., our salvation   Is 33.02
LORD: " 'Execute justice in the m.,   Jer 21.12
Your love is like a m. cloud,   Hos 6.04
early in the m. to hire laborers   Mt 20.01
When m. came, all the chief priests   27.01
dawns and the m. star rises in   2Pe 1.19
of David, the bright m. star."   Rev 22.16

MORSEL
bread, and dip your m. in the wine."   Ru 2.14
or have eaten my m. alone,   Job 31.17
shall give this m. when I have   Jn 13.26

MORTAL
'Can m. man be righteous before God?   Job 4.17
therefore reign in your m. bodies,   Rom 6.12
and the m. puts on immortality, then   1Co 15.54
so that what is m. may be swallowed   2Co 5.04
committing what is not a m. sin,   1Jn 5.16

MOTHER
"Honor your father and your m.,   Ex 20.12
a city which is a m. in Israel;   2Sa 20.19
to the worm, 'My m.,' or 'My sister,'   Job 17.14
father and my m. have forsaken me,   Ps 27.10
foolish son is a sorrow to his m.   Pro 10.01
As one whom his m. comforts,   Is 66.13
about you. 'Like m., like daughter.'   Eze 16.44
When his m. Mary had been betrothed   Mt 1.18
loves father or m. more than me is   10.37
"Who is my m., and who are my brothers?"   12.48
to the disciple, "Behold your m.!"   Jn 19.27
above is free, and she is our m.   Gal 4.26
"Honor your father and m." (this is   Eph 6.02

MOUNTAIN —S
and came to Horeb, the m. of God.   Ex 3.01
His holy m., beautiful in elevation,   Ps 48.02
devil took him to a very high m.,   Mt 4.08
the crowds, he went up on the m.,   5.01
and led them up a high m. apart.   17.01

MOUNTAIN —S (cont.)
neither on this m. nor in Jerusalem	Jn 4.21
high m., and showed me the holy	Rev 21.10
righteousness is like the m. of God,	Ps 36.06
Before the m. were brought forth, or	90.02
They sacrifice on the tops of the m.,	Hos 4.13
who are in Judea flee to the m.;	Mt 24.16
to say to the m., 'Fall on us';	Lk 23.30
have all faith, so as to remove m.,	1Co 13.02

MOURN —ING
a time to m., and a time to dance;	Ecc 3.04
"Blessed are those who m., for they shall	Mt 5.04
wedding guests m. as long as the	9.15
Ought you not rather to m.?	1Co 5.02
m. as though they were not m.,	7.30

MOURNING (n)
turned for me my m. into dancing;	Ps 30.11
the oil of gladness instead of m.,	Is 61.03
I will turn their m. into joy, I will	Jer 31.13
I will turn your feasts into m.,	Amo 8.10

MOUTH —S
Men have gaped at me with their m.,	Job 16.10
by the m. of babes and infants, thou	Ps 8.02
Let the words of my m. and the	19.14
My m. is filled with thy praise, and	71.08
Set a guard over my m., O LORD,	141.03
He who guards his m. preserves his	Pro 13.03
A fool's m. is his ruin, and his lips	18.07
thread, and your m. is lovely.	Sol 4.03
for the m. of the LORD has spoken."	Is 1.20
And he touched my m., and said,	6.07
He made my m. like a sharp sword, in	49.02
that proceeds from the m. of God.' "	Mt 4.04
abundance of the heart the m. speaks.	12.34
for I will give you a m. and wisdom,	Lk 21.15
so that every m. may be stopped, and	Rom 3.19
hot, I will spew you out of my m.	Rev 3.16
They have m., but do not speak;	Ps 115.05
promises, stopped the m. of lions,	Heb 11.33

MOVE —D —ING
set up an image that will not m.	Is 40.20
him we live and m. and have our	Ac 17.28
in his heart, "I shall not be m.;	Ps 10.06
I shall not be greatly m.	62.02
Mount Zion, which cannot be m.,	125.01
M. with pity, he stretched out his	Mk 1.41
deeply m. again, came to the tomb;	Jn 11.38
that no one be m. by these afflictions.	1Th 3.03
but men m. by the Holy Spirit spoke	2Pe 1.21
of God was m. over the face of the	Gen 1.02

MULTIPLIED —IES —Y
Thou hast m. the nation, thou hast	Is 9.03

And because wickedness is m.,	Mt 24.12
But the word of God grew and m.	Ac 12.24
A fool m. words, though no man	Ecc 10.14
"Be fruitful and m. and fill the	Gen 1.22
will supply and m. your resources	2Co 9.10

MULTITUDE —S
'From men,' we are afraid of the m.;	Mt 21.26
death and will cover a m. of sins.	Jas 5.20
to the Lord, m. both of men and women,	Ac 5.14
are peoples and m. and nations and	Rev 17.15

MURDER
m., adultery, fornication, theft,	Mt 15.19
Full of envy, m., strife, deceit,	Rom 1.29

MURDERER
The m. rises in the dark, that he	Job 24.14
He was a m. from the beginning, and	Jn 8.44
another, "No doubt this man is a m.	Ac 28.04
But let none of you suffer as a m.,	1Pe 4.15
Any one who hates his brother is a m.,	1Jn 3.15

MURMUR —ED
"Do not m. among yourselves.	Jn 6.43
And the people m. against Moses,	Ex 15.24
And the Pharisees and the scribes m.,	Lk 15.02

MUSIC
instruments for m. to the LORD	2Ch 7.06
for themselves instruments of m.;	Amo 6.05
the house, he heard m. and dancing.	Lk 15.25

MUSTARD
have faith as a grain of m. seed,	Mt 17.20

MUSTER —ING*
and m. an army like the army that	1Ki 20.25
of hosts is m. a host for battle.	Is 13.04

MYRRH
gold and frankincense and m.	Mt 2.11
offered him wine mingled with m.;	Mk 15.23

MYSTERIES —Y
is a God in heaven who reveals m.,	Dan 2.28
and stewards of the m. of God.	1Co 4.01
understand all m. and all knowledge,	13.02
I want you to understand this m.,	Rom 11.25
I tell you a m. We shall not all	1Co 15.51
This is a great m., and I take it to	Eph 5.32
to proclaim the m. of the gospel,	6.19
knowledge of God's m., of Christ,	Col 2.02
they must hold the m. of the faith	1Ti 3.09

MYTHS
to do with godless and silly m.	1Ti 4.07

N

NAILS
in his hands the print of the n.,   Jn 20.25

NAKED —NESS
And the man and his wife were both n.,   Gen 2.25
I was n. and you clothed me, I was   Mt 25.36
the linen cloth and ran away n.   Mk 14.52
or n., or peril, or sword?   Rom 8.35

NAME —S (n)
The man called his wife's n. Eve,   Gen 3.20
Abram called on the n. of the LORD.   13.04
but your n. shall be Abraham;   17.05
this is my n. for ever, and thus I   Ex 3.15
blessed be the n. of the LORD."   Job 1.21
The n. of the God of Jacob protect   Ps 20.01
As thy n., O God, so thy praise   48.10
May his n. endure for ever, his fame   72.17
is within me, bless his holy n.!   103.01
Our help is in the n. of the LORD,   124.08
and shall call his n. Immanuel.   Is 7.14
I am the LORD, that is my n.;   42.08
"Call his n. Not my people, for you   Hos 1.09
and you shall call his n. Jesus,   Mt 1.21
art in heaven, Hallowed be thy n.   6.09
did we not prophesy in your n.,   7.22
two or three are gathered in my n.,   18.20
them in the n. of the Father and   28.19
works that I do in my Father's n.,   Jn 10.25
And his n., by faith in his n., has   Ac 3.16
is no other n. under heaven given   4.12
so that my n. may be proclaimed in   Rom 9.17
and above every n. that is named,   Eph 1.21
of lips that acknowledge his n.   Heb 13.15
but under that n. let him glorify   1Pe 4.16
with a new n. written on the stone   Rev 2.17
Now these are the n. of the   Gen 46.08
The n. of the twelve apostles are   Mt 10.02
whose n. are in the book of life.   Php 4.03

NARROW
covering too n. to wrap oneself in   Is 28.20
"Enter by the n. gate; for the   Mt 7.13

NATION —S
And I will make of you a great n.,   Gen 12.02
Blessed is the n. whose God is the   Ps 33.12
Righteousness exalts a n.,   Pro 14.34
For n. will rise against n., and   Mt 24.07
found this man perverting our n.,   Lk 23.02
that Jesus should die for the n.,   Jn 11.51
men from every n. under heaven.   Ac 2.05
from one every n. of men to live   17.26
a holy n., God's own people, that you   1Pe 2.09
to every n. and tribe and tongue   Rev 14.06
"Two n. are in your womb, and two   Gen 25.23
Why do the n. conspire, and the   Ps 2.01
Say among the n., "The LORD reigns!   96.10
Praise the LORD, all n.! Extol him,   117.01
Draw near, O n., to hear, and   Is 34.01
And n. shall come to your light, and   60.03
appointed you a prophet to the n."   Jer 1.05
world, as a testimony to all n.;   Mt 24.14

and make disciples of all n.,   28.19
a house of prayer for all the n.'?   Mk 11.17
must first be preached to all n.   13.10
by angels, preached among the n.,   1Ti 3.16
All n. shall come and worship thee,   Rev 15.04
By its light shall the n. walk;   21.24

NATIVE —S
each of us in his own n. language?   Ac 2.08
And the n. showed us unusual kindness,   28.02

NATURE
of like n. with you, and bring you   Ac 14.15
the law do by n. what the law   Rom 2.14
Does not n. itself teach you that   1Co 11.14
For this perishable n. must put on   15.53
our inner n. is being renewed every   2Co 4.16
to beings that by n. are no gods;   Gal 4.08
and put on the new n., created after   Eph 4.24
and bears the very stamp of his n.,   Heb 1.03

NECESSARY
Was it not n. that the Christ   Lk 24.26
hence it is n. for this priest also   Heb 8.03

NECESSITIES* —Y*
these hands ministered to my n.,   Ac 20.34
being under no n. but having his   1Co 7.37
For n. is laid upon me. Woe to me   9.16

NECK —S
round his n. and to be drowned in   Mt 18.06
a yoke upon the n. of the disciples   Ac 15.10
who risked their n. for my life,   Rom 16.04

NEED —FUL
knows what you n. before you ask   Mt 6.08
one thing is n. Mary has chosen   Lk 10.42

NEED (n)
distributed them to all, as any had n.   Ac 2.45
"I have no n. of you," nor again the   1Co 12.21
find grace to help in time of n.   Heb 4.16

NEEDLE
the eye of a n. than for a rich   Mt 19.24

NEGLECT
and n. justice and the love of God: Lk 11.42
Do not n. the gift you have, which   1Ti 4.14
we escape if we n. such a great   Heb 2.03

NEIGHBOR —HOOD
bear false witness against your n.   Ex 20.16
Better is a n. who is near than a   Pro 27.10
You shall love your n. as yourself."   Mt 19.19
said to Jesus, "And who is my n.?"   Lk 10.29
Love does no wrong to a n.;   Rom 13.10
who are you that you judge your n.?   Jas 4.12
they begged him to leave their n.   Mt 8.34

NESTS
and birds of the air have n.;   Mt 8.20
come and make n. in its branches."   13.32

NET —S

brother, casting a n. into the sea;	Mt 4.18
is like a n. which was thrown into	13.47
were so many, the n. was not torn.	Jn 21.11
Immediately they left their n. and	Mt 4.20

NEW

O sing to the LORD a n. song;	Ps 96.01
there is nothing n. under the sun.	Ecc 1.09
I create n. heavens and a n. earth;	Is 65.17
I will make a n. covenant with the	Jer 31.31
and put a n. spirit within them;	Eze 11.19
Neither is n. wine put into old	Mt 9.17
when I drink it n. with you in my	26.29
A n. teaching! With authority	Mk 1.27
A n. commandment I give to you, that	Jn 13.34
"This cup is the n. covenant in my	1Co 11.25
is in Christ, he is a n. creation;	2Co 5.17
is the mediator of a n. covenant,	Heb 9.15
Then I saw a n. heaven and a n. earth;	Rev 21.01

NEWS

This day is a day of good n.;	2Ki 7.09
poor have good n. preached to them.	Mt 11.05
preach the good n. of the kingdom	Lk 4.43
preached good n. about the kingdom	Ac 8.12
feet of those who preach good n.!"	Rom 10.15

NIGHT —S

'But the n. is long, and I am full	Job 7.04
on his law he meditates day and n.	Ps 1.02
Her lamp does not go out at n.	Pro 31.18
of the n.? Watchman, what of the n.?"	Is 21.11
the moon give light to you by n.,	60.19
so that day and n. will not come	Jer 33.20
the child and his mother by n.,	Mt 2.14
this very n., before the cock crows,	26.34
This n. your soul is required of	Lk 12.20
But if any one walks in the n.,	Jn 11.10
immediately went out; and it was n.	13.30

they earnestly worship n. and day.	Ac 26.07
Jesus on the n. when he was	1Co 11.23
the fish three days and three n.	Jon 1.17
And he fasted forty days and forty n.,	Mt 4.02

NINETY-NINE

not leave the n. on the hills and	Mt 18.12

NOBLE

powerful, not many were of n. birth;	1Co 1.26
of bishop, he desires a n. task.	1Ti 3.01

NOISE —Y

Make a joyful n. to the LORD, all	Ps 100.01
will pass away with a loud n.,	2Pe 3.10
I am a n. gong or a clanging cymbal.	1Co 13.01

NOON —DAY

we stumble at n. as in the twilight,	Is 59.10
"I will make the sun go down at n.,	Amo 8.09
and grope at n. as in the night.	Job 5.14

NOSTRILS

into his n. the breath of life;	Gen 2.07
and the spirit of God is in my n.;	Job 27.03
These are a smoke in my n.,	Is 65.05

NOTHING

"Is it n. to you, all you who pass	Lam 1.12
and n. will be impossible to you."	Mt 17.20
"I can do n. on my own authority;	Jn 5.30
I glorify myself, my glory is n.;	8.54
Hitherto you have asked n. in my name;	16.24
Lord Jesus that n. is unclean in	Rom 14.14
to bring to n. things that are,	1Co 1.28
who were of repute added n. to me;	Gal 2.06

NOURISHED

n. and knit together through its	Col 2.19
n. on the words of the faith and of	1Ti 4.06

O

OBEDIENCE

so by one man's o. many will be	Rom 5.19
me to win o. from the Gentiles, by	15.18
he learned o. through what he	Heb 5.08

OBEDIENT

to Nazareth, and was o. to them;	Lk 2.51
Slaves, be o. to those who are your	Eph 6.05
himself and became o. unto death,	Php 2.08

OBEY —ED

if you will o. my commandments	Deu 11.13
that even winds and sea o. him?"	Mt 8.27
"We must o. God rather than men.	Ac 5.29
are slaves of the one whom you o.,	Rom 6.16
thought captive to o. Christ,	2Co 10.05
we love God and o. his commandments.	1Jn 5.02
By faith Abraham o. when he was	Heb 11.08

OBJECT —S (n)

so-called god or o. of worship,	2Th 2.04
observed the o. of your worship, I	Ac 17.23

OBSERVANCE

by the o. of which a man shall live,	Neh 9.29
you yourself live in o. of the law.	Ac 21.24

OBSERVE —D

" 'O the sabbath day, to keep it	Deu 5.12
teaching them to o. all that I have	Mt 28.20
You o. days, and months, and seasons,	Gal 4.10
said to him, "All these I have o.;	Mt 19.20
is not coming with signs to be o.;	Lk 17.20

OBTAIN —ED

merciful, for they shall o. mercy.	Mt 5.07
you could o. the gift of God with	Ac 8.20

OBTAIN —ED (cont.)
Israel failed to o. what it sought.   Rom 11.07
but to o. salvation through our   1Th 5.09
no one fail to o. the grace of God;   Heb 12.15
you will o. the unfading crown of   1Pe 5.04
Through him we have o. access to   Rom 5.02
I have already o. this or am   Php 3.12

ODOR —S
the LORD smelled the pleasing o.,   Gen 8.21
by this time there will be an o.,   Jn 11.39
I will not smell your pleasing o.   Lev 26.31

OFFENSE
blessed is he who takes no o. at me."   Lk 7.23
Give no o. to Jews or to Greeks or   1Co 10.32

OFFER —ED (v)
O. right sacrifices, and put your   Ps 4.05
and o. the gift that Moses commanded,   Mt 8.04
on the cheek, o. the other also;   Lk 6.29
and thus let us o. to God acceptable   Heb 12.28
to o. spiritual sacrifices acceptable   1Pe 2.05
Now concerning food o. to idols: 1Co 8.01
o. up Isaac, and he who had received   Heb 11.17

OFFERING (n)
to you about the o. for the saints,   2Co 9.01
the sacrificial o. of your faith,   Php 2.17
For by a single o. he has perfected   Heb 10.14

OFFICE
Matthew sitting at the tax o.;   Mt 9.09
to the divine o. which was given   Col 1.25
one aspires to the o. of bishop,   1Ti 3.01
by death from continuing in o.;   Heb 7.23

OFFSPRING
I will bring your o. from the east,   Is 43.05
"And to your o.," which is Christ.   Gal 3.16
I am the root and the o. of David,   Rev 22.16

OFTEN
How o. would I have gathered your   Mt 23.37
Do this, as o. as you drink it, in   1Co 11.25

OIL
thou anointest my head with o.,   Ps 23.05
lamps, they took no o. with them;   Mt 25.03
his wounds, pouring on o. and wine;   Lk 10.34
thee with the o. of gladness   Heb 1.09

OINTMENT —S
alabaster jar of very expensive o.,   Mt 26.07
the Lord with o. and wiped his   Jn 11.02
returned, and prepared spices and o.   Lk 23.56

OLD
Now Abraham and Sarah were o.,   Gen 18.11
Yet God my King is from of o.,   Ps 74.12
Who declared it of o.? Was it not   Is 45.21
of unshrunk cloth on an o. garment,   Mt 9.16
treasure what is new and what is o."   13.52
can a man be born when he is o.?   Jn 3.04

"You are not yet fifty years o.,   8.57
We know that our o. self was   Rom 6.06
the o. has passed away, behold, the   2Co 5.17
Put off your o. nature which   Eph 4.22
God spoke of o. to our fathers by   Heb 1.01

OLIVE
a wild o. shoot, were grafted in   Rom 11.17

OPEN —ED
O Lord, o. thou my lips, and my   Ps 51.15
saying, 'Lord, lord, o. to us.'   Mt 25.11
"Their throat is an o. grave,   Rom 3.13
I have set before you an o. door,   Rev 3.08
Then the eyes of both were o.,   Gen 3.07
heavens were o. and he saw the   Mt 3.16
to him who knocks it will be o.   7.08
Then I saw heaven o., and behold,   Rev 19.11

OPENLY
could no longer o. enter a town,   Mk 1.45
him, "I have spoken o. to the world;   Jn 18.20
Christ quite o. and unhindered.   Ac 28.31

OPINION —S
but I give my o. as one who by the   1Co 7.25
him, but not for disputes over o.   Rom 14.01

OPPORTUNITY
he sought an o. to betray him.   Mt 26.16
finding o. in the commandment,   Rom 7.08
freedom as an o. for the flesh,   Gal 5.13
and give no o. to the devil.   Eph 4.27

OPPOSE —D —S —ING
so these men also o. the truth,   2Ti 3.08
for these are to each other, to   Gal 5.17
"God o. the proud, but gives grace   Jas 4.06
You might even be found o. God!"   Ac 5.39

OPPRESS —ED
"You shall not o. your neighbor or   Lev 19.13
who o. the poor, who crush the needy,   Amo 4.01
He was o., and he was afflicted, yet   Is 53.07
to set at liberty those who are o.,   Lk 4.18

ORACLES
are entrusted with the o. of God.   Rom 3.02
as one who utters o. of God;   1Pe 4.11

ORDAIN —ED
thou wilt o. peace for us, thou hast   Is 26.12
he is the one o. by God to be,   Ac 10.42
as many as were o. to eternal life   13.48
and it was o. by angels through an   Gal 3.19

ORDER
should be done decently and in o.   1Co 14.40
But each in his own o.: Christ the first   15.23
ever, after the o. of Melchizedek."   Heb 5.06

ORDINANCE —S
shall observe it as an o. for ever.   Ex 12.14
the o. of the LORD are true, and   Ps 19.09

ORDINANCE —S (cont.)
commandments and o. of the LORD	Lk 1.06
the law of commandments and o.,	Eph 2.15

OUGHT
these you o. to have done, without	Mt 23.23
law, and by that law he o. to die,	Jn 19.07
more highly than he o. to think,	Rom 12.03
and we o. to lay down our lives for	1Jn 3.16

OURSELVES
and let us make a name for o.,	Gen 11.04
but we o., who have the first	Rom 8.23
For what we preach is not o.,	2Co 4.05
we deceive o., and the truth is not	1Jn 1.08

OUTER
be thrown into the o. darkness;	Mt 8.12
Though our o. nature is wasting	2Co 4.16
go continually into the o. tent,	Heb 9.06

OUTSIDE
mother and his brothers stood o.,	Mt 12.46
you cleanse the o. of the cup and	23.25
God judges those o. Drive out the	1Co 5.13
for sin are burned o. the camp.	Heb 13.11

OUTSIDER —S
position of an o. say the "Amen" to	1Co 14.16
Conduct yourselves wisely toward o.,	Col 4.05
you may command the respect of o.,	1Th 4.12

OUTSTRETCHED
with a strong hand and an o. arm,	Ps 136.12
power and my o. arm have made the	Jer 27.05

OVERCOME —S
and the darkness has not o. it.	Jn 1.05
of good cheer, I have o. the world."	16.33
Do not be o. by evil, but o. evil	Rom 12.21
Who is it that o. the world but he	1Jn 5.05

OVERFLOW —S
their hearts o. with follies.	Ps 73.07
saints but also o. in many thanksgivings	2Co 9.12

OVERTAKE —N
light, lest the darkness o. you;	Jn 12.35
No temptation has o. you that is	1Co 10.13
if a man is o. in any trespass, you	Gal 6.01

OVERWHELM —ED
the rivers, they shall not o. you;	Is 43.02
or he may be o. by excessive sorrow.	2Co 2.07

OWN
and his o. people received him not.	Jn 1.11
I know my o. and my o. know me,	10.14

OX —EN
an ass or an o. that has fallen	Lk 14.05
not muzzle an o. when it is	1Co 9.09
Is it for o. that God is concerned?	9.09

P

PAIN
in p. you shall bring forth children,	Gen 3.16
my p. is not assuaged, and if I	Job 16.06
How long must I bear p. in my soul,	Ps 13.02
For all his days are full of p.,	Ecc 2.23
I writhe in p.! Oh, the walls	Jer 4.19
For if I cause you p., who is there	2Co 2.02
he endures p. while suffering	1Pe 2.19
mourning nor crying nor p. any more,	Rev 21.04

PALACE —S
gathered in the p. of the high	Mt 26.03
fully armed, guards his own p.,	Lk 11.21
From ivory p. stringed instruments	Ps 45.08

PALLET
let down the p. on which the	Mk 2.04
"Rise, take up your p., and walk."	Jn 5.08

PALM
branches of p. trees and went out	Jn 12.13
with p. branches in their hands,	Rev 7.09

PALMS
graven you on the p. of my hands;	Is 49.16

PANGS
or p. of conscience, for having shed	1Sa 25.31
Many are the p. of the wicked;	Ps 32.10

p. have seized me, like the p. of a	Is 21.03
up, having loosed the p. of death,	Ac 2.24

PANIC
Do not be afraid of sudden p.,	Pro 3.25
LORD: We have heard a cry of p.,	Jer 30.05

PARABLE —S
I will open my mouth in a p.;	Ps 78.02
"Hear then the p. of the sower.	Mt 13.18
did not speak to them without a p.,	Mk 4.34
So he told them this p.:	Lk 15.03
and through the prophets gave p.	Hos 12.10
This is why I speak to them in p.,	Mt 13.13
Jesus spoke to them in p., saying,	22.01

PARALYTIC —S*
And behold, they brought to him a p.,	Mt 9.02
and p., and he healed them.	4.24

PARALYZED
my servant is lying p. at home,	Mt 8.06
many who were p. or lame were	Ac 8.07

PARDON —ED
The LORD would not p. him,	Deu 29.20
O LORD, p. my guilt, for it is great.	Ps 25.11
our God, for he will abundantly p.	Is 55.07
for I will p. those whom I leave as	Jer 50.20
is ended, that her iniquity is p.,	Is 40.02

PARENT* —S

who loves the p. loves the child.	1Jn 5.01
Now his p. went to Jerusalem every	Lk 2.41
wife or brothers or p. or children,	18.29
who sinned, this man or his p.,	Jn 9.02
obey your p. in the Lord, for this	Eph 6.01

PART —S

brought only a p. and laid it at	Ac 5.02
You have neither p. nor lot in this	8.21
hardening has come upon p. of Israel,	Rom 11.25
greater honor to the inferior p.,	1Co 12.24
Now I know in p.; then I shall	13.12
apportioned a tenth p. of everything.	Heb 7.02
For thou didst form my inward p.,	Ps 139.13
LORD will lay bare their secret p.	Is 3.17
took his garments and made four p.,	Jn 19.23
more presentable p. do not require.	1Co 12.24

PARTAKERS

for you are all p. with me of	Php 1.07

PARTIALITY

you shall not show p.; and you shall	Deu 16.19
and show no p., but truly teach the	Lk 20.21
I perceive that God shows no p.,	Ac 10.34

PARTNER —S

the unbelieving p. desires to	1Co 7.15
to their p. in the other boat to	Lk 5.07
eat the sacrifices p. in the altar?	1Co 10.18
sometimes being p. with those so	Heb 10.33

PARTY

the p. of the Sadducees, and filled	Ac 5.17
the circumcision p. criticized him,	11.02
belonged to the p. of the Pharisees	15.05
selfishness, dissension, p. spirit,	Gal 5.20

PASS —ED

I will p. over you, and no plague	Ex 12.13
All that p. by despoil him;	Ps 89.41
For my days p. away like smoke, and	102.03
And the idols shall utterly p. away.	Is 2.18
When you p. through the waters I	43.02
nothing to you, all you who p. by?	Lam 1.12
I will never again p. by them;	Amo 7.08
you, till heaven and earth p. away,	Mt 5.18
possible, let this cup p. from me;	26.39
He had to p. through Samaria.	Jn 4.04
Who are you to p. judgment on the	Rom 14.04
men p. through the river on foot.	Ps 66.06
he saw him he p. by on the other	Lk 10.31
but has p. from death to life.	Jn 5.24
forbearance he had p. over former	Rom 3.25
the old has p. away, behold, the new	2Co 5.17
that we have p. out of death into	1Jn 3.14

PASSOVER

"This is the ordinance of the p.:	Ex 12.43
and keep the p. to the LORD your	Deu 16.01
they killed the p. lamb for all	Ez 6.20
them, and they prepared the p.	Mt 26.19

after the P. to bring him out to	Ac 12.04
he kept the P. and sprinkled the	Heb 11.28

PASTURE —S

we thy people, the flock of thy p.,	Ps 79.13
people, and the sheep of his p.	100.03
and scatter the sheep of my p.!"	Jer 23.01
are my sheep, the sheep of my p.,	Eze 34.31
he makes me lie down in green p.	Ps 23.02

PATH —S

Thou dost show me the p. of life;	Ps 16.11
to my feet and a light to my p.	119.105
searchest out my p. and my lying	139.03
The wise man's p. leads upward to	Pro 15.24
in the sea, a p. in the mighty waters,	Is 43.16
some seeds fell along the p.,	Mt 13.04
He leads me in p. of righteousness	Ps 23.03
by p. his feet have not trod.	Is 41.03
of the Lord, make his p. straight."	Mt 3.03
in their p. are ruin and misery,	Rom 3.16
and make straight p. for your feet,	Heb 12.13

PATIENCE

have p. with me, and I will pay you	Mt 18.26
and bring forth fruit with p.	Lk 8.15
do not see, we wait for it with p.	Rom 8.25
p., kindness, goodness, faithfulness,	Gal 5.22
faith and p. inherit the promises,	Heb 6.12

PATIENT —LY

is my end, that I should be p.?	Job 6.11
Love is p. and kind; love is not	1Co 13.04
the LORD and wait p. for him;	Ps 37.07

PATTERN

according to the p. that he had	Ac 7.44
Follow the p. of the sound words	2Ti 1.13
according to the p. which was shown	Heb 8.05

PEACE

And Jethro said to Moses, "Go in p."	Ex 4.18
'P. be to you, and p. be to your house,	1Sa 25.06
"Agree with God, and be at p.;	Job 22.21
who speak p. with their neighbors,	Ps 28.03
do good; seek p., and pursue it.	34.14
for he will speak p. to his people,	85.08
Everlasting Father, Prince of P.	Is 9.06
Thou dost keep him in perfect p.,	26.03
'P., p.,' when there is no p.	Jer 6.14
We looked for p., but no good came,	8.15
not come to bring p., but a sword.	Mt 10.34
guide our feet into the way of p."	Lk 1.79
say, 'P. be to this house!'	10.05
P. I leave with you; my p. I give to	Jn 14.27
good news of p. by Jesus Christ	Ac 10.36
we have p. with God through our	Rom 5.01
not a God of confusion but of p.	1Co 14.33
For he is our p., who has made us	Eph 2.14
And let the p. of Christ rule in	Col 3.15

PEARL* —S

who, on finding one p. of great value,	Mt 13.46
do not throw your p. before swine,	7.06
hair or gold or p. or costly	1Ti 2.09

PEN
is like the p. of a ready scribe.   Ps 45.01
rather not write with p. and ink;   3Jn 13

PENALTY
persons the due p. for their error.   Rom 1.27

PEOPLE —S
they are one p., and they have all   Gen 11.06
will give this p. favor in the   Ex 3.21
'Let my p. go, that they may hold a   5.01
to be a p. of his own possession, as   Deu 4.20
LORD binds up the hurt of his p.,   Is 30.26
Comfort, comfort my p., says your God.   40.01
Therefore my p. shall know my name;   52.06
And they shall be called the holy p.,   62.12
I have given my p. Israel to inherit: Jer 12.14
said to them, "You are not my p.,"   Hos 1.10
'This p. honors me with their lips,   Mt 15.08
and "God has visited his p.!"   Lk 7.16
and his own p. received him not.   Jn 1.11
ask, then, has God rejected his p.?   Rom 11.01
the power of it. Avoid such p.   2Ti 3.05
nation and tribe and tongue and p.;   Rev 14.06
who have separated you from the p.   Lev 20.24
prepared in the presence of all p.,   Lk 2.31
and the p. imagine vain things?   Ac 4.25

PERCEIVE —D
see and see, but do not p.'   Is 6.09
you shall indeed see but never p.   Mt 13.14
their eyes and p. with their heart,   Jn 12.40
"Truly I p. that God shows no   Ac 10.34
and p. that they were uneducated,   4.13
been clearly p. in the things that   Rom 1.20

PERDITION
of them is lost but the son of p.,   Jn 17.12
the bottomless pit and go to p.;   Rev 17.08

PERFECT
The law of the LORD is p., reviving   Ps 19.07
Thou dost keep him in p. peace,   Is 26.03
be p., as your heavenly Father is p.   Mt 5.48
Jesus said to him, "If you would be p., 19.21
but when the p. comes, the imperfect   1Co 13.10
obtained this or am already p.;   Php 3.12
their salvation p. through suffering.   Heb 2.10
and every p. gift is from above,   Jas 1.17
but p. love casts out fear.   1Jn 4.18

PERFECTION
Now if p. had been attainable   Heb 7.11

PERIL
or nakedness, or p., or sword?   Rom 8.35

PERISH —ES —ING
"Let the day p. wherein I was born,   Job 3.03
all flesh would p. together,   34.15
but the way of the wicked will p.   Ps 1.06
Flight shall p. from the swift, and   Amo 2.14
the sword will p. by the sword.   Mt 26.52
"Teacher, do you not care if we p.?"   Mk 4.38

spare, but I p. here with hunger!   Lk 15.17
But not a hair of your head will p.   21.18
him should not p. but have eternal   Jn 3.16
"Your silver p. with you, because   Ac 8.20
Do not labor for the food which p.,   Jn 6.27
flower falls, and its beauty p.   Jas 1.11
Give strong drink to him who is p.,   Pro 31.06
cross is folly to those who are p.,   1Co 1.18

PERISHABLE
What is sown is p., what is raised   1 Co 15.42
When the p. puts on the imperishable,   15.54

PERMIT —S —TED
he would not p. the demons to   Mk 1.34
some time with you, if the Lord p.   1Co 16.07
For they are not p. to speak,   14.34

PERPETUAL
This shall be a p. statute for him   Ex 28.43
turned away in p. backsliding?   Jer 8.05

PERPLEXED
when he heard him, he was much p.;   Mk 6.20
And all were amazed and p.,   Ac 2.12
p., but not driven to despair;   2Co 4.08
my tone, for I am p. about you.   Gal 4.20

PERSECUTE —D
Let those be put to shame who p. me,   Jer 17.18
revile you and p. you and utter   Mt 5.11
and pray for those who p. you,   5.44
persecuted me, they will p. you;   Jn 15.20
him, "Saul, Saul, why do you p. me?"   Ac 9.04
Bless those who p. you; bless and   Rom 12.14
And this was why the Jews p. Jesus,   Jn 5.16
because I p. the church of God.   1Co 15.09
how I p. the church of God violently   Gal 1.13
life in Christ Jesus will be p.,   2Ti 3.12

PERSECUTION —S
tribulation or p. arises on account   Mt 13.21
and stirred up p. against Paul and   Ac 13.50
or p., or famine, or nakedness, or   Rom 8.35
with p., and in the age to come   Mk 10.30
in all your p. and in the afflictions   2Th 1.04

PERSISTENTLY
I spoke to you p. you did not   Jer 7.13
which I p. sent to you by my servants   29.19
I have spoken to you p., but you have   35.14

PERSON —S
Let every p. be subject to the   Rom 13.01
For what p. knows a man's thoughts   1Co 2.11
in p. not in heart, we endeavored   1Th 2.17
they inquired what p. or time was   1Pe 1.11
Now such p. we command and exhort   2Th 3.12
certain p. have made shipwreck of   1Ti 1.19
eight p., were saved through water.   1Pe 3.20

PERSUADE —D
the fear of the Lord, we p. men;   2Co 5.11
And some of them were p., and joined   Ac 17.04

PERSUADE —D (cont.)
for I am p. that none of these — Ac 26.26
I know and am p. in the Lord Jesus — Rom 14.14

PERVERSE
"O faithless and p. generation, — Mt 17.17
of a crooked and p. generation, — Php 2.15

PERVERT —ED —ING
Does God p. justice? Or does the — Job 8.03
you and want to p. the gospel of — Gal 1.07
persons who p. the grace of our — Jud 4
righteous, so justice goes forth p. — Hab 1.04
"We found this man p. our nation, — Lk 23.02

PESTILENCE
upon us with p. or with the sword." — Ex 5.03
So the LORD sent a p. upon Israel — 2Sa 24.15
LORD: 'Those who are for p., to p., — Jer 15.02

PETITION —S*
but makes his p. three times a day." — Dan 6.13
May the LORD fulfil all your p.! — Ps 20.05

PHYSICIAN —S
who are well have no need of a p., — Mt 9.12
this proverb, 'P., heal yourself; — Lk 4.23
Luke the beloved p. and Demas greet — Col 4.14
with lies; worthless p. are you all. — Job 13.04
had suffered much under many p., — Mk 5.26

PIECE —S
I too was formed from a p. of clay. — Job 33.06
dash them in p. like a potter's — Ps 2.09
hammer which breaks the rock in p.? — Jer 23.29
All her images shall be beaten to p., — Mic 1.07
they paid him thirty p. of silver. — Mt 26.15
full of broken p. and of the fish. — Mk 6.43

PIERCE —D
(and a sword will p. through your — Lk 2.35
they have p. my hands and feet— — Ps 22.16
of the soldiers p. his side with a — Jn 19.34

PIGEONS
and the seats of those who sold p. — Mt 21.12

PILLAR —S
back, and she became a p. of salt. — Gen 19.26
by day in a p. of cloud to lead — Ex 13.21
the p. and bulwark of the truth. — 1Ti 3.15
The p. of heaven tremble, and are — Job 26.11
John, who were reputed to be p., — Gal 2.09
sun, and his legs like p. of fire. — Rev 10.01

PINIONS
them, bearing them on its p., — Deu 32.11
he will cover you with his p., — Ps 91.04

PIT
him into this p. here in the — Gen 37.22
yet thou wilt plunge me into a p., — Job 9.31
He drew me up from the desolate p., — Ps 40.02

Yet they have dug a p. for my life. — Jer 18.20
man, both will fall into a p." — Mt 15.14
of the shaft of the bottomless p.; — Rev 9.01

PITIED —IES
said to him, "Call her name Not p., — Hos 1.06
we are of all men most to be p. — 1Co 15.19
As a father p. his children, so the — Ps 103.13

PITY (n)
And out of p. for him the lord of — Mt 18.27
And Jesus in p. touched their eyes, — 20.34
Moved with p., he stretched out his — Mk 1.41

PLACE (n)
for the p. on which you are standing — Ex 3.05
And who shall stand in his holy p.? — Ps 24.03
Thou art a hiding p. for me, — 32.07
How lovely is thy dwelling p., — 84.01
our dwelling p. in all generations. — 90.01
Lift up your hands to the holy p., — 134.02
Enlarge the p. of your tent, and let — Is 54.02
"I dwell in the high and holy p., — 57.15
him and said, "This is a lonely p., — Mt 14.15
Come, see the p. where he lay. — 28.06
and found the p. where it was — Lk 4.17
when I go and prepare a p. for you, — Jn 14.03
they were all together in one p. — Ac 2.01
who in every p. call on the name — 1Co 1.02
for a dwelling p. of God in the — Eph 2.22

PLAGUE —S (n)
"Yet one p. more I will bring upon — Ex 11.01
to smite the earth with every p., — Rev 11.06
O Death, where are your p.? O Sheol, — Hos 13.14
of diseases and p. and evil spirits, — Lk 7.21

PLAIN (adj)
make it p. upon tablets, so he may — Hab 2.02
be known about God is p. to them, — Rom 1.19
Now the works of the flesh are p.: — Gal 5.19

PLAN —S (n)
"who carry out a p., but not mine; — Is 30.01
to the definite p. and foreknowledge — Ac 2.23
as a p. for the fulness of time, to — Eph 1.10
see what is the p. of the mystery — 3.09
Without counsel p. go wrong, — Pro 15.22
p. formed of old, faithful and sure. — Is 25.01
For I know the p. I have for you, — Jer 29.11
Do I make my p. like a worldly man, — 2Co 1.17

PLANT —ED —S (v)
Again you shall p. vineyards upon — Jer 31.05
And the LORD God p. a garden in — Gen 2.08
He is like a tree p. by streams of — Ps 1.03
Scarcely are they p., scarcely sown, — Is 40.24
He is like a tree p. by water, — Jer 17.08
Father has not p. will be rooted — Mt 15.13
a householder who p. a vineyard, — 21.33
I p., Apollos watered, but God gave — 1Co 3.06
So neither he who p. nor he who — 3.07
Who p. a vineyard without eating — 9.07

PLANT (n)
grew up before him like a young p.,   Is 53.02
"You pity the p., for which you did   Jon 4.10
"Every p. which my heavenly Father   Mt 15.13

PLAY —ED —S
this fellow to p. the madman in my   1Sa 21.15
stringed harp I will p. to thee,   Ps 144.09
child shall p. over the hole of   Is 11.08
and will p. the harlot with all the   23.17
left their God to p. the harlot.   Hos 4.12
I have p. the fool, and have erred   1Sa 26.21
how will any one know what is p.?   1Co 14.07
than one who p. the great man but   Pro 12.09

PLEA —S*
with an empty p. turn aside him   Is 29.21
me, O LORD, and hearken to my p.   Jer 18.19
they rely on empty p., they speak   Is 59.04

PLEAD —ING —S
will you p. the case for God?   Job 13.08
for the LORD will p. their cause   Pro 22.23
p. your case before the mountains,   Mic 6.01
arguing and p. about the kingdom of   Ac 19.08
how he p. with God against Israel?   Rom 11.02

PLEASANT
was good, and that the land was p.;   Gen 49.15
P. words are like a honeycomb,   Pro 16.24
you have planted p. vineyards,   Amo 5.11
seems painful rather than p.;   Heb 12.11

PLEASE —D —S —ING
who are in the flesh cannot p. God.   Rom 8.08
For Christ did not p. himself;   15.03
just as I try to p. all men in   1Co 10.33
not to p. men, but to p. God who tests   1Th 2.04
Son, with whom I am well p."   Mt 3.17
peace among men with whom he is p.!"   Lk 2.14
Whatever the LORD p. he does,   Ps 135.06
May my meditation be p. to him,   104.34
sacrifice acceptable and p. to God.   Php 4.18
for such sacrifices are p. to God.   Heb 13.16

PLEASURE —S
I kept my heart from no p.,   Ecc 2.10
of your fast you seek your own p.,   Is 58.03
Father's good p. to give you the   Lk 12.32
on the earth in luxury and in p.;   Jas 5.05
cares and riches and p. of life,   Lk 8.14
slaves to various passions and p.,   Tit 3.03
to enjoy fleeting p. of sin.   Heb 11.25

PLENTIFUL —LY
his disciples, "The harvest is p.,   Mt 9.37
of a rich man brought forth p.;   Lk 12.16

PLENTY
The seven years of p. that prevailed   Gen 41.53
then your barns will be filled with p.,   Pro 3.10
"You shall eat in p. and be satisfied,   Joe 2.26
the secret of facing p. and hunger,   Php 4.12

PLOT —S —TED (v)
conspire, and the peoples p. in vain?   Ps 2.01
What do you p. against the LORD?   Nah 1.09
A worthless man p. evil, and his   Pro 16.27
passed, the Jews p. to kill him,   Ac 9.23

PLOW —ED (v)
You shall not p. with an ox and an   Deu 22.10
plowman should p. in hope and the   1Co 9.10
You have p. iniquity, you have   Hos 10.13

PLOW (n)
his hand to the p. and looks back   Lk 9.62

PLOWING (n)
will be neither p. nor harvest.   Gen 45.06

PLUCK —ED
and a time to p. up what is planted,   Ecc 3.02
over them to p. up and break down,   Jer 31.28
will plant you, and not p. you up;   42.10
p. it out and throw it away;   Mt 5.29
they began to p. ears of grain and   12.01
were as a brand p. out of the   Amo 4.11
you would have p. out your eyes   Gal 4.15

PLUNDER —ED —S* (v)
they shall p. the people of the   Is' 11.14
all who p. her shall be sated, says   Jer 50.10
man's house and p. his goods,   Mt 12.29
But this is a people robbed and p.,   Is 42.22
the plunderer p., and the destroyer   21.02

PLUNDERING (n)
accepted the p. of your property,   Heb 10.34

POINT —S (n)
son, for he was at the p. of death.   Jn 4.47
Christ from a human p. of view,   2Co 5.16
resisted to the p. of shedding   Heb 12.04
fails in one p. has become guilty   Jas 2.10
But on some p. I have written to   Rom 15.15

POOR
and the p. shall not give less, than   Ex 30.15
For the p. will never cease out of   Deu 15.11
The LORD makes p. and makes rich;   1Sa 2.07
So the p. have hope, and injustice   Job 5.16
I was a father to the p.,   29.16
This p. man cried, and the LORD   Ps 34.06
As for me, I am p. and needy;   40.17
Blessed is he who considers the p.!   41.01
Better is a p. man who walks in his   Pro 19.01
righteousness he shall judge the p.,   Is 11.04
hast been a stronghold to the p.,   25.04
the cause of the p. and needy;   Jer 22.16
the head of the p. into the dust   Amo 2.07
and bring the p. of the land to an   8.04
"Blessed are the p. in spirit,   Mt 5.03
and the p. have good news preached   11.05
you possess and give to the p.,   19.21
For you always have the p. with you,   26.11
me to preach good news to the p.   Lk 4.18
half of my goods I give to the p.;   19.08

POOR (cont.)

contribution for the p. among the	Rom 15.26
as p., yet making many rich;	2Co 6.10
yet for your sake he became p.,	8.09
both rich and p., both free and	Rev 13.16

PORTENT —S

And a great p. appeared in heaven,	Rev 12.01
are signs and p. in Israel from	Is 8.18

PORTION

For the LORD's p. is his people,	Deu 32.09
This is the wicked man's p. from God,	Job 20.29
The LORD is my chosen p. and my cup;	Ps 16.05
land you shall possess a double p.;	Is 61.07
Mary has chosen the good p.,	Lk 10.42

POSITION —S

you do not regard the p. of men.	Mt 22.16
on a man's p. and not on his heart.	2Co 5.12
for kings and all who are in high p.,	1Ti 2.02

POSSESS —ED —ING

to give you this land to p."	Gen 15.07
for the LORD shall p. the land.	Ps 37.09
descendants will p. the nations and	Is 54.03
sell what you p. and give to the	Mt 19.21
truths to those who p. the Spirit.	1Co 2.13
know that "all of us p. knowledge."	8.01
Do all p. gifts of healing? Do all	12.30
him many who were p. with demons;	Mt 8.16
nothing, and yet p. everything.	2Co 6.10

POSSESSION —S

of Canaan, for an everlasting p.;	Gen 17.08
and the ends of the earth your p.	Ps 2.08
no p. in Israel; I am their p.	Eze 44.28
inheritance until we acquire p. of it,	Eph 1.14
had a better p. and an abiding one.	Heb 10.34
sorrowful; for he had great p.	Mt 19.22
he will set him over all his p.	24.47
and they sold their p. and goods	Ac 2.45

POSSIBLE

but with God all things are p."	Mt 19.26
All things are p. to him who	Mk 9.23
that if p. I may attain the resurrection	Php 3.11

POSTERITY

P. shall serve him; men shall tell	Ps 22.30
to Abraham and to his p. for ever."	Lk 1.55
Of this man's p. God has brought to	Ac 13.23

POTTER

are the clay, and thou art our p.;	Is 64.08
as it seemed good to the p. to do.	Jer 18.04
Has the p. no right over the clay,	Rom 9.21

POUR —ED —S

p. out your heart before him;	Ps 62.08
P. out thy anger on the nations	79.06
I p. out my complaint before him, I	142.02
I will p. my Spirit upon your	Is 44.03
P. out your heart like water before	Lam 2.19
when I p. out my Spirit upon the	Eze 39.29

that I will p. out my spirit on all	Joe 2.28
that I will p. out my Spirit upon	Ac 2.17
I am p. out like water, and all my	Ps 22.14
until the Spirit is p. upon us from	Is 32.15
because he p. out his soul to death,	53.12
which is p. out for many for the	Mt 26.28
Spirit had been p. out even on the	Ac 10.45
love has been p. into our hearts	Rom 5.05
which he p. out upon us richly	Tit 3.06
p. unmixed into the cup of his	Rev 14.10
scorn me; my eye p. out tears to God,	Job 16.20
Day to day p. forth speech, and	Ps 19.02

POVERTY

she out of her p. has put in	Mk 12.44
so that by his p. you might become	2Co 8.09

POWER —S

'My p. and the might of my hand	Deu 8.17
Behold, God is exalted in his p.;	Job 36.22
He gives p. to the faint, and to him	Is 40.29
by thy great p. and by thy outstretched	Jer 32.17
is he who made the earth by his p.,	51.15
the p., and the might, and the glory,	Dan 2.37
nor by p., but by my Spirit, says	Zec 4.06
kingdom and the p. and the glory,	*Mt 6.13
man seated at the right hand of P.,	26.64
the kingdom of God come with p."	Mk 9.01
and the p. of the Most High will	Lk 1.35
returned in the p. of the Spirit	4.14
and the p. of the Lord was with him	5.17
at the right hand of the p. of God."	22.69
he gave p. to become children of	Jn 1.12
hast given him p. over all flesh,	17.02
shall receive p. when the Holy	Ac 1.08
"By what p. or by what name did you	4.07
And Stephen, full of grace and p.,	6.08
saying 'Give me also this p.,	8.19
it is the p. of God for salvation	Rom 1.16
Greeks, are under the p. of sin,	3.09
so that by the p. of the Holy	15.13
Christ the p. of God and the wisdom	1Co 1.24
will also raise us up by his p.	6.14
transcendent p. belongs to God and	2Co 4.07
may have p. to comprehend with all	Eph 3.18
May you be strengthened with all p.,	Col 1.11
religion but denying the p. of it.	2Ti 3.05
the universe by his word of p.	Heb 1.03
I will give him p. over the nations.	Rev 2.26
and glory and p. belong to our God,	19.01
and the p. of death shall not	Mt 16.18
present, nor things to come, nor p.,	Rom 8.38
if I have prophetic p., and understand	1Co 13.02
principalities and p. in the	Eph 3.10
authorities, and p. subject to him.	1Pe 3.22

PRACTICE —D —ING (v)

for they preach, but do not p.	Mt 23.03
of the saints, p. hospitality.	Rom 12.13
of those who p. magic arts brought	Ac 19.19
"Beware of p. your piety before men	Mt 6.01

PRACTICE —S (n)

Consider the p. of Israel;	1Co 10.18

PRACTICE —S (n) (cont.)

Esther fixed these p. of Purim,	Est 9.32
put off the old nature with its p.	Col 3.09

PRAETORIUM

governor took Jesus into the p.,	Mt 27.27
him to be guarded in Herod's p.	Ac 23.35

PRAISE —D —ING (v)

Let heaven and earth p. him,	Ps 69.34
people yet unborn may p. the LORD:	102.18
O my soul! P. the LORD!	104.35
kings of the earth shall p. thee,	138.04
Great is the LORD, and greatly to be p.,	145.03
for all men p. God for what had	Ac 4.21
a multitude of the heavenly host p.	Lk 2.13
walking and leaping and p. God.	Ac 3.08

PRAISE (n)

He is your p.; he is your God;	Deu 10.21
I will sing p. to thy name. O Most	Ps 9.02
righteous! P. befits the upright.	33.01
my mouth shall show forth thy p.	51.15
walls Salvation, and your gates P.	Is 60.18
thou hast brought perfect p.'?"	Mt 21.16
the p. of men more than the p. of God.	Jn 12.43
His p. is not from men but from God.	Rom 2.29
Christ, to the glory and p. of God.	Php 1.11

PRAY —ED —ING

and they p. to the LORD toward the	1Ki 8.44
profit do we get if we p. to him?'	Job 21.15
my servant Job shall p. for you,	42.08
and my God, for to thee do I p.	Ps 5.02
P. for the peace of Jerusalem!	122.06
he comes to his sanctuary to p.,	Is 16.12
do not p. for this people, or lift	Jer 7.16
'P. for us to the LORD our God, and	42.20
enemies and p. for those who	Mt 5.44
"And when you p., you must not be	6.05
up into the hills by himself to p.	14.23
"Sit here, while I go yonder and p."	26.36
Watch and p. that you may not enter	26.41
teach us to p., as John taught his	Lk 11.01
"Two men went up into the temple to p.,	18.10
And I will p. the Father, and he	Jn 14.16
do not know how to p. as we ought,	Rom 8.26
For if I p. in a tongue, my spirit	1Co 14.14
P. at all times in the Spirit, with	Eph 6.18
p. constantly,	1Th 5.17
in every place the men should p.,	1Ti 2.08
Then Abraham p. to God; and God	Gen 20.17
So Moses p. for the people.	Num 21.07
Then Jonah p. to the LORD his God	Jon 2.01
farther he fell on his face and p.,	Mt 26.39
and they p. and laid their hands	Ac 6.06
to the people, and p. constantly to God.	10.02
were gathered together and were p.	12.12
and Silas were p. and singing	16.25
p. earnestly night and day that we	1Th 3.10

PRAYER —S

regard to the p. of thy servant	1Ki 8.28
and the LORD accepted Job's p.	Job 42.09

"Hear my p., O LORD, and give ear to	Ps 39.12
O thou who hearest p.! To thee shall	65.02
but the p. of the upright is his	Pro 15.08
a house of p. for all peoples.	Is 56.07
so that no p. can pass through	Lam 3.44
seeking him by p. and supplications	Dan 9.03
And whatever you ask in p.,	Mt 21.22
for your p. is heard, and your wife	Lk 1.13
ourselves to p. and to the ministry	Ac 6.04
you may devote yourselves to p.;	1Co 7.05
with all p. and supplication.	Eph 6.18
consecrated by the word of God and p.	1Ti 4.05
The p. of a righteous man has great	Jas 5.16
the breaking of bread and the p.	Ac 2.42
keep sane and sober for your p.	1Pe 4.07
which are the p. of the saints;	Rev 5.08

PREACH —ED

From that time Jesus began to p.,	Mt 4.17
And p. as you go, saying, 'The	10.07
for they p., but do not practice.	23.03
anointed me to p. good news to the	Lk 4.18
so I am eager to p. the gospel to	Rom 1.15
And how can men p. unless they are	10.15
me to baptize but to p. the gospel,	1Co 1.17
but we p. Christ crucified, a	1.23
p. the word, be urgent in season and	2Ti 4.02
this gospel is p. in the whole	Mt 26.13
because he p. Jesus and the resurrection.	Ac 17.18
in what terms I p. to you the	1Co 15.01
And he came and p. peace to you who	Eph 2.17

PREACHER

The words of the P., the son of	Ecc 1.01
he would be the p. for this people!	Mic 2.11
seems to be a p. of foreign	Ac 17.18
how are they to hear without a p.?	Rom 10.14

PREACHING (n)

Macedonia, Paul was occupied with p.,	Ac 18.05
that in my p. I may make the gospel	1Co 9.18
then our p. is in vain and your	15.14
of scripture, to p., to teaching.	1Ti 4.13

PRECEPT —S

For it is p. upon p., p. upon p.,	Is 28.10
the p. of the LORD are right,	Ps 19.08
I will meditate on thy p.,	119.15
teaching as doctrines the p. of men.' "	Mt 15.09
according to human p. and doctrines?	Col 2.22

PRECIOUS

How p. is thy steadfast love, O God!	Ps 36.07
How p. to me are thy thoughts, O God!	139.17
a p. cornerstone of a sure foundation:	Is 28.16
p. stones, wood, hay, stubble—	1Co 3.12
but with the p. blood of Christ,	1Pe 1.19

PREPARE —D

p. to meet your God, O Israel!"	Amo 4.12
my messenger to p. the way before	Mal 3.01
P. the way of the Lord, make his	Mt 3.03
has done it to p. me for burial.	26.12
that I go to p. a place for you?	Jn 14.02

PREPARE —D (cont.)

whom it has been p. by my Father."	Mt 20.23
the kingdom p. for you from the	25.34
which he has p. beforehand for glory,	Rom 9.23
for he has p. for them a city.	Heb 11.16

PRESCRIBED

Who has p. for him his way, or who	Job 36.23

PRESENCE

went away from the p. of the LORD,	Gen 4.16
bread of the P. on the table	Ex 25.30
"My p. will go with you, and I will	33.14
Cast me not away from thy p.,	Ps 51.11
strength, seek his p. continually!	105.04
whither shall I flee from thy p.?	139.07
being might boast in the p. of God.	1Co 1.29
before the p. of his glory with	Jud 24
will shelter them with his p.	Rev 7.15
from his p. earth and sky fled away,	20.11

PRESENT (adj)

a very p. help in trouble.	Ps 46.01
know how to interpret the p. time?	Lk 12.56
sufferings of this p. time are not	Rom 8.18
For Demas, in love with this p. world,	2Ti 4.10

PRESERVE —D

P. me, O God, for in thee I take	Ps 16.01
whoever loses his life will p. it.	Lk 17.33
and thy care has p. my spirit.	Job 10.12

PRESS —ED (v)

or p. down his tongue with a cord?	Job 41.01
let us p. on to know the LORD;	Hos 6.03
I p. on toward the goal for the	Php 3.14
good measure, p. down, shaken	Lk 6.38
I am hard p. between the two.	Php 1.23

PRETEND —ED

There are friends who p. to be friends,	Pro 18.24
power and with p. signs and wonders,	2Th 2.09

PRETENSE —IONS*

and for a p. make long prayers.	Mk 12.40
whether in p. or in truth, Christ is	Php 1.18
through the p. of liars whose consciences	1Ti 4.02

PREVAIL —ED

for not by might shall a man p.	1Sa 2.09
Let not man p.; let the nations be	Ps 9.19
of death shall not p. against it.	Mt 16.18
Moses held up his hand, Israel p.;	Ex 17.11
of the Lord grew and p. mightily.	Ac 19.20

PREY (n)

slothful man will not catch his p.,	Pro 12.27
Can the p. be taken from the mighty,	Is 49.24
no one makes a p. of you by	Col 2.08

PRICE

not for p. or reward," says the LORD	Is 45.13
milk without money and without p.	55.01
p. of him on whom a p. had been set	Mt 27.09
you were bought with a p. So glorify	1Co 6.20

PRIDE

P. goes before destruction, and a	Pro 16.18
and the p. of men shall be humbled;	Is 2.11
lay low his p. together with the	25.11
will weep in secret for your p.;	Jer 13.17
"I abhor the p. of Jacob, and hate	Amo 6.08
envy, slander, p., foolishness.	Mk 7.22
our confidence and p. in our hope.	Heb 3.06

PRIEST —S

he was p. of God Most High.	Gen 14.18
the p. and the prophet reel with	Ps 28.07
prophet and p. ply their trade	Jer 14.18
law shall not perish from the p.,	18.18
I reject you from being a p. to me.	Hos 4.06
but go, show yourself to the p.,	Mt 8.04
there was a p. named Zechariah, of	Lk 1.05
Now by chance a p. was going down	10.31
faithful high p. in the service of	Heb 2.17
"Thou art a p. for ever, after the	5.06
we have a great p. over the house	10.21
Saul had killed the p. of the LORD.	1Sa 22.21
Moses and Aaron were among his p.,	Ps 99.06
Her p. I will clothe with salvation,	132.16
I will take for p. and for Levites,	Is 66.21
people and some of the senior p.,	Jer 19.01
Her p. have done violence to my law	Eze 22.26
elders and chief p. and scribes,	Mt 16.21
The former p. were many in number,	Heb 7.23
them a kingdom and p. to our God,	Rev 5.10

PRIESTHOOD

but he holds his p. permanently,	Heb 7.24
to be a holy p., to offer spiritual	1Pe 2.05
a royal p., a holy nation, God's own	2.09

PRINCE —S

"Who made you a p. and a judge over	Ex 2.14
him to be p. over my people Israel.	1Sa 9.16
but without people a p. is ruined.	Pro 14.28
Everlasting Father, P. of Peace."	Is 9.06
out demons by the p. of demons."	Mt 9.34
following the p. of the power of	Eph 2.02
who shows no partiality to p.,	Job 34.19
The p. of the peoples gather as the	Ps 47.09
Put not your trust in p.,	146.03
And I will make boys their p.,	Is 3.04
And the p. were enraged at Jeremiah,	Jer 37.15
but Michael, one of the chief p.,	Dan 10.13
their p. shall fall by the sword	Hos 7.16
them no more; all their p. are rebels.	9.15
where are all your p., to defend	13.10
you said, "Give me a king and p."?	13.10
Your p. are like grasshoppers, your	Nah 3.17

PRINCIPALITIES

nor p., nor things present, nor	Rom 8.38
known to the p. and powers in the	Eph 3.10

PRISON —S

he ground at the mill in the p.	Ju 16.21
opening of the p. to those who are	Is 61.01
people, that you have put me in p.?	Jer 37.18
John heard in p. about the deeds	Mt 11.02

PRISON —S (cont.)
I was in p. and you came to me.'Mt 25.36
Lord opened the p. doors andAc 5.19
So Peter was kept in p.; but earnest12.05
a favor, Felix left Paul in p.24.27
shut up many of the saints in p.,26.10
on account of which I am in p.,Col 4.03
Remember those who are in p.,Heb 13.03
and preached to the spirits in p.,1Pe 3.19
you up to the synagogues and p.,Lk 21.12

PRISONER —S
a p. for Christ Jesus on behalf ofEph 3.01
and now a p. also for Christ Jesus—Phm 9
The LORD sets the p. free;Ps 146.07
Return to your stronghold, O p. ofZec 9.12
The soldier's plan was to kill the p.,Ac 27.42
my kinsmen and my fellow p.;Rom 16.07

PRIVATE —LY
went up, not publicly but in p.Jn 7.10
disciples came to Jesus p. and said,Mt 17.19
but p. to his own disciples heMk 4.34
before them (but p. before thoseGal 2.02

PRIZE
but only one receives the p.?1Co 9.24
goal for the p. of the upward callPhp 3.14

PROCEED —ED —S
does not p. from faith is sin.Rom 14.23
words which p. out of his mouth;Lk 4.22
for I p. and came forth from God;Jn 8.42
out of the mouth p. from the heart,Mt 15.18
who p. from the Father, he will bearJn 15.26

PROCLAIM —ED —ING —S
The heavens p. his righteousness;Ps 97.06
"P. all these words in the citiesJer 11.06
and p. to it the message that IJon 3.02
whispered, p. upon the housetops.Mt 10.27
to p. the acceptable year of theLk 4.19
whom I p. to you, is the Christ."Ac 17.03
you p. the Lord's death until he1Co 11.26
Him we p., warning every man andCol 1.28
seen and heard we p. also to you,1Jn 1.03
forgiveness of sins is p. to you,Ac 13.38
your faith is p. in all the world.Rom 1.08
pretense or in truth, Christ is p.;Php 1.18
I did not come p. to you the1Co 2.01
and the firmament p. his handiwork.Ps 19.01

PROCLAMATION
Then King Asa made a p. to all Judah,1Ki 15.22
sacred and imperishable p. of eternal*Mk 16.08

PRODUCES
The earth p. of itself, first theMk 4.28
that suffering p. endurance,Rom 5.03

PROFANE —D —S (v)
and not p. the name of their God;Lev 21.06
in the temple p. the sabbath,Mt 12.05
He even tried to p. the temple,Ac 24.06

your trade you p. your sanctuaries;Eze 28.18
and p. the blood of the covenant byHeb 10.29
every one who p. it shall be put toEx 31.14

PROFANING (n)
be guilty of p. the body and blood1Co 11.27

PROFIT —S* (v)
For what will it p. a man, if heMt 16.26
What does it p., my brethren, if aJas 2.14
'It p. a man nothing that he shouldJob 34.09

PROFITABLE
"Can a man be p. to God? Surely heJob 22.02
inspired by God and p. for teaching,2Ti 3.16

PROMISE —D (v)
and I p. that I will bring you upEx 3.17
They p. them freedom, but they2Pe 2.19
to Abraham what he has p. him."Gen 18.19
will do this thing that he has p.:Is 38.07
perform the mercy p. to our fathers,Lk 1.72
Israel a Savior, Jesus, as he p.Ac 13.23
which he p. beforehand through hisRom 1.02
God, who never lies, p. ages agoTit 1.02
not having received what was p.,Heb 11.13
which God has p. to those who loveJas 1.12
And this is what he has p. us,1Jn 2.25

PROMISE —S (n)
the p. of the LORD proves true;2Sa 22.31
Thy p. is well tried, and thyPs 119.140
I send the p. of my Father upon you;Lk 24.49
to wait for the p. of the Father,Ac 1.04
for hope in the p. made by God to26.06
p. to Abraham and his descendants,Rom 4.13
receive the p. of the SpiritGal 3.14
partakers of the p. in Christ JesusEph 3.06
patiently endured, obtained the p.Heb 6.15
not slow about his p. as some count2Pe 3.09
Are his p. at an end for all time?Ps 77.80
For all the p. of God find their2Co 1.20
faith and patience inherit the p.Heb 6.12

PRONOUNCE —D
"By you Israel will p. blessing,Gen 48.20
judgment you p. you will be judged,Mt 7.02
Therefore do not p. judgment before1Co 4.05
Is this blessing p. only upon theRom 4.09

PROOF —S
Why do you put the LORD to the p.?"Ex 17.02
commanded, for a p. of the people."Mt 8.04
since you desire p. that Christ is2Co 8.24
alive after his passion by many p.,Ac 1.03

PROPER —LY
is it p. for a woman to pray to God1Co 11.13
to which was borne at the p. time.1Ti 2.06
manifest at the p. time by the6.15
when each part is working p., makesEph 4.16

PROPERTY
met him at the p. of Naboth the2Ki 9.21

PROPERTY (cont.)

and entrusted to them his p.;	Mt 25.14
wife Sapphira sold a piece of p.,	Ac 5.01
accepted the plundering of your p.,	Heb 10.34

PROPHECY

if p., in proportion to our faith;	Rom 12.06
to another p., to another the	1Co 12.10
as for p., it will pass away;	13.08
while p. is not for unbelievers but	14.22
of Jesus is the spirit of p.	Rev 19.10

PROPHESIED —IES —Y

spirit rested upon them, they p.	Num 11.25
which Jeremiah p. against all the	Jer 25.13
So I p. as I was commanded;	Eze 37.07
prophets and the law p. until John;	Mt 11.13
and they spoke with tongues and p.	Ac 19.06
The prophets who p. of the grace	1Pe 1.10
He who p. is greater than he who	1Co 14.05
the prophets p. falsely, and the	Jer 5.31
"P. to these bones, and say to them,	Eze 37.04
GOD has spoken; who can but p.?"	Amo 3.08
me, 'Go, p. to my people Israel.'	7.15
did we not p. in your name, and cast	Mt 7.22
saying, "P. to us, you Christ! Who	26.68
pour out my Spirit; and they shall p.	Ac 2.18
brethren, earnestly desire to p.,	1Co 14.39

PROPHESYING (n)

do not despise p.,	1Th 5.20

PROPHET —S

your brother shall be your p.	Ex 7.01
"If a p. arises among you, or a	Deu 13.01
established as a p. of the LORD.	1Sa 3.20
and sent a message by Nathan the p.;	2Sa 12.25
I only, am left a p. of the LORD;	1Ki 18.22
"Is there no p. of the LORD here,	2Ki 3.11
appointed you a p. to the nations."	Jer 1.05
"I am no p., nor a prophet's son;	Amo 7.14
On that day every p. will be	Zec 13.04
the Lord had spoken by the p.:	Mt 1.22
He who receives a p. because he is a p.	10.41
I tell you, and more than a p.	11.09
"A p. is not without honor except	13.57
"This is the p. Jesus from Nazareth	21.11
be called the p. of the Most High;	Lk 1.76
"Are you the p.?" And he answered,	Jn 1.21
magician, a Jewish false p., named	Ac 13.06
If any one thinks that he is a p.,	1Co 14.37
and from the mouth of the false p.,	Rev 16.13
that all the LORD's people were p.,	Num 11.29
Then Elijah said to the p. of Baal.	1Ki 18.25
my anointed ones, do my p. no harm!"	Ps 105.15
has raised up p. for us in Babylon,	Jer 29.15
Where are your p. who prophesied to	37.19
Your p. have seen for you false and	Lam 2.14
raised up some of your sons for p.,	Amo 2.11
come to abolish the law and the p.;	Mt 5.17
"Beware of false p., who come to	7.15
"The law and the p. were until John;	Lk 16.16
the law and the p. bear witness to	Rom 3.21
Are all p.? Are all teachers? Do	1Co 12.29

and the spirits of p. are subject to p.	14.32
O saints and apostles and p.,	Rev 18.20

PROPHETESS

Now Deborah, a p., the wife of	Ju 4.04
And I went to the p., and she	Is 8.03
And there was a p., Anna, the	Lk 2.36
calls herself a p. and is teaching	Rev 2.20

PROSPERITY

Behold, is not their p. in their hand?	Job 21.16
I will extend p. to her like a	Is 66.12
shall again overflow with p.,	Zec 1.17

PROSTITUTE —S

and make them members of a p.?	1Co 6.15
harlots, and sacrifice with cult p.,	Hos 4.14

PROSTRATE

Then I lay p. before the LORD as	Deu 9.18
I am utterly bowed down and p.;	Ps 38.06
princes, and they shall p. themselves;	Is 49.07

PROUD

For God abases the p., but he saves	Job 22.29
against all that is p. and lofty,	Is 2.12
be not p., for the LORD has spoken.	Jer 13.15
scattered the p. in the imagination	Lk 1.51
So do not become p., but stand in	Rom 11.20

PROVE —D

P. me, O LORD, and try me;	Ps 26.02
and so p. to be my disciples.	Jn 15.08
it was to p. at the present time	Rom 3.26
that you may p. what is the will of	12.02
impossible that God should p. false,	Heb 6.18
which comes upon you to p. you,	1Pe 4.12
p. neighbor to the man who fell	Lk 10.36

PROVERB —S

a p., and a byword, among all the	Deu 28.37
you will quote to me this p.,	Lk 4.23
Your maxims are p. of ashes,	Job 13.12
The p. of Solomon, son of David, king	Pro 1.01

PROVIDE

"God will p. himself the lamb for a	Gen 22.08
O God, thou didst p. for the needy.	Ps 68.10
And God is able to p. you with	2Co 9.08

PROVISION

and make no p. for the flesh, to	Rom 13.14

PROVOKE —D

God, so as to p. him to anger,	Deu 4.25
Shall we p. the Lord of jealousy?	1Co 10.22
and p. the Holy One of Israel.	Ps 78.41
his spirit was p. within him as he	Ac 17.16
And with whom was he p. forty years?	Heb 3.17

PROVOKING (n)

no p. of one another, no envy of one	Gal 5.26

PRUDENCE
that p. may be given to the simple, Pro 1.04
the dishonest steward for his p.; Lk 16.08

PSALM —S
the earth; sing praises with a p.! Ps 47.07
addressing one another in p. and Eph 5.19
and as you sing p. and hymns and Col 3.16

PUBLIC —LY
powerfully confuted the Jews in p., Ac 18.28
and made a p. example of them, Col 2.15
attend to the p. reading of scripture, 1Ti 4.13
went up, not p. but in private. Jn 7.10
Christ was p. portrayed as crucified? Gal 3.01
sometimes being p. exposed to abuse Heb 10.33

PUBLISH —ES
p. it not in the streets of Ashkelon; 2Sa 1.20
who p. peace, who brings good Is 52.07

PUNISH —ED
then I will p. their transgression Ps 89.32
I will p. the world for its evil, Is 13.11
their iniquity, and p. their sins; Hos 8.13
"that on the day I p. Israel for Amo 3.14
and will p. him, and put him with Mt 24.51
being ready to p. every disobedience, 2Co 10.06
as p., and yet not killed; 6.09
courage when you are p. by him. Heb 12.05

PUNISHMENT
"My p. is greater than I can bear. Gen 4.13
Add to them p. upon p.; Ps 69.27
What will you do on the day of p., Is 10.03
Be not cut off in her p., Jer 51.06
The days of p. have come, the days Hos 9.07
And they will go away into eternal p., Mt 25.46
suffer the p. of eternal destruction 2Th 1.09
How much worse p. do you think will Heb 10.29
For fear has to do with p., 1Jn 4.18

PURE
with the p. thou dost show thyself p., 2Sa 22.27
Can a man be p. before his Maker? Job 4.17
the LORD are promises that are p., Ps 12.06
the commandment of the LORD is p., 19.08

"Blessed are the p. in heart, Mt 5.08
and may be p. and blameless for the Php 1.10
whatever is p., whatever is lovely, 4.08
issues from a p. heart and a good 1Ti 1.05
To the p. all things are p., but to the Tit 1.15
Religion that is p. and undefiled Jas 1.27
the street of the city was p. gold, Rev 21.21

PURGE
P. me with hyssop, and I shall be Ps 51.07

PURIFIED —IES —Y
Having p. your souls by your 1Pe 1.22
hopes in him p. himself as he is 1Jn 3.03
and p. your hearts, you men of Jas 4.08

PURPOSE —S (n)
to God who fulfils his p. for me. Ps 57.02
has made everything for its p., Pro 16.04
let the p. of the Holy One of Is 5.19
and I will accomplish all my p.,' 46.10
rejected the p. of God for themselves, Lk 7.30
No, for this p. I have come to this Jn 12.27
who are called according to his p. Rom 8.28
that God's p. of election might 9.11
the law, then Christ died to no p. Gal 2.21
For a good p. it is always good to 4.18
to the eternal p. which he has Eph 3.11
unchangeable character of his p., Heb 6.17
you have seen the p. of the LORD, Jas 5.11
will disclose the p. of the heart. 1Co 4.05

PURPOSED
and as I have p., so shall it stand, Is 14.24
I have p., and I will do it. 46.11
for I have spoken, I have p.; Jer 4.28

PURSE —S*
Carry no p., no bag, no sandals; Lk 10.04
yourselves with p. that do not 12.33

PURSUE
a driven leaf and p. dry chaff? Job 13.25
Why do you, like God, p. me? 19.22
and do good; seek peace, and p. it. Ps 34.14
they did not p. it through faith, Rom 9.32
Let us then p. what makes for peace 14.19
let him seek peace and p. it. 1Pe 3.11

Q

QUAKE
the cherubim; let the earth q.! Ps 99.01
mountains might q. at thy presence— Is 64.01

QUAKING (n)
"Son of man, eat your bread with q., Eze 12.18

QUARRELING (n)
but q. is like the bars of a castle. Pro 18.19
and a wife's q. is a continual 19.13
licentiousness, not in q. and jealousy. Rom 13.13
people that there is q. among you, 1Co 1.11
holy hands without anger or q.; 1Ti 2.08

QUARRY (n)
and to the q. from which you were Is 51.01

QUEEN —S
and he told it to Q. Esther, Est 2.22
to make cakes for the q. of heaven; Jer 7.18
The q. of the South will arise at Mt 12.42
of Candace the q. of the Ethiopians, Ac 8.27
'A q. I sit, I am no widow, mourning Rev 18.07
and their q. your nursing mothers. Is 49.23

QUENCH —ED
Many waters cannot q. love, neither can Sol 8.07

QUENCH —ED (cont.)
bruised reed or q. a smoldering　　　Mt 12.20
Do not q. the Spirit,　　　　　　　1Th 5.19
Night and day it shall not be q.;　　Is 34.10
not die, and the fire is not q.　　　Mk 9.48

QUESTION —ED (v)
"Why do you q. thus in your hearts?　Mk 2.08
priest then q. Jesus about his　　　Jn 18.19

QUESTION —S (n)
and they asked him a q.,　　　　　Mt 22.23
together, Jesus asked them a q.,　　　22.41
apostles and the elders about this q.　Ac 15.02
raising any q. on the ground of　　1Co 10.25
listening to them and asking them q.;　Lk 2.46

QUESTIONING (n)
things without grumbling or q.,　　Php 2.14

QUICK —LY
Let every man be q. to hear,　　　Jas 1.19
Make friends q. with your accuser,　Mt 5.25
"What you are going to do, do q."　Jn 13.27
that you are so q. deserting him　　Gal 1.06
not to be q. shaken in mind or　　2Th 2.02

QUIET —LY
"Be q., for this day is holy;　　　Neh 8.11
The whole earth is at rest and q.;　Is 14.07
we may lead a q. and peaceable　　1Ti 2.02
jewel of a gentle and q. spirit,　　1Pe 3.04
one should wait q. for the salvation　Lam 3.26
shame, resolved to divorce her q.　Mt 1.19
to aspire to live q., to mind　　　1Th 4.11

R

RABBI
places, and being called r. by men.　Mt 23.07
"R. (which means Teacher), where are　Jn 1.38

RACE
know that in a r. all the runners　1Co 9.24
good fight, I have finished the r.,　2Ti 4.07
perseverance the r. that is set　　Heb 12.01
But you are a chosen r., a royal　　1Pe 2.09

RAGE —S —ING (v)
Spirit, 'Why did the Gentiles r.,　　Ac 4.25
the fool only r. and laughs, and　　Pro 29.09
quenched r. fire, escaped the edge　Heb 11.34

RAGE (n)
the wise men, was in a furious r.,　Mt 2.16

RAIMENT
Thou changest them like r., and they　Ps 102.26
lightning, and his r. white as snow.　Mt 28.03

RAIN (v)
let the skies r. down righteousness;　Is 45.08
he may come and r. salvation upon　Hos 10.12

RAIN (n)
I will send r. upon the earth　　　Gen 7.04
the early r. and the latter r.,　　Deu 11.14
he gives r. upon the earth and　　Job 5.10
"Has the r. a father, or who has　　38.28
and the clouds return after the r.;　Ecc 12.02
and sends r. on the just and on the　Mt 5.45
and the r. fell, and the floods came,　7.25

RAISE —D
I will r. up for them a prophet　　Deu 18.18
On a bare hill r. a signal, cry　　Is 13.02
and r. you from your graves, O my　Eze 37.12
these stones to r. up children to　Mt 3.09
Heal the sick, r. the dead, cleanse　10.08
and r. up children for his brother.'　22.24

and in three days I will r. it up."　Jn 2.19
and I will r. him up at the last　　6.40
'God will r. up for you a prophet　Ac 7.37
and will also r. us up by his　　1Co 6.14
whom he did not r. if it is true　　15.15
God was able to r. men even from　Heb 11.19
the Son of man is r. from the dead."　Mt 17.09
This Jesus God r. up, and of that we　Ac 2.32
as Christ was r. from the dead by　Rom 6.04
is preached as r. from the dead,　1Co 15.12
one will ask, "How are the dead r.?　15.35
If then you have been r. with Christ,　Col 3.01

RANSOM —ED (v)
But God will r. my soul from the　Ps 49.15
thy blood didst r. men for God　　Rev 5.09
that you were r. from the futile　　1Pe 1.18

RANSOM —ED (n)
The r. of a man's life is his wealth,　Pro 13.08
I give Egypt as your r., Ethiopia　Is 43.03
to give his life as a r. for many."　Mt 20.28
who gave himself as a r. for all,　1Ti 2.06
And the r. of the LORD shall return,　Is 35.10

RASH
Be not r. with your mouth, nor let　Ecc 5.02
to be quiet and do nothing r.　　Ac 19.36

RAVEN —S
the owl and the r. shall dwell in　Is 34.11
Consider the r.: they neither sow　Lk 12.24

READ —S
sabbath day. And he stood up to r.;　Lk 4.16
to be known and r. by all men;　　2Co 3.02
this letter be r. to all the　　　1Th 5.27
tablets, so he may run who r. it.　Hab 2.02
Blessed is he who r. aloud the　　Rev 1.03

READY
Therefore you also must be r.;　　Mt 24.44

READY (cont.)

'Come; for all is now r.'	Lk 14.17
of the house, r. for any good work.	2Ti 2.21
for a salvation r. to be revealed	1Pe 1.05

REAP —ED —S

sow in tears r. with shouts of joy!	Ps 126.05
and they shall r. the whirlwind.	Hos 8.07
neither sow nor r. nor gather into	Mt 6.26
You knew that I r. where I have not	25.26
that I may r. some harvest among	Rom 1.13
a man sows, that he will also r.	Gal 6.07
and r., for the hour to r. has come,	Rev 14.15
you have r. injustice, you have	Hos 10.13
true, 'One sows and another r.'	Jn 4.37

REAPER —S

field, like sheaves after the r.,	Jer 9.22
overtake the r. and the treader of	Amo 9.13
that sower and r. may rejoice together.	Jn 4.36
gleaned in the field after the r.;	Ru 2.03
of the age, and the r. are angels.	Mt 13.39

REASON —ED* (v)

let us r. together, says the LORD:	Is 1.18
like a child, I r. like a child;	1Co 13.11

REBEL —LED (v)

do not r. against him, for he will	Ex 23.21
But they r. and grieved his holy	Is 63.10

REBELLION

For he adds r. to his sin;	Job 34.37
unless the r. comes first, and the	2Th 2.03
harden your hearts as in the r.,	Heb 3.08

REBUILD

and r. the house of the LORD, the	Ez 1.03
r.the walls of Jerusalem,	Ps 51.18

REBUKE —D (v)

O LORD, r. me not in thy anger, nor	Ps 6.01
Peter took him and began to r. him,	Mt 16.22
Do not r. an older man but exhort	1Ti 5.01
he rose and r. the winds and the	Mt 8.26
the disciples saw it, they r. them.	Lk 18.15
but was r. for his own transgression;	2Pe 2.16

REBUKE —S (n)

At thy r. they fled; at the sound	Ps 104.07
a scoffer does not listen to r.	Pro 13.01
dost chasten man with r. for sin,	Ps 39.11

RECEIVE —D —S

a prophet shall r. a prophet's	Mt 10.41
the blind r. their sight and the	11.05
you will r., if you have faith."	21.22
does not r. the kingdom of God	Mk 10.15
Father's name, and you do not r. me;	Jn 5.43
said to them, "R. the Holy Spirit.	20.22
But you shall r. power when the	Ac 1.08
is more blessed to give than to r.' "	20.35
what have you that you did not r.?	1Co 4.07
that we might r. adoption as sons.	Gal 4.05

did not r. what was promised,	Heb 11.39
and we r. from him whatever we ask,	1Jn 3.22
to r. glory and honor and power, for	Rev 4.11
I should have r. what was my own	Mt 25.27
days drew near for him to be r. up,	Lk 9.51
and his own people r. him not.	Jn 1.11
And from his fulness have we all r.,	1.16
ministry which I r. from the Lord	Ac 20.24
by his blood, to be r. by faith.	Rom 3.25
For I r. from the Lord what I also	1Co 11.23
of first importance what I also r.,	15.03
but r. me as an angel of God, as	Gal 4.14
I have r. full payment, and more;	Php 4.18
As therefore you r. Christ Jesus	Col 2.06
the tradition that you r. from us.	2Th 3.06
"Whoever r. one such child in my	Mt 18.05
For every one who asks r.,	Lk 11.10
and he who r. me r. him who sent me."	Jn 13.20
compete, but only one r. the prize?	1Co 9.24

RECKON —ED

whom the Lord will not r. his sin."	Rom 4.08
and he r. it to him as righteousness.	Gen 15.06
'And he was r. with transgressors';	Lk 22.37
his faith is r. as righteousness.	Rom 4.05

RECOGNIZE —D

we r. no other practice, nor do the	1Co 11.16
And when the men of that place r. him,	Mt 14.35

RECOMPENSE (n)

a year of r. for the cause of Zion.	Is 34.08
the LORD, and my r. with my God."	49.04
Is evil a r. for good? Yet they have	Jer 18.20
for the LORD is a God or r.,	51.56
come, the days of r. have come;	Hos 9.07
bringing my r., to repay every one	Rev 22.12

RECONCILE —D —ING

and might r. us both to God in one	Eph 2.16
and through him to r. to himself	Col 1.20
first be r. to your brother, and	Mt 5.24
enemies we were r. to God by the	Rom 5.10
through Christ r. us to himself	2Co 5.18
was in Christ r. the world to	5.19

RED

The first came forth r., all his body	Gen 25.25
My face is r. with weeping, and on	Job 16.16
though they are r. like crimson,	Is 1.18
Why is thy apparel r., and thy garments	63.02
fair weather; for the sky is r.'	Mt 16.02
And out came another horse, bright r.;	Rev 6.04

REDEEM —ED

and I will r. you with an outstretched	Ex 6.06
all the first-born of my sons I r.'	13.15
of an ass you shall r. with a lamb,	34.20
R. Israel, O God, out of all his	Ps 25.22
Thou didst with thy arm r. thy people,	77.15
that he was the one to r. Israel.	Lk 24.21
to r. those who were under the law,	Gal 4.05
for us to r. us from all iniquity	Tit 2.14
love the people whom thou hast r.,	Ex 15.13

REDEEM —ED (cont.)

thou hast r. me, O LORD, faithful God.	Ps 31.05
"Fear not, for I have r. you;	Is 43.01
and you shall be r. without money.	52.03
he has visited and r. his people,	Lk 1.68
Christ r. us from the curse of the	Gal 3.13
these have been r. from mankind as	Rev 14.04

REDEEMED (n)

Let the r. of the LORD say so, whom	Ps 107.02
but the r. shall walk there.	Is 35.09

REDEEMER*

For I know that my R. lives,	Job 19.25
sight, O LORD, my rock and my r.	Ps 19.14
your R. is the Holy One of Israel.	Is 41.14
Our R.—the LORD of hosts is his	47.04
LORD, am your Savior and your R.,	60.16

REDEMPTION

give for the r. of his life	Ex 21.30
He sent r. to his people;	Ps 111.09
love, and with him is plenteous r.	130.07
looking for the r. of Jerusalem.	Lk 2.38
because your r. is drawing near."	21.28
through the r. which is in Christ	Rom 3.24
as sons, the r. of our bodies.	8.23
In him we have r. through his blood,	Eph 1.07
blood, thus securing an eternal r.	Heb 9.12

REED —S

a bruised r. he will not break, and	Is 42.03
A r. shaken by the wind?	Mt 11.07
and took the r. and struck him on	27.30
with vinegar, and put it on a r.,	27.48
it among the r. at the river's	Ex 2.03

REFINE —D

I will r. them and test them, for	Jer 9.07
Behold, I have r. you, but not like	Is 48.10
r. as in a furnace, and his voice	Rev 1.15

REFINING* (n)

in vain the r. goes on, for the	Jer 6.29

REFRAIN —S

and a time to r. from embracing;	Ecc 3.05
no right to r. from working for a	1Co 9.06
and will r. from burdening you in	2Co 11.09
and he who r. from marriage will do	1Co 7.38

REFRESH —ED

in the Lord. R. my heart in Christ.	Phm 20
for they r. my spirit as well as	1Co 16.18
on Onesiphorus, for he often r. me;	2Ti 1.16
saints have been r. through you.	Phm 7

REFUGE

my God, my rock, in whom I take r.,	2Sa 22.03
This God is my strong r., and has	22.33
Preserve me, O God, for in thee I take r.	Ps 16.01
Be thou a rock of r. for me,	31.02
God is our r. and strength, a very	46.01
shadow of thy wings I will take r.,	57.01

not remembered the Rock of your r.;	Is 17.10
No r. will remain for the shepherds,	Jer 25.35
have fled for r. might have strong	Heb 6.18

REFUSE —D —S (v)

See that you do not r. him who is	Heb 12.25
Pharaoh stubbornly r. to let us go,	Ex 13.15
but r. to walk according to his law.	Ps 78.10
they have r. to return to me.	Hos 11.05
If any one r. to obey what we say	2Th 3.14

REGARD —ED —S (v)

I r. not myself; I loathe my life.	Job 9.21
he will r. the prayer of the	Ps 102.17
of hosts, him you shall r. as holy;	Is 8.13
In that day men will r. their Maker,	17.07
for you do not r. the position of	Mt 22.16
I neither fear God nor r. man,	Lk 18.04
we r. no one from a human point of	2Co 5.16
do not r. lightly the discipline of	Heb 12.05
for he has r. the low estate of his	Lk 1.48
uncircumcision be r. as circumcision?	Rom 2.26
we are r. as sheep to be slaughtered."	8.36
the LORD is high, he r. the lowly;	Ps 138.06

REGION —S

And in that r. there were shepherds	Lk 2.08
have any room for work in these r.,	Rom 15.23

REIGN —ED —S (v)

him, "Are you indeed to r. over us?	Gen 37.08
The LORD will r. for ever and ever."	Ex 15.18
that said, 'Shall Saul r. over us?'	1Sa 11.12
that a godless man should not r.,	Job 34.30
a king will r. in righteousness, and	Is 32.01
do not want this man to r. over us.'	Lk 19.14
righteousness r. in life through	Rom 5.17
sin therefore r. in your mortal	6.12
And would that you did r.,	1Co 4.08
For he must r. until he has put all	15.25
and they shall r. for ever and	Rev 22.05
as sin r. in death, grace also might	Rom 5.21
The LORD r.; let the earth rejoice;	Ps 97.01
who says to Zion, "Your God r."	Is 52.07

REJECT —ED —S

God will not r. a blameless man, nor	Job 8.20
and r. not your mother's teaching;	Pro 1.08
commands of men who r. the truth.	Tit 1.14
we escape if we r. him who warns	Heb 12.25
r. authority, and revile the glorious	Jud 8
Hast thou not r. us, O God?	Ps 60.10
He was despised and r. by men;	Is 53.03
You have r. me, says the LORD, you	Jer 15.06
the builders r. has become the	Mt 21.42
and the lawyers r. the purpose of	Lk 7.30
things and be r. by this generation.	17.25
God has not r. his people whom he	Rom 11.02
he was r., for he found no chance	Heb 12.17
r. by men but in God's sight chosen	1Pe 2.04
you hears me, and he who r. you r. me,	Lk 10.16

REJOICE —D —S —ING

R. in the LORD, O you righteous!	Ps 33.01

REJOICE —D —S —ING (cont.)

But the king shall r. in God;	Ps 63.11
be glad, and let the earth r.;	96.11
of those who seek the LORD r.!	105.03
let us r. and be glad in it.	118.24
Do not r. when your enemy falls, and	Pro 24.17
us be glad and r. in his salvation."	Is 25.09
the desert shall r. and blossom;	35.01
And you shall r. in the LORD;	41.16
Let not the buyer r., nor the seller	Eze 7.12
R. greatly, O daughter of Zion!	Zec 9.09
R. and be glad, for your reward is	Mt 5.12
and we r. in our hope of sharing	Rom 5.02
R. in your hope, be patient in	12.12
it does not r. at wrong, but r.	1Co 13.06
is proclaimed; and in that I r.	Php 1.18
Finally, my brethren, r. in the Lord.	3.01
R. in the Lord always; again I will say, R.	4.04
Now I r. in my sufferings for your	Col 1.24
R. always,	1Th 5.16
R. over her, O heaven, O saints and	Rev 18.20
same hour he r. in the Holy Spirit	Lk 10.21
and my spirit r. in God my Savior,	1.47
r. greatly at the bridegroom's voice;	Jn 3.29
at wrong, but r. in the right.	1Co 13.06
the LORD are right, r. the heart;	Ps 19.08
as sorrowful, yet always r.;	2Co 6.10

REJOICING (n)

the presence of his glory with r.,	Jud 24

RELEASE (v)

accustomed to r. for the crowd any	Mt 27.15
know that I have power to r. you,	Jn 19.10

RELIEF

to send r. to the brethren who	Ac 11.29
part in the r. of the saints—	2Co 8.05

RELIES* —Y —ING

of the LORD and r. upon his God?	Is 50.10
and do not r. on your own insight.	Pro 3.05
to Egypt for help and r. on horses,	Is 31.01
"We r. on the LORD our God," is it	36.07
they r. on empty pleas, they speak	59.04
was to make us r. not on ourselves	2Co 1.09
you are r. on Egypt, that broken	Is 36.06

RELIGION

confess, is the mystery of our r.:	1Ti 3.16
holding the form of r. but denying	2Ti 3.05
R. that is pure and undefiled	Jas 1.27

REMAIN —ED —EST —S

R. this night, and in the morning, if	Ru 3.13
to Babylon and r. there until the	Jer 27.22
r. here, and watch with me."	Mt 26.38
you see the Spirit descend and r.,	Jn 1.33
Every one should r. in the state in	1Co 7.20
But to r. in the flesh is more	Php 1.24
seen God and r. alive after seeing	Gen 16.13
at first baptized, and there he r.	Jn 10.40
they will perish, but thou r.;	Heb 1.11
While the earth r., seedtime and	Gen 8.22

law that the Christ r. for ever.	Jn 12.34
strengthen what r. and is on the	Rev 3.02

REMEMBER —ED —ING —S

I will r. my covenant which is	Gen 9.15
"R. the sabbath day, to keep it holy.	Ex 20.08
You shall r. the LORD your God, for	Deu 8.18
R. not the sins of my youth, or my	Ps 25.07
R. also your Creator in the days of	Ecc 12.01
and I will r. their sin no more."	Jer 31.34
R. Lot's wife.	Lk 17.32
R. Jesus Christ, risen from the dead,	2Ti 1.04
R. then what you received and heard;	Rev 3.03
and God r. his covenant with	Ex 2.24
He has r. his steadfast love and	Ps 98.03
be moved; he will be r. for ever.	112.06
and have not r. the Rock of your	Is 17.10
r. the words of the Lord Jesus, how	Ac 20.35
our frame; he r. that we are dust.	Ps 103.14

REMEMBRANCE

For in death there is no r. of thee;	Ps 6.05
the fool there is no enduring r.,	Ecc 2.16
and a book of r. was written before	Mal 3.16
Israel, in r. of his mercy,	Lk 1.54
is for you. Do this in r. of me."	1Co 11.24

REMIND

to r. you of my ways in Christ, as I	1Co 4.17
Now I would r. you, brethren, in what	15.01
let him r. himself that as he is	2Co 10.07

REMNANT

to preserve for you a r. on earth,	Gen 45.07
prayer for the r. that is left."	2Ki 19.04
hast given us such a r. as this,	Ez 9.13
A r. will return, the r. of Jacob,	Is 10.21
thoroughly as a vine the r. of Israel;	Jer 6.09
only a r. of them will be saved;	Rom 9.27
at the present time there is a r.,	11.05

REMOVE —D

r. this cup from me; yet not what	Mk 14.36
him not seek to r. the marks of	1Co 7.18
so as to r. mountains, but have not	13.02
The righteous will never be r.,	Pro 10.30
covenant of peace shall not be r.,	Is 54.10
turns to the Lord the veil is r.	2Co 3.16
block of the cross has been r.	Gal 5.11

REND

a time to r., and a time to sew;	Ecc 3.07
thou wouldst r. the heavens and	Is 64.01
and r. your hearts and not your	Joe 2.13

RENDER

What shall I r. to the LORD for all	Ps 116.12
R. true judgments, show kindness and	Zec 7.09
"R. therefore to Caesar the things	Mt 22.21
For he will r. to every man according	Rom 2.06

RENEW* —ED* —EST*

to Gilgal and there r. the kingdom."	1Sa 11.14
the LORD shall r. their strength,	Is 40.31

RENEW —ED —EST (cont.)

gladness, he will r. you in his love;	Zep 3.17
your youth is r. like the eagle's.	Ps 103.05
inner nature is being r. every day.	2Co 4.16
and thou r. the face of the ground.	Ps 104.30

REPAIR

Israel money to r. the house of	2Ch 24.05
they shall r. the ruined cities, the	Is 61.04

REPAY

Do not say, "I will r. evil";	Pro 20.22
then he will r. every man for what	Mt 16.27
R. no one evil for evil, but take	Rom 12.17
is mine, I will r., says the Lord."	12.19
to r. every one for what he has	Rev 22.12

REPENT —ED —S

myself, and r. in dust and ashes."	Job 42.06
I will r. of the evil that I	Jer 18.08
R. and turn from all your	Eze 18.30
God may yet r. and turn from his	Jon 3.09
"R., for the kingdom of heaven is	Mt 3.02
"R., and be baptized every one of	Ac 2.38
they should r. and turn to God and	26.20
for he found no chance to r.,	Heb 12.17
they would have r. long ago in	Mt 11.21
for they r. at the preaching of	12.41
he r. and brought back the thirty	27.03
of God over one sinner who r."	Lk 15.10

REPENTANCE

Bear fruit that befits r.,	Mt 3.08
"I baptize you with water for r.,	3.11
also God has granted r. unto life."	Ac 11.18
perform deeds worthy of their r.	26.20
kindness is meant to lead you to r.?	Rom 2.04
produces a r. that leads to	2Co 7.10
a foundation of r. from dead works	Heb 6.01
but that all should reach r.	2Pe 3.09

REPORT (n)

And the r. of this went through all	Mt 9.26
"Lord, who has believed our r.,	Jn 12.38

REPROACH —ES (n)

Thou knowest my r., and my shame	Ps 69.19
fear not the r. of men, and be not	Is 51.07
to be a r., a byword, a taunt, and a	Jer 24.09
and a r. among all the nations	29.18
Now a bishop must be above r.,	1Ti 3.02
so that they may be without r.	5.07
"The r. of those who reproached	Rom 15.03

REPROOF

but he who rejects r. goes astray.	Pro 10.17
for r., for correction, and for	2Ti 3.16

REPROVE —S

exhort and r. with all authority.	Tit 2.15
Those whom I love, I r. and chasten;	Rev 3.19
happy is the man whom God r.;	Job 5.17
for the LORD r. him whom he loves,	Pro 3.12

REPUTE

among you seven men of good r.,	Ac 6.03
and dishonor, in ill r. and good r.	2Co 6.08
who were of r.) the gospel which I	Gal 2.02

REQUIRE —D —S

brother I will r. the life of man.	Gen 9.05
does the LORD r. of you but to do	Mic 6.08
For there our captors r. of us songs,	Ps 137.03
it shall be r. of this generation.	Lk 11.51
this night your soul is r. of you;	12.20
is given, of him will much be r.;	12.48
of suffering is r. of your brotherhood	1Pe 5.09
what the law r. is written on	Rom 2.15

REQUITE

For thou dost r. a man according to	Ps 62.12
lead him and r. him with comfort,	Is 57.18
the Lord will r. him for his deeds.	2Ti 4.14

RESCUE —D —S

I will r. my sheep from their	Eze 34.10
will carry off, and none shall r.	Hos 5.14
The Lord will r. me from every evil	2Ti 4.18
knows how to r. the godly from	2Pe 2.09
and r. him out of all his afflictions,	Ac 7.10
yet from them all the Lord r. me.	2Ti 3.11
He delivers and r., he works	Dan 6.27

RESIST —S*

Do not r. one who is evil. But if	Mt 5.39
you always r. the Holy Spirit.	Ac 7.51
fault? For who can r. his will?"	Rom 9.19
R. him, firm in your faith, knowing	1Pe 5.09
he who r. the authorities r. what God	Rom 13.02

RESPECT (n)

with r. to the hope and the resurrection	Ac 23.06
r. to whom r. is due, honor to whom	Rom 13.07
made like his brethren in every r.,	Heb 2.17
who in every r. has been tempted	4.15

REST —ED —S (v)

on the seventh day you shall r.;	Ex 23.12
in the night his mind does not r.	Ecc 2.23
of the LORD shall r. upon him,	Is 11.02
your peace shall r. upon him;	Lk 10.06
and he r. on the seventh day from	Gen 2.02
sabbath they r. according to the	Lk 23.56
"The spirit of Elijah r. on Elisha."	2Ki 2.15
but the wrath of God r. upon him.	Jn 3.36
of glory and of God r. upon you.	1Pe 4.14

REST (n)

the ark came to r. upon the mountains	Gen 8.04
Return, O my soul, to your r.;	Ps 116.07
even there you will have no r."	Is 23.12
returning and r. you shall be	30.15
in it, and find r. for your souls.	Jer 6.16
heavy-laden, and I will give you r.	Mt 11.28
we who have believed enter that r.,	Heb 4.03

RESTORE —D —S

R. to me the joy of thy salvation,	Ps 51.12

RESTORE —D —S (cont.)

R. us, O God; let thy face shine,	Ps 80.03
thou didst r. the fortunes of Jacob.	85.01
R. us to thyself, O LORD, that we may	Lam 5.21
that I will r. to you double.	Zec 9.12
come, and he is to r. all things;	Mt 17.11
at this time r. the kingdom to	Ac 1.06
spiritual should r. him in a spirit	Gal 6.01
impossible to r. again to repentance	Heb 6.04
will himself r., establish, and	1Pe 5.10
And the LORD r. the fortunes of Job,	Job 42.10
how shall its saltness be r.?	Mt 5.13
and it was r., whole like the other	12.13
he r. my soul. He leads me in	Ps 23.03

RESTRAIN —ED —S

to r. her is to r. the wind or to	Pro 27.16
Wilt thou r. thyself at these	Is 64.12
Who can r. her lust? None who	Jer 2.24
he r. his anger often, and did not	Ps 78.38
I have kept still and r. myself;	Is 42.14
but he who r. his lips is prudent.	Pro 10.19

RESTRAINT

benefit, not to lay any r. upon you,	1Co 7.35
kept under r. until faith should be	Gal 3.23

RESURRECTION

him, who say that there is no r.;	Mt 22.23
tombs after his r. they went into	27.53
be repaid at the r. of the just."	Lk 14.14
sons of God, being sons of the r.	20.36
to her, "I am the r. and the life;	Jn 11.25
he preached Jesus and the r.	Ac 17.18
Sadducees say that there is no r.,	23.08
respect to the r. of the dead I am	24.21
united with him in a r. like his.	Rom 6.05
But if there is no r. of the dead,	1Co 15.13
know him and the power of his r.,	Php 3.10
that the r. is past already.	2Ti 2.18
the r. of the dead, and eternal	Heb 6.02
were ended. This is the first r.	Rev 20.05

RETURN —ED —S

we will r. with you to your people."	Ru 1.10
R. every man to his home, for this	1Ki 12.24
"If you r. in peace, the LORD has	22.28
If you r. to the Almighty and	Job 22.23
R., O LORD! How long? Have	Ps 90.13
R., O my soul, to your rest;	116.07
A remnant will r., the remnant of	Is 10.21
And the ransomed of the LORD shall r.,	35.10
righteousness a word that shall not r.:	45.23
let him r. to the LORD, that he may	55.07
it shall not r. to me empty, but it	55.11
for they shall r. to me with their	Jer 24.07
who does not r. empty-handed.	50.09
"Come, let us r. to the LORD;	Hos 6.01
they have refused to r. to me.	11.05
R. to me, and I will r. to you, says	Mal 3.07
worthy, let your peace r. to you.	Mt 10.13
'After this I will r., and I will	Ac 15.16
Do not r. evil for evil or reviling	1Pe 3.09
And the shepherds r., glorifying	Lk 2.20

And Jesus r. in the power of the	4.14
but have now r. to the Shepherd and	1Pe 2.25
Like a dog that r. to his vomit is	Pro 26.11
and the spirit r. to God who gave	Ecc 12.07

RETURNING* (n)

"In r. and rest you shall be saved;	Is 30.15

REVEAL —ED —S

to whom the Son chooses to r. him.	Mt 11.27
was pleased to r. his Son to me, in	Gal 1.16
God will r. that also to you.	Php 3.15
there God had r. himself to him	Gen 35.07
And the glory of the LORD shall be r.,	Is 40.05
has the arm of the LORD been r.?	53.01
Then the mystery was r. to Daniel	Dan 2.19
is covered that will not be r.,	Mt 10.26
understanding and r. them to babes;	11.25
that Jesus was r. to the disciples	Jn 21.14
of God is r. through faith for	Rom 1.17
the glory that is to be r. to us.	8.18
God has r. to us through the Spirit.	1Co 2.10
restraint until faith should be r.	Gal 3.23
Lord Jesus is r. from heaven with	2Th 1.07
ready to be r. in the last time.	1Pe 1.05
and be glad when his glory is r.	4.13
for thy judgments have been r."	Rev 15.04
a God in heaven who r. mysteries,	Dan 2.28

REVELATION

a light for r. to the Gentiles, and	Lk 2.32
according to the r. of the mystery	Rom 16.25
came through a r. of Jesus Christ.	Gal 1.12
mystery was made known to me by r.,	Eph 3.03

REVILE —D —S

"You shall not r. God, nor curse a	Ex 22.28
you when men r. you and persecute	Mt 5.11
the enemy no occasion to r. us.	1Ti 5.14
he was r., he did not r. in return;	1Pe 2.23
mountains and r. me upon the hills,	Is 65.07
with him also r. him in the same	Mt 27.44
When r., we bless; when persecuted,	1Co 4.12
and an impious people r. thy name.	Ps 74.18

REVIVE —D —ING

who seek God, let your hearts r.	Ps 69.32
Wilt thou not r. us again, that thy	85.06
commandment came, sin r. and I died;	Rom 7.09
the LORD is perfect, r. the soul;	Ps 19.07

REWARD —ING —S (v)

So may the LORD r. you with good	1Sa 24.19
his head, and the LORD will r. you.	Pro 25.22
r. every man according to his ways	Jer 32.19
and that he r. those who seek him.	Heb 11.06

REWARD (n)

there is a r. for the righteous;	Ps 58.11
sows righteousness gets a sure r.	Pro 11.18
behold, his r. is with him, and his	Is 40.10
for your r. is great in heaven, for	Mt 5.12
I say to you, they have their r.	6.02
shall receive a prophet's r.,	10.41

REWARD (n) (cont.)

receiving the due r. of our deeds;	Lk 23.41
What then is my r.? Just this:	1Co 9.18
receive the inheritance as your r.;	Col 3.24
confidence, which has a great r.	Heb 10.35

RIB* —S*

and the r. which the LORD God had	Gen 2.22
took one of his r. and closed up	2.21
it had three r. in its mouth between	Dan 7.05

RICH

The LORD makes poor and makes r.;	1Sa 2.07
The r. rules over the poor, and the	Pro 22.07
A r. man is wise in his own eyes,	28.11
in your bedchamber curse the r.;	Ecc 10.20
and with a r. man in his death,	Is 53.09
let not the r. man glory in his	Jer 9.23
r. in treasures, your end has come,	51.13
but I am r., I have gained wealth	Hos 12.08
be hard for a r. man to enter the	Mt 19.23
there came a r. man from Arimathea,	27.57
Many r. people put in large sums.	Mk 12.41
and the r. he has sent empty away.	Lk 1.53
himself, and is not r. toward God."	12.21
Already you have become r.! Without	1Co 4.08
as poor, yet making many r.; as	2Co 6.10
Christ, that though he was r., yet	8.09
who is r. in mercy, out of the great	Eph 2.04
to be r. in good deeds, liberal and	1Ti 6.18
the world to be r. in faith and	Jas 2.05
both r. and poor, both free and	Rev 13.16

RICHES

if r. increase, set not your heart	Ps 62.10
I delight as much as in all r.	119.14
He who trusts in his r. will wither,	Pro 11.28
and in their r. you shall glory.	Is 61.06
is he who gets r. but not by right	Jer 17.11
the delight in r. choke the word,	Mt 13.22
upon the r. of his kindness and	Rom 2.04
make known the r. of his glory for	9.23
depth of the r. and wisdom and	11.33
according to the r. of his grace	Eph 1.07
the unsearchable r. of Christ,	3.08
on uncertain r. but on God who	1Ti 6.17

RIDDLE —S

them, "Let me now put a r. to you;	Ju 14.12
the words of the wise and their r.	Pro 1.06
who understands r., shall arise.	Dan 8.23

RIDER —S

horse and his r. he has thrown into	Ex 15.01
white horse, and its r. had a bow;	Rev 6.02
here come r., horsemen in pairs!"	Is 21.09
overthrow the chariots and their r.;	Hab 2.22
the flesh of horses and their r.,	Rev 19.18

RIDES —T*

song to him who r. upon the clouds;	Ps 68.04
to him who r. in the heavens, the	68.33
who r. on the wings of the wind,	104.03

RIGHT (adj)

Thou didst stretch out thy r. hand,	Ex 15.12
put a new and r. spirit within me.	Ps 51.10
His r. hand and his holy arm have	98.01
O Jerusalem, let my r. hand wither!	137.05
If your r. eye causes you to sin,	Mt 5.29
know what your r. hand is doing,	6.03
one at your r. hand and one at your	20.21
will say to those at his r. hand,	25.34
but judge with r. judgment."	Jn 7.24
exalted at the r. hand of God,	Ac 2.33
at the r. time Christ died for the	Rom 5.06
I can will what is r., but I cannot	7.18
Come to your r. mind, and sin no	1Co 15.34
Barnabas the r. hand of fellowship,	Gal 2.09
sat down at the r. hand of the	Heb 1.03

RIGHTEOUS

Suppose there are fifty r. within	Gen 18.24
'Can mortal man be r. before God?	Job 4.17
born of a woman, that he can be r.?	15.14
for the LORD knows the way of the r.,	Ps 1.06
God is a r. judge, and a God who has	7.11
For the LORD is r., he loves r. deeds;	11.07
LORD are true, and r. altogether.	19.09
R. art thou, O LORD, and right are	119.137
no man living is r. before thee.	143.02
but the r. will flourish like a	Pro 11.28
The thoughts of the r. are just;	12.05
No ill befalls the r., but the wicked	12.21
Be not r. overmuch, and do not make	Ecc 7.16
a r. God and a Savior; there is	Is 45.21
and all our r. deeds are like a	64.06
O LORD of hosts, who triest the r.,	Jer 20.12
I will cause a r. Branch to spring	33.15
"If a man is r. and does what is	Eze 18.05
the r. turns from his righteousness,	33.18
they sell the r. for silver,	Amo 2.06
but the r. shall live by his faith.	Hab 2.04
not to call the r., but sinners."	Mt 9.13
and separate the evil from the r.,	13.49
also outwardly appear r. to men,	23.28
but the r. into eternal life."	25.46
ninety-nine r. persons who need no	Lk 15.07
who through faith is r. shall live."	Rom 1.17
written: "None is r., no, not one;	3.10
how holy and r. and blameless was	1Th 2.10
but my r. one shall live by faith,	Heb 10.38
The prayer of a r. man has great	Jas 5.16
the Father, Jesus Christ the r.;	1Jn 2.01
and the r. still do right, and the	Rev 22.11

RIGHTEOUSNESS

and he reckoned it to him as r.	Gen 15.06
but in r. shall you judge your	Lev 19.15
Not because of your r. or the	Deu 9.05
I hold fast my r., and will not let	Job 27.06
rewarded me according to my r.;	Ps 18.20
He loves r. and justice; the earth	33.05
The heavens declare his r.,	50.06
May he judge thy people with r.,	72.02
r. and peace will kiss each other.	85.10
R. and justice are the foundation	89.14
Open to me the gates of r., that I	118.19

RIGHTEOUSNESS (cont.)

I walk in the way of r., in the	Pro 8.20
He who is steadfast in r. will live,	11.19
R. exalts a nation, but sin is a	14.34
for r., but behold, a cry!	Is 5.07
R. shall be the girdle of his waist,	11.05
And the effect of r. will be peace,	32.17
gone forth in r. a word that shall	45.23
and do r., for soon my salvation	56.01
your r. shall go before you, the	58.08
turned back, and r. stands afar off;	59.14
He put on r. as a breastplate, and a	59.17
be called: 'The LORD is our r.'	Jer 23.06
iniquity, to bring in everlasting r.,	Dan 9.24
Sow for yourselves r., reap the fruit	Hos 10.12
and r. like an ever-flowing stream.	Amo 5.24
seek r., seek humility; perhaps	Zep 2.03
those who hunger and thirst for r.,	Mt 5.06
But seek first his kingdom and his r.,	6.33
But now the r. of God has been	Rom 3.21
his faith is reckoned as r.	4.05
free gift of r. reign in life	5.17
to God as instruments of r.	6.13
and drink but r. and peace and joy	14.17
our r. and sanctification and	1Co 1.30
him we might become the r. of God.	2Co 5.21
faith, we wait for the hope of r.	Gal 5.05
not having a r. of my own, based on	Php 3.09
aim at r., godliness, faith, love,	1Ti 6.11
Thou hast loved r. and hated	Heb 1.09
we might die to sin and live to r.	1Pe 2.24
and a new earth in which r. dwells.	2Pe 3.13

RIGHTS

maintain the r. of the poor and	Pro 31.09
do not defend the r. of the needy.	Jer 5.28
give to his wife her conjugal r.,	1Co 7.03
made no use of any of these r.,	9.15

RING —S

man took a gold r. weighing a half	Gen 24.22
Like a gold r. in a swine's snout is	Pro 11.22
and make you like a signet r.;	Hag 2.23
and put a r. on his hand, and shoes	Lk 15.22
a man with gold r. and in fine	Jas 2.02

RIPE

But when the grain is r., at once	Mk 4.29
harvest of the earth is fully r."	Rev 14.15

RISE —N —S

R. up, come to our help! Deliver	Ps 44.26
I r. before dawn and cry for help;	119.147
when I sit down and when I r. up;	139.02
Woe to those who r. early in the	Is 5.11
the sun of righteousness shall r.,	Mal 4.02
"R., take the child and his mother,	Mt 2.13
forgiven,' or to say, 'R. and walk'!	9.05
For nation will r. against nation,	24.07
'After three days I will r. again.'	27.63
children will r. against parents	Mk 13.12
no prophet is to r. from Galilee."	Jn 7.52
the first to r. from the dead,	Ac 26.23
the dead in Christ will r. first;	1Th 4.16

glory of the LORD has r. upon you.	Is 60.01
not here; for he has r., as he said.	Mt 28.06
"The Lord has r. indeed, and has	Lk 24.34
Light r. in the darkness for the	Ps 112.04
the morning star r. in your hearts.	2Pe 1.19

RIVER —S

A r. flowed out of Eden to water	Gen 2.10
There is a r. whose streams make	Ps 46.04
peace would have been like a r.,	Is 48.18
baptized by him in the r. Jordan,	Mt 3.06
water like a r. out of his mouth	Rev 12.15
also, on either side of the r.,	22.02
He turned their r. to blood,	Ps 78.44
r. in the desert, to give drink to	Is 43.20
shall flow r. of living water.' "	Jn 7.38
journeys, in danger from r.,	2Co 11.26

ROAD —S

They thrust the poor off the r.;	Job 24.04
spread their garments on the r.,	Mt 21.08
a priest was going down that r.;	Lk 10.31
told what had happened on the r.,	24.35
they have made their r. crooked,	Is 59.08

ROAR —S (v)

let the sea r., and all that fills	Ps 96.11
nations, they r. like the roaring of	Is 17.12
'The LORD will r. from on high,	Jer 25.30
Does a lion r. in the forest, when	Amo 3.04
And the LORD r. from Zion, and	Joe 3.16

ROARING

perplexity at the r. of the sea and	Lk 21.25
devil prowls around like a r. lion,	1Pe 5.08

ROB —BED

Will man r. God? Yet you are	Mal 3.08
"R. no one by violence or by false	Lk 3.14
But this is a people r. and plundered,	Is 42.22
I r. other churches by accepting	2Co 11.08

ROBBER —S

way, that man is a thief and a r.;	Jn 10.01
but Barabbas!" Now Barabbas was a r.	18.40
but you make it a den of r."	Mt 21.13
Then two r. were crucified with him,	27.38
to Jericho, and he fell among r.,	Lk 10.30
nor r. will inherit the kingdom of	1Co 6.10

ROBE

he made him a long r. with sleeves.	Gen 37.03
justice was like a r. and a turban.	Job 29.14
me with the r. of righteousness, as	Is 61.10
shall take hold of the r. of a Jew,	Zec 8.23
him, they stripped him of the r.,	Mt 27.31
right side, dressed in a white r.;	Mk 16.05
servants, 'Bring quickly the best r.,	Lk 15.22
crown of thorns and the purple r.,	Jn 19.05
He is clad in a r. dipped in blood,	Rev 19.13

ROCK

you there on the r. at Horeb;	Ex 17.06
and struck the r. with his rod	Num 20.11

ROCK (cont.)

"The R., his work is perfect;	Deu 32.04
For their r. is not as our R., even	32.31
there is no r. like our God.	1Sa 2.02
He said, "The LORD is my r.,	2Sa 22.02
O LORD, my r. and my redeemer.	Ps 19.14
Be thou a r. of refuge for me, a	31.02
He only is my r. and my salvation,	62.02
and a r. of stumbling to both	Is 8.14
the LORD GOD is an everlasting r.	26.04
which breaks the r. in pieces?	Jer 23.29
who built his house upon the r.;	Mt 7.24
and on this r. I will build my	16.18
tomb, which he had hewn in the r.;	27.60
a r. that will make them fall;	Rom 9.33
them, and the R. was Christ.	1Co 10.04

ROCKY

Other seeds fell on r. ground,	Mt 13.05

ROD —S

his hand Moses took the r. of God.	Ex 4.20
But Aaron's r. swallowed up their	7.12
Write each man's name upon his r.,	Num 17.02
He who spares the r. hates his son,	Pro 13.24
and I said, "I see a r. of almond."	Jer 1.11
I will make you pass under the r.,	Eze 20.37
Shall I come to you with a r.,	1Co 4.21
and Aaron's r. that budded, and the	Heb 9.04
shall rule them with a r. of iron,	Rev 2.27
will rule them with a r. of iron;	19.15
had a measuring r. of gold to	21.15
Three times I have been beaten with r.;	2Co 11.25

ROLL —ED (v)

and the skies r. up like a scroll.	Is 34.04
But let justice r. down like waters,	Amo 5.24
"Who will r. away the stone for us	Mk 16.03
like a weaver I have r. up my life;	Is 38.12
and came and r. back the stone,	Mt 28.02
like a scroll that is r. up,	Rev 6.14

ROOF

Make a r. for the ark, and finish it	Gen 6.16
Samuel called to Saul upon the r.,	1Sa 9.26
upon the r. of the king's house,	2Sa 11.02
to have you come under my r.;	Mt 8.08
they removed the r. above him;	Mk 2.04

ROOM —S

make r. for me to dwell in.'	Is 49.20
go into your r. and shut the door	Mt 6.06
Teacher says, Where is my guest r.,	Mk 14.14
they went up to the upper r.,	Ac 1.13
In my Father's house are many r.;	Jn 14.02

ROOT (n)

but the r. of the righteous will	Pro 12.03
In that day the r. of Jesse shall	Is 11.10
and like a r. out of dry ground;	53.02
axe is laid to the r. of the trees;	Mt 3.10
yet he has no r. in himself, but	13.21
and if the r. is holy, so are the	Rom 11.16
"The r. of Jesse shall come, he who	15.12

of money is the r. of all evils;	1Ti 6.10
that no "r. of bitterness" spring up	Heb 12.15
I am the r. and the offspring of	Rev 22.16

ROOTED

being r. and grounded in love,	Eph 3.17
r. and built up in him and established	Col 2.07

ROPE —S

and instead of a girdle, a r.;	Is 3.24
guard, letting Jeremiah down by r.	Jer 38.06

ROUSE —D —ING*

R. thyself! Why sleepest thou, O	Ps 44.23
R. yourself, r. yourself, stand up, O	Is 51.17
thee when once thy anger is r.?	Ps 76.07
For lo, I am r. the Chaldeans, that	Hab 1.06
Your r. scepter is a scepter of	Ps 45.06
thy righteousness to the r. son!	72.01
If you really fulfil the r. law,	Jas 2.08
a r. priesthood, a holy nation, God's	1Pe 2.09
who have not yet received r. power,	Rev 17.12

RUIN —S (n)

A foolish son is r. to his father,	Pro 19.13
and a flattering mouth works r.	26.28
a r., without inhabitant.	Jer 46.19
A r., r., r. I will make it; there	Eze 21.27
and the r. of that house was great."	Lk 6.49
in their paths are r. and misery,	Rom 3.16
eat cause the r. of one for whom	14.15
plunge men into r. and destruction.	1Ti 6.09
And your ancient r. shall be	Is 58.12
I will make Jerusalem a heap of r.,	Jer 9.11
I will rebuild its r.,	Ac 15.16

RULE (v)

husband, and he shall r. over you."	Gen 3.16
Thou dost r. the raging of the sea;	Ps 89.09
and stars to r. over the night,	136.09
and babes shall r. over them.	Is 3.04
and princes will r. in justice.	32.01
he who rises to r. the Gentiles;	Rom 15.12
wife does not r. over her own body,	1Co 7.04
peace of Christ r. in your hearts,	Col 3.15
Let the elders who r. well be	1Ti 5.17
one who is to r. all the nations	Rev 12.05

RULE —S (n)

we might share the r. with you!	1Co 4.08
This is my r. in all the churches.	7.17
destroying every r. and every	15.24
be upon all who walk by this r.,	Gal 6.16
far above all r. and authority and	Eph 1.21
he competes according to the r.	2Ti 2.05

RULER —S

God, nor curse a r. of your people.	Ex 22.28
A r. who lacks understanding is a	Pro 28.16
Many seek the favor of a r.,	29.26
is our judge, the LORD is our r.,	Is 33.22
is in the land, and r. is against r.	Jer 51.46
a r. came in and knelt before him,	Mt 9.18
the house of a r. who belonged to	Lk 14.01

RULER —S (cont.)

named Nicodemus, a r. of the Jews.	Jn 3.01
now shall the r. of this world be	12.31
'Who made you a r. and a judge	Ac 7.27
All your r. have fled together,	Is 22.03
know that the r. of the Gentiles	Mt 20.25
but the r. scoffed at him, saying,	Lk 23.35
and the r. were gathered together,	Ac 4.26
the market place before the r.;	16.19
For r. are not a terror to good	Rom 13.03
None of the r. of this age understood	1Co 2.08
the world r. of this present	Eph 6.12
submissive to r. and authorities,	Tit 3.01

RUMOR —S

Hark, a r.! Behold, it comes!—	Jer 10.22
comes upon disaster, r. follows r.;	Eze 7.26
will hear of wars and r. of wars;	Mt 24.06

RUN

r. in the way of thy commandments	Ps 119.32

for their feet r. to evil, and they	Pro 1.16
All streams r. to the sea, but the	Ecc 1.07
that they may r. after strong drink,	Is 5.11
they shall r. and not be weary, they	40.31
Do the mountain waters r. dry,	Jer 18.14
tablets, so he may r. who reads it.	Hab 2.02
"R., say to that young man, 'Jerusalem	Zec 2.04
prize? So r. that you may obtain it.	1Co 9.24
should be running or had r. in vain.	Gal 2.02
that I did not r. in vain or labor	Php 2.16
and let us r. with perseverance the	Heb 12.01

RUST

earth, where moth and r. consume and	Mt 6.19
and their r. will be evidence against	Jas 5.03

RUTHLESS

r. men seek my life; they do not	Ps 54.03
lay low the haughtiness of the r.	Is 13.11
For the r. shall come to nought and	29.20
foolish, faithless, heartless, r.	Rom 1.31

S

SABBATH —S

The LORD has given you the s.,	Ex 16.29
"Remember the s. day, to keep it	20.08
The s. of the land shall provide	Lev 25.06
"On the s. day two male lambs a	Num 28.09
today? It is neither new moon nor s."	2Ki 4.23
who keeps the s., not profaning it,	Is 56.02
a burden on the s. day or bring it	Jer 17.21
And the s., that we may offer wheat	Amo 8.05
through the grainfields on the s.;	Mt 12.01
For the Son of man is lord of the s."	12.08
it is lawful to do good on the s."	12.12
Now after the s., toward the dawn	28.01
"The s. was made for man, not man	Mk 2.27
And when the s. was past, Mary	16.01
And he was teaching them on the s.;	Lk 4.31
you circumcise a man upon the s.	Jn 7.22
cross on the s. (for that s. was a	19.31
near Jerusalem, a s. day's journey away;	Ac 1.12
is read every s. in the synagogues."	15.21
argued in the synagogue every s.,	18.04
a festival or a new moon or a s.	Col 2.16
there remains a s. rest for the	Heb 4.09
of Israel, 'You shall keep my s.,	Ex 31.13
Moreover I gave them my s.,	Eze 20.12

SACKCLOTH

and put s. upon his loins, and	Gen 37.34
I have sewed s. upon my skin, and	Job 16.15
When I made s. my clothing, I became	Ps 69.11
in the streets they gird on s.	Is 15.03
and loose the s. from your loins	20.02
and to spread s. and ashes under	58.05
For this gird you with s.,	Jer 4.08
are gashes, and on the loins is s.	48.37
with fasting and s. and ashes.	Dan 9.03
repented long ago in s. and ashes.	Mt 11.21
and the sun become black as s.,	Rev 6.12

SACRED

the east, shall be s. to the LORD.	Jer 31.40
the altar that makes the gift s.?	Mt 23.19
the s. and imperishable proclamation	*Mk 16.08
and of the s. stone that fell from	Ac 19.35
with the s. writings which are	2Ti 3.15

SACRIFICE —D —S (v)

that we may s. to the LORD our God.'	Ex 3.18
"You shall not s. to the LORD your	Deu 17.01
to s. to the LORD your God; and the	1Sa 15.15
your gifts and s. your sons by	Eze 20.31
what pagans s. they offer to	1Co 10.20
when they s. the passover lamb, his	Mk 14.12
our paschal lamb, has been s.	1Co 5.07
already on the point of being s.;	2Ti 4.06
he who s. a lamb, like him who	Is 66.03
Therefore he s. to his net and	Hab 1.16

SACRIFICE —S (n)

and Jacob offered a s. on the	Gen 31.54
'It is the s. of the LORD's passover,	Ex 12.27
"When you offer a s. of peace offerings	Lev 19.05
the ram as a s. of peace offering	Num 6.17
nor for s., but to be a witness	Jos 22.28
behold, to obey is better than s.,	1Sa 15.22
morning I prepare a s. for thee,	Ps 5.03
S. and offering thou dost not	40.06
Offer to God a s. of thanksgiving,	50.14
The s. acceptable to God is a	51.17
up of my hands as an evening s.!	141.02
The s. of the wicked is an abomination	Pro 15.08
then to offer the s. of fools;	Ecc 5.01
worship with s. and burnt offering,	Is 19.21
I desire steadfast love and not s.,	Hos 6.06
means, 'I desire mercy, and not s.'	Mt 9.13
people from offering s. to them.	Ac 14.18
present your bodies as a living s.,	Rom 12.01

SACRIFICE —S (n) (cont.)

a fragrant offering and s. to God.	Eph 5.02
a s. acceptable and pleasing to God.	Php 4.18
bound to offer s. for his own sins	Heb 5.03
put away sin by the s. of himself.	9.26
God a more acceptable s. than Cain,	11.04
offer up a s. of praise to God,	13.15
Offer right s., and put your trust	Ps 4.05
and ate s. offered to the dead;	106.28
"What to me is the multitude of your s.?	Is 1.11
offerings, and to make s. for ever."	Jer 33.18
Pilate had mingled with their s.	Lk 13.01
to offer gifts and s. for sins.	Heb 5.01
offer spiritual s. acceptable to	1Pe 2.05

SAD

Even in laughter the heart is s.,	Pro 14.13
But when he heard this he became s.,	Lk 18.23
and they stood still, looking s.	24.17

SAFE

'I shall be s., though I walk in	Deu 29.19
refuge, and has made my way s.	2Sa 22.33
You shall know that your tent is s.,	Job 5.24
Oh to be s. under the shelter of	Ps 61.04
he who trusts in the LORD is s.	Pro 29.25
And if in a s. land you fall down,	Jer 12.05
and holy man, and kept him s.	Mk 6.20
irksome to me, and is s. for you.	Php 3.01

SAFETY

the LORD, he dwells in s. by him;	Deu 33.12
His sons are far from s., they are	Job 5.04
O LORD, makest me dwell in s.	Ps 4.08
flee for s., stay not, for I bring	Jer 4.06
and I will make you lie down in s.	Hos 2.18

SAIL —ED (v)

you all those who s. with you.'	Ac 27.24
and as they s. he fell asleep.	Lk 8.23

SAINT* —S

Greet every s. in Christ Jesus.	Php 4.21
As for the s. in the land, they are	Ps 16.03
he will not forsake his s. The righteous	37.28
he preserves the lives of his s.;	97.10
of the LORD is the death of his s.	116.15
But the s. of the Most High shall	Dan 7.18
bodies of the s. who had fallen	Mt 27.52
he has done to thy s. at Jerusalem;	Ac 9.13
shut up many of the s. in prison,	26.10
in Rome, who are called to be s.:	Rom 1.07
intercedes for the s. according to	8.27
Contribute to the needs of the s.,	12.13
her in the LORD as befits the s.,	16.02
know that the s. will judge the	1Co 6.02
wants of the s. but also overflows	2Co 9.12
glorious inheritance in the s.,	Eph 1.18
I am the very least of all the s.,	3.08
for the equipment of the s.,	4.12
but now made manifest to his s.	Col 1.26
of our Lord Jesus with all his s.	1Th 3.13
hospitality, washed the feet of the s.,	1Ti 5.10
hearts of the s. have been refreshed	Phm 7

once for all delivered to the s.	Jud 3
which are the prayers of the s.;	Rev 5.08
thy servants, the prophets and s.,	11.18
the endurance and faith of the s.	13.10
O s. and apostles and prophets, for	18.20
is the righteous deeds of the s.	19.08

SAKE

of righteousness for his name's s.	Ps 23.03
Nay, for thy s. we are slain all the	44.22
pleased, for his righteousness' s.,	Is 42.21
For the s. of my servant Jacob, and	45.04
For my own s., for my own s., I do	48.11
Return for the s. of thy servants,	63.17
that for thy s. I bear reproach.	Jer 15.15
It is not for your s. that I will	Eze 36.32
persecuted for righteousness' s.,	Mt 5.10
his life for my s. will find it.	10.39
of God for the s. of your tradition?	15.03
but for the s. of the elect those	24.22
me for the s. of the works themselves.	Jn 14.11
And for their s. I consecrate myself,	17.19
"For thy s. we are being killed all	Rom 8.36
Christ for the s. of my brethren,	9.03
for the s. of food, destroy the work	14.20
We are fools for Christ's s., but you are	1Co 4.10
informed you, and for conscience' s.—	10.28
as your servants for Jesus' s.	2Co 4.05
For our s. he made him to be sin	5.21
yet for your s. he became poor, so	8.09
For the s. of Christ, then, I am	12.10
For his s. I have suffered the loss	Php 3.08
wine for the s. of your stomach	1Ti 5.23
yet for love's s. I prefer to appeal	Phm 9
do suffer for righteousness' s.,	1Pe 3.14
your sins are forgiven for his s.	1Jn 2.12
and bearing up for my name's s.,	Rev 2.03

SALT

and she became a pillar of s.	Gen 19.26
is tasteless be eaten without s.,	Job 6.06
wilderness, in an uninhabited s. land.	Jer 17.06
shall sprinkle s. upon them and	Eze 43.24
"You are the s. of the earth;	Mt 5.13
seasoned with s., so that you may	Col 4.06
No more can s. water yield fresh.	Jas 3.12

SALUTE

And if you s. only your brethren,	Mt 5.47
As you enter the house, s. it.	10.12
And they began to s. him, "Hail, King	Mk 15.18
no sandals, and s. no one on the road.	Lk 10.04

SALVATION

I wait for thy s., O LORD.	Gen 49.18
and scoffed at the Rock of his s.	Deu 32.15
be my God, the rock of my s.,	2Sa 22.47
Tell of his s. from day to day.	1Ch 16.23
my heart shall rejoice in thy s.	Ps 13.05
The LORD is my light and my s.;	27.01
Restore to me the joy of thy s.,	51.12
O God of our s., who art the hope	65.05
Our God is a God of s.; and to God	68.20
Surely his s. is at hand for those	85.09

SALVATION (cont.)

joyful noise to the rock of our s.!	Ps 95.01
tell of his s. from day to day.	96.02
up the cup of s. and call on the	116.13
and my song; he has become my s.	118.14
My soul languishes for thy s.;	119.81
S. is far from the wicked, for they	119.155
Her priests I will clothe with s.,	132.16
draw water from the wells of s.	Is 12.03
us be glad and rejoice in his s."	25.09
that my s. may reach to the end of	49.06
my s. has gone forth, and my arms	51.05
who publishes s., who says to Zion,	52.07
and a helmet of s. upon his head;	59.17
you shall call your walls S.,	60.18
clothed me with the garments of s.,	61.10
quietly for the s. of the LORD.	Lam 3.26
up a horn of s. for us in the	Lk 1.69
for mine eyes have seen thy s.	2.30
"Today s. has come to this house,	19.09
what we know, for s. is from the Jews.	Jn 4.22
And there is s. in no one else, for	Ac 4.12
of God for s. to every one who has	Rom 1.16
For s. is nearer to us now than	13.11
behold, now is the day of s.	2Co 6.02
of truth, the gospel of your s.,	Eph 1.13
out your own s. with fear and	Php 2.12
may obtain the s. which in Christ	2Ti 2.10
sake of those who are to obtain s.?	Heb 1.14
if we neglect such a great s.?	2.03
of better things that belong to s.	6.09
you obtain the s. of your souls.	1Pe 1.09
that by it you may grow up to s.;	2.02
to write to you of our common s.,	Jud 3
"S. belongs to our God who sits	Rev 7.10

SANCTIFICATION

righteousness and s. and redemption;	1Co 1.30

SANCTIFIED —Y

and it shall be s. by my glory;	Ex 29.43
and the Levites s. themselves to	1Ch 15.14
those who are s. by faith in me.'	Ac 26.18
acceptable, s. by the Holy Spirit.	Rom 15.16
you were s., you were justified in	1Co 6.11
those who are s. have all one	Heb 2.11
the Father and s. by the Spirit	1Pe 1.02
may know that I, the LORD, s. you.	Ex 31.13
Now s. yourselves, and s. the house	2Ch 29.05
"Those who s. and purify themselves	Is 66.17
S. them in the truth; thy word is	Jn 17.17
God of peace himself s. you wholly;	1Th 5.23

SANCTUARIES —Y

and the s. of Israel shall be laid	Amo 7.09
the s., O LORD, which thy hands have	Ex 15.17
And let them make me a s.,	25.08
and reverence my s.: I am the LORD.	Lev 19.30
The inner s. he prepared in the	1Ki 6.19
my hands toward thy most holy s.	Ps 28.02
Terrible is God in his s., the God of	68.35
until I went into the s. of God;	73.17
He built his s. like the high heavens	78.69
strength and beauty are in his s.	96.06

Praise God in his s.; praise him in	150.01
possessed thy s. a little while;	Is 63.18
beginning is the place of our s.	Jer 17.12
And begin at my s." So they began	Eze 9.06
when my s. is in the midst of them	37.28
the place of his s. was overthrown.	Dan 8.11
at Bethel, for it is the king's s.,	Amo 7.13
between the s. and the altar.	Mt 23.35
copy and shadow of the heavenly s.;	Heb 8.05
for worship and an earthly s.	9.01
not into a s. made with hands, a	9.24
to enter the s. by the blood of	10.19
into the s. by the high priest as	13.11

SAND

descendants as the s. of the sea,	Gen 32.12
them, they are more than the s.	Ps 139.18
and s. is weighty, but a fool's	Pro 27.03
the burning s. shall become a pool,	Is 35.07
who built his house upon the s.;	Mt 7.26
of Israel be as the s. of the sea,	Rom 9.27
grains of s. by the seashore.	Heb 11.12

SANDAL —S

drew off his s. and gave it to the	Ru 4.07
thong of whose s. I am not worthy	Jn 1.27
patched s. on their feet, and	Jos 9.05
and the needy for a pair of s.,	Amo 8.06
whose s. I am not worthy to carry;	Mt 3.11
two tunics, nor s., nor a staff;	10.10
"Dress yourself and put on your s."	Ac 12.08

SANG

And Miriam s. to them: "Sing to the	Ex 15.21
and they s. responsively, praising	Ez 3.11
when the morning stars s. together,	Job 38.07
his words; they s. his praise.	Ps 106.12
and they s. a new song, saying,	Rev 5.09

SANK

the valleys s. down to the place	Ps 104.08
mire, and Jeremiah s. in the mire.	Jer 38.06
the everlasting hills s. low.	Hab 3.06

SAPPHIRE —S

of fire and of s. and of sulphur,	Rev 9.17
and lay your foundations with s.	Is 54.11

SATED

But before they had s. their craving,	Ps 78.30
He who is s. loathes honey, but to	Pro 27.07
it is s. with blood, it is gorged	Is 34.06
You will be s. with contempt instead of	Hab 2.16

SATISFIED —Y

and you shall eat, and not be s.	Lev 26.26
We shall be s. with the goodness of	Ps 65.04
Sheol and Abaddon are never s.,	Pro 27.20
Three things are never s.;	30.15
his eyes are never s. with riches,	Ecc 4.08
or s. me with the fat of your	Is 43.24
the travail of his soul and be s.;	53.11
may suck and be s. with her	66.11
people shall be s. with my goodness,	Jer 31.14

SATISFIED —Y (cont.)

them, and still you were not s.	Eze 16.28
They shall eat, but not be s.;	Hos 4.10
righteousness, for they shall be s.	Mt 5.06
they all ate and were s. And they took	14.20
they all ate and were s.; and they took	15.37
us the Father, and we shall be s."	Jn 14.08
I myself am s. about you, my	Rom 15.14
With long life I will s. him,	Ps 91.16
labor for that which does not s.?	Is 55.02
For I will s. the weary soul, and	Jer 31.25

SAVE —D —S —ING

He shall s. my people from the hand	1Sa 9.16
said, "How can this man s. us?"	10.27
Turn, O LORD, s. my life; deliver me	Ps 6.04
O s. thy people, and bless thy	28.09
s. me in thy steadfast love!	31.16
by its great might it cannot s.	33.17
do I trust, nor can my sword s. me.	44.06
incline thy ear to me, and s. me!	71.02
S. us, we beseech thee, O LORD!	118.25
I am thine, s. me; for I have sought	119.94
rod you will s. his life from	Pro 23.14
is our king; he will s. us.	Is 33.22
of God. He will come and s. you."	35.04
on praying to a god that cannot s.	45.20
like a mighty man who cannot s.?	Jer 14.09
I will s. you from afar, and your	30.10
to s. you and to deliver you from	42.11
I will s. my flock, they shall no	Eze 34.22
Where now is your king, to s. you;	Hos 13.10
And I will s. the lame and gather	Zep 3.19
for he will s. his people from	Mt 1.21
to sink he cried out, "Lord, s. me."	14.30
For whoever would s. his life will	16.25
it in three days, s. yourself!	27.40
whether Elijah will come to s. him."	27.49
to s. life or to kill?" But they were	Mk 3.04
came to seek and to s. the lost."	Lk 19.10
the Christ? S. yourself and us!"	23.39
the world but to s. the world.	Jn 12.47
jealous, and thus s. some of them.	Rom 11.14
we preach to s. those who believe.	1Co 1.21
that I might by all means s. some.	9.22
came into the world to s. sinners.	1Ti 1.15
for all time to s. those who draw	Heb 7.25
but has not work? Can his faith s. him?	Jas 2.14
s. some, by snatching them out of	Jud 23
Thus the LORD s. Israel that day	Ex 14.30
And David s. neither man nor woman	1Sa 27.11
To thee they cried, and were s.;	Ps 22.05
Yet he s. them for his name's sake,	106.08
returning and rest you shall be s.	Is 30.15
'The LORD has s. his people, the	Jer 31.07
who endures to the end will be s.	Mt 10.22
astonished, saying, "Who then can be s.?"	19.25
"He s. others; he cannot s. himself.	27.42
days, no human being would be s.;	Mk 13.20
believes and is baptized will be s.;	*16.16
the woman, "Your faith has s. you;	Lk 7.50
"Lord, will those who are s. be few?"	13.23
the world might be s. through him.	Jn 3.17
day by day those who were being s.	Ac 2.47

a message by which you will be s.,	11.14
said, "Men, what must I do to be s.?"	16.30
reconciled, shall we be s. by his life.	Rom 5.10
For in this hope we were s.	8.24
only a remnant of them will be s.;	9.27
confesses with his lips and so is s.	10.10
and so all Israel will be s.;	11.26
by which you are s., if you hold	1Co 15.02
Christ (by grace you have been s.),	Eph 2.05
to love the truth and so be s.	2Th 2.10
Yet woman will be s. through	1Ti 2.15
who s. us and called us with a holy	2Ti 1.09
the righteous man is scarcely s.,	1Pe 4.18
that the LORD s. not with sword	1Sa 17.47
also hears their cry, and s. them.	Ps 145.19
thy s. power among all nations.	67.02
may know the s. acts of the LORD."	Mic 6.05

SAVIOR

(Therefore the LORD gave Israel a s.,	2Ki 13.05
the Holy One of Israel, your S.	Is 43.03
and besides me there is no s.	43.11
am your S. and your Redeemer, the	60.16
its s. in time of trouble, why	Jer 14.08
and my spirit rejoices in God my S.,	Lk 1.47
this day in the city of David a S.,	2.11
this is indeed the S. of the world."	Jn 4.42
God has brought to Israel a S.,	Ac 13.23
heaven, and from it we await a S.,	Php 3.20
of God our S. and of Christ Jesus	1Ti 1.01
who is the S. of all men, especially	4.10
appearing of our S. Christ Jesus,	2Ti 1.10
our great God and S. Jesus Christ.	Tit 2.13
kindness of God our S. appeared,	3.04
through Jesus Christ our S.,	3.06
his Son as the S. of the world.	1Jn 4.14

SCALES (n)

just balance and s. are the LORD's;	Pro 16.11
accounted as the dust on the s.;	Is 40.15
something like s. fell from his	Ac 9.18

SCARLET

and bound on his hand a s. thread,	Gen 38.28
Your lips are like a s. thread,	Sol 4.03
LORD: though your sins are like s.,	Is 1.18
do you mean that you dress in s.,	Jer 4.30
him and put a s. robe upon him,	Mt 27.28
with water and s. wool and hyssop,	Heb 9.19
sitting on a s. beast which was	Rev 17.03

SCATTER —ED —S

And I will s. you among the nations,	Lev 26.33
For God will s. the bones of the	Ps 53.05
s. the peoples who delight in war.	68.30
I will s. you like chaff driven by	Jer 13.24
if a man should s. seed upon the	Mk 4.26
lest we be s. abroad upon the face	Gen 11.04
So the people were s. abroad	Ex 5.12
Let God arise, let his enemies be s.;	Ps 68.01
your God and s. your favors among	Jer 3.13
"You have s. my flock, and have	23.02
The LORD himself has s. them,	Lam 4.16
My sheep were s., they wandered	Eze 34.06

SCATTER —ED —S (cont.)

the sheep of the flock will be s.'	Mt 26.31
he has s. the proud in the imagination	Lk 1.51
it has come, when you will be s.,	Jn 16.32
Now those who were s. went about	Ac 8.04
he who does not gather with me s.	Mt 12.30
the wolf snatches them and s. them.	Jn 10.12
"He s. abroad, he gives to the poor;	2Co 9.09

SCEPTER

The s. shall not depart from Judah,	Gen 49.10
and a s. shall rise out of Israel;	Num 24.17
Your royal s. is a s. of equity;	Ps 45.06
Ephraim is my helmet; Judah is my s.	60.07
say, 'How the mighty s. is broken,	Jer 48.17
righteous s. is the s. of thy kingdom.	Heb 1.08

SCHEMES (n)

and the s. of the wily are brought	Job 5.13
caught in the s. which they have	Ps 10.02
it was against me they devised s.,	Jer 11.19

SCOFF —ED —S*

how the impious s. at thee all the	Ps 74.22
and s. at the Rock of his salvation.	Deu 32.15
heard all this, and they s. at him.	Lk 16.14
but the rulers s. at him, saying,	23.35
how the enemy s., and an impious	Ps 74.18

SCOFFER —S

but a s. does not listen to rebuke.	Pro 13.01
"S." is the name of the proud,	21.24
come to nought and the s. cease,	Is 29.20
sinners, nor sits in the seat of s.;	Ps 1.01
How long will s. delight in their	Pro 1.22
'Behold, you s., and wonder, and	Ac 13.41
that s. will come in the last days	2Pe 3.03
"In the last time there will be s.,	Jud 18

SCOFFING (n)

Beware lest wrath entice you into s.;	Job 36.18
will come in the last days with s.,	2Pe 3.03

SCORCH* —ED —ING

it was allowed to s. men with fire;	Rev 16.08
but when the sun rose they were s.;	Mt 13.06
and his speech is like a s. fire.	Pro 16.27
burden of the day and the s. heat.'	Mt 20.12
rises with its s. heat and withers	Jas 1.11
you did not s. or despise me, but	Gal 4.14
s. by men, and despised by the	Ps 22.06
like a harlot, because you s. hire.	Eze 16.31

SCORN (n)

but they laughed them to s., and	2Ch 30.10
the innocent laugh them to s.,	Job 22.19
LORD is to them an object of s.,	Jer 6.10

SCORPION* —S

asks for an egg, will give him a s.?	Lk 11.12
was like the torture of a s., when	Rev 9.05
to tread upon serpents and s.,	Lk 10.19

SCOURGE —D (v)

some you will s. in your synagogues	Mt 23.34

for you to s. a man who is a Roman	Ac 22.25
to be mocked and s. and crucified,	Mt 20.19
and having s. Jesus, delivered him	27.26

SCRIBE —S

He was a s. skilled in the law of	Ez 7.06
told Ezra the s. to bring the book	Neh 8.01
is like the pen of a ready s.	Ps 45.01
and gave it to Baruch the s.,	Jer 36.32
And a s. came up and said to him,	Mt 8.19
"Therefore every s. who has been	13.52
is the wise man? Where is the s.?	1Co 1.20
chief priests and s. of the people,	Mt 2.04
had authority, and not as their s.	7.29
Then some of the s. and Pharisees	12.38
Then Pharisees and s. came to Jesus	15.01
"The s. and the Pharisees sit on	23.02
"How can the s. say that the Christ	Mk 12.35
"Beware of the s., who like to go	Lk 20.46
and elders and s. were gathered	Ac 4.05

SCRIPTURE —S

"Today this s. has been fulfilled	Lk 4.21
you that this s. must be fulfilled	22.37
believed the s. and the word which	Jn 2.22
Has not the s. said that the Christ	7.42
it is that the s. may be fulfilled,	13.18
for as yet they did not know the s.,	20.09
"Brethren, the s. had to be fulfilled,	Ac 1.16
For what does the s. say? "Abraham	Rom 4.03
by us to live according to s.,	1Co 4.06
And the s., foreseeing that God	Gal 3.22
But the s. consigned all things to	3.22
attend to the public reading of s.,	1Ti 4.13
All s. is inspired by God and	2Ti 3.16
no prophecy of s. is a matter of	2Pe 1.20
neither the s. nor the power of	Mt 22.29
You search the s., because you	Jn 5.39
examining the s. daily to see if	Ac 17.11
showing by the s. that the Christ	18.28
destruction, as they do the other s.	2Pe 3.16

SCROLL

a s. was found on which this was	Ez 6.02
and the skies roll up like a s.	Is 34.04
"Take a s. and write on it all the	Jer 36.02
the entire s. was consumed in the	36.23
eat this s. that I give you and	Eze 3.03
and saw, and behold, a flying s.!	Zec 5.01
on the throne a s. written within	Rev 5.01
He had a little s. open in his hand.	10.02

SEA —S

dominion over the fish of the s.,	Gen 1.26
LORD drove the s. back by a strong	Ex 14.21
By his power he stilled the s.;	Job 26.12
"Or who shut in the s. with doors,	38.08
May he have dominion from s. to s.,	Ps 72.08
Thy way was through the s.,	77.19
The s. is his, for he made it;	95.05
let the s. roar, and all that fills	96.11
Some went down to the s. in ships,	107.23
The s. looked and fled, Jordan	114.03
the tongue of the s. of Egypt;	Is 11.15

SEA —S (cont.)

abundance of the s. shall be turned	Is 60.05
up out of the s. the shepherds of	63.11
Your branches passed over the s.,	Jer 48.32
The s. has come up on Babylon;	51.42
For vast as the s. is your ruin;	Lam 2.13
ships of the s. with their mariners	Eze 27.09
Does one plow the s. with oxen?	Amo 6.12
our sins into the depths of the s.	Mic 7.19
and dwelt in Capernaum by the s.,	Mt 4.13
arose a great storm on the s.,	8.24
of the house and sat beside the s.	13.01
disciples saw him walking on the s.,	14.26
'Be taken up and cast into the s.,'	21.21
sent Paul off on his way to the s.,	Ac 17.14
throwing out the wheat into the s.	27.38
Moses in the cloud and in the s.,	1Co 10.02
danger at s., danger from false	2Co 11.26
and a third of the s. became blood,	Rev 8.09
he set his right foot on the s.,	10.02
I saw a beast rising out of the s.,	13.01
And the s. gave up the dead in it,	20.13
passed away, and the s. was no more.	21.01
for he has founded it upon the s.,	Ps 24.02

SEAL —ED —S (v)

"Do not s. up the words of the	Rev 22.10
transgression would be s. up in a bag,	Job 14.17
a garden locked, a fountain s.	Sol 4.12
the words of a book that is s.	Is 29.11
were s. with the promised Holy	Eph 1.13
whom you were s. for the day of	4.30
does not rise; who s. up the stars;	Job 9.07

SEAL —S (n)

him has God the Father set his s."	Jn 6.27
as a sign or s. of the righteousness	Rom 4.11
for you are the s. of my apostleship	1Co 9.02
he has put his s. upon us and given	2Co 1.22
bearing this s.: "The Lord knows	2Ti 2.19
When he opened the second s.,	Rev 6.03
on the back, sealed with seven s.;	5.01

SEARCH —ED —ES (v)

out my iniquity and s. for my sin,	Job 10.06
Who can s. out our crimes? We have	Ps 64.06
night; I meditate and s. my spirit:	77.06
S. me, O God, and know my heart!	139.23
to seek and to s. out by wisdom	Ecc 1.13
"I the Lord s. the mind and try the	Jer 17.10
people groan as they s. for bread;	Lam 1.11
I myself will s. for my sheep, and	Eze 34.11
"Go and s. diligently for the child,	Mt 2.08
You s. the scriptures, because you	Jn 5.39
he established it, and s. it out.	Job 28.27
in Rome he s. for me eagerly and	2Ti 1.17
for the Lord s. all hearts, and	1Ch 28.09
evil comes to him who s. for it.	Pro 11.27
And he who s. the hearts of men	Rom 8.27
For the Spirit s. everything,	1Co 2.10
that I am he who s. mind and heart,	Rev 2.23

SEASON —ED (v)

its saltness, how will you s. it?	Mk 9.50

s. with salt, pure and holy;	Ex 30.35
s. with salt, so that you may know	Col 4.06

SEASON —S (n)

that yields its fruit in its s.,	Ps 1.03
For everything there is a s.,	Ecc 3.01
were prolonged for a s. and a time.	Dan 7.12
When the s. of fruit drew near, he	Mt 21.34
perhaps by agreement for a s.,	1Co 7.05
for in due s. we shall reap, if we	Gal 6.09
be urgent in s. and out of s.,	2Ti 4.02
signs and for s. and for days and	Gen 1.14
hast made the moon to mark the s.;	Ps 104.19
know times or s. which the Father	Ac 1.07
But as to the times and the s.,	1Th 5.01

SEAT —S (n)

shall make a mercy s. of pure gold;	Ex 25.17
set the mercy s. above on the ark;	40.20
nor sits in the s. of scoffers;	Ps 1.01
and gave him a s. above the s.	Jer 52.32
I sit in the s. of the gods, in the	Eze 28.02
and the Pharisees sit on Moses' s.;	Mt 23.02
he was sitting on the judgment s.,	27.19
love the best s. in the synagogues	Lk 11.43
on the judgment s. at a place	Jn 19.13
took his s. upon the throne, and	Ac 12.21
before the judgment s. of God;	Rom 14.10
before the judgment s. of Christ,	2Co 5.10
glory overshadowing the mercy s.	Heb 9.05
"Have a s. here, please," while you	Jas 2.03
money-changers and the s. of those	Mt 21.12

SECRET —S

"The s. things belong to the Lord	Deu 29.29
So the s. of his strength was not	Ju 16.09
thee, when I was being made in s.,	Ps 139.15
and bread eaten in s. is pleasant."	Pro 9.17
and do not disclose another's s.;	25.09
Lord will lay bare their s. parts.	Is 3.17
I did not speak in s., in a land of	45.19
will weep in s. for your pride;	Jer 13.17
revealing his s. to his servants	Amo 3.07
who sees in s. will reward you.	Mt 6.04
been given the s. of the kingdom	Mk 4.11
nor is anything s., except to come	4.22
For no man works in s. if he seeks	Jn 7.04
which was kept s. for long ages	Rom 16.25
But we impart a s. and hidden	1Co 2.07
of the things that they do in s.;	Eph 5.12
learned the s. of facing plenty	Php 4.12
For he knows the s. of the heart.	Ps 44.21
to know the s. of the kingdom of	Mt 13.11
God judges the s. of men by Christ	Rom 2.16
the s. of his heart are disclosed;	1Co 14.25

SECRETARY

the household, and Shebna the s.,	Is 36.03
Baruch the s. and Jeremiah the	Jer 36.26
in the house of Jonathan the s.,	37.15

SECRETLY

Then they s. instigated men, who	Ac 6.11
of false brethren s. brought in,	Gal 2.04

SECRETLY (cont.)

who will s. bring in destructive	2Pe 2.01
has been s. gained by some who	Jud 4

SECT*

ringleader of the s. of the Nazarenes.	Ac 24.05
to the Way, which they call a s.,	24.14
regard to this s. we know that	28.22

SECURE (adj)

rejoices; my body also dwells s.	Ps 16.09
upon a rock, making my steps s.	40.02
You felt s. in your wickedness, you	Is 47.10
bound with cords and made s.;	Eze 27.24
to be made s. until the third day,	Mt 27.64

SECURITY

He gives them s., and they are	Job 24.23
and s. within your towers!"	Ps 122.07
I am oppressed; be thou my s.!	Is 38.14
abundance of prosperity and s.	Jer 33.06
people say, "There is peace and s.,"	1Th 5.03

SEED

and between your s. and her s.;	Gen 3.15
rain for the s. with which you sow	Is 30.23
giving s. to the sower and bread to	55.10
the s. of man and the s. of beast.	31.27
you shall not sow s.; you shall	35.07
man who sowed good s. in his field;	Mt 13.24
of mustard s. which a man took and	13.31
faith as a grain of mustard s.,	17.20
to each kind of s. its own body.	1Co 15.38
He who supplies s. to the sower and	2Co 9.10
of perishable s. but of imperishable,	1Pe 1.23

SEEK —S

"S. out for me a woman who is a	1Sa 28.07
and they s. my life, to take it away."	1Ki 19.10
S. the LORD and his strength,	1Ch 16.11
observe and s. out all the commandments	28.08
If you s. him, he will be found by	28.09
He set himself to s. God in the	2Ch 26.05
I would s. God, and to God would I	Job 5.08
the generation of those who s. him,	Ps 24.06
do good; s. peace, and pursue it.	34.14
my mind to s. and to search out by	Ecc 1.13
a time to s., and a time to lose;	3.06
s. justice, correct oppression;	Is 1.17
"S. the LORD while he may be found,	55.06
But s. the welfare of the city	Jer 29.07
when you s. me with all your heart,	29.13
And do you s. great things for	45.05
they will s. peace, but there shall	Eze 7.25
I will s. the lost, and I will bring	34.16
return and s. the LORD their God,	Hos 3.05
S. good, and not evil, that you may	Amo 5.14
s. righteousness, s. humility; perhaps	Zep 2.03
But s. first his kingdom and his	Mt 6.33
s., and you will find; knock, and	7.07
"Why does this generation s. a sign?	Mk 8.12
of man came to s. and to save the	Lk 19.10
"Why do you s. the living among the	24.05
because I s. not my own will but	Jn 5.30

'You will s. me and you will not	7.36
that they should s. God, in the hope	Ac 17.27
demand signs and Greeks s. wisdom,	1Co 1.22
Let no one s. his own good, but the	10.24
s. the things that are above, where	Col 3.01
but always s. to do good to one	1Th 5.15
days men will s. death and will	Rev 9.06
one who does justice and s. truth;	Jer 5.01
As a shepherd s. out his flock when	Eze 34.12
Whoever s. to gain his life will	Lk 17.33
such the Father s. to worship him.	Jn 4.23
one understands, no one s. for God.	Rom 3.11

SEER —S

Samuel answered Saul, "I am the s.;	1Sa 9.19
"O s., go, flee away to the land of	Amo 7.12
who say to the s., "See not"; and to	Is 30.10
the s. shall be disgraced, and the	Mic 3.07

SEIZE —D —S

"S. the prophets of Baal; let not	1Ki 18.40
they s. flocks and pasture them.	Job 24.02
I shall seize the man; s. him."	Mt 26.48
heard it, they went out to s. him,	Mk 3.21
encouragement to s. the hope set	Heb 6.18
so that no one may s. your crown.	Rev 3.11
For Herod had s. John and bound him	Mt 14.03
And amazement s. them all, and they	Lk 5.26
they s. one Simon of Cyrene, who was	23.26
they s. Paul and Silas and dragged	Ac 16.19
dismayed, and shuddering s. my flesh.	Job 21.06
Hot indignation s. me because of	Ps 119.53
a spirit s. him, and he suddenly	Lk 9.39

SELF-CONTROL

A man without s. is like a city	Pro 25.28
athlete exercises s. in all things.	1Co 9.25
gentleness, s.; against such	Gal 5.23
a spirit of power and love and s.	2Ti 1.07

SELFISH —NESS

where jealousy and s. ambition exist,	Jas 3.16
Do nothing from s. or conceit, but in	Php 2.03

SELL —ING —S

said, "First s. me your birthright."	Gen 25.31
Buy truth, and do not s. it;	Pro 23.23
because they s. the righteous for	Amo 2.06
s. what you possess and give to the	Mt 19.21
has no sword s. his mantle and buy	Lk 22.36
one can buy or s. unless he has	Rev 13.17
those who were s. oxen and sheep	Jn 2.14
joy he goes and s. all that he has	Mt 13.44

SEND —EST —ING —S

Oh s. out thy light and thy truth;	Ps 43.03
"Whom shall I s., and who will go	Is 6.08
"Behold, I s. my messenger to	Mal 3.01
the harvest to s. out laborers	Mt 9.38
"Behold, I s. you out as sheep in	10.16
The Son of man will s. his angels,	13.41
Therefore I s. you prophets and	23.34
And behold, I s. the promise of my	Lk 24.49
any one whom I s. receives me;	Jn 13.20

SEND —EST —ING —S (cont.)

whom the Father will s. in my name,	Jn 14.26
but if I go, I will s. him to you.	16.07
As thou didst s. me into the world,	17.18
has sent me, even so I s. you."	20.21
For Christ did not s. me to baptize	1Co 1.17
When thou s. forth thy Spirit, they	Ps 104.30
s. his own Son in the likeness of	Rom 8.03
and s. rain on the just and on the	Mt 5.45
Therefore God s. upon them a strong	2Th 2.11

SENSE

and they gave the s., so that the	Neh 8.08
Good s. makes a man slow to anger,	Pro 19.11
like a dove, silly and without s.,	Hos 7.11
where would be the s. of smell?	1Co 12.17

SENSELESS

and their s. minds were darkened.	Rom 1.21
do with stupid, s. controversies;	2Ti 3.22

SENTENCE

"This man deserves the s. of death,	Jer 26.11
So Pilate gave s. that their demand	Lk 23.24
him, asking for s. against him.	Ac 25.15
execute his s. upon the earth with	Rom 9.28
commandment, are summed up in this s.,	13.09
we received the s. of death;	2Co 1.09

SEPARATE —D —S

and s. himself to the LORD for the	Num 6.12
s. yourselves from the peoples of	Ez 10.11
come out and s. the evil from the	Mt 13.49
Who shall s. us from the love of	Rom 8.35
so that they s. from each other;	Ac 15.39
came he drew back and s. himself,	Gal 2.12
were at that time s. from Christ,	Eph 2.12
and a whisperer s. close friends.	Pro 16.28
as a shepherd s. the sheep from	Mt 25.32

SEPARATION

the law for his s. as a Nazirite."	Num 6.21
have made a s. between you and	Is 59.02
to make a s. between the holy and	Eze 42.20

SEPULCHRE

destruction, their throat is an open s.,	Ps 5.09
there, sitting opposite the s.	Mt 27.61
the other Mary went to see the s.	28.01

SERPENT —S

"The s. beguiled me, and I ate."	Gen 3.13
So Moses made a bronze s., and set it	Num 21.09
They have venom like the venom of a s.,	Ps 58.04
the way of a s. on a rock, the way	Pro 30.19
for a fish, will give him a s.?	Mt 7.10
lifted up the s. in the wilderness,	Jn 3.14
that as the s. deceived Eve by his	2Co 11.03
that ancient s., who is the Devil	Rev 20.02
down his rod, and they became s.	Ex 7.12
For behold, I am sending among you s.,	Jer 8.17
so be wise as s. and innocent as	Mt 10.16
You s., you brood of vipers, how are	23.33
their tails are like s., with heads, and	Rev 9.19

SERVANT —S

So the s. put his hand under the	Gen 24.09
So Moses rose with his s. Joshua,	Ex 24.13
of a hired s. shall not remain	Lev 19.13
for your hired s. and the sojourner	25.06
So Moses the s. of the LORD died	Deu 34.05
'Speak, LORD, for thy s. hears.' "	1Sa 3.09
Give thy s. therefore an understanding	1Ki 3.09
"Have you considered my s. Job,	Job 1.08
back thy s. also from presumptuous	Ps 19.13
Turn not thy s. away in anger, thou	27.09
Gladden the soul of thy s.,	86.04
O LORD, I am thy s.; I am thy s.,	116.16
a heritage to Israel his s.,	136.22
Enter not into judgment with thy s.;	143.02
By mere words a s. is not disciplined,	Pro 29.19
"You are my s., I have chosen you	Is 41.09
or blind as the s. of the LORD?	42.19
and Israel, for you are my s.;	44.21
"The LORD has redeemed his s. Jacob!"	48.20
Behold, my s. shall prosper, he shall	52.13
my s., make many to be accounted	53.11
Is he a homeborn s.? Why then	Jer 2.14
And the s. was healed at that	Mt 8.13
his teacher, nor a s. above his master;	10.24
"Behold, my s. whom I have chosen, my	12.18
"Who then is the faithful and wise s.,	24.45
'Well done, good and faithful s.,	25.21
must be last of all and s. of all."	Mk 9.35
thou thy s. depart in peace,	Lk 2.29
No s. can serve two masters;	16.13
I am, there shall my s. be also;	Jn 12.26
glorified his s. Jesus, whom you	Ac 3.13
Paul, a s. of Jesus Christ, called to	Rom 1.01
for he is God's s. for your good.	13.04
Christ became a s. to the circumcised	15.08
himself, taking the form of a s.,	Php 2.07
the s. of God, and the song of the	Rev 15.03
For to me the people of Israel are s.,	Lev 25.55
Remember thy s., Abraham, Isaac,	Deu 9.27
And my s. will be with your s.,	2Ch 2.08
and slew the s. with the edge of	Job 1.15
The LORD redeems the life of his s.;	Ps 34.22
and my s. shall dwell there.	Is 65.09
hand of the LORD is with his s.,	66.14
sent to you all my s. the prophets,	Jer 35.15
father's hired s. have bread	Lk 15.17
you, say, 'We are unworthy s.;	17.10
No longer do I call you s.,	Jn 15.15
S. through whom you believed, as the	1Co 3.05
as s. of Christ and stewards of the	4.01
themselves as s. of righteousness.	2Co 11.15
Are they s. of Christ? I am a	11.23
through love be s. of one another.	Gal 5.13
for evil; but live as s. of God.	1Pe 2.16
S., be submissive to your masters	2.18

SERVE —D —S —ING

Let peoples s. you, and nations bow	Gen 27.29
you shall s. God upon this mountain."	Ex 3.12
Moses, and said, "Go, s. the LORD;	10.24
You shall s. the LORD your God, and	23.25
choose this day whom you will s.,	Jos 24.15
"Nay, but we will s. the LORD."	24.21

SERVE —D —S —ING (cont.)

Almighty, that we should s. him?	Job 21.15
S. the LORD with fear, with trembling	Ps 2.11
S. the LORD with gladness!	100.02
the beasts of the field to s. him.	Jer 27.06
But they shall s. the LORD their	30.09
not go after other gods to s. them,	35.15
your God and him only shall you s.' "	Mt 4.10
You cannot s. God and mammon.	6.24
came not to be s. but to s.,	20.28
the word of God to s. tables.	Ac 6.02
whom I s. with my spirit in the	Rom 1.09
so that we s. not under the old	7.06
"The elder will s. the younger."	9.12
aglow with the Spirit, s. the Lord.	12.11
and those who s. at the altar share	1Co 9.13
to s. a living and true God,	1Th 1.09
which those who s. the tent have	Heb 13.10
nor is he s. by human hands, as	Ac 17.25
If any one s. me, he must follow me;	Jn 12.26
he who thus s. Christ is acceptable	Rom 14.18
Who s. as a soldier at his own	1Co 9.07
for his sake is s. the saints,	Heb 6.10
that they were s. not themselves	1Pe 1.12

SERVICE

for the s. of God at Jerusalem, as	Ez 6.18
"Has not man a hard s. upon earth,	Job 7.01
And when his time of s. was ended,	Lk 1.23
think he is offering s. to God.	Jn 16.02
in the priestly s. of the gospel	Rom 15.16
and there are varieties of s.,	1Co 12.05
his life to complete your s. to me.	Php 2.30
No soldier on s. gets entangled in	2Ti 2.04
high priest in the s. of God,	Heb 2.17

SERVING (n)

Martha was distracted with much s.;	Lk 10.40

SEVENTY

seven times, but s. times seven.	Mt 18.22
After this the Lord appointed s. others,	Lk 10.01

SEVERE —LY

for the famine was s. in the land.	Gen 12.10
There is s. discipline for him who	Pro 15.10
You knew that I was a s. man,	Lk 19.22
for in a s. test of affliction,	2Co 8.02
not have to be s. in my use of the	13.10
not to put it too s.—to you all.	2.05

SHADE —S (n)

LORD is your s. on your right hand	Ps 121.05
It will be for a s. by day from the	Is 4.06
like the s. of a great rock in a	32.02
in the s. of its branches birds of	Eze 17.23
He sat under it in the s.,	Jon 4.05
the air can make nests in its s."	Mk 4.32
Do the s. rise up to praise thee?	Ps 88.10
they are s., they will not arise;	Is 26.14

SHADOW —S

for our days on earth are a s.	Job 8.09
he flees like a s., and continues not.	14.02

hide me in the s. of thy wings,	Ps 17.08
abides in the s. of the Almighty,	91.01
My days are like an evening s.;	102.11
life, which he passes like a s.?	Ecc 6.12
to seek shelter in the s. of Egypt!	Is 30.02
return and dwell beneath my s.,	Hos 14.07
in darkness and in the s. of death,	Lk 1.79
These are only a s. of what is to	Col 2.17
a copy and s. of the heavenly	Heb 8.05
no variation or s. due to change.	Jas 1.17
Until the day breathes and the s. flee,	Sol 2.17

SHAFT —S

the key of the s. of the bottomless	Rev 9.01
weapons, making his arrows fiery s.	Ps 7.13
pierce with thy s. the head of his	Hab 3.14

SHAKE —N —S

S. yourself from the dust, arise;	Is 52.02
I will s. the heavens and the earth	Hag 2.06
s. off the dust from your feet as	Mt 10.14
more I will s. not only the earth	Heb 12.26
my fortress; I shall not be s.	Ps 62.06
foundations of the earth are s.	82.05
to behold? A reed s. by the wind?	Mt 11.07
s. together, running over, will be	Lk 6.38
not to be quickly s. in mind or	2Th 2.02
a kingdom that cannot be s.,	Heb 12.28
the nations as one s. with a sieve,	Amo 9.09

SHAKING*

be a great s. in the land of Israel;	Eze 38.19

SHAME —D —S* (v)

in the world to s. the wise,	1Co 1.27
"As a thief is s. when caught, so	Jer 2.26
companion of gluttons s. his father.	Pro 28.07

SHAME (n)

I trust, let me not be put to s.;	Ps 25.02
Let them be put to s. and confusion	40.14
they will be put to s., for God has	53.05
Let not the downtrodden be put to s.;	74.21
Let the godless be put to s.,	119.78
to himself brings s. to his mother.	Pro 29.15
of sackcloth; instead of beauty, s.	Is 3.24
Instead of your s. you shall have a	61.07
Let us lie down in our s., and let	Jer 3.25
s. is upon all faces, and baldness	Eze 7.18
I will change their glory into s.	Hos 4.07
change their s. into praise and	Zep 3.19
in him will not be put to s."	Rom 9.33
believes in him will be put to s."	10.11
pride in you, I was not put to s.;	2Co 7.14
belly, and they glory in their s.,	Php 3.19
despising the s., and is seated at	Heb 12.02
behavior in Christ may be put to s.	1Pe 3.16
up the foam of their own s.;	Jud 13

SHARE —S (v)

Is it not to s. your bread with the	Is 58.07
to those who s. the faith of	Rom 4.16
have come to s. in their spiritual	15.27
that we might s. the rule with you!	1Co 4.08

SHARE —S (v) (cont.)

at the altar s. in the sacrificial	1Co 9.13
For as we s. abundantly in Christ's	2Co 1.05
taught the word s. all good things	Gal 6.06
and may s. his sufferings, becoming	Php 3.10
were ready to s. with you not only	1Th 2.08
For we s. in Christ, if only we hold	Heb 3.14
so far as you s. Christ's sufferings,	1Pe 4.13
holy is he who s. in the first	Rev 20.06

SHARE —ING (n)

give me the s. of property that	Lk 15.12
but take your s. of suffering for	2Ti 1.08
take away his s. in the tree of	Rev 22.19
in our hope of s. the glory of God.	Rom 5.02

SHARP —ER*

Your arrows are s. in the heart of	Ps 45.05
sledge, new, s., and having teeth;	Is 41.15
He made my mouth like a s.	49.02
mouth issued a s. two-edged sword,	Rev 1.16
s. than any two-edged sword, piercing	Heb 4.12

SHATTER —ED —S

will you set upon a man to s. him,	Ps 62.03
"We are s. but we will rebuild the	Mal 1.04
He s. the mighty without investigation,	Job 34.24
For he s. the doors of bronze, and	Ps 107.16

SHAVE —D —N

nor s. off the edges of their	Lev 21.05
and when he had s. himself and	Gen 41.14
and s. his head, and fell upon the	Job 1.20
"For every head is s. and every	Jer 48.37
is the same as if her head were s.	1Co 11.05

SHEAF —VES

and lo, my s. arose and stood upright;	Gen 37.07
shall bring the s. of the first	Lev 23.10
"Let her glean even among the s.,	Ru 2.15
of joy, bringing his s. with him.	Ps 126.06
gathered them as s. to the threshing	Mic 4.12

SHEATH

Peter, "Put your sword into its s.;	Jn 18.11

SHED

man, by man shall his blood be s.;	Gen 9.06
for having s. blood without cause	1Sa 25.31
and they make haste to s. blood,	Pro 1.16
and hands that s. innocent blood,	6.17
make haste to s. innocent blood;	Is 59.07
the righteous blood s. on earth,	Mt 23.35
s. from the foundation of the world,	Lk 11.50
"Their feet are swift to s. blood,	Rom 3.15
For men have s. the blood of saints	Rev 16.06

SHEDDING (n)

and without the s. of blood there	Heb 9.22

SHEEP

Then Abimelech took s. and oxen,	Gen 20.14
the firstlings of cow and s.	Ex 34.19
as s. that have no shepherd;	2Ch 18.16

hast made us like s. for slaughter,	Ps 44.11
Then he led forth his people like s.,	78.52
I have gone astray like a lost s.;	119.176
or like s. with none to gather them,	Is 13.14
All we like s. have gone astray;	53.06
and like a s. that before its	53.07
"My people have been lost s.;	Jer 50.06
"Israel is a hunted s. driven away	50.17
Should not shepherds feed the s.?	Eze 34.02
I, I myself will search for my s.,	34.11
I judge between s. and s., rams	34.17
you are my s., the s. of my pasture,	34.31
to the lost s. of the house of	Mt 10.06
send you out as s. in the midst of	10.16
much more value is a man than a s.!	12.12
separates the s. from the goats,	25.32
selling oxen and s. and pigeons,	Jn 2.14
calls his own s. by name and leads	10.03
and I lay down my life for the s.	10.15
And I have other s., that are not	10.16
He said to him, "Tend my s."	21.16
the great shepherd of the s.,	Heb 13.20

SHEEPFOLD —S

not enter the s. by the door but	Jn 10.01
Why did you tarry among the s.,	Ju 5.16
though they stay among the s.—	Ps 68.13

SHEKEL

the ephah small and the s. great,	Amo 8.05
open its mouth you will find a s.;	Mt 17.27

SHELTER (n)

be safe under the s. of thy wings!	Ps 61.04
dwells in the s. of the Most High,	91.01

SHEPHERD —ING (v)

I commanded to s. my people Israel,	2Sa 7.07
S. thy people with thy staff, the	Mic 7.14
was s. the flock with his brothers;	Gen 37.02

SHEPHERD —S (n)

'You shall be s. of my people	2Sa 5.02
The LORD is my s., I shall not want;	Ps 23.01
Death shall be their s.; straight	49.14
He will feed his flock like a s.,	Is 40.11
What s. can stand before me?	Jer 49.19
As a s. seeks out his flock when	Eze 34.12
helpless, like sheep without a s.	Mt 9.36
is written, 'I will strike the s.,	26.31
I am the good s. The good s. lays down	Jn 10.11
there shall be one flock, one s.	10.16
the great s. of the sheep, by the	Heb 13.20
And when the chief S. is manifested	1Pe 5.04
The s. also have no understanding;	Is 56.11
I will give you s. after my own	Jer 3.15
For the s. are stupid, and do not	10.21
prophesy against the s. of Israel,	Eze 34.02
there were s. out in the field,	Lk 2.08
And the s. returned, glorifying and	2.20

SHIELD

"Fear not, Abram, I am your s.;	Gen 15.01
art a s. about me, my glory, and the	Ps 3.03

SHIELD (cont.)
My s. is with God, who saves the Ps 7.10
my s., and the horn of my salvation, 18.02
The LORD is my strength and my s.; 28.07
Take hold of s. and buckler, and 35.02
For the LORD God is a sun and s.; 84.11
Thou art my hiding place and my s.; 119.114
above all taking the s. of faith, Eph 6.16

SHINE —D* —S —ING
The LORD make his face to s. upon Num 6.25
Let thy face s. on thy servant; Ps 31.16
thou God of vengeance, s. forth! 94.01
A man's wisdom makes his face s., Ecc 8.01
Arise, s.; for your light has Is 60.01
Let your light so s. before men, Mt 5.16
righteous will s. like the sun in 13.43
"Let light s. out of darkness," who 2Co 4.06
among whom you s. as lights in the Php 2.15
need of sun or moon to s. upon it, Rev 21.23
of deep darkness, on them has light s. Is 9.02
perfection of beauty, God s. forth. Ps 50.02
The light s. in the darkness, and Jn 1.05
He was a burning and s. lamp, 5.35
and the true light is already s. 1Jn 2.08

SHIP —S
the way of a s. on the high seas, Pro 30.19
can go, nor stately s. can pass. Is 33.21
Some went down to the sea in s., Ps 107.23
Wail, O s. of Tarshish, for your Is 23.14
all who had s. at sea grew rich by Rev 18.19

SHOES
put off your s. from your feet, for Ex 3.05
take off your s. from your feet, Is 20.02
and put your s. on your feet; Eze 24.17
and the needy for a pair of s.— Amo 2.06
on his hand, and s. on his feet; Lk 15.22

SHONE
that the skin of Moses' face s.; Ex 34.35
and his face s. like the sun, and Mt 17.02
glory of the Lord s. around them, Lk 2.09
who has s. in our hearts to give 2Co 4.06

SHOOK
earth tremble, who s. kingdoms, Is 14.16
he looked and s. the nations; Hab 3.06
and the earth s., and the rocks Mt 27.51
His voice then s. the earth; but now Heb 12.26

SHOOT —S (n)
come forth a s. from the stump of Is 11.01
the s. of my planting, the work of 60.21
a wild olive s., were grafted in Rom 11.17
For as the earth brings forth its s., Is 61.11

SHORT
For the bed is too s. to stretch Is 28.20
"In a s. time you think to make me Ac 26.28
sinned and fall s. of the glory of Rom 3.23
appointed time has grown very s.; 1Co 7.29
he knows that his time is s.!" Rev 12.12

SHORTENED
steps are s. and his own schemes Job 18.07
Is my hand s., that it cannot Is 50.02
Behold, the LORD's hand is not s., 59.01

SHOUT —ED (v)
the people shall s. with a great s.; Jos 6.05
S. to God with loud songs of joy! Ps 47.01
they s. and sing together for joy. 65.13
break forth and s., thou who Gal 4.27
But they s. all the more, "Crucify Mk 15.14

SHOUT —ING —S (n)
Raise a s. against her round about, Jer 50.15
Philistines heard the noise of the s., 1Sa 4.06
he hears not the s. of the driver. Job 39.07
sow in tears reap with s. of joy! Ps 126.05

SHOWER —S (n)
you say at once, 'A s. is coming'; Lk 12.54
like s. that water the earth! Ps 72.06

SHRINE —S
into the inner s. behind the curtain, Heb 6.19
does not live in s. made by man, Ac 17.24
who made silver s. of Artemis, 19.24

SHUN
S. immorality. Every other sin 1Co 6.18
beloved, s. the worship of idols. 10.14

SICK
Hope deferred makes the heart s., Pro 13.12
with apples; for I am s. with love. Sol 2.05
healing, my heart is s. within me. Jer 8.18
a physician, but those who are s. Mt 9.12
Heal the s., raise the dead, cleanse 10.08
I was s. and you visited me, I was 25.36

SICKLE
is ripe, at once he puts in the s., Mk 4.29
"Put in your s., and reap, for the Rev 14.15

SIEGEWORKS
they have cast up s. against me, Job 19.12

SIGH —ED (v)
S., but not aloud; make no mourning Eze 24.17
in this tent, we s. with anxiety; 2Co 5.04
And he s. deeply in his spirit, and Mk 8.12

SIGH —ING —S* (n)
our years come to an end like a s. Ps 90.09
and sorrow and s. shall flee away. Is 35.10
for us with s. too deep for words. Rom 8.26

SIGHT
Now the earth was corrupt in God's s., Gen 6.11
turn aside and see this great s., Ex 3.03
Precious in the s. of the LORD is Ps 116.15
Better is the s. of the eyes than Ecc 6.09
receive their s. and the lame walk, Mt 11.05
walk by faith, not by s. 2Co 5.07
not known by s. to the churches of Gal 1.22

SIGHT (cont.)

acceptable in the s. of God our	1Ti 2.03
but in God's s. chosen and precious;	1Pe 2.04

SIGN —S (n)

"This is the s. of the covenant	Gen 9.12
The blood shall be a s. for you,	Ex 12.13
Show me a s. of thy favor, that	Ps 86.17
Lord himself will give you a s.	Is 7.14
It will be a s. and a witness to	19.20
an everlasting s. which shall not	55.13
and I will set a s. among them.	66.19
it except the s. of the prophet	Mt 12.39
given to it except the s. of Jonah."	16.04
then will appear the s. of the Son	24.30
Now the betrayer had given them a s.,	26.48
And this will be a s. for you:	Lk 2.12
now the second s. that Jesus did	Jn 4.54
"John did no s., but everything	10.41
circumcision as a s. or seal of the	Rom 4.11
tongues are a s. not for believers	1Co 14.22
let them be for s. and for seasons	Gen 1.14
interpret the s. of the times,	Mt 16.03
not coming with s. to be observed;	Lk 17.20
seek me, not because you saw s.,	Jn 6.26
did many other s. in the presence	20.30
and wonders and s. which God did	Ac 2.22
by the power of s. and wonders,	Rom 15.19
For Jews demand s. and Greeks seek	1Co 1.22
The s. of a true apostle were	2Co 12.12
bore witness by s. and wonders and	Heb 2.04
performing s., who go abroad to the	Rev 16.14

SIGNAL (n)

He will raise a s. for a nation	Is 5.26
On a bare hill raise a s.,	13.02

SIGNET

were the s. ring on my right hand,	Jer 22.24
"You were the s. of perfection, full	Eze 28.12

SILENCE

For if you keep s. at such a time	Est 4.14
"Let me have s., and I will speak,	Job 13.13
For God alone my soul waits in s.;	Ps 62.01
a time to keep s., and a time	Ecc 3.07
Sit in s., and go into darkness, O	Is 47.05
all the earth keep s. before him.	Hab 2.20
should keep s. in the churches.	1Co 14.34
Let a woman learn in s. with all	1Ti 2.11
there was s. in heaven for about	Rev 8.01

SILENT

Be not s., O God of my praise!	Ps 109.01
a man of understanding remains s.	Pro 11.12
before me: "I will not keep s.,	Is 65.06
I cannot keep s.; for I hear	Jer 4.19
Be s., all flesh, before the LORD;	Zec 2.13
But Jesus was s. And the high priest	Mt 26.63
if these were s., the very stones	Lk 19.40

SILVER

the s. cup, in the mouth of the sack	Gen 44.02
the innocent will divide the s.	Job 27.17

Their idols are s. and gold,	Ps 115.04
before the s. cord is snapped, or	Ecc 12.06
their idols of s. and their idols	Is 2.20
their s. and gold with them, for the	60.09
the poor for s. and the needy for	Amo 8.06
they paid him thirty pieces of s.	Mt 26.15
"I have no s. and gold, but I give	Ac 3.06
"Your s. perish with you, because	8.20
s., precious stones, wood, hay,	1Co 3.12
Your gold and s. have rusted, and	Jas 5.03
perishable things such as s. or gold,	1Pe 1.18

SIMPLE —MINDED*

The LORD preserves the s.;	Ps 116.06
it imparts understanding to the s.	119.130
The s. believes everything, but the	Pro 14.15
but the s. go on, and suffer for it.	22.03
they deceive the hearts of the s.	Rom 16.18

SIN —NED (v)

there is no man who does not s.—	2Ch 6.36
Job did not s. or charge God with	Job 1.22
If I s., thou dost mark me, and dost	10.14
man not to s., and he does not s.,	Eze 3.21
And now they s. more and more, and	Hos 13.02
If your right eye causes you to s.,	Mt 5.29
shall my brother s. against me,	18.21
S. no more, that nothing worse	Jn 5.14
But if you marry, you do not s.,	1Co 7.28
it is weak, you s. against Christ.	8.12
For if we s. deliberately after	Heb 10.26
Both we and our fathers have s.;	Ps 106.06
Your first father s., and your	Is 43.27
Our fathers s., and are no more;	Lam 5.07
who s., this man or his parents,	Jn 9.02
since all have s. and fall short of	Rom 3.23
If we say we have not s.,	1Jn 1.10

SIN —S (n)

s. is couching at the door;	Gen 4.07
"The LORD also has put away your s.;	2Sa 12.13
For he adds rebellion to his s.;	Job 34.37
and my s. is ever before me.	Ps 51.03
thou didst pardon all their s.	85.02
but s. is a reproach to any people.	Pro 14.34
The devising of folly is s.,	24.09
Let not your mouth lead you into s.,	Ecc 5.06
who draw s. as with cart ropes,	Is 5.18
that they may add s. to s.;	30.01
yet he bore the s. of many,	53.12
price of your s. throughout all	Jer 17.03
I will remember their s. no more."	31.34
every s. and blasphemy will be	Mt 12.31
but is guilty of an eternal s."—	Mk 3.29
"Let him who is without s. among	*Jn 8.07
him, "You were born in utter s.,	9.34
the world of s. and of righteousness	16.08
Greeks, are under the power of s.,	Rom 3.09
the law comes knowledge of s.	3.20
Therefore as s. came into the world	5.12
but where s. increased, grace	5.20
For he who has died is freed from s.	6.07
Let not s. therefore reign in your	6.12
or the wages of s. is death,	6.23

SIN —S (n) (cont.)

For s., finding opportunity in the	Rom 7.11
to the law of s. which dwells in	7.23
he condemned s. in the flesh,	8.03
does not proceed from faith is s.	14.23
The sting of death is s.,	1Co 15.56
is Christ then an agent of s.?	Gal 2.17
scripture consigned all things to s.,	3.22
Be angry but do not s.;	Eph 4.26
enjoy the fleeting pleasures of s.	11.25
his Son cleanses us from all s.	1Jn 1.07
There is s. which is mortal;	5.16
for many for the forgiveness of s.	Mt 26.28
he had passed over former s.;	Rom 3.25
died for our s. in accordance with	1Co 15.03
to fill up the measure of their s.	1Th 2.16
Therefore confess your s. to one	Jas 5.16
love covers a multitude of s.	1Pe 4.08
Son to be the expiation for our s.	1Jn 4.10

SINCERE —LY

sent spies, who pretended to be s.,	Lk 20.20
astray from a s. and pure devotion	2Co 11.03
and a good conscience and s. faith.	1Ti 1.05
not s. but thinking to afflict me	Php 1.17

SINFUL

Ah, s. nation, a people laden with	Is 1.04
this adulterous and s. generation,	Mk 8.38
delivered into the hands of s. men,	Lk 24.07
might become s. beyond measure.	Rom 7.13
the likeness of s. flesh and for	8.03

SING —ING

"I will s. to the Lord, for he has	Ex 15.01
the earth; s. praises with a psalm!	Ps 47.07
S. to God, s. praises to his name;	68.04
O s. to the Lord a new song;	96.01
"S., O barren one, who did not bear;	Is 54.01
who s. idle songs to the sound of	Amo 6.05
S. aloud, O daughter of Zion;	Zep 3.14
I will s. with the spirit and I	1Co 14.15
and as you s. psalms and hymns and	Col 3.16
and they s. a new song before the	Rev 14.03
were praying and s. hymns to God,	Ac 16.25

SINGING (n)

Come into his presence with s.!	Ps 100.02
return, and come to Zion with s.,	Is 35.10

SINGLE —NESS

well for them to remain s. as I do.	1Co 7.08
If all were a s. organ, where would	12.19
For by a s. offering he has perfected	Heb 10.14
in s. of heart, as to Christ;	Eph 6.05

SINNER —S

As is the good man, so is the s.;	Ecc 9.02
heaven over one s. who repents	Lk 15.07
'God, be merciful to me a s.!'	18.13
am I still being condemned as a s.?	Rom 3.07
Sweep me not away with s.,	Ps 26.09
Let not your heart envy s., but	Pro 23.17

not to call the righteous, but s."	Mt 9.13
a friend of tax collectors and s.!'	11.19
is betrayed into the hands of s.	26.45
Even s. lend to s., to receive	Lk 6.34
we were yet s. Christ died for us.	Rom 5.08
came into the world to save s.	1Ti 1.15
endured from s. such hostility	Heb 12.03
you s., and purify your hearts, you	Jas 4.08

SINNING (n)

tempted as we are, yet without s.	Heb 4.15

SISTER

of Sarah his wife, "She is my s."	Gen 20.02
and you are the s. of your sisters,	Eze 16.45
is my brother, and s., and mother."	Mt 12.50
his mother, and his mother's s.,	Jn 19.25
son of Paul's s. heard of their	Ac 23.16
I commend to you our s. Phoebe,	Rom 16.01
the brother or s. is not bound.	1Co 7.15
If a brother or s. is ill-clad and	Jas 2.15

SKIES —Y

Can you, like him, spread out the s.,	Job 37.18
Yet he commanded the s. above,	Ps 78.23
and the s. roll up like a scroll.	Is 34.04
and let the s. rain down righteousness;	45.08
interpret the appearance of the s.,	Mt 16.03
presence earth and s. fled away,	Rev 20.11

SKILFUL —LY

Esau was a s. hunter, a man of the	Gen 25.27
them, and guided them with s. hand.	Ps 78.72
he seeks out a s. craftsman to set	Is 40.20
send for the s. women to come;	Jer 9.17
play s. on the strings, with loud	Ps 33.03

SKILLED

They are s. in doing evil, but how	Jer 4.22
those who are s. in lamentation,	Amo 5.16
like a s. master builder I laid a	1Co 3.10

SKIN —S

answered the Lord, "S. for s.! All that	Job 2.04
Thou didst clothe me with s. and flesh,	10.11
My s. turns black and falls from me,	30.30
change his s. or the leopard his	Jer 13.23
if it is, the s. burst, and the wine	Mt 9.17
went about in s. of sheep and	Heb 11.37

SKULL

(which means the place of a s.),	Mt 27.33

SLAIN

thy sake we are s. all the day	Ps 44.22
Your s. are not s. with the sword	Is 22.02
breath, and breathe upon these s.,	Eze 37.09
"Worthy is the Lamb who was s.,	Rev 5.12
And the rest were s. by the sword	19.21

SLANDER —ED (v)

Do not s. a servant to his master,	Pro 30.10
when s., we try to conciliate; we	1Co 4.13

SLANDER (n)
fornication, theft, false witness, s.	Mt 15.19
s., gossip, conceit, and disorder.	2Co 12.20

SLAUGHTER —ED —S (v)
and you shall s. the ram, and shall	Ex 29.16
we are regarded as sheep to be s."	Rom 8.36
"He who s. an ox is like him who	Is 66.03

SLAUGHTER (n)
Thou has made us like sheep for s.,	Ps 44.11
like a lamb that is led to the s.,	Is 53.07
set them apart for the day of s.	Jer 12.03
fattened your hearts in a day of s.	Jas 5.05

SLAVE —S
and became a s. at forced labor.	Gen 49.15
When you buy a Hebrew s., he shall	Ex 21.02
them, Joseph, who was sold as a s.	Ps 105.17
A s. who deals wisely will rule	Pro 17.02
borrower is the s. of the lender.	22.07
"Is Israel a s.? Is he a homeborn	Jer 2.14
be first among you must be your s.;	Mt 20.27
and struck the s. of the high	26.51
one who commits sin is a s. to sin.	Jn 8.34
the Lord as a s. is a freedman of	1Co 7.22
I have made myself a s. to all,	9.19
there is neither s. nor free,	Gal 3.28
you are no longer a s. but a son,	4.07
no longer as a s. but more than a s.,	Phm 16
who were once s. of sin have	Rom 6.17
we were s. to the elemental spirits	Gal 4.03
S., be obedient to those who are	Eph 6.05
treat your s. justly and fairly,	Col 4.01
Bid s. to be submissive to their	Tit 2.09

SLAVERY
the spirit of s. to fall back into	Rom 8.15
not submit again to a yoke of s.	Gal 5.01

SLAY —S
and took the knife to s. his son.	Gen 22.10
Behold, he will s. me; I have no	Job 13.15
O that thou wouldst s. the wicked,	Ps 139.19
and he will s. the dragon that is	Is 27.01
and shall s. them with the sword.	Jer 20.04
them here and s. them before me."	Lk 19.27
Lord Jesus will s. him with the	2Th 2.08
so that men should s. one another;	Rev 6.04
if any one s. with the sword, with	13.10

SLEEP —EST* —ING —S (v)
Israel will neither slumber nor s.	Ps 121.04
and he said to them, "Why do you s.?	Lk 22.46
We shall not all s., but we shall	1Co 15.51
So then let us not s., as others do,	1Th 5.06
Rouse thyself! Why s. thou, O Lord?	Ps 44.23
for the girl is not dead but s."	Mt 9.24
to the disciples and found them s.;	26.40
none stumbles, none slumbers or s.,	Is 5.27

SLEEP (n)
caused a deep s. to fall upon the	Gen 2.21
Then Jacob awoke from his s. and said,	28.16

Love not s., lest you come to	Pro 20.13
Sweet is the s. of a laborer,	Ecc 5.12
sank into a deep s. as Paul talked	Ac 20.09

SLOW
s. to anger, and abounding in	Ex 34.06
Good sense makes a man s. to anger,	Pro 19.11
The Lord is not s. about his promise	2Pe 3.09

SLUGGARD
Go to the ant, O s.; consider her	Pro 6.06
the s. buries his hand in the dish,	19.24
hinges, so does a s. on his bed.	26.14

SLUMBER —ED* —S* (v)
Israel will neither s. nor sleep.	Ps 121.04
was delayed, they all s. and slept.	Mt 25.05
none s. or sleeps, not a waistcloth	Is 5.27

SMALL —EST
And though your beginning was s.,	Job 8.07
"Behold, I am of s. account; what	40.04
I am s. and despised, yet I do not	Ps 119.141
Behold, I will make you s. among the	Ob 2
crowd, because he was s. of stature.	Lk 19.03
testifying both to s. and great,	Ac 26.22
forest is set ablaze by a s. fire!	Jas 3.05
it is the s. of all seeds, but when	Mt 13.32

SMITE
The sun shall not s. you by day,	Ps 121.06
And the Lord will s. Egypt, smiting	Is 19.22
He shall s. them with the edge of	Jer 21.07
know that I am the Lord, who s.	Eze 7.09
the Lord will s. all the peoples	Zec 14.12

SMITH —S
created the s. who blows the fire	Is 54.16
and the s., and had brought them to	Jer 24.01

SMITTEN
stricken, s. by God, and afflicted.	Is 53.04
Why hast thou s. us so that there	Jer 14.19

SMOKE (n)
And Mount Sinai was wrapped in s.,	Ex 19.18
Out of his nostrils comes forth s.,	Job 41.20
For my days pass away like s.,	Ps 102.03
was filled with s. from the glory	Rev 15.08
they see the s. of her burning;	18.09

SMOOTH —LY —S*
is a hairy man, and I am a s. man.	Gen 27.11
with her s. talk she compels him.	Pro 7.21
thou dost make s. the path of the	Is 26.07
the rough ways shall be made s.;	Lk 3.05
sparkles in the cup and goes down s.	Pro 23.31
and he who s. with the hammer him who	Is 41.07

SNARE —S (n)
their gods shall be a s. to you."	Ju 2.03
s. of the fowlers; the s. is broken,	Ps 124.07
a trap and a s. to the inhabitants	Is 8.14
come upon you suddenly like a s.;	Lk 21.34

SNARE —S (n) (cont.)
their feast become a s. and a trap,   Rom 11.09
reproach and the s. of the devil.   1Ti 3.07
Therefore s. are round about you,   Job 22.10
woman whose heart is s. and nets,   Ecc 7.26

SNATCH —ED —ES*
who seek to s. away my life; let   Ps 40.14
no one shall s. them out of my   Jn 10.28
They were s. away before their time;   Job 22.16
Behold, he s. away; who can hinder   9.12
one comes and s. away what is sown   Mt 13.19
and the wolf s. them and scatters   Jn 10.12

SNOW
He gives s. like wool; he scatters   Ps 147.16
they shall be as white as s.;   Is 1.18
lightning, and his raiment white as s.   Mt 28.03
white as white wool, white as s.;   Rev 1.14

SOBER
Festus, but I am speaking the s. truth. Ac 26.25
but to think with s. judgment, each   Rom 12.03
but let us keep awake and be s.   1Th 5.06

SOFT
A s. answer turns away wrath, but a   Pro 15.01
To see a man clothed in s. raiment?   Mt 11.08

SOIL (n)
Noah was the first tiller of the s.   Gen 9.20
fell on good s. and brought forth   Mt 13.08

SOJOURN —ED
Abram went down to Egypt to s.   Gen 12.10
stranger shall s. with you and   Ex 12.48
many days in the land where you s.'   Jer 35.07
By faith he s. in the land of   Heb 11.09

SOJOURNER —S
"I am a stranger and a s. among you;   Gen 23.04
Love the s. therefore; for you were   Deu 10.19
They slay the widow and the s.,   Ps 94.06
I am a s. on earth; hide not thy   119.19
The LORD watches over the s.,   146.09
you are no longer strangers and s.,   Eph 2.19

SOJOURNING (n)
the years of my s. are a hundred   Gen 47.09

SOLD
and s. his birthright to Jacob.   Gen 25.33
Joseph, whom you s. into Egypt.   45.04
And the LORD s. them into the hand   Ju 4.02
For we are s., I and my people, to   Est 7.04
"You were s. for nothing, and you   Is 52.03
went and s. all that he had and   Mt 13.46
wife Sapphira s. a piece of property,   Ac 5.01
but I am carnal, s. under sin.   Rom 7.14

SOLDIER —S
the king sent a s. of the guard   Mk 6.27
made four parts, one for each s.   Jn 19.23
Who serves as a s. at his own   1Co 9.07

and fellow worker and fellow s.,   Php 2.25
as a good s. of Christ Jesus.   2Ti 2.03
Even her hired s. in her midst are   Jer 46.21
The s. also mocked him, coming up   Lk 23.36

SOLEMN —LY
seventh day is a sabbath of s. rest,   Ex 31.15
Thy s. processions are seen, O God,   Ps 68.24
no delight in your s. assemblies.   Amo 5.21
For I s. warned your fathers when I   Jer 11.07
things, as we s. forewarned you.   1Th 4.06

SOLID FOOD*
I fed you with milk, not s. f.; for   1Co 3.02
God's word. You need milk, not s. f.;   Heb 5.12
But s. f. is for the mature, for those   5.14

SON —S
"You are my s., today I have   Ps 2.07
as a father the s. in whom he   Pro 3.12
A wise s. hears his father's instruction,   13.01
woman shall conceive and bear a s.,   Is 7.14
child is born, to us a s. is given;   9.06
and out of Egypt I called my s.   Hos 11.01
am no prophet, nor a prophet's s.;   Amo 7.14
saying, "This is my beloved S.,   Mt 3.17
but the S. of man has nowhere to   8.20
one knows the S. except the Father,   11.27
Is not this the carpenter's s.?   13.55
Afterward he sent his s. to them,   21.37
said, "Truly this was the S. of God!"   27.54
her first-born s. and wrapped him   Lk 2.07
father against s. and s. against father,   12.53
as of the only S. from the Father.   Jn 1.14
the world that he gave his only S.,   3.16
his mother, "Woman, behold your s.!"   19.26
sending his own S. in the likeness   Rom 8.03
into the fellowship of his S.,   1Co 1.09
but a s., and if a s. then an heir.   Gal 4.07
how as a s. with a father he has   Php 2.22
to the kingdom of his beloved S.,   Col 1.13
faithful over God's house as a s.   Heb 3.06
He who has the S. has life;   1Jn 5.12
be his God and he shall be my s.   Rev 21.07
Lo, s. are a heritage from the LORD,   Ps 127.03
s. who will not hear the instruction   Is 30.09
Take wives and have s. and daughters;   Jer 29.06
to them, "S. of the living God."   Hos 1.10
for they shall be called s. of God.   Mt 5.09
while the s. of the kingdom will be   8.12
said to him, "Then the s. are free.   17.26
A man had two s.; and he went   21.28
Boanerges, that is, s. of thunder;   Mk 3.17
"The s. of this age marry and are   Lk 20.34
as we wait for adoption as s.,   Rom 8.23
we might receive adoption as s.   Gal 4.05
at work in the s. of disobedience.   Eph 2.02
For you are all s. of light and   1Th 5.05
God is treating you as s.; for what   Heb 12.07

SONG —S
The LORD is my strength and my s.,   Ex 15.02
Sing to him a new s.,   Ps 33.03
and they sang a new s.,   Rev 5.09

SONG —S (cont.)
"Sing us one of the s. of Zion!"   Ps 137.03
them shall come s. of thanksgiving,   Jer 30.19
away from me the noise of your s.;   Amo 5.23
psalms and hymns and spiritual s.,   Eph 5.19

SONSHIP*
you have received the spirit of s.   Rom 8.15
Israelites, and to them belong the s.,   9.04

SORELY
my lord, I am a woman s. troubled;   1Sa 1.15
My soul also is s. troubled. But   Ps 6.03
keep silent, and afflict us s.?   Is 64.12

SORES
with loathsome s. from the sole of   Job 2.07
man named Lazarus, full of s.,   Lk 16.20

SORROW —S
For my life is spent with s., and   Ps 31.10
foolish son is a s. to his mother.   Pro 10.01
S. is better than laughter, for by   Ecc 7.03
and s. and sighing shall flee away.   Is 35.10
and give them gladness for s.   Jer 31.13
the LORD has added s. to my pain;   45.03
but your s. will turn into joy.   Jn 16.20
that I have great s. and unceasing   Rom 9.02
may be overwhelmed by excessive s.   2Co 2.07
me also, lest I should have s. upon s.   Php 2.27
a man of s., and acquainted with   Is 53.03

SORROWFUL
"My soul is very s., even to death;   Mt 26.38
as s., yet always rejoicing;   2Co 6.10

SORRY
And the LORD was s. that he had   Gen 6.06
my iniquity, I am s. for my sin.   Ps 38.18

SOUGHT
I s. the LORD, and he answered me,   Ps 34.04
When he slew them, they s. for him;   78.34
I was ready to be s. by those who   Is 65.01
And I s. for a man among them who   Eze 22.30
that moment he s. an opportunity   Mt 26.16
And he s. to see who Jesus was, but   Lk 19.03
Israel failed to obtain what it s.   Rom 11.07
repent, though he s. it with tears.   Heb 12.17

SOUL —S
March on, my s., with might!   Ju 5.21
their heart and with all their s.,   1Ki 2.04
"And now my s. is poured out within   Job 30.16
LORD is perfect, reviving the s.;   Ps 19.07
Our s. waits for the LORD;   33.20
My s. thirsts for God, for the   42.02
My s. longs, yea, faints for the   84.02
Bless the LORD, O my s.; and all   103.01
Like cold water to a thirsty s.,   Pro 25.25
My s. failed me when he spoke.   Sol 5.06
my chosen, in whom my s. delights;   Is 42.01
he poured out his s. to death,   53.12

hear, that your s. may live;   55.03
my s. shall exult in my God;   61.10
For I will satisfy the weary s.,   Jer 31.25
the body but cannot kill the s.;   Mt 10.28
with whom my s. is well pleased.   12.18
your heart, and with all your s.,   22.37
"My s. is very sorrowful, even to   26.38
said, "My s. magnifies the Lord,   Lk 1.46
This night your s. is required of   12.20
wilt not abandon my s. to Hades,   Ac 2.27
believed were of one heart and s.,   4.32
your spirit and s. and body be   1Th 5.23
and steadfast anchor of the s.,   Heb 6.19
know that it is well with your s.   3Jn 2
Behold, all s. are mine; the s.   Eze 18.04
and you will find rest for your s.   Mt 11.29
strengthening the s. of the disciples,   Ac 14.22
which is able to save your s.   Jas 1.21
obtain the salvation of your s.   1Pe 1.09
Shepherd and Guardian of your s.   2.25
They entice unsteady s. They have   2Pe 2.14
Also I saw the s. of those who had   Rev 20.04

SOUND (v)
s. the alarm on my holy mountain!   Joe 2.01
s. no trumpet before you, as the   Mt 6.02
For the trumpet will s.,   1Co 15.52

SOUND (n)
And they heard the s. of the LORD   Gen 3.08
And as the s. of the trumpet grew   Ex 19.19
Hearken to the s. of my cry, my King   Ps 5.02
when the s. of the grinding is low,   Ecc 12.04
wills, and you hear the s. of it,   Jn 3.08
the bugle gives an indistinct s.,   1Co 14.08
was like the s. of many waters;   Rev 1.15
and the s. of the millstone shall   18.22

SOUND (adj)
So, if your eye is s., your whole   Mt 6.22
A s. tree cannot bear evil fruit,   7.18
body be kept s. and blameless at   1Th 5.23
else is contrary to s. doctrine,   1Ti 1.10
that they may be s. in the faith,   Tit 1.13

SOW —N —S (v)
iniquity and s. trouble reap the   Job 4.08
May those who s. in tears reap with   Ps 126.05
In the morning s. your seed, and at   Ecc 11.06
fallow ground, and s. not among thorns.   Jer 4.03
For they s. the wind, and they shall   Hos 8.07
S. for yourselves righteousness,   10.12
You shall s., but not reap; you shall   Mic 6.15
they neither s. nor reap nor gather   Mt 6.26
saying: "A sower went out to s.   13.03
man, reaping where you did not s.,   25.24
What you s. does not come to life   1Co 15.36
You have s. much, and harvested   Hag 1.06
If we have s. spiritual good among   1Co 9.11
What is s. is perishable, what is   15.42
righteousness is s. in peace by   Jas 3.18
he who s. sparingly will also reap   2Co 9.06
not mocked, for whatever a man s.,   Gal 6.07

SPAN
yet their s. is but toil and	Ps 90.10
marked off the heavens with a s.,	Is 40.12
add one cubit to his s. of life?	Mt 6.27

SPARE —S
"Cry aloud, s. not, lift up your	Is 58.01
S. not her young men; utterly destroy	Jer 51.03
I will not s., I will not repent;	Eze 24.14
"S. thy people, O LORD, and make not	Joe 2.17
have bread enough and to s.,	Lk 15.17
He who did not s. his own Son but	Rom 8.32
troubles, and I would s. you that.	1Co 7.28
I come again I will not s. them—	2Co 13.02
For if God did not s. the angels	2Pe 2.04
He who s. the rod hates his son, but	Pro 13.24

SPARROW —S
Even the s. finds a home, and the	Ps 84.03
Are not two s. sold for a penny?	Mt 10.29

SPEAK —ING —S
You shall s. all that I command you;	Ex 7.02
and the LORD would s. with Moses.	33.09
'S., LORD, for thy servant hears.' "	1Sa 3.09
But oh, that God would s.,	Job 11.05
But I would s. to the Almighty, and	13.03
God the LORD will s., for he will s. peace	Ps 85.08
They shall s. of the glory of thy	145.11
Do not s. in the hearing of a fool,	Pro 23.09
to keep silence, and a time to s.;	Ecc 3.07
s. to us smooth things, prophesy	Is 30.10
S. tenderly to Jerusalem, and cry to	40.02
whatever I command you you shall s.	Jer 1.07
your feet, and I will s. with you."	Eze 2.01
I the LORD will s. the word which I will s.,	12.25
how you are to s. or what you are	Mt 10.19
the deaf hear and the dumb s."	Mk 7.37
for we cannot but s. of what we	Ac 4.20
Do all s. with tongues? Do all	1Co 12.30
I would rather s. five words with	14.19
the sight of God we s. in Christ.	2Co 2.17
we too believe, and so we s.,	4.13
let every one s. the truth with his	Eph 4.25
more bold to s. the word of God	Php 1.14
so we s., not to please men, but to	1Th 2.04
to s. evil of no one, to avoid	Tit 3.02
So s. and so act as those who are	Jas 2.12
I am s. the truth in Christ, I am	Rom 9.01
that no one s. by the Spirit of	1Co 12.03
humanly s., I fought with beasts at	15.32
proof that Christ is in me.	2Co 13.03
Rather, s. the truth in love, we are	Eph 4.15
figuratively s., he did receive him	Heb 11.19
abundance of the heart the mouth s.	Mt 12.34
blood that s. more graciously than	Heb 12.24

SPEAR —S
LORD saves not with sword and s.;	1Sa 17.47
But Saul cast his s. at him to	20.33
soldiers pierced his side with a s.,	Jn 19.34
and their s. into pruning hooks;	Is 2.04
and your pruning hooks into s.;	Joe 3.10

SPECIAL
my s. possession on the day when I	Mal 3.17
each has his own s. gift from God,	1Co 7.07

SPEECH
may not understand one another's s."	Gen 11.07
but I am slow of s. and of tongue."	Ex 4.10
Day to day pours forth s., and	Ps 19.02
Put away from you crooked s.,	Pro 4.24
Fine s. is not becoming to a fool;	17.07
and had an impediment in his s.;	Mk 7.32
he prolonged his s. until midnight.	Ac 20.07
and my s. and my message were not	1Co 2.04
is weak, and his s. of no account.	2Co 10.10
Let your s. always be gracious,	Col 4.06
an example in s. and conduct,	1Ti 4.12

SPEEDILY
Incline thy ear to me, rescue me s.!	Ps 31.02
My deliverance draws near s.,	Is 51.05
tell you, he will vindicate them s.	Lk 18.08

SPEND
Why do you s. your money for that	Is 55.02
and whatever more you s.,	Lk 10.35
most gladly s. and be spent for	2Co 12.15

SPIES (n)
David sent out s., and learned of a	1Sa 26.04
and sent s., who pretended to be	Lk 20.20
given friendly welcome to the s.	Heb 11.31

SPIRIT
and the S. of God was moving over	Gen 1.02
"My s. shall not abide in man for	6.03
And the S. of God came upon him,	Num 24.02
"The s. of Elijah rests on Elisha."	2Ki 2.15
Then a s. came forward and stood	2Ch 18.20
Thou gavest thy good S. to instruct	Neh 9.20
My s. is broken, my days are extinct,	Job 17.01
The s. of God has made me, and the	33.04
acceptable to God is a broken s.;	Ps 51.17
Whither shall I go from thy S.?	139.07
and the s. returns to God who gave	Ecc 12.07
until the S. is poured upon us from	Is 32.15
in all these is the life of my s.	38.16
Who has directed the S. of the LORD,	40.13
the S. of the LORD gave them rest.	63.14
Then the S. lifted me up, and as the	Eze 3.12
and a new s. I will put within you;	36.26
My S. abides among you; fear not.	Hag 2.05
to be with child of the Holy S.;	Mt 1.18
and he saw the S. of God descending	3.16
"Blessed are the poor in s.,	5.03
But if it is by the S. of God that	12.28
a loud voice and yielded up his s.	27.50
and of the Son and of the Holy S.,	28.19
and the Holy S. was upon him.	Lk 2.25
And Jesus, full of the Holy S.,	4.01
"The S. of the Lord is upon me,	4.18
into thy hands I commit my s.!"	23.46
one is born of water and the S.,	Jn 3.05
God is s., and those who worship	4.24
the Holy S., whom the Father will	14.26

SPIRIT (cont.)

When the S. of truth comes, he will	Jn 16.13
said to them, "Receive the Holy S.	20.22
the Holy S. to the apostles whom	Ac 1.02
will pour out my S. upon all flesh,	2.17
Paul, filled with the Holy S.,	13.09
bound in the S., not knowing what	20.22
code but in the new life of the S.	Rom 7.06
the flesh but according to the S.	8.04
If the S. of him who raised Jesus	8.11
it is the S. himself bearing	8.16
but the S. himself intercedes for	8.26
flag in zeal, be aglow with the S.,	12.11
acceptable, sanctified by the Holy S.	15.16
and that God's S. dwells in you?	1Co 3.16
the Lord becomes one s. with him.	6.17
is Lord" except by the Holy S.	12.03
For by one S. we were all baptized	12.13
given us his S. in our hearts as a	2Co 1.22
Now the Lord is the S., and	3.17
has given us the S. as a guarantee.	5.05
has sent the S. of his Son into	Gal 4.06
walk by the S., and do not gratify	5.16
But the fruit of the S. is love,	5.22
will from the S. reap eternal life.	6.08
sealed with the promised Holy S.,	Eph 1.13
There is one body and one S.,	4.04
salvation, and the sword of the S.,	6.17
love, any participation in the S.,	Php 2.01
Do not quench the S.,	1Th 5.19
you by the Holy S. who dwells	2Ti 1.14
the eternal S. offered himself	Heb 9.14
the body apart from the s. is dead,	Jas 2.26
By this you know the S. of God:	1Jn 4.02
And the S. is the witness, because	5.07
the S., the water, and the blood:	5.08
I was in the S. on the Lord's day,	Rev 1.10
hear what the S. says to the	2.07
The S. and the Bride say, "Come."	22.17

SPIRITUAL

to you some s. gift to strengthen	Rom 1.11
of the heart, s. and not literal.	2.29
to God, which is your s. worship.	12.01
interpreting s. truths to those who	1Co 2.13
could not address you as s. men,	3.01
If we have sown s. good among you,	9.11
Now concerning s. gifts, brethren, I	12.01
body, it is raised a s. body.	15.44
against the s. hosts of wickedness	Eph 6.12
yourselves built into a s. house,	1Pe 2.05

SPIT

and when he had s. on his eyes and	Mk 8.23
and s. upon him, and scourge him, and	10.34
And some began to s. on him,	14.65

SPITTING* (n)

I hid not my face from shame and s.	Is 50.06

SPLENDOR

On the glorious s. of thy majesty,	Ps 145.05
be presented before him in s.,	Eph 5.27

SPLIT —S*

earth shook, and the rocks were s.;	Mt 27.51
The great city was s. into three	Rev 16.19
and he who s. logs is endangered by	Ecc 10.09

SPOIL —ED (v)

Even so will I s. the pride of	Jer 13.09
of clay was s. in the potter's hand,	18.04

SPOIL —S (n)

and the booty and the s. to Moses,	Num 31.12
The women at home divide the s.,	Ps 68.12
to divide the s. with the proud.	Pro 16.19
the s. of the poor is in your	Is 3.14
to take s. and seize plunder, and to	10.06
divide the s. with the strong;	53.12
who despoil you shall become a s.,	Jer 30.16
shall become a s. to the nations;	Eze 26.05
he trusted, and divides his s.	Lk 11.22
patriarch gave him a tithe of the s.	Heb 7.04

SPORT

"Because you have made s. of me.	Num 22.29
who looked on while Samson made s.	Ju 16.27
Of whom are you making s.? Against	Is 57.04

SPOT —S

without s. or wrinkle or any such	Eph 5.27
of a lamb without blemish or s.	1Pe 1.19
found by him without s. or blemish,	2Pe 3.14
his skin or the leopard his s.?	Jer 13.23

SPREAD —S

my roots s. out to the waters, with	Job 29.19
s. out the skies, hard as a molten	37.18
or s. forth our hands to a strange	Ps 44.20
"Can God s. a table in the wilderness?	78.19
O Lord; I s. out my hands to thee.	88.09
He s. a cloud for a covering, and	105.39
When you s. forth your hands, I will	Is 1.15
I s. out my hands all the day to a	65.02
with a table s. before it on which	Eze 23.41
there is s. upon the mountains a	Joe 2.02
and s. dung upon your faces, the	Mal 2.03
So his fame s. throughout all Syria,	Mt 4.24
Most of the crowd s. their garments	21.08
and so death s. to all men because	Rom 5.12
it as a swimmer s. his hands out	Is 25.11
and through us s. the fragrance of	2Co 2.14

SPRING —S (v)

sang this song: "S. up, O well!	Num 21.17
Faithfulness will s. up from the	Ps 85.11
cause righteousness to s. up also;	Is 45.08
Branch to s. forth for David;	Jer 33.15
appeal does not s. from error or	1Th 2.03
now it s. forth, do you not perceive	Is 43.19
so judgment s. up like poisonous	Hos 10.04

SPRING —S (n)

the flint into a s. of water.	Ps 114.08
like a s. of water, whose waters	Is 58.11
become in him a s. of water	Jn 4.14
Does a s. pour forth from the same	Jas 3.11

SPRING —S (n) (cont.)

Thou makest s. gush forth in the	Ps 104.10
a parched land into s. of water.	107.35
for from it flow the s. of life.	Pro 4.23
are like doves beside s. of water,	Sol 5.12
and the thirsty ground s. of water;	Is 35.07
These are waterless s. and mists	2Pe 2.17

SPRINKLE —D

the blood and s. part of the blood	Lev 4.06
I will s. clean water upon you, and	Eze 36.25
lifeblood is s. upon my garments,	Is 63.03
with our hearts s. clean from an	Heb 10.22

SPRINKLING (n)

For if the s. of defiled persons	Heb 9.13
Christ and for s. with his blood:	1Pe 1.02

SPROUT —ED

I will make a horn to s. for David;	Ps 132.17
open, that salvation may s. forth,	Is 45.08
making it bring forth and s.,	55.10
and the seed should s. and grow,	Mk 4.27
after them s. seven ears, thin and	Gen 41.06

SPURN —ED —S

if you s. my statutes, and if your	Lev 26.15
"Will the Lord s. for ever, and	Ps 77.07
Do not s. us, for thy name's sake;	Jer 14.21
Israel has s. the good; the enemy	Hos 8.03
the man who has s. the Son of God,	Heb 10.29
that is not good; he s. not evil.	Ps 36.04

SPY (v)

Moses sent them to s. out the land	Num 13.17
slipped in to s. out our freedom	Gal 2.04

STAFF

with only my s. I crossed this	Gen 32.10
When I break your s. of bread,	Lev 26.26
that pass under the herdsman's s.,	27.32
thy rod and thy s., they comfort me.	Ps 23.04
rod of my anger, the s. of my fury!	Is 10.05
Shepherd thy people with thy s.,	Mic 7.14
And I took my s. Grace, and I broke	Zec 11.10
two tunics, nor sandals, nor a s.;	Mt 10.10
for their journey except a s.;	Mk 6.08
in worship over the head of his s.	Heb 11.21
given a measuring rod like a s.,	Rev 11.01

STAGGER —ED* —S

have made Egypt s. in all her	Is 19.14
with wine and s. with strong drink;	28.07
s., but not with strong drink!	29.09
they reeled and s. like drunken men,	Ps 107.27
The earth s. like a drunken man, it	Is 24.20

STAGGERING

taken from your hand the cup of s.;	Is 51.22

STAND —ING —S (v)

s. firm, and see the salvation of	Ex 14.13
"Who is able to s. before the LORD,	1Sa 6.20
at last he will s. upon the earth;	Job 19.25

Why dost thou s. afar off, O LORD?	Ps 10.01
And who shall s. in his holy place?	24.03
of the world s. in awe of him!	33.08
iniquities, Lord, who could s.?	130.03
speak a word, but it will not s.,	Is 8.10
word of our God will s. for ever.	40.08
from the sword, go, s. not still!	Jer 51.50
s. upon your feet, and I will speak	Eze 2.01
and who can s. when he appears?	Mal 3.02
they love to s. and pray in the	Mt 6.05
divided against itself will s.;	12.25
who s. in the presence of God;	Lk 1.19
you must s. before Caesar; and lo, God	Ac 27.24
to this grace in which we s.,	Rom 5.02
we shall all s. before the judgment	14.10
you received, in which you s.,	1Co 15.01
s. fast therefore, and do not submit	Gal 5.01
day, and having done all, to s.	Eph 6.13
S. therefore, having girded your	6.14
that you may s. mature and fully	Col 4.12
Behold, I s. at the door and knock;	Rev 3.20
there are some s. here who will	Mt 16.28
Now Simon Peter was s. and warming	Jn 18.25
but s. by the cross of Jesus were	19.25
she turned round and saw Jesus s.,	20.14
So Paul, s. in the middle of the	Ac 17.22
as long as the outer tent is still s.	Heb 9.08
I saw a Lamb s., as though it had	Rev 5.06
nor s. in the way of sinners, nor	Ps 1.01
The counsel of the LORD s. for ever,	33.11
but my heart s. in awe of thy words	119.161
and righteousness s. afar off;	Is 59.14
But God's firm foundation s.,	2Ti 2.19

STAND (n)

but on a s., and it gives light to	Mt 5.15

STANDARD —S

Raise a s. toward Zion, flee for	Jer 4.06
heart to the s. of teaching to	Rom 6.17
were wise according to worldly s.,	1Co 1.26

STAR —S

a s. shall come forth out of Jacob,	Num 24.17
from heaven, O Day S., son of Dawn!	Is 14.12
we have seen his s. in the East,	Mt 2.02
for s. differs from s. in glory.	1Co 15.41
and the morning s. rises in your	2Pe 1.19
and I saw a s. fallen from heaven	Rev 9.01
of David, the bright morning s.'	22.16
toward heaven, and number the s.,	Gen 15.05
when the morning s. sang together,	Job 38.07
moon and the s. which thou hast	Ps 8.03
He determines the number of the s.,	147.04
the heavens, who gaze at the s.,	Is 47.13
moon and the s. for light by night,	Jer 31.35
and the s. will fall from heaven,	Mt 24.29
as many as the s. of heaven and as	Heb 11.12
wandering s. for whom the nether	Jud 13
in his right hand he held seven s.,	Rev 1.16
on her head a crown of twelve s.;	12.01

STATE (n)

and the last s. of that man becomes	Mt 12.45

STATE (n) (cont.)
remain in the s. in which he was	1Co 7.20
in whatever s. I am, to be content.	Php 4.11

STATURE
to grow both in s. and in favor	1Sa 2.26
increased in wisdom and in s.,	Lk 2.52
crowd, because he was small of s.	19.03
measure of the s. of the fulness	Eph 4.13

STATUTE —S
made for them a s. and an ordinance	Ex 15.25
thee, who frame mischief by s.?	Ps 94.20
commandments, my s., and my laws."	Gen 26.05
Keep my s., and do them;	Lev 20.08
and I will meditate on thy s.	Ps 119.48
violated the s., broken the everlasting	Is 24.05
they did not walk in my s., and were	Eze 20.21

STAY —ED (v)
and s. themselves on the God of	Is 48.02
here shall your proud waves be s.'?	Job 38.11
whose mind is s. on thee, because he	Is 26.03

STEADFAST —LY
Their heart was not s. toward him;	Ps 78.37
to the Lord with s. purpose;	Ac 11.23
be s., immovable, always abounding	1Co 15.58
as a sure and s. anchor of the	Heb 6.19
Behold, we call those happy who were s.	Jas 5.11
Continue s. in prayer, being watchful	Col 4.02

STEADFAST LOVE
but showing s. l. to thousands of those	Deu 5.10
God, who keepest covenant and s. l.,	Neh 9.32
Thou hast granted me life and s. l.;	Job 10.12
But I have trusted in thy s. l.; my	Ps 13.05
but s. l. surrounds him who trusts in	32.10
By day the LORD commands his s. l.;	42.08
Lord, where is thy s. l. of old, which	89.49
who crowns you with s. l. and mercy,	103.04
Let them thank the LORD for his s. l.,	107.08
good, for his s. l. endures for ever.	136.01
I will recount the s. l. of the LORD,	Is 63.07
that I am the LORD who practice s. l.,	Jer 9.24
For I desire s. l. and not sacrifice,	Hos 6.06
slow to anger, and abounding in s. l.,	Joe 2.13

STEADFASTNESS
May the God of s. and encouragement	Rom 15.05
of love and s. of hope in our Lord	1Th 1.03
of God and to the s. of Christ.	2Th 3.05
faith, love, s., gentleness.	1Ti 6.11
You have heard of the s. of Job,	Jas 5.11

STEAL
"You shall not s.	Ex 20.15
and where thieves break in and s.,	Mt 6.19
You shall not s., You shall not	19.18
preach against stealing, do you s.?	Rom 2.21
You shall not s., You shall not	13.09
Let the thief no longer s.,	Eph 4.28

STEP —S (n)
whom victory meets at every s.?	Is 41.02

For then thou wouldest number my s.,	Job 14.16
The s. of a man are from the LORD,	Ps 37.23
upon a rock, making my s. secure.	40.02
way, but the LORD directs his s.	Pro 16.09
A man's s. are ordered by the LORD;	20.24
of the poor, the s. of the needy."	Is 26.06
Did we not take the same s.?	2Co 12.18
that you should follow in his s.	1Pe 2.21

STEWARD —S
then is the faithful and wise s.,	Lk 12.42
stewardship, for you can no longer be s.'	16.02
as God's s., must be blameless;	Tit 1.07
of Christ and s. of the mysteries	1Co 4.01
as good s. of God's varied grace:	1Pe 4.10

STILL
after the fire a s. small voice.	1Ki 19.12
He leads me beside s. waters;	Ps 23.02
"Be s., and know that I am God.	46.10
"Peace! Be s.!" And the wind	Mk 4.39
them, "My Father is working s.,	Jn 5.17

STING*
victory? O death, where is thy s.?"	1Co 15.55
The s. of death is sin, and the	15.56

STIR —RED —S (v)
S. up thy might, and come to save us!	Ps 80.02
I will s. up the spirit of a	Jer 51.01
whose baker ceases to s. the fire,	Hos 7.04
Jerusalem, all the city was s.,	Mt 21.10
your zeal has s. up most of them.	2Co 9.02
Hatred s. up strife, but love covers	Pro 10.12
"He s. up the people, teaching	Lk 23.05

STOCKS
Thou puttest my feet in the s.,	Job 13.27
released Jeremiah from the s.,	Jer 20.03
and fastened their feet in the s.	Ac 16.24

STONE —D —ING (v)
"We s. you for no good work but for	Jn 10.33
they s. Paul and dragged him out of	Ac 14.19
once I was s. Three times I have been	2Co 11.25
They were s., they were sawn in two,	Heb 11.37
prophets and s. those who are sent	Mt 23.37
And as they were s. Stephen,	Ac 7.59

STONE —S (n)
thy arm, they are as still as a s.,	Ex 15.16
I will give you the tables of s.,	24.12
serve other gods, of wood and s.	Deu 28.36
Then Samuel took a s. and set it up	1Sa 7.12
Philistine with a sling and with a s.,	17.50
The s. which the builders rejected	Ps 118.22
and a s. of offense, and a rock of	Is 8.14
in Zion for a foundation a s.,	28.16
committing adultery with s. and tree.	Jer 3.09
the heart of s. and give you a	Eze 36.26
a s. was cut out by no human hand,	Dan 2.34
you have built houses of hewn s.,	Amo 5.11
him for a loaf, will give him a s.?	Mt 7.09
'The very s. which the builders	21.42

STONE —S (n) (cont.)

be left here one s. upon another,	Mt 24.02
rolled a great s. to the door of	27.60
and came and rolled back the s.,	28.02
This is the s. which was rejected	Ac 4.11
stumbled over the stumbling s.,	Rom 9.32
on tablets of s. but on tablets of	2Co 3.03
"The very s. which the builders	1Pe 2.07
and I will give him a white s.,	Rev 2.17
a time to cast away s., and a time	Ecc 3.05
clear it of s., lift up an ensign	Is 62.10
able from these s. to raise up	Mt 3.09
command these s. to become loaves	4.03
what wonderful s. and what wonderful	Mk 13.01
precious s., wood, hay, stubble—	1Co 3.12
and like living s. be yourselves	1Pe 2.05

STORE —D —ING* (v)

for I have nowhere to s. my crops?'	Lk 12.17
put something aside and s. it up,	1Co 16.02
now exist have been s. up for fire,	2Pe 3.07
heart you are s. up wrath for	Rom 2.05

STOREHOUSE —S

Bring the full tithes into the s.,	Mal 3.10
they have neither s. nor barn,	Lk 12.24
the land, Joseph opened all the s.,	Gen 41.56

STORM

me about in the roar of the s.	Job 30.22
he made the s. be still, and the	Ps 107.29
there arose a great s. on the sea,	Mt 8.24

STRAIGHT

make thy way s. before me.	Ps 5.08
of the blameless keeps his way s.,	Pro 11.05
What is crooked cannot be made s.,	Ecc 1.15
make s. in the desert a highway for	Is 40.03
way of the Lord, make his paths s."	Mt 3.03
and the crooked shall be made s.,	Lk 3.05
and go to the street called S.,	Ac 9.11
and make s. paths for your feet, so	Heb 12.13

STRANGE

after the s. gods of the land,	Deu 31.16
forth our hands to a s. god,	Ps 44.20
"We have seen s. things today."	Lk 5.26
"By men of s. tongues and by the	1Co 14.21
away by diverse and s. teachings;	Heb 13.09

STRANGER —S

"I am a s. and a sojourner among	Gen 23.04
And when a s. shall sojourn with	Ex 12.48
my maidservants count me as a s.;	Job 19.15
I have become a s. to my brethren,	Ps 69.08
thou be like a s. in the land,	Jer 14.08
I was a s. and you welcomed me,	Mt 25.35
A s. they will not follow, but they	Jn 10.05
you shall serve s. in a land that	Jer 5.19
and s. to the covenants of promise,	Eph 2.12
that they were s. and exiles on	Heb 11.13
neglect to show hospitality to s.,	13.02

STRAW

He counts iron as s., and bronze	Job 41.27
What has s. in common with wheat?	Jer 23.28

STREAM —S (n)

an overflowing s. that reaches up	Is 30.28
the nations like an overflowing s.;	66.12
righteousness like an ever-flowing s.	Amo 5.24
like a tree planted by s. of water,	Ps 1.03
As a hart longs for flowing s.,	42.01
a river whose s. make glad the	46.04
All s. run to the sea, but the sea	Ecc 1.07

STREET —S

Wisdom cries aloud in the s.; in the	Pro 1.20
and the doors on the s. are shut;	Ecc 12.04
synagogues and at the s. corners,	Mt 6.05
and the s. of the city was pure	Rev 21.21
publish it not in the s. of Ashkelon;	2Sa 1.20
out into the s. and gathered all	Mt 22.10

STRENGTH

for as the man is, so is his s."	Ju 8.21
the secret of his s. was not known.	16.09
ascribe to the LORD glory and s.!	1Ch 16.28
Is my s. the s. of stones, or is my	Job 6.12
With him are s. and wisdom; the	12.16
The LORD is the s. of his people,	Ps 28.08
God is our refuge and s.,	46.01
s. and beauty are in his sanctuary.	96.06
The LORD is my s. and my song;	118.14
The glory of young men is their s.,	Pro 20.29
for s., and not for drunkenness!	Ecc 10.17
lift up your voice with s.,	Is 40.09
let the peoples renew their s.;	41.01
your mind, and with all your s.'	Mk 12.30
He has shown s. with his arm, he has	Lk 1.51
let you be tempted beyond your s.,	1Co 10.13
Lord and in the s. of his might.	Eph 6.10
him who has given me s. for this,	1Ti 1.12
me and gave me s. to proclaim the	2Ti 4.17
won s. out of weakness, became	Heb 11.34
it by the s. which God supplies;	1Pe 4.11

STRENGTHEN —ED —S

s. me according to thy word!	Ps 119.28
S. the weak hands, and make firm the	Is 35.03
your cords and s. your stakes.	54.02
you some spiritual gift to s. you,	Rom 1.11
who is able to s. you according to	16.25
restore, establish, and s. you.	1Pe 5.10
Awake, and s. what remains and is on	Rev 3.02
May you be s. with all power,	Col 1.11
well that the heart be s. by grace,	Heb 13.09
can do all things in him who s. me.	Php 4.13

STRETCH —ED —ES

I will s. out my hands to the LORD;	Ex 9.29
I s. out my hands to thee;	Ps 143.06
and s. themselves upon their	Amo 6.04
who alone s. out the heavens, and	Job 9.08
line shall be s. out over Jerusalem	Zec 1.16
The carpenter s. a line, he marks it	Is 44.13

STRICKEN
and my heart is s. within me.   Ps 109.22
yet we esteemed him s., smitten by   Is 53.04

STRICT —EST* —LY
according to the s. manner of the law   Ac 22.03
according to the s. party of our religion   26.05
Then he s. charged the disciples to   Mt 16.20

STRIFE
and with continual s. in his bones;   Job 33.19
Hatred stirs up s., but love   Pro 10.12
and pressing anger produces s.   30.33
s., deceit, malignity, they are   Rom 1.29
there is jealousy and s. among you,   1Co 3.03
s., jealousy, anger, selfishness,   Gal 5.20

STRIKE —S
and you shall s. the rock, and water   Ex 17.06
"S. the shepherd, that the sheep may   Zec 13.07
lest you s. your foot against a   Mt 4.06
"Lord, shall we s. with the sword?"   Lk 22.49
But if any one s. you on the right   Mt 5.39
puts on airs, or s. you in the face.   2Co 11.20

STRIPE* —S
for burn, wound for wound, s. for s.   Ex 21.25
and with his s. we are healed.   Is 53.05

STRIPPED
And Moses s. Aaron of his garments,   Num 20.28
He has s. from me my glory, and   Job 19.09
I will go s. and naked; I will make   Mic 1.08
And they s. him and put a scarlet   Mt 27.28
who s. him and beat him, and departed,   Lk 10.30

STRIVE —N* —S* —ING
"S. to enter by the narrow door;   Lk 13.24
s. to excel in building up the   1Co 14.12
For to this end we toil and s.,   1Ti 4.10
Let us therefore s. to enter that   Heb 4.11
S. for peace with all men, and for   12.14
for you have s. with God and with   Gen 32.28
"Woe to him who s. with his Maker,   Is 45.09
with one mind s. side by side for   Php 1.27

STRIVING (n)
all is vanity and a s. after wind.   Ecc 1.14

STRONG —ER
"Drink no wine nor s. drink,   Lev 10.09
Out of the s. came something sweet."   Ju 14.14
The LORD, s. and mighty, the LORD,   Ps 24.08
Be s., and let your heart take   31.24
with a s. hand and an outstretched   136.12
The name of the LORD is a s. tower;   Pro 18.10
Wine is a mocker; s. drink a brawler;   20.01
wise man is mightier than a s. man,   24.05
swift, nor the battle to the s.,   Ecc 9.11
a fearful heart, "Be s., fear not!   Is 35.04
shall divide the spoil with the s.;   53.12
not truth has grown s. in the land;   Jer 9.03
Their Redeemer is s.; the LORD of   50.34
can one enter a s. man's house and   Mt 12.29

shall drink no wine nor s. drink,   Lk 1.15
And the child grew and became s.,   2.40
We who are s. ought to bear with   Rom 15.01
weak in the world to shame the s.,   1Co 1.27
We are weak, but you are s.   4.10
your faith, be courageous, be s.   16.13
for when I am weak, then I am s.   2Co 12.10
Therefore God sends upon them a s.   2Th 2.11
generals and the rich and the s.,   Rev 6.15
he that has clean hands grows s. and s.   Job 17.09
the weakness of God is s. than men.   1Co 1.25

STRONGHOLD —S
a s. to the needy in his distress, a   Is 25.04
O LORD, my strength and my s., my   Jer 16.19
have divine power to destroy s.   2Co 10.04

STRUCK
Then they spat in his face, and s. him;   Mt 26.67
s. down, but not destroyed;   2Co 4.09

STRUCTURE
in whom the whole s. is joined   Eph 2.21

STUBBORN —LY
righteousness; for you are a s. people.   Deu 9.06
a s. and rebellious generation, a   Ps 78.08
Like a s. heifer, Israel is s.;   Hos 4.16
every one who s. follows his own   Jer 23.17

STUMBLE
and foes, they shall s. and fall.   Ps 27.02
and if you run, you will not s.   Pro 4.12
we s. at noon as in the twilight,   Is 59.10
he does not s., because he sees the   Jn 11.09
Zion a stone that will make men s.,   Rom 9.33
anything that makes your brother s.   14.21
for they s. because they disobey   1Pe 2.08

STUMP
whose s. remains standing when it   Is 6.13
forth a shoot from the s. of Jesse,   11.01

STUPID
But a s. man will get understanding,   Job 11.12
but he who hates reproof is s.   Pro 12.01
Surely I am too s. to be a man.   30.02
For the shepherds are s., and do   Jer 10.21
Every man is s. and without knowledge;   51.17
Have nothing to do with s., senseless,   2Ti 2.23
But avoid s. controversies, genealogies,   Tit 3.09

SUBDUE
multiply, and fill the earth and s. it;   Gen 1.28
to s. nations before him and ungird   Is 45.01
but I pommel my body and s. it,   1Co 9.27

SUBJECT —ED
the demons are s. to us in your   Lk 10.17
Let every person be s. to the   Rom 13.01
of prophets are s. to prophets.   1Co 14.32
As the church is s. to Christ,   Eph 5.24
much more be s. to the Father of   Heb 12.09
for the creation was s. to futility,   Rom 8.20

SUBJECT —ED (cont.)
When all things are s. to him, 1Co 15.28
angels that God s. the world to Heb 2.05

SUBJECTION
all things in s. under his feet. 1Co 15.27
in putting everything in s. to him, Heb 2.08

SUBMISSIVE
his children s. and respectful in 1Ti 3.04
and s. to their husbands, that the Tit 2.05
Servants, be s. to your masters with 1Pe 2.18

SUBMIT
did not s. to God's righteousness. Rom 10.03
and do not s. again to a yoke of Gal 5.01
Why do you s. to regulations, Col 2.20
S. yourselves therefore to God. Jas 4.07

SUBSTANCE
Thy eyes beheld my unformed s.; Ps 139.16
to come; but the s. belongs to Christ. Col 2.17

SUCCEED —S*
strength; but wisdom helps one to s. Ecc 10.10
perhaps you may be able to s., Is 47.12
Will he s.? Can a man escape Eze 17.15
on law did not s. in fulfilling Rom 9.31
and a maid when she s. her mistress. Pro 30.23

SUCCESS
grant me s. today, I pray thee, and Gen 24.12
LORD, we beseech thee, give us s.! Ps 118.25

SUCK (v)
He will s. the poison of asps; Job 20.16
You shall s. the milk of nations, Is 60.16

SUCK —ING (n)
those who give s. in those days! Mt 24.19
and the breasts that never gave s.!' Lk 23.29
"Can a woman forget her s. child, Is 49.15

SUFFER —ED —S
the simple go on, and s. for it. Pro 22.03
not the son s. for the iniquity of Eze 18.19
Jerusalem and s. many things from Mt 16.21
Son of man will s. at their hands." 17.12
Christ should s. these things and Lk 24.26
worthy to s. dishonor for the name Ac 5.41
provided we s. with him in order Rom 8.17
member suffers, all s. together; 1Co 12.26
in him but also s. for his sake, Php 1.29
and therefore I s. as I do. But I 2Ti 1.12
you may have to s. various trials, 1Pe 1.06
But even if you do s. for righteousness 3.14
But let none of you s. as a murderer, 4.15
Do not fear what you are about to s. Rev 2.10
his sake I have s. the loss of all Php 3.08
obedience through what he s.; Heb 5.08
So Jesus also s. outside the gate 13.12
because Christ also s. for you, 1Pe 2.21
for whoever has s. in the flesh 4.01
And after you have s. a little while, 5.10
yet if one s. as a Christian, let 4.16

SUFFERING —S (n)
knowing that s. produces endurance, Rom 5.03
your share of s. for the gospel in 2Ti 1.08
endure s., do the work of an 4.05
their salvation perfect through s. Heb 2.10
that the s. of this present time Rom 8.18
resurrection, and may share his s., Php 3.10
in so far as you share Christ's s., 1Pe 4.13

SUFFICE
life is costly, and can never s., Ps 49.08
Lebanon would not s. for fuel, Is 40.16
that is past s. for doing what the 1Pe 4.03

SUFFICIENT
own trouble be s. for the day. Mt 6.34
to life. Who is s. for these things? 2Co 2.16
Not that we are s. of ourselves to 3.05
"My grace is s. for you, for my 12.09

SUMMER
s. and winter, day and night, shall Gen 8.22
the winter house with the s. house; Amo 3.15
me: behold, a basket of s. fruit. 8.01
leaves, you know that s. is near. Mt 24.32

SUMMON —ED
matter of justice, who can s. him? Job 9.19
S. thy might, O God; show thy Ps 68.28
Who will s. me? What shepherd can Jer 50.44
If I s. him and he answered me, I Job 9.16
Then Herod s. the wise men secretly Mt 2.07

SUN
"S., stand thou still at Gibeon, and Jos 10.12
LORD has set the s. in the heavens, 1Ki 8.12
rising of the s. to its setting. Ps 50.01
For the LORD God is a s. and shield; 84.11
The s. shall not smite you by day, 121.06
Praise him, s. and moon, praise him, 148.03
there is nothing new under the s. Ecc 1.09
that under the s. the race is not 9.11
the s. will be dark at its rising Is 13.10
The s. shall be no more your light 60.19
"I will make the s. go down at noon, Amo 8.09
he makes his s. rise on the evil Mt 5.45
shine like the s. in the kingdom 13.43
and his face shone like the s., 17.02
those days the s. will be darkened, 24.29
from heaven, brighter than the s., Ac 26.13
There is one glory of the s., 1Co 15.41
do not let the s. go down on your Eph 4.26
Then I saw an angel standing in the s., Rev 19.17
they need no light of lamp or s., 22.05

SUPPER
'Prepare s. for me, and gird yourself Lk 17.08
There they made him a s.; Martha Jn 12.02
his breast at the s. and had said, 21.20
after s., saying, "This cup is the 1Co 11.25
to the marriage s. of the Lamb.' Rev 19.09

SUPPLICATION —S
The LORD has heard my s.; the LORD Ps 6.09

SUPPLICATION —S (cont.)

Hear the voice of my s., as I cry	Ps 28.02
a spirit of compassion and s.,	Zec 12.10
the Spirit, with all prayer and s.	Eph 6.18
by prayer and s. with thanksgiving	Php 4.06
be attentive to the voice of my s.!	Ps 130.02
I urge that s., prayers, intercessions,	1Ti 2.01
Jesus offered up prayers and s.,	Heb 5.07

SUPPLIED —IES —Y (v)

my needs were s. by the brethren	2Co 11.09
by every joint with which it is s.,	Eph 4.16
Does he who s. the Spirit to you	Gal 3.05
it by the strength which God s.;	1Pe 4.11
And my God will s. every need of yours	Php 4.19
to face and s. what is lacking in your	1Th 3.10

SUPPORT —ED (v)

Those who s. Egypt shall fall, and	Eze 30.06
remember it is not you that s. the	Rom 11.18
So we ought to s. such men, that we	3Jn 8
salvation, and thy right hand s. me,	Ps 18.35

SURETY

is there that will give s. for me?	Job 17.03
This makes Jesus the s. of a better	Heb 7.22

SURPASS —ED ES* —ING

excellently, but you s. them all."	Pro 31.29
Solomon's wisdom s. the wisdom of	1Ki 4.30
because of the splendor that s. it.	2Co 3.10
love of Christ which s. knowledge,	Eph 3.19
because of the s. grace of God in	2Co 9.14
because of the s. worth of knowing	Php 3.08

SURROUND —ED —S

his archers s. me. He slashes open	Job 16.13
They s. me like a flood all day	Ps 88.17
the multitudes s. you and press	Lk 8.45
you see Jerusalem s. by armies,	21.20
since we are s. by so great a cloud	Heb 12.01
steadfast love s. him who trusts	Ps 32.10

SURVIVE —D —S

and those who s. will be very few	Is 16.14
of the LORD none escaped or s.;	Lam 2.22
man has built on the foundation s.,	1Co 3.14

SURVIVOR —S

and no s. where he used to live.	Job 18.19
no remnant or s. from the evil	Jer 42.17
and out of Mount Zion a band of s.	Is 37.32
them I will send s. to the nations,	66.19

SWALLOW —ED —ING*

let me alone till I s. my spittle?	Job 7.19
He will s. up death for ever, and	Is 25.08
written: "Death is s. up in victory."	1Co 15.54
is mortal may be s. up by life.	2Co 5.04
straining out a gnat and s. a camel!	Mt 23.24

SWEAR

And Abraham said, "I will s."	Gen 21.24
And you shall not s. by my name	Lev 19.12

shall bow, every tongue shall s."	Is 45.23
Do not s. at all, either by heaven,	Mt 5.34
a curse on himself and to s.,	26.74
had no one greater by whom to s.,	Heb 6.13
do not s., either by heaven or by	Jas 5.12

SWEEP —S

a lamp and s. the house and seek	Lk 15.08
to s. her away with the flood.	Rev 12.15
waters, and the flood s. over me.	Ps 69.02

SWEET

the s. psalmist of Israel:	2Sa 23.01
"Though wickedness is s. in his mouth,	Job 20.12
We used to hold s. converse together;	Ps 55.14
"Stolen water is s., and bread	Pro 9.17
S. is the sleep of a laborer,	Ecc 5.12
How s. is your love, my sister, my	Sol 4.10
bitter for s. and s. for bitter!	Is 5.20

SWIFT —ER

the sun the race is not to the s.,	Ecc 9.11
justice and is s. to do righteousness."	Is 16.05
The s. cannot flee away, nor the	Jer 46.06
Flight shall perish from the s.,	Amo 2.14
"Their feet are s. to shed blood,	Rom 3.15
upon themselves s. destruction.	2Pe 2.01
My days are s. than a weaver's	Job 7.06

SWINE

do not throw your pearls before s.,	Mt 7.06
Now a herd of many s. was feeding	8.30
fed on the pods that the s. ate;	Lk 15.16

SWORD —S

and a flaming s. which turned every	Gen 3.24
us with pestilence or with the s."	Ex 5.03
LORD saves not with s. and spear;	1Sa 17.47
"Shall the s. devour for ever?	2Sa 2.26
And the king said, "Bring me a s."	1Ki 3.24
rash words are like s. thrusts,	Pro 12.18
not lift up s. against nation,	Is 2.04
For my s. has drunk its fill in the	34.05
He made my mouth like a sharp s.,	49.02
And I will send s., famine, and	Jer 24.10
nor by s., nor by war, nor by horses,	Hos 1.07
"Awake, O s., against my shepherd,	Zec 13.07
not come to bring peace, but a s.	Mt 10.34
the s. will perish by the s.	26.52
him who has no s. sell his mantle	Lk 22.36
or nakedness, or peril, or s.?	Rom 8.35
he does not bear the s. in vain;	13.04
and the s. of the Spirit, which is	Eph 6.17
sharper than any two-edged s.,	Heb 4.12
mouth issued a sharp two-edged s.,	Rev 1.16
wounded by the s. and yet lived;	13.14
beat their s. into plowshares, and	Is 2.04
Beat your plowshares into s.,	Joe 3.10
a great crowd with s. and clubs,	Mt 26.47
said, "Look, Lord, here are two s."	Lk 22.38

SYNAGOGUE —S

country he taught them in their s.,	Mt 13.54
and he went to the s., as his custom	Lk 4.16

SYNAGOGUE —S (cont.)
And he argued in the s. every sabbath, Ac 18.04
that in every s. I imprisoned and 22.19
and are not, but are a s. of Satan. Rev 2.09

councils, and flog you in their s., Mt 10.17
and the best seats in the s., 23.06
They will put you out of the s.; Jn 16.02
he is read every sabbath in the s." Ac 15.21

T

TABERNACLE —S
concerning the pattern of the t., Ex 25.09
And they brought the t. to Moses, 39.33
glory of the LORD filled the t. 40.34
as the cloud rested over the t., Num 9.18
of weeks, and the feast of t. 2Ch 8.13

TABLE —S
Thou preparest a t. before me in Ps 23.05
God spread a t. in the wilderness? 78.19
who set a t. for Fortune and fill Is 65.11
he sat at t. with the twelve Mt 26.20
dogs under the t. eat the children's Mk 7.28
was sitting at t. in the Pharisee's Lk 7.37
and sit at t. in the kingdom of God. 13.29
betrays me is with me on the t. 22.21
and drink at my t. in my kingdom, 22.30
When he was at t. with them, he took 24.30
partake of the t. of the Lord and 1Co 10.21
lampstand and the t. and the bread Heb 9.02
I will give you the t. of stone, Ex 24.12
"Cut two t. of stone like the first 34.01
he wrote them upon two t. of stone. Deu 4.13
For all t. are full of vomit, no Is 28.08
overturned the t. of the money-changers Mt 21.12
the word of God to serve t. Ac 6.02

TABLET —S
write them on the t. of your heart. Pro 3.03
engraved on the t. of their heart, Jer 17.01
make it plain upon t., so he may run Hab 2.02

TAIL —S
prophet who teaches lies is the t.; Is 9.15
a torch between each pair of t. Ju 15.04

TALENT —S
But he who had received the one t. Mt 25.18
him who owed him ten thousand t.; 18.24

TALK —ED —ING (v)
And my tongue will t. of thy Ps 71.24
I will no longer t. much with you, Jn 14.30
to see you and t. with you face to 2Jn 12
two men t. with him, Moses and Lk 9.30
us while he t. to us on the road, 24.32
deep sleep as Paul t. still longer; Ac 20.09
because he had been t. with God. Ex 34.29
While they were t. and discussing Lk 24.15

TALK (n)
Job opens his mouth in empty t., Job 35.16
The t. of a fool is a rod for his Pro 14.03
but mere t. tends only to want. 14.23
how to entangle him in his t. Mt 22.15
not consist in t. but in power. 1Co 4.20

Let no evil t. come out of your Eph 4.29
and their t. will eat its way like 2Ti 2.17

TARRY
my deliverer; do not t., O my God! Ps 40.17
Those who t. long over wine, those Pro 23.30
off, and my salvation will not t.; Is 46.13
which t. not for men nor wait for Mic 5.07
one shall come and shall not t.; Heb 10.37

TASK
it seemed to me a wearisome t., Ps 73.16
Whatever your t., work heartily, as Col 3.23
of bishop, he desires a noble t. 1Ti 3.01

TASKMASTERS
whom Pharaoh's t. had set over Ex 5.14
peace and your t. righteousness. Is 60.17

TASTE —D (v)
O t. and see that the LORD is good! Ps 34.08
who will not t. death before they Mt 16.28
my word, he will never t. death.' Jn 8.52
by an oath to t. no food till we Ac 23.14
handle, Do not t., Do not touch" Col 2.21
of God he might t. death for every Heb 2.09
who have t. the heavenly gift, and 6.04
for you have t. the kindness of the 1Pe 2.03

TASTE (n)
Cannot my t. discern calamity? Job 6.30
How sweet are thy words to my t., Ps 119.103
but if salt has lost its t., Mt 5.13

TAUGHT
I have t. you the way of wisdom; Pro 4.11
All your sons shall be t. by the LORD, Is 54.13
though I have t. them persistently Jer 32.33
Yet it was I who t. Ephraim to walk, Hos 11.03
his mouth and t. them, saying: Mt 5.02
for he t. them as one who had 7.29
he entered the synagogue and t. Mk 1.21
to pray, as John t. his disciples." Lk 11.01
'And they shall all be t. by God.' Jn 6.45
but speak thus as the Father t. me. 8.28
doctrine which you have been t.; Rom 16.17
human wisdom but t. by the Spirit, 1Co 2.13
Let him who is t. the word share Gal 6.06
in the faith, just as you were t., Col 2.07

TAUNT (v)
All the day my enemies t. me, Ps 102.08

TAUNT (n)
We have become a t. to our neighbors, Ps 79.04

TAX —ES

Do not even the t. collectors do	Mt 5.46
Matthew sitting at the t. office;	9.09
"Does not your teacher pay the t.?"	17.24
Show me the money for the t."	22.19
and the other a t. collector.	Lk 18.10
he was a chief t. collector,	19.02
Is it lawful to pay t. to Caesar,	Mt 22.17
For the same reason you also pay t.,	Rom 13.06

TEACH —ES —ING

and will t. you what you shall do.	Ex 4.15
and you shall t. them diligently to	Deu 6.07
"T. me, and I will be silent;	Job 6.24
Will any t. God knowledge, seeing	21.22
O Lord; t. me thy paths.	Ps 25.04
T. me thy way, O Lord; and lead me	27.11
therefore t. me wisdom in my secret	5.106
So t. us to number our days that we	90.12
T. me to do thy will, for thou art	143.10
shall each man t. his neighbor and	Jer 31.34
and t. the way of God truthfully,	Mt 22.16
t. us to pray, as John taught his	Lk 11.01
Spirit will t. you in that very	12.12
all that Jesus began to do and t.,	Ac 1.01
charged you not to t. in this name,	5.28
you then who t. others, will you not	Rom 2.21
as I t. them everywhere in every	1Co 4.17
nature itself t. you that for a	11.14
Command and t. these things.	1Ti 4.11
t. what befits sound doctrine.	Tit 2.01
And they shall not t. every one his	Heb 8.11
no need that any one should t. you;	1Jn 2.27
For your iniquity t. your mouth,	Job 15.05
aright; his God t. him.	Is 28.26
he who t., in his teaching;	Rom 12.07
every man and t. every man in all	Col 1.28
families by t. for base gain what	Tit 1.11

TEACHER —S

yet your T. will not hide himself	Is 30.20
"T., I will follow you wherever you	Mt 8.19
"A disciple is not above his t.,	10.24
Why trouble the T. any further?"	Mk 5.35
said to him, "Rabbi (which means T.),	Jn 1.38
that you are a t. come from God;	3.02
"Are you a t. of Israel, and yet you	3.10
You call me T. and Lord; and you are	13.13
dignified, hospitable, an apt t.,	1Ti 3.02
a preacher and apostle and t.,	2Ti 1.11
more understanding than all my t.,	Ps 119.99
third t., then workers of miracles,	1Co 12.28
evangelists, some pastors and t.,	Eph 4.11
Let not many of you become t.,	Jas 3.01
there will be false t. among you,	2Pe 2.01

TEACHING (n)

May my t. drop as the rain, my	Deu 32.02
My son, do not forget my t.,	Pro 3.01
is a lamp and the t. a light,	6.23
Give ear to the t. of our God,	Is 1.10
it, they were astonished at his t.	Mt 22.33
A new t.! With authority	Mk 1.27
Lord's feet and listened to his t.	Lk 10.39

"My t. is not mine, but his who sent	Jn 7.16
to the apostles' t. and fellowship,	Ac 2.42
the standard of t. to which you	Rom 6.17
of scripture, to preaching, to t.	1Ti 4.13
Christ and the t. which accords	6.03
by God and profitable for t.,	2Ti 3.16

TEAR —S (v)

You shall t. down their altars, and	Ex 34.13
he will t. the new, and the piece	Lk 5.36
"Let us not t. it, but cast lots for	Jn 19.24
If he t. down, none can rebuild;	Job 12.14

TEAR —S (n)

wipe away every t. from their eyes	Rev 7.17
every night I flood my bed with t.;	Ps 6.06
My t. have been my food day and	42.03
who sow in t. reap with shouts of	126.05
will wipe away t. from all faces,	Is 25.08
You cover the Lord's altar with t.,	Mal 2.13
began to wet his feet with her t.,	Lk 7.38
day to admonish every one with t.	Ac 20.31
anguish of heart and with many t.,	2Co 2.04
you and now tell you even with t.,	Php 3.18
though he sought it with t.	Heb 12.17

TEETH

their t. are spears and arrows,	Ps 57.04
Like vinegar to the t., and smoke	Pro 10.26
the children's t. are set on edge.'	Jer 31.29
the children's t. are set on edge'?	Eze 18.02
cleanness of t. in all your cities,	Amo 4.06
men will weep and gnash their t."	Mt 8.12

TEMPEST

and the t. carries them off like	Is 40.24
and a great t. is stirring from the	Jer 25.32
with a t. in the day of the whirlwind;	Amo 1.14
and no small t. lay on us, all hope	Ac 27.20
and darkness and gloom, and a t.,	Heb 12.18

TEMPLE

glory of the Lord filled the t.	2Ch 7.01
back to the t. which is in Jerusalem,	Ez 6.05
The Lord is in his holy t., the	Ps 11.04
and his train filled the t.	Is 6.01
one speaking to me out of the t.;	Eze 43.06
The songs of the t. shall become	Amo 8.03
seek will suddenly come to his t.;	Mal 3.01
set him on the pinnacle of the t.,	Mt 4.05
greater than the t. is here.	12.06
entered the t. of God and drove	21.12
out to him the buildings of the t.	24.01
I am able to destroy the t. of God,	26.61
he had seen a vision in the t.;	Lk 1.22
by the Spirit he came into the t.;	2.27
days they found him in the t.,	2.46
"Two men went up into the t. to pray,	18.10
continually in the t. blessing God.	24.53
But he spoke of the t. of his body.	Jn 2.21
whose t. was in front of the city,	Ac 14.13
you are God's t. and that God's	1Co 3.16
knowledge, at table in an idol's t.,	8.10
For we are the t. of the living God;	2Co 6.16

TEMPLE (cont.)

grows into a holy t. in the Lord;	Eph 2.21
Then God's t. in heaven was opened,	Rev 11.19
for its t. is the Lord God the	21.22

TEMPT —ED

'You shall not t. the Lord your God.' "	Mt 4.07
together to t. the Spirit of the	Ac 5.09
lest Satan t. you through lack of	1Co 7.05
to yourself, lest you too be t.	Gal 6.01
himself has suffered and been t.,	Heb 2.18
respect has been t. as we are,	4.15

TEMPTATION —S

And lead us not into t., But deliver	Mt 6.13
to the man by whom the t. comes!	18.07
that you may not enter into t.;	26.41
No t. has overtaken you that is not	1Co 10.13
who desire to be rich fall into t.,	1Ti 6.09
For it is necessary that t. come,	Mt 18.07

TENANTS

he sent his servants to the t.,	Mt 21.34

TEND —ED —S

He said to him, "T. my sheep."	Jn 21.16
T. the flock of God that is your	1Pe 5.02
With upright heart he t. them, and	Ps 78.72
Who t. a flock without getting some	1Co 9.07

TENT —S

drunk, and lay uncovered in his t.	Gen 9.21
So Abram moved his t., and came	13.18
the LORD, and pitched his t. there.	26.25
When they go into the t. of meeting,	Ex 30.20
Let me dwell in thy t. for ever!	Ps 61.04
stretched out the heavens like a t.,	104.02
an immovable t., whose stakes will	Is 33.20
from me like a shepherd's t.;	38.12
Enlarge the place of your t.,	54.02
My t. is destroyed, and all my cords	Jer 10.20
"Our fathers had the t. of witness	Ac 7.44
if the earthly t. we live in is	2Co 5.01
and the true t. which is set up	Heb 8.02
more perfect t. (not made with	9.11
who dwell in t. and have cattle.	Gen 4.20
To your t., O Israel! Look now	1Ki 12.16
not wickedness dwell in your t.	Job 11.14
I will again make you dwell in t.,	Hos 12.09

TERMS

an embassy and asks t. of peace.	Lk 14.32
I am speaking in human t.,	Rom 6.19
in what t. I preached to you the	1Co 15.01
they work on the same t. as we do.	2Co 11.12

TERRIBLE

t. in glorious deeds, doing wonders?	Ex 15.11
and the t. God, who is not partial	Deu 10.17
God is clothed with t. majesty.	Job 37.22
T. is God in his sanctuary, the God	Ps 68.35
Let them praise thy great and t. name!	99.03

TERRIFIED —Y

Therefore I am t. at his presence;	Job 23.15

they were t., saying, "It is a ghost!"	Mt 14.26
the rest were t. and gave glory to	Rev 11.13
do right and let nothing t. you.	1Pe 3.06

TERRITORY

And the t. of the Canaanites extended	Gen 10.19
Or is their t. greater than your t.,	Amo 6.02

TERROR —S

I will send my t. before you, and	Ex 23.27
a time of healing, but behold, t.	Jer 8.15
Be not a t. to me; thou art my	17.17
are not a t. to good conduct, but	Rom 13.03
there will be t. and great signs	Lk 21.11

TEST —ED —S (v)

t. my heart and my mind.	Ps 26.02
Let us t. and examine our ways, and	Lam 3.40
the fire will t. what sort of work	1Co 3.13
But let each one t. his own work,	Gal 6.04
but t. everything; hold fast what	1Th 5.21
but t. the spirits to whether	1Jn 4.01
After these things God t. Abraham,	Gen 22.01
All this I have t. by wisdom;	Ecc 7.23
a t. stone, a precious cornerstone,	Is 28.16
though perishable is t. by fire,	1Pe 1.07
into prison, that you may be t.,	Rev 2.10
The LORD t. the righteous and the	Ps 11.05
to please God who t. our hearts.	1Th 2.04

TEST —ING (n)

put the LORD your God to the t.,	Deu 6.16
now, I will make a t. of pleasure;	Ecc 2.01
malice, said, "Why put me to the t.,	Mt 22.18
We must not put the Lord to the t.,	1Co 10.09
put me to the t. and saw my works	Heb 3.09
know that the t. of your faith	Jas 1.03

TESTIFIED —IES —Y

And he t. with many other words and	Ac 2.40
because we t. of God that he raised	1Co 15.15
the Holy Spirit t. to me in every	Ac 20.23
thee, and our sins t. against us;	Is 59.12
me because I t. of it that its	Jn 7.07
and to t. that he is the one	Ac 10.42
I t. again to every man who receives	Gal 5.03
Now this I affirm and t. in the Lord,	Eph 4.17
have seen and t. that the Father	1Jn 4.14

TESTIFYING

be ashamed then of t. to our Lord,	2Ti 1.08

TESTIMONIES —Y

these are the t., the statutes, and	Deu 4.45
Thy t. are my delight, they are my	Ps 119.24
for thy t. are my meditation.	119.99
that are upon the ark of the t.,	Ex 25.22
the t. of the LORD is sure, making	Ps 19.07
Bind up the t., seal the teaching	Is 8.16
to bear t. before them and the	Mt 10.18
world, as a t. to all nations;	24.14
And this is the t. of John,	Jn 1.19
heard, yet no one receives his t.;	3.32
I know that the t. which he bears	5.32

TESTIMONIES —Y (cont.)
my t. is true, for I know whence I	Jn 8.14
and we know that his t. is true.	21.24
gave their t. to the resurrection	Ac 4.33
to you the t. of God in lofty	1Co 2.01
who in his t. before Pontius	1Ti 6.13
This t. is true. Therefore rebuke	Tit 1.13
for this is the t. of God that he	1Jn 5.09
For the t. of Jesus is the spirit	Rev 19.10

THANK —ED
"I t. thee, Father, Lord of heaven	Mt 11.25
them Paul t. God and took courage.	Ac 28.15

THANKS (n)
O give t. to the LORD, for he is	Ps 106.01
All thy works shall give t. to thee,	145.10
having given t. he broke them and	Mt 15.36
he had given t. he gave it to them,	26.27
and giving t. to God in the presence	Ac 27.35
But t. be to God, that you who were	Rom 6.17
T. be to God through Jesus Christ	7.25
because of that for which I give t.?	1Co 10.30
For you may give t. well enough,	14.17
But t. be to God, who gives us the	15.57
T. be to God for his inexpressible	2Co 9.15
give t. in all circumstances;	1Th 5.18
"We give t. to thee, Lord God	Rev 11.17

THANKSGIVING
Offer to God a sacrifice of t.,	Ps 50.14
Let us come into his presence with t.;	95.02
"Amen" to your t. when he does not	1Co 14.16
through us will produce t. to God;	2Co 9.11

THICK
near to the t. cloud where God was	Ex 20.21
T. clouds enwrap him, so that he	Job 22.14
Clouds and t. darkness are round	Ps 97.02

THIEF —VES
If a t. is found breaking in, and is	Ex 22.02
If you see a t., you are a friend	Ps 50.18
of the night the t. was coming,	Mt 24.43
way, that man is a t. and a robber;	Jn 10.01
Let the t. no longer steal, but	Eph 4.28
will come like a t. in the night.	1Th 5.02
and where t. break in and steal,	Mt 6.19

THIGH
and Jacob's t. was put out of joint	Gen 32.25
robe and on his t. he has a name	Rev 19.16

THING —S
And he said, "You have asked a hard t.;	2Ki 2.10
she has done a beautiful t. to me.	Mt 26.10
and said to him, "You lack one t.;	Mk 10.21
one t. is needful. Mary has chosen	Lk 10.42
and the t. was taken up at once to	Ac 10.16
is a very small t. that I should	1Co 4.03
with God a t. to be grasped,	Php 2.06
but one t. I do, forgetting what	3.13
It is a fearful t. to fall into the	Heb 10.31
and creeping t. and beasts of the	Gen 1.24

t. too wonderful for me, which I did	Job 42.03
Glorious t. are spoken of you, O	Ps 87.03
speak to us smooth t., prophesy illusions,	Is 30.10
"Remember not the former t.,	43.18
but with God all t. are possible."	Mt 19.26
to Caesar the t. that are Caesar's,	22.21
nor t. present, nor t. to come, nor	Rom 8.38
I have become all t. to all men,	1Co 9.22
Love bears all t., believes all t.,	13.07
of praise, think about these t.	Php 4.08
said, "Behold, I make all t. new."	Rev 21.05

THINK
"T. not that I have come to abolish	Mt 5.17
said "Why do you t. evil in your	9.04
saying, "What do you t. of the Christ?	22.42
short time you t. to make me a	Ac 26.28
but to t. with sober judgment, each	Rom 12.03

THINKING (n)
futile in their t. and their	Rom 1.21
do not be children in your t.;	1Co 14.20

THIRST —S (v)
they shall not hunger or t.,	Is 49.10
who hunger and t. for righteousness,	Mt 5.06
I shall give him will never t.;	Jn 4.14
who believes in me shall never t.	6.35
(to fulfil the scripture), "I t."	19.28
To the present hour we hunger and t.,	1Co 4.11
no more, neither t. any more;	Rev 7.16
My soul t. for God, for the living	Ps 42.02
every one who t., come to the	Is 55.01

THIRSTY
Like cold water to a t. soul,	Pro 25.25
For I will pour water on the t. land,	Is 44.03
I was t. and you gave me drink, I	Mt 25.35
if he is t., give him drink;	Rom 12.20

THISTLE —S
Thorn and t. shall grow up on their	Hos 10.08
from thorns, or figs from t.?	Mt 7.16
But if it bears thorns and t.,	Heb 6.08

THONG —S
the t. of whose sandals I am not	Mk 1.07
to undo the t. of the yoke, to let	Is 58.06

THORN —S
a t. was given me in the flesh, a	2Co 12.07
Are grapes gathered from t.,	Mt 7.16
As for what was sown among t.,	13.22
a crown of t. they put it on his	27.29

THOUGHT —S (n)
is no work or t. or knowledge or	Ecc 9.10
perceived the t. of their hearts,	Lk 9.47
but take t. for what is noble in	Rom 12.17
and take every t. captive to obey	2Co 10.05
arm yourselves with the same t.,	1Pe 4.01
O LORD! Thy t. are very deep!	Ps 92.05
knows the t. of man, that they are	94.11
How precious to me are thy t., O God!	139.17

THOUGHT —S (n) (cont.)
For my t. are not your t., neither | Is 55.08
For out of the heart come evil t., | Mt 15.19
comprehends the t. of God except | 1Co 2.11

THREAD
and bound on his hand a scarlet t., | Gen 38.28
the t. of your life is cut. | Jer 51.13

THRESH
the LORD will t. out the grain, | Is 27.12
the thresher t. in hope of a share | 1Co 9.10

THRESHING FLOOR
that the woman came to the t. f." | Ru 3.14
is like a t. f. at the time when it is | Jer 51.33
will clear his t. f. and gather his wheat | Mt 3.12

THREW
the blood and t. it upon the people, | Ex 24.08
into vessels but t. away the bad. | Mt 13.48
and t. it into the great wine press | Rev 14.19

THROAT
their t. is an open sepulchre, they | Ps 5.09
"Their t. is an open grave, they use | Rom 3.13

THRONE —S
Solomon sits upon the royal t. | 1Ki 1.46
temple, the LORD's t. is in heaven; | Ps 11.04
and build your t. for all generations.' " | 89.04
who sits on the t. of judgment | Pro 20.08
I saw the Lord sitting upon a t., | Is 6.01
"Heaven is my t. and the earth is | 66.01
man shall sit on his glorious t., | Mt 19.28
draw near to the t. of grace, | Heb 4.16
at the right hand of the t. of God. | 12.02
Round the t. were twenty-four | Rev 4.04
Therefore as they before the t. of God, | 7.15
from the t. of God and of the Lamb | 22.01
put down the mighty from their t., | Lk 1.52

THRONG
in the mighty t. I will praise thee. | Ps 35.18
As he went ashore he saw a great t.; | Mt 14.14

THUNDER —S (n)
and the LORD sent t. and hail, | Ex 9.23
Boanerges, that is, sons of t.; | Mk 3.17
there were peals of t., loud noises, | Rev 8.05
Mightier than the t. of many waters, | Ps 93.04
called out, the seven t. sounded. | Rev 10.03

TIDINGS
mountain, O Zion, herald of good t.; | Is 40.09
peace, who brings good t. of good, | 52.07
to bring good t. to the afflicted; | 61.01

TILL —ED —S (v)
there was no man to t. the ground; | Gen 2.05
you, and you shall be t. and sown; | Eze 36.09
He who t. his land will have plenty | Pro 12.11

TIME —S
the kingdom for such a t. as this?" | Est 4.14

and a t. for every matter under | Ecc 3.01
has appointed a t. for every | 3.17
For man does not know his t. | 9.12
The Teacher says, My t. is at hand; | Mt 26.18
"The t. is fulfilled, and the kingdom | Mk 1.15
of the world in a moment of t., | Lk 4.05
you at this t. restore the kingdom | Ac 1.06
"In a short t. you think to make me | 26.28
at the right t. Christ died for the | Rom 5.06
how it is full t. now for you to | 13.11
the appointed t. has grown very | 1Co 7.29
behold, now is the acceptable t.; | 2Co 6.02
But when the t. had fully come, God | Gal 4.04
as a plan for the fulness of t., | Eph 1.10
making the most of the t., | 5.16
interpret the signs of the t. | Mt 16.03
for you to know t. or seasons | Ac 1.07
But as to the t. and the seasons, | 1Th 5.01
at the end of the t. for your sake. | 1Pe 1.20

TITHE (v)
"You shall t. all the yield of your | Deu 14.22
for you t. mint and dill and cummin, | Mt 23.23

TITHE —S (n)
gave him a t. of the spoils. | Heb 7.04
Bring the full t. into the storehouse, | Mal 3.10
I give t. of all that I get.' | Lk 18.12

TODAY
which t. is alive and tomorrow is | Mt 6.30
"T. this scripture has been fulfilled | Lk 4.21
"T. salvation has come to this | 19.09
day, as long as it is called "t.," | Heb 3.13
same yesterday and t. and for ever. | 13.08

TOGETHER
were gathered t. he called Seas. | Gen 1.10
"Do you walk t., unless they have | Amo 3.03
What therefore God has joined t., | Mt 19.06
your children t. as a hen gathers | 23.37
shaken t., running over, will be put | Lk 6.38
There will be two women grinding t.; | 17.35
they were all t. in one place. | Ac 2.01
t. with all his household; | 18.08
groaning in travail t. until now; | Rom 8.22
If one member suffers, all suffer t.; | 1Co 12.26
to die t. and to live t. | 2Co 7.03
made us alive t. with Christ (by | Eph 2.05
joined and knit t. by every joint | 4.16
and in him all things hold t. | Col 1.17
feasts, as they boldly carouse t., | Jud 12

TOIL —ED (v)
they grow; they neither t. nor spin; | Mt 6.28
For to this end we t. and strive, | 1Ti 4.10
we t. all night and took nothing! | Lk 5.05

TOIL (n)
in t. you shall eat of it all the | Gen 3.17
their span is but t. and trouble; | Ps 90.10
In all t. there is profit, but mere | Pro 14.23
I hated all my t. in which I had | Ecc 2.18
What gain has the worker from his t.? | 3.09

TOIL (n) (cont.)

All the t. of man is for his mouth,   Ecc 6.07
in t. and hardship, through many a   2Co 11.27

TOMORROW

is alive and t. is thrown into the   Mt 6.30
"Therefore do not be anxious about t.,   6.34
us eat and drink, for t. we die."   1Co 15.32
whereas you do not know about t.   Jas 4.14

TONGUE —S

Keep your t. from evil, and your   Ps 34.13
Let my t. cleave to the roof of my   137.06
A gentle t. is a tree of life, but   Pro 15.04
and the t. of the dumb sing for joy.   Is 35.06
have taught their t. to speak lies;   Jer 9.05
Come, let us smite him with the t.,   18.18
in their mouth a deceitful t.   Zep 3.13
and every t. shall give praise to   Rom 14.11
He who speaks in a t. edifies   1Co 14.04
If any speak in a t., let there be only   14.27
and every t. confess that Jesus   Php 2.11
So the t. is a little member and   Jas 3.05
nation and tribe and t. and people;   Rev 14.06
who whet their t. like swords, who   Ps 64.03
Do all speak with t.? Do all interpret?   1Co 12.30
men gnawed their t. in anguish   Rev 16.10

TOOTH

t. for t., hand for hand, foot for foot,   Ex 21.24
fracture, eye for eye, t. for t.;   Lev 24.20
for an eye and a t. for a t.   Mt 5.38

TORCH —ES

and put a t. between each pair of   Ju 15.04
and her salvation as a burning t.   Is 62.01
with lanterns and t. and weapons.   Jn 18.03

TORRENT —S

the t. would have gone over us;   Ps 124.04
and shall become an overflowing t.;   Jer 47.02
the t. of perdition assailed me;   Ps 18.04

TOUCH —ED

garden, neither shall you t. it,   Gen 3.03
t. no unclean thing; go out from   Is 52.11
"If I only t. his garment, I shall   Mt 9.21
they might only t. the fringe of   14.36
handle, Do not taste, Do not t."   Col 2.21
he t. the hollow of his thigh;   Gen 32.25
for the hand of God has t. me!   Job 19.21
And he t. his ear and healed him.   Lk 22.51
looked upon and t. with our hands,   1Jn 1.01

TOWER —S

and a t. with its top in the   Gen 11.04
against every high t., and against   Is 2.15
of you, desiring to build a t.,   Lk 14.28
walls, and security within your t.!"   Ps 122.07

TOWN

and enter no t. of the Samaritans,   Mt 10.05
and persecute from t. to t.,   23.34

TRADE (v)

'T. with these till I come.'   Lk 19.13
a year there and t. and get gain";   Jas 4.13

TRADE (n)

my Father's house a house of t."   Jn 2.16
for by t. they were tentmakers.   Ac 18.03
and all whose t. is on the sea,   Rev 18.17

TRADITION —S

transgress the t. of the elders?   Mt 15.02
deceit, according to human t.,   Col 2.08
accord with t. that you   2Th 3.06
maintain the t. even as I have   1Co 11.02
was I for the t. of my fathers.   Gal 1.14
and hold to the t. which you were   2Th 2.15

TRAIN* —ED (v)

T. up a child in the way he should   Pro 22.06
T. yourself in godliness;   1Ti 4.07
and so t. the young women to love   Tit 2.04
Ephraim was a t. heifer that loved   Hos 10.11
who has been t. for the kingdom of   Mt 13.52
their faculties t. by practice to   Heb 5.14

TRAMPLE —D —S

they that t. the head of the poor   Amo 2.07
Thou didst t. the sea with thy   Hab 3.15
lest they t. them underfoot and   Mt 7.06
in my anger and t. them in my   Is 63.03
so that he t. kings under foot;   41.02

TRANSGRESS —ED

"Come to Bethel, and t.; to Gilgal,   Amo 4.04
"And why do you t. the commandment   Mt 15.03
that no man t., and wrong his   1Th 4.06
and your mediators t. against me.   Is 43.27
But at Adam they t. the covenant;   Hos 6.07

TRANSGRESSING

t., and denying the LORD, and turning   Is 59.13

TRANSGRESSION —S

Make me know my t. and my sin.   Job 13.23
Blessed is he whose t. is forgiven,   Ps 32.01
Are you not children of t.,   Is 57.04
What is the t. of Jacob? Is it not   Mic 1.05
there is no law there is no t.   Rom 4.15
but was rebuked for his own t.;   2Pe 2.16
For I know my t., and my sin is   Ps 51.03
far does he remove our t. from us.   103.12
But he was wounded for our t.,   Is 53.05
Repent and turn from all your t.,   Eze 18.30
It was added because of t.,   Gal 3.19

TRANSGRESSOR —S

down, then I prove myself a t.   Gal 2.18
But t. shall be altogether destroyed;   Ps 37.38
Then I will teach t. thy ways,   51.13
and was numbered with the t.;   Is 53.12
me, 'And he was reckoned with t.';   Lk 22.37

TRAP

Arrogant men have hidden a t. for me,   Ps 140.05

TRAP (cont.)

They set a t.; they catch men.	Jer 5.26
feast become a snare and a t.,	Rom 11.09

TRAVAIL

I will cry out like a woman in t.,	Is 42.14
fruit of the t. of his soul and be	53.11
When a woman is in t. she has sorrow,	Jn 16.21
groaning in t. together until now;	Rom 8.22
I am again in t. until Christ be	Gal 4.19
upon them as t. comes upon a woman	1Th 5.03

TREACHEROUS

For the t. deal treacherously, the	Is 24.16
Why do all who are t. thrive?	Jer 12.01
Moreover, wine is t.; the arrogant	Hab 2.05
t., reckless, swollen with conceit,	2Ti 3.04

TREAD —ING —S

authority to t. upon serpents and	Lk 10.19
he will t. the wine press of the	Rev 19.15
an ox when it is t. out the grain.	1Co 9.09
no treader t. out wine in the	Is 16.10
like his that t. in the wine press?	63.02

TREASURE —S (n)

For where your t. is, there will	Mt 6.21
heaven is like t. hidden in a	13.44
and you will have t. in heaven;	19.21
But we have this t. in earthen	2Co 4.07
have laid up t. for the last days.	Jas 5.03
are hid all the t. of wisdom and	Col 2.03

TREASURY

not lawful to put them into the t.,	Mt 27.06

TREAT —ED

t. me as one of your hired servants." '	Lk 15.19
Masters, t. your slaves justly and	Col 4.01
t. younger men like brothers,	1Ti 5.01
t. them shamefully, and killed them.	Mt 22.06

TREE —S

but of the t. of the knowledge of	Gen 2.17
"For there is hope for a t.,	Job 14.07
He is like a t. planted by streams	Ps 1.03
She is a t. of life to those who	Pro 3.18
eunuch say, "Behold, I am a dry t."	Is 56.03
who say to a t., 'You are my father,'	Jer 2.27
committing adultery with stone and t.	3.09
a t. in the midst of the earth;	Dan 4.10
every t. therefore that does not	Mt 3.10
Every t. that does not bear good	7.19
for the t. is known by its fruit.	12.33
"How did the fig t. wither at once?"	21.20
"From the fig t. learn its lesson:	24.32
up into a sycamore t. to see him,	Lk 19.04
to you, I saw you under the fig t.,	Jn 1.50
you killed by hanging him on a t.	Ac 5.30
the richness of the olive t.,	Rom 11.17
be every one who hangs on a t."—	Gal 3.13
our sins in his body on the t.,	1Pe 2.24
grant to eat of the t. of life,	Rev 2.07
share in the t. of life and in the	22.19

axe is laid to the root of the t.;	Mt 3.10
but they look like t., walking.	Mk 8.24

TREMBLE

make their loins t. continually.	Ps 69.23
T., O earth, at the presence of the	114.07
Therefore I will make the heavens t.,	Is 13.13
T., you women who are at ease,	32.11
Do you not t. before me? says the LORD;	Jer 5.22

TREMBLING (n)

Serve the LORD with fear, with t.	Ps 2.11
Fear and t. come upon me, and horror	55.05
weakness and in much fear and t.;	1Co 2.03
the fear and t. with which you	2Co 7.15
with fear and t., in singleness of	Eph 6.05
own salvation with fear and t.;	Php 2.12

TRESPASS —ES (n)

But the free gift is not like the t.	Rom 5.15
Law came in, to increase the t.;	5.20
through their t. salvation has	11.11
Brethren, if a man is overtaken in any t.,	Gal 6.01
For if you forgive men their t.,	Mt 6.14
death for our t. and raised for	Rom 4.25
were dead through the t. and sins	Eph 2.01

TRIAL —S

bring you to t. and deliver you up,	Mk 13.11
resurrection of the dead I am on t."	Ac 23.06
I stand here on t. for hope in the	26.06
my condition was a t. to you,	Gal 4.14
Blessed is the man who endures t.,	Jas 1.12
the hour of t. which is coming on	Rev 3.10
have continued with me in my t.;	Lk 22.28
you may have to suffer various t.,	1Pe 1.06

TRIBES

All these are the twelve t. of Israel;	Gen 49.28
to raise up the t. of Jacob and to	Is 49.06
judging the twelve t. of Israel.	Mt 19.28
and all t. of the earth will wail	Rev 1.07
the peoples and t. and tongues and	11.09

TRIBULATION —S*

and when t. or persecution arises	Mt 13.21
For then there will be great t.,	24.21
In the world you have t.; but be of	Jn 16.33
Shall t., or distress, or persecution,	Rom 8.35
be patient in t., be constant in	12.12
in Jesus the t. and the kingdom	Rev 1.09
who have come out of the great t.;	7.14
through many t. we must enter the	Ac 14.22

TRIED —EST —Y

Would that Job were t. to the end,	Job 34.36
I have t. you in the furnace of	Is 48.10
thou who t. the minds and hearts,	Ps 7.09
my heart! T. me and know my thoughts!	139.23
search the mind and t. the heart,	Jer 17.10
incompetent to t. trivial cases?	1Co 6.02

TRIUMPH —ED —ING* —S (v)

of Israel shall t. and glory."	Is 45.25

TRIUMPH —ED —ING* —S (v) (cont.)
the LORD, for he has t. gloriously;	Ex 15.01
example of them, t. over them in him.	Col 2.15
yet mercy t. over judgment.	Jas 2.13

TRIUMPH —S (n)
in Christ always leads us in t.,	2Co 2.14
Great t. he gives to his king, and	Ps 18.50

TROD —DEN
by paths his feet have not t.	Is 41.03
I t. them in my anger and trampled	63.03
thrown out and t. under foot by	Mt 5.13
Jerusalem will be t. down by the	Lk 21.24

TROOPS
I dwelt like a king among his t.,	Job 29.25
Behold your t. are women in your	Nah 3.13
and he sent his t. and destroyed	Mt 22.07

TROUBLE —D (v)
"I will t. the hearts of many peoples,	Eze 32.09
to them, "Why do you t. the woman?	Mt 26.10
Why t. the Teacher any further?"	Mk 5.35
are some who t. you and want to	Gal 1.07
he began to be sorrowful and t.	Mt 26.37
"Now is my soul t. And what shall I	Jn 12.27
"Let not your hearts be t.;	14.01

TROUBLE —S (n)
thou hide thyself in times of t.?	Ps 10.01
In the day of my t. I seek the Lord;	77.02
yet their span is but toil and t.;	90.10
although man's t. lies heavy upon	Ecc 8.06
Israel, its savior in time of t.,	Jer 14.08
the day's own t. be sufficient for	Mt 6.34
Yet it was kind of you to share my t.	Php 4.14
Redeem Israel, O God, out of all his t.	Ps 25.22
the former t. are forgotten and	Is 65.16
who marry will have worldly t.,	1Co 7.28

TRUE
thou art God, and thy words are t.,	2Sa 7.28
"Is your heart t. to my heart as	2Ki 10.15
the promise of the LORD proves t.;	Ps 18.30
for ever, and thy law is t.	119.142
But the LORD is the t. God;	Jer 10.10
that are t. and make for peace,	Zec 8.16
"Teacher, we know that you are t.,	Mt 22.16
The t. light that enlightens every	Jn 1.09
his seal to this, that God is t.	3.33
when the t. worshipers will worship	4.23
"I am the t. vine, and my Father is	15.01
they know thee the only t. God,	17.03
we know that his testimony is t.	21.24
nor is t. circumcision something	Rom 2.28
Let God be t. though every man be	3.04
The signs of a t. apostle were	2Co 12.12
in God in t. righteousness and	Eph 4.24
that is good and right and t.),	5.09
whatever is t., whatever is honorable,	Php 4.08
to serve a living and t. God,	1Th 1.09
a copy of the t. one, but into	Heb 9.24
that this is the t. grace of God;	1Pe 5.12

and is t., and is no lie, just as it	1Jn 2.27
Amen, the faithful and t. witness,	Rev 3.14
upon it is called Faithful and T.,	19.11

TRUMPET —S
not, lift up your voice like a t.;	Is 58.01
sound no t. before you, as the	Mt 6.02
For the t. will sound, and the dead	1Co 15.52
with the sound of the t. of God.	1Th 4.16
With t. and the sound of the horn	Ps 98.06
and seven t. were given to them.	Rev 8.02

TRUST —ED —S (v)
T. in the LORD, and do good;	Ps 37.03
I t. in the steadfast love of God	52.08
in God I t. without a fear.	56.11
I will t., and will not be afraid;	Is 12.02
who t. in chariots because they are	31.01
"Behold, you t. in deceptive words	Jer 7.08
but Jesus did not t. himself to	Jn 2.24
but he t. to him who judges justly.	1Pe 2.23
He t. in God; let God deliver him	Mt 27.43
not work but t. him who justifies	Rom 4.05

TRUST (n)
and put your t. in the LORD.	Ps 4.05
Put not your t. in princes, in a son	146.03

TRUTH
Lead me in thy t., and teach me, for	Ps 25.05
Oh send out thy light and thy t.;	43.03
thou desirest t. in the inward	51.06
T. is lacking, and he who departs	Is 59.15
bless himself by the God of t.,	65.16
among us, full of grace and t.;	Jn 1.14
him must worship in spirit and t."	4.24
and the t. will make you free."	8.32
the way, and the t., and the life;	14.06
even the Spirit of t., whom the world	14.17
Sanctify them in the t.; thy word is t.	17.17
who is of the t. hears my voice."	18.37
Pilate said to him, "What is t.?"	18.38
exchanged the t. about God for a	Rom 1.25
I am speaking the t. in Christ,	9.01
unleavened bread of sincerity and t.	1Co 5.08
statement of the t. we would	2Co 4.02
having girded your loins with t.,	Eph 6.14
guard the t. that has been entrusted	2Ti 1.14
receiving the knowledge of the t.,	Heb 10.26
obedience to the t. for a sincere	1Pe 1.22
established in the t. that you have.	2Pe 1.12
ourselves, and the t. is not in us.	1Jn 1.08
because the Spirit is the t.	5.07

TUMULT —S
He scorns the t. of the city;	Job 39.07
my soul is in t., my heart is wrung	Lam 1.20
lest there be a t. among the	Mt 26.05
And when you hear of wars and t.,	Lk 21.09
t., labors, watching, hunger;	2Co 6.05

TUNIC —S
But the t. was without seam, woven	Jn 19.23
nor two t., nor sandals, nor a staff;	Mt 10.10

TURBAN —S
Bind on your t., and put your shoes   Eze 24.17
garments, the t., and the veils.   Is 3.23

TURN —ED
T. thou to me, and be gracious to me;   Ps 25.16
T. not thy servant away in anger,   27.09
T. again, O God of hosts!   80.14
"T. back, O children of men!"   90.03
O Jordan, that you t. back?   114.05
T. to him from whom you have deeply   Is 31.06
"T. to me and be saved, all the ends   45.22
And he will t. the hearts of   Mal 4.06
unless you t. and become like   Mt 18.03
the field not t. back to take his   24.18
how can you t. back again to the   Gal 4.09
a flaming sword which t. every way,   Gen 3.24

He t. the sea into dry land; men passed   Ps 66.06
t. back, praising God with a loud   Lk 17.15
and how you t. to God from idols, to   1Th 1.09

TWELVE
All these are the t. tribes of   Gen 49.28
The names of the t. apostles are   Mt 10.02
they took up t. baskets full of   14.20
judging the t. tribes of Israel.   19.28
appeared to Cephas, then to the t.   1Co 15.05
of the city had t. foundations,   Rev 21.14

TWICE
I fast t. a week, I give tithes of   Lk 18.12
after admonishing him once or t.,   Tit 3.10
in late autumn, t. dead, uprooted;   Jud 12

U

UNBELIEF
works there, because of their u.   Mt 13.58
"I believe; help my u.!"   Mk 9.24
broken off because of their u.,   Rom 11.20
I had acted ignorantly in u.,   1Ti 1.13
were unable to enter because of u.   Heb 3.19

UNBELIEVER —S
brother has a wife who is an u.,   1Co 7.12
and an u. or outsider enters, he is   14.24
a believer in common with an u.?   2Co 6.15
If one of the u. invites you to   1Co 10.27
Do not be mismated with u. For   2Co 6.14

UNCHASTITY
wife, except on the ground of u.,   Mt 5.32

UNCIRCUMCISED
Any u. male who is not circumcised   Gen 17.14
into you the u. and the unclean.   Is 52.01
the house of Israel is u. in heart."   Jer 9.26
So, if a man who is u. keeps the   Rom 2.26
entrusted with the gospel to the u.,   Gal 2.07
Greek and Jew, circumcised and u.,   Col 3.11

UNCIRCUMCISION
law, your circumcision becomes u.   Rom 2.25
circumcision counts for anything nor u.,   1Co 7.19
nor u., but a new creation.   Gal 6.15

UNCLEAN —NESS
Or if any one touches an u. thing,   Lev 5.02
bring a clean thing out of an u.?   Job 14.04
Thus they became u. by their acts,   Ps 106.39
for I am a man of u. lips, and I dwell   Is 6.05
them authority over u. spirits,   Mt 10.01
not call any man common or u.   Ac 10.28
but it is u. for any one who thinks it u.   Rom 14.14
the Lord, and touch nothing u.;   2Co 6.17
But nothing u. shall enter it, nor   Rev 21.27
of dead men's bones and all u.   Mt 23.27
to practice every kind of u.   Eph 4.19
For God has not called us for u.,   1Th 4.07

UNCOVER —ED —S
then, go and u. his feet and lie   Ru 3.04
will punish, he will u. your sins.   Lam 4.22
Now I will u. her lewdness in the   Hos 2.10
Your nakedness shall be u.,   Is 47.03
to pray to God with her head u.?   1Co 11.13
He u. the deeps out of darkness, and   Job 12.22

UNDERSTAND —S
thunder of his power who can u.?"   Job 26.14
Can any one u. the spreading of the   36.29
I have uttered what I did not u.,   42.03
Make me u. the way of thy precepts,   Ps 119.27
not know, my people does not u."   Is 1.03
the latter days you will u. this.   Jer 30.24
I heard, but I did not u.   Dan 12.08
You shall indeed hear but never u.,   Mt 13.14
their minds to u. the scriptures,   Lk 24.45
Why do you not u. what I say?   Jn 8.43
I do not u. my own actions.   Rom 7.15
I want you to u. this mystery,   11.25
and u. all mysteries and all   1Co 13.02
By faith we u. that the world was   Heb 11.03
are some things in them hard to u.,   2Pe 3.16
are taken away, while no one u.   Is 57.01
that he u. and knows me, that I am   Jer 9.24
no one u., no one seeks for God.   Rom 3.11

UNDERSTANDING (n)
The shepherds also have no u.;   Is 56.11
"Are you also still without u.?   Mt 15.16
the wise and u. and revealed them   Lk 10.21
they are darkened in their u.,   Eph 4.18
peace of God, which passes all u.,   Php 4.07
of assured u. and the knowledge of   Col 2.02
God has come and has given us u.,   1Jn 5.20

UNDERSTOOD
Have you not u. from the foundations   Is 40.21
None of the rulers of this age u. this;   1Co 2.08
even as I have been fully u.   13.12
as you have u. in part, that you can   2Co 1.14
you heard and u. the grace of God   Col 1.06

UNFAITHFUL
him, and put him with the u. — Lk 12.46
What if some were u.? — Rom 3.03

UNFRUITFUL
choke the word, and it proves u. — Mt 13.22
my spirit prays but my mind is u. — 1Co 14.14

UNGODLINESS
against all u. and wickedness of — Rom 1.18
lead people into more and more u., — 2Ti 2.16

UNGODLY
God gives me up to the u., — Job 16.11
will scatter the bones of the u.; — Ps 53.05
"Both prophet and priest are u.; — Jer 23.11
right time Christ died for the u. — Rom 5.06
for the u. and sinners, for the — 1Ti 1.09
u. persons who pervert the grace of — Jud 4

UNHOLY
for the u. and profane, for murderers — 1Ti 1.09
to their parents, ungrateful, u., — 2Ti 3.02

UNITE —D
to u. all things in him, things in — Eph 1.10
For if we have been u. with him in — Rom 6.05
but that you be u. in the same — 1Co 1.10
But he who is u. to the Lord — 6.17

UNITY
attain to the u. of the faith and — Eph 4.13

UNKNOWN*
plenty will be u. in the land by — Gen 41.31
this inscription, 'To an u. god.' — Ac 17.23
what therefore you worship as u., — 17.23
as u., and yet well known; — 2Co 6.09

UNLEAVENED
Seven days you shall eat u. bread; — Ex 12.15
You shall keep the feast of u. bread; — 23.15
first day of U. Bread the disciples — Mt 26.17
but with the u. bread of sincerity — 1Co 5.08

UNPUNISHED
assured, an evil man will not go u., — Pro 11.21
You shall not go u., but you must — Jer 49.12

UNRIGHTEOUS —NESS
and the u. man his thoughts; — Is 55.07

know that the u. will not inherit — 1Co 6.09
for all, the righteous for the u., — 1Pe 3.18
sins and cleanse us from all u. — 1Jn 1.09

UNSEARCHABLE
praised, and his greatness is u. — Ps 145.03
weary, his understanding is u. — Is 40.28
How u. are his judgments and how — Rom 11.33
Gentiles the u. riches of Christ, — Eph 3.08

UNTIMELY
as to one u. born, he appeared also — 1Co 15.08

UNWITTINGLY
If any one sins u. in any of the — Lev 4.02

UPHOLD —ING* —S
and u. me with a willing spirit. — Ps 51.12
appalled, but there was no one to u.; — Is 63.05
On the contrary, we u. the law. — Rom 3.31
u. the universe by his word of power. — Heb 1.03
but the Lord u. the righteous. — Ps 37.17

UPPER
you a large u. room furnished and — Mk 14.15
they went up to the u. room, — Ac 1.13

UPRIGHT
lo, my sheaf arose and stood u.; — Gen 37.07
God, who saves the u. in heart. — Ps 7.10
Good and u. is the Lord; therefore — 25.08
For the word of the Lord is u.; — 33.04
I found, that God made man u., — Ecc 7.29
an u. and God-fearing man, who is — Ac 10.22
u., and godly lives in this world, — Tit 2.12

UPWARD
The wise man's path leads u. to life, — Pro 15.24
of man goes u. and the spirit of — Ecc 3.21
root downward, and bear fruit u.; — Is 37.31
my eyes are weary with looking u. — 38.14
prize of the u. call of God in — Php 3.14

UTTERANCE
tongues, as the Spirit gave them u. — Ac 2.04
that u. may be given me in opening — Eph 6.19
by prophetic u. when the elders — 1Ti 4.14

UTTERMOST
dwell in the u. parts of the sea, — Ps 139.09
salvation to the u. parts of the — Ac 13.47

V

VAIN
name of the Lord your God in v.; — Ex 20.07
consternation, "Men are all a v. hope." — Ps 116.11
In my v. life I have seen everything; — Ecc 7.15
But I said, "I have labored in v., — Is 49.04
They shall not labor in v., or bear — 65.23
In v. you beautify yourself. — Jer 4.30
to you, filling you with v. hopes; — 23.16
You have said, 'It is v. to serve God. — Mal 3.14

in v. do they worship me, teaching — Mt 15.09
and the peoples imagine v. things? — Ac 4.25
his grace toward me was not in v. — 1Co 15.10
the Lord your labor is not in v. — 15.58
should be running or had run in v. — Gal 2.02
did not run in v. or labor in v. — Php 2.16

VALLEY
through the v. of the shadow of — Ps 23.04

VALLEY (cont.)

oracle concerning the v. of vision.	Is 22.01
Every v. shall be lifted up, and	40.04
the v. shall perish, and the plain	Jer 48.08
set me down in the midst of the v.;	Eze 37.01
multitudes, in the v. of decision!	Joe 3.14
Every v. shall be filled, and every	Lk 3.05

VALUE

Are you not of more v. than they?	Mt 6.26
Of how much more v. is a man than a	12.12
who, on finding one pearl of great v.,	13.46
Or what is the v. of circumcision?	Rom 3.01
godliness is of v. in every way,	1Ti 4.08

VANISH —ED —ES

made their days v. like a breath,	Ps 78.33
for the heavens will v. like smoke,	Is 51.06
growing old is ready to v. away.	Heb 8.13
the sky v. like a scroll that is	Rev 6.14
for a little time and then v.	Jas 4.14

VANITIES —Y

Turn my eyes from looking at v.;	Ps 119.37
the Preacher, v. of v.! All is v.	Ecc 1.02
V. of v., says the Preacher;	12.08
he was determined to go after v.	Hos 5.11

VARIOUS

to another v. kinds of tongues, to	1Co 12.10
sins and swayed by v. impulses,	2Ti 3.06
In many and v. ways God spoke of	Heb 1.01
you may have to suffer v. trials,	1Pe 1.06

VEIL (n)

put off your v., strip off your	Is 47.02
ought to have a v. on her head,	1Co 11.10
Moses is read a v. lies over their	2Co 3.15

VENGEANCE

God of v., thou God of v., shine forth!	Ps 94.01
For the LORD has a day of v.,	Is 34.08
For this is the v. of the LORD:	Jer 50.15
I will execute v. upon the nations	Mic 5.15
"V. is mine, I will repay, says the	Rom 12.19
inflicting v. upon those who do not	2Th 1.08

VENTURE —S* (v)

For I will not v. to speak of	Rom 15.18
Not that we v. to class or compare	2Co 10.12
"If one v. a word with you, will you	Job 4.02

VESSEL —S

them in pieces like a potter's v.	Ps 2.09
and he reworked it into another v.,	Jer 18.04
city, as one breaks a potter's v.,	19.11
same lump one v. for beauty and	Rom 9.21
then he will be a v. for noble use,	2Ti 2.21
the good into v. but threw away	Mt 13.48
have this treasure in earthen v.,	2Co 4.07

VEXATION

"O that my v. were weighed, and all	Job 6.02
Remove v. from your mind, and put	Ecc 11.10

VICTORIES —Y

with mighty v. by his right hand.	Ps 20.06
the LORD gave v. to David wherever	2Sa 8.06
Give v. to the king, O LORD;	Ps 20.09
The war horse is a vain hope for v.,	33.17
earth have seen the v. of our God.	98.03
so my own arm brought me v.,	Is 63.05
wick, till he brings justice to v.;	Mt 12.20
"Death is swallowed up in v."	1Co 15.54
gives us the v. through our Lord	15.57
and this the v. that overcomes	1Jn 5.04

VIEW (n)

no one from a human point of v.,	2Co 5.16
will take no other v. than mine;	Gal 5.10

VILLAGE —S

And whatever town or v. you enter,	Mt 10.11
And as he entered a v., he was met	Lk 17.12
Bethlehem, the v. where David was?"	Jn 7.42
up against the land of unwalled v.;	Eze 38.11
be inhabited as v. without walls,	Zec 2.04
went about all the cities and v.,	Mt 9.35
gospel to many v. of the Samaritans.	Ac 8.25

VINDICATE —D —S*

For the LORD will v. his people,	Ps 135.14
And will not God v. his elect,	Lk 18.07
v. in the Spirit, seen by angels,	1Ti 3.16
he who v. me is near. Who will contend	Is 50.08

VINDICATION

From thee let my v. come! Let thy eyes	Ps 17.02
The LORD works v. and justice for	103.06
The nations shall see your v.,	Is 62.02
The LORD has brought forth our v.;	Jer 51.10

VINE

my dream there was a v. before me,	Gen 40.09
And the trees said to the v.,	Ju 9.12
Thou didst bring a v. out of Egypt;	Ps 80.08
fall, as leaves fall from the v.,	Is 34.04
one of you will eat of his own v.,	36.16
thoroughly as a v. the remnant of	Jer 6.09
bear fruit, and become a noble v.	Eze 17.08
man under his v. and under his fig	Mic 4.04
fruit of the v. until that day	Mt 26.29
"I am the true v., and my Father is	Jn 15.01

VINEDRESSER —S

true vine, and my Father is the v.	Jn 15.01
foreigners shall be your plowmen and v.;	Is 61.05

VINEGAR

my thirst they gave me v. to drink.	Ps 69.21
Like v. to the teeth, and smoke to	Pro 10.26
took a sponge, filled it with v.,	Mt 27.48

VINEYARD —S

of the soil. He planted a v.;	Gen 9.20
possession of the v. of Naboth the	1Ki 21.15
but, my own v. I have not kept!	Sol 1.06
For the v. of the LORD of hosts is	Is 5.07
Many shepherds have destroyed my v.,	Jer 12.10

VINEYARD —S (cont.)

a vine in a v. transplanted by the	Eze 19.10
to hire laborers for his v.	Mt 20.01
was a householder who planted a v.,	21.33
Who plants a v. without eating any	1Co 9.07
houses and planted v. for myself;	Ecc 2.04
let us go out early to the v.,	Sol 7.12
Again you shall plant v. upon the	Jer 31.05
you have planted pleasant v.,	Amo 5.11
though they plant v., they shall not	Zep 1.13

VINTAGE

for the v. will fail, the fruit	Is 32.10
and gathered the v. of the earth,	Rev 14.19

VIOLATED

for having v. their first pledge.	1Ti 5.12
A man who has v. the law of Moses	Heb 10.28

VIOLENCE

and the earth was filled with v.	Gen 6.11
From oppression and v. he redeems	Ps 72.14
v. covers them as a garment.	73.06
the ways of all who get gain by v.;	Pro 1.19
wickedness and drink the wine of v.	4.17
V. shall no more be heard in your	Is 60.18
and v. is in the land, and ruler is	Jer 51.46
V. has grown up into a rod of	Eze 7.11
Put away v. and oppression, and	45.09
kingdom of heaven has suffered v.,	Mt 11.12
great city be thrown down with v.,	Rev 18.21

VIOLENT —LY

not v. but gentle, not quarrelsome,	1Ti 3.03
preached, and every one enters it v.	Lk 16.16
church of God v. and tried to	Gal 1.13

VIPER —S

which is crushed a v. is hatched.	Is 59.05
when a v. came out because of the	Ac 28.03
he said to them, "You brood of v.!	Mt 3.07

VIRGIN —S

O v. daughter of Babylon; sit on the	Is 47.01
The v. Israel has done a very	Jer 18.13
'Fallen, no more to rise, is the v. Israel;	Amo 5.02
"Behold, a v. shall conceive and	Mt 1.23
to a v. betrothed to a man whose	Lk 1.27
beautiful young v. be sought out	Est 2.02

VISION —S

of the LORD came to Abram in a v.,	Gen 15.01
in those days; there was no frequent v.	1Sa 3.01
speak in a v. to thy faithful one;	Ps 89.19
oracle concerning the valley of v.	Is 22.01
prophets obtain no v. from the LORD.	Lam 2.09
me in the v. by the Spirit of God	Eze 11.24
to Daniel in a v. of the night.	Dan 2.19
For the v. is for days yet to come."	10.14
commanded them, "Tell no one the v.,	Mt 17.09
he had seen a v. in the temple;	Lk 1.22
And while Peter was pondering the v.,	Ac 10.19
And a v. appeared to Paul in the	16.09

disobedient to the heavenly v.,	26.19
and your young men shall see v.,	2.17
I will go on to v. and revelations	2Co 12.01
of angels, taking his stand on v.,	Col 2.18

VISIT —ED —EST —ING (v)

"God will v. you, and you shall	Gen 50.25
dost v. him every morning, and test	Job 7.18
thee sick or in prison and v. thee?'	Mt 25.39
I will v. you after passing through	1Co 16.05
went up to Jerusalem to v. Cephas,	Gal 1.18
to v. orphans and widows in their	Jas 1.27
The LORD v. Sarah as he had said,	Gen 21.01
the LORD had v. the people of	Ex 4.31
how God first v. the Gentiles,	Ac 15.14
and Paul v. him and prayed, and	28.08
Thou v. the earth and waterest it,	Ps 65.09
v. the iniquity of the fathers upon	Ex 20.05

VISIT (n)

not to make you another painful v.	2Co 2.01
that our v. to you was not in vain;	1Th 2.01

VOICE

"The v. is Jacob's v., but the	Gen 27.22
saw no form; there was only a v.	Deu 4.12
after the fire a still small v.	1Ki 19.12
"Can you lift up your v. to the clouds,	Job 38.34
the morning thou dost hear my v.;	Ps 5.03
yet their v. goes out through all	19.04
has heard the v. of my supplications.	28.06
he utters his v., the earth melts.	46.06
and the v. of the turtledove is	Sol 2.12
And I heard the v. of the Lord	Is 6.08
A v. cries: "In the wilderness	40.03
lift up your v. with strength, O	40.09
from the city! A v. from the temple!	66.06
A v. on the bare heights is heard,	Jer 3.21
When he utters his v. there is a	10.13
and I heard the v. of one speaking.	Eze 1.28
like the v. of God Almighty when he	10.05
"A v. was heard in Ramah, wailing	Mt 2.18
"The v. of one crying in the	3.03
and lo, a v. from heaven, saying,	3.17
and a v. from the cloud said, "This	17.05
hour Jesus cried with a loud v.,	27.46
will hear the v. of the Son of God,	Jn 5.25
His v. you have never heard, his	5.37
the sheep hear his v.,	10.03
who is of the truth hears my v."	18.37
"The v. of a god, and not of man!"	Ac 12.22
may with one v. glorify the God	Rom 15.06
His v. then shook the earth;	Heb 12.26
one hears my v. and opens the door,	Rev 3.20

VOID

The earth was without form and v.,	Gen 1.02
you have made v. the word of God.	Mt 15.06
is null and the promise is v.	Rom 4.14
God, so as to make the promise v.	Gal 3.17

VOMIT (n)

The dog turns back to his own v.,	2Pe 2.22

VOTE* (n)
to death I cast my v. against them.   Ac 26.10

VOW —S (n)
a pillar and made a v. to me.   Gen 31.13

for the Nazirite who takes a v.   Num 6.21
he cut his hair, for he had a v.   Ac 18.18
have four men who are under a v.;   21.23
Make your v. to the LORD your God,   Ps 76.11
confirm your v. and perform your v.!   Jer 44.25

W

WAG —GING
mouths at me, they w. their heads;   Ps 22.07
they hiss and w. their heads at the   Lam 2.15
passed by derided him, w. their heads   Mt 27.39

WAGE (v)
by them you may w. the good   1Ti 1.18
the flesh that w. war against your   1Pe 2.11

WAGES (n)
The w. of a hired servant shall not   Lev 19.13
A wicked man earns deceptive w.,   Pro 11.18
the laborers and pay them their w.,   Mt 20.08
and be content with your w."   Lk 3.14
for the laborer deserves his w.;   10.07
his w. are not reckoned as a gift   Rom 4.04
For the w. of sin is death, but the   6.23
receive his w. according to his   1Co 3.08

WAIL —ED —ING
W., for the day of the LORD is near;   Is 13.06
"Son of man, w. over the multitude   Eze 32.18
the earth will w. on account of   Rev 1.07
we w., and you did not mourn.'   Mt 11.17
and people weeping and w. loudly.   Mk 5.38

WAIT —ED —ING —S
I w. for thy salvation, O LORD.   Gen 49.18
for thee I w. all the day long.   Ps 25.05
all you who w. for the LORD!   31.24
I w. for the LORD, my soul waits, and   130.05
I will w. for the LORD, who is   Is 8.17
we w. for thee. Be our arm   33.02
and w. continually for your God."   Hos 12.06
I will w. for the God of my salvation;   Mic 7.07
If it seem slow, w. for it;   Hab 2.03
but to w. for the promise of the   Ac 1.04
And now why do you w.? Rise and be   22.16
we w. for it with patience.   Rom 8.25
we w. for the hope of righteousness.   Gal 5.05
and to w. for his Son from heaven,   1Th 1.10
his promise we w. for new heavens   2Pe 3.13
w. for the mercy of our Lord Jesus   Jud 21
and when I w. for light, darkness   Job 30.26
I w. patiently for the LORD;   Ps 40.01
God's patience w. in the days of   1Pe 3.20
w. for the promise from you."   Ac 23.21
w. for and hastening the coming of   2Pe 3.12
For God alone my soul w. in silence,   Ps 62.05
my soul w., and in his word I hope;   130.05
Therefore the LORD w. to be gracious   Is 30.18
For the creation w. with eager   Rom 8.19
the farmer w. for the precious   Jas 5.07

WAKE —ENS
I w. again, for the LORD sustains me.   Ps 3.05

time now for you to w. from sleep.   Rom 13.11
that whether we w. or sleep we   1Th 5.10
he w. my ear to hear as those who   Is 50.04

WALK —ED —ING —S
w. before me, and be blameless.   Gen 17.01
You shall w. in all the way which   Deu 5.33
Even though I w. through the valley   Ps 23.04
W. about Zion, go round about her,   48.12
O LORD, that I may w. in thy truth;   86.11
feet, but do not w.; and they do not   115.07
and w. in the way of insight."   Pro 9.06
let us w. in the light of the LORD.   Is 2.05
but the redeemed shall w. there.   35.09
W. by the light of your fire, and by   50.11
who w. in a way that is not good,   65.02
Yet it was I who taught Ephraim to w.,   Hos 11.03
and to w. humbly with your God?   Mic 6.08
forgiven,' or to say, 'Rise and w.'?   Mt 9.05
their sight and the lame w.,   11.05
follows me will not w. in darkness,   Jn 8.12
W. while you have the light, lest   12.35
of Jesus Christ of Nazareth, w."   Ac 3.06
we too might w. in newness of life.   Rom 6.04
for we w. by faith, not by sight.   2Co 5.07
let us also w. by the Spirit.   Gal 5.25
And w. in love, as Christ loved us   Eph 5.02
but if we w. in the light, as he is   1Jn 1.07
By its light shall the nations w.;   Rev 21.24
Enoch w. with God; and he was not   Gen 5.24
God's house we w. in fellowship.   Ps 55.14
The people who w. in darkness have   Is 9.02
but w. in their own counsels and   Jer 7.24
of the boat and w. on the water   Mt 14.29
in which you once w.,   Eph 2.02
of the LORD God w. in the garden   Gen 3.08
w. in the midst of the fire, and   Dan 3.25
but they look like trees, w."   Mk 8.24
eat, you are no longer w. in love.   Rom 14.15
LORD your God w. in the midst of   Deu 23.14
Blessed is the man who w. not in   Ps 1.01
He who in integrity w. securely,   Pro 10.09

WALL —S
waters being a w. to them on their   Ex 14.22
and the w. fell down flat, so that   Jos 6.20
thought, "I will pin David to the w."   1Sa 18.11
and by my God I can leap over a w.   2Sa 22.30
LORD and the w. around Jerusalem.   1Ki 3.01
let us build the w. of Jerusalem.   Neh 2.17
So we built the w.; and all the w. was   4.06
him, all of you, like a leaning w.,   Ps 62.03
and all your w. of precious stones.   Is 54.12
We grope for the w. like the blind,   59.10
break down the w. that you have   Eze 13.14

WALL —S (cont.)

beside a w. built with a plumb	Amo 7.07
night and let him down over the w.,	Ac 9.25
strike you, you whitewashed w.!	23.03
basket through a window in the w.,	2Co 11.33
down the dividing w. of hostility,	Eph 2.14
high w., with twelve gates, and at	Rev 21.12
Peace be within your w., and security	Ps 122.07
up salvation as w. and bulwarks.	Is 26.01
Foreigners shall build up your w.,	60.10
you shall call your w. Salvation,	60.18
Oh, the w. of my heart! My heart is	Jer 4.19
By faith the w. of Jericho fell	Heb 11.30

WANDER —ED —ING

they w. about each in his own	Is 47.15
Therefore the people w. like sheep;	Zec 10.02
to the truth and w. into myths.	2Ti 4.04
from these have w. away into vain	1Ti 1.06
up to Assyria, a wild ass w. alone;	Hos 8.09
w. over deserts and mountains, and	Heb 11.38

WANT —ING*

is my shepherd, I shall not w.;	Ps 23.01
For I do not do what I w.,	Rom 7.15
in the balances and found w.;	Dan 5.27

WANT —S (n)

go into exile for w. of knowledge;	Is 5.13
are afflicted for w. of a shepherd.	Zec 10.02
when I was with you and was in w.,	2Co 11.09
Not that I complain of w.;	Php 4.11
supplies the w. of the saints but	9.12

WANTON —LY

broken their w. heart which has	Eze 6.09
Her prophets are w., faithless men;	Zep 3.04
when they grow w. against Christ	1Ti 5.11
fornication and were w. with her,	Rev 18.09
glancing w. with their eyes, mincing	Is 3.16

WAR (v)

those who w. against you shall be	Is 41.12
to you soon and w. against them	Rev 2.16

WAR —S (n)

The LORD is a man of w.;	Ex 15.03
a man of w., prudent in speech, and	1Sa 16.18
The w. horse is a vain hope for	Ps 33.17
yet w. was in his heart; his words were	55.21
a time for w., and a time for peace.	Ecc 3.08
there is no discharge from w.,	8.08
Wisdom is better than weapons of w.,	9.18
have his life as a prize of w.	Jer 21.09
this horn made w. with the saints,	Dan 7.21
nor by w., nor by horses, nor by	Hos 1.07
shall they learn w. any more;	Mic 4.03
another law at w. with the law of	Rom 7.23
are not carrying on a worldly w.,	2Co 10.03
that are at w. in your members?	Jas 4.01
Now w. arose in heaven, Michael and	Rev 12.07
they will make w. on the Lamb, and	17.14
He makes w. cease to the end of the	Ps 46.09

will hear of w. and rumors of w.;	Mt 24.06
What causes w., and what causes	Jas 4.01

WARM (adj)

Again, if two lie together, they are w.;	Ecc 4.11
my compassion grows w. and tender,	Hos 11.08

WARN —ED —ING

"Go down and w. the people, lest	Ex 19.21
W. the nations that he is coming;	Jer 4.16
But I will w. you whom to fear: fear	Lk 2.05
brothers, so that he may w. them,	16.28
and I w. them now while absent, as I	2Co 13.02
as an enemy, but w. him as a brother.	2Th 3.15
Moreover by them is thy servant w.;	Ps 19.11
For I solemnly w. your fathers when	Jer 11.07
And being w. in a dream not to	Mt 2.12
Who w. you to flee from the wrath	3.07
refused him who w. them on earth,	Heb 12.25
w. every man and teaching every man	Col 1.28

WARNING —S (n)

a w. and a horror, to the nations	Eze 5.15
things happened to them as a w.,	1Co 10.11
Now these things are w. for us,	10.06

WARRIOR —S

the Gileadite was a mighty w.,	Ju 11.01
chariot and horse, army and w.;	Is 43.17
But the LORD is with me as a dread w.;	Jer 20.11
A sword upon her w., that they may be	50.36
and in the multitude of your w.,	Hos 10.13

WASH —ED

They shall w. their hands and their	Ex 30.21
I w. my hands in innocence, and go	Ps 26.06
W. me thoroughly from my iniquity,	51.02
Though you w. yourself with lye and	Jer 2.22
O Jerusalem, w. your heart from	4.14
anoint your head and w. your face,	Mt 6.17
For they do not w. their hands when	15.02
and began to w. the disciples' feet,	Jn 13.05
who has bathed does not need to w.,	13.10
and w. away your sins, calling on	Ac 22.16
Blessed are those who w. their robes,	Rev 22.14
when my steps were w. with milk,	Job 29.06
Lord shall have w. away the filth	Is 4.04
took water and w. his hands before	Mt 27.24
But you were w., you were sanctified,	1Co 6.11
w. the feet of the saints, relieved	1Ti 5.10

WASHING (n)

the w. of cups and pots and vessels	Mk 7.04
her by the w. of water with the	Eph 5.26
by the w. of regeneration and	Tit 3.05

WASTE

LORD will lay w. the earth and	Is 24.01
divided against itself is laid w.,	Mt 12.25
But Saul laid w. the church, and	Ac 8.03

WASTED —S —ING

"Why was the ointment thus w.?	Mk 14.04
Man w. away like a rotten thing,	Job 13.08
Though our outer nature is w. away,	2Co 4.16

WATCH —ES —ING (v)

"The LORD w. between you and me,	Gen 31.49
W. therefore, for you do not know on	Mt 24.42
remain here, and w. with me."	26.38
W. and pray that you may not enter	26.41
Unless the LORD w. over the city,	Ps 127.01
for I am w. over my word to perform	Jer 1.12
to the Pharisees, they were w. him.	Lk 14.01

WATCH —ING (n)

whose eyes keep w. on the nations—	Ps 66.07
he who keeps w. over your soul	Pro 24.12
keeping w. over Jesus, saw the	Mt 27.54
keeping w. over their flock by	Lk 2.08
are keeping w. over your souls, as	Heb 13.17
tumults, labors, w., hunger;	2Co 6.05

WATCHMAN —MEN

the w. stays awake in vain.	Ps 127.01
"W., what of the night? W., what of	Is 21.11
I have made a w. for the house of	Eze 33.07
The prophet is the w. of Ephraim,	Hos 9.08
His w. are blind, they are all	Is 56.10
walls, O Jerusalem, I have set w.;	62.06

WATER —ED

out of Eden to w. the garden,	Gen 2.10
like showers that w. the earth!	Ps 72.06
and you shall be like a w. garden,	Is 58.11
Apollos w., but God gave the growth.	1Co 3.06

WATER —S (n)

and all the w. that was in the Nile	Ex 7.20
But the people thirsted there for w.,	17.03
and w. shall come out of it, that	17.06
sprinkle the w. of expiation upon	Num 8.07
how he made the w. of the Red Sea	Deu 11.04
He asked w. and she gave him milk,	Ju 5.25
You have given no w. to the weary	Job 22.07
a tree planted by streams of w.,	Ps 1.03
the river of God is full of w.;	65.09
went through fire and through w.;	66.12
the rock, and w. gushed forth;	105.41
He turns a desert into pools of w.,	107.35
Drink w. from your own cistern,	Pro 5.15
"Stolen w. is sweet, and bread eaten	9.17
Like cold w. to a thirsty soul, so	25.25
fountain, a well of living w.,	Sol 4.15
dross, your wine mixed with w.	Is 1.22
you will draw w. from the wells of	12.03
To the thirsty bring w.,	21.14
for I give w. in the wilderness,	43.20
their fish stink for lack of w.,	50.02
and the fire causes w. to boil—	64.02
cisterns, that can hold no w.	Jer 2.13
LORD, the fountain of living w.	17.13
And there was no w. in the cistern,	38.06
and all knees will be weak as w.	Eze 21.07
I will sprinkle clean w. upon you,	36.25
baptize you with w. for repentance,	Mt 3.11
a cup of cold w. because he is a	10.42
walked on the w. and came to Jesus;	14.29
he took w. and washed his hands	27.24
pierced his side, and out came w.	* 27.49

carrying a jar of w. will meet you;	Mk 14.13
that he commands even wind and w.,	Lk 8.25
tasted the w. now become wine, and	Jn 2.09
one is born of w. and the Spirit,	3.05
where do you get that living w.?	4.11
the washing of w. with the word,	Eph 5.26
No longer drink only w.,	1Ti 5.23
same opening fresh w. and brackish?	Jas 3.11
the Spirit, the w., and the blood;	1Jn 5.08
guide them to springs of living w.;	Rev 7.17
the fountain of the w. of life.	21.06
was moving over the face of the w.	Gen 1.02
bring a flood of w. upon the earth,	6.17
ark floated on the face of the w.	7.18
the w. being a wall to them on	Ex 14.22
He binds up the w. in his thick	Job 26.08
He leads me beside still w.;	Ps 23.02
I have come into deep w.,	69.02
He turned their w. into blood,	105.29
spread out the earth upon the w.,	136.06
By the w. of Babylon, there we sat	137.01
Cast your bread upon the w.,	Ecc 11.01
Many w. cannot quench love, neither	Sol 8.07
the LORD as the w. cover the sea.	Is 11.09
Happy are you who sow beside all w.,	32.20
measured the w. in the hollow of	40.12
one who thirsts, come to the w.;	55.01
me, the fountain of living w.,	Jer 2.13
trouble the w. with your feet, and	Eze 32.02
like a chip on the face of the w.	Hos 10.07
But let justice roll down like w.,	Amo 5.24
On that day living w. shall flow	Zec 14.08
harlot who is seated upon many w.,	Rev 17.01

WAVES (n)

and trampled the w. of the sea;	Job 9.08
righteousness like the w. of the sea;	Is 48.18
boat was being swamped by the w.;	Mt 8.24
wild w. of the sea, casting up the	Jud 13

WAY —S

to guard the w. to the tree of life.	Gen 3.24
of cloud to lead them along the w.,	Ex 13.21
This God—his w. is perfect;	2Sa 22.31
given to a man whose w. is hid,	Job 3.23
Who has prescribed for him his w.,	36.23
Teach me thy w., O LORD; and lead me	Ps 27.11
Commit your w. to the LORD;	37.05
Thy w., O God, is holy.	77.13
and lead me in the w. everlasting!	139.24
There is a w. which seems right to	Pro 14.12
A man's mind plans his w.,	16.09
Train up a child in the w. he should go,	22.06
For every matter has its time and w.,	Ecc 8.06
"This is the w., walk in it," when	Is 30.21
"My w. is hid from the LORD, and my	40.27
And I will make all my mountains a w.,	49.11
let the wicked forsake his w.,	55.07
paths, where the good w. is;	Jer 6.16
"Learn not the w. of the nations,	10.02
give them one heart and one w.,	32.39
to prepare the w. before me,	Mal 3.01
to their own country by another w.	Mt 2.12
Prepare the w. of the LORD, make his	3.03

WAY —S (cont.)

gate is wide and the w. is easy,	Mt 7.13
"What were you discussing on the w.?"	Mk 9.33
men, but truly teach the w. of God.	12.14
"I am the w., and the truth, and the	Jn 14.06
he found any belonging to the W.,	Ac 9.02
evil of the W. before the congregation,	19.09
no little stir concerning the W.	19.23
accurate knowledge of the W.,	24.22
show you a still more excellent w.	1Co 12.31
walking in his w. and by fearing	Deu 8.06
the integrity of your w. your hope?	Job 4.06
Make me to know thy w., O LORD;	Ps 25.04
Then I will teach transgressors thy w.,	51.13
He made known his w. to Moses,	103.07
I will make straight all his w.;	Is 45.13
These have chosen their own w.,	66.03
Amend your w. and your doings, and I	Jer 7.03
Let us test and examine our w.,	Lam 3.40
Is it not your w. that are not just?	Eze 18.25
and the rough w. shall be made	Lk 3.05
and how inscrutable his w.!	Rom 11.33
to remind you of my w. in Christ,	1Co 4.17
disgraceful, underhanded w.;	2Co 4.02
and various w. God spoke of old to	Heb 1.01

WEAK —NESS

Give justice to the w. and the	Ps 82.03
Strengthen the w. hands, and make	Is 35.03
and I will strengthen the w.,	Eze 34.16
is willing, but the flesh is w."	Mt 26.41
by so toiling one must help the w.,	Ac 20.35
As for the man who is w. in faith,	Rom 14.01
bear with the failings of the w.,	15.01
chose what is w. in the world to	1Co 1.27
We are w., but you are strong.	4.10
encouraged, if his conscience is w.,	8.10
the w. I became w., that I might win the w.	9.22
That is why many of you are w. and ill,	11.30
Who is w., and I am not w.?	2Co 11.29
for when I am w., then I am strong.	12.10
help the w., be patient with them	1Th 5.14
Likewise the Spirit helps us in our w.;	Rom 8.26
and the w. of God is stronger than	1Co 1.25
It is sown in w., it is raised in	15.43
For he was crucified in w.,	2Co 13.04
since he himself is beset with w.	Heb 5.02

WEALTH

W. hastily gotten will dwindle, but	Pro 13.11
W. brings many new friends, but a	19.04
Do not toil to acquire w.;	23.04
the w. of the nations shall come to	Is 60.05
"Your w. and your treasures I will	Jer 15.13
will put an end to the w. of Egypt,	Eze 30.10
Christ greater w. than the treasures	Heb 11.26
power and w. and wisdom and might	Rev 5.12

WEANED

Those who are w. from the milk,	Is 28.09
When she had w. Not pitied, she	Hos 1.08

WEAPON —S

"You are my hammer and w. of war:	Jer 51.20

Wisdom is better than w. of war,	Ecc 9.18
with the w. of righteousness for	2Co 6.07
for the w. of our warfare are not	10.04

WEAR —ING —S

they will all w. out like a garment.	Ps 102.26
drink?' or 'What shall we w.?'	Mt 6.31
but to w. sandals and not put on	Mk 6.09
shorn or shaven, let her w. a veil.	1Co 11.06
w. the crown of thorns and the	Jn 19.05
I am suffering and w. fetters,	2Ti 2.09
to the one who w. the fine clothing	Jas 2.03

WEARIED —IES

you have w. me with your iniquities.	Is 43.24
The toil of a fool w. him,	Ecc 10.15

WEARY (adj)

as in a dry and w. land where no	Ps 63.01
shade of a great rock in a w. land.	Is 32.02
My eyes are w. with looking upward.	38.14
He does not faint or grow w.,	40.28
they shall run and not be w.,	40.31
sustain with a word him that is w.	50.04
iniquity and are too w. to repent.	Jer 9.05
and I am w. with holding it in, and	20.09
And let us not grow w. in well-doing,	Gal 6.09

WEDDING

"Can the w. guests mourn as long as	Mt 9.15
'The w. is ready, but those invited	22.08

WEEDS

came and sowed w. among the wheat,	Mt 13.25
grain, then the w. appeared also.	13.26

WEEK —S

dawn of the first day of the w.,	Mt 28.01
I fast twice a w., I give tithes of	Lk 18.12
On the first day of the w.,	Ac 20.07
On the first day of every w.,	1Co 16.02
And you shall observe the feast of w.,	Ex 34.22
and for three w. he argued with	Ac 17.02

WEEP

you shall w. no more. He will surely	Is 30.19
that I might w. day and night for	Jer 9.01
Awake, all you drunkards, and w.;	Joe 1.05
Tell it not in Gath, w. not at all;	Mic 1.10
there men will w. and gnash their	Mt 8.12
"Blessed are you that w. now,	Lk 6.21
we wailed, and you did not w.'	7.32
do not w. for me, but w. for yourselves	23.28
you will w. and lament, but the	Jn 16.20
rejoice, w. with those who w.	Rom 12.15
of the earth w. and mourn for her,	Rev 18.11

WEEPING (n)

W. may tarry for the night, but joy	Ps 30.05
My eyes are spent with w.; my soul is	Lam 2.11

WEIGH —ED —S

and let the others w. what is said.	1Co 14.29
a measure and w. the mountains in	Is 40.12
eyes, but the LORD w. the spirit.	Pro 16.02

WEIGHT

A full and just w. you shall have,	Deu 25.15
When he gave to the wind its w.,	Job 28.25
LORD, but a just w. is his delight.	Pro 11.01
worth their w. in fine gold, how	Lam 4.02
us an eternal w. of glory beyond	2Co 4.17
let us also lay aside every w.,	Heb 12.01

WELCOME —D (v)

we see thee a stranger and w. thee,	Mt 25.38
w. him, but not for disputes over	Rom 14.01
W. one another, therefore, as Christ	15.07
they were w. by the church and the	Ac 15.04
him who eats; for God has w. him.	Rom 14.03

WELFARE

for in its w. you will find your w.	Jer 29.07
be genuinely anxious for your w.	Php 2.20

WELL —S (n)

sang this song: "Spring up, O w.!	Num 21.17
flowing water from your own w.	Pro 5.15
an adventuress is a narrow w.	23.27
a w. of living water, and flowing	Sol 4.15
As a w. keeps its water fresh, so	Jer 6.07
or an ox that has fallen into a w.,	Lk 14.05
Jacob's w. was there, and so Jesus,	Jn 4.06
water from the w. of salvation.	Is 12.03

WEPT

Babylon, there we sat down and w.,	Ps 137.01
And he went out and w. bitterly.	Mt 26.75
and saw the city he w. over it,	Lk 19.41
Jesus w.	Jn 11.35

WHEAT

They have sown w. and have reaped	Jer 12.13
and sell the refuse of the w.?"	Amo 8.06
and gather his w. into the granary,	Mt 3.12
weeds among the w., and went away.	13.25
a grain of w. falls into the earth	Jn 12.24

WHEEL —S

or the w. broken at the cistern,	Ecc 12.06
and there he was working at his w.	Jer 18.03
as it were a w. within a w.	Eze 1.16
clogging their chariot w. so that	Ex 14.25
had four bronze w. and axles of	1Ki 7.30
and their w. like the whirlwind.	Is 5.28
and the w. were full of eyes round	Eze 10.12

WHIRLING

the wind and w. dust before the	Is 17.13
Wrath has gone forth, a w. tempest;	Jer 23.19
"Go in among the w. wheels	Eze 10.02

WHIRLWIND

Elijah went up by a w. into heaven.	2Ki 2.11
LORD answered Job out of the w.:	Job 38.01
wind, and they shall reap the w.	Hos 8.07

WHITE —ER

they shall be as w. as snow;	Is 1.18
his raiment was w. as snow,	Dan 7.09

cannot make one hair w. or black.	Mt 5.36
his garments became w. as light.	17.02
lightning, and his raiment w. as snow.	28.03
fields are already w. for harvest.	Jn 4.35
and his hair were w. as w. wool, w. as	Rev 1.14
a w. horse, and its rider had a bow;	6.02
Then I saw a great w. throne and	20.11
me, and I shall be w. than snow.	Ps 51.07

WHITHER

W. shall I go from thy Spirit?	Ps 139.07
know whence it comes or w. it goes;	Jn 3.08

WHOLE

may his glory fill the w. earth!	Ps 72.19
With my w. heart I seek thee;	119.10
for this is the w. duty of man.	Ecc 12.13
the w. earth is full of his glory."	Is 6.03
return to me with their w. heart.	Jer 24.07
than that your w. body be thrown	Mt 5.29
it was restored, w. like the other.	12.13
if he gains the w. world and	16.26
preached throughout the w. world,	24.14
We know that the w. creation has	Rom 8.22
Put on the w. armor of God, that you	Eph 6.11
For in him the w. fulness of deity	Col 2.09
also for the sins of the w. world,	1Jn 2.02
and the w. earth followed the beast	Rev 13.03

WICKED

for I will not acquit the w.	Ex 23.07
If I am w., woe to me! If I am	Job 10.15
The w. man writhes in pain all his	15.20
Why do the w. live, reach old age,	21.07
The w. are not so, but are like	Ps 1.04
The w. shall depart to Sheol, all	9.17
and I will not sit with the w.	26.05
Many are the pangs of the w.;	32.10
Fret not yourself because of the w.,	37.01
But to the w. God says: "What right	50.16
earth, and let the w. be no more!	104.35
Salvation is far from the w.,	119.155
he has cut the cords of the w.	129.04
The way of the w. is like deep	Pro 4.19
a heart that devises w. plans,	6.18
The LORD is far from the w.,	15.29
The w. is a ransom for the righteous,	21.18
The w. flee when no one pursues, but	28.01
Be not w. overmuch, neither be a	Ecc 7.17
Woe to the w.! It shall be	Is 3.11
grave with the w. and with a rich	53.09
let the w. forsake his way, and the	55.07
But the w. are like the tossing sea	57.20
Why does the way of the w. prosper?	Jer 12.01
But if you warn the w., and he does	Eze 3.19
and said to him, 'You w. servant!	Mt 18.32
'You w. and slothful servant!	25.26
Drive out the w. person from among	1Co 5.13
the licentiousness of the w.	2Pe 2.07

WICKEDNESS

saw that the w. of man was great	Gen 6.05
"Though w. is sweet in his mouth,	Job 20.12
so w. is broken like a tree.'	24.20

WICKEDNESS (cont.)

art not a God who delights in w.;	Ps 5.04
you love righteousness and hate w.	45.07
God than dwell in the tents of w.	84.10
the bread of w. and drink the wine	Pro 4.17
A man is not established by w.,	12.03
I choose: to loose the bonds of w.,	Is 58.06
We acknowledge our w., O LORD,	Jer 14.20
And because w. is multiplied, most	Mt 24.12
coveting, w., deceit, licentiousness,	Mk 7.22
Repent therefore of this w. of yours,	Ac 8.22
who by their w. suppress the truth.	Rom 1.18
to sin as instruments of w.,	6.13
hosts of w. in the heavenly places.	Eph 6.12
rank growth of w. and receive with	Jas 1.21

WIDE

for the gate is w. and the way is	Mt 7.13
for a w. door for effective work	1Co 16.09
Corinthians; our heart is w.	2Co 6.11

WIDOW —S

A w., or one divorced, or a woman	Lev 21.14
he upholds the w. and the fatherless;	Ps 146.09
his brother must marry the w.,	Mt 22.24
And a poor w. came, and put in two	Mk 12.42
She who is a real w., and is left	1Ti 5.05
I am no w., mourning I shall never	Rev 18.07
I have made their w. more in number	Jer 15.08
because their w. were neglected in	Ac 6.01

WIFE —VES

his mother and cleaves to his w.,	Gen 2.24
Now Adam knew Eve his w., and she	4.01
And Abram took Sarai his w.,	12.05
I am repulsive to my w., loathsome	Job 19.17
A good w. is the crown of her	Pro 12.04
A good w. who can find?	31.10
Enjoy life with the w. whom you love,	Ecc 9.09
Surely, as a faithless w. leaves her	Jer 3.20
morning, and at evening my w. died.	Eze 24.18
to yourself a w. of harlotry and	Hos 1.02
do not fear to take Mary your w.,	Mt 1.20
said, 'Whoever divorces his w.,	5.31
which of the seven will she be w.?	22.28
Remember Lot's w.	Lk 17.32
with his w. Sapphira sold a piece	Ac 5.01
have his own w. and each woman her	1Co 7.02
brother has a w. who is an unbeliever,	7.12
A w. is bound to her husband as	7.39
the head of the w. as Christ is	Eph 5.23
and mother and be joined to his w.,	5.31
you the Bride, the w. of the Lamb."	Rev 21.09
allowed you to divorce your w.,	Mt 19.08
W., be subject to your husbands, as	Eph 5.22

WILD

than any other w. creature that	Gen 3.01
grapes, but it yielded w. grapes.	Is 5.02
But w. beasts will lie down there,	13.21
Be like a w. ass in the desert!	Jer 48.06
a w. ass wandering alone; Ephraim has	Hos 8.09
Even the w. beasts cry to thee	Joe 1.20
his food was locusts and w. honey.	Mt 3.04

a w. olive shoot, were grafted in	Rom 11.17
them in the same w. profligacy,	1Pe 4.04

WILDERNESS

that they may serve me in the w.;	Ex 7.16
the way of the w. toward the Red	13.18
on from the w. of Sin by stages,	17.01
I wrought in Egypt and in the w.,	Num 14.22
you these forty years in the w.,	Deu 8.02
thou didst march through the w.,	Ps 68.07
"Can God spread a table in the w.?	78.19
who led his people through the w.,	136.16
Then justice will dwell in the w.,	Is 32.16
"In the w. prepare the way of the	40.03
and will make her w. like Eden,	51.03
the sword found grace in the w.;	Jer 31.02
Now it is transplanted in the w.,	Eze 19.13
And I will cast you forth into the w.,	29.05
Like grapes in the w., I found	Hos 9.10
It was I who knew you in the w.,	13.05
and led you forty years in the w.,	Amo 2.10
preaching in the w. of Judea,	Mt 3.01
you go out into the w. to behold?	11.07
And he was in the w. forty days,	Mk 1.13
But he withdrew to the w. and prayed.	Lk 5.16
leave the ninety-nine in the w.,	15.04
Our fathers ate the manna in the w.;	Jn 6.31
for they were overthrown in the w.	1Co 10.05
on the day of testing in the w.,	Heb 3.08

WILL (n)

I delight to do thy w., O my God;	Ps 40.08
Teach me to do thy w., for thou art	143.10
Thy w. be done, On earth as it is in	Mt 6.10
he who does the w. of my Father	7.21
So it is not the w. of my Father	18.14
unless I drink it, thy w. be done."	26.42
of the flesh nor of the w. of man,	Jn 1.13
and your w. is to do your father's	8.44
"The w. of the Lord be done."	Ac 21.14
by God's w. I may now at last	Rom 1.10
so that by God's w. I may come to	15.32
of Christ Jesus by the w. of God,	2Co 1.01
according to the w. of our God and	Gal 1.04
and insight the mystery of his w.,	Eph 1.09
understand what the w. of the Lord is.	5.17
rivalry, but others from good w.	Php 1.15
For this is the w. of God, your	1Th 4.03
And by that w. we have been sanctified	Heb 10.10
Of his own w. he brought us forth	Jas 1.18
passions but by the w. of God.	1Pe 4.02
he who does the w. of God abides	1Jn 2.17

WILLING —LY

and uphold me with a w. spirit.	Ps 51.12
the spirit indeed is w., but the flesh	Mt 26.41
as an exaction but as a w. gift.	2Co 9.05
charge, not by constraint but w.,	1Pe 5.02

WIN —S*

through me to w. obedience from	Rom 15.18
to all, that I might w. the more.	1Co 9.19
for, but may w. a full reward.	2Jn 8
Good sense w. favor, but the way of	Pro 13.15

WIND —S

And God made a w. blow over the	Gen 8.01
speech of a despairing man is w.?	Job 6.26
That they are like straw before the w.,	21.18
By his w. the heavens were made	26.13
chaff which the w. drives away.	Ps 1.04
who ridest on the wings of the w.,	104.03
is vanity and a striving after w.	Ecc 1.14
He who observes the w. will not sow;	11.04
The prophets will become w.;	Jer 5.13
The w. shall shepherd all your	22.22
For they sow the w., and they shall	Hos 8.07
A reed shaken by the w.?	Mt 11.07
got into the boat, the w. ceased.	14.32
The w. blows where it wills, and you	Jn 3.08
like the rush of a mighty w.,	Ac 2.02
about with every w. of doctrine,	Eph 4.14
is driven and tossed by the w.	Jas 1.06
that no w. might blow on earth or	Rev 7.01
Lord GOD: Come from the four w.,	Eze 37.09
and the w. blew and beat upon that	Mt 7.25
that even w. and sea obey him?"	8.27
gather his elect from the four w.,	Mk 13.27

WINDOW —S

Noah opened the w. of the ark	Gen 8.06
bound the scarlet cord in the w.	Jos 2.21
"Out of the w. she peered, the	Ju 5.28
Eutychus was sitting in the w.	Ac 20.09
a basket through a w. in the wall,	2Co 11.33
and the w. of the heavens were	Gen 7.11
look through the w. are dimmed,	Ecc 12.03
cloud, and like doves to their w.?	Is 60.08

WINE

"Drink no w. nor strong drink, you	Lev 10.09
I leave my w. which cheers gods	Ju 9.13
heart is like w. that has no vent;	Job 32.19
and w. to gladden the heart of man,	Ps 104.15
W. is a mocker, strong drink a	Pro 20.01
Those who tarry long over w.,	23.30
and drink your w. with a merry	Ecc 9.07
For your love is better than w.,	Sol 1.02
who are heroes at drinking w.,	Is 5.22
Be drunk, but not with w.;	29.09
Come, buy w. and milk without money	55.01
"let us get w., let us fill ourselves	56.12
"I have trodden the w. press alone,	63.03
fill cups of mixed w. for Destiny;	65.11
hand this cup of the w. of wrath,	Jer 25.15
to drink no w. all our days, ourselves,	35.08
the nations drank of her w.,	51.07
No priest shall drink w.,	Eze 44.21
the mountains shall drip sweet w.,	Joe 3.18
"But you made the Nazirites drink w.,	Amo 2.12
Moreover, w. is treacherous;	Hab 2.05
shall drink their blood like w.,	Zec 9.15
Neither is new w. put into old	Mt 9.17
they offered him w. to drink,	27.34
eating no bread and drinking no w.;	Lk 7.33
his wounds, pouring on oil and w.;	10.34
tasted the water now become w.,	Jn 2.09
said, "They are filled with new w."	Ac 2.13
meat or drink w. or do anything	Rom 14.21

And do not get drunk with w.,	Eph 5.18
use a little w. for the sake of	1Ti 5.23
shall drink the w. of God's wrath,	Rev 14.10

WINESKIN* —S

have become like a w. in the smoke,	Ps 119.83
like new w., it is ready to burst.	Job 32.19
Neither is new wine put into old w.;	Mt 9.17

WINGS

hide me in the shadow of thy w.,	Ps 17.08
I say, "O that I had w. like a dove!	55.06
If I take the w. of the morning and	139.09
each had six w.: with two he covered	Is 6.02
sound of the w. of the cherubim	Eze 10.05
hen gathers her brood under her w.,	Mt 23.37
noise of their w. was like the	Rev 9.09

WINNOW —ED —ING —S

and gathering where you did not w.;	Mt 25.24
I have w. them with a w. fork	Jer 15.07
His w. fork is in his hand, and he	Mt 3.12
A wise king w. the wicked, and	Pro 20.26

WINTER (n)

may not be in w. or on a sabbath.	Mt 24.20
stay with you or even spend the w.,	1Co 16.06

WIPE —D —S

Lord GOD will w. away tears from	Is 25.08
we w. off against you; nevertheless	Lk 10.11
and to w. them with the towel with	Jn 13.05
he will w. away every tear from	Rev 21.04
and w. them with the hair of her	Lk 7.38
w. Jerusalem as one w. a dish,	2Ki 21.13

WISDOM

gave Solomon w. and understanding	1Ki 4.29
"With God are w. and might; he has	Job 12.13
"But where shall w. be found? And where	28.12
Beware lest you say, 'We have found w.;	32.13
teach me w. in my secret heart.	Ps 51.06
of the LORD is the beginning of w.;	111.10
W. cries aloud in the street;	Pro 1.20
The LORD by w. founded the earth;	3.19
The beginning of w. is this:	4.07
W. abides in the mind of a man of	14.33
you may gain w. for the future.	19.20
For in much w. is much vexation, and	Ecc 1.18
When I applied my mind to know w..	8.16
the spirit of w. and understanding,	Is 11.02
of salvation, w., and knowledge;	33.06
established the world by his w.,	Jer 10.12
he gives w. to the wise and knowledge	Dan 2.21
Yet w. is justified by her deeds."	Mt 11.19
man get this w. and these mighty	13.54
and became strong, filled with w.;	Lk 2.40
increased in w. and in stature,	2.52
Therefore also the W. of God said,	11.49
the riches and w. and knowledge of	Rom 11.33
"I will destroy the w. of the wise,	1Co 1.19
Christ Jesus, whom God made our w.,	1.30
of God in lofty words or w.	2.01
the Spirit the utterance of w.,	12.08

WISDOM (cont.)

you a spirit of w. and of revelation	Eph 1.17
his works in the meekness of w.	Jas 3.13
But the w. from above is first pure,	3.17

WISE

"Should a w. man answer with windy	Job 15.02
LORD is sure, making w. the simple;	Ps 19.07
Whoever is w., let him give heed to	107.43
Be not w. in your own eyes;	Pro 3.07
A w. son makes a glad father, but a	10.01
who keeps silent is considered w.;	17.28
How the w. man dies just like the	Ecc 2.16
to the strong, nor bread to the w.,	9.11
Where then are your w. men? Let them	Is 19.12
who turns w. men back, and makes	44.25
Who is the man so w. that he can	Jer 9.12
w. men from the East came to	Mt 2.01
will be like a w. man who built	7.24
so be w. as serpents and innocent	10.16
things from the w. and understanding	11.25
were foolish, and five were w.	25.02
Claiming to be w., they became	Rom 1.22
Lest you be w. in your own conceits,	11.25
to the only w. God be glory for	16.27
Where is the w. man? Where is the	1Co 1.20
the thoughts of the w. are futile."	3.20
sake, but you are w. in Christ.	4.10
walk, not as unwise men but as w.,	Eph 5.15
Who is w. and understanding among	Jas 3.13

WISH (v)

So whatever you w. that men would	Mt 7.12
to him, "Sir, we w. to see Jesus."	Jn 12.21
I w. that all were as I myself am.	1Co 7.07
I w. those who unsettle you would	Gal 5.12

WITHER —ED —S

O Jerusalem, let my right hand w.!	Ps 137.05
and they w., and the tempest carries	Is 40.24
"How did the fig tree w. at once?"	Mt 21.20
there was a man with a w. hand.	12.10
they had no root they w. away.	13.06
The grass w., the flower fades, when	Is 40.07
is cast forth as a branch and w.;	Jn 15.06
The grass w., and the flower falls,	1Pe 1.24

WITHSTAND

who was I that I could w. God?"	Ac 11.17
may be able to w. in the evil day,	Eph 6.13

WITNESS —ED* —ES (v)

Thus you w. against yourselves, that	Mt 23.31
shall be signed and sealed and w.,	Jer 32.44
For it is w. of him, "Thou art a	Heb 7.17
Their partiality w. against them;	Is 3.09

WITNESS —ES (n)

God is w. between you and me."	Gen 31.50
you bear false w. against your	Deu 5.20
my w. is in heaven, and he that	Job 16.19
Be not a w. against your neighbor	Pro 24.28
I made him a w. to the peoples, a	Is 55.04

fornication, theft, false w., slander.	Mt 15.19
to bear w. to the light, that all	Jn 1.07
needed no one to bear w. of man;	2.25
I bear w. to myself, and the Father	8.18
the world, to bear w. to the truth.	18.37
who is bearing w. to these things,	21.24
with us a w. to his resurrection."	Ac 1.22
had the tent of w. in the wilderness,	7.44
did not leave himself without w.,	14.17
blood of Stephen thy w. was shed,	22.20
so you must bear w. also at Rome."	23.11
For God is my w., whom I serve with	Rom 1.09
himself bearing w. with our spirit	8.16
while God also bore w. by signs and	Heb 2.04
Holy Spirit also bears w. to us;	10.15
And the Spirit is the w.,	1Jn 5.07
and from Jesus Christ the faithful w.,	Rev 1.05
of the tent of the w. in heaven was	15.05
evidence of two w. or of three	Deu 17.06
"You are my w.," says the LORD, "and	Is 43.10
their w. neither see nor know, that	44.09
by the evidence of two or three w.	Mt 18.16
though many false w. came forward.	26.60
You are w. of these things.	Lk 24.48
and you also are w., because you	Jn 15.27
you shall be my w. in Jerusalem	Ac 1.08
from the dead. To this we are w.	3.15
and the w. laid down their garments	7.58
to us who were chosen by God as w.,	10.41
by the evidence of two or three w.	2Co 13.01
You are w., and God also, how holy	1Th 2.10
confession in the presence of many w.	1Ti 6.12
surrounded by so great a cloud of w.,	Heb 12.01
There are three w., the Spirit,	1Jn 5.08

WOE

"W. to you, Chorazin! W. to you,	Mt 11.21
but w. to the man by whom the	18.07
"But w. to you, scribes and Pharisees,	23.13
but w. to that man by whom the Son	26.24
"W., w., w. to those who dwell on	Rev 8.13
the third w. is soon to come.	11.14

WOLF —VES

The w. shall dwell with the lamb,	Is 11.06
sees the w. coming and leaves the	Jn 10.12
but inwardly are ravenous w.	Mt 7.15
out as sheep in the midst of w.;	10.16
departure fierce w. will come in	Ac 20.29

WOMAN —EN

she shall be called W., because she	Gen 2.23
"Is there not a w. among the	Ju 14.03
know that you are a w. of worth.	Ru 3.11
is born of a w. is of few days,	Job 14.01
A gracious w. gets honor, and	Pro 11.16
house shared with a contentious w.	21.09
but a w. who fears the LORD is to	31.30
but a w. among all these I have not	Ecc 7.28
a young w. shall conceive and bear	Is 7.14
will cry out like a w. in travail,	42.14
"Can a w. forget her sucking child,	49.15
on the earth: a w. protects a man."	Jer 31.22

WOMAN —EN (cont.)

who looks at a w. lustfully has	Mt 5.28
leaven which a w. took and hid in	13.33
"O w., great is your faith!	15.28
what sort of w. this is who is	Lk 7.39
And a w. who had had a flow of	8.43
a w. in the crowd raised her voice	11.27
There came a w. of Samaria to draw	Jn 4.07
w. who had been caught in adultery,	* 8.03
When a w. is in travail she has	16.21
mother, "W., behold your son!"	19.26
Thus a married w. is bound by law	Rom 7.02
well for a man not to touch a w.	1Co 7.01
the head of a w. is her husband, and	11.03
but w. is the glory of man.	11.07
born of w., born under the law,	Gal 4.04
Let a w. learn in silence with all	1Ti 2.11
honor on the w. as the weaker sex,	1Pe 3.07
a w. clothed with the sun, with the	Rev 12.01
and I saw a w. sitting on a scarlet	17.03
Hebrew w. are not like the Egyptian w.;	Ex 1.19
there were no w. so fair as Job's	Job 42.15
Give not your strength to w.,	Pro 31.03
do not know, O fairest among w.,	Sol 1.08
day the Egyptians will be like w.,	Is 19.16
Tremble, you w. who are at ease,	32. 11
Behold your troops are w. in your	Nah 3.13
Old men and old w. shall again sit	Zec 8.04
those born of w. there has risen	Mt 11.11
men, besides w. and children.	14.21
Two w. will be grinding at the mill;	24.41
But the angel said to the w.,	28.05
loud cry, "Blessed are you among w.,	Lk 1.42
Moreover, some w. of our company	24.22
with the w. and Mary the mother of	Ac 1.14
were baptized, both men and w.	8.12
and not a few of the leading w.	17.04
these w. are two covenants. One is from	Gal 4.24
help these w., for they have labored	Php 4.03
as befits w. who profess religion.	2.10
households and capture weak w.,	2Ti 3.06
W. received their dead by resurrection	Heb 11.35
So once the holy w. who hoped in	1Pe 3.05
not defiled themselves with w.,	Rev 14.04

WOMB

to her, "Two nations are in your w.,	Gen 25.23
"Naked I came from my mother's w.,	Job 1.21
From the w. of the morning like dew	Ps 110.03
knit me together in my mother's w.	139.13
Redeemer, who formed you from the w.:	Is 44.24
The LORD called me from the w.,	49.01
cause to bring forth, shut the w.?	66.09
"Before I formed you in the w. I knew	Jer 1.05
Spirit, even from his mother's w.	Lk 1.15
blessed is the fruit of your w.!	1.42
that opens the w. shall be called	2.23
"Blessed is the w. that bore you,	11.27
into his mother's w. and be born?"	Jn 3.04

WON

which his right hand had w.	Ps 78.54
w. strength out of weakness, became	Heb 11.34
may be w. without a word by the	1Pe 3.01

WONDER —ED (v)

why do you w. at this, or why do you	Ac 3.12
and w. that there was no one to	Is 59.16
uneducated, common men, they w.;	Ac 4.13
When Moses saw it he w. at the sight;	7.31

WONDERFUL

Thy testimonies are w.; therefore	Ps 119.129
Such knowledge is too w. for me;	139.06
Three things are too w. for me;	Pro 30.18
name will be called "W. Counselor,	Is 9.06
for thou hast done w. things,	25.01
scribes saw the w. things that he	Mt 21.15
w. stones and what w. buildings!"	Mk 13.01
may declare the w. deeds of him	1Pe 2.09
"Great and w. are thy deeds, O Lord	Rev 15.03

WONDERS (n)

with all the w. which I will do in	Ex 3.20
Thou art the God who workest w.,	Ps 77.14
land of Egypt with signs and w.,	Jer 32.21
arise and show great signs and w.,	Mt 24.24
see signs and w. you will not	Jn 4.48
works and w. and signs which God	Ac 2.22
what signs and w. God had done	15.12
by the power of signs and w.,	Rom 15.19
and with pretended signs and w.,	2Th 2.09

WONDROUS

and consider the w. works of God.	Job 37.14
I may behold w. things out of thy	Ps 119.18
and on thy w. works, I will meditate.	145.05

WOOD —EN

Make yourself an ark of gopher w.;	Gen 6.14
will serve gods of w. and stone,	Deu 4.28
hewers of w. and drawers of water	Jos 9.21
For lack of w. the fire goes out;	Pro 26.20
work of men's hands, w. and stone;	Is 37.19
for an offering w. that will not	40.20
I fall down before a block of w.?"	44.19
instead of w., bronze, instead of	60.17
The children gather w., the fathers	Jer 7.18
and boys stagger under loads of w.	Lam 5.13
countries, and worship w. and stone.'	Eze 20.32
My people inquire of a thing of w.,	Hos 4.12
they do this when the w. is green,	Lk 23.31
silver, precious stones, w., hay,	1Co 3.12
who carry about their w. idols,	Is 45.20
the LORD: You have broken w. bars,	Jer 28.13
him who says to a w. thing, Awake;	Hab 2.19

WOOL

He gives snow like w.; he scatters	Ps 147.16
crimson, they shall become like w.	Is 1.18
shall have nothing of w. on them,	Eze 44.17
the hair of his head like pure w.;	Dan 7.09
water and scarlet w. and hyssop,	Heb 9.19
white as white w., white as snow;	Rev 1.14

WORD

The w. that God puts in my mouth,	Num 22.38
The w. of the LORD came to Samuel:	1Sa 15.10
whose w. saved the king, is standing	Est 7.09

WORD (cont.)

By the w. of the LORD the heavens	Ps 33.06
In God, whose w. I praise, in God I	56.04
he sent forth his w., and healed	107.20
I have laid up thy w. in my heart,	119.11
And take not the w. of truth	119.43
thy salvation; I hope in thy w.	119.81
Thy w. is a lamp to my feet and a	119.105
and a w. in season, how good it is!	Pro 15.23
A w. fitly spoken is like apples of	25.11
Every w. of God proves true;	30.05
For the w. of the king is supreme,	Ecc 8.04
This is the w. which the LORD spoke	Is 16.13
but the w. of our God will stand	40.08
so shall my w. be that goes forth	55.11
Now the w. of the LORD came to me	Jer 1.04
For the w. of the LORD has become	20.08
the burden is every man's own w.,	23.36
The w. that came to Jeremiah	25.01
"Is there any w. from the LORD?"	37.17
The w. which Jeremiah the prophet	51.59
the w. of the LORD came to Ezekiel	Eze 1.03
I will speak the w. and perform it,	12.25
dry bones, hear the w. of the LORD.	37.04
but by every w. that proceeds from	Mt 4.04
he cast out the spirits with a w.,	8.16
one hears the w. of the kingdom	13.19
this is he who hears the w.,	13.22
you have made void the w. of God.	15.06
he was preaching the w. to them.	Mk 2.02
eyewitnesses and ministers of the w.,	Lk 1.02
in peace, according to thy w.;	2.29
In the beginning was the W.,	Jn 1.01
And the W. became flesh and dwelt	1.14
in him, "If you continue in my w.,	8.31
you say, 'If any one keeps my w.,	8.52
a man loves me, he will keep my w.,	14.23
in the truth, thy w. is truth.	17.17
of those who heard the w. believed;	Ac 4.04
and to the ministry of the w.	6.04
went about preaching the w.	8.04
But the w. of God grew and multiplied.	12.24
witness to the w. of his grace,	14.03
The w. is near you, on your lips and	Rom 10.08
For the w. of the cross is folly to	1Co 1.18
our w. to you has not been Yes and	2Co 1.18
like so many, peddlers of God's w.;	2.17
cunning to tamper with God's w.,	4.02
whole law is fulfilled in one w.,	Gal 5.14
the washing of water with the w.,	Eph 5.26
the Spirit, which is the w. of God.	6.17
holding fast the w. of life,	Php 2.16
Let the w. of Christ dwell in you	Col 3.16
gospel came to you not only in w.,	1Th 1.05
But the w. of God is not fettered.	2Ti 2.09
preach the w., be urgent in season	4.02
the universe by his w. of power.	Heb 1.03
For the w. of God is living and	4.12
But be doers of the w., and not hearers	Jas 1.22
the living and abiding w. of God;	1Pe 1.23
but the w. of the Lord abides for ever."	1.25
hands, concerning the w. of life—	1Jn 1.01
and the w. of God abides in you, and	2.14
he is called is The W. of God.	Rev 19.13

WORK —ED —ING —S (v)

go and w. in the vineyard today.'	Mt 21.28
night comes, when no one can w.	Jn 9.04
who does not w. but trusts him who	Rom 4.05
Are all teachers? Do all w. miracles?	1Co 12.29
we w. with you for your joy, for you	2Co 1.24
So death is at w. in us, but life in	4.12
w. out your own salvation with fear	Php 2.12
w. heartily, as serving the Lord and	Col 3.23
command: If any one will not w.,	2Th 3.10
I w. harder than any of them, though	1Co 15.10
we w. night and day, that we might	1Th 2.09
w. salvation in the midst of the	Ps 74.12
"My Father is w. still, and I am w."	Jn 5.17
W. together with him, then, we	2Co 6.01
avail, but faith w. through love.	Gal 5.06
when each part is w. properly,	Eph 4.16
w. in you that which is pleasing in	Heb 13.21
For no man w. in secret if he seeks	Jn 7.04
everything God w. for good with	Rom 8.28

WORK —S (n)

from all his w. which he had done	Gen 2.03
"Six days you shall do your w.,	Ex 23.12
"The Rock, his w. is perfect;	Deu 32.04
man, that all men may know his w.	Job 37.07
the w. of thy fingers, the moon and	Ps 8.03
requite a man according to his w.	62.12
heavens are the w. of thy hands.	102.25
Commit your w. to the LORD, and	Pro 16.03
Consider the w. of God; who can	Ecc 7.13
making'? or 'Your w. has no handles'?	Is 45.09
we are all the w. of thy hand.	64.08
he who does the w. of the LORD	Jer 48.10
They are worthless, a w. of delusion;	51.18
'Our God,' to the w. of our hands.	Hos 14.03
And he could do no mighty w. there,	Mk 6.05
does a mighty w. in my name will	9.39
sent me, and to accomplish his w.	Jn 4.34
"This is the w. of God, that you	6.29
accomplished the w. which thou	17.04
to be proud of my w. for God.	Rom 15.17
each man's w. will become manifest;	1Co 3.13
abounding in the w. of the Lord,	15.58
boasting of w. already done in	2Co 10.16
But let each one test his own w.,	Gal 6.04
by the power at w. within us is	Eph 3.20
nearly died for the w. of Christ,	Php 2.30
complete, equipped for every good w.	2Ti 3.17
do the w. of an evangelist, fulfil	4.05
overlook your w. and the love	Heb 6.10
consider the wondrous w. of God.	Job 37.14
"He is the first of the w. of God;	40.19
How great are thy w., O LORD!	Ps 92.05
I will meditate on thy wondrous w.	119.27
All thy w. shall give thanks to	145.10
their w. are nothing; their molten	Is 41.24
"For I know their w. and their	66.18
see your good w. and give glory to	Mt 5.16
he did not do many mighty w. there,	13.58
and greater w. than these will he	Jn 5.20
I am not doing the w. of my Father,	10.37
to every man according to his w.;	Rom 2.06
On the principle of w.? No, but on the	3.27

WORK —S (n) (cont.)

righteousness apart from w.:	Rom 4.06
cast off the w. of darkness and	13.12
For all who rely on w. of the law	Gal 3.10
Now the w. of the flesh are plain:	5.19
one another to love and good w.,	Heb 10.24
so faith apart from w. is dead.	Jas 2.26
" 'I know your w., your toil and	Rev 2.02

WORKER —S

What gain has the w. from his toil?	Ecc 3.09
For we are fellow w. for God;	1Co 3.09
then w. of miracles, then healers,	12.28
and the rest of my fellow w.,	Php 4.03

WORKING (n)

and there are varieties of w.,	1Co 12.06

WORKMAN —MEN

A w. made it; it is not God.	Hos 8.06
a w. who has no need to be ashamed,	2Ti 2.15
with the w. of like occupation, and	Ac 19.25

WORKMANSHIP

Are not you my w. in the Lord?	1Co 9.01
For we are his w., created in	Eph 2.10

WORLD

and who laid on him the whole w.?	Job 34.13
and he judges the w. with righteousness,	Ps 9.08
foundations of the w. were laid bare.	18.15
their words to the end of the w.	19.04
hadst formed the earth and the w.,	90.02
inhabitants of the w. learn righteousness.	Is 26.09
established the w. by his wisdom,	Jer 10.12
make you to dwell in the nether w.,	Eze 26.20
kingdoms of the w. and the glory	Mt 4.08
"You are the light of the w.	5.14
cares of the w. and the delight in	13.22
in the new w., when the Son of man	19.28
gospel is preached in the whole w.,	26.13
"Go into all the w. and preach the	*Mk 16.15
every man was coming into the w.	Jn 1.09
who takes away the sin of the w.!	1.29
so loved the w. that he gave his	3.16
the light has come into the w.,	3.19
is indeed the Savior of the w."	4.42
saying, "I am the light of the w.;	8.12
whom the w. cannot receive, because	14.17
"If the w. hates you, know that it	15.18
In the w. you have tribulation;	16.33
"My kingship is not of this w.;	18.36
have turned the w. upside down	Ac 17.06
faith is proclaimed in all the w.	Rom 1.08
means the reconciliation of the w.,	11.15
conformed to this w. but be transformed	12.02
foolish in the w. to shame the	1Co 1.27
form of this w. is passing away.	7.31
reconciling the w. to himself,	2Co 5.19
crucified to me, and I to the w.	Gal 6.14
before the foundation of the w.,	Eph 1.04
you shine as lights in the w.,	Php 2.15
keep oneself unstained from the w.	Jas 1.27

And the w. passes away, and the lust	1Jn 2.17
kingdom of the w. has become the	Rev 11.15

WORLDLY

man is anxious about w. affairs,	1Co 7.33
suspect us of acting in w. fashion.	2Co 10.02
since many boast of w. things,	11.18
renounce irreligion and w. passions,	Tit 2.12
w. people, devoid of the Spirit.	Jud 19

WORM —S

and the son of man, who is a w.!"	Job 25.06
But I am a w., and no man;	Ps 22.06
Fear not, you w. Jacob, you men of	Is 41.14
where their w. does not die, and the	Mk 9.48
and he was eaten by w. and died.	Ac 12.23

WORMWOOD

O you who turn justice to w.,	Amo 5.07
The name of the star is W.	Rev 8.11

WORSHIP —ED —ING (v)

(for you shall w. no other god, for	Ex 34.14
drawn away to w. other gods and	Deu 30.17
of his name; w. the LORD in holy array.	Ps 29.02
O come, let us w. and bow down, let	95.06
the East, and have come to w. him."	Mt 2.02
'You shall w. the Lord your God and	4.10
we w. what we know, for salvation is	Jn 4.22
him must w. in spirit and truth."	4.24
what therefore you w. as unknown,	Ac 17.23
who w. God in spirit, and glory in	Php 3.03
and all who dwell on earth will w. it,	Rev 13.08
of this book, W. God."	22.09
And they w. the LORD there.	1Sa 1.28
and w. other gods and served them." ' "	Jer 22.09
and they fell down and w. him.	Mt 2.11
and the elders fell down and w.	Rev 5.14
w. with fasting and prayer night	Lk 2.37
While they were w. the Lord and	Ac 13.02

WORSHIP (n)

to God, which is your spiritual w.	Rom 12.01
Therefore, my beloved, shun the w. of	1Co 10.14
so-called god or object of w.,	2Th 2.04

WORSHIPER —S

if any one is a w. of God and does	Jn 9.31
perfect the conscience of the w.,	Heb 9.09
when the true w. will worship the	Jn 4.23

WORTHLESS

w. physicians are you all.	Job 13.04
who make their boast in w. idols;	Ps 97.07
For Egypt's help is w. and empty,	Is 30.07
They are w., a work of delusion;	Jer 10.15
Woe to my w. shepherd, who deserts	Zec 11.17
And cast the w. servant into the	Mt 25.30

WORTHY

I am not w. of the least of all the	Gen 32.10
who is w. to be praised, and I am	Ps 18.03
whose sandals I am not w. to carry;	Mt 3.11
I am not w. to have you come under	8.08

WORTHY (cont.)

and follow me is not w. of me.	Mt 10.38
but those invited were not w.	22.08
I am no longer w. to be called your	Lk 15.19
were counted w. to suffer dishonor	Ac 5.41
perform deeds w. of their repentance.	26.20
to lead a life w. of the calling	Eph 4.01
if there is anything w. of praise,	Php 4.08
of whom the world was not w.—	Heb 11.38
"Who is w. to open the scroll and	Rev 5.02
"W. is the Lamb who was slain, to	5.12

WOUND —S (n)

burn for burn, w. for w., stripe for	Ex 21.25
cold day, and like vinegar on a w.	Pro 25.20
beast, whose mortal w. was healed.	Rev 13.12
Faithful are the w. of a friend;	Pro 27.06
and went to him and bound up his w.,	Lk 10.34
By his w. you have been healed.	1Pe 2.24

WOUNDED

But he was w. for our transgressions,	Is 53.05
of my people is my heart w., I mourn,	Jer 8.21

WRATH

and my w. will burn, and I will kill	Ex 22.24
He has kindled his w. against me,	Job 19.11
for his w. is quickly kindled.	Ps 2.12
Refrain from anger, and forsake w.!	37.08
Riches do not profit in the day of w.,	Pro 11.04
W. is cruel, anger is overwhelming;	27.04
hand of the LORD the cup of his w.,	Is 51.17
me victory, and my w. upheld me.	63.05
Therefore I am full of the w. of the	Jer 6.11
At his w. the earth quakes, and the	10.10
my hand this cup of the wine of w.,	25.15
The LORD gave full vent to his w.,	Lam 4.11
Thus will I spend my w. upon the wall,	Eze 13.15
I have taken them away in my w.	Hos 13.11
His w. is poured out like fire, and	Nah 1.06
Make it known; in w. remember	Hab 3.02
A day of w. is that day, a day of	Zep 1.15

you to flee from the w. to come?	Mt 3.07
but the w. of God rests upon him.	Jn 3.36
For the w. of God is revealed from	Rom 1.18
For the law brings w., but where there is	4.15
be saved by him from the w. of God.	5.09
we were by nature children of w.,	Eph 2.03
For God has not destined us for w.,	1Th 5.09
the seven bowls of the w. of God."	Rev 16.01

WRITE

LORD said to Moses, "W. these words;	Ex 34.27
w. them on the tablet of your heart.	Pro 3.03
W. in a book all the words that I	Jer 30.02
and I will w. it upon their hearts;	31.33
"Son of man, w. down the name of	Eze 24.02
LORD answered me: "W. the vision;	Hab 2.02
to w. an orderly account for you,	Lk 1.03
I, Paul, w. this greeting with my own	1Co 16.21
To w. the same things to you is not	Php 3.01
and w. them on their hearts, and I	Heb 8.10
and w. them on their minds,"	10.16

WRONG (n)

justice, I hate robbery and w.;	Is 61.08
and no w. was found on his lips.	Mal 2.06
wrongly, bear witness to the w.;	Jn 18.23
Love does no w. to a neighbor;	Rom 13.10
not burden you? Forgive me this w.!	2Co 12.13

WRONGDOER —S

For the w. will be paid back for	Col 3.25
the wicked, be not envious of w.!	Ps 37.01

WROUGHT

Jacob and Israel, 'What has God w.!'	Num 23.23
they will tell what God has w.,	Ps 64.09
I muse on what thy hands have w.	143.05
We have w. no deliverance in the	Is 26.18
mighty works are w. by his hands!	Mk 6.02
that his deeds have been w. in God.	Jn 3.21
what Christ has w. through me to	Rom 15.18

Y

YEAR —S

"Three times in the y. you shall	Ex 23.14
at the time appointed every y.,	Est 9.27
rejoice among the days of the y.,	Job 3.06
Thou crownest the y. with thy	Ps 65.11
In the y. that King Uzziah died I	Is 6.01
Add y. to y.; let the feasts	29.01
to proclaim the y. of the LORD's	61.02
and my y. of redemption has come.	63.04
continually offered y. after y.,	Heb 10.01
of Israel ate the manna forty y.,	Ex 16.35
"For six y. you shall sow your land	23.10
If the y. are many you shall	Lev 25.16
days of man, or thy y. as man's y.,	Job 10.05
For a thousand y. in thy sight are	Ps 90.04
the same, and thy y. have no end.	102.27
and y. will be added to your life.	Pro 9.11
In the midst of the y. renew it;	Hab 3.02

and months, and seasons, and y.!	Gal 4.10
Lord one day is as a thousand y.,	2Pe 3.08
and a thousand y. as one day.	3.08
and bound him for a thousand y.,	Rev 20.02

YES

ready to say Y. and No at once?	2Co 1.17
of God find their Y. in him.	1.20
but let your y. be y. and your no	Jas 5.12

YESTERDAY

for we are but of y., and know	Job 8.09
are but as y. when it is past, or	Ps 90.04
is the same y. and today and for	Heb 13.08

YIELD —ED (v)

but y. yourselves to the LORD, and	2Ch 30.08
and our land will y. its increase.	Ps 85.12

YIELD —ED (v) (cont.)

But do not y. to them;	Ac 23.21
Do not y. your members to sin as	Rom 6.13
to them we did not y. submission	Gal 2.05
a loud voice and y. up his spirit.	Mt 27.50

YOKE (n)

he will put a y. of iron upon your	Deu 28.48
For the y. of his burden, and the	Is 9.04
nations an iron y. of servitude to	Jer 28.14
will break the y. from off their	30.08
one who eases the y. on their jaws,	Hos 11.04
Take my y. upon you, and learn from	Mt 11.29
For my y. is easy, and my burden is	11.30
submit again to a y. of slavery.	Gal 5.01
are under the y. of slavery regard	1Ti 6.01

YOUNG

"I am y. in years, and you are aged;	Job 32.06
How can a y. man keep his way pure?	Ps 119.09
Y. men and maidens together, old men	148.12
The glory of y. men is their	Pro 20.29
Rejoice, O y. man, in your youth, and	Ecc 11.09
or a y. stag upon rugged mountains.	Sol 2.17
Behold, a y. woman shall conceive	Is 7.14
their y. shall lie down together;	11.07
and y. men shall fall exhausted;	40.30
Spare not her y. men; utterly destroy	Jer 51.03

Y. men are compelled to grind at	Lam 5.13
and your y. men shall see visions.	Joe 2.28
The y. man said to him, "All these I	Mt 19.20
they saw a y. man sitting on the	Mk 16.05
and your y. men shall see visions,	Ac 2.17
And a y. man named Eutychus was	20.09
and so train the y. women to love	Tit 2.04

YOUNGER —EST

told, "The elder will serve the y."	Rom 9.12
Likewise you that are y. be subject	1Pe 5.05
greatest among you become as the y.,	Lk 22.26

YOUTH —S

of man's heart is evil from his y.;	Gen 8.21
let his flesh become fresh with y.;	Job 33.25
Remember not the sins of my y.,	Ps 25.07
O God, from my y. thou hast taught	71.17
so that your y. is renewed like	103.05
Creator in the days of your y.,	Ecc 12.01
will forget the shame of your y.,	Is 54.04
how to speak, for I am only a y."	Jer 1.06
not remember the days of your y.,	Eze 16.22
these I have observed from my y."	Mk 10.20
"My manner of life from my y.,	Ac 26.04
Let no one despise your y.,	1Ti 4.12
Even y. shall faint and be weary,	Is 40.30
y. without blemish, handsome and	Dan 1.04

Z

ZEAL

For z. for thy house has consumed	Ps 69.09
The z. of the LORD of hosts will do	Is 9.07
Where are thy z. and thy might?	63.15
"Z. for thy house will consume me."	Jn 2.17
that they have a z. for God,	Rom 10.02
he who gives aid, with z.; he who does	12.08
Never flag in z., be aglow with the	12.11
and your z. has stirred up most of	2Co 9.02
as to z. a persecutor of the church,	Php 3.06

ZEALOUS* —LY*

they are all z. for the law,	Ac 21.20
being z. for God as you all are	22.03
so extremely z. was I for the	Gal 1.14
his own who are z. for good deeds.	Tit 2.14
you if you are z. for what is	1Pe 3.13
be the more z. to confirm your call	2Pe 1.10
be z. to be found by him without	3.14
and chasten; so be z. and repent.	Rev 3.19
charged them, the more z. they	Mk 7.36

Proper Names

A

AARON
The LORD said to A., "Go into — Ex 4.27
But the LORD spoke to Moses and A., — 6.13
A. also and his sons I will consecrate, — 29.44
These are the names of the sons of A.: Num 3.02
of Israel wept for A. thirty days. — 20.29
is called by God, just as A. was. — Heb 5.04

ABEDNEGO
against Shadrach, Meshach, and A. — Dan 3.19
and A., servants of the Most High — 3.26

ABEL
Now A. was a keeper of sheep, and — Gen 4.02
to Cain, "Where is A. your brother?" — 4.09
By faith A. offered to God a more — Heb 11.04

ABIATHAR
named A., escaped and fled after — 1Sa 22.20
Are not Zadok and A. the priests — 2Sa 15.35
when A. was high priest, and ate the — Mk 2.26

ABIGAIL
When A. saw David, she made haste, — 1Sa 25.23
Then David sent and wooed A., — 25.39

ABIJAH
and A. his son reigned in his — 2Ch 12.16
And A. pursued Jeroboam, and took — 13.19
So A. slept with his fathers, and — 14.01

ABIMELECH (1)
And A. king of Gerar sent and took — Gen 20.02
and God healed A., and also — 20.17
sheep and oxen and gave them to A., — 21.27

ABIMELECH (2)
Now A. the son of Jerubbaal went to — Ju 9.01
A. ruled over Israel three years. — 9.22
"Who is A., and who are we of — 9.28
Thus God requited the crime of A., — 9.56

ABISHAI
Joab's brother A. the son of — 1Sa 26.06
So Joab and A. his brother slew — 2Sa 3.30
And David said to A., "Now Sheba — 20.06

ABNER
of his army was A. the son of Ner, — 1Sa 14.05
and A. sat by Saul's side, but David's — 20.25
A. was making himself strong in the — 2Sa 3.06
But A. was not with David at Hebron, — 3.22
"Should A. die as a fool dies? — 3.33

ABRAHAM
Abram, but your name shall be A.; — Gen 17.05
Now A. and Sarah were old, advanced — 18.11
of the valley, God remembered A., — 19.29
After these things God tested A., — 22.01

A. said, "God will provide himself — 22.08
LORD had blessed A. in all things. — 24.01
A. breathed his last and died in a — 25.08
A. was the father of Isaac, — 25.19
"I am the God of A. your father; — 26.24
the son of David, the son of A. — Mt 1.01
yourselves, 'We have A. as our father'; — 3.09
'I am the God of A., and the God — 22.32
'Father A., have mercy upon me, and — Lk 16.24
They answered him, "A. is our father." — Jn 8.39
"A. believed God, and it was — Rom 4.03
of faith who are the sons of A. — Gal 3.07
but God gave it to A. by a promise. — 3.18
By faith A. obeyed when he was — Heb 11.08
Was not A. our father justified by — Jas 2.21
as Sarah obeyed A., calling him — 1Pe 3.06

ABSALOM
Now A., David's son, had a beautiful — 2Sa 13.01
"A. has slain all the king's sons, — 13.30
So A. dwelt apart in his own house, — 14.24
'A. is king at Hebron!'" — 15.10
surrounded A. and struck him, and — 18.15
"O my son A., O A., my son, my — 19.04

ACHAIA
But when Gallio was proconsul of A., — Ac 18.12
were the first converts in A., — 1Co 16.15
saints who are in the whole of A.: — 2Co 1.01

ACHISH
and went to A. the king of Gath. — 1Sa 21.10
And David dwelt with A. at Gath, — 27.03

ADAM
God made for A. and for his wife — Gen 3.21
the son of A., the son of God. — Lk 3.38
Yet death reigned from A. to Moses, — Rom 5.14
For as in A. all die, so also in — 1Co 15.22
"The first man A. became a living — 15.45

ADMAH
How can I make you like A.! — Hos 11.08

ADONIJAH
Now A. the son of Haggith exalted — 1Ki 1.05
A. is king, although you, my lord the — 1.18
And A. feared Solomon; and he — 1.50

ADULLAM
and escaped to the cave of A.; — 1Sa 22.01
glory of Israel shall come to A. — Mic 1.15

AGABUS
a prophet named A. came down from — Ac 21.10

AGAG
But Saul and the people spared A., — 1Sa 15.09
Samuel hewed A. in pieces before — 15.33

AGRIPPA
A. the king and Bernice arrived at   Ac 25.13
And A. said to Paul, "In a short   26.28

AHAB
So Elijah went to show himself to A.   1Ki 18.02
And A. rode and went to Jezreel.   18.45
And after this A. said to Naboth,   21.02
"Arise, go down to meet A. king of   21.18

AHAZ
A. the son of Jotham, king of Judah,   2Ki 16.01
So A. sent messengers to Tiglathpileser   16.07
Again the LORD spoke to A.,   Is 7.10

AHIJAH
the prophet A. the Shilonite found   1Ki 11.29

AHIMELECH
came David to Nob to A. the priest;   1Sa 21.01
to A. the son of Ahitub,   22.09

AHINOAM (1)
Saul's wife was A. the daughter of   1Sa 14.50

AHINOAM (2)
David also took A. of Jezreel;   1Sa 25.43

AHITHOPHEL
was all the counsel of A. esteemed,   2Sa 16.23
A. was the king's counselor, and   1Ch 27.33

AI
Joshua sent men from Jericho to A.,   Jos 7.02
The men of Bethel and A.,   Ez 2.28
"Wail, O Heshbon, for A. is laid waste! Jer 49.03

AIJALON
and thou Moon in the valley of A."   Jos 10.12
was buried at A. in the land of   Ju 12.12

ALEXANDER
Some of the crowd prompted A.,   Ac 19.33

ALPHAEUS (1)
James the son of A., and Thaddaeus;   Mt 10.03

ALPHAEUS (2)
Levi the son of A. sitting at the   Mk 2.14

AMAZIAH (1)
and A. his son reigned in his stead.   2Ki 12.21
Israel captured A. king of Judah,   14.13

AMAZIAH (2)
and A. said to Amos, "O seer, go,   Amo 7.12

AMOS
The words of A., who was among the   Amo 1.01
Then A. answered Amaziah, "I am no   7.14

AMOZ
The vision of Isaiah the son of A.,   Is 1.01

AMPHIPOLIS*
passed through A. and Apollonia,   Ac 17.01

ANANIAS (1)
But a man named A. with his wife   Ac 5.01

ANANIAS (2)
a disciple at Damascus named A.   Ac 9.10

ANANIAS (3)
And the high priest A. commanded   Ac 23.02

ANATHOTH
A. with its pasture lands, and Almon   Jos 21.18
Jeremiah of A. who is prophesying   Jer 29.27

ANDREW
is called Peter and A. his brother,   Mt 4.18
Bethsaida, the city of A. and Peter.   Jn 1.44

ANNAS
high-priesthood of A. and Caiaphas,   Lk 3.02
First they led him to A.; for he was   Jn 18.13

ANTIOCH
found him, be brought him to A.   Ac 11.26
the church at A. there were   13.01
send them to A. with Paul and   15.22
Cephas came to A. I opposed him to   Gal 2.11
sufferings, what befell me at A.,   2Ti 3.11

ANTIPATRIS*
and brought him by night to A.   Ac 23.31

APOLLOS
Now a Jew named A.,   Ac 18.24
While A. was at Corinth, Paul passed   19.01
I planted, A. watered, but God gave   1Co 3.06

AQUILA
and with him Priscilla and A.   Ac 18.18
A. and Prisca, together with the   1Co 16.19

AR
I have given A. to the sons of Lot   Deu 2.09
Because A. is laid waste in a night   Is 15.01

ARABAH
the Canaanites who live in the A.,   Deu 11.30
went all that night through the A.;   2Sa 2.29
of Hammath to the Brook of the A." Amo 6.14

ARABIA
The oracle concerning A.   Is 21.13
before me, but I went away into A.;   Gal 1.17
Now Hagar is Mount Sinai in A.;   4.25

ARAM
Asshur, Arpachshad, Lud, and A.   Gen 10.22
(Jacob fled to the land of A.,   Hos 12.12
the LORD belong the cities of A.,   Zec 9.01

ARARAT
to rest upon the mountains of A.   Gen 8.04

ARCHELAUS*
he heard that A. reigned over   Mt 2.22

ARCHIPPUS
And say to A., "See that you fulfil   Col 4.17

AREOPAGUS*
of him and brought him to the A.,   Ac 17.19
standing in the middle of the A.,   17.22

ARETAS*
under King A. guarded the city of   2Co 11.32

ARIEL
Ho A., A., the city where David   Is 29.01

ARIMATHEA
Joseph of A., a respected member of   Mk 15.43

ARISTARCHUS
dragging with them Gaius and A.,   Ac 19.29
A., Demas, and Luke, my fellow   Phm 24

ARMAGEDDON*
place which is called in Hebrew A.   Rev 16.16

ARNON
for the A. is the boundary of Moab,   Num 21.13
the edge of the valley of the A.,   Jos 12.02
of Moab at the fords of the A.   Is 16.02
Tell it by the A.,   Jer 48.20

ARTAXERXES
associates wrote to A. king of Persia;   Ez 4.07
"A., king of Kings, to Ezra the   7.12

ARTEMIS
"Great is A. of the Ephesians!"   Ac 19.28

ASA
king of Israel A. began to reign   1Ki 15.09
the heart of A. was wholly true to   15.14

ASAPH
Joah the son of A., the recorder   2Ki 18.18

ASHDOD
carried it from Ebenezer to A.;   1Sa 5.01
Jews who had married women of A.,   Neh 13.23
came to A. and fought against it   Is 20.01
cut off the inhabitants from A.,   Amo 1.08
a mongrel people shall dwell in A.;   Zec 9.06

ASHER
so she called his name A.   Gen 30.13
of Phanuel, of the tribe of A.;   Lk 2.36

ASHKELON
he went down to A. and killed   Ju 14.19
and A. shall become a desolation;   Zep 2.04
A. shall be uninhabited;   Zec 9.05

ASHTAROTH
Og king of Bashan, who dwelt in A.   Jos 9.10
lands and A. with its pasture   1Ch 6.71

ASIA
Spirit to speak the word in A.   Ac 16.06
throughout all A. this Paul has   19.26
the first convert in A. for Christ.   Rom 16.05
affliction we experienced in A.;   2Co 1.08
the seven churches that are in A.:   Rev 1.04

ASSYRIA
From that land he went into A.,   Gen 10.11
the king of A. captured Samaria,   2Ki 17.06
Sennacherib king of A. came up   18.13
A. also has joined them; they are   Ps 83.08
the bee which is in the land of A.   Is 7.18
Ah, A., the rod of my anger, the   10.05
will be a highway from Egypt to A.,   19.23
A. shall not save us, we will not   Hos 14.03

ATHENS
"Men of A., I perceive that in   Ac 17.22
to be left behind at A. alone,   1Th 3.01

AUGUSTUS*
from Caesar A. that all the world   Lk 2.01

B

BAAL
Israel yoked himself to B. of Peor.   Num 25.03
Then Elijah said to the prophets of B.,   1Ki 18.25
Thus Jehu wiped out B. from Israel.   2Ki 10.28
prophesied by B. and led my people   Jer 23.13
They turn to B.; they are like a   Hos 7.16

BAALPEOR*
have seen what the LORD did at B.,   Deu 4.03
But they came to B.,   Hos 9.10

BAALZEBUB
inquire of B., the god of Ekron,   2Ki 1.02

BABEL*
The beginning of his kingdom was B.,   Gen 10.10
Therefore its name was called B.,   11.09

BABYLON
the king of B. had carried captive   Ez 2.01
By the waters of B.,   Ps 137.01
he answered, "Fallen, fallen is B.;   Is 21.09
Go forth from B., flee from Chaldea,   48.20
to B. you shall go; and there   Jer 20.06
into exile to B. the rest of the   39.09
Judah who were being exiled to B.   40.01
Do not fear the king of B.,   42.11
"Flee from the midst of B.,   50.08
"I will requite B. and all the   51.24
For the LORD is laying B. waste   51.55
'Thus shall B. sink, to rise no more,   51.64
king said, "Is not this great B.,   Dan 4.30
She who is at B., who is likewise   1Pe 5.13
fallen is B. the great, she who made   Rev 14.08
"B. the great, mother of harlots and   17.05
"Fallen, fallen is B. the great!   18.02

BABYLONIA		**BELIAL***	
brought up from B. to Jerusalem.	Ez 1.11	What accord has Christ with B.?	2Co 6.15

BALAAM
And God came to B. at night and   Num 22.20
And B. said to the ass, "Because you   22.29
"The oracle of B. the son of Beor,   24.03
they have followed the way of B.,   2Pe 2.15
there who hold the teaching of B.,   Rev 2.14

BELSHAZZAR
King B. made a great feast for a   Dan 5.01
first year of B. king of Babylon   7.01

BELTESHAZZAR
them names: Daniel he called B.,   Dan 1.07

BALAK
"B. the son of Zippor, king of Moab,   Num 22.10
And B. did as Balaam had said, and   23.30

BENHADAD
but B. king of Syria escaped on a   1Ki 20.20

BARABBAS
a notorious prisoner, called B.   Mt 27.16
Then he released for them B.,   27.26

BENJAMIN
but his father called his name B.   Gen 35.18
Of the people of B., their generations,   Num 1.36

BARAK
and summoned B. the son of Abinoam   Ju 4.06
And behold, as B. pursued Sisera,   4.22

BERNICE
the king and B. arrived at Caesarea   Ac 25.13

BEROEA
Paul and Silas away by night to B.:   Ac 17.10

BAR-JESUS*
a Jewish false prophet, named B.   Ac 13.06

BETHANY
Jesus was at B. in the house of   Mt 26.06
Jesus came to B., where Lazarus was,   Jn 12.01

BARNABAS
by the apostles B. (which means,   Ac 4.36
And Paul and B. spoke out boldly,   13.46
went up again to Jerusalem with B.,   Gal 2.01

BETHEL
He called the name of that place B.;   Gen 28.19
where God had spoken with him, B.   35.15
he placed in B. the priests of the   1Ki 12.32
Now there dwelt an old prophet in B.   13.11
He met God at B., and there God   Hos 12.04
"Come to B., and transgress;   Amo 4.04
but never again prophesy at B.,   7.13

BARTHOLOMEW
Philip and B.; Thomas and Matthew   Mt 10.03

BARTIMAEUS*
B., a blind beggar, the son of   Mk 10.46

BARUCH
And B. the son of Neriah did all   Jer 36.08
spoke to B. the son of Neriah, when   45.01

BETHLEHEM
They told him, "In B. of Judea;   Mt 2.05
city of David, which is called B.,   Lk 2.04
from David, and comes from B.,   Jn 7.42

BASHAN
Moses had given a possession in B.;   Jos 22.07
me, strong bulls of B. surround me;   Ps 22.12
out, and lift up your voice in B.;   Jer 22.20
you cows of B., who are in the   Amo 4.01

BETHSAIDA
woe to you, B.! for if   Mt 11.21
And they came to B. And some   Mk 8.22
Now Philip was from B., the city   Jn 1.44

BATHSHEBA
B., and went in to her, and lay with   2Sa 12.24
King David answered, "Call B. to me." 1Ki 1.28

BILDAD
B. the Shuhite, and Zophar the   Job 2.11

BILHAH
And B. conceived and bore Jacob a   Gen 30.05

BEELZEBUL
called the master of the house B.,   Mt 10.25
And if I cast out demons by B.,   12.27

BOANERGES*
of James, whom he surnamed B.,   Mk 3.17

BEERSHEBA
So they made a covenant at B.   Gen 21.32
they arose and went together to B.;   22.19
and came to B., and offered sacrifices   46.01

BOAZ
So B. took Ruth and she became his   Ru 4.13

BOZRAH
For the LORD has a sacrifice in B.,   Is 34.06
in crimsoned garments from B.,   63.01
shall devour the strongholds of B."   Amo 1.12

BEL
B. bows down, Nebo stoops, their   Is 46.01
And I will punish B. in Babylon,   Jer 51.44

C

CAESAR
lawful to pay taxes to C., or not?   Mk 12.14
year of the reign of Tiberius C.,   Lk 3.01
up to them. I appeal to C."   Ac 25.11
you must stand before C.;   27.24

CAESAREA
into the district of C. Philippi,   Mt 16.13
the disciples from C. went with us,   Ac 21.16
that Paul was being kept at C.,   25.04

CAIAPHAS
high priest, who was called C.,   Mt 26.03

CAIN
and C. a tiller of the ground.   Gen 4.02
C. rose up against his brother Abel,   4.08
more acceptable sacrifice than C.,   Heb 11.04

CANA
was a marriage at C. in Galilee,   Jn 2.01
So he came again to C. in Galilee,   4.46

CANAAN
Abram dwelt in the land of C.,   Gen 13.12
famine is severe in the land of C.;   47.04
saying, "To you I will give the land of C., 1Ch 16.18
they sacrificed to the idols of C.;   Ps 106.38
famine throughout all Egypt and C.,   Ac 7.11

CARCHEMISH
Is not Calno like C.? Is not   Is 10.09

CARMEL
the prophets together at Mount C.   1Ki 18.20
Elijah went up to the top of C.;   18.42
came to the man of God at Mount C.   2Ki 4.25
Your head crowns you like C.,   Sol 7.05
mourn, and the top of C. withers.   Amo 1.02

CENCHREAE
At C. he cut his hair, for he had a   Ac 18.18

CEPHAS
shall be called C." (which means   Jn 1.42

to Apollos," or "I belong to C.,"   1Co 1.12
I went up to Jerusalem to visit C.,   Gal 1.18

CHEMOSH
You are undone, O people of C.!   Num 21.29
The people of C. is undone; for your   Jer 48.46

CHILION
of his two sons were Mahlon and C.;   Ru 1.02

CILICIA
And he went through Syria and C.,   Ac 15.41
"I am a Jew, from Tarsus in C.,   21.39
into the regions of Syria and C.   Gal 1.21

CLAUDIUS
this took place in the days of C.   Ac 11.28
because C. had commanded all the   18.02

CLEOPAS*
named C., answered him "Are you the Lk 24.18

CORINTH
this he left Athens and went to C.   Ac 18.01
While Apollos was at C., Paul passed   19.01

CORNELIUS
At Caesarea there was a man named C., Ac 10.01
"C., a centurion, an upright and   10.22

CRISPUS
C., the ruler of the synagogue,   Ac 18.08

CYPRUS
the land of C. it is revealed to   Is 23.01
of pines from the coasts of C.,   Eze 27.06
When we had come in sight of C.,   Ac 21.03
we sailed under the lee of C.,   27.04

CYRENE
upon a man of C., Simon by name;   Mt 27.32

CYRUS
"Thus says C. king of Persia, 'The   2Ch 36.23
who says of C., 'He is my shepherd,   Is 44.28

D

DAGON
a great sacrifice to D. their god,   Ju 16.23
the house of D. and set it up beside D. 1Sa 5.02

DAMASCUS
Then David put garrisons in Aram of D. 2Sa 8.05
Ahaz went to D. to meet Tiglathpileser 2Ki 16.10
For the head of Syria is D., and the   Is 7.08
An oracle concerning D. Behold, D.   17.01
"For three transgressions of D.,   Amo 1.03
letters to the synagogues at D.,   Ac 9.02
I journeyed to D. to take those   22.05
but declared first to those at D.,   26.20
At D., the governor under King   2Co 11.32
Arabia; and again I returned to D.   Gal 1.17

DAN
therefore she called his name D.   Gen 30.06
D. shall judge his people as one of   49.16
from D. to Beersheba, including the   Ju 20.01
Bethel, and the other he put in D.   1Ki 12.29

DANIEL
even if Noah, D., and Job were in it,   Eze 14.20
And God gave D. favor and compassion Dan 1.09
Then this D. became distinguished   6.03
and D. was brought and cast into   6.16

DARIUS
the reign of D. king of Persia.   Ez 4.05
Then D. the king made a decree, and   6.01

DAVID

D. took the lyre and played it with	1Sa 16.23
Now D. was the son of an Ephrathite	17.12
So D. prevailed over the Philistine	17.50
Jonathan was knit to the soul of D.,	18.01
Saul was afraid of D., because the	18.12
Now D. fled and escaped, and he came	19.18
they anointed D. king over the	2Sa 2.04
And sons were born to D. at Hebron:	3.02
So D. went and brought up the ark	6.12
D. said to Nathan, "I have sinned	12.13
And D. built there an altar to the	24.25
D. said to Solomon, "My son, I had it	1Ch 22.07
aloud, "Have mercy on us, Son of D."	Mt 9.27
of the house and lineage of D.,	Lk 2.04
the Christ is descended from D.,	Jn 7.42
the Root of D., has conquered, so	Rev 5.05

DEBORAH

Now D., a prophetess, the wife of	Ju 4.04
Then sang D. and Barak the son of	5.01

DECAPOLIS

Galilee and the D. and Jerusalem	Mt 4.25

DELILAH

And D. said to Samson, "Please tell	Ju 16.06
So D. took new ropes and bound him	16.12

DEMAS

D., and Luke, my fellow workers.	Phm 24

DEMETRIUS

For a man named D., a silversmith,	Ac 19.24

DERBE

of it and fled to Lystra and D.,	Ac 14.06
And he came also to D. and Lystra.	16.01

DIBON

The daughter of D. has gone up to	Is 15.02
parched ground, O inhabitant of D.!	Jer 48.18

E

EBEDMELECH

When E. the Ethiopian, a eunuch, who	Jer 38.07

EBENEZER

they carried it from E. to Ashdod;	1Sa5.01

EDEN

a garden in E., in the east;	Gen 2.08
in the land of Nod, east of E.	4.16
will make her wilderness like E.,	Is 51.03
You were in E., the garden of God;	Eze 28.13

EDOM

country of Seir; Esau is E.	Gen 36.08
In his days E. revolted from the	2Ki 8.20
they had sought the gods of E.	2Ch 25.20
Upon E. I cast my shoe; over Philistia	Ps 60.08
great slaughter in the land of E.	Is 34.06
Who is this that comes from E.,	63.01
the remnant of E. and all the	Amo 9.12

EGYPT

When Abram entered E. the Egyptians	Gen 12.14
of silver; and they took Joseph to E.	37.28
and came into E., Jacob and all his	46.06
Thus Israel dwelt in the land of E.,	47.27
the sons of Israel, out of E."	Ex 3.10
the LORD has brought you out of E.	13.09
a people has come out of E.	Num 22.11
Thou didst bring a vine out of E.:	Ps 80.08
An oracle concerning E. Behold, the	Is 19.01
be a highway from E. to Assyria,	19.23
who go down to E. for help and	31.01
you rely on E. for chariots and	36.09
"A beautiful heifer is E., but a	Jer 46.20
they played the harlot in E.;	Eze 23.03
bring to nought the pride of E.	32.12
and flee to E., and remain there	Mt 2.13
By faith he left E., not being	Heb 11.27
allegorically called Sodom and E.,	Rev 11.08

ELEAZAR

E., Aaron's son, took to wife one of	Ex 6.25
to Aaron and to E. and Ithamar,	Lev 10.06
So E. and Ithamar served as priests	Num 3.04

ELI

Now E. the priest was sitting on	1Sa 1.09
E. fell over backward from his seat	4.18

ELIEZER

E. (for he said, "The God of my	Ex 18.04
The sons of Moses: Gershom and E.	1Ch 23.15

ELIHU

Now E. had waited to speak to Job	Job 32.04

ELIJAH

Now E. the Tishbite, of Tishbe in	1Ki 17.01
And the hand of the LORD was on E.;	18.46
And E. went up by a whirlwind into	2Ki 2.11
"Behold, I will send you E. the	Mal 4.05
but I tell you that E. has already	Mt 17.12
Are you E.?" He said, "I am not."	Jn 1.21
E. was a man of like nature with	Jas 5.17

ELIPHAZ

E. the Temanite, Bildad the Shuhite,	Job 2.11

ELISHA

"The spirit of Elijah rests on E."	2Ki 2.15
the great things that E. has done."	8.04
So E. died, and they buried him.	13.20

ELIZABETH

of Aaron, and her name was E.	Lk 1.05
And when E. heard the greetings of	1.41

EPHESUS

not only at E. but almost throughout	Ac 19.26

EPHESUS (cont.)
speaking, I fought with beasts at E.?   1Co 15.32
angel of the church in E. write: Rev 2.01

ER
But E., Judah's first-born, was   Gen 38.07

ERASTUS
E., the city treasurer, and our   Rom 16.23

ESAU
E. was a skilful hunter, a man of   Gen 25.27
Thus E. despised his birthright.   25.34
my brother E. is a hairy man, and I   27.11
"Jacob I loved, but E. I hated."   Rom 9.13
be immoral or irreligious like E.,   Heb 12.16

ESTHER
that is E., the daughter of his   Est 2.07
Jew and Queen E. enjoined upon the   9.31

ETHIOPIA
because of E. their hope and of   Is 20.05
Egypt, and anguish shall be in E.,   Eze 30.04
E. was her strength, Egypt too, and   Nah 3.09

EUPHRATES
And the fourth river is the E.   Gen 2.14

EUTYCHUS*
young man named E. was sitting in   Ac 20.09

EVE
The man called his wife's name E.,   Gen 3.20
serpent deceived E. by his cunning,   2Co 11.03

EZEKIEL
of the LORD came to E. the priest,   Eze 1.03

EZRA
For E. had set his heart to study   Ez 7.10
and they told E. the scribe to bring   Neh 8.01

F

FELIX
him safely to F. the governor."   Ac 23.24
"There is a man left prisoner by F.;   25.14

FESTUS
F. replied that Paul was being kept   Ac 25.04
F. laid Paul's case before the king,   25.14
"I am not mad, most excellent F.,   26.25

G

GABRIEL
"I am G., who stand in the presence   Lk 1.19

GAD
so she called his name G.   Gen 30.11

GAIUS
dragging with them G. and Aristarchus,   Ac 19.29

GALATIA
through the region of G. and Phrygia,   Ac 18.23
with me, To the churches of G.:   Gal 1.02

GALILEE
Then Jesus came from G. to the   Mt 3.13
And he went about all G., teaching   4.23
up, I will go before you to G."   26.32
officers and the leading men of G.   Mk 6.21
beginning from G. after the baptism   Ac 10.37

GALLIO
But when G. was proconsul of Achaia,   Ac 18.12

GAMALIEL
a Pharisee in the council named G.   Ac 5.34
up in this city at the feet of G.,   22.03

GATH
Saul that David had fled to G.,   1Sa 27.04
Tell it not in G., publish it not   2Sa 1.20
then go down to G. of the Philistines.   Amo 6.02
Tell it not in G., weep not at all;   Mic 1.10

GAZA
Samson went to G., and there he saw   Ju 16.01
Baldness has come upon G., Ashkelon   Jer 47.05
"For three transgressions of G.,   Amo 1.06
goes down from Jerusalem to G."   Ac 8.26

GERIZIM
upon Mount G. to bless the people: Deu 27.12

GETHSEMANE
with them to a place called G.,   Mt 26.36

GEZER
so Solomon rebuilt G.) and Lower   1Ki 9.17
war with the Philistines at G.;   1Ch 20.04

GIBEAH
Saul also went to his home at G.,   1Sa 10.26
Ramah trembles, G. of Saul has fled   Is 10.29
Blow the horn in G., the trumpet   Hos 5.08

GIBEON
"Sun, stand thou still at G.,   Jos 10.12
At G. the LORD appeared to Solomon   1Ki 3.05

GIDEON
Then G. built an altar there to the   Ju 6.24
And G. sent messengers throughout   7.24
time would fail me to tell of G.,   Heb 11.32

GILBOA
his three sons fallen on Mount G.   1Sa 31.08
the Philistines killed Saul on G.;   2Sa 21.12

GILEAD
Is there no balm in G.? Is there no	Jer 8.22
is iniquity in G. they shall	Hos 12.11

GILGAL
So Joshua went up from G.,	Jos 10.07
let us go to G. and there renew the	1Sa 11.14
if in G. they sacrifice bulls, their	Hos 12.11
to G., and multiply transgression;	Amo 4.04

GOG
"Son of man, set your face toward G.,	Eze 38.02
G. and Magog, to gather them for	Rev 20.08

GOLGOTHA
a place called G. (which means the	Mt 27.33

GOLIATH
Philistines a champion named G.	1Sa 17.04

GOMER
went and took G. the daughter of	Hos 1.03

GOMORRAH
the LORD destroyed Sodom and G.	Gen 13.10
like Sodom, and become like G.	Is 1.09
of Sodom and G. than for that town	Mt 10.15

GREECE
And the he-goat is the king of G.;	Dan 8.21
much encouragement, he came to G.	Ac 20.02

H

HABAKKUK
of God which H. the prophet saw.	Hab 1.01

HAGAR
took H. the Egyptian, her maid, and	Gen 16.03
H. bore Abram a son; and Abram	16.15
Now H. is Mount Sinai in Arabia;	Gal 4.25

HAGGAI
LORD came by H. the prophet to	Hag 1.01

HANANIAH
the prophet H. took the yoke-bars	Jer 28.10
son of H., seized Jeremiah the prophet,	37.13

HARAN
but when they came to H.,	Gen 11.31
left Beersheba, and went toward H.	28.10

HAZAEL
Now H. king of Syria oppressed	2Ki 13.22

HEBRON
Now the name of H. formerly was	Jos 14.15
And sons were born to David at H.:	2Sa 3.02
then say, 'Absalom is king at H.!' "	15.10

HERMON
Tabor and H. joyously praise thy	Ps 89.12
It is like the dew of H.,	133.03

HEROD (1)
Judea in the days of H. the king,	Mt 2.01

HEROD (2)
and H. being tetrarch of Galilee,	Lk 3.01

HERODIAS
him in prison, for the sake of H.,	Mt 14.03

HEZEKIAH
H. the son of Ahaz, king of Judah,	2Ki 18.01
Isaiah said to H., "Hear the word	20.16

HILKIAH
"Go up to H. the high priest, that	2Ki 22.04

HIRAM
And H. King of Tyre sent messengers	2Sa 5.11
So H. supplied Solomon with all the	1Ki 5.10

HOREB
and came to H., the mountain of God.	Ex 3.01
God made a covenant with us in H.	Deu 5.02

HOSEA
that came to H. the son of Beeri,	Hos 1.01

I

ICONIUM
Now at I. they entered together	Ac 14.01
at I., and at Lystra, what persecutions	2Ti 3.11

ILLYRICUM*
as far round as I. I have fully	Rom 15.19

ISAAC
to him, whom Sarah bore him, I.	Gen 21.03
for through I. shall your descendants	21.12
and bound I. his son, and laid him	22.09
and take a wife for my son I."	24.04
the God of I., and the God of Jacob."	Ex 3.06

ISAIAH
by one man, our forefather I.,	Rom 9.10
offered up I., and he who had	Heb 11.17

ISAIAH
to the prophet I. the son of Amoz.	2Ki 19.02
And the LORD said to I., "Go forth	Is 7.03

ISCARIOT
and Judas I., who betrayed him.	Mt 10.04

ISHMAEL
old when Hagar bore I. to Abram.	Gen 16.16

ISRAEL (1)
but I. shall be your name." Gen 35.10
I. is my first-born son, Ex 4.22

ISRAEL (2)
Moses spoke thus to the people of I.; Ex 6.09
Then Moses led I. onward from the 15.22
Thou, LORD God of hosts, art God of I. Ps 59.05
O Shepherd of I., thou who leadest 80.01
And he will redeem I. from all his 130.08
the Holy One of I. your Savior. Is 43.03
I. was holy to the LORD, the first Jer 2.03

Like a stubborn heifer, I. is stubborn; Hos 4.16
For I. has forgotten his Maker, and 8.14
and I. shall surely go into exile Amo 7.17
the lost sheep of the house of I. Mt 10.06
time restore the kingdom to I.?" Ac 1.06
God has brought to I. a savior, 13.23
I. failed to obtain what it sought. Rom 11.07

ITALY
come from I. with his wife Priscilla, Ac 18.02
decided that we should sail for I., 27.01
who come from I. send you greetings. Heb 13.24

J

JABESHGILEAD
was the men of J. who buried Saul," 2Sa 2.04

JACOB
so his name was called J. Isaac was Gen 25.26
J. said to his father, "I am Esau 27.19
Then J. kissed Rachel, and wept 29.11
And J. was left alone; and a man wrestled 32.24
Now the sons of J. were twelve. 35.22

JAIRUS
of the synagogue, J. by name; Mk 5.22

JAMES (1)
J. the son of Zebedee and John his Mt 4.21
him Peter and J. and John his 17.01

JAMES (2)
his brothers J. and Joseph and Mt 13.55
"Tell this to J. and to the brethren." Ac 12.17
apostles except J. the Lord's Gal 1.19

JASON
and attacked the house of J., Ac 17.05

JEHOAHAZ
J. the son of Jehu began to reign 2Ki 13.01

JEHOIACHIN
And he carried away J. to Babylon; 2Ki 24.15
graciously freed J. king of Judah 25.27

JEHOIADA
Then J. the priest took a chest, and 2Ki 12.09

JEHOIAKIM
father, and changed his name to J. 2Ki 23.34

JEHORAM
J. the son of Ahab became king over 2Ki 3.01

JEHOSHAPHAT
J. made ships of Tarshish to go to 1Ki 22.48

JEHU
Then J. mounted his chariot, and 2Ki 9.16
So J. slew all that remained of the 10.11
But J. was not careful to walk in 10.31

JEPHTHAH
Now J. the Gileadite was a mighty Ju 11.01

JEREMIAH
The words of J., the son of Hilkiah, Jer 1.01
Then J. spoke to all the princes 26.12
And J. ordered Baruch, saying, "I am 36.05
J. set out from Jerusalem to go to 37.12
they had put J. into the cistern-- 38.07

JERICHO
When Joshua was by J., he lifted up Jos 5.13
"Remain at J. until your beards 2Sa 10.05
And they came to J.; and as Mk 10.46
going down from Jerusalem to J., Lk 10.30
the walls of J. fell down after Heb 11.30

JEROBOAM
J. the son of Nebat, an Ephraimite 1Ki 11.26

JERUSALEM
carried the ark of God back to J.; 2Sa 15.29
Solomon desired to build in J., 1Ki 9.19
"In J. will I put my name." 2Ki 21.04
and I will wipe J. as one wipes a 21.13
He carried away all J., 24.14
built the house of the LORD in J.; 1Ch 6.32
So I came to J. and was there three Neh 2.11
they have laid J. in ruins. Ps 79.01
Pray for the peace of J.! 122.06
from Zion, he who dwells in J.! 135.21
O J., let my right hand wither! 137.05
Praise the LORD, O J.! 147.12
Speak tenderly to J., and cry to Is 40.02
garments, O. J., the holy city; 52.01
singing, you waste places of J.; 52.09
I create J. a rejoicing, and her 65.18
J. has become a filthy thing among Lam 1.17
Zion, and utters his voice from J.; Amo 1.02
land, and will again choose J." Zec 2.12
was troubled, and all J. with him; Mt 2.03
"Behold, we are going up to J.; 20.18
"O J., J., killing the prophets and 23.37
And when they drew near to J, Mk 11.01
looking for the redemption of J. Lk 2.38
the boy Jesus stayed behind in J. 2.43
was going down from J. to Jericho, 10.30

JERUSALEM (cont.)
you say that in J. is the place	Jn 4.20
my witnesses in J. and in all	Ac 1.08
apostles and elders who were at J.	16.04
they told Paul not to go on to J.	21.04
so that from J. and as far round as	Rom 15.19
I went up to J. to visit Cephas,	Gal 1.18
But the J. above is free, and she is	4.26
the heavenly J., and to innumerable	Heb 12.22
the New J. which comes down from	Rev 3.12
the holy city J. coming down out	21.10

JESHURUN
my servant, J. whom I have chosen	Is 44.02

JESSE
And J. said to David his son, "Take	1Sa 17.17
forth a shoot from the stump of J.,	Is 11.01

JETHRO
Moses went back to J. his father-in-law	Ex 4.18

JEZEBEL
Ahab told J. all that Elijah had	1Ki 19.01
like Ahab, whom J. his wife incited.	21.25

JOAB
And J. the son of Zeruiah, and the	2Sa 2.13
David arrived with J. from a raid,	3.22

JOB
"Does J. fear God for nought?	Job 1.09
heard of the steadfastness of J.,	Jas 5.11

JOEL
The word of the LORD that came to J.,	Joe 1.01
what was spoken by the prophet J.:	Ac 2.16

JOHN (1)
In those days came J. the Baptist,	Mt 3.01
he heard that J. had been arrested,	4.12
"Go and tell J. what you hear and	11.04
From the days of J. the Baptist	11.12
he sent and had J. beheaded in the	14.10
"Some say J. the Baptist, others say	16.14
sent from God, whose name was J.	Jn 1.06

JOHN (2)
son of Zebedee, and J. his brother;	Mt 10.2
Now Peter and J. were going up to	Ac 3.01
to me, James and Cephas and J.,	Gal 2.09

JOHN (3)
to take with them J. called Mark.	Ac 15.27

JOHN (4)
I J. am he who heard and saw these	Rev 22.08

JONAH
But J. rose to flee to Tarshish	Jon 1.03
and J. was in the belly of the fish	1.17
except the sign of the prophet J.	Mt 12.39

JONATHAN
And Saul, and J. his son, and the	1Sa 13.16
So the people ransomed J.,	14.45
Then J. made a covenant with David,	18.03
And J. spoke well of David to Saul	19.04
"J. lies slain upon thy high places.	2Sa 1.25

JORDAN
pass over the J. before the LORD,	Num 32.21
which Moses gave you beyond the J.;	Jos 1.14
waters of the J. were cut off	4.07
"Go and wash in the J. seven times,	2Ki 5.10
looked and fled, J. turned back.	Ps 114.03
baptized by him in the river J.,	Mt 3.06
place in Bethany beyond the J.,	Jn 1.28

JOSEPH (1)
The sons of Rachel: J. and Benjamin.	Gen 35.24
Now Israel loved J. more than any	37.03
So when J. came to his brothers,	37.23
Now J. was handsome and good-looking.	39.06
And J. stored up grain in great	41.49
So J. went up to bury his father;	50.07

JOSEPH (2)
the father of J. the husband of	Mt 1.16
Mary had been betrothed to J.,	1.18

JOSEPH (3)
And J. took the body, and wrapped it	Mt 27.59

JOSHUA
And Moses said to J., "Choose for us	Ex 17.09
When J. was by Jericho, he lifted up	Jos 5.13
So the LORD was with J.; and his fame	6.27
Then J. gathered all the tribes of	24.01

JOSIAH
the land made J. his son king in	2Ki 21.24
Moreover J. put away the mediums	23.24

JOTHAM
but J. the youngest son of Jerubbaal	Ju 9.05

JUDAH
therefore she called his name J.;	Gen 29.35
And J. said to Israel his father,	43.08

JUDAS (1)
and J. Iscariot, who betrayed him.	Mt 10.04

JUDAS (2)
After him J. the Galilean arose in	Ac 5.37

JUDEA
in Bethlehem of J. in the days of	Mt 2.01
preaching in the wilderness of J.,	3.01
Jesus had come from J. to Galilee,	Jn 4.47
and in all J. and Samaria and to	Ac 1.08
delivered from the unbelievers in J.,	Rom 15.31

JULIUS
and J. treated Paul kindly, and gave	Ac 27.03

K

KIDRON
and the king crossed the brook K., 2Sa 15.23
his disciples across the K. valley, Jn 18.01

KIRIATHJEARIM
bends around to Baalah (that is K.); Jos 15.09

day that the ark was lodged at K. 1Sa 7.02
to bring the ark of God from K. 1Ch 13.05

KISH
So K. said to Saul his son, "Take 1Sa 9.03

L

LABAN
a brother whose name was L.; Gen 24.29
flee to L. my brother in Haran, 27.43
But God came to L. the Aramean in a 31.24
Early in the morning L. arose, 31.55

LAMECH
And L. took two wives; the name of Gen 4.19

LAODICEA
for you, and for those at L., Col 2.01
you read also the letter from L. 4.16
angel of the church in L. write: Rev 3.14

LAZARUS (1)
his gate lay a poor man named L., Lk 16.20

LAZARUS (2)
"Our friend L. has fallen asleep, Jn 11.11
with a loud voice, "L., come out." 11.43
where L. was, whom Jesus had raised 12.01

LEAH
the name of the older was L., Gen 29.16
and he loved Rachel more than L., 29.30

LEBANON
"A thistle on L. sent to a cedar on L., 2Ki 14.09
know how to cut timber in L. 2Ch 2.08
the LORD breaks the cedars of L. Ps 29.05
tree, and grow like a cedar in L. 92.12
the glory of L. shall be given to Is 35.02
L. would not suffice for fuel, nor 40.16

"Go up to L., and cry out, and lift Jer 22.20
Behold, I will liken you to a cedar in L., Eze 31.03

LEVI
therefore his name was called L. Gen 29.34
Simeon and L. are brothers; 49.05
of the sons of L. according to Ex 6.16
To the tribe of L. alone Moses gave Jos 13.14

LOIS*
grandmother L. and your mother 2Ti 1.05

LOT
and Haran was the father of L. Gen 11.27
and L. lifted up his eyes, and saw 13.10
Likewise as it was in the days of L.— Lk 17.28
and if he rescued righteous L., 2Pe 2.07

LUKE
L. the beloved physician and Demas Col 4.14
Demas, and L., my fellow workers. Phm 24

LUZ
And Jacob came to L. (that is, Gen 35.06
name of the city was formerly L.) Ju 1.23

LYDIA
who heard us was a woman named L., Ac 16.14

LYSIAS
"When L. the tribune comes down, I Ac 24.22

LYSTRA
And he came also to Derbe and to L. Ac 16.01
and at L., what persecutions I 2Ti 3.11

M

MACEDONIA
"Come over to M. and help us." Ac 16.09
he determined to return through M. 20.03
For even when we came into M., 2Co 7.05

MAGOG
send fire on M. and on those who Eze 39.06
Gog and M., to gather them for Rev 20.08

MAHLON
his two sons were M. and Chilion; Ru 1.02

MANASSEH
the name of the first-born M., Gen 41.51
of Egypt were born M. and Ephraim, 46.20
These are the families of M.; Num 26.34

MARK
of John whose other name was M., Ac 12.12
Barnabas took M. with him and 15.39
and so does my son M. 1Pe 5.13

MARTHA
But M. was distracted with much Lk 10.40
Now Jesus loved M. and her sister Jn 11.05
M. served, but Lazarus was one of 12.02

MATTHEW
a man called M. sitting at the tax Mt 9.09
and Thomas, Bartholomew and M., Ac 1.13

MATTHIAS
for them, and the lot fell on M.; Ac 1.26

MEGIDDO

and Pharaoh Neco slew him at M.,	2Ki 23.29
joined battle in the plain of M.	2Ch 35.22

MELCHIZEDEK

And M. king of Salem brought out	Gen 14.18
for ever, after the order of M.	Heb 5.06
arises in the likeness of M.,	7.15

MESHACH

Babylon: Shadrach, M., and Abednego.	Dan 3.12
M., and Abednego, fell bound into	3.23

METHUSELAH

Thus all the days of M. were nine	Gen 5.27

MICAH (1)

And the man M. had a shrine, and he	Ju 17.05

MICAH (2)

"M. of Moresheth prophesied in the	Jer 26.18
that came to M. of Moresheth in	Mic 1.01

MICAIAH

"Bring quickly M. the son of Imlah."	1Ki 22.09
And M. said, "Therefore hear the	22.19

MICHAEL

"At that time shall arise M.,	Dan 12.01
when the archangel M., contending	Jud 9
M. and his angels fighting against	Rev 12.07

MIDIAN

And the LORD said to Moses in M.,	Ex 4.19
the priest of M., Moses' father-in-law,	18.01
the young camels of M. and Ephah;	Is 60.06
of the land of M. did tremble.	Hab 3.07

MIRIAM

And M. sang to them: "Sing to the	Ex 15.21
M. and Aaron spoke against Moses	Num 12.01

MIZPAH

said, "Gather all Israel at M.,	1Sa 7.05

As for me, I will dwell at M.,	Jer 40.10
Gedaliah the son of Ahikam, at M.	41.01

MOAB

Woe to you, O M.! You are undone,	Num 21.29
Now then, M., to the spoil!"	2Ki 3.23
An oracle concerning M. Because Ar	Is 15.01
Concerning M. Thus says the LORD	Jer 48.01

MORDECAI

M. adopted her as his own daughter.	Est 2.07
But M. did not bow down or do	3.02
For M. the Jew was next in rank to	10.03

MOSES

and she named him M., for she said,	Ex 2.10
to kill M. But M. fled from Pharaoh,	2.15
Now M. was keeping the flock of his	3.01
God said to M., "I AM WHO I AM."	3.14
So M. and Aaron went to Pharaoh and	7.10
Then M. stretched forth his rod	9.23
Then M. led Israel onward from the	15.22
And M. went up to God, and the LORD	19.03
And M. was on the mountain forty	24.18
M. erected the tabernacle;	40.18
M. and Aaron were among his priests,	Ps 99.06
"Remember the law of my servant M.,	Mal 4.04
appeared to them M. and Elijah,	Mt 17.03
For the law was given through M.;	Jn 1.17
Yet death reigned from Adam to M.,	Rom 5.14
baptized into M. in the cloud and	1Co 10.02
just as M. also was faithful in	Heb 3.02
Now M. was faithful in all God's	3.05
And they sing the song of M.,	Rev 15.03

MOUNT OF OLIVES

to Bethphage, to the M. o. O.,	Mt 21.1
at the descent of the M. o. O., the	Lk 19.37

MOUNT SINAI

And M. S. was wrapped in smoke,	Ex 19.18
glory of the LORD settled on M. S.,	24.16
The LORD said to Moses on M. S.,	Lev 25.1
One is from M. S., bearing children	Gal 4.24

N

NAAMAN

Therefore the leprosy of N. shall	2Ki 5.27

NABOTH

Now N. the Jezreelite had a vineyard	1Ki 21.01

NAHUM

book of the vision of N. of Elkosh.	Nah 1.01

NAIN*

he went to a city called N.,	Lk 7.11

NAOMI

and the name of his wife N.,	Ru 1.02

NAPHTALI

so she called his name N.	Gen 30.08
N. is a hind let loose, that bears	49.21

NATHAN

And the LORD sent N. to David.	2Sa 12.01

NATHANAEL

Jesus saw N. coming to him, and said	Jn 1.47

NAZARETH

prophet Jesus from N. of Galilee."	Mt 21.11
"Can anything good come out of N.?"	Jn 1.46
"Jesus of N., the King of the Jews."	19.19
'I am Jesus of N. whom you are	Ac 22.08

NEBO
Bel bows down, N. stoops, their idols   Is 46.01

NEBUCHADNEZZAR
In his days N. king of Babylon came   2Ki 24.01

NEBUCHADREZZAR
for N. king of Babylon is making   Jer 21.02
"Son of man, N. king of Babylon made   Eze 29.18

NEGEB
had, and Lot with him, into the N.   Gen 13.01
like the water-courses in the N.!   Ps 126.04
The cities of the N. are shut up,   Jer 13.19

NEHEMIAH
And N., who was the governor, and   Neh 8.09

NICODEMUS
named N., a ruler of the Jews.   Jn 3.01

NILE
water from the N. and pour it upon   Ex 4.09
"Who is this, rising like the N.,   Jer 46.07
'The N. is mine, and I made it,'   Eze 29.09

NIMROD
"Like N. a mighty hunter before the   Gen 10.09

NINEVEH
"Arise, go to N., that great city,   Jon 1.02
An oracle concerning N. The book of   Nah 1.01
The men of N. will arise at the   Mt 12.41

NOAH
called his name N., saying, "Out of   Gen 5.29
They went into the ark with N.,   7.15
But God remembered N. and all the   8.01
the day when N. entered the ark,   Mt 24.38
By faith N., being warned by God   Heb 11.07

O

OBADIAH
O. took a hundred prophets and hid   1Ki 18.04
So O. went to meet Ahab, and told   18.16

OG
and O. the king of Bashan came out   Num 21.33

OLIVET
and lodged on the mount called O.   Lk 21.37
Jerusalem from the mount called O.,   Ac 1.12

OMRI
so Tibni died, and O. became king.   1Ki 16.22
O. did what was evil in the sight   16.25

ONESIMUS*
and with him O., the faithful and   Col 4.09
O., whose father I have become in   Phm 10

P

PADDAN-ARAM
him away to P. to take a wife from   Gen 28.06
Leah, whom she bore to Jacob in P.,   46.15

PAMPHYLIA
Phrygia and P., Egypt and the parts   Ac 2.10
who had withdrawn from them in P.,   15.38

PATMOS*
island called P. on account of the   Rev 1.09

PAUL
But Saul, who is also called P.,   Ac 13.09
they stoned P. and dragged him out   14.19
So P., standing in the middle of   17.22
Lord said to P. one night in a   18.09
a favor, Felix left P. in prison.   24.27
On seeing them P. thanked God and   28.15
What is P.? Servants through whom   1Co 3.05
P., an ambassador and now a prisoner   Phm 9

PEOR
Balak took Balaam to the top of P.,   Num 23.28
men who followed the Baal of P.;   Deu 4.03

PERSIA
the first year of Cyrus king of P.,   2Ch 36.22
three more kings shall arise in P.,   Dan 11.02

PETER
who is called P. and Andrew his   Mt 4.18
you are P., and on this rock I will   16.18
Now P. was sitting outside in the   26.69
be called Cephas" (which means P.).   Jn 1.42
breakfast, Jesus said to Simon P.,   21.15
Then P., filled with the Holy Spirit,   Ac 4.08
P. was sleeping between two soldiers,   12.06
worked through P. for the mission   Gal 2.08

PHARAOH
LORD afflicted P. and his house   Gen 12.17
Joseph said to P., "The dream of P.   41.25
Then P. said to Joseph, "Your father   47.05
"Go in, tell P. king of Egypt to let   Ex 6.11
When P. let the people go, God did   13.17

PHILEMON*
To P. our beloved fellow worker   Phm 1

PHILIP (1)
P. and Bartholomew; Thomas and   Mt 10.03
"Before P. called you, when you were   Jn 1.48
and yet you do not know me, P.?   14.09

PHILIP (2)
P. and the eunuch, and he baptized   Ac 8.38
the house of P. the evangelist,   21.08

PHILIPPI
into the district of Caesarea P.,	Mt 16.13
in Christ Jesus who are at P.,	Php 1.01
and been shamefully treated at P.,	1Th 2.02

PILATE
delivered him to P. the governor.	Mt 27.02
Then P. ordered it to be given to	27.58
P. answered, "What I have written I	Jn 19.22

and denied in the presence of P.,	Ac 3.13
before Pontius P. made the good	1Ti 6.13

POTIPHAR
and P., an officer of Pharaoh, the	Gen 39.01

PRISCILLA (PRISCA)
Syria, and with him P. and Aquila.	Ac 18.18
Aquila and P., together with the	1Co 16.19

R

RACHEL
So Jacob served seven years for R.,	Gen 29.20
Jacob's anger was kindled against R.,	30.02
Now R. had taken the household gods	31.34

RAHAB
only R. the harlot and all who are	Jos 6.17
By faith R. the harlot did not	Heb 11.31

RAMAH
and he came to Samuel at R., and told	1Sa 19.18
they buried him in his house at R.	25.01
R. trembles, Gibeah of Saul has fled	Is 10.29
the LORD: "A voice is heard in R.,	Jer 31.15

RAMOTHGILEAD
and said, "Go up to R. and triumph;	1Ki 22.12
that he may go up and fall at R.?'	22.20

REBEKAH
R. had a brother whose name was	Gen 24.29
and R. his wife conceived.	25.21

RED SEA
led Israel onward from the R. S.,	Ex 15.22
LORD your God did to the R. S.,	Jos 4.23
who divided the R. S. in sunder,	Ps 136.13
crossed the R. S. as if on dry	Heb 11.29

REHOBOAM
"Say to R. the son of Solomon, king	1Ki 12.23
him and defied R. the son of	2Ch 13.07

REUBEN
a son, and she called his name R.;	Gen 29.32
And R. said to them, "Shed no blood;	37.22
R., you are my first-born, my might,	49.03

RUTH
mother-in-law, but R. clung to her.	Ru 1.14
So Boaz took R. and she became his	4.13

S

SALIM*
was baptizing at Aenon near S., because	Jn 3.23

SAMARIA
S., after the name of Shemer, the	1Ki 16.24
Ahab became king over Israel in S.,	2Ki 3.01
And there was a great famine in S.,	6.25
And the head of Ephraim is S.,	Is 7.09
I have spurned your calf, O S.	Hos 8.05
yourselves upon the mountains of S.,	Amo 3.09
feel secure on the mountain of S.,	6.01
He had to pass through S.	Jn 4.04
all Judea and S. and to the end of	Ac 1.08
and Galilee and S. had peace and	9.31

SAMSON
bore a son, and called his name S.;	Ju 13.24
And S. said, "With the jawbone of an	15.16
And Delilah said to S., "Please tell	16.06
And S. grasped the two middle	16.29

SAMUEL
S. was ministering before the LORD,	1Sa 2.18
And S. said, "Speak, for thy servant	3.10
And S. grew, and the LORD was with	3.19

Then S. took a vial of oil and	10.01
And S. said to all Israel, "Behold, I	12.01
And S. rose up, and went to Ramah.	16.13
Now S. died; and all Israel	25.01
of David and S. and the prophets—	Heb 11.32

SANBALLAT
But when S. the Horonite and Tobiah	Neh 2.10

SARAH
her name, Sarai, but S. shall be her	Gen 17.15
And S. conceived, and bore Abraham a	21.02
your father and to S. who bore you;	Is 51.02
By faith S. herself received power	Heb 11.11

SAUL (1)
and he had a son whose name was S.,	1Sa 9.02
there they made S. king before the	11.15
"I repent that I have made S. king;	15.11
And David came to S., and entered	16.21
"S. has slain his thousands, And	18.07
S. was afraid of David, because the	18.12
"Is S. also among the prophets?"	19.24
and there lay S. sleeping within	26.07
Therefore S. took his own sword, and	31.04

SAUL (2)
And S. was consenting to his death.   Ac 8.01
"S., S., why do you persecute me?"   9.04
But S., who is also called Paul,   13.09

SETH
bore a son and called his name S.,   Gen 4.25

SHADRACH
S., Meshach, and Abednego, fell bound   Dan 3.23

SHEBA
the queen of S. heard of the fame   1Ki 10.01
look, the travelers of S. hope.   Job 6.19
all those from S. shall come.   Is 60.06

SHECHEM
Rehoboam went to S., for all Israel   1Ki 12.01
they murder on the way to S.,   Hos 6.09

SHEM
S. and Ham and Japheth, and Noah's   Gen 7.13

SHILOH
people of Israel assembled at S.,   Jos 18.01
the yearly feast of the LORD at S.,   Ju 21.19
to Samuel at S. by the word of the   1Sa 3.21
He forsook his dwelling at S.,   Ps 78.60

SHITTIM
Joshua rose and set out from S.   Jos 3.01

SIDON
kings of Tyre, all the kings of S.,   Jer 25.22
"Son of man, set your face toward S.,   Eze 28.21
you had been done in Tyre and S.,   Mt 11.21
about Tyre and S. a great multitude,   Mk 3.08

SILOAM
the tower in S. fell and killed   Lk 13.04
in the pool of S." (which means   Jn 9.07

SILVANUS
S. and Timothy and I, was not Yes   2Co 1.19

SIMEON (1)
son also"; and she called his name S.   Gen 29.33

SIMEON (2)
and S. blessed them and said to   Lk 2.34

SIMON (1)
S. who is called Peter and Andrew   Mt 4.18
him, "Blessed are you, S. Bar-Jona!   16.17

SIMON (2)
in the house of S. the leper,   Mt 26.06

SIMON (3)
upon a man of Cyrene, S. by name;   Mt 27.32

SIMON (4)
Now when S. saw that the Spirit was   Ac 8.18

SISERA
the commander of his army was S.,   Ju 4.02
S. called out all his chariots, nine   4.13
and there lay S. dead, with the tent   4.22

SODOM
Now the men of S. were wicked,   Gen 13.13
"If I find at S. fifty righteous in   18.26
LORD rained on S. and Gomorrah   19.24
God overthrew S. and Gomorrah and   Jer 50.40
done in you had been done in S.,   Mt 11.23
went out from S. fire and brimstone   Lk 17.29
allegorically called S. and Egypt,   Rev 11.08

SOLOMON
"S. your son shall reign after me,   1Ki 1.13
lord King David has made S. king;   1.43
S. loved the LORD, walking in the   3.03
and all that S. desired to build,   9.01
The proverbs of S., son of David,   Pro 1.01
even S. in all his glory was not   Mt 6.29
something greater than S. is here.   12.42
But it was S. who built a house for   Ac 7.47

SOSTHENES
And they all seized S., the ruler   Ac 18.1

SPAIN
see you in passing as I go to S.,   Rom 15.24

STEPHANAS
baptize also the household of S.   1Co 1.16

STEPHEN
whole multitude, and they chose S.,   Ac 6.05
And as they were stoning S., he prayed,   7.59

SYCHAR*
called S., near the field that   Jn 4.05

SYMEON
S. has related how God first   Ac 15.14

SYRIA
the king of S. will come up against   1Ki 20.22
the LORD had given victory to S.   2Ki 5.01
you relied on the king of S.,   2Ch 16.07
"S. is in league with Ephraim," his   Is 7.02
the remnant of S. will be like the   17.03
So his fame spread through out all S.,   Mt 4.24
when Quirinius was governor of S.   Lk 2.02

T

TABITHA
to the body he said, "T., rise."   Ac 9.40

TABOR
'Go, gather your men at Mount T.,   Ju 4.06
Mizpah, and a net spread upon T.   Hos 5.01

TAMAR
first-born, and her name was T.   Gen 38.06

TARSHISH
Jehoshaphat made ships of T. to go   1Ki 22.48
the ships of T. first, to bring your   Is 60.09
rose to flee to T. from the   Jon 1.03

TARSUS
Judas for a man of T. named Saul;   Ac 9.11
from T. in Cilicia, a citizen of no   21.39

TEKOA
Blow the trumpet in T., and raise   Jer 6.01
who was among the shepherds of T.,   Amo 1.01

THEBES
T. shall be breached, and its walls   Eze 30.16
Are you better than T. that sat by   Nah 3.08

TIGLATHPILESER
Damascus to meet T. king of Assyria,   2Ki 15.29

TIMOTHY
named T., the son of a Jewish woman   Ac 16.01
Therefore I sent to you T.,   1Co 4.17
and we sent T., our brother and   1Th 1.01
O T., guard what has been entrusted   1Ti 6.2

TITUS
comforted us by the coming of T.,   2Co 7.06
As for T., he is my partner and   8.23
Barnabas, taking T. along with me.   Gal 2.01
To T., my true child in a common   Tit 1.04

TOBIAH
Remember T. and Sanballat, O my   Neh 6.14

TROAS
Setting sail therefore from T.,   Ac 16.11
When I came to T. to preach the   2Co 2.12

TYRE
And Hiram king of T. sent messengers   2Sa 5.11

U

UR
his birth, in U. of the Chaldeans.   Gen 11.28

URIAH
When U. came to him, David asked how   2Sa 11.07
U. said to David, "The ark and   11.11
and sent it by the hand of U.   11.14

UZ
There was a man in the land of U.,   Job 1.01
of the land of U. and all the   Jer 25.20

UZZIAH
year that king U. died I saw the   Is 6.01

Z

ZACCHAEUS
And there was a man named Z.;   Lk 19.02

ZADOK
So Z. and Abiathar carried the ark   2Sa 15.29
"Call to me Z. the priest, Nathan   1Ki 1.32

ZEBULUN
so she called his name Z.   Gen 30.20
Z. shall dwell at the shore of the   49.13

ZECHARIAH (1)
LORD came to Z. the son of Berechiah,   Zec 1.07

ZECHARIAH (2)
Judea, there was a priest named Z.,   Lk 1.05
And his father Z. was filled with   1.67

ZEDEKIAH
stead, and changed his name to Z.   2Ki 24.17
eyes, and put out the eyes of Z.,   25.07

ZEPHANIAH (1)
Z. the priest read this letter in   Jer 29.29

ZEPHANIAH (2)
which came to Z. the son of Cushi,   Zep 1.01

ZERUBBABEL
"The hands of Z. have laid the   Zec 4.09

ZEUS*
they called Z., and Paul, because   Ac 14.12
And the priest of Z., whose temple   14.13

ZIKLAG
When David came to Z.,   1Sa 30.26
I seized him and slew him at Z.,   2Sa 4.10

ZILLAH
Z. bore Tubalcain;   Gen 4.22

ZIMRI
all the kings of Z., all the kings of   Jer 25.25

ZION
of the city of David, which is Z.   1Ki 8.01
out of Mount Z. a band of survivors   2Ki 19.31
of the city of David, which is Z.   2Ch 5.02
The LORD is great in Z.; he is exalted   Ps 99.02
"Sing us one of the songs of Z.!"   137.03
"For out of Z. shall go forth the   Is 2.03
and come to Z. with singing, with   35.10
O Z., herald of good tidings;   40.09
I will put salvation in Z.,   46.13

ZION (cont.)

"And he will come to Z. as Redeemer, Is 59.20
earth: Say to the daughter of Z., 62.11
of the land: "Is the LORD not in Z.? Jer 8.19
Blow the trumpet in Z.; sound the alarm Joe 2.01
And the LORD roars from Z., and utters 3.16
"Woe to those who are at ease in Z., Amo 6.01
Sing aloud, O daughter of Z.; Zep 3.14
says the LORD: I will return to Z., Zec 8.03
Rejoice greatly, O daughter of Z.! 9.09
"Tell the daughter of Z., Behold, your Mt 21.05
I am laying in Z. a stone that Rom 9.33

come to Mount Z. and to the city Heb 12.22
on Mount Z. stood the Lamb, and with Rev 14.01

ZIPPORAH

and he gave Moses his daughter Z. Ex 2.21

ZOAR

Now Lot went up out of Z., Gen 19.30
his fugitives flee to Z., Is 15.05
a cry is heard as far as Z. Jer 48.04

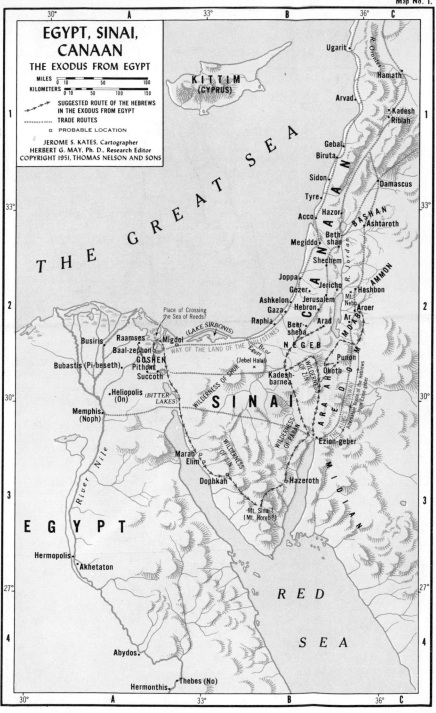

Map No. 1.

EGYPT, SINAI, CANAAN
THE EXODUS FROM EGYPT

MILES 0 10 50 100
KILOMETERS 0 10 50 100 150

SUGGESTED ROUTE OF THE HEBREWS
IN THE EXODUS FROM EGYPT
TRADE ROUTES
□ PROBABLE LOCATION

JEROME S. KATES, Cartographer
HERBERT G. MAY, Ph. D., Research Editor
COPYRIGHT 1951, THOMAS NELSON AND SONS

CANAAN
AND THE TRIBAL ALLOTMENTS

MILES

0 5 10   20   30   40

KILOMETERS

0 5 10   20   30   40   50

□ PROBABLE LOCATION

JEROME S. KATES, Cartographer
HERBERT G. MAY, Ph. D., Research Editor
COPYRIGHT 1951, THOMAS NELSON AND SONS

THE GREAT SEA

(MEDITERRANEAN)

34° 35° 36°

A B C

1

33°

2

32°

3

31°

4

Mearah
Sidon
Zarephath
Baal-gad
Damascus
Ijon
Tyre
Kanah
Dan (Leshem)
DAN
Hammon
Kartan
Kedesh
MAACAH
Misrephoth-maim
Iron
Achzib
Abdon
Merom
Hazor
Acco
Beth-anath
GESHUR
Achshaph
Neiel
Hukkok
Golan
Ashtaroth
Cabul
SEA OF
CHINNERETH
Bethlehem
Madon
ZEBULUN
Sarid
Mt.Tabor
ISSACHAR
HAVOTH-JAIR
Dor
Shonen
Edrei
Megiddo
Jezreel
Beth-shean
Debir
Ramoth-gilead
Taanach
Ram
To Salecah →
En-gannim
Dothan
Jabesh-gilead
Thebez
Tirzah
Zarethan
Zaphon
Mt.Ebal
Shechem
Mahanaim
Mt.Gerizim
Succoth
R. Jabbok
Gilgal
Taanath-shiloh
Rakkon
Kanah
Tappuah
Ataroth
Adam
Aphek
Shiloh
Joppa
Jehud
Timnath-serah
Betonim
Jogbehah
Beth-dagon
Bethel
Naarah
Beth-nimrah
Beeroth
Ai
Jericho
Rabbah
L.Beth-horon
Gezer
BENJAMIN
Gilgal
Shittim
Mephaath
Jabneel
Kiriath-jearim
Heshbon
Ekron
Zorah
Jerusalem
Mt.
Nebo
Bezer
Ashdod
Timnah
Beth-shemesh
Medeba
Libnah
Azekah
Bethlehem
Baal-meon
Ashkelon
Gath
Adullam
Kedemoth
Achzib
Beth-anoth
Dibon
Mattanah
Eglon
Lachish
Hebron
Aroer
Gaza
Debir
En-gedi
City of Moab
Hormah
Ziklag
Carmel
Gerar
En-rimmon
Maon
Ar
Sharuhen
Ashan
Jattir
Beer-sheba
Arad
Moladah
Kir-hareseth
NEGEB
Aroer
(THE SOUTH)
Ezem
Rehoboth
Hazazon-tamar
Br. Zered
Beeroth
Tophel
Azmon
Bozrah
Hazar-addar
Punon
Kadesh-barnea
Sela
Teman

ASHER
NAPHTALI
Mt. Lebanon
Mt. Hermon
BASHAN
MANASSEH
(MACHIR)
MANASSEH
G
A
D
EPHRAIM
DAN
JUDAH
SIMEON
PHILISTIA
PLAIN OF SHARON
Mt. Carmel
Jordan R.
SALT SEA
R. Arnon
REUBEN
MOAB
AMMON
EDOM
ARABAH
WILDERNESS OF ZIN
Brook of Egypt
Ascent of Akrabbim

34° 35° 36°

A B C

ISRAEL and JUDAH

In the Time of
AHAB and JEHOSHAPHAT (ca. 860 B.C.)

The Kingdom of ISRAEL

The Kingdom of JUDAH

In the Time of
JEROBOAM II and UZZIAH (ca. 750 B.C.)

●●●●●●●●●●● The Boundary of ISRAEL
●●●●●●●●●●● The Boundary of JUDAH

▫ PROBABLE LOCATION

MILES
0 5 10   20   30   40

KILOMETERS
0 5 10 20 30 40 50 60

JEROME S. KATES, Cartographer
HERBERT G. MAY, Ph. D., Research Editor
COPYRIGHT 1951, THOMAS NELSON AND SONS

THE GREAT SEA

PHOENICIA

Sidon
Zarephath
Tyre
Ijon
Abel-beth-maacah
Dan
Kedesh
MAACAH
Hazor
GESHUR
Acco
Cabul
Br. Kishon
Mt. Carmel
GALILEE
SEA OF CHINNERETH
Gath-hepher
Aphek
Karnaim
BASHAN
SYRIA OF DAMASCUS
Damascus
R. Abana
R. Pharpar
Mt. Lebanon
Entrance to Hamath
Mt. Hermon

Dor
Megiddo
Taanach
Ibleam
Arubboth
Dothan
Jezreel
V. of Jezreel
Beth-shean
Shunem
Mt. Tabor
Lo-debar
Beth-arbel
Ramoth-gilead
Abel-meholah
Tishbeh
Br. Cherith

I S R A E L
Samaria
Tirzah
Shechem
SAMARIA
HILL COUNTRY OF EPHRAIM
[Shiloh]
Baal-shalishah
Zarethan
Penuel
Mahanaim
R. Jabbok
The Jordan
The Arabah
G I L E A D
A M M O N

Joppa
Jabneel (Jabneh)
Gibbethon
Ekron
Gezer
Mizpah
Bethel
Gilgal
Gibeah
Ramah
Jericho
Gilgal
Shittim
Rabbah
Anathoth
Ashdod
Beth-shemesh
Jerusalem
Nebo
Bezer
Libnah
Ashkelon
Gath
Moresheth
Azekah
Bethlehem
Baal-meon
Medeba
Jahaz
Achzib
Eglon
Tekoa
Zior
Ataroth
Kiriathaim
Dibon
Gaza
Lachish
Hebron
En-gedi
Aroer
Debir
Ziklag
JUDAH
WILDERNESS OF JUDAH
SEA OF THE ARABAH
SALT SEA
R. Arnon
M O A B
Gerar
Beer-sheba
Arad
V. of Salt
Kir-haresheth

PHILISTIA
Eglon

Hazazon-tamar
Br. Zered

Brook of Egypt

A R A B A H
E D O M
Mt. Seir

Bozrah

Kadesh-barnea

To Ezion-geber (Elath)
Sela
Teman

THE NEAR EAST
ca. 730 B.C.

MILES
0   50   100   200   300
KILOMETERS
0   50 100   200   300   400

SUBJECT TO ASSYRIA under TIGLATH-PILESER III
(Various Arabian Tribes also acknowledged
overlordship of TIGLATH-PILESER III)

EGYPT

JEROME S. KATES, Cartographer
HERBERT G. MAY, Ph. D., Research Editor
COPYRIGHT 1951, THOMAS NELSON AND SONS

(CASPIAN
SEA)

BITTER SEA (PERSIAN GULF)

MEDIA

Ecbatana

ARARAT (URARTU)

(L. Van)

(L. Urmia)

NAIRI
Turushpa

NAMRI

ASSYRIA

Arbela

Nineveh
Calah
Asshur
Gozan

ELAM

Shushan
(Susa)

Sippar
Cuthah
Babylon
Borsippa
Nippur

BABYLON

Erech
Ur

R. Tigris

R. Euphrates

TUBAL
Melidia

Carchemish
Haran

Samal
Arpad
Calneh
Aleppo

Hamath
Hazar-enan
Riblah
Damascus

Dumah

ARABIA

Tema

KUE

MESHECH

R. Halys

PHRYGIA

LYDIA

Sardis

Arvad
Gebal
Sidon
Tyre

Samaria
ISRAEL
Jerusalem
Gaza

AMMON
MOAB
EDOM
Sela

Ezion-geber

MIDIAN

RED SEA

SINAI

KITTIM
(CYPRUS)

CAPHTOR
(CRETE)

THE GREAT SEA

GREECE

Athens

LIBYA

Sais
Zoan
Bubastis
On
Memphis
(Noph)
Heracleopolis
Hermopolis

EGYPT

R. Nile

Thebes

Syene

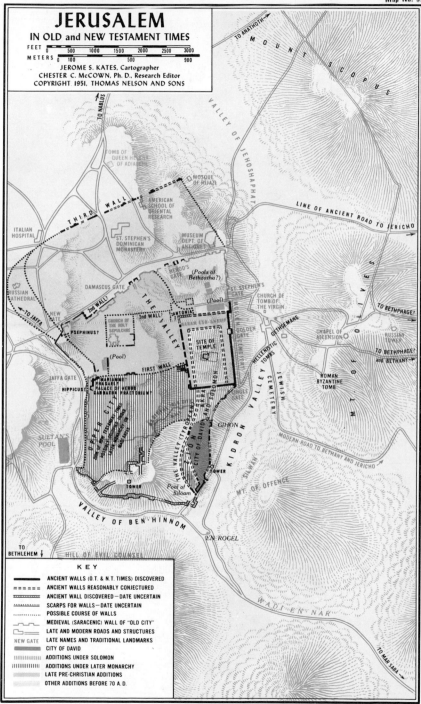

JERUSALEM
IN OLD and NEW TESTAMENT TIMES

FEET 0   500   1000   1500   2000   2500   3000
METERS 0   100   500   900

JEROME S. KATES, Cartographer
CHESTER C. McCOWN, Ph. D., Research Editor
COPYRIGHT 1951, THOMAS NELSON AND SONS

KEY

——— ANCIENT WALLS (O.T. & N.T. TIMES) DISCOVERED
══════ ANCIENT WALLS REASONABLY CONJECTURED
▨▨▨▨▨ ANCIENT WALL DISCOVERED—DATE UNCERTAIN
∴∴∴∴∴ SCARPS FOR WALLS—DATE UNCERTAIN
·········· POSSIBLE COURSE OF WALLS
⊏⊐⊏⊐ MEDIEVAL (SARACENIC) WALL OF "OLD CITY"
▭▭ LATE AND MODERN ROADS AND STRUCTURES
NEW GATE LATE NAMES AND TRADITIONAL LANDMARKS
▦▦ CITY OF DAVID
▥▥▥ ADDITIONS UNDER SOLOMON
▥▥▥ ADDITIONS UNDER LATER MONARCHY
▓▓ LATE PRE-CHRISTIAN ADDITIONS
░░ OTHER ADDITIONS BEFORE 70 A.D.

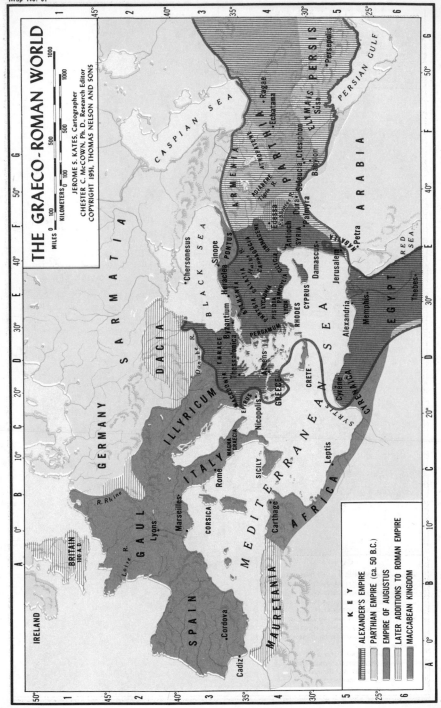

THE GRAECO-ROMAN WORLD

JEROME S. KATES, Cartographer
CHESTER C. McCOWN, Ph.D., Research Editor
COPYRIGHT 1951, THOMAS NELSON AND SONS

MILES 0 100 500 1000
KILOMETERS 0 100 500 1000

K E Y

ALEXANDER'S EMPIRE
PARTHIAN EMPIRE (ca. 50 B.C.)
EMPIRE OF AUGUSTUS
LATER ADDITIONS TO ROMAN EMPIRE
MACCABEAN KINGDOM

IRELAND

BRITAIN
100 A.D.

GERMANY

SARMATIA

CASPIAN SEA

DACIA

BLACK SEA

R. Rhine

GAUL

Lyons

Marseilles

SPAIN

Cordova

Cadiz

CORSICA

ITALY

Rome

SICILY

MAGNA
GRAECIA

ILLYRICUM

EPIRUS

MACEDONIA

Thessalonica

THRACE

Byzantium

Heraclea

Chersonesus

Sinope

PONTUS

ARMENIA

MEDIA

ATROPATENE

Ecbatana

Ragae

PARTHIA

ADIABENE
Tigris R.

Nineveh

MESOPOTAMIA

Dura

Seleucia Ctesiphon

Babylon

ELYMAIS

PERSIS

Susa

Persepolis

PERSIAN GULF

GREECE

Athens

Nicopolis

CRETE

MYSIA

PERGAMUM

LYDIA

BITHYNIA

GALATIA

PAPHLAGONIA

CAPPADOCIA

PHRYGIA

PISIDIA

LYCIA

PAMPHYLIA

CILICIA

Tarsus

Antioch

SYRIA

Palmyra

Damascus

Jerusalem

NABATEA

Petra

ARABIA

RHODES

CYPRUS

MEDITERRANEAN SEA

SYRTIS

CYRENAICA

Cyrene

Alexandria

Memphis

EGYPT

Thebes

RED SEA

AFRICA

Carthage

Leptis

MAURETANIA

CASPIAN SEA

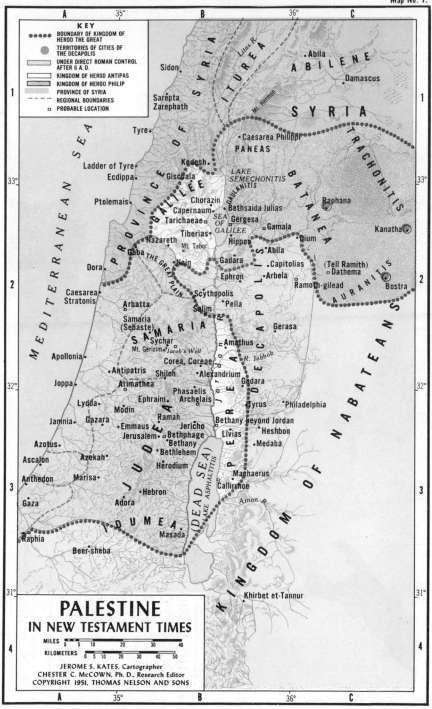

KEY

●●●● BOUNDARY OF KINGDOM OF
    HEROD THE GREAT
● TERRITORIES OF CITIES OF
    THE DECAPOLIS
▨ UNDER DIRECT ROMAN CONTROL
    AFTER 6 A.D.
▢ KINGDOM OF HEROD ANTIPAS
▨ KINGDOM OF HEROD PHILIP
▨ PROVINCE OF SYRIA
–·–·– REGIONAL BOUNDARIES
▢ PROBABLE LOCATION

PALESTINE
IN NEW TESTAMENT TIMES

MILES
0 5 10   20   30   40
KILOMETERS
0 5 10   20   30   40   50

JEROME S. KATES, Cartographer
CHESTER C. McCOWN, Ph. D., Research Editor
COPYRIGHT 1951, THOMAS NELSON AND SONS

THE MISSIONARY JOURNEYS OF PAUL

1 –·–·–·– ACTS 13:1—15:35
1 – – – – ACTS 15:36—18:22
2 ·············· Possible Alternative Routes
3 –·–·–·– ACTS 18:23—21:17
3 – – – – Possible Alternative Routes
II CORINTHIANS 2:1; 12:14; 13:1,2
ACTS 27:1—28:16

MILES 0 25 50 100 200
KILOMETERS 0 50 100 200 300

JEROME S. KATES, Cartographer
CHESTER C. McCOWN, Ph.D. Research Editor
-COPYRIGHT 1951, THOMAS NELSON AND SONS

PALESTINE
TOPOGRAPHY

MILES
0 5 10   20   30

KILOMETERS
0 10 20   30   40

AREA BELOW SEA LEVEL

VOLCANIC DEBRIS

JEROME S. KATES, Cartographer
HERBERT G. MAY, Ph. D., Research Editor
COPYRIGHT 1951,
THOMAS NELSON AND SONS

A   35°   B   36°   C

1

33°

THE GREAT SEA
(MEDITERRANEAN)

Sidon
Zarephath
Tyre
Achzib
Acco
Dor
Caesarea

Mt. Lebanon
R. Litani
Mt. Hermon
Damascus
R. Abana
R. Pharpar

Dan

(LAKE HULEH)

TRACHONITIS

GALILEE
HILL COUNTRY OF NAPHTALI

PLAIN OF GENNESARET
SEA OF CHINNERETH (GALILEE)

Ashtaroth

BASHAN
Edrei
Ramoth-gilead

Mt. Carmel
R. Kishon
V. of Iphtah-el
Nazareth
Mt. Tabor
×Mt. Moreh
V. of Megiddo
V. of Jezreel
Mt. Gilboa

(R. Yarmuk)

MT. GILEAD

Ham

Dothan

Br. Cherith

Mt. Ebal
Shechem
×Mt. Gerizim

R. Jabbok

PLAIN OF SHARON

Br. of Kanah

32°

MOUNT EPHRAIM

The Jordan

PLAIN OF THE JORDAN

Rabbah

Joppa

V. of Aijalon
Mt. Gaash
Bethel
Mt. Ephron
Jericho
V. of Sorek
Jerusalem
Br. Kidron

PLAINS OF MOAB
×Mt. Pisgah
×Mt. Nebo
Medeba

Ashdod
Ashkelon

THE SHEPHELAH
V. of Elah
V. of Zephathah
Gath
Tekoa
Hebron

HILL COUNTRY OF JUDAH

WILDERNESS OF JUDAH

Nahaliel

WILDERNESS OF KEDEMOTH

Gaza
Debir
Ziph
Maon

Aroer
R. Arnon

WILDERNESS
OF
MOAB

3

SALT SEA
OF THE ARABAH
(SEA

Beer-sheba
V. of Salt

Kir-hareseth

NEGEB

Waters of Nimrim

31°

Mt. Halak

ASCENT OF AKRABBIM

Br. Zered

Bozrah

4

WILDERNESS
OF
ZIN

Kadesh-barnea

ARABAH

MT. SEIR

Sela

A   35°   B   36°   C

Map No. 10.

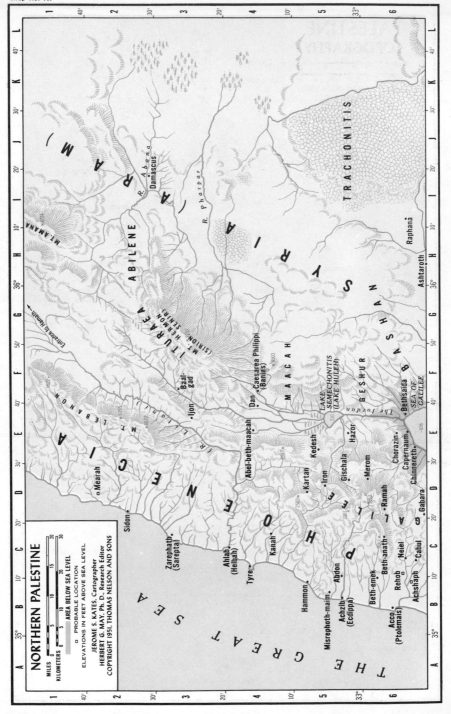

NORTHERN PALESTINE

MILES
KILOMETERS

□ PROBABLE LOCATION
ELEVATIONS IN FEET ABOVE SEA LEVEL

JEROME S. KATES, Cartographer
HERBERT G. MAY, Ph. D., Research Editor
COPYRIGHT 1951, THOMAS NELSON AND SONS

AREA BELOW SEA LEVEL

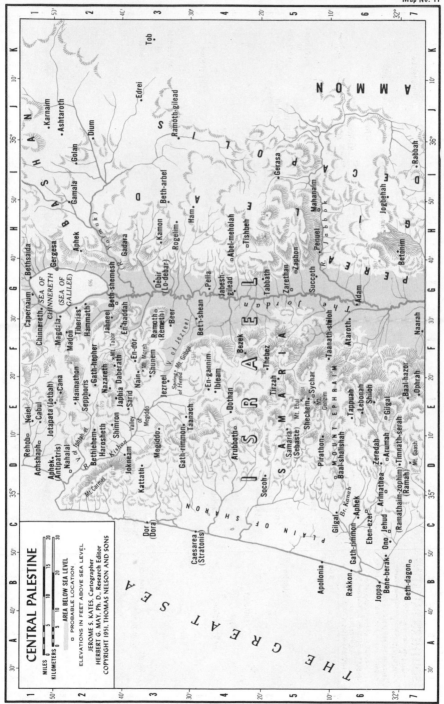

Map No. 11

CENTRAL PALESTINE

MILES
KILOMETERS

ELEVATIONS IN FEET ABOVE SEA LEVEL
AREA BELOW SEA LEVEL
□ PROBABLE LOCATION

JEROME S. KATES, Cartographer
HERBERT G. MAY, Ph. D., Research Editor
COPYRIGHT 1951, THOMAS NELSON AND SONS

THE GREAT SEA

PLAIN OF SHARON

ISRAEL

SAMARIA

MOUNT EPHRAIM

GILEAD

BASHAN

AMMON

SEA OF CHINNERETH (SEA OF GALILEE)

The Jordan

Valley of Jezreel

Mt. Carmel

Caesarea (Stratonis)
Dor (Dora)
Apollonia
Rakkon
Joppa
Bene-berak
Beth-dagon
Ono
Jehud
Gath-rimmon
Eben-ezer
Gilgal
Br. Kanah
Aphek
Socoh
Arubboth
Pirathon
Samaria (Sebaste)
Baal-shalishah
Tappuah
Zeredah
Arumah
Arimathea
(Ramathaim-zophim) (Ramah)
Timnath-serah
Mt. Gaash
Ophrah
Baal-hazor
Gilgal
Shiloh
Lebonah
Shechem
Mt. Ebal
Mt. Gerizim
Sychar
Tirzah
Thebez
Bezek
En-gannim
Ibleam
Dothan
Gath-rimmon
Taanach
Megiddo
Jokneam
Kattath
Haresheth
Shimron
Jabia Daberath
Sarid
Nain
En-dor
Shunem
Spring of Herod
Mt. Gilboa
Mt. Moreh
Jezreel
Ramoth (Remeth)
Beth-shean
Beer
Ramoth (Remeth)
Pella
Jabesh-gilead
Beth-arbel
Kamon
Rogelim
Ham
Gadara
Abel-meholah
Tishbeh
Zarethan
Zaphon
Tabbath
Succoth
Adam
Penuel
Mahanaim
R. Jabbok
Jogbehah
Betonim
Rabbah
Naarah
Atarotah
Taanath-shiloh
Debir (Lo-debar)
Gerasa
Ramoth-gilead
Edrei
Tob
Karnaim
Ashtaroth
Dium
Golan
Gamala
Aphek
Bethsaida
Capernaum
Chinnereth
Magdala
Tiberias
Hammath
Madon
Cana
Gath-hepher
Hannathon
Seppboris
Nazareth
Mt. Tabor
Jahneel
Er-haddah
Beth-shemesh
Gergesa
Rehob
Neiel
Cabul
Iotapata (Jotbah)
Nahalal
Bethlehem
Achshaph
Aphek (Antipatris)
Mt. Carmel
R. Kishon

Jabesh

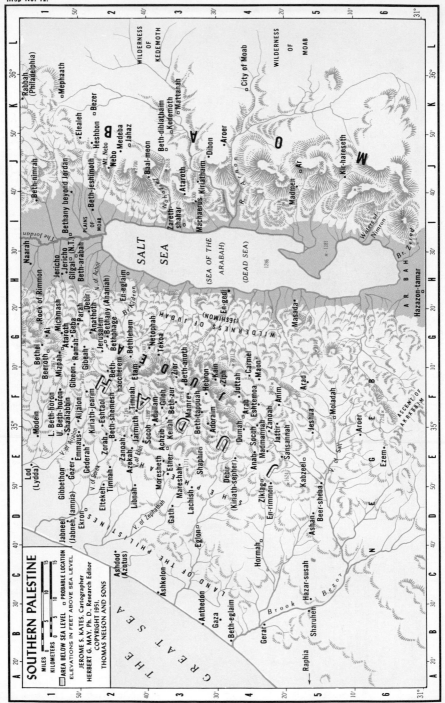

Map No. 12.

SOUTHERN PALESTINE

MILES
0   5   10   15
KILOMETERS
0   5   10   15

□ AREA BELOW SEA LEVEL   □ PROBABLE LOCATION
ELEVATIONS IN FEET ABOVE SEA LEVEL

JEROME S. KATES, Cartographer
HERBERT G. MAY, Ph. D. Research Editor
COPYRIGHT 1951,
THOMAS NELSON AND SONS

DATE DUE

MAY 1 2			
APR. 3 1977			
GAYLORD			PRINTED IN U.S.A.